HARRY C. TREXLER LIBRARY

Gift of

Dr. & Mrs. Bernard Frank

MUHLENBERG
COLLEGE

American Jewish Year Book

American Jewish Year Book 1987

VOLUME 87

Prepared by THE AMERICAN JEWISH COMMITTEE

Editor
DAVID SINGER
Associate Editor
RUTH R. SELDIN

THE AMERICAN JEWISH COMMITTEE
NEW YORK
THE JEWISH PUBLICATION SOCIETY
PHILADELPHIA

COPYRIGHT © 1987 BY THE AMERICAN JEWISH COMMITTEE
AND THE JEWISH PUBLICATION SOCIETY

All rights reserved. No part of this book may be reproduced in any form without permission in writing from the publisher, except by a reviewer who may quote brief passages in a review to be printed in a magazine or newspaper.

ISBN 0-8276-0290-1

Library of Congress Catalogue Number: 99-4040

PRINTED IN THE UNITED STATES OF AMERICA
BY THE HADDON CRAFTSMEN, INC., SCRANTON, PA.

Preface

The present volume contains three feature articles. In "New Perspectives in American Jewish Sociology," Nathan Glazer elucidates the main issues in the debate on the future of American Jewry. In "The Bitburg Controversy," Deborah E. Lipstadt examines the events and reactions surrounding President Ronald Reagan's 1985 visit to a military cemetery in Germany. U.O. Schmelz's "The Population of Reunited Jerusalem, 1967–1985" is a demographic survey of the Holy City's diverse multiethnic, multireligious inhabitants.

A special supplement to this volume, marking the 80th anniversary of the American Jewish Committee, includes essays by Henry L. Feingold and David M. Gordis.

Regular articles on Jewish life in the United States are Murray Friedman's "Intergroup Relations" and "The United States, Israel, and the Middle East," by George E. Gruen and Marc Brandriss. The article on Jewish population in the United States is presented this year in a new format, the work of a team of researchers associated with the recently established North American Jewish Data Bank: Barry A. Kosmin, Paul Ritterband, and Jeffrey Scheckner.

Jewish life around the world is reported on in a series of articles about Israel, Canada, Great Britain, France, the Netherlands, West Germany, East Germany, the Soviet Union, and the countries of the Soviet bloc. Estimates for world Jewish population are provided by researchers on the faculty of the Hebrew University of Jerusalem.

Carefully compiled directories of national Jewish organizations, periodicals, and federations and welfare funds, as well as religious calendars and obituary notices, round out the 1987 AMERICAN JEWISH YEAR BOOK.

We are very grateful to our colleagues Robert Rosenbaum and Michele Anish for their proofreading efforts and to Diane Hodges for compiling the index. We also acknowledge the aid of Cyma M. Horowitz, director of the Blaustein Library, Lotte Zajac, and all our other co-workers in Information and Research Services.

THE EDITORS

Contributors

HENRIETTE BOAS: journalist, Amsterdam, Holland.

MARC BRANDRISS: director, Zionist affairs department, Hadassah, New York.

SERGIO DELLAPERGOLA: senior lecturer, Jewish demography and statistics, Institute of Contemporary Jewry, Hebrew University of Jerusalem, Israel.

HENRY L. FEINGOLD: professor, history, Baruch College and Graduate School, City University of New York.

MURRAY FRIEDMAN: director, Middle Atlantic region, AJC, Philadelphia.

ZVI GITELMAN: professor, political science, University of Michigan.

NATHAN GLAZER: professor, education and sociology, Harvard University.

DAVID M. GORDIS: executive vice-president, AJC, New York.

GEORGE E. GRUEN: director, Israel and Middle East affairs, AJC, New York.

LIONEL E. KOCHAN: Bearsted Reader in Jewish History, University of Warwick, England.

MIRIAM KOCHAN: writer, translator, Oxford, England.

BARRY A. KOSMIN: director of research, Council of Jewish Federations, New York.

DEBORAH E. LIPSTADT: director, Brandeis-Bardin Institute, California.

ARNOLD MANDEL: novelist, reporter, literary critic, Paris, France.

RALPH MANDEL: journalist, translator, Jerusalem, Israel.

PAUL RITTERBAND: professor, sociology and Jewish studies, City College and Graduate School, City University of New York.

FRIEDO SACHSER: reporter, editor, Cologne, West Germany.

JEFFREY SCHECKNER: research associate, Council of Jewish Federations, New York.

U.O. SCHMELZ: professor, Jewish demography and statistics, Institute of Contemporary Jewry, Hebrew University of Jerusalem, Israel.

HAROLD M. WALLER: associate professor, political science, McGill University, Canada.

Contents

PREFACE		v
CONTRIBUTORS		vii

SPECIAL ARTICLES

New Perspectives in American Jewish Sociology	*Nathan Glazer*	3
The Bitburg Controversy	*Deborah E. Lipstadt*	21
The Population of Reunited Jerusalem, 1967–1985	*U.O. Schmelz*	39

UNITED STATES

CIVIC AND POLITICAL

Intergroup Relations	*Murray Friedman*	117
The United States, Israel, and the Middle East	*George E. Gruen and Marc Brandriss*	137

DEMOGRAPHIC

Jewish Population in the United States, 1986	*Barry A. Kosmin, Paul Ritterband, and Jeffrey Scheckner*	164

OTHER COUNTRIES

CANADA	Harold M. Waller	195

WESTERN EUROPE

Great Britain	Lionel and Miriam Kochan	208
France	Arnold Mandel	219
The Netherlands	Henriette Boas	224

CENTRAL EUROPE

Federal Republic of Germany	Friedo Sachser	241
German Democratic Republic	Friedo Sachser	261

EASTERN EUROPE

Soviet Union	Zvi Gitelman	263
Soviet Bloc Nations	Zvi Gitelman	271

ISRAEL	Ralph Mandel	277

WORLD JEWISH POPULATION, 1984	U.O. Schmelz and Sergio DellaPergola	331

SPECIAL SUPPLEMENT

THE AMERICAN JEWISH COMMITTEE
80TH ANNIVERSARY

In Appreciation		340
The Continued Vitality of the American Jewish Committee at 80	Henry L. Feingold	341
Looking Ahead: The American Jewish Committee at 80	David M. Gordis	353
Honors and Awards		362
80th-Anniversary Planning Committee		364

DIRECTORIES, LISTS, AND OBITUARIES

NATIONAL JEWISH ORGANIZATIONS
United States 367
Canada 412

JEWISH FEDERATIONS, WELFARE FUNDS,
COMMUNITY COUNCILS 415

JEWISH PERIODICALS
United States 427
Canada 435

OBITUARIES: UNITED STATES 436

SUMMARY JEWISH CALENDAR,
5747–5751 (Oct. 1986–Aug. 1991) 448

CONDENSED MONTHLY CALENDAR,
1986–1988 (5746–5749) 450

SELECTED ARTICLES OF INTEREST IN RECENT VOLUMES
OF THE AMERICAN JEWISH YEAR BOOK 477

INDEX 481

Special Articles

New Perspectives in American Jewish Sociology

by Nathan Glazer

For the first time in the 40- or 50-year history of the sociology of American Jews, we have among the central figures engaged in that enterprise a substantial and meaningful debate over the future of the American Jewish community. It is a debate that can be identified in a number of ways, but all of them come down to one central question, which has perhaps been given its most useful naming in Steven Cohen and Paul Ritterband's forthcoming work on the Jews of Greater New York[1]—the argument between the "assimilationists" and the "transformationists." The terms themselves are interesting, perhaps tendentious, because who in Jewish life (or indeed in the study of Jewish life) is for assimilation? Indeed, the "assimilationists" in this polarity are not for assimilation, but say that it is happening. And who is not for transformation? And yet I cannot find better terms.

Still another formulation that we owe to Cohen, this time in collaboration with Leonard Fein, contrasts "integrationism" and "survivalism."[2] Until 1967, Cohen and Fein argue, integration into American society was "the highest priority on the collective agenda of the Jews; since then it has been survival." We borrow the terms for a somewhat different purpose, to refer to the chief anxieties of the two opposing groups of sociologists. "Integrationists," like "transformationists," see no major threat to Jewish survival in American Jewish integration into American society; "survivalists," parallel to "assimilationists," do.

Perhaps the most neutral and sober formulation is that which contrasts those who expect "straight-line" change as we move from generation to generation, with those who see the possibility of a U-shaped curve of Jewish "identity" and "commitment" as against a straight descent.

However the matter is put, what we are in fact asking is whether American Jewry is headed for assimilation or whether it is engaged in transforming the terms in which Jewishness and Judaism are to be understood. In

---

Note: This paper was delivered as a keynote address at the conference on "New Perspectives in American Jewish Sociology," sponsored by the American Jewish Committee, May 28–29, 1986.

[1] I will have to return a number of times to Cohen and Ritterband's as yet unpublished work. A good part of its import is already available in Steven M. Cohen, *American Modernity and Jewish Identity* (New York, 1983).

[2] Steven M. Cohen and Leonard Fein, "From Integration to Survival: American Jewish Anxieties in Transition," *The Annals,* July 1985, pp. 75–88.

other words, is there a straight-line process of reduction in Jewish knowledge, commitment to Jewish causes, involvement in the Jewish religion, connection to the Jewish community—American or international—with each passing generation or with the passage of time since immigration to America, or is there, rather, despite obvious changes, many of which can be presented in the language of decline—lesser quantities or intensities of one kind of measurement or another and a distancing from connection and involvement—the emergence of something new? Settling this issue requires meticulous attention to concepts, assumptions, and measures about which we have become increasingly sophisticated in recent years.

What are the issues in the debate? One that has perhaps engaged the greatest interest of the Jewish community is the extent and meaning of intermarriage. Has it increased over time, and by generation, and by how much? The central question of numbers in turn leads to many subordinate issues that are relevant to the "assimilationist"–"transformationist" debate. How many of the non-Jewish spouses convert to Judaism or, indeed—but this information is unavailable—how many of the Jewish spouses convert to another faith? How do the intermarried relate to the Jewish community? How fertile are these marriages? How many of the children of these marriages are raised as Jews? And regardless of how many are raised as Jews, what is the nature of their Jewish "identity" or "commitment"?

All this is relevant to the question of the future size of the Jewish population, which is another part of the debate discussed below. Will there be "enough" Jews, and what is enough? Although the sensational projections of decline voiced a few years ago are now not heard, it is clear that American Jews stand at a point where the maintenance of their absolute numbers in the United States, let alone their proportion in the general population, is unlikely.

Another key element in the debate is the effect of increased levels of education, occupation, and income on Jewish identity and commitment. On this issue, common and elite wisdom have diverged. It is doubtful that ordinary Jews have ever felt that they should be more poorly educated, engage in occupations of lesser status, and receive lesser incomes in order to maintain the strength of Judaism and the Jewish community. Nor have the leaders of the Jewish community ever taken this position. But sociologists, ironically, have almost taken it for granted—before some recent research, that is—that the inevitable result of rising education, occupation, and income would be increased assimilation, however measured. (One important tendency in Zionist thought, too, has looked doubtfully on prosperity in the Diaspora, arguing that it could never be counted on in the face of anti-Semitism. In this line of thought, prosperity also undermined the factors—poverty and distress—that spurred *aliyah* and contributed to the very Jewish exceptionalism that Zionism sought to overcome.) In any case, since the prosperity of American Jews has been indisputable, one key element in the current debate is its effect on the balance between assimilation and transformation, integration and survival.

A fourth related issue is the effect of a decline in anti-Semitism on the balance between assimilation and transformation. Certainly such a decline should, by the logic of the terms and concepts, make assimilation easier or more possible. But has it?

A fifth issue in the debate involves causality in the opposite direction: the effect of the balance of assimilation and transformation on the relationship of American Jews to Israel. The chief function of Jewish community organization in this country would appear to be support of Israel. Indeed, this support almost fully defines the range of interests of Jewish community organizations in politics. At the same time, Israel occupies a major place in the content of Jewish life; it defines much of the curriculum of the Jewish school and much of the subject matter of the Jewish sermon. Assimilation certainly must mean, if it means anything, increasing indifference to the fate of Israel and the connection between American Jews and Israel. But what about transformation? Does that in the end mean anything different?

Before we fully engage in this debate, it is interesting to see what is not much in question, what is not even included in it. A discussion of new perspectives must include some mention of old perspectives that are no longer central.

One subject that is not included in the current debate is concern over the economic position of Jews in the United States. Undoubtedly Jews have economic problems. Young Jews, like all young Americans, have difficulty getting the kind of education they want, paying for it, and establishing themselves in the professions. Established Jews are affected, as are all Americans, by the ups or downs of the American economy. Older Jews, again, like all other Americans, may struggle on insufficient pensions and Social Security. But one must always ask: compared to whom? The economic issue, a central concern of Jewish organizational life until the 1960s and one that still aroused Jewish communities in the 1960s—recall the estimates of the Jewish poor during the war on poverty—and that engaged Jewish organizations in the form of the fight over affirmative action in the 1970s, is simply not an issue in the late 1980s. Whatever the weaknesses that afflict the American economy generally—huge budget deficits, an enormous trade deficit, the growing number of poorly paid service jobs, the inability of so many young people to get the education or training that make possible any job—they do not particularly affect Jews. Insofar as the debate between "assimilationists" and "transformationists" is concerned, the key issue is not the impact of economic shocks on the balance between assimilation and transformation; rather, it is the effect on American Jews of relatively unbroken and untroubled prosperity, whatever the condition of the American economy.

Note, for example, that there has been surprisingly little concern over the decline of the Rustbelt or Snowbelt, despite the fact that some of the largest Jewish communities—Chicago, Detroit, Cleveland, St. Louis, etc.—are located in those areas. Obviously the businessmen and professionals who make up the majority of Jewish employed persons in those communities, as in all others,[3] must have been adversely affected by the changes taking place, even if not as seriously as blue-collar workers and small merchants. Yet it is interesting that this great national misfortune seems to have gone unnoted in studies of American Jews, which leads one to think it was for them not as great a misfortune.

Whether or not sociologists study a question is not the only index to its importance, of course, and economic troubles and dangers may be a more important matter than we imagine. But whether research on an issue is funded is one index to the seriousness with which an issue is taken by communal leaders, and we have seen no spate of inquiry into the economic position of Jews. It is a perspective that is, for the moment, abandoned.

Yet a second issue about which one hears much less than in the past—but more, it is true, than about the economic dangers to American Jews—is anti-Semitism. The major Jewish community organizations that have been created to fight anti-Semitism are not without functions in this area. There has recently been great concern about anti-Semitism in the black community and some concern about the exploitation of the difficulties of farmers by anti-Semites. There is an old populist anti-Semitism (connected with anti-Eastern, anti-big-business sentiment) that can be tapped in farming areas, and some people are trying to do so. The concern about anti-Semitism among blacks is more substantial: after all, there are more blacks than farmers, and Jews live in closer contact with them. But as those contacts diminish, concern over black anti-Semitism inevitably becomes less urgent.

Recall that in the period of the summer riots in the late 1960s, one concern of Jewish organizations was the fate of Jewish shopkeepers in black areas. (There appeared to be less concern over the fate of Jewish property owners, whether slumlords, landlords, or home owners.) But there is precious little Jewish presence in the black ghetto these days. When one hears of shopkeepers being killed in poor black neighborhoods—an index to the

---

[3]The percentage of Jewish manual workers as reported in recent Jewish community studies ranges from 4 percent (Washington, D.C.) to a surprising 14 percent (Phoenix, Arizona), with Chicago and Cleveland at 10 percent, which seems to be the mean. See Gary Tobin and Alvin Chenkin, "Recent Jewish Community Population Studies: A Roundup," AJYB, vol. 85, 1985, pp. 154–178.

perilousness of their situation—they tend to be Chinese or more likely Korean. The Jews are all out. Even the tensions of the 1960s and the 1970s between Jewish teachers, administrators, and social workers and incoming blacks seem to me—by the index of public attention—markedly reduced. Perhaps there are simply fewer Jews in these occupations. Many of the Jewish teachers and administrators involved in the great New York school war over decentralization in 1968 must by now have retired. The transition to teachers, principals, and administrators who better reflect the dominant racial and ethnic makeup of students in various communities has been substantial.

So neither the Jewish economic position nor anti-Semitism seems to engage Jewish sociologists much these days. I should point out that in paying less attention to these areas, Jewish sociologists are, in part, at least, following the funding priorities of Jewish communal organizations. Both may be out of touch with Jewish popular feeling. I note that even in a community like Los Angeles, which we would think does not have to worry much about anti-Semitism, a survey shows considerable concern.[4] What one is seeing, I suspect, is a general uneasiness and anxiety among Jews, still unabated despite the absence of many concrete acts of prejudice and discrimination. But perhaps the Jewish masses know something that their leaders and scholars do not.

Let me point to still another reflection of this popular uneasiness. In talks to Jewish community groups, I heard a number of positive comments about a review I had written of Charles Silberman's *A Certain People* in the *New York Times Book Review*.[5] "I am glad you took him to task for his optimism," I was told. But then it immediately emerged that the speakers were criticizing Silberman for his optimism about anti-Semitism—with which I agreed! They had not noted that my criticism of Silberman had to do with his optimism about the quality of Jewish life.

Which brings us to the central issues in the current debate.

II

Since numbers are clearly a necessary base for the maintenance of Jewish life, I begin with the question "How many Jews will there be?" How large that base must be is, of course, itself arguable. It is known that the

---

[4]The percentage who perceive a lot or some anti-Jewish prejudice or discrimination is high: 79 percent mention private clubs; 63 percent, employment; 38 percent, housing; and 37 percent, education. Can Jews really have faced that much discrimination in Los Angeles? See Neil Sandberg, *Jewish Life in Los Angeles: A Window to Tomorrow* (Lanham, Md., 1986), p. 159.

[5]*New York Times Book Review*, Sept. 2, 1985, pp. 2, 17–18.

percentage of Jews in the American population has been dropping. Sidney Goldstein suggests that the percentage peaked in 1937, at 3.7 percent.[6] Schmelz and DellaPergola give a figure for 1980 of 2.54 percent of the American population.[7] No one suggests that this population proportion will go up in the future. American Jewish fertility has been below general American fertility for 60 years. Jewish immigration will remain very low; that from the Soviet Union remains a question mark, that from Israel remains small, and there is no need to explore other, much smaller possible sources of additional Jews, whether from South Africa or some other country with a Jewish population that may be experiencing problems. A good part of U.S. population growth is now contributed by a sizable flow of peoples from Asia and Latin America, which includes few Jews, and for that reason alone the Jewish proportion of the population will decline. (By 1990 there will be more Asians than Jews in the United States.) The 30-percent reduction over 50 years in the proportion of Jews in the American population means—if these estimates are correct—that the American Jewish population is smaller by 2,500,000 Jews than it would have been had the percentage of 1937 been maintained. Clearly, one can easily maintain a gloomy "assimilationist" perspective on the basis of the population figures alone.

On the other hand, one can argue that numbers alone hardly tell the entire story, whatever the particular story that we want to tell—whether of sheer survival, or of the ability to maintain Jewish institutions of all kinds, or of the possibility of influencing American politics, or of defending the interests of Israel or—should they ever appear threatened—the interests of the American Jewish population itself. Despite the decline in the proportion of Americans who are Jews, the Jewish community is still very large and will remain so for some time, even on the basis of pessimistic assumptions. (Schmelz and DellaPergola's lowest estimate for the year 2000 is 4,639,000.[8]) Jewish community institutions are on the whole more extensive and stronger than in the 1930s, and Jewish political strength is substantially greater. This may be attributable in part to changes in the American polity itself. Even quite small groups, such as Greek-Americans, and groups with very few representatives in Congress, such as Hispanic-Americans—there are three times as many Jewish as Hispanic congressmen—exert substantial political influence. Because ethnic and other subgroup claims are no longer seen as threats to Americanism—a word which itself has gone somewhat

---

[6]Sidney Goldstein, "Jews in the United States: Perspectives from Demography," AJYB, vol. 81, 1981, p. 8.
[7]U.O. Schmelz and Sergio DellaPergola, "The Demographic Consequences of U.S. Jewish Population Trends," AJYB, vol. 83, 1983, p. 144.
[8]Ibid., p. 179.

out of favor—the majority is tolerant of, even acquiescent to, minority demands.

So the argument as to the meaning of numbers is not decided by the numbers themselves. Yet the numbers themselves are of considerable importance. We see their weight when we consider the effect of numbers—births—on Jewish schools. American Jews show, even more than other Americans, an exceptional capacity to control their fertility on the basis of individual decisions that maximize individual interest. The result for all Americans of such a capacity is widely varying numbers of children being born, depending on a range of factors: the impact of the Great Depression, lowering marriages and births; the impact of World War II, delaying them; the postwar baby boom, making up for depression and war; the decade of the sixties with its remarkable drop in births for reasons that remain unexplained; and the recent modest resurgence of births with the onset of a period of rather late marriage and late childbearing.

Amid all these shifts, Jews seem to exaggerate the overall behavior of the American population. One is reminded of the mock Hasidic song, *"Ven der rebbe tantzt, shpringen alle hasidim."* As all this variation takes place, Jewish birthrates remain steadily below general white American rates. Or, as Calvin Goldscheider has put it: "Jews have tended in the past to be in the forefront of major socioeconomic revolutions. American Jews are located in social statuses and geographic locations that are most responsive to changes in marriage and the family. The high proportion of Jews with college- and graduate-level educations, their disproportionate concentrations in major metropolitan areas, and their middle-class backgrounds and values place them in the avant-garde of social change."[9]

The effects of shifting birthrates are striking indeed. In 1980, 21.7 percent of American whites, but only 16.2 percent of Jews, were under the age of 14. On the other end, only 11.8 percent of the American white population, but 15.5 percent of the Jewish, were over 65. Cohorts vary widely: the peak years of births, 1956–1960, contributed a substantial part of the current American Jewish population, 10 percent; just a decade later, a five-year period of low growth (1966–1970) contributed less than half of that, 4.7 percent. This variation in cohort size is another factor depressing Jewish births, since a wide disparity may develop at any given time between the number of marriageable males and females, assuming that females are generally two-and-a-half years younger at marriage (or at least were in 1970–1971—I suspect that there have been changes in marriage practices in the intervening 15 years). This disparity means, according to Schmelz and DellaPergola, that there have been since 1981—and this will continue

---

[9]Calvin Goldscheider, *Jewish Continuity and Change: Emerging Patterns in America* (Bloomington, 1986), p. 59.

through the decade—125 marriageable males for every 100 females, or only 80 marriageable Jewish females for every 100 males.[10]

We could pursue the argument over numbers and fertility further and point out, from the more optimistic side, other findings: that marriage is delayed rather than rejected; that childbearing is delayed rather than abjured; that the fourth generation expects to have larger families than the third or even the second; and that, perhaps most interestingly, higher education and working status no longer depress, as demographers had assumed they must, the expected family size of Jewish women.[11]

III

Differences in evaluating marriage and fertility trends of American Jews, serious as they are, pale when we come to the issue of intermarriage. Here is a matter that has always been of high concern to the masses of Jews, but that has been a major issue for American Jewish and other Jewish demographers and sociologists only since the 1970s.

Until the National Jewish Population Survey (NJPS) of 1970–1971, it appeared from most studies that the Jewish intermarriage rate, while rising, was still very low when compared to that of other American ethnic and religious groups. However, the NJPS showed remarkably high rates for those marrying most recently (1965–1971): 41 percent of Jewish males marrying wives not born Jews and 10.3 percent of Jewish females marrying husbands not born Jews, for a combined rate of 29.2 percent. It is important to observe, though, that conversions reduce this "outmarriage" rate to a lower "mixed marriage" rate—30 percent of non-Jewish wives of Jewish men were converting, as were a few non-Jewish husbands of Jewish wives, bringing down the rate of mixed marriage to 22.5 percent. Furthermore, most of the children born to outmarried Jewish women were being raised as Jews despite their unconverted husbands. When all outmarriages are considered, it appears that half the children were being raised as Jews.[12]

In this argument over figures there are many unknowns: the NJPS is already 15 years old, and there have been no other large national studies; each local Jewish community that has been studied shows a different pattern; and Jewish community studies (as well as the NJPS) do worst in finding the intermarrieds who want least to identify with the Jewish community, who live in non-Jewish neighborhoods, and who are unconnected to Jewish organizations. There is also an argument as to whether the

---

[10]Schmelz and DellaPergola, op. cit., pp. 144–145, 150.
[11]Goldscheider, op. cit., pp. 58–73, 90–107; Sandberg, op. cit., table 46.
[12]Schmelz and DellaPergola, op. cit., pp. 165–169.

1966–1971 figures showing such a huge rise are dependable, in view of the small sample on which they are based. Bernard Lazerwitz argues that they are not, and using figures for the entire decade of the 1960s brings the combined rate down to 14 percent.[13] Between "assimilationists" and "transformationists" a good deal of discretion is exercised as to which figures to emphasize. Even more controversial are the meanings to be attached to the figures. Yet the figures, as indicated in the NJPS, can be surprising. Note that the NJPS population size of 5,800,000 included all those in Jewish households—and those in Jewish households included 430,000 non-Jews! (These are the non-Jewish spouses and children. It is not clear whether account has been taken in these figures of those spouses who had converted and those children who were being raised as Jews.[14])

Certainly our understanding of the intermarriage issue has been made considerably deeper and more complex by the work of Jewish demographers in recent years. We now know that we must take into account conversions, the numbers of children being raised as Jews, the proportions of marriageable males and females at given times, the great differences among communities, and the like.

Around the question of intermarriage and what it means, the issue between "assimilationists" and "transformationists," integrationists and survivalists, is most sharply engaged. Interestingly enough, the two variant views on intermarriage were put forth almost simultaneously in two books on American Jews that were included in leading series on ethnic groups in America, published in the late 1960s. Sidney Goldstein and Calvin Goldscheider, in *Jewish Americans: Three Generations in a Jewish Community* — part of the series on "Ethnic Groups in American Life," edited by Milton Gordon—were perhaps the first to argue, in a careful analysis of a 1962 survey of the Jewish community of Providence, R.I., that the meaning and significance of intermarriage were changing. The "imports," they maintained, were larger than the "exports": "In every instance in which the non-Jewish partner had converted to Judaism, the children were being raised as Jews. In all, 136 children in the sample belonged in this category. Among the couples in which the non-Jewish partner had not converted to Judaism, 84 children were being raised as Jews, and 60 as non-Jews."[15] Goldstein and Goldscheider added some important qualifications to the generally optimistic note of these observations, but whatever the qualifications, their tone was strikingly different from that of Marshall Sklare,

---

[13]For this dispute, see Charles Silberman, *A Certain People: American Jews and Their Lives Today* (New York, 1985), pp. 287–297.

[14]Schmelz and DellaPergola, op. cit., pp. 142–143.

[15]Sidney Goldstein and Calvin Goldscheider, *Jewish Americans: Three Generations in a Jewish Community* (Englewood Cliffs, N.J., 1968), pp. 168–169.

writing in the parallel series "Ethnic Groups in Comparative Perspective," edited by Peter Rose. Sklare argued in his work *America's Jews:*

> Intermarriage is an issue that all minorities face. If the minority is assimilationist in orientation, intermarriage is experienced as an opportunity. If the group is survivalist intermarriage is experienced as a threat. . . . [T]he threat exists both on a collective as well as on an individual basis. In its collective aspects, intermarriage menaces the continuity of the group. In its individual aspects it menaces the continuity of generations within the family, the ability of family members to identify with one another, and the satisfaction of such members with their family roles. . . . American Jews experience intermarriage more as a threat than an opportunity.[16]

Regardless of the theoretical viewpoint taken by particular scholars in the field, there is no denying that attitudes toward intermarriage have become more accepting over time. They have changed strikingly since, for example, Sklare's Lakeville study of 1957–1958 (the book was published ten years later): 43 percent of the population in that prosperous suburb said that they would be "somewhat unhappy" if their child married a non-Jew, while another 29 percent indicated that they would be "very unhappy."[17] In Boston, 20 years later, negative attitudes toward intermarriage had dropped substantially, and particularly so among the younger age group: 43 percent of those over the age of 60 were very negative, compared to only 5 percent of those aged 18–29.[18]

What about a comparative historical perspective on intermarriage? Should we be looking at the situation today with alarm, comparing it to that in Central Europe in the 1920s and 1930s? Is not the entire context that determines the attitude toward intermarriage, and possibly its effects as well, drastically different at present from what prevailed then? In the earlier period, the purpose of intermarriage—we believe—was to escape Judaism and its penalties. It was part of a complex that included conversion and the conversion of Jewish spouses to Christianity. It was inconceivable in that context that non-Jewish spouses would convert to Judaism. The "transformationists" do have an important point here. They argue that intermarriage no longer means or is the result of a desire to escape from Judaism or the Jewish people. As Goldscheider points out: "No ideological base for intermarriage was uncovered which favors out-marriages among Jews, nor is there any evidence that intermarriage reflects values emphasizing assimilation. Younger Jews in their late teens and early twenties see little connection between intermarriage and total assimilation."[19] The intermarried show no

---

[16]Marshall Sklare, *America's Jews* (New York, 1971), p. 100.
[17]Marshall Sklare and Joseph Greenblum, *Jewish Identity on the Suburban Frontier* (New York, 1967), p. 307.
[18]Goldscheider, op. cit., p. 15.
[19]Ibid., p. 172.

particular tendency toward greater assimilation. Half of their children are being raised as Jews. Why then the alarm?

In Central Europe in the 1920s and 1930s, intermarriage was the result of the exclusion of Jews from the surrounding society and of their efforts to join it. It reflected "self-hatred," a term that is just not heard today. At present in the United States, intermarriage is the result of the acceptance of Jews by the surrounding society and of Jewish unself-consciousness in taking part in it. Doing so inevitably leads to education with non-Jews, work with non-Jews, and political participation and social life with non-Jews. A perfectly understandable integration results—no consequence of a desire to assimilate. And after all, integration and upward social mobility are what Jews have wanted. They have sought to leave the central cities, where their children have attended such schools as New York's City College, and move to the suburbs, from which they hoped their children could aspire to Harvard and Yale, with understandable consequences.

I believe that the differences pointed out by the "transformationists" between intermarriage in Central Europe and intermarriage in the United States are important. These scholars, however, may not have as strong a case on the consequences of intermarriage. The converted may be better Jews than those born within the fold, and indeed often are, but it seems undeniable that their children have alternatives before them that the children of families in which both parents were born Jewish do not—they have legitimate alternative identities.

The argument that non-Jewish American acceptance of Jews is a cause of higher rates of intermarriage is something of a double-edged sword when it comes to the future of the institutions of the Jewish community and support of the policies that the community feels are crucial. That acceptance, after all, while involving elements of appreciation of different ethnic and religious heritages, is not as sympathetic to the notion of the maintenance over time of ethnic separateness. "Separatism" is not a positive term in the United States; "integration" certainly is, as "assimilation" used to be. Jews, in their resistance to the prospect of assimilation while insisting on integration, can find little solace in the attitudes of their fellow Americans, despite the ethnic revival and the rise of ethnic studies. White American groups are not expected to worry about intermarriage; they are expected to welcome it. It may be an issue for an individual first- or second-generation parent, but it is not an issue for any white ethnic community. There are no studies sponsored by the community, and for the sake of the community, of intermarriage among Italians, or Greeks, or Poles. If we turn around the identity question and say the Jewish concern is for the religion, Judaism, we again find no equivalent: Catholics want their children to be raised as Catholics, but they are so far from an ethnic definition of Catholicism that converts and children raised as Catholics have no problem, I believe, within the Catholic Church, regardless of ethnic background. Jews have not been interested in conversion—indeed have resisted it—for a thousand years or more. They convert now not to demonstrate the glory or superiority of Judaism or to increase the number of Jews as such, but to retain the number of Jews there might have been in the absence of intermarriage. Conversion exists almost solely in the context of intermarriage.

The point of these reflections is that while we can understand why the rate of intermarriage goes up, and can expect it to continue to go up—what after all would restrain it in view of the educational level, occupations, and activities of Jews?—we can also expect it to be a problem for American Jews, and one that their fellow citizens will not find easy to understand. The dilemma is that the kind of life Jews wish to lead in America, and the one that their fellow Americans would not seek to begrudge them—one in which they are free from prejudice and discrimination and free to pursue whatever education and careers they wish—will inevitably undermine a community committed to particularistic practices, institutions, and policies.

The argument of the "assimilationists" is that the strongest basis for Jewish commitment is given by birth within the community. American Jews are not, and, I believe, cannot be, a community of choice. As such, Judaism and Jewishness would have no more force than Unitarianism. A minority of Jews, in fact, takes the position that birth alone makes a Jew, and takes it so strongly that it is suspicious of most conversions. There are directly religious—*halakhic*—grounds for this suspicion, but it may well be that wrapped up in that unreasoning, and to my mind unenlightened, view is a piece of unexplicated basic sociological wisdom: the community of birth is stronger than the community of choice.

The "transformationists," of course, do not dispute that wisdom. They are aware that depth of Jewish commitment can range from the deep to the barely perceptible, and much of their work has been devoted to studying that commitment and how it varies by age, generation, education, and class. They maintain that the level of commitment is enough to sustain the Jewish community, with its manifold institutions and varied activities. But the question of what is enough is another issue that divides the two schools.

IV

With regard to the question of commitment, the "assimilationists" point to the decline of traditional observances and practices and to the growing acceptance of intermarriage. The "transformationists" respond to this by arguing that the content of Judaism and Jewishness is changing in America, but that this does not constitute a threat to the continuity of the community and the maintenance of a vital Jewish life within it. Recent books by Goldscheider[20] and Cohen[21] offer the strongest statements of this point of view, which finds popular expression in Silberman's *A Certain People*. It is challenged by Silberman's critics, Arthur Hertzberg,[22] Samuel Heilman,[23] and Ruth R. Wisse,[24] and to a somewhat lesser degree the author of the present essay,[25] but the strongest proponents of an alternative view within the field of American Jewish sociology have been Sklare[26] and Charles Liebman.[27] Herbert Gans makes a similar but more general argument, not from the perspective of one committed to the maintenance of a strong Jewish life but as a sociologist of ethnicity who sees all groups in the United States ending up with a purely "symbolic" ethnicity, one which provides an identity perhaps, but one without any specific content that meaningfully separates those who maintain an ethnic identity from other Americans.[28] This position is familiar, which is not to say it is not persuasive. We have heard it since St. John de Crèvecoeur's *Letters from an American Farmer*, Israel Zangwill's *The Melting Pot*, and the writings of Robert E. Park and his school. So let us put forth the "transformationist" case, which is newer, having been formulated only in recent years.

The "transformationists"—I draw this summary account from Goldscheider and Cohen, without any claim that they subscribe to every element of the synthetic position I present—point out that American Jews remain different in family structure, occupations, education, political values, and social behavior from non-Jewish Americans. They argue that these differences have nothing to do with discrimination or the failure of American Jews to integrate. Indeed, some of these differences—as in the greater amount of education and the concentration in the professions—are due to the very openness of American society. The ability to integrate leads, paradoxically, not to American Jews paralleling American educational achievement and occupational structure, but to their diverging on the basis of open opportunity. Furthermore, these differences are sustained by and help to sustain a pattern of social life in which Jews interact for the most part with

---

[20]Ibid.
[21]Cohen, op. cit.
[22]*New York Review of Books*, Nov. 21, 1985, pp. 18–21.
[23]*New Yorker*, Oct. 7, 1985, pp. 16–19.
[24]*Commentary*, Nov. 1985, pp. 108–114.
[25]*New York Times Book Review*, op. cit.
[26]Sklare and Greenblum, op. cit.; Sklare, op. cit.
[27]Charles Liebman, *The Ambivalent American Jew* (Philadelphia, 1973).
[28]Herbert Gans, "Symbolic Ethnicity: The Future of Ethnic Groups and Cultures in America," in Herbert Gans et al. (eds.), *On the Making of Americans: Essays in Honor of David Riesman* (Philadelphia, 1979), pp. 193–220.

other Jews. Once again this should not be seen as a product of exclusion. The "transformationists" no longer speak, as the American Jewish Committee once did, of the "five o'clock shadow," the separation of Jews from non-Jews at the end of the business day, as a problem. Rather, this separation is the product of the social life Jews choose for themselves, which is with other Jews.

But while social life sustains Jewish community cohesion and occupational concentration, that is not the whole story. The Jewish religion and the commitment to the State of Israel—an expression of unity with the Jewish people—are the two pillars of Jewish communal life. We see a near universal commitment to Israel[29] and the emergence of a common norm of practice that selects some Jewish customs and rituals, some almost universally. The two most frequent such observances are the Passover seder and lighting candles on Hanukkah.[30] The second generation showed a strong decline in ritual observance from the first, but in the third the decline is moderated, and between third and fourth there are no indications of continued decline.

Combined measures of Jewish identification show that the fourth generation is not falling away. Indeed, an error can be made in evaluating the observances of later generations—who are of course young—because involvement in the Jewish community, identification with it, and the practice of what has become the norm of Judaism and Jewishness for the majority of Jewish Americans are all related to family life-cycle stage. One may think that the third or fourth generation is assimilating, failing to take into account that much of it consists of young people in college or beginning their careers, who are as yet without families or children. But if we divide the Jewish group by life-cycle stages, we see an inverted U-shaped curve, with ritual observance and affiliation rising when children reach school age, and declining somewhat in later stages of the life cycle.

Sklare is skeptical. As far back as his Lakeville study, he pointed to the rather instrumental character of the religious observances that are retained: "Five criteria emerge as important in explaining retention of specific home rituals. Thus, the highest retention will occur when a ritual (1) is capable of effective redefinition in modern terms, (2) does not demand social isolation or the adoption of a unique life style, (3) accords with the religious culture of the larger community and provides a 'Jewish' alternative when such is felt to be needed, (4) is centered on the child, and (5) is performed annually or infrequently."[31]

My impression is that Sklare does not consider this to be enough. Neither does Liebman, who pointed out in the preface to *The Ambivalent American*

---

[29]Cohen, op. cit., pp. 154–170.
[30]Ibid., p. 56.
[31]Sklare and Greenblum, op. cit., p. 57.

Jew: "The American Jew is torn between two sets of values—those of integration and acceptance into American society and those of Jewish group survival. These values appear to me to be incompatible. But most American Jews do not view them in this way."[32] Liebman's observations are sharp and incisive. For him the undoubted reality of a continuing Jewish identity in the third and fourth generations—and beyond—but one that is maintained by means of a much reduced norm of some Jewish practices combined with a political commitment to Israel, is not enough.

We may now ask, enough for what? It is enough to maintain a Jewish identity and community in the United States for a long time. Of that I am convinced. The "assimilationists" have been somewhat hasty in telescoping a process that undoubtedly occurs: distancing from historical origins and adoption of new practices that reduce the differences between Jews and non-Jews. Perhaps that ultimately will assimilate Jews, making them indistinguishable from others, whether in their own consciousness or in that of others. That may yet happen. But on the basis of present social trends it is hard to see *how* it will happen. One reason is that in the United States ethnic identity and religious identification have become in large part expected norms of individual identification. To be an "unhyphenated American"—the term is Stanley Lieberson's—is somewhat exceptional, despite the enormous mixture of backgrounds. It is revealing that only in 1980, some 50 years after the end of mass immigration, was a question on ancestry —in effect, ethnicity—added to the census. I suspect that we will keep and refine this question. And it is further revealing that the overwhelming majority of white Americans answer it, perhaps with some prodding from the census-taker, and do so by (necessarily) putting together a few different ancestries.

As Daniel Bell asks in a perceptive essay[33] in which he argues against the expectation of assimilation in America, "What is there to assimilate to?" He observes: "For better or worse, the very breakup of the cultural hegemony of the WASPs and the growth of ethnicity as a legitimate dimension of American life have forced the *politicization* of group identity. To the extent that government becomes the source of group rights and protections, . . . ethnic-group identity becomes salient in the competition for place and privilege in the society. In that sense, Jews are 'forced' to maintain an identity, and to define themselves in ethnic terms." That goes some way toward explaining what is happening. While Jews do not seek group privileges from the government in the same sense that blacks and Hispanics do, they do ask for active governmental aid for Israel, and they do need to be organized in order to make certain that the group rights of others do not affect their own ability to obtain access to education and the professions.

---

[32]Liebman, op. cit., p. vii.
[33]Daniel Bell, "Where Are We?" *Moment,* May 1986, pp. 15–22.

But this is only part of the story, of course, and the "transformationists" are right to point to more. There is among most Jews a real desire to maintain identity and continuity. It is not a very strong desire, however, and it adapts itself to the needs of integration in the United States, as Liebman points out. It makes few demands and is largely cut off from historic Judaism[34] in terms of belief and practice. And now those who claim to be the heirs to historic Judaism—the small minority of Orthodox Jews in the United States—are engaged in an offensive, not only pointing out all these shortcomings but asserting that the unity of the Jewish people will be broken if this form of adaptive Jewishness and Judaism remains the norm for American Jews. The "transformationists" have had little to say about this prediction as they meticulously describe the Judaism and Jewishness of the overwhelming majority of American Jews. But those who decry adaptive Judaism as a betrayal—as not enough—will not be content to stay on the sidelines and accept a role as simply another wing of Judaism in America. I believe that this development will have a powerful impact on the evolution of Judaism.

Just how it will work out I do not know. Yet I think the surprising aggressiveness of the Orthodox group, the strength given it by the official position Orthodoxy holds in Israel, perhaps the additional factor of a new historical context in which Christian fundamentalism—not to mention various kinds of self-confident sectarianism—has developed surprising strength in the United States, all suggest that the transformational implication—I do not say assertion—that Judaism and Jewishness have reached a stable and reproducible form in the United States is premature.

My reference to the split that may be created by Orthodoxy's refusal to accept the legitimacy of the two major branches of American Judaism is not for the purpose of suggesting that Orthodoxy will win in America, or be crushed, or that American Jews and Israelis will be divided by the inability

---

[34]In another essay ("On Jewish Forebodings," *Commentary*, August 1985, pp. 32–36) I used the term "historic Judaism" to refer to Orthodox Judaism—as I do here—and was properly reminded by a correspondent that Solomon Schechter applied that term to Conservative Judaism. In an essay in *Moment* (May 1986), Nathan Rotenstreich again uses "historic Judaism" to refer to a Judaism that adapts itself to historic change, whereas "ahistoric Judaism" applies to an unadapting Orthodoxy! Still, Orthodox Judaism, I believe, has a claim to this description because it is most closely linked to the Judaism that developed historically and that was the only Judaism before the spread of Enlightenment and the impact of modernity. I fully understand the argument which maintains that Orthodoxy's refusal to adapt to changing history makes it different from the Judaism to which it claims direct connection; that in refusing to change, its essence changes. Nevertheless, Orthodoxy puts forth a claim that no other variant can maintain. And its claim seems to be able to find substantial reverberation among Jews today, giving Orthodoxy greater vitality than one would have guessed possible 30 years ago. It is no mere fossil, as it would have been reasonable to consider it a few decades ago.

to define a common peoplehood. It is rather to note—and this is important for both sides in the dispute—how unfinished the story is, how unclear it is what may yet happen. What we have seen thus far, as Cohen, for one, perceptively points out, is already the result of history, that is, of specific shaping and shaking events, as well as simply the result of the passing of the generations. Thus, the sharp drop in ritual observance between the first and second generations resulted not only from the impact of a new land but also from the impact of the specific historical context in which the second generation was being raised. It is the case that specific historical events have tended to affect one American Jewish generation more than another, simply because the American Jewish community is today overwhelmingly descended from one major wave of immigration that lasted from the 1880s to the 1920s. As a result, the 1920s, 1930s, and 1940s had their most marked impact on the second generation, while the 1950s, 1960s, and 1970s had it on the third generation. It is not yet clear what will be the shaping historical events for the fourth generation.

V

If I have wavered between the two sides in the debate between "assimilationists" and "transformationists"—and for the purposes of exposition I may well have exaggerated the polarization—it is because I find much merit in both. It is hard to see how Judaism and Jewishness of most Americans connects with the Judaism and Jewishness of their grandfathers and great-grandfathers. At the same time, what has been achieved so far is remarkable, and was hardly expected in, let us say, the 1940s and 1950s. There have been some surprises, such as the remarkable growth of Jewish studies on university campuses and the stabilization in identity, affiliation, and ritual practice that seems to have occurred in the fourth generation. There is no reason to believe there will not be further surprises in the future. In the meantime, the development of the controversy between optimists and pessimists is forcing us to consider and sharpen questions to which we perhaps gave too easy answers in the past.

The Bitburg Controversy

by DEBORAH E. LIPSTADT

ON MAY 5, 1985, DURING a state visit to West Germany, President Ronald Reagan stopped for a few minutes at a small cemetery outside the city of Bitburg. What should have been a routine visit of little concern to anyone except perhaps the residents of the area, had by that point become a major international event. The imbroglio over the visit to the Bitburg cemetery—which in itself lasted no more than ten minutes and during which Reagan said nothing publicly—threatened to seriously affect American-German relations, be a spur to anti-Semitism, politically alienate American Jews from the Reagan administration, and, indeed, color the way in which Reagan's entire presidency would be viewed in history. For over a month the details of the visit and the debate over whether it should proceed as planned occupied the pages—often the front pages—of virtually every major American newspaper. This article will examine the events surrounding the Bitburg visit, seeking to explain how it became one of the most explosive political events of 1985.[1]

Origins of the Controversy

The origins of the entire issue lay in West German Chancellor Helmut Kohl's consternation at having been excluded from the 40th-anniversary commemoration of the landing at Normandy beach in June 1944. Kohl told a number of Western leaders of his anger and, in compensation, President François Mitterrand of France agreed to accompany Kohl to the World War I cemetery at Verdun for a wreath-laying ceremony. There, the leaders of the two former adversaries held hands in a symbolic act of reconciliation.

In fall 1984, during the course of a visit to Washington, Chancellor Kohl asked President Reagan to accompany him to a German cemetery during a planned visit to Germany the following spring and to join him in laying

---

Note: This article is based primarily on an examination of news stories and editorials appearing in major newspapers in the United States. In addition, personal interviews were conducted with Hyman Bookbinder, Marshall Breger, Abraham Foxman, Milton Himmelfarb, Benjamin Meed, and Menachem Rosensaft.

[1]Two volumes that bring together a wealth of material about the Bitburg controversy are Geoffrey Hartman (ed.), *Bitburg in Moral and Political Perspective* (Bloomington, 1986) and Ilya Levkov (ed.), *Bitburg and Beyond* (New York, 1986).

a wreath, as Mitterrand had done. Reagan impulsively agreed, without consulting his advisers, the State Department, or officials in the American embassy in Bonn. Throughout this affair, State Department and Foreign Service personnel, who would have been more sensitive to the historical connotations and implications, played a limited role. Reagan and Kohl, perhaps, did not grasp that the visit of two former adversaries to a cemetery in which World War II soldiers were buried would be regarded differently than a visit to Verdun. Some observers subsequently argued that while Reagan may have been naive about the residue of emotions regarding World War II, Kohl was not. His intention, they maintained, was to use the visit to the cemetery as a means of "normalizing" Germany's past and wiping the historical slate clean. Those who were less critical of Kohl argued that he wanted to impress upon the world that *his* Germany was not the Germany of the past. That was why he was so anxious for Reagan to visit a German war cemetery.

Even at this point the proposed visit posed some thorny questions. President Reagan and, for that matter, all the former Allied leaders had to determine how the anniversary of the end of World War II could be commemorated without appearing to rebuke West Germany, a leading member of the Western alliance. Reagan, well aware of the strong support he had received from Chancellor Kohl in the past, was anxious to avoid any insult to him. Moreover, Reagan was convinced that the Russians would use the anniversary of the end of the war for their own political purposes, and thus wanted to stress the theme of reconciliation and the strength of the Western alliance.

West Germans in general, and Chancellor Kohl in particular, faced a different sort of problem: how to mark the anniversary of a national catastrophe, the worst defeat in Germany's history. Was the commemoration of V-E Day (May 8) a time for joy or sadness? Kohl seemed to be intent on marking the occasion as a victory of democracy over fascism and not as the defeat of Germany. (Ironically, by so doing, he was following the lead of the East Germans and the other Communist-bloc countries, who were planning to commemorate Germany's "liberation" from Nazi rule.) On the other hand, there were those, such as Alfred Dregger, floor leader of Kohl's Christian Democratic Union party in the German Bundestag, who contended that V-E Day marked the loss of the eastern third of Germany and the division of the nation into two states. He, therefore, saw no reason to celebrate. Other Germans simply hoped that the 40th-anniversary commemoration would represent the final spasm of historical torment for their country, and that President Reagan's visit would demonstrate that Germany was now an important part of the Western alliance.

The controversy over Bitburg began with a debate over an entirely different issue. In January 1985 President Reagan was asked whether he would visit Dachau or some other concentration camp site during his forthcoming visit to Germany. Reporters were told that he would not, because he wanted "to focus on the future." Moreover, the press was told that a visit to a concentration camp would not "contribute to the theme of reconciliation and friendship."[2] Four days later the White House officially announced that Reagan would commemorate V-E Day in Germany. On February 14, the White House, in the first of what would turn out to be a long series of reversals, indicated that Reagan would not be in Germany on May 8; his official visit would begin on May 1 but would end prior to May 8. The decision to leave Germany immediately before V-E Day was apparently an attempt by the White House to avoid having to confront some of the historical problems associated with the commemoration. Little did the Reagan administration imagine that it would soon become mired in a conflict in which history assumed an unprecedented contemporary importance.

At a White House press conference on March 21, President Reagan again indicated that he would not visit a concentration camp during his stay in Germany because "instead of reawakening memories . . . we should observe this as the day when, forty years ago, peace began." Referring to the German people, Reagan observed that "none of them who were adults and participating in any way" in World War II were still alive, and "very few . . . even remember the war." Moreover, Reagan contended, "a guilt feeling . . . [has] been imposed upon them, and I just think it's unnecessary."[3]

A number of editorials, including one appearing in the *New York Times*, noted with dismay that Reagan's statement about German adults during World War II no longer being alive was made by a man who was 34 years old in 1945, had served in the military, and claimed in many of his speeches to remember the war clearly. Other, more acerbic, critics observed that Reagan's combat zone had been Hollywood, and that this might have colored his understanding and memory of what World War II was all about. The question was also raised as to whom the president had in mind when he spoke about guilt feeling being "imposed"? Was this some sort of slap at the Jewish community? Moreover, various commentators asked, was it not appropriate for Germans, particularly those who had been adults during the war, to feel guilt pangs?

At this point the reaction of the organized Jewish community was rather muted. Most Jewish leaders remained silent, and those who did comment tried to ease the situation by opining that President Reagan had probably just misspoken—a not unfamiliar failing on his part. Among the few Jewish figures who did speak out against Reagan was Menachem Rosensaft,

---

[2]*New York Times*, Jan. 24, 1985.
[3]From a transcript of President Reagan's news conference in Washington, as recorded by the *New York Times*, Mar. 22, 1985.

founding chairman of the International Network of Children of Jewish Holocaust Survivors, whose comments were published on the op-ed page of the *New York Times* on March 30. Another critic was Israel Singer, executive director of the World Jewish Congress, who not only criticized Reagan for his remarks but also contended that Jewish organizations were being "entirely too quiescent" on the matter.[4]

On April 1, in an interview with the *Washington Post*, President Reagan reiterated his explanation as to why he had decided not to visit Dachau. The bulk of the German people, he argued, were small children or not yet born when the Holocaust had occurred. Moreover, he maintained, a visit to a concentration camp would be "out of line" with the sense of celebration associated with V-E Day. Apparently aware that his refusal to go to a concentration camp would anger some Americans, particularly Jews, Reagan went on to stress his determination that "we . . . never forget the Holocaust," and reminded the interviewer of his support for a national Holocaust museum.[5] Rather than placating his critics, however, Reagan's comments about the Holocaust museum were interpreted by some as a sop designed to appease them. Privately, many observers felt that Reagan's remarks were indicative of his failure to understand the historical significance of the Holocaust. On the whole, however, the leadership of the American Jewish community still remained silent. They believed that the wisest course of action was to say nothing—at least publicly—in order to defuse the situation.

Bitburg Becomes an Issue

On April 11 the White House press office released the itinerary for President Reagan's European trip. Included was a stop at the German military cemetery at Bitburg where Reagan, in the company of Chancellor Kohl, was to lay a wreath "in a spirit of reconciliation, in a spirit of forty years of peace, in a spirit of economic and military compatibility."[6] (Initially, a White House aide claimed that both Germans and Americans were buried at Bitburg, but this was quickly shown not to be the case.)

This decision stirred a new burst of criticism. Hyman Bookbinder, Washington representative of the American Jewish Committee, Kenneth Bialkin, chairman of the Conference of Presidents of Major American Jewish Organizations, Elie Wiesel, chairman of the U.S. Holocaust Memorial Council, and Rabbi Alexander Schindler, president of the Union of American Hebrew Congregations, were among the Jewish figures who condemned the planned visit to a German military cemetery in strongly worded statements

---

[4]*Long Island Jewish World*, Apr. 12–18, 1985.
[5]*Washington Post*, Apr. 2, 1985.
[6]*New York Times*, Apr. 12, 1985.

and op-ed columns. Had Reagan's refusal to visit a concentration camp not been coupled with a commitment to visit the Bitburg cemetery, the issue would probably not have become as controversial as it did; certainly it would not have provoked the same degree of anger in the American Jewish community. It was not only Jews, however, who were angry. Among others, the American Legion joined in the protest. Apparently stung, the White House announced that the plans for the Bitburg visit were under review.

The Bitburg visit, which was already emerging as a major political issue, became even more controversial when, within hours of the original announcement, reports began to circulate that SS soldiers were buried in the cemetery. First estimates mentioned 30 graves; ultimately it was revealed that 49 SS members were interred there. When asked about the matter, West German government spokesman Peter Boenisch described it as of "secondary importance"; the major issue, he argued, was reconciliation.

On April 16, Michael Deaver, the White House aide in charge of planning the trip and a close confidant of President Reagan, left for Germany in order to find ways of "broadening the visit." A number of newspaper columnists cynically observed that Deaver, who was famous for finding dramatic settings in which Reagan might appear, had gone to Germany in search of a concentration camp that provided the right camera angle. Still, the vast majority of American newspapers supported the attempt to add a concentration camp or another symbolic site to Reagan's German trip.

At this point only a few journalists defended the Bitburg visit on its merits —as opposed to those who believed that it had to go forward because it had already been scheduled. The *Wall Street Journal* acknowledged that Reagan might have acted "insensitive[ly]," but accused his critics of "political cynicism." While it did not go so far as to openly support the trip, it did demonstrate an ambivalence about calling for its cancellation. Jody Powell, former Carter White House press secretary, writing in the *Washington Post*, argued that the wreath Reagan would lay at the cemetery would just acknowledge the "terrible loss . . . shared by all sides in war." It would be a "reaffirmation of the basic humanity that should unite us all." William F. Buckley, Jr., argued that there was "no political vice practiced under Hitler that is not also practiced under the German pro-consuls of Stalin and his successors." Asserting that Hitler's Germany was no more than another criminal state and that the Soviet Union was "very much alive," Buckley contended that a visit to Bitburg would indicate our support of a democratic Germany. Columnist George Will expressed the belief that the reason why it was not "improper" to go to Bitburg was that in "1945, at the moment of most intense passion and maximum power to act upon passion, the victors rejected the doctrine of collective guilt."[7]

---

[7]*Wall Street Journal*, Apr. 19, 1985; *Washington Post*, Apr. 17, 1985; *New York Daily News*, Apr. 25, 1985; *Newsweek*, Apr. 29, 1985.

President Reagan tried to defuse the controversy when, in a speech delivered to the Conference on Religious Liberty on April 16, he reversed his position and announced that he would go to a concentration camp. He explained that his previous decision not to visit Dachau was due to a "mistaken impression that such a visit was outside the official agenda."[8] In fact, in March he had said he was not going because it would impose unnecessary guilt feeling on the German population. Rather than mollify the critics, therefore, the two conflicting explanations further heightened the tensions concerning the visit.

The announcement of a stopover at a concentration camp did not satisfy Jewish community leaders. Elie Wiesel, speaking as chairman of the U.S. Holocaust Memorial Council, described the planned addition as a "trade-off" which was unacceptable. Some members of the council, which had been established by Congress in 1980, called for a mass resignation, but cooler heads prevailed.

On April 17, 53 members of the U.S. Senate (42 Democrats and 11 Republicans) sent a petition to President Reagan, urging him not to go to the Bitburg cemetery. On April 18, Elie Wiesel, in a speech delivered in the Capitol Rotunda on the occasion of the National Civic Day of Commemoration of the Holocaust, turned to Secretary of State George Shultz and asked him to "tell those who need to know that our pain is genuine, our outrage deep."[9] The pain and outrage only increased when, on the same day, President Reagan, in a group press interview, described the SS men buried at Bitburg as "victims of Nazism also. . . . They were victims, just as surely as the victims in the concentration camps." In the same interview Reagan equated his visit to Bitburg with visits by German leaders to the U.S. national cemetery in Arlington, Virginia. Reagan blamed the whole controversy on "someone [who] dug up the fact that there are about thirty graves of SS troops there." Reagan went on to describe the SS men as "young soldiers that were conscripted, forced into military service in the closing days of the Third Reich."[10] Reagan claimed that the average age of the SS men was about 18, but offered no explanation of how he had determined this or the fact that they had been drafted at war's end. Former members of the SS hastened to correct the president by pointing out that no one could be drafted into the SS. One had to volunteer.

In the same interview Reagan indicated what was probably his real reason for refusing to reconsider the visit to the Bitburg cemetery. Not to go would "leave me looking as if I caved in in the face of some unfavorable

---

[8]*Washington Post*, Apr. 17, 1985.
[9]*New York Times*, Apr. 19, 1985.
[10]Ibid.

attention."[11] This point was emphasized repeatedly by various administration officials in the days that followed. Given the nature of American-Soviet relations, they argued, it was critically important that Reagan not appear weak or subject to public pressure. Moreover, White House officials vividly remembered how former president Jimmy Carter had backed down on the production and deployment of the neutron bomb, despite the fact that then German chancellor Helmut Schmidt had gone out of his way to support the stationing of the bombs in Germany. To do the same to Chancellor Kohl, who had exposed himself to domestic political risks in order to deploy American missiles on German soil, they contended, was an unacceptable way to treat a loyal ally and a good friend.

Protests Mount

The Reagan interview set off a storm of protest even among those who were generally staunch supporters of the president. Former UN ambassador Jeane Kirkpatrick maintained that it was entirely wrong to argue that all were "equally guilty . . . equally dangerous . . . equally victims."[12] Others criticizing President Reagan included Senate majority leader Robert Dole, House minority leader Trent Lott, the Reverend Jerry Falwell, and Archbishop John O'Connor of New York. Two leading congressional conservatives, Newt Gingrich (R., Ga.) and Vin Weber (R., Minn.) described the decision to go to Bitburg as "morally wrong"; calling Bitburg the "Watergate of symbolism," they also expressed concern about its potential negative effect on the Republican party.[13] Former president Richard Nixon and former secretary of state Henry Kissinger were among the few prominent Republicans to openly support the Bitburg visit.[14] Nixon argued that for Reagan to back out of the visit would be a sign of "weakness" that would undermine his "credibility." Kissinger felt similarly.

Palpably strained relations now existed between the White House and the American Jewish community, with prominent Jewish leaders forcefully attacking President Reagan. Union of American Hebrew Congregations president Rabbi Alexander Schindler described Reagan's remarks in the *New York Times* interview as a "distortion of history, a perversion of language, and a callous offense to the Jewish community."[15] Rabbi Henry Siegman, executive director of the American Jewish Congress, observed, "The president would be well advised both morally and politically to tell

---

[11]Ibid.
[12]*New York Times,* Apr. 20, 1985.
[13]*Washington Post,* May 1, 1985.
[14]*New York Post,* Apr. 29, 1985.
[15]*New York Times,* Apr. 19, 1985.

the American people that he has made a terrible mistake and is man enough to undo it."[16] Howard Friedman, president of the American Jewish Committee, stated: "There is simply no parallel between genocide and the tragedy of lives lost in war. Surely the president of the United States, as the leader of this country, should understand this elementary distinction."[17] Rabbi David Saperstein, head of the Religious Action Center of Reform Judaism, contended that the president's statement "desecrate[d] the memory of the six million Jews who died in the camps."[18]

There was also open tension at this point between U.S. and West German officials, as well as between the U.S. State Department and the White House advance team. Each group tried to shift the blame to someone else as the greatest political fiasco of the Reagan administration up to that point continued to grow. West German officials, anxious to prove that they were not the ones who had prevented President Reagan from visiting Dachau, said that they were perplexed by Reagan's initial refusal to visit a concentration camp. They explained that they had proposed Dachau because they believed that Reagan would want to acknowledge the Holocaust at some point, if only for "domestic political considerations."[19]

Clearly, though, Chancellor Kohl also had a domestic agenda in mind. A crucial election was scheduled to be held in North Rhine–Westphalia during the second week in May, and many people were convinced that Kohl had insisted on the Bitburg visit and the scheduling of a summit immediately prior to the election in order to enhance the electorate's perception of him as an international statesman.

The Bonn government, believing that Washington was now trying to make it appear responsible for the Bitburg controversy, criticized Michael Deaver and the White House advance team. German officials complained that Deaver had not consulted with the Bonn government when the original plans were made. Ironically, officials at the State Department and the American embassy in West Germany had the same complaint. Press reports also revealed that Deaver, during his initial visit to Germany, had spent a considerable amount of time ordering a BMW luxury car. Critics contended that Deaver had been more concerned about his BMW than about the details of President Reagan's trip. In truth, however, Reagan had told Deaver and his other aides that he was not anxious to visit Dachau. One aide explained to the press: "He is a cheerful politician . . . and does not like to grovel in a grisly scene like Dachau. . . . He was reluctant to go. . . . And nobody pushed him."[20]

---

[16]Ibid.
[17]Ibid.
[18]Ibid.
[19]*Washington Post,* Apr. 18, 1985.
[20]*New York Times,* Apr. 18, 1985.

Writing in the *Washington Post,* Lou Cannon echoed the view of many of his fellow journalists when he observed that the White House seemed to have lost its public-relations touch.[21] There were growing fears in the White House that President Reagan's image as a political leader had been seriously compromised by the uproar over Bitburg. Jane Mayer, writing in the *Wall Street Journal,* wondered why no one on the White House staff had argued strenuously with Reagan about the possible political implications of not visiting a concentration camp.[22] Donald Regan, the new White House chief of staff, further complicated the situation when he described Reagan, in an interview, as anguished over the criticism that had been directed against him by the Jewish community. After all, Regan observed, Reagan had spent all his life in Hollywood dealing with members of the Jewish faith and had always supported Israel and Jewish causes. Protestations such as these seemed to confirm the White House's inability to understand why Reagan's critics felt as they did.

On April 19, in what has been described as one of the most dramatic public encounters ever to take place in the White House, Elie Wiesel, on the occasion of being awarded a Congressional Gold Medal of Achievement, turned to President Reagan and virtually begged him to cancel the visit to the Bitburg cemetery. (The award ceremony had long been scheduled for this date.) Noting that the Jewish tradition required the individual to "speak truth to power," Wiesel—whose appearance was carried live by a number of television networks—said, "That place, Mr. President, is not your place. Your place is with the victims of the SS."[23] Prior to the public gathering, Wiesel and a small group of Jewish leaders, including Peggy Tishman, president of the Federation of Jewish Philanthropies of New York, and Malcolm Hoenlein, director of the New York Jewish Community Relations Council, had met with Reagan and Vice-President George Bush in the Oval Office and implored them to cancel the visit. Both the private and the public appeals were to no avail, however.

After the ceremony the White House announced that the Bergen-Belsen concentration camp had been added to President Reagan's itinerary. According to the White House, Reagan had phoned Chancellor Kohl to inform him of the decision. Any subsequent change, White House aides declared, would have to come at Kohl's initiative. That possibility seemed highly unlikely in light of a letter that German politician Alfred Dregger sent Sen. Howard Metzenbaum (D., Ohio). Metzenbaum had circulated a petition to President Reagan, signed by 53 senators, asking him not to go to Bitburg. Dregger described the attempt to have Reagan cancel the visit as an "insult to my brother, and his fallen comrades" who had been killed

---

[21] *Washington Post,* Apr. 20, 1985.
[22] *Wall Street Journal,* Apr. 24, 1985.
[23] *New York Times,* Apr. 20, 1985.

in hostilities on the eastern front.[24] To critics of the visit it seemed that once again the fate of the victims and that of the perpetrators were being equated, this time by a prominent German politician.

Even as attempts were being made by various parties to find a way to resolve the Bitburg controversy, others were trying to understand how the White House could have let itself become mired in such a situation. One contributing element, perhaps, was the fact that Marshall Breger, the White House aide who served as a liaison to the Jewish community, was not involved in the initial planning of the trip and, furthermore, was in Israel when the Bitburg stop was announced. Only upon his return to Washington on April 17 did Breger become aware of the depth of the Jewish community's anger. Some Jewish figures, including Israel Singer of the World Jewish Congress and David Brody, Washington representative of the Anti-Defamation League of B'nai B'rith, maintained that even if Breger had been in the country there was little he could have done to change matters, since he, like his predecessors as liaison to the Jewish community, was removed from the main decision-making arena.[25] It is ironic that the Bitburg controversy occurred during Breger's watch, since Jewish leaders, including those who strongly disagreed with Breger's conservative political views, believed that he had been instrumental in gaining them unusually good access to the president and his advisers. New York CRC head Malcolm Hoenlein, for one, argued that Breger was taking a "bum rap. People are blaming him for something he didn't do."[26]

Breger's role also became mired in controversy as a result of two things he did in the hours immediately preceding Wiesel's address at the White House. In the first place, he told Wiesel that President Reagan's schedule would not permit him to remain at the ceremony for more than a few minutes, and if Wiesel wanted to have Reagan present during his remarks, he would have to curtail them. Breger also called Sen. Frank Lautenberg (D., N.J.) before the ceremony to ask him to use his personal influence to convince Wiesel not to criticize Reagan publicly. Breger strongly believed that from a tactical point of view this would be a more effective means of convincing Reagan to alter his plans, since it would not appear that Reagan was caving in to pressure. Wiesel and Lautenberg, however, publicly attacked the White House official for an attempt at "censorship."[27] In interviews after Bitburg, many Jewish leaders felt that Breger had made a legitimate argument about political tactics. While they may have disagreed with his approach at the time, they expressed respect for him and for what he had accomplished in the White House.

---

[24]*Christian Science Monitor,* Apr. 22, 1985; *New York Times,* Apr. 22, 1985.
[25]*Washington Post,* May 4, 1985.
[26]Ibid.
[27]*New York Post,* Apr. 25, 1985; *New York Times,* Apr. 26, 1985.

Protests by American Jews reached a peak on April 21, when thousands of Holocaust survivors and others assembled in Philadelphia for the inaugural assembly of the American Gathering and Federation of Jewish Holocaust Survivors. In a speech delivered at the opening plenary assembly, Menachem Rosensaft, founding chairman of the International Network of Children of Jewish Holocaust Survivors, termed President Reagan's words and actions "obscene and morally repugnant." If Reagan insisted on going through with his visit to Bitburg, Rosensaft said, "We do not need him and we do not want him at Bergen-Belsen." Sen. Arlen Specter (R., Pa.) offered those at the gathering some hope when he said that the issue was "not over with finality." In fact, however, it was. The White House had decided, despite the growing wave of criticism, that international political considerations made it inexpedient to cancel the Bitburg visit.

A Range of Views

Public opinion polls revealed that Americans in general were hardly enthusiastic about the Bitburg visit, but did not oppose it to the same degree as did the Jewish community. A *Washington Post*-ABC poll, released on April 23, found 52 percent of Americans wanting President Reagan to cancel the visit; 44 percent wished to have Reagan "go ahead with his plans." A *USA Today* poll published on April 26 reported a 52-percent disapproval rate among the general American population, compared with an 88-percent disapproval rate among American Jews. A Gallup poll, taken immediately after the Bitburg visit, reported similar findings. At the same time, a *Washington Post*-ABC poll published on May 15 found that 60 percent of Americans felt that "Jews were making too big a deal out of Reagan's visit." Moreover, a *New York Times*-CBS poll conducted the day after the Bitburg visit revealed that 38 percent of the American public believed that "Jewish leaders in the United States had protested too much over his visit."[28]

Whatever the divisions among the general public about the Bitburg visit, they were not reflected in Congress. On April 25, 257 members of the House of Representatives called on Chancellor Kohl to release President Reagan from his commitment to go to Bitburg. (The White House did not seek to stop Republicans in the House from joining in the appeal.) The next day the Senate passed a resolution sponsored by over 80 senators, recommending that Reagan "reassess his planned itinerary." Among the resolution's sponsors was Republican majority leader Sen. Robert Dole. The press interpreted Dole's action as evidence of the White House's desire to indicate

---

[28] *Washington Post,* Apr. 24, 1985; May 15, 1985; *USA Today,* Apr. 26, 1985; press release, CBS News, May 7, 1985.

to Kohl that it would still like to find a way to avoid the Bitburg visit. In private conversations with journalists, members of the White House staff made this point explicit.

On the same day that the House of Representatives called on Chancellor Kohl to free President Reagan from his commitment, the West German Bundestag defeated a motion introduced by the opposition Green party to eliminate the stop at Bitburg; the motion was voted down 398 to 24. In the course of the debate Kohl thanked Reagan for his "noble gesture."[29] A motion by the opposition Social Democrats, accusing Kohl of injuring U.S.-German relations, failed by the narrow margin of 162–155, despite Kohl's majority of 54 seats in the Bundestag.

Reports began to appear in the press about an escalation of anti-Semitism in Germany. *Quick,* a popular German magazine, ran a cover story blaming the Bitburg controversy on the "influence of Jews" and their power over the "big media" in the United States. The article suggested that "legendary Jewish power had once again influenced the course of Washington and its President."[30] In point of fact, however, there was no shortage of Christian voices opposed to President Reagan's Bitburg visit. Rabbi A. James Rudin, director of interreligious affairs at the American Jewish Committee, observed that this was not an instance where Jews had to "solicit Christian names." "They called us," Rudin observed, "my phone was ringing off the hook."[31]

On April 28 an "open letter" to President Reagan appeared in the *New York Times.* The letter was organized by Sister Carol Rittner, a faculty member at Mercy College in Detroit, who feared that the public might blame American Jews for the Bitburg controversy, accusing them of "throwing their weight around." Working with staff members of the National Council of Churches and three leading Christian scholars who had written about the Holocaust—Harry Cargas, Franklin Littell, and Robert McAfee Brown—Rittner secured the support of 143 Protestant and Catholic leaders, who stated in the letter:

> We are shocked by the insensitivity and inaccuracy of your explanation that the German soldiers buried [in Bitburg] "were victims, just as surely as the victims in the concentration camps." The failure to distinguish between perpetrators and victims, between the death of combatants in battle and the slaughter of innocents in the Nazi concentration camps does injustice not only to the memory of the dead but to the most basic tenets of Jewish and Christian morality.[32]

While the mainline Christian denominations expressed considerable opposition to the Bitburg visit, the evangelical and fundamentalist churches

---

[29]*New York Times,* Apr. 26, 1985; *Washington Post,* Apr. 26, 1985.
[30]*New York Post,* Apr. 26, 1985; *New York Daily News,* Apr. 26, 1985.
[31]William Bole, "Bitburg: The American Scene," in Hartman, op. cit., p. 66.
[32]A. Roy Eckardt, "The Christian World Goes to Bitburg," in Hartman, op. cit., p. 86ff.

were largely silent about the matter. The only leader on the Christian Right who publicly criticized President Reagan was the Reverend Jerry Falwell. Two other well-known figures, Billy Graham and Pat Robertson, refused to take a public position, although they did approach the White House privately. Some analysts, including Rabbi Yechiel Eckstein, head of the Holy Land Fellowship of Christians and Jews, an organization devoted to promoting understanding between Jews and evangelical Christians, attributed the silence of the Christian Right to a lack of established ties, such as those that existed between the American Jewish community and the major Catholic and Protestant churches. But even Eckstein was bitter at being rebuffed by Christian leaders with whom he had worked on other issues.[33] The American Legion was joined by other veterans' groups—the Jewish War Veterans, the American Ex-Prisoners of War, the Catholic War Veterans, and the American Veterans Committee—in protesting the Bitburg visit. Only the Veterans of Foreign Wars did not speak out, arguing that it could not oppose a foreign-policy decision made by the commander-in-chief of the armed forces. Among ethnic organizations opposing President Reagan's decision were the Sons of Italy, the Ukrainian National Association, the United Hellenic American Congress, the Mexican American Legal Defense Fund, and the Japanese American Citizens League. The congressional black caucus also publicly took a stance against the visit, as did AFL-CIO president Lane Kirkland.

Support for President Reagan was voiced by some conservative spokesmen. William F. Buckley, Jr., in his syndicated column of April 25, argued that the visit to Bitburg was no more an endorsement of Nazism than a visit to a Civil War cemetery would be an endorsement of slavery. After the visit Buckley declared that Reagan had done the "right thing," and that his critics owed him "apologies which he will never get."[34] Richard Viguerie, editor of *Conservative Digest*, argued that the debate over Bitburg was focusing too much attention on the Nazi Holocaust at the expense of atrocities currently being committed by the Soviet Union.[35]

Until the day of the Bitburg visit the Israeli government remained silent about the matter, when Prime Minister Peres said: "I believe that President Reagan is a true friend of the Jewish people and the state of Israel. . . . It is precisely for this reason that we feel deep pain at the terrible error of his visit to Bitburg. . . . There can be no reconciliation regarding the past."[36]

---

[33]Eckardt, op. cit.; William Bole, "Bitburg—Who Spoke Out, Who Didn't," *Present Tense*, Summer 1985, pp. 16–19.
[34]*New York Daily News*, May 9, 1985.
[35]*New York Daily News*, Apr. 25, 1985; William Bole, "Bitburg: The American Scene," op. cit., p. 75.
[36]*New York Times*, May 7, 1985.

By the final days of April it was clear that neither Kohl nor Reagan would succumb to the critics. However, up until the president's actual departure, the White House tried to find some way to mollify the Jewish community and soften the impact of the ceremony at Bitburg. Through the good offices of Billy Graham, a delegation from the American Jewish Committee was invited to the White House on April 29, to meet with Michael Deaver. AJC officials who had just returned from Germany—where the Committee had close, long-standing relationships at the highest levels—reported to Deaver that Chancellor Kohl was apparently receptive to the idea of adding a visit to the grave of Konrad Adenauer, the man regarded as the architect of postwar German democracy. Deaver reportedly said that this information would make it easier for him to adjust the president's itinerary. Before the group left the White House, President Reagan and Donald Regan greeted them and thanked them for their cooperation.[37]

Reagan in Germany

On May 1 President Reagan arrived in Germany and within hours another controversy erupted. Peter Boenisch, a West German government spokesman, quoted Reagan as saying that he "regretted" that some Americans believed in collective German guilt for the killing of millions during World War II. According to Boenisch, Reagan had told this to Chancellor Kohl in an hour-long meeting that the two had held shortly after Reagan's arrival. White House spokesman Larry Speakes issued a strong denial, as did Secretary of State Shultz. When Shultz was asked if Reagan had essentially apologized for the fact that some Americans opposed the Bitburg visit, Shultz told reporters, "Americans are free to speak out on this and other subjects." Boenisch ultimately conceded that he had "interpreted" rather than quoted Reagan's remarks.[38]

Another controversy emerged regarding comments made by Richard R. Burt, assistant secretary of state for European and Canadian affairs. Burt, who was then expected to be named ambassador to Bonn, told reporters that Chancellor Kohl had said to President Reagan, "We must never forget and we can never forgive." Burt was accused by German officials of "turn[ing] West German policy on its head."[39]

On May 3, White House spokesmen traveling with President Reagan announced that the stop at the Bitburg cemetery would be limited to ten minutes and would include a wreath-laying ceremony. The announcement

---

[37]Marc H. Tanenbaum, "The American Jewish Committee at the White House," in Levkov, op. cit., pp. 330–334.
[38]*New York Post,* May 3, 1985; *New York Times,* May 3, 1985.
[39]*New York Times,* May 3, 1985.

came in the wake of conjecture that Reagan would not lay a wreath in order to diminish the significance of the visit. However, the White House spokesmen told the press there would be no point in going if a wreath were not laid.

The Bonn government was desperately trying to find a representative of Germans who had opposed Hitler to be present at the Bitburg cemetery. Yet, even this became a matter of controversy. Berthold von Stauffenberg, a West German army colonel whose father, Claus von Stauffenberg, had been one of the officers involved in the unsuccessful attempt to assassinate Hitler on July 20, 1944, told reporters that he would attend the ceremony only because the government had requested him to do so; personally he found the Bitburg visit "repugnant." Other relatives of resisters to Hitler simply refused to take part. Von Stauffenberg's brother, Franz Ludwig, a member of parliament in Kohl's conservative alliance, instructed his staff to decline any invitation to Bitburg. Marianne von Schwanenfeld, widow of one of the officers executed after the attempted coup, said she had no intention of "honoring the SS."

Alfred von Hofacker, whose father, Caesar, had been among the anti-Hitler plotters, participated with leaders of the American Jewish Congress in an "alternative" wreath-laying ceremony on May 3 at the Munich graves of Hans and Sophie Scholl, young students killed by the Nazis in 1943 for their resistance activities as part of the White Rose group. Also participating in the American Jewish Congress ceremony were several black leaders, including activist Dick Gregory, New York representatives Charles Rangel and Major R. Owens, and City Clerk David Dinkins of New York. At the ceremony, Henry Siegman, executive director of the American Jewish Congress, described those buried at Bitburg as "killers."[40]

This was not the only protest organized and led by American Jews on German soil on the eve of the Bitburg visit. On May 4, the Sabbath immediately preceding President Reagan's scheduled stop at the Bergen-Belsen concentration camp, a group of American Jews led by Rabbi Avraham Weiss of New York camped out in the Bergen-Belsen documentation center. On Saturday night German policemen came to remove them. In a voice cracking with emotion, Friedrich Wilhelm Thieke, a white-haired police official, told the protesters: "We have come peacefully. We have no weapons. You must leave and we have orders to escort you out."[41]

On Sunday, May 5, within a half hour after the departure of Chancellor Kohl and President Reagan, a group of 50 American Jews, many of them

---

[40]*New York Amsterdam News*, May 4, 1985; *New York Times*, May 4, 1985; *New York Post*, May 4, 1985; Henry Siegman, "To Be True to Their Cause," remarks at graves of Sophie and Hans Scholl, Munich, May 3, 1985, as quoted in Levkov, op. cit., p. 84.
[41]*New York Times*, May 7, 1985.

children of Holocaust survivors, entered Bergen-Belsen to stage their own protest demonstration at the site of the Jewish monument in the center of the camp. Menachem Rosensaft, the leader of the group, said that Reagan and Kohl "can either honor the memory of the victims of Belsen or they can honor the SS. They cannot do both."[42]

Originally, the protesters had hoped to be present at Bergen-Belsen when Reagan and Kohl entered. They had been denied permission, however, not by the Bonn government, which actually was quite helpful in trying to make the necessary arrangements, but by White House representatives. When this fact became clear, help was solicited from Democratic senators Joseph Biden of Delaware and Daniel Patrick Moynihan of New York. On Saturday, May 4, Moynihan devoted his previously scheduled national broadcast (a response to the president's weekly Saturday radio speech) to the "incredible" fact that "despite the full cooperation of the West German government, the American government has denied these American citizens the right to be present at Bergen-Belsen when our President is there, also." But all this was to no avail.

Ironically, the very White House representatives who had barred the way to the children of survivors had been desperately searching for American-Jewish and German-Jewish leaders to accompany Reagan and Kohl to Bergen-Belsen. The search proved to be in vain; not one Jewish leader was willing to participate.

President Reagan stayed at Bergen-Belsen for over an hour, while his visit to the Bitburg cemetery lasted approximately ten minutes. The wreath left at Bergen-Belsen read "From the People of the United States"; the one left at Bitburg read "From the President of the United States." Reagan's speech at the concentration camp made reference to the fact that the Jews who were buried there had died for "no reason other than their very existence."[43] Reagan quoted the Talmud and Anne Frank, who had died at Bergen-Belsen. It was an uncharacteristically somber speech for Reagan, a speech crafted with the imbroglio of the preceding months in mind. It tried to heal the wounds that had been opened up and to demonstrate that Ronald Reagan understood the unique horror that was the Holocaust.

Reagan's speech at the American air base which he visited immediately after laying the wreath at the cemetery came closest to an admission that a mistake had been made. He noted that no one could visit the cemetery "without deep and conflicting emotions. . . . This visit has stirred many emotions. . . . Some old wounds have been reopened and this I regret very much because this should be a time of healing."

---

[42]Menachem Rosensaft, "A Jew at Bergen-Belsen," in Levkov, op. cit., p. 138.
[43]Ronald Reagan, "Never Again," speech delivered at Bergen-Belsen, May 5, 1985, reprinted in Levkov, op. cit., p. 131.

Aftermath

Jewish community leaders clearly felt that now was the time for damage control and that nothing further was to be gained from continuing to criticize President Reagan. Abraham Foxman, associate national director of the Anti-Defamation League of B'nai B'rith, described Reagan in a statement issued right after the Bitburg visit as a "well-meaning American President who had demonstrated his sympathy with the Jewish people by his support of Israel, his dramatic use of the Air Force to rescue Ethiopian Jews and his outspoken support of Soviet Jewry."[44] Morris B. Abram, chairman of the National Conference on Soviet Jewry and a Reagan appointee to the U.S. Civil Rights Commission, argued in a May 10 op-ed piece in the *New York Times* that "Bitburg was the mistake of a friend—not the sin of an enemy."[45] Decidedly dissenting from this approach was Israel Singer, executive director of the World Jewish Congress, who accused key leaders of the American Jewish community of engaging in a "whitewash" and acting as "defenders" of the Reagan administration.[46]

In Germany, while the Bitburg visit certainly unleashed manifestations of anti-Semitism, it also prompted expressions of true contrition. Thus, on May 8, in a speech to the Bundestag commemorating the 40th anniversary of V-E Day, German president Richard von Weizsäcker stated: "All of us, whether guilty or not, whether old or young, must accept the past. We are all affected by its consequences and liable for it. . . . We must understand that there can be no reconciliation without remembrance."[47]

Still, it was painfully clear that reconciliation had not been achieved by the Bitburg visit. "What should have been obvious from the beginning," wrote Marvin Kalb a week after the event, "is that reconciliation is a long process—not a single photo opportunity, an event, a moment frozen in time. Bitburg, exposing clumsiness and poor political judgment in Bonn and Washington, in the process lifted the scab on dark corners of recent German history. . . ."[48]

For many Jews, the episode not only lifted the scab, it painfully reopened the wound.

---

[44]Abraham H. Foxman, "Thoughts After Bitburg," *ADL News,* reprinted in Levkov, op. cit., p. 381.
[45]*New York Times,* May 10, 1985.
[46]*Long Island Jewish World,* May 10–16, 1985.
[47]Speech by President von Weizsäcker, reprinted in Hartman, op. cit., p. 262.
[48]*New York Times,* May 14, 1985.

The Population of Reunited Jerusalem, 1967–1985

by U.O. SCHMELZ

JERUSALEM IS A CITY with a long and fascinating history, a city held sacred by three faiths. Even in the modern period, Jerusalem's religious importance has been a fundamental determinant of the city's development.

The course of Jerusalem's general and demographic evolution in the 20th century has been uneven. Prior to World War I, Jerusalem was the largest city—in terms of total and Jewish populations—of what became Mandatory Palestine. Indeed, Jerusalem had a Jewish majority among its total population going back to the second half of the 19th century. But World War I caused a great loss of inhabitants, especially Jews, due to departures and mortality. Though Jerusalem became the country's capital when Palestine was constituted as a British Mandate (1918–1948), the city's Jewish and total populations experienced lesser relative growth than Tel Aviv (and Yafo)—which overtook Jerusalem in numbers in about 1930—and Haifa. This was due to limited economic opportunities in Jerusalem and—from the Jewish standpoint—the city's location within a compact Arab region. Jerusalem had 62,700 inhabitants, including 34,100 Jews, according to the census of 1922; there were 93,100 inhabitants, including 53,800 Jews, according to the census of 1931. The last estimates of the Mandatory government put the corresponding figures at 164,400 and 99,300, as of 1946.

Israel's War of Independence in 1948 included among its important aspects the siege of the Jewish part of Jerusalem by the Arabs and the area's subsequent relief by Israeli forces. As a result of the war there was a partition into two cities—an Israeli Jerusalem and a Jordanian Jerusalem. Both sides experienced population losses through out-migration during the war. On the Jewish side, this was soon overcome when a portion of the mass of immigrants who flocked into the newly created State of Israel were directed to Jerusalem.

During the 19 years of partition, Jerusalem was Israel's official capital city. Yet, Jewish Jerusalem led an uncomfortable existence during this period, constricted as it was on three sides by an inimical armistice line that left it connected to the main body of the state by only a narrow corridor. While no Jews could live in Jordanian Jerusalem, 99 percent of Israeli Jerusalem's inhabitants were Jewish. Their number leaped from the 82,900 permanent residents—the *de facto* number was smaller—who were enumerated in November 1948, to 138,600 by 1951, in an enlarged city territory, and then to 165,000 according to the 1961 census, and an estimated 196,800 in September 1967. In 1961, 60,500 inhabitants were counted in Jordanian Jerusalem.

The Six Day War of June 1967 led to the reunification of Jerusalem and to a considerable enlargement of the municipal territory on the former Jordanian side. Thus, urban areas that had sprung up outside the narrow Jordanian city boundaries, together with a hemicycle of Arab villages, elements of a Bedouin tribe in course of sedentarization, and a camp of 1948 Arab refugees were all included in the enlarged city territory. The war led to the departure of numerous Arabs, primarily during the summer months of 1967, many of them wives and children going to join family heads elsewhere in the Middle East.

At the end of September 1967, a special census held in "East Jerusalem," i.e., the ex-Jordanian areas, counted 68,600 persons. Adding an estimate for those areas of Jerusalem that already formed part of Israel, a total population of 267,800 is arrived at, including 196,800 (73.5 percent) Jews. Had it not been for the enlargement of the city territory on the ex-Jordanian side, the proportion of Jews would have amounted to 81 percent. Since the 1967 census, the whole of enlarged Jerusalem has been included in the official statistics of Israel's population.

This article will describe the sociodemographic characteristics of Jerusalem between 1967 and 1985, with emphasis on data from the population census of 1983. The article forms part of a larger study of Jerusalem's demographic evolution since the middle of the 19th century.*

Israel's Population, 1967–1985

The general evolution of population in Israel during 1967–1985 provides the framework for an examination of the specific evolution in Jerusalem. Between September 1967 and the end of 1985, the total population of Israel rose from 2,765,000 to 4,266,000 (i.e., by about 1,500,000, or 54 percent) and the Jewish population from 2,374,000 to 3,517,000 (i.e., by 1,143,000, or 48 percent (table 1).[1] The number of non-Jews in the state experienced an abrupt increase because of the addition of East Jerusalem, rising from 312,000 at the end of 1966 to 391,000 in September 1967, and then grew

---

*Part of the research was carried out at the Hebrew University's Institute of Contemporary Jewry. The author wishes to thank Judith Even, Nitza Genuth, and Arin Poller for their assistance. The whole study will be published as volume 20 in the Jewish Population Studies series of the Institute of Contemporary Jewry (in conjunction with the Jerusalem Institute for Israel Studies).

[1]See Appendix for tables.

gradually to 749,000 in 1985 (i.e., by another 92 percent). The annual growth rates were 2.4 percent for the total population, 2.2 percent for Jews, and 3.6 percent for non-Jews. Categorized by religion, the latter are almost exclusively Muslims, Christians, and Druze.

JEWS

After 1967 the number of Israel's Jews grew, primarily owing to natural increase. The striking fertility differential that existed in Israel in the mid-1950s between Asian-African Jews and European Jews had by 1985 virtually disappeared. While the Asian-African Jews rapidly reduced their fertility, European Jews slightly raised theirs, thus constituting an exception to the great fertility decline that swept over the developed countries beginning in the 1960s. The current fertility of Israel's total Jews—an average of 2.8 children per woman (regardless of marital status)—markedly exceeds not only that of Diaspora Jews but also the levels observed among the general populations of developed countries. The level suffices for natural increase to a not insubstantial extent—1.4 percent in recent years. With regard to patterns of nuptiality, fertility, and very low mortality, similar levels have beeen attained between the two previously diverse major origin groups of Israel's Jews, more so than in many other spheres. It should be noted that above 20 percent of recent marriages between Jews are origin-mixed in respect to these two major groups.

About half a million Jews immigrated to Israel during 1967–1985, of whom nearly 80 percent came from Europe-America, about 165,000 from the Soviet Union alone.[2] In recent years, however, owing to the virtual stoppage of Jewish departures from the USSR, immigration has been at a very low level (minor spurts such as refugees from Ethiopia notwithstanding). Nor is any real change likely, unless large numbers of Jews are again allowed to leave the Soviet Union—and on the further condition that they actually come to Israel and do not opt for other destinations—or that *aliyah* (immigration) increases significantly from the free and affluent countries of the West. The external migration balance—immigrants minus emigrants—of Israel's Jews during the whole span 1967–1985 amounted to about 285,000, but has been small in the most recent years.

NON-JEWS

The rapid growth of Israel's non-Jewish population has been essentially due to high natural increase, though the addition of East Jerusalem and, later, of the Golan Druze has contributed as well. The migration balance

---

[2]The entire Soviet Union is classified under "Europe" in Israel's official immigration statistics.

of all non-Jews in Israel is close to nil. Their mortality is low, thanks to Israel's well-developed health services. A conspicuous difference has long prevailed between the high fertility of Muslims and Druze, on the one hand, and the rather low fertility of Christians, on the other, though the latter, too, are overwhelmingly Arab. The average fertility of Muslims reached peaks above 9 children per woman in the 1960s, but has dropped with dramatic speed since the 1970s—it is already below 5 and still decreasing. This momentous change can be attributed to the replacement, in the reproductive age groups, of the generation born in the Mandatory period by that born since the establishment of Israel. This turnover of generations has been accompanied by, among many other things, a substantial rise in education, in which women have also participated. Whereas the natural increase of Israeli Muslims was 4.5 percent on average in the 1960s and that of all non-Jews above 4 percent, the corresponding figures for 1985 were only 3.1 and 2.9 percent, respectively. Despite this strong reduction, however, the natural increase of Israel's non-Jews is still twice as high as that of Jews. But the differential continues to narrow.

The non-Jewish population of Israel is now distributed as follows: Muslims—77 percent; Christians—13 percent; and Druze—10 percent. The relative share of Christians is slowly shrinking due to their smaller natural increase.

Since the termination of massive Jewish immigration and partly also due to the incorporation of East Jerusalem, the proportion of Jews in Israel's total population receded from 88 percent in 1966 to 82 percent in 1985.

The Arabs in the administered areas still have relatively high fertility and natural increase, but—unlike the Arabs in the state territory of Israel—they have a long-standing tendency to emigrate for economic reasons. (Since 1967, nationalistic motives have also played a role in this regard.) This emigration slows down their population growth, one result being that the proportion of Jews in the entire territory of what was Mandatory Palestine has remained about 63–64 percent throughout the period 1967–1985.

General Evolution of Jerusalem

Within the general Israeli framework, reunited and enlarged Jerusalem, with a 1985 population above 450,000, is a widespread city with an area of more than 100 square kilometers. Since 1967 intensive building activity has taken place, decisively changing the townscape. Most evident are the large-scale public-housing projects for Jews on the perimeter of the new municipal territory, but there has also been a great deal of building by Arabs. Movement is now free and unfettered to and from Jerusalem in all directions within Israel and the administered areas. The latter are legally and administratively distinct, but there are no limitations to the flow of persons and goods, nor any control posts on the road. This is both practically and psychologically important for Jerusalem, which is situated along the previous armistice line, at a junction between territories inhabited predominantly either by Jews or Arabs.

Jerusalem's traditional geographic handicap of inland location in a mountainous terrain has become less important in an age of good roads and fast traffic. As the nation's capital, Jerusalem functions as a center for public services, in addition to being a holy city and tourist attraction of international renown. Yet, the comparative deficiency of other economic branches remains a source of obvious weakness for Jerusalem's economy.

Coexistence of diverse groups continues to be the rule in Jerusalem's population and society, but the practical expressions of it are now somewhat modified, compared to late Mandatory times. There is more economic cooperation between Jews and Arabs, both in the exchange of goods and services and in the employment of Arabs by Jews. (Jews are not hired by Arabs, however.) Residential separation between religious groups, which is an age-old practice in the Levant, continues to predominate in Jerusalem as between Jews and Arabs, as well as between Christians and Muslims. In the Mandatory period, huge separate zones of Arabs and Jews crystallized, practically bisecting the city before its actual partition during 1948–1967. Since 1967 a pattern of alternating medium-sized areas has formed in the ex-Jordanian zone, each of which is inhabited almost exclusively by people of one group or another.

Among Jews, the earlier tendency in the direction of separate residential location for people from a particular geographical region abroad has been much reduced and is largely confined to long-established and rather poor families, especially their older members. A growing portion of the Jewish population, particularly among the younger generation, lives in large housing projects or smaller condominiums, regardless of family origin. For this segment, it is life-style and financial means that determine residential location in the modern parts of the city. Some overlap still exists between those categorized as living in less privileged surroundings and being of Asian-African origin, reflecting the socioeconomic conditions of many of the immigrants who came from Asia-Africa in the first two decades of the state. Another long-existing social and residential differentiation—that between the ultra-Orthodox and other Jews—is assuming increased prominence in Jerusalem, with the growing ultra-Orthodox subpopulation expanding its accustomed residential areas and establishing itself in new ones.

Physically, Jerusalem's Arabs live at a distance from other Arabs in the state territory of Israel but are surrounded by those of Judea, in the administered areas. Culturally, they are in an intermediate position: they have lived in the Israeli context and have been exposed to Israeli influences for a shorter time than other Arabs in Israel—only since 1967—but they are more intensively exposed to those influences than are the Arabs of the administered areas. By now half of Jerusalem's Arab residents have been born under Israeli administration. Since its reunification, Jerusalem has had by far the largest population of Arabs, and, among them, of Muslims, of any town in the state territory of Israel.

Jerusalem's sphere of influence has widened as modern transportation has diminished the importance of distances in a small country like Israel. In particular, Jerusalem is now the nucleus of what amounts functionally to a metropolitan area, or rather two such areas that partly overlap. The one consists of the Jewish satellite towns and settlements in the former "corridor" to the west, as well as in Judea and parts of Samaria, which are closely linked to the city. The other consists of the Arab towns and villages in Judea which do the following: look to the Arab sector in Jerusalem as their own major urban center; find in the Jewish sector of the city important suppliers of goods and services, as well as customers and employers; and have recourse to governmental or Jewish institutions (e.g., hospitals) in Jerusalem.

Population Dynamics in Jerusalem

The main sources of demographic data on the population of Jerusalem and Israel since 1967 are the following: the national censuses of May 1972 and June 1983,[3] including special tabulations which the author prepared from the data files deposited with the Hebrew University;[4] and statistics of vital events, internal migration, and immigration, as well as up-dated estimates, all prepared by the Israel Central Bureau of Statistics.[5] With special reference to Jerusalem are the following: the census of East Jerusalem, conducted in September 1967,[6] and special studies which the author made of fertility of Jews according to degree of religiosity.[7] The data in the

---

[3]See the publications of the Israel Central Bureau of Statistics, issued bilingually in Hebrew and English: *Census of Population and Housing 1972*, 17 vols.; *1983 Census of Population and Housing*, publication in progress. Numerous ultra-Orthodox Jews in Jerusalem refused to be enumerated in both these censuses, but a part of the data for them could be supplemented from other sources.

[4]Marked as such in the statistical tables of this article.

[5]See the publications of the Israel Central Bureau of Statistics, issued bilingually in Hebrew and English: the data are summarized annually in *Statistical Abstract of Israel;* specific publications are issued on vital statistics, immigration, etc.; see also *Population in Localities 30 V 1977* (Special Publication no. 673).

[6]Israel Central Bureau of Statistics, *East Jerusalem: Census of Population and Housing 1967*, 2 vols. (Hebrew and English).

[7]See the articles by U.O. Schmelz: "Fertility of Jewish Women in the Metropolitan Areas of Israel, 1972," in U.O. Schmelz and G. Nathan (eds.), *Studies in the Population of Israel in Honor of Roberto Bachi* (Jerusalem, 1986), Scripta Hierosolymitana, vol. 30; "Religiosity and Fertility Among Israel's Jews," in U.O. Schmelz and S. DellaPergola (eds.), *Papers in Jewish Demography 1985*, forthcoming.

statistical tables appearing in this article are taken from the above-mentioned official sources (including some unpublished figures), unless stated otherwise.

The demography of Israel at the beginning of this period is described in Roberto Bachi's *The Population of Israel* (Jerusalem, 1977). Accounts of the demography of Jerusalem are contained in several articles written by the author.[8]

RELIGIOUS GROUPS

The growth of major religious groups in Jerusalem between September 1967 and the end of 1985 can be seen from table 2. During that period the Jewish population grew more rapidly in Jerusalem than in the other two main cities (Tel Aviv and Haifa), their conurbations,* or the whole state (table 3). Accordingly, Jerusalem's share among all Jews in Israel increased somewhat from 8.3 percent in 1967 to 9.3 percent in 1985. This marked a reversal of the trend that had seen the continued reduction of Jerusalem's proportion during the Mandatory period and the first two decades of the state. Muslims, due to their high natural increase, grew relatively more than the other population groups in Jerusalem. The doubling of their size in the city during 1967–1985 corresponded to their rate of increase in the whole of Israel. The number of Christians in Jerusalem declined for some time after 1967 but then reversed itself, and is now back at the 1961 level (for both zones of the formerly partitioned city added together). In 1985 Jerusalem accounted for the following shares among Israel's population: total— 10.7 percent; Jews—9.3 percent; Muslims—20.0 percent; and Christians— 14.3 percent. (There are hardly any Druze in Jerusalem.) The city's proportion among Israel's total population increased from 9.7 percent in September 1967 to 10.7 percent at the end of 1985.

With regard to the characteristics and behavioral patterns of Muslims and Christians in Jerusalem, the influences of specific subgroups should be noted. Jerusalem's Muslims now include many ex-villagers whose localities were incorporated into the enlarged city territory in 1967, but whose adaptation to urban standards could not be other than gradual. In contrast, Jerusalem's Christian population includes a number of non-Arabs of considerable educational attainments, some of them ecclesiastical personnel, who are demographically atypical.

---

[8]See the articles by U.O. Schmelz: "Jerusalem's Jewish Population in the Decade Since the City's Reunification," in U.O. Schmelz, P. Glikson, and S. DellaPergola (eds.), *Papers in Jewish Demography* (Jerusalem, 1977), pp. 379–397; "Demography of Muslims and Christians in Jerusalem," *Hamizrah Hehadash*, vol. 28, no. 1–2, 1979, pp. 39–73 (Hebrew); "A United Jerusalem: Demographic Characteristics of the Main Population Groups," in A. Shmueli, D. Grossman, and R. Zeevy (eds.), *Judea and Samaria* (Jerusalem, 1977), pp. 467–478 (Hebrew).

*Conurbation: a metropolitan area.

It is generally agreed that nearly all of Jerusalem's Muslims are Arabs, but this is not the case with Christians. A rough estimate of the proportion of Arabs among the city's Christians can be obtained from the 1983 census data on language use. In the census, 68 percent of the Christian residents of Jerusalem aged 15 and over reported Arabic as their principal spoken language and can therefore be considered, virtually without exception, to be Arabs. Since the proportion of Arabs must be greater among Christian children than among Christian adults—because of the Arabs' greater fertility and the immigration of non-Arab adults (e.g., religious functionaries)—the proportion of Arabs among all Christians in Jerusalem is apparently above 70 percent.

Jerusalem is once again the city in Israel with both the largest total and Jewish populations. Jerusalem overtook Haifa in 1967; it outpaced Tel Aviv-Yafo around 1975 in total population size and in 1984 in the number of Jews. Population size in the city of Haifa has been almost stationary since the early 1970s, and the growth of the Haifa conurbation has also been moderate. The population of the city of Tel Aviv-Yafo has been slowly but steadily shrinking since the mid-1960s, due to persistent suburbanization involving residential moves to the surrounding towns. By contrast, by 1985 the conurbation of Tel Aviv—according to the wider delimitation adopted for the 1983 census—comprised 38 percent of Israel's total population and as many as 45 percent of Israel's Jews.

COMPONENTS OF POPULATION CHANGE

Table 4 analyzes the components of change in population size, and presents average annual rates for three subperiods of the entire span 1967–1985. Throughout these years Jews experienced stronger growth in Jerusalem than in the whole country and the two conurbations, especially that of Haifa, and the differences widened in the course of time. This was essentially due to higher rates of birth and natural increase in Jerusalem, which remained rather stable in the city, while declining somewhat in Israel as a whole and more markedly in the two conurbations. By 1983–1985 the natural increase of Jews in Jerusalem was twice as high as that in the Tel Aviv conurbation and three times as high as that in the Haifa conurbation.

The mortality of all Israel's Jews is very low in international comparison. The death rate for Jews per 1,000 of their population (all ages together) is now even lower in Jerusalem than in the other mentioned locations[9] because of the younger age composition of Jerusalem's Jews.

---

[9]The term "locations" is used here in comparing Tel Aviv and Haifa (these cities alone or with their surrounding areas) and total Israel with Jerusalem.

Around 1970 the external migration balance was still important for Jewish population growth, and Jerusalem's relative increment thereof corresponded to that in the whole country. This was unlike the situation in previous decades when the city absorbed a smaller proportion of new immigrants than its share in Israel's Jewish population. The special appeal of reunited Jerusalem attracted immigrants, including those from Western countries. Over the last decade, however, *aliyah* has been no more than a secondary factor with regard to population growth in Jerusalem, as in Israel as a whole. Another change from the past was that, in the first decade after reunification, Jerusalem had a positive balance of internal migration vis-à-vis other localities in Israel, because of the transfer of certain government offices to the capital and generally improved conditions in the city. However, in the last ten years Jerusalem's internal migration balance has again become somewhat negative, though with a significant difference as compared with the past. In the earlier period it was the economic advantages in the coastal belt, particularly in Tel Aviv and its surrounding areas, that drained Jewish population away from Jerusalem. At present, a large segment of the out-migrants, especially young couples, move to satellite towns and smaller settlements in Judea and Samaria, some of which are just beyond the municipal boundaries, as part of a process of suburbanization to what are primarily dormitory localities. This reduces the growth in the number of inhabitants of Jerusalem proper, while furthering the processes of metropolitanization.

In the past decade, the not inconsiderable net growth of Jews in the municipal territory of Jerusalem—slightly above 2 percent per annum—has been entirely due to natural increase, whereas the overall migratory balance has been nil. Not only has the balance of the internal migrations of Jews within Israel been smaller, relative to population, in Jerusalem than in the Tel Aviv conurbation, but the volume (i.e., the sum of entrances and departures) has also been relatively lower in Jerusalem than in the two conurbations and the whole of Israel.

Non-Jews in Jerusalem, most of whom are Muslims, show greater natural increase than Jews, but the differential has narrowed from 36 versus 22 per 1,000 of population in 1972–1975 to 28 versus 22 in 1983–1985. The birthrate of Jerusalem's Jews has fluctuated at about 28 per 1,000 of population, whereas that of the city's non-Jews has declined from 44 to 32 in that interval. However, the relative drop in the death rate of the city's non-Jews has been even more striking—from at least 11 per 1,000 in the quinquennium after the city's reunification, and still 8 in 1972–1975, to only 4 by 1983–1985. The current death rate of Jerusalem's non-Jews is the same as that which prevails among Israel's non-Jews generally, and is, paradoxically, in both instances markedly lower than that of Jews, in consequence of the non-Jews' much younger age structure. The registered infant mortality rate of non-Jews in Jerusalem was reduced from 68 per 1,000 live-born in 1972 to 21 by 1984.

The birthrate of Muslims declined from 47 per 1,000 of population in 1972–1975 to 36 in 1982–1984, and that of Christians from 22 to 15. Over the same years the death rate of Muslims dropped from 7 to 4 per 1,000 of population and that of the Christians from 11 to 9. This last figure, which is comparatively high, is indicative of aging among the Christian population in Jerusalem (see below). Analysis of the 1967 census suggests that, in the preceding years, of 1,000 Muslim newborn in East Jerusalem, 177 had died before reaching age 5; the corresponding figure for Christians was 131. In 1973–1975 the registered infant-mortality rates (deaths in the first year of life) for these communities were down to 54 and 26 per 1,000 live-born, respectively, and by 1982–1984 to only 21 and 15, compared to 11 among Jewish infants in Jerusalem.

FERTILITY

The substantial birthrate of Jerusalem's Jews has been due to their relatively elevated fertility level, which has been consistently higher than that in the whole country and especially that in Tel Aviv and Haifa. This is the case not only with regard to the total Jewish population but also when comparisons are made by region of birth (table 5). In this regard, interesting changes have taken place. For a long period the fertility ranking by birth region among Jews in Palestine/Israel was as follows: Asian-African-born; Israeli-born; and European-born. A fertility differential clearly existed between the Asian-African-born and the European-born, though on a generally diminishing scale, while the Israeli-born (who are of mixed origin) occupied an intermediate position, reflecting the tendency toward convergence. Beginning in the 1950s the fertility of the Israeli-born actually began to approach that of the European-born, at first because most were themselves of European origin and later for social reasons. This pattern continues to prevail in Israel as a whole, as well as in Tel Aviv and Haifa. In contrast, the fertility ranking in Jerusalem had changed by 1983, with the Israeli-born coming first, the European-born next, though at a considerable distance, and the Asian-African-born, last. In 1983 the total fertility rates (TFRs)[10] in Jerusalem of Israeli-born Jewish women whose fathers were born, respectively, in Israel or Europe stood as high as 4.37 and 4.23 children on

---

[10]"Total fertility rate" indicates the average number of children that a woman would bear during her lifetime if the age-specific fertility rates remained the same as in the year(s) under consideration. Under conditions of very low mortality, the "replacement level" is 2.1 children per woman (regardless of marital status).

average, while Israeli-born women with Asian-African fathers attained only 3.47. The main explanation lies in the greater fertility of very religious Jews, particularly the ultra-Orthodox,[11] and their strong representation in Jerusalem, especially among Jews of European birth or parentage, as well as among the Israeli-born whose fathers were also born in the country.

The striking fertility differences among Jerusalem's Jews according to degree of religiosity (when women's origin and age are controlled) and the high average levels of cumulative number of births attained by very religious women at ages 30–34 are illustrated in table 6, based on the results of three specific studies.[12] The data sugest that the completed fertility of the very religious was about 6 children, at least twice that of Jews of low religiosity. It was mainly this fact and the frequency of the ultra-Orthodox in Jerusalem which raised the fertility level of the city's total Jews by almost 30 percent above that in the whole of Israel, as of 1983. The data also seem to point to a rising fertility trend among the very religious of European origin.

According to the 1967 census of East Jerusalem, the average completed fertility of 45–49-year-old married women was as follows: Muslim—9.7; Christian—6.0. The total fertility rate of all Muslim women in Jerusalem amounted to 7.5 in 1972, but only 4.9 in 1983; the corresponding figures for all Christians (Arabs and others) were 2.8 in 1972, but merely 1.8—i.e., below replacement level—in 1983. Thus, the fertility of Muslims and total non-Jews in Jerusalem, as in the whole of Israel, is now below that of the very religious Jews in Jerusalem, while Christian fertility in Israel and especially in Jerusalem falls short of that of total Jews.

Demographic Characteristics

COUNTRIES OF BIRTH AND ORIGIN

The percentage of Israeli-born among Jews continues to be greater in Jerusalem than in the whole state, or in Tel Aviv and Haifa, or in the entire conurbations of these two cities (table 7). However, the respective differences have narrowed. By 1983, 63 percent of Jerusalem's Jews were native-born. This proportion is continually increasing, particularly since *aliyah* is low at present. Of Jerusalem's Israeli-born Jews, 38 percent, considerably

---

[11]For the ultra-Orthodox, see the discussion below.
[12]Ecological studies for 1970–1974 and 1983, respectively, compared fertility in areas of varying religiosity in Jerusalem, as indicated by the percentages of votes cast for religious parties in parliamentary elections. An interview study of maternity cases, conducted in 1975–1976 by Professors M. Davis and S. Harlap, made it possible to investigate differential fertility according to selected religious behaviors (e.g., woman going to the *mikveh*, husband being a yeshivah student or rabbi). Cf. footnote 7.

more than in the other mentioned locations, had fathers who were also born in the country; they constituted 24 percent of Jerusalem's total Jews. In contrast, the proportion of the foreign-born is generally receding, owing to the substantial level of natural increase among Jews in Israel, especially in Jerusalem, and the great reduction in *aliyah*. The latter reason applies with particular force to the Asian-African-born, who have been a minority of *olim* (immigrants) during the last two decades. In 1972, the Asian-African-born were still a slight majority of the foreign-born Jews in Jerusalem, but a minority in the whole state and especially in the two conurbations. By 1983, owing to the preponderantly European-American provenance of the immigration since 1972, the Asian-African-born had turned into a minority among the foreign-born in all the locations mentioned, and their proportions were rather similar in Jerusalem, the Tel Aviv conurbation, and the whole state, though far smaller in the Haifa conurbation.

Table 7 also shows the geographical origin of Jews, i.e., their distribution according to personal birth region of the foreign-born or father's birth region for the Israeli-born. However, "Israeli origin"—i.e., the Israeli-born whose fathers were also born in the country—is really an indeterminate group (since the censuses did not ask about birthplace of grandfather). If it is set aside and origin is examined only for the two generations for which it could be geographically ascertained from the census—the foreign-born and the Israeli-born whose fathers were born abroad—we find that in 1983 the Asian-African-origin group exceeded the European group[13] in Jerusalem and the whole of Israel, but not in the Tel Aviv and Haifa conurbations. By 1983 the Europeans had surpassed in numbers the Asian-Africans among *foreign-born* Jews in Jerusalem—as in the Mandatory period and unlike in 1961 and 1972—but Europeans remained a minority according to *origin,* because of their lower fertility in the past. Jews who were born in Asia or were of Asian origin continued to be more numerous in Jerusalem than corresponding Jews from Africa.

The relative share of persons born in Central and Western Europe or America among all the European-American-born Jews continued to be much greater in Jerusalem than in the other locations. In 1983 the breakdown was as follows: Jerusalem—54 percent; Tel Aviv conurbation—24 percent; Haifa conurbation—21 percent; and State of Israel—28 percent.

Table 8 illustrates the present heterogeneity of Jerusalem's and Israel's Jewish population with regard to geographical origin. The following

---

[13]Jews from America (or Australia) have been relatively few in numbers in Palestine/Israel, especially prior to the Six Day War, and most have themselves been of European extraction. Therefore they are usually grouped together with Jews from Europe in the available statistics. When, for simplicity's sake, the text of this article refers to "European Jews," American Jews are meant to be included.

countries of birth each accounted for more than 5 percent of the foreign-born Jews in Jerusalem, according to the 1983 census: Morocco—14.2 percent; USSR—11.7 percent; North America and Oceania—10.5 percent; Iraq—8.8 percent; Rumania—7.3 percent; Iran—7.2 percent; and Poland —7.1 percent. All these countries recurred with a representation of at least 5 percent in the origin distribution of both the foreign-born and the Israeli-born with foreign-born fathers. In comparing countries of origin of the Israeli-born with birth countries of the foreign-born, the above-mentioned Asian-African countries had augmented frequencies, whereas the USSR, Rumania, and North America-Oceania had reduced frequencies. This can be explained by differences in the proportions of Israeli-born—due to disparities in length of residence in Israel and past fertility—among those originating in the two groups of countries.

The frequency distribution of countries of birth and origin of Jews in Jerusalem largely corresponded to that in the whole of Israel, except that the latter included Yemen (above 5 percent only according to origin) but did not include either Iran or North America and Oceania. While Jews born in North America-Oceania amounted to only 2.6 percent of all the foreign-born in Israel, they were as many as 10.5 percent of the foreign-born in Jerusalem. By contrast, Polish and Rumanian Jews were far less represented in Jerusalem than in Israel as a whole.

Foreign-born Jews are differentiated not only by countries/continents of birth and their correlates—e.g., fertility and educational attainment (see below)—but also by years of immigration (table 9). The difference between time of arrival and any later date, e.g., that of a census, indicates the remaining immigrants' duration of stay in Israel. Since its reunification, Jerusalem has exercised a special attraction for new immigrants; consequently, they have formed a larger share of all foreign-born Jews there than in the other two main cities and the respective conurbations, or in Israel as a whole. This applies to arrivals since 1965 in the censuses of both 1972 and 1983. For every 100 foreign-born Jews in Israel in 1983, the proportions of those who had arrived only since 1965 were 23 and 25 percent, respectively, in the conurbations of Tel Aviv and Haifa, 27 percent in total Israel, but as high as 38 percent in Jerusalem. The most recent immigrants, those who had arrived during the time span 1980–May 1983, accounted for 3.6 percent of Israel's Jewish population and 8.2 percent of Jerusalem's. In keeping with the general composition of the immigrants since 1965 by provenance, 81 percent of the post-1965 arrivals who resided in Jerusalem in 1983 had come from Europe or America. Conversely, immigrants who had come since 1965 constituted nearly 54 percent of all the European-American-born in Jerusalem as compared to only 22 percent of all the African-born, and 13 percent of all the Asian-born. In Jerusalem, as of 1983, 58 percent of the Asian-born had arrived during 1948–1954, and 74 percent of the African-born during 1948–1964.

AGE

The age structure of Muslims in Jerusalem, as in Israel as a whole, is younger than that of Jews. In turn, the age composition of Jews in Jerusalem is younger than that of Christians in the city and the whole country, as well as Jews in Israel and in the two conurbations. This can be easily seen from table 10 by comparing the median ages of the various populations. In all the populations presented in that table, the median age rose somewhat from 1972 to 1983. This was largely due, especially among Jerusalem's Jews, to a diminished proportion in ages 15–24 and an augmented one in ages 25–34. Many of those who were around age 20 in 1972, and thus around age 30 in 1983, had been born about 1950, when the natural increase of Asian-African Jews was very high and European Jews were experiencing a baby boom. In contrast, those who were around age 20 in 1983 were born about 1960, when the natural increase of Jews was generally lower. In 1972 and 1983, the proportion (31–32 percent) of children aged 0–14 among Jerusalem's Jews had shrunk somewhat, as compared to earlier periods, but continued to be larger than in the other mentioned locations. Unlike in the past, Jerusalem's proportion of elderly (aged 65+) was smaller than in the rest of Israel, though it rose a little, as it did generally in the country—in Jerusalem, from 7.4 percent in 1972 to 8.7 percent in 1983. The dependency ratio among Jerusalem's Jews—i.e., the ratio of young dependents (aged 0–19) plus elderly (65+) to the number of persons in the productive ages (20–64)—increased from 95 per 100 in 1972 to 98 per 100 in 1983. This rise was similar to that for Israel's total Jews, but the actual ratios were somewhat higher in Jerusalem.

Israeli-born Jews as a group are much younger than the foreign-born, since any children born in Israel to the latter are classified among the Israeli-born. The age composition of the foreign-born in Israel is thus influenced not only by their own ages at arrival, but also by the duration of their stay in Israel. A group that receives few migratory reinforcements must age rapidly, since its Israeli-born children are not classified together with their parents, and because of the cumulative effects of mortality and emigration. If the four main origin groups of Jews (combining the foreign-born and Israeli-born) are compared, the Israeli-origin group is by far the youngest—58 percent children below age 15 in Jerusalem in 1983—because it is composed of Israeli-born persons only. The Asian- and especially the African-origin groups are younger than the European-, in accordance with the former's greater fertility in the past. The proportions of the origin groups among Jews vary with age. Israeli origin is most represented among children—44 percent at ages 0–14 in Jerusalem as of 1983. Conversely, persons of European origin account for a large share of the elderly—63 percent at ages 65 and over in Jerusalem as of 1983. Altogether, 93 percent of the 0–14-year-old Jewish children in the city were Israeli-born (regardless of origin).

Similarly, the proportions of the religious groups—Jewish, Muslim, and Christian—vary with age, in keeping with their different levels of fertility and migration. In Jerusalem, as of 1983, Jews formed 71 percent of the total population, but only 64 percent of the children and as many as 83 percent of the elderly. The corresponding figures for Muslims were 25 percent, 33 percent, and 12 percent, respectively, while for Christians they were 3.3 percent, 2.4 percent, and 4.6 percent. The age composition of Muslims is similarly young in Jerusalem and in the whole of Israel, whereas Christians are more aged in Jerusalem than in Israel as a whole (median ages of 29.4 and 23.8 years, respectively, in 1983).

The demographic characteristics of Jerusalem's total population are, of course, weighted averages of those of the city's Jews and non-Jews, respectively, and, with regard to the latter, especially, of the predominant Muslims. In terms of age structure, Jerusalem's population as a whole is more youthful than that of local Jews, but less so than that of the Muslims.

SEX

The sex composition of all Jews in Jerusalem, the conurbations of Tel Aviv and Haifa, and the whole of Israel, as well as of all Muslims in Jerusalem, was fairly balanced (49–51 percent males) as of 1983; only Christians had a marked surplus of women in Jerusalem, as they did in the whole state (table 11). There was a surplus of boys among the children of all these populations, according to the biologically determined sex ratio at the time of birth.[14] Similarly, the surplus of women among the elderly that was found in all the populations compared has an essentially biological foundation in the age-specifically lower mortality of females. Among adults aged 15–64, the excess of women in all the Jewish groups compared was slight, but marked among the Christians. The excess of adult Christian women, especially among the elderly in Jerusalem, is probably due to greater out-migration of men in the past and some in-migration of women,[15] as well. The absolute differences were 5,651 women to 4,410 men among all Jerusalem Christians aged 15 and over in 1983. The majority of the

---

[14]Slightly more boys than girls are born in human populations, so that one usually finds a male surplus among children.

[15]Including the wives of some religiously mixed immigrant couples.

Israeli-born Jews in Jerusalem were males (51.4 percent as of 1983), since nearly half of them were children below age 15; in contrast, foreign-born Jews, who were overwhelmingly adults and included 21 percent elderly, had a minority (47.2 percent) of males.

MARITAL STATUS

Regarding marital status (ages 15 and over), in 1983 the proportions of single persons of both sexes in different population groups ranked in the following ascending order: Jews in Israel; Jews in Jerusalem; Muslims and Christians in Jerusalem (table 12). The proportions of the currently married tended to diminish inversely. Two major determinants operate directly in this context: age structure and marriage patterns (the propensity to marry and age at first marriage). There were relatively more single persons among the enumerated Jews in Jerusalem than in the whole state, both in 1972 and 1983, because their age composition was younger and because they married later and were somewhat more likely to not marry at all. This can be seen from their lower sex-age-specific proportions of ever-married persons, especially among women, in table 13. Generally, there has been some rise in marriage age and some decrease in the propensity for marriage among Israel's Jews since the late 1970s. The greater proportion of highly educated persons in Jerusalem (see below), as well as opportunities for professional and clerical jobs in public services in the city, which give economic independence to many young women, have perhaps influenced the reduction in the age-specific proportions of the ever-married that has been observable among Jews there.[16]

It may seem paradoxical that the sex-age-specific proportions of the ever-married among Jews declined from 1972 to 1983 among Jews in Jerusalem, as in the whole of Israel (table 13), while some reduction took place in the overall share of single persons among adult Jews in each sex (table 12), meaning that the overall share of the ever-married actually rose. The apparent contradiction is explainable by shifts in age composition, especially with regard to the principal marriageable ages, between approximately 20 and 30 (see above). In Jerusalem, had the age composition of 1972 remained unchanged, the percent single among all Jewish men would have risen to 37.8 percent by 1983; instead, the percent single actually shrank from 35.4 percent to 34.6 percent. Similarly, the corresponding figures for Jewish women in Jerusalem were 28.3 percent in 1972 and 26.6 percent in 1983, but the proportion single rises to 30.5 percent for the latter year when the data are age-standardized.

---

[16]The underrepresentation of the ultra-Orthodox in population censuses (cf. footnote 3) must be remembered in this context. The marriage age of the ultra-Orthodox is low.

The larger proportions of single persons among the Muslims of Jerusalem, compared to the Jews, were decisively due to younger age composition, since the Muslims' marriage age was earlier than that of the Jews (which factor operated in the opposite direction). About 1983, the marriage age of Muslim women was even lower in Jerusalem, despite its urban character, than in the whole of Israel. Among the populations here compared, Christians in Jerusalem had the highest shares of single persons, the aging of their population notwithstanding (cf. table 10). This was due to later marriage age and to the unusual frequency of permanent celibacy among clergy, monks and nuns, and other religiously minded Christians who spurned marriage.

HOUSEHOLD SIZE

The average number of persons per private household was greater in the Jewish population of Jerusalem than in the whole state and the conurbations of Tel Aviv and Haifa. In a comparison by religion, average household size in Jerusalem was in the following descending order: Muslims; Christians; Jews (table 14). Greater household size is strongly connected with high fertility, though other factors—such as age structure of the population, marriage age of the younger generation, and patterns of coresidence—also play a role. Recorded household size generally decreased between the 1972 and 1983 censuses—except among Jerusalem's Muslims—but this was in part due to a downward bias in the 1983 census results (caused by a change in the enumeration technique). Whereas households of 6 or more persons were a limited minority among Jewish households, they still were 56 percent of all Muslim households in Jerusalem as of 1983. On the other hand, one-person households have been relatively more numerous among Jerusalem's Jews and Christians than among the city's Muslims and Israel's total Jews.

For all the religious groups of Jerusalem, average household size increases with age of household head up to a peak at about ages 40–49, due to family formation and growth; at later ages of the household head it decreases, because of residential separation of grown-up children and eventual instances of widowhood. Households in Jerusalem headed by women are a minority; in 1983 they were found in the following proportions: total population—22 percent; Jews—23 percent; Muslims—15 percent; and Christians—33 percent. Among Jews, average household size was greatest if the head was born in Asia or Africa (averages of 3.8–3.9 persons) and lowest for the European-born (2.7). This difference was due mainly to the much greater fertility of the former group in the past, but it was also influenced by disparities in the age distribution of the respective household heads. At any rate, the difference has considerably narrowed in the course of time.

As a religious and educational center, Jerusalem has comparatively greater percentages of persons who live in institutions than is usual in Israel; the 1983 figures for Jerusalem were as follows: total population—4.5 percent; Jews—5.4 percent; Muslims—1.2 percent; and Christians—9.7 percent.

Sociocultural Characteristics

EDUCATION

Jerusalem's Jews formerly comprised greater proportions both of illiterates and of highly educated persons than the Jews of Tel Aviv, Haifa, and Israel as a whole. The first difference has disappeared: in 1983 the percentage of Jews with 0–4 years of schooling was even slightly lower in Jerusalem than in the other locations. However, a considerably greater share of highly educated persons among Jerusalem's Jews persists (table 15). It is connected in part with the prominence of public services in the city, since the professional positions, and by now usually the upper positions in administrative services, require higher education.

There has been great educational progress in Jerusalem generally, as in Israel as a whole, over the past 20–25 years. The percentage of adults in Jerusalem with 0–4 years of schooling dropped from 1961 (1967 for non-Jews) to 1972 and 1983, as follows: Jews—19 percent, 11 percent, and 7 percent; Muslims—50 percent, 44 percent, and 27 percent; and Christians—25 percent, 26 percent, and 11 percent. Conversely, the share of persons with 13 or more years of study rose as follows: Jews—19 percent, 26 percent, and 35 percent; Muslims—4 percent, 5 percent, and 13 percent; and Christians—10 percent, 12 percent, and 27 percent.

Educational attainment is, on the whole, inversely related to age, since there has been a marked trend toward improved education for the young over time. However, the proviso must be added that the almost complete shares of persons with 13+ years of schooling—and even more so with 16 + years or academic degrees—are reached only after age 30. Changes in the educational distribution of an adult population are slowed down by the fact that education is usually acquired in childhood and in the earlier adult ages. Almost all persons beyond these ages at the time of any given census preserve their respective educational attainments for many decades until their eventual decease. Thus, an adult population's educational level is raised mainly by the replacement of the less educated elderly, who die, by more educated young persons, whereas its improvement is retarded by the educational inertia of persons beyond early adulthood. The process is accelerated if the population has high natural increase, so that relatively many youngsters join the adult sector. This demographic factor, together with the existence of compulsory schooling, explains the rapid decrease in the share of uneducated persons among Jerusalem's Muslims. It also implies that the educational distribution of any population may be considerably influenced by age structure. We therefore present in table 15A age-standardized data on the respective educational attainments of the principal population groups in Jerusalem as of 1983.

Aside from the educational differentials between the total of Jews and the other religious groups, especially Muslims, there are differentials among Jews themselves. Lack of or low education is now mainly confined to aging women born in Asia-Africa. Even among those with 13+ years of study, there is still a marked gap between the European-origin group, where a majority has attained this level, and the other Jewish groups according to origin and place of birth (abroad or in Israel). Another relevant factor used to be sex differences in education, particularly for persons belonging to Islamic societies or who had lived in them. According to the 1967 census, a majority (62 percent) of Muslim women in Jerusalem had little or no schooling (0–4 years of study). The corresponding proportions were 65 percent of all Jewish women born in Asia-Africa who had immigrated as adults, and even above 90 percent for Yemenite Jewish women, according to Israel's 1961 census. By 1983, the percentages of persons with 0–4 years of schooling among Jerusalem's Muslims aged 15–24 were already low and with little sex differential: males—4.6 percent; females—6.0 percent. Such differentials do, however, persist among the entire population of adult Muslims (tables 15 and 15A), because of the above-explained slowing effect.

In 1983, 17 percent of adult Jews in Jerusalem (both sexes together) held academic degrees, as compared to 13 percent among Christians and only 6 percent among Muslims. The corresponding proportions for Jews aged 25–34 or 35–44 were 26 percent and 27 percent, respectively; 13 percent of Jews at the latter age had postgraduate degrees.

LANGUAGE USE

In a society that is heterogeneous in terms of its members' geographical origins, the use of many languages signifies differentiation, whereas use of a *lingua franca* is one of the mechanisms of societal integration. In Israel, there are several *linguae francae:* Hebrew and Arabic, various international languages, and widespread Jewish Diaspora tongues such as Yiddish or Ladino. The 1983 census contained the question "What language(s) do you speak daily?" and up to two languages per person could be registered. Table

16 shows what percentages of adult Jews, Muslims, and Christians in Jerusalem used any of the more common languages as principal tongue or at all (i.e., as principal or second tongue) in daily speech.

The successful revival of Hebrew as a living language and its practical use as the national language of Israel's Jews is generally recognized as a remarkable cultural achievement. In 1983, as many as 84 percent of adult Jews in Jerusalem reported Hebrew as their principal spoken language. This left limited room for Hebrew as a second language of Jews, and in fact English and Arabic were somewhat more frequent in this capacity. In all, 50 percent of Jews reported everyday use of a second language. Arabic, English, French, Spanish, and Russian may have been either the mother tongue of Jews who migrated from countries where one of these was the national language, or they were used in Israel as relatively frequent media of communication with others who were familiar with one of these languages. Yiddish is, of course, an international Jewish language, though its use has much decreased compared to that of the national languages in countries where Jews live, including Hebrew in Israel. Spanish includes the traditional Judeo-Spanish, i.e., Ladino; the two variants could not be distinguished in the census returns because the same Hebrew word, if not qualified by additional terms, may mean either of them.

Among the other somewhat common everyday languages of Jerusalem's Jews, several groups can be distinguished: Rumanian, Persian, and Bokharian serve, among others, new immigrants; German and Hungarian are used by immigrant groups of long standing in Israel, but who, according to the findings of recurrent studies, evince less propensity than others to abandon the everyday use of their mother tongues; and the same apparently applies to speakers of Kurdish. A noteworthy feature of the recent linguistic situation of Jews in Israel, and for that matter in Jerusalem, is the near disappearance of Polish as an everyday language.

In 1983 all adult Jews in Jerusalem were distributed as follows, according to everyday speaking of Hebrew (in percent): as only language—44.8 percent; as first language—39.4 percent; as second language—9.7 percent; no Hebrew—6.1 percent. The differences between the sexes were limited; 87 percent of Jewish men and 82 percent of Jewish women spoke Hebrew as the principal language. Everyday use of Hebrew as either the only or as the first language depends not only on personal predilection but also on surroundings, e.g., the need to communicate in another language with elderly relatives, or to speak at work with new immigrants, foreign-business relations, or Arabs. While Hebrew is now the principal language of virtually all Israeli-born Jews of either sex (98 percent in Jerusalem as of 1983 for both sexes together), it is not as prominent among the foreign-born (71 percent). Among the latter its use decreases in the more advanced age groups and is somewhat smaller among women than men. These distinctions prevail in Jerusalem as in the whole of Israel. Research has shown that the transition to use of Hebrew—in general or principally—is facilitated for foreign-born Jews not only by increasing duration of stay in Israel but also by lower age at arrival, in particular since immigrant children receive their schooling in Hebrew. Moreover, transition to Hebrew by foreign-born Jews is facilitated by higher education and participation in the labor force. Sex differences in the latter respect largely account for the limited overall differential that does exist between the sexes in everyday use of Hebrew.[17]

Muslims in Jerusalem speak almost exclusively Arabic as the first language. English somewhat exceeded Hebrew among the relatively few—only 19 percent—who reported a second everyday language in 1983. The reported extent of Hebrew speaking among Muslims, virtually always as second language, is markedly lower in Jerusalem (9 percent) than in the whole of Israel (30 percent). While it is true that the Muslims of Jerusalem have lived in the Israeli context for a shorter time than those elsewhere in the state, the 17 years from the Six Day War to the 1983 census were a not inconsiderable period. Additional reasons for the difference may therefore be sought in other considerations. For one thing, the census question did not relate to knowledge or intermittent use, but to daily speaking of languages; opportunity for this is limited, since the rather compact body of non-Jews in Jerusalem (more than 100,000 by 1983), with the Arabs of Judea surrounding them, lead a largely self-contained existence, economically as well as culturally. Another consideration is that Jerusalem's Jews comprise a sizable share from Arabic-speaking countries as well as many adults among the long-established Ashkenazi families who know some Arabic, while many of the younger Jewish generation learned it at school.[18] As elsewhere among Muslims in Israel, daily speaking of Hebrew in Jerusalem, though nearly always as a second language, was most frequent among young men, for work-related reasons—22 percent at ages 25–34.

Among Jerusalem's Christians, as of 1983, 78 percent spoke Arabic, 68 percent as a first language, and 10 percent as a second language, while 54 percent used a second daily language. Hebrew was reportedly used by more than 12 percent of all Christians in Jerusalem and by 18 percent of 25–34-year-old men, mostly as a second language. Non-Arab Christians are very

---

[17]Roberto Bachi, "A Statistical Analysis of the Revival of Hebrew in Israel," in R. Bachi (ed.), *Studies in Social Sciences* (Jerusalem, 1956), Scripta Hierosolymitana, vol. 3, pp. 179–247; U.O. Schmelz and R. Bachi, "Hebrew as Everyday Language of the Jews in Israel—Statistical Appraisal," in *Salo Wittmayer Baron Jubilee Volume* (Jerusalem, 1974), pp. 745–785; U.O. Schmelz, "New Immigrants' Progress in Hebrew—Statistical Data from Israel," in *Contemporary Jewry—Studies in Honor of Moshe Davis* (Jerusalem, 1984), pp. 191–216.

[18]The possibility of some reporting bias against Hebrew by Arab nationalists in Jerusalem also cannot be ruled out.

heterogeneous as to provenance, and numerous Arab Christians have affinities, economic or cultural, to foreign institutions. Thus, other not infrequent languages in daily use by Christians were English, to a far lesser extent French, and, indicative of specific national communities, Armenian and Greek.

Labor-Force Characteristics

PARTICIPATION IN LABOR FORCE

Of the 278,000 Jerusalem residents aged 15 and over in 1983, 143,600 (or 52 percent for both sexes together) participated in the civilian labor force. The corresponding percentages, by religious group, were as follows: Jews —57 percent; Muslims—34 percent; and Christians—38 percent (table 17). These differences are largely explained by the low labor-force participation of Arab women (see below), but dissimilarities in age structure also play an important role. Thus, Muslims at ages 15 and over include comparatively many adolescents who do not yet work, while Christians are an aging group.

In measuring the labor force active in Jerusalem, commuting must also be taken into account. This is mainly of two types: by Israelis commuting between Jerusalem and other localities and by Arabs commuting from the administered areas. Of the total labor force of Israeli inhabitants, 90 percent gave identifiable returns to the question on locale of employment in the 1983 census. Among them, while the overall numbers of Jerusalemites commuting elsewhere and of inhabitants of other localities commuting to Jerusalem virtually equaled out at 8 percent, there was a somewhat positive balance for Jerusalem among Jews and a somewhat negative balance among non-Jews.[19] The extent of commuting to Jerusalem by Jews may be on the increase as residential moves to dormitory localities outside the municipal boundaries continue. In addition, sample surveys carried out in the administered areas in 1984–1985 yielded information on about 17,000–18,000 Arabs from these areas working in Jerusalem.

The participation of Jewish men in the labor force was somewhat smaller in Jerusalem, both in 1972 and 1983, than in the conurbations of Tel Aviv and Haifa, as well as in the whole of Israel (table 17). The difference was, partly at least, connected with more prolonged study (university, yeshivah, etc.) among Jerusalem's Jewish young men. However, both in 1972 and 1983, labor-force participation of Jewish women was distinctly greater in Jerusalem than in the other mentioned locations, especially the two conurbations. This in turn is related to the particular prominence of public services in Jerusalem, which offer professional and clerical occupations

---

[19] About 2,000 non-Jewish residents of Jerusalem worked in the administered areas.

convenient to women. (Mention should be made in this context that the proportion of those employed part-time among the Jewish labor force—both sexes together—is greater in Jerusalem than in the conurbations and total Israel.) Labor-force participation of women increased in the interval between the 1972 and 1983 censuses. By the latter year half of Jerusalem's Jewish women aged 15 and over were in the labor force. However, between the two censuses the proportion of labor-force participants among men dropped slightly in Jerusalem and the other mentioned locations. As for Jews of both sexes together, the percentage in the labor force was somewhat greater in Jerusalem than in the other locations, due to the influence of the local women, and the respective differences widened from 1972 to 1983.

The labor-force participation of Muslim and especially Christian men in Jerusalem was somewhat smaller than that of Jewish men. Christians are, as already noted, a comparatively aging group, of whom a not negligible proportion live in institutions and engage in religious pursuits only. The labor-force participation of Christian and especially of Muslim women, as reported in the censuses, was very low. Insofar as Muslim women are concerned, this is partly attributable to the large number of children that they have, on average, as well as to their low educational attainment, which bars them from many occupations. More generally, though, it reflects the customary tendency of Arab society, especially in the urban sector, not to allow women to work outside the home. Christian women are better educated, which qualifies not a few of them for professional jobs in the Arab sector; in Jerusalem, however, they are a comparatively aged group and some fulfill only religious tasks outside the labor force. In part, the low labor-force participation of Arab women, as measured by censuses and surveys, is probably due to a downward reporting bias, since, for the just mentioned social reasons, it is difficult to elicit information about Arab women's "work" (apart from accepted domestic tasks).

In Jerusalem, as elsewhere in Israel, labor-force participation rises after ages 15–24, when a great many individuals are still exclusively engaged in studies or, among Jews, perform their compulsory military service for several years; it decreases again in advanced ages, and earlier among women than men. In the 1983 census, at the peak ages 35–54, 92–94 percent of Jewish men in Jerusalem belonged to the annual labor force; the corresponding peak proportion for Jewish women in the city was 74 percent at ages 25–34. Age-standardized percentages of labor-force participation in 1983 show rather small differences among Jewish men according to origin and birthplace (table 17A).

ECONOMIC BRANCHES AND OCCUPATIONS

The mainstay of Jerusalem's economy continues to be public services (administrative and professional). The proportion of those employed in public services among the city's Jewish labor force, as divided by economic branch, was as follows in 1972: total—49 percent; men—39.5 percent; women—64.5 percent. The corresponding figures for 1983 were as follows: total—49 percent; men—38 percent; women—62 percent.[20] These percentages far exceeded the corresponding ones in the Tel Aviv and Haifa conurbations and in Israel as a whole (table 18). The relative share of public-service employment among Christians in Jerusalem is similar to that among Jews, also for each sex separately. The corresponding figures for total Muslims and for Muslim men are much lower; the respective figure for employed Muslim women is high, but relates to a very small group (see above). Altogether, 46 percent of Jerusalem's total labor force was employed in public services as of 1983. Among Jews employed in Jerusalem, the proportion in public services is greatest at middle age, and for men at a somewhat higher middle age than for women. Age-standardized data show the highest percentages employed in this branch in the European-origin group, with origin-specific differences greater among men than women (table 18A).

Industrial establishments are rarer in Jerusalem, relative to population, than in the two conurbations and in the country as a whole. Moreover, those that exist have relatively fewer workers and less output (in money terms).[21] In consequence, industry in Jerusalem accounted for only about half the share of the employed—11 percent in 1983—that it did in the other mentioned locations. In Jerusalem, 16 percent of all employed men, but only 6 percent of all women, worked in industry. According to age-standardized data, employment in industry was for either sex somewhat more frequent among foreign-born than among Israeli-born Jews. Industry, including crafts, accounted for somewhat larger shares among employed Muslims and Christians than among Jews in Jerusalem.

Nearly a quarter of the 1983 labor force was engaged in commerce and finance in Jerusalem, with little difference by religious group. Nor were there great differences in this respect between Jerusalem, the conurbations, and Israel as a whole. But the share of commerce, as distinct from finance, was greater among employed Muslims and Christians than among Jews in Jerusalem, and greater among Jewish men than Jewish women. The persons employed in commerce were comparatively aged. According to age-standardized data for Jews, commerce was particularly frequent among Asian-born men.

---

[20]The increased labor-force participation of women as of 1983 explains why the proportion employed in public services did not change in the total Jewish labor force (both sexes together), compared to 1972, though it receded slightly for each of the sexes if they are considered separately.

[21]As substantiated by surveys of industry carried out by the Israel Central Bureau of Statistics.

Relatively more Muslim men worked in construction than did Jews or Christians. Insofar as this relates to manual labor, it is connected to the existing educational differentials. A large proportion of workers from the administered areas were also employed in Jerusalem in the construction of buildings and roads.

With regard to personal occupation, Jerusalem's Jews have a greater share of academic and other professional workers, and of managers, than the two conurbations and the whole country (table 19). The differences are much smaller with regard to clerical workers. As of 1983, all these white-collar occupations together accounted for 63 percent of employed Jews resident in Jerusalem; the corresponding figures for men and women were 54 and 75 percent, respectively, some rise having occurred for each sex since 1972. Age-standardized data show higher proportions for the total of these white-collar occupations and for their upper bracket (academic, other professional, and managerial) per 100 employed of European-origin than of Asian-African origin, of each sex (table 19A). The ranking of the two origin groups was reversed with regard to the frequency of clerical occupations among them, while Jews of Israeli origin occupied an intermediate position in both respects.

In contrast, skilled workers in industry, building, and transport constituted far smaller percentages among the employed Jews of Jerusalem than in the other mentioned locations, in keeping with the city's limited industrial development. The occupational distribution of employed Christians in Jerusalem somewhat resembled that of Jews, though with smaller proportions in academic and managerial jobs. The distribution of Muslims, however, who are a far less educated group, was quite different; nearly 40 percent were skilled, and nearly 10 percent unskilled, manual workers.

The overwhelming majority of the labor force in Israel is made up of employees. The distribution by employment status in Jerusalem as of 1983 was as follows: employees—87.9 percent; self-employed—7.4 percent; employers—3.3 percent; others—1.5 percent. There were no great differences in this respect between religious groups, except that non-Jews had somewhat more self-employed persons and fewer employers than did Jews. The proportion of employees was even greater among women who participated in the labor force than among men.

About 40 percent of the non-Jews who both resided and worked in Jerusalem were employed in predominantly Jewish subquarters of the city, insofar as this is ascertainable from the 1983 census.[22] In addition, a

---

[22] The 1983 census data on this topic are deficient and can only be used with reservation. Among Jerusalem's employed non-Jews, 21 percent did not report the locality where they were working (though it is obvious that this was mostly Jerusalem); and of those who indicated that they were working in Jerusalem, 20 percent did not report a sufficiently detailed address for identification of the particular subquarter.

significant proportion of Arabs from the administered areas, particularly Judea, who were working in Jerusalem, were hired by Jews or for public-housing projects and road construction in Jewish neighborhoods.

Living Conditions

Considerable improvement in living conditions took place between 1972 and 1983 among Jerusalem's Jews and non-Jews, as well as in the two conurbations and in Israel as a whole. When comparing the respective census data in table 20, it should be remembered that the areas of the Tel Aviv and Haifa conurbations, as defined for statistical purposes, were widened in the 1983 census.

HOUSING

In 1983, 23 percent of Jewish households in Jerusalem and rather similar percentages in the other mentioned locations lived in apartments that had been built as recently as 1975 and after. This usually implied more modern dwelling facilities and, if a whole neighborhood was newly constructed, improved amenities. The corresponding figures for Jerusalem's non-Jews were much lower. However, Jerusalem's Jews exceeded those of the other locations in the share of households that had moved since 1975 into the apartments which they occupied in June 1983. The respective share in Jerusalem—55 percent—implied, on the whole, not only rapid residential mobility but also upward socioeconomic mobility. The corresponding figure —42 percent—for Jerusalem's non-Jews was also very considerable for a span of only 8½ years.

Small dwellings of up to two rooms became much less frequent in all locations from 1972 to 1983; at the latter date, they accommodated about a quarter of the Jewish households in Jerusalem, the conurbations, and the whole of Israel, but still constituted upward of half the dwellings of Jerusalem's non-Jews. On the other hand, large apartments of four rooms or more had become more common. By 1983 they amounted to roughly similar proportions—around 20 percent—in all the mentioned locational and religious categories. The average number of persons per dwelling room had been reduced to about 1 in all the mentioned locational categories of Jews, but remained more than 2 among the non-Jews of Jerusalem. In 1983 a dwelling density of less than 1 person per room was found in about 40 percent of Jewish households in Jerusalem, the conurbations, and Israel as a whole, whereas it was rare among the city's Muslims.

The proportion of households that owned the apartments they lived in showed an increase. In 1983 between two-thirds and three-quarters of the households in all the mentioned categories owned the apartments in which they were enumerated, except for Christians in Jerusalem, many of whom resided in buildings that were the property of institutions. Apartments with at least two lavatories, which were more likely to be found in recently erected buildings, were somewhat more frequently inhabited by Jewish households in Jerusalem than in the other locations, as of 1983.

STANDARD OF LIVING

Possession of telephones and cars had much increased between the two censuses. Both in 1972 and 1983, Jerusalem's Jewish households resembled those in the other mentioned locations regarding possession of one or more cars, and in this respect far surpassed the non-Jewish households in the city. Whereas by 1983 telephones were very common in Jerusalem's Jewish households, they were comparatively rare among Muslims, with Christians in an intermediate position.

Because of Israel's strong inflation between 1972 and 1983, household incomes reported in the two censuses cannot be compared in direct money terms. Also, the approach for measuring income was different in the two censuses—gross annual income in 1972 and net monthly income in 1983—though in either case the published figures related to households of employees only. For these reasons, table 20 presents index numbers showing the relative differences in income between the various locational and religious categories and between Israel's total Jewish employee-headed households at the time of each census. The data suggest that the income differentials—per household and especially per capita—between the categories that are compared in the table narrowed during 1972–1983.[23] According to the 1983 census, the mean net monthly income per standard person in households headed by employees—who are the overwhelming majority of Israel's labor force (see above)—was similar among Jews in Jerusalem, the conurbations, and the whole of Israel. Taking the countrywide figures as the basis (=100.0), the index numbers for respective locations were as follows: Jerusalem—104; Tel Aviv conurbation—106; Haifa conurbation—108. The corresponding incomes were much lower among Christians and especially Muslims in Jerusalem: 54 and 35, respectively. The low level of the Muslim figure is partly explained by the Muslims' much greater household size, which reduces the per capita income, but even the entire household income of Muslim employees was not much more than half that of their Jewish counterparts. This is connected to the large educational differential between the two groups and the low labor-force-participation rates of Arab and especially Muslim women.

---

[23]The narrowing of the per capita income differences in 1983 was influenced by the use of the "standard person" concept, which adjusts with decreasing weights for the number of persons in a household.

Some Specific Subpopulations

ULTRA-ORTHODOX JEWS

There is a conspicuous differentiation within Jewish society in Jerusalem between the ultra-Orthodox and all other Jews. The ultra-Orthodox constitute a large segment of the very religious Jews. They are not only punctilious in religious observance but also strictly follow traditionalist modes of life, including distinctive styles of dress. The ultra-Orthodox live together in common neighborhoods, for ritual and social reasons, and try to avoid contact with persons who do not share their way of life. In the political sphere, ultra-Orthodox groups express non-Zionist or anti-Zionist views. It is now usual to denote the ultra-Orthodox in Jerusalem and Israel generally by the term *haredim*. In fact, complicated divisions and power contests exist between subgroups of the ultra-Orthodox—according to geographical origin, ideological tenets, and loyalty to certain leaders—but they share many common features that set them off from the majority of Jewish society.

The considerable representation of the ultra-Orthodox in Jerusalem is an undoubted fact of everyday life, Jerusalem being one of the two cities in Israel —the other is Bene-Berak—where the ultra-Orthodox live in large absolute and relative numbers. Yet it is by no means easy to measure statistically the frequency of the ultra-Orthodox, since there are no generally accepted criteria for defining them and no direct data sources. Population censuses and other official demographic statistics cannot be a direct source, because they do not presume to inquire into people's attitudes in religious, let alone political, matters. Statistics of school enrollment and election results are not conclusive. Agudat Israel and Shas, the two overtly ultra-Orthodox parties at the time of the 1984 parliamentary elections, together won about 14.5 percent of the Jewish vote in Jerusalem,[24] but this does not convey the full proportion of the ultra-Orthodox, since some of them boycotted the balloting at the instigation of extremist leaders, and others voted for different parties. In estimating the ultra-Orthodox subpopulation—including children—one must take into account its particularly young age structure; because of high fertility, the ultra-Orthodox comprise a greater share of Jewish children than of total Jews (of all ages together) or, more narrowly, those aged 18 and over, who are entitled to vote in elections.

In order to arrive at an admittedly very rough approximation of a figure for the ultra-Orthodox in Jerusalem, the author ascertained the number of

---

[24]Shas is not only an ultra-Orthodox party but also an "ethnic" party, made up of Sephardim and members of oriental (Asian/African-origin) communities. For this reason Shas may have won votes from persons of such ethnicity who are religious, though not themselves ultra-Orthodox.

Jews who, according to the 1983 population census, lived in tracts (according to a detailed division) where at least 30 percent of the valid votes in the 1984 parliamentary elections were cast for Agudat Israel and Shas. Knowledge of local conditions indicates that most, if not all, the Jews in each of these tracts actually belonged to ultra-Orthodox society according to their mode of life. Any individuals who were not ultra-Orthodox themselves in some of these particular tracts were, roughly speaking, offset by smaller clusters of the ultra-Orthodox elsewhere (whose presence there is documented, among other signs, by additional votes cast for the two mentioned parties). The resulting estimate of an ultra-Orthodox subpopulation of around 20 percent of Jerusalem's Jews—or something like 60,000 people in absolute numbers—can convey the order of magnitude of this phenomenon among Jerusalem's Jews as of a few years ago. Since the Jewish population of Jerusalem now grows mainly by natural increase, and since the ultra-Orthodox have more children—and are also less prone to migrate from the city—their share of the Jewish population seems bound to increase, unless there is considerable in-migration of other Jews.

NON-JEWS

An obvious differentiation among Jerusalem's Arabs, according to mode of life, is that between urban population and ex-villagers or ex-Bedouin, but since these matters are connected with locale of residence, they will be considered below in the section on spatial distribution.

Christians are divided into many churches and sects. The significance of this division is not only religious but relates to residential location and mode of life as well, since some of the sects form distinct nuclei within the city. This is true especially in the Old City, where the Armenian Quarter is a conspicuous example. Since the religious breakdown of Jerusalem's Christian residents from the 1983 population census has not been published, the following data are from the 1972 census: Catholics (Roman, Greek, etc.) —48.2 percent; Orthodox (Greek, etc.)—32.3 percent; Armenians—10.1 percent; Syrians—0.7 percent; Copts—1.3 percent; Ethiopians—0.4 percent; Protestants—3.6 percent; others and unspecified—3.4 percent.[25]

Spatial Distribution

In the period since reunification, Jerusalem's population not only grew substantially—by 71 percent (cf. table 2)—but also underwent considerable

---

[25]The data for Armenians, Syrians, and Copts include both the Orthodox and the Catholic (Uniate) sections of each of these denominations; the data presented for Catholics and Orthodox do not, however, include Armenians, Syrians, or Copts.

geographical redistribution within the enlarged city territory. This was rendered possible by large-scale building activity, particularly publicly initiated Jewish housing projects. Residential separation between Jews and Arabs persists, but its spatial pattern has been altered.

RESIDENTIAL EXPANSION

Soon after the Six Day War, a Jewish land bridge was created between the north of what had been the Israeli city (see map 1)[26] and the institutional sites—the Hebrew University campus and Hadassah Hospital—on Mount Scopus (in the center of Sq 29), which had been practically inaccessible to Jews during the years of the city's division. This was achieved through the establishment of Jewish housing projects in the previously unbuilt Sq 28 (Ramat Eshkol, across the defunct armistice line) and in the western section of Sq 29 (French Hill). At the time of the 1972 census, 8,300 Jews already lived there; by 1985 their number had grown to 23,200. The Mount Scopus campus and the hospital were renovated and expanded and resumed their functions.

During the 1970s and the first half of the 1980s, the Jewish Quarter in the Old City was restored and to a large extent rebuilt. With great care, usable portions of old buildings were joined to newly erected ones. By this blend of the old and new, modern apartments with up-to-date facilities were created, while a good deal of the appearance and atmosphere of the historic quarter was retained. Also, many Jewish religious sites were reconstructed and put to use again, the most important being the Western Wall of the Temple Mount (the so-called Wailing Wall), now with a large open-air expanse for prayer and ceremonies in front of it. The Arabs who had installed themselves in this quarter during the Jordanian period were indemnified so that they could acquire dwellings elsewhere. By now more than 2,000 Jews live in the Old City, a select socioeconomic group, very distinct from the inhabitants of the other, long-neglected sections of the Old City.

Since the early 1970s, four big Jewish residential clusters have been set up on empty land along the outer perimeter of enlarged East Jerusalem. At the time of the 1972 census, they were just being started and were virtually

---

[26]Map 1 shows the division of Jerusalem's municipal territory into "subquarters" (abbreviated "Sqs"), as used in the official statistics and last updated on the occasion of the 1983 population census. However, the numeration of the subquarters has been changed here from the official one so as to more specifically express the spatial structure of Jerusalem according to geographic, chronological, and demographic considerations. This modified numeration starts with the Jewish Quarter of the walled Old City, which alone has been inhabited almost continuously since biblical times.

Map 1
Jerusalem Subquarters, 1983

Old City:
1 Jewish Quarter
2 Muslim Quarter
3 Armenian Quarter
4 Christian Quarter

Urban Core:
5 Town Center
6 Musrara (Morashah)
7 Me'ah She'arim, Beit Yisra'el, Bukharim
8 Kerem Avraham, Mekor Barukh
9 Nahla'ot
10 Rehaviah

Central, South:
11 Talbieh (Komemi'ut)
12 Katamon (Gonen), German Colony (Emek Refa'im)
13 Bak'a (Ge'ulim)
14 Talpiot
15 Rassco
16 Katamonim

West:
17 Romemah
18 Givat Sha'ul
19 Kiryat Moshe, Beit ha-Kerem
20 Nayot, Ha-Kiryah
21 Bayit va-Gan
22 Kiryat ha-Yovel (north)
23 Kiryat ha-Yovel (south)
24 Kiryat Menahem, Malha (Manhat)

North and East:
25 American Colony, Sheikh Jarrah
26 Et-Tur
27 Shu'afat, Beit Hanina, refugee camp
28 Ramat Eshkol
29 French Hill (Givat Shapira), Mount Scopus
30 Neveh Ya'akov
31 Ramot

South
32 Silwan, Abu Tor (east)
33 Sur Bahir, Beit Safafa (south)
34 East Talpiot
35 Gilo

uninhabited, but by the 1983 census they already housed 51,000 Jews, and by the end of 1985 the figure had increased to 70,000, according to the updating notifications received by the Israel Population Registry. These new residential clusters are Neveh Ya'akov (Sq 30) and Ramot (Sq 31), in the north, the former with an extension—Pisgat Ze'ev—now being constructed to connect it with Mount Scopus. In the south are East Talpiot (Sq 34) and Gilo (Sq 35), the last mentioned now the largest of them all with an estimated population of 24,000 in 1985.

In addition, there has been a good deal of residential building in already existing Jewish neighborhoods, particularly in the west, where the populations of Kiryat Moshe, Beit ha-Kerem, Bayit va-Gan, and Nayot (Sqs 19–21) more than doubled, from 16,000 to 37,400, between 1967 and 1985.

As already stated, 23 percent of all Jewish households in Jerusalem reported in the 1983 census that their apartments had been built since 1975, while only 12 percent of all non-Jewish households in the city did so. Yet, there was also a considerable amount of new housing constructed by Arabs in, or close to, already existing Arab neighborhoods. This took place particularly in the north (Shu'afat and Beit Hanina, Sq 27), where a quarter of the non-Jewish households reported in 1983 that their apartments had been built since 1975.

In addition, several new industrial zones, though of limited dimensions, were set up at the outskirts of Jerusalem, particularly in Talpiot, Har Hotzvim, and Atarot (in Sqs 14, 7, and 27).

The above-outlined new constructions for residential and other purposes have not only widely extended the built-up area but have also improved its appearance. The new housing developments consist mainly of condominiums, however, in which even the minority of one-family houses are built relatively close to one another. This has been due to considerations of security, economy (in land and infrastructure), and the saving of construction time. Jews who aspire to a house and garden of their own, on comparatively easy terms, often move to the new Jewish suburbia of Jerusalem that is springing up outside the municipal territory (see below).

SEPARATION OF RELIGIOUS GROUPS

The spatial pattern of residential separation between Jews and Arabs has changed since 1967 (tables 21 and 22; maps 2A and 2B). Arabs have stayed within the ex-Jordanian territory, whereas Jews have not only returned to the Old City and Mount Scopus but have also established the three tiers of new residential neighborhoods that were mentioned above: Neveh Ya'akov and Ramot at the northern outskirts of the city territory (Sqs 30 and 31); still in the north but more inwardly located, Ramat Eshkol and French Hill

(Sqs 28 and 29), as a connection between Mount Scopus and the bulk of the Jewish area; and East Talpiot and Gilo at the southern outskirts (Sqs 34 and 35).

Map 2B shows that a kind of checker pattern has emerged in the north, east, and south, made up of sizable sections that are each inhabited predominantly by Jews or by Muslims and Christians. Of the 35 subquarters into which Jerusalem is now divided for statistical purposes, there were only 6 in which the proportion of either Jews or non-Jews (i.e., the sum of Muslims and Christians) did not exceed 95 percent in 1983; in 25 subquarters the respective proportions exceeded 98 percent. Even the few exceptions were mostly due to discrepancies between the subquarter boundaries and the habitational limits of the population groups, or to the existence of small enclaves, rather than to actual residential intermingling. Intermingling exists only on a small scale, usually with Christians living among Jews.[27]

Comparison of tables 22 and 23 indicates the changes in the spatial distribution of population that took place in Jerusalem between 1967 and 1985; maps 2A and 2B show the religious composition of population within each subquarter in 1967 and 1983.[28] The general tendency was centrifugal, with a growing spread toward the city boundaries, particularly in the north and south, where wide stretches had previously been unbuilt.

Table 23 (and maps 3A and 3B) shows the differences in residential density of population (thousands of inhabitants per square kilometer) between the various subquarters. Density is greatest in the Old City (Sqs 1–4) and in the Jewish urban core (Sqs 5–10). In the latter, a decreasing trend prevails due to net out-movement of population, except for the ultra-Orthodox Sqs 7 and 8. Density is comparatively low in the large peripheral regions of Jerusalem.

JEWISH AREAS

The Jewish population underwent a far-reaching redistribution across large sections of the extended city territory. Between 1967 and 1985, the urban core of Jewish Jerusalem (Sqs 5–10) lost population not only relatively, from 43 to 21 percent of total Jews, but also absolutely, from 84,000 to 68,000 (tables 22 and 23). This happened, on the one hand, because of

---

[27]Including instances of mixed households.
[28]The data for Jews in map 2A are the author's estimates based on figures of the Israel Central Bureau of Statistics for proximate years and ultimately on the 1961 and 1972 censuses; the data for Muslims and Christians in map 2A are nearly all taken from the 1967 census of East Jerusalem (see footnote 6). The aggregates of these data have supplied the information for map 3A.

72 / AMERICAN JEWISH YEAR BOOK, 1987

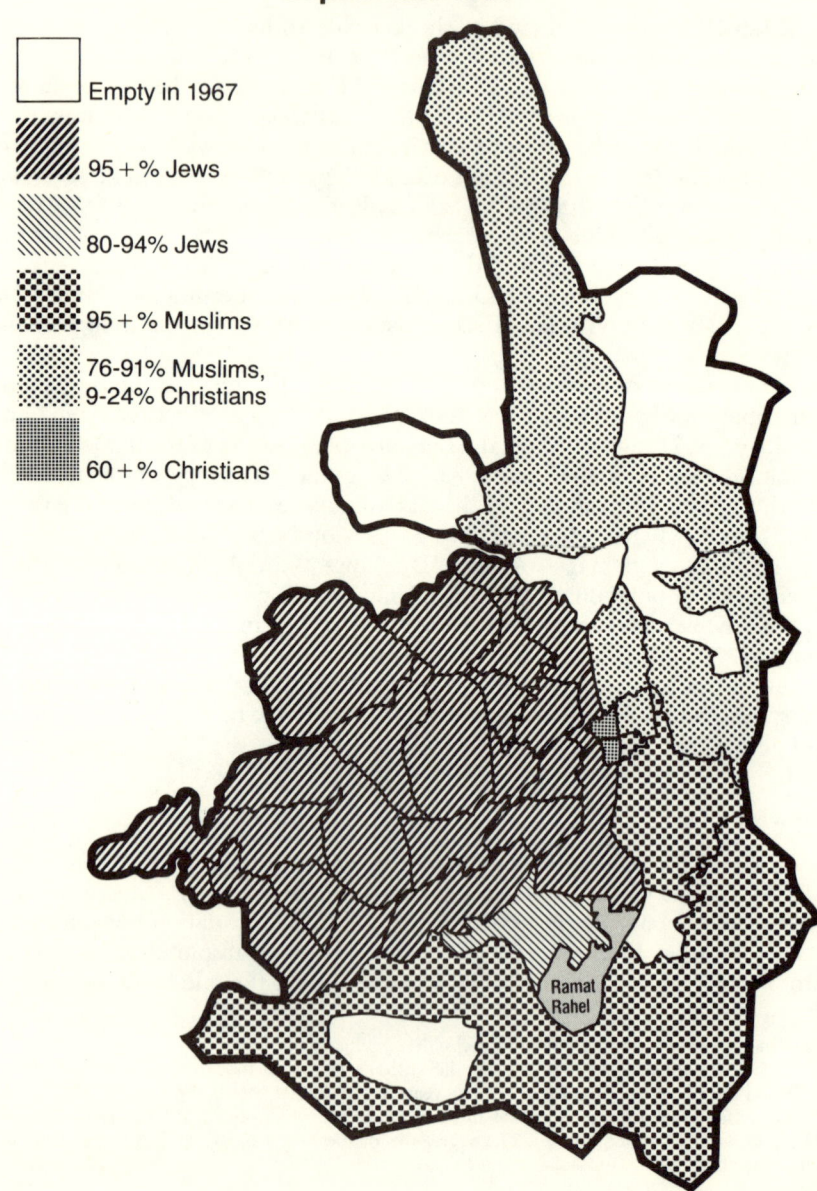

**Map 2A
Jerusalem: Religious Composition,
September 1967**

- Empty in 1967
- 95+% Jews
- 80-94% Jews
- 95+% Muslims
- 76-91% Muslims, 9-24% Christians
- 60+% Christians

Ramat Rahel

THE POPULATION OF JERUSALEM / 73

Map 2B
Jerusalem: Religious Composition, 1983

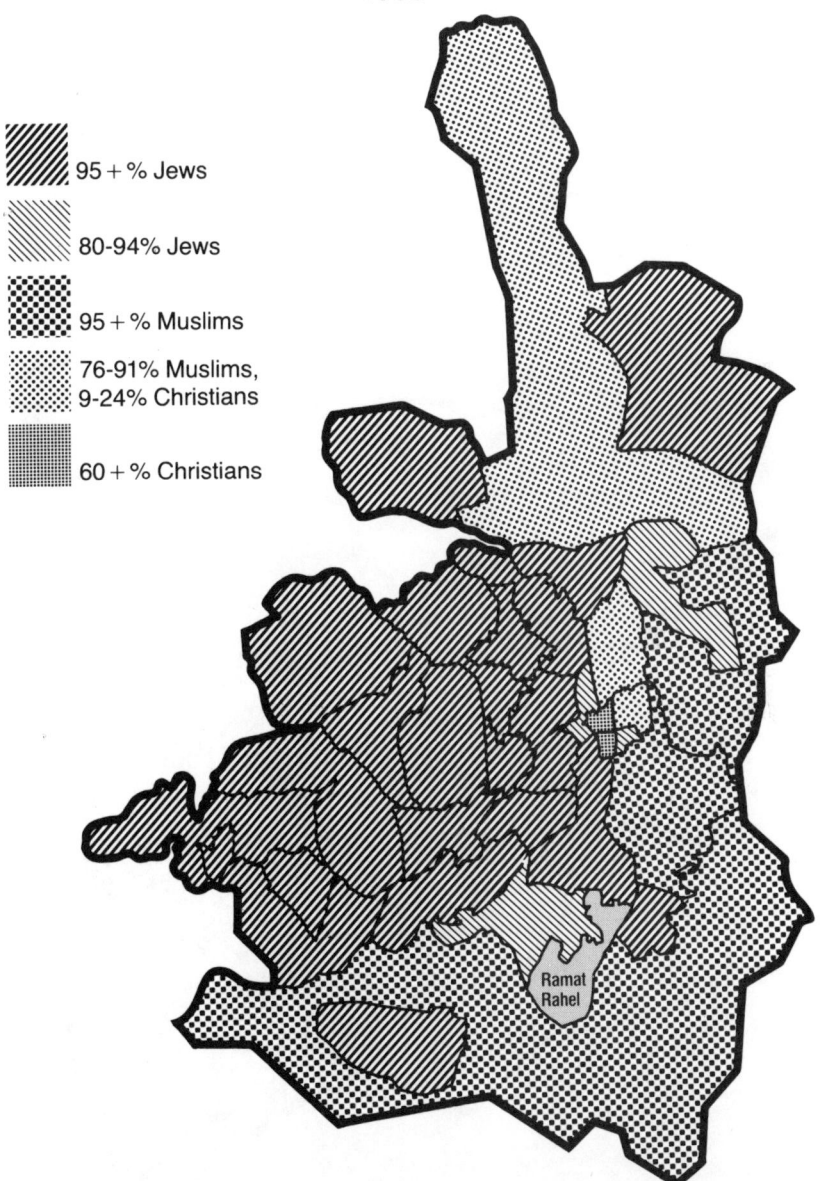

- 95 + % Jews
- 80-94% Jews
- 95 + % Muslims
- 76-91% Muslims, 9-24% Christians
- 60 + % Christians

Ramat Rahel

74 / AMERICAN JEWISH YEAR BOOK, 1987

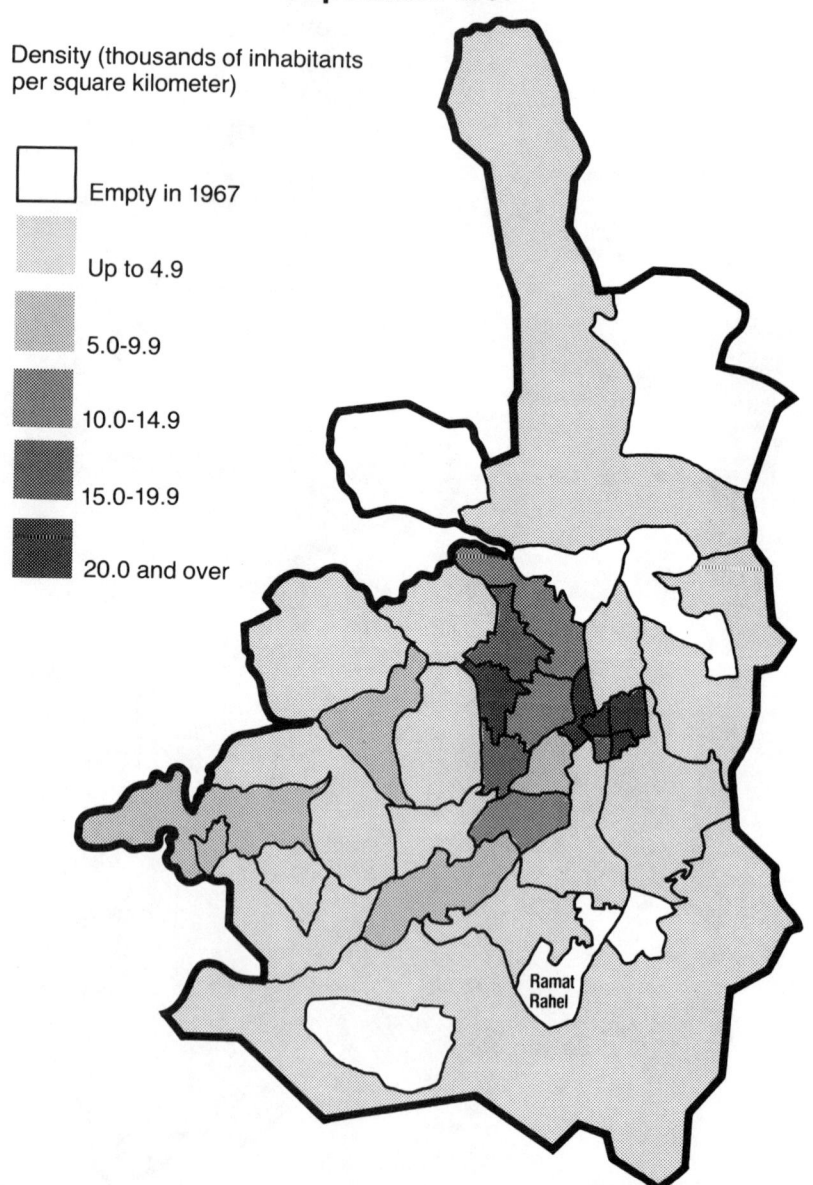

Map 3A
Jerusalem: Population Density, September 1967

Density (thousands of inhabitants per square kilometer)

- Empty in 1967
- Up to 4.9
- 5.0-9.9
- 10.0-14.9
- 15.0-19.9
- 20.0 and over

Ramat Rahel

THE POPULATION OF JERUSALEM / 75

Map 3B
Jerusalem: Population Density, 1985

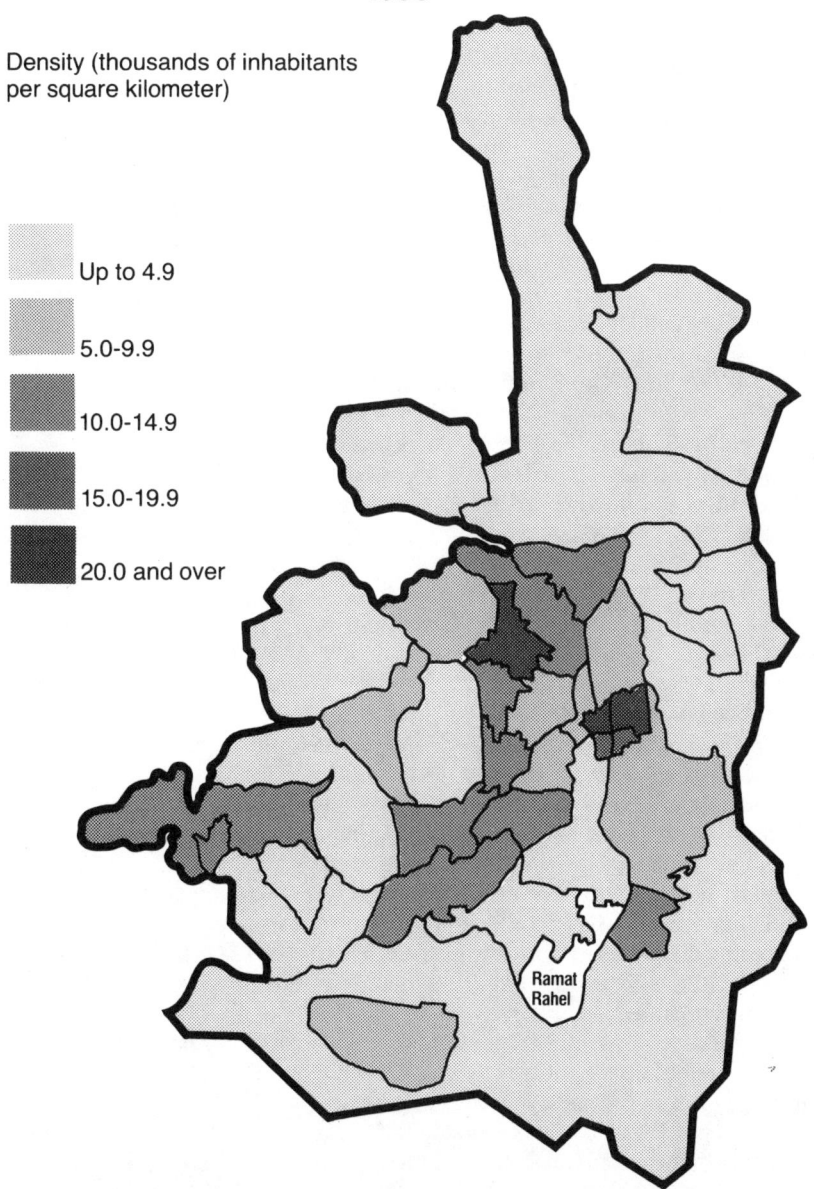

Density (thousands of inhabitants per square kilometer)

- Up to 4.9
- 5.0-9.9
- 10.0-14.9
- 15.0-19.9
- 20.0 and over

Ramat Rahel

the increasing sprawl of the downtown area, with business premises and offices spreading throughout the urban core, and, on the other hand, continual out-movement of residents, particularly younger couples, from low-grade neighborhoods in the area toward more attractive ones elsewhere. However, the process of replacing older houses with new business and office structures has moved at a slow pace. A special case is Sq 6, whose southern part (the Mamilla region) is scheduled for rebuilding and has been gradually abandoned by its population. At the same time, within the Jewish urban core, the population has grown in the now mainly ultra-Orthodox Sqs 7 and 8 (Me'ah She'arim, etc., Kerem Avraham, etc.) because of the strong natural increase there.

Many other areas of what had been the Israeli zone of divided Jerusalem have also lost population, relatively or even absolutely. This is true of the following: Talbieh, Katamon, Bak'a, and Talpiot (Sqs 11–14), which were first established in the late Ottoman or Mandatory periods; the Katamonim (Sq 16), with new-immigrant housing set up in the 1950s and early 1960s; and Sqs 22–24 in the southwest (Kiryat ha-Yovel, etc.) that accommodated new immigrants in the late 1950s and throughout the 1960s.

In contrast, marked growth of Jewish population during 1967–1985 took place in the following areas: Kiryat Moshe, Beit ha-Kerem, and Bayit va-Gan (Sqs 19 and 21), which started as garden suburbs in the Mandatory period and still preserve a comfortable residential character; Rassco (Sq 15), which in the 1960s attracted intelligentsia of European origin, among them many young Israeli-born Jews; Nayot (Sq 20), a relatively new upper-class neighborhood; and Romemah and Givat Sha'ul (Sqs 17 and 18), which contain growing numbers of new housing projects for the ultra-Orthodox with their large families.

The main thrust of Jewish residential development has been beyond the former Israeli zone of divided Jerusalem—to Sqs 28–31, 34, and 35, as already stated. Not only new immigrants have been directed there since the 1970s; a great many families of the existing Jewish population, particularly younger couples, have moved there as well. This is due to the larger size of apartments, the superior structural and town-planning aspects of the new housing, and cost-benefit considerations (comparatively low prices, though a greater distance from most places of work). By 1985, the Jewish population of these new residential areas already approached 100,000, or 30 percent of Jerusalem's total Jews.

While date of immigration of the foreign-born continues to be an important determinant of the residential distribution of the Jewish population, financial resources and ages of the adults are increasingly significant factors in this regard. The obvious tendency of younger couples to move to peripheral locations better suited for child rearing is reinforced by the lower prices of apartments in new and more distant places, and facilitated by public mortgage loans that are allocated specifically to new couples.

A similar process, leading to increased spread of the Jewish population within Jerusalem, applies to the housing needs of the younger generation among the ultra-Orthodox. Up to the first decade of the state, the ultra-Orthodox were mainly concentrated in certain sections of Sq 7 (Me'ah She'arim, etc.). Since then they have experienced a population explosion, due to high fertility and also to greater success than before in retaining their younger generation within the fold. At first they filled Sq 8 (Kerem Avraham, Mekor Barukh), gradually replacing the previous Jewish inhabitants. When this area became insufficient and the demand for improved living standards grew, special housing projects for ultra-Orthodox families were erected in Sanhedria Murhevet (in Sq 28), Kiryat Matersdorf, and Kiryat Zanz near Romemah (Sq 17), as well as in Har Nof and in parts of Givat Sha'ul and Bayit va-Gan (Sqs 18 and 21), plus Ramat Polin (in Sq 31).

One of the consequences of sustained residential out-movement, which is primarily undertaken by younger adults with children, is the aging of the population that remains in the older neighborhoods. This process is very conspicuous in the urban core of Jewish Jerusalem (Sqs 5–10). Of the 36 tracts distinguished there for statistical purposes, in 1983 no fewer than 29 had a proportion of the elderly (aged 65+ years) in excess of 10 percent, as compared to an 8.7-percent city average for Jews at the time. Moreover, 17 of these tracts had between 15 and 35 percent elderly.

Jerusalem's Jews were distributed in 1985 as follows: Old City—0.8 percent; business center (Sq 5)—1.5 percent; lower-class neighborhoods largely built before 1948 (Sqs 6–9)—17.0 percent; upper-class neighborhoods first set up before 1948, partly as garden suburbs, but most of them now with large additions of buildings (Sqs 10–14, 17–19, 21)—30.5 percent; housing projects started 1948–1967, some having been expanded since then (Sqs 15, 16, 20, 22–24)—21.6 percent; housing projects initiated from 1967 onward (Sqs 28–31, 34, 35)—28.6 percent.

Region of birth of the foreign-born and origin of the Israeli-born are still consequential for the sociodemographic character of particular residential areas in Jerusalem because of the discrepant backgrounds of the Jews who came, respectively, from Asia-Africa and Europe-America. The gaps express themselves, as noted above, in demographic patterns (e.g., fertility and age composition), educational attainments, occupational distribution, etc. The origin-related sociodemographic disparities have, however, narrowed in the course of time, even among the foreign-born and much more so in the second generation, which is already Israeli-born. Among the determinants of residential profile, education is important because of its manifold implications for demographic behavior and other socioeconomic characteristics (e.g., occupation and income). Age structure is not only *per se* a basic aspect of a population, but it influences labor-force participation, income levels, and life-styles.

The period in which most apartments in a neighborhood were built is relevant for structural characteristics, number and size of rooms, and the original availability of modern facilities, as well as for the prevalence of ownership by residents. Up to the Mandatory period, building for rental was common, whereas since then, owning—actual or prospective—of apartments by their residents (often in condominiums) has been usual in Jerusalem, as in Israel generally. Moreover, the time when a neighborhood was chiefly constructed, especially if this occurred after the establishment of the state, is reflected in the foreign-born residents' distribution by immigration period, since in any given period the new arrivals were largely directed to vacant apartments in neighborhoods just being built. The distance of a neighborhood from the center of town influences possession of cars, which in Israel is an indicator of socioeconomic status. The degree of religiosity in a neighborhood influences fertility, and thereby age composition, with its various concomitants.

A factor of demographic dynamics that is apt to override others is an area's migration balance. In Jerusalem, for instance, Sq 9 (the Nahla'ot) has long had a major concentration of oriental Jews, who once were very fertile and had a high proportion of young people. By 1983 the neighborhood had a rather aging population—median age of 30.9 years, compared to the city average for Jews of 25.1—because the younger generation had been leaving for more attractive neighborhoods. All these and other factors influence one another in complex interrelationships which together create a particular residential profile.

According to data from the 1983 census and other information, the group of Jerusalem Jewish subquarters that ranked highest sociodemographically included the adjacent areas numbered 10 (Rehaviah), 11 (Talbieh), and 20 (Nayot, etc.). These are also the subquarters with the greatest proportions of European and American Jews. Rehaviah and Talbieh have been upper-class neighborhoods since their establishment in Mandatory times; Nayot is rather new and has only a small population (Sq 20 is mainly institutional). After these comes a group of more outlying subquarters: 15 (Rassco), 19 (Beit ha-Kerem), and 29 (French Hill). At the bottom of the ranking is the following group of Jewish subquarters: 9 (Nahla'ot)—with its already-mentioned traditional concentration of oriental Jews;[29] (7) (Me'ah She'arim, etc.)—the original concentration of the ultra-Orthodox Ashkenazim, including several oriental Jewish neighborhoods as well; and 6 (Musrara)—

---

[29]Though some process of "gentrification" is now under way in parts of the Nahla'ot.

at the border with the ex-Jordanian zone, along the course of the armistice line that had divided Jerusalem.[30] All three of these areas were built in Ottoman or early Mandatory times and have largely become slums.

NON-JEWISH AREAS

The spatial-distribution trends of the non-Jewish population in Jerusalem since 1967 have been characterized by moves from the crowded Old City to the northern, eastern, and southern areas outside it (respectively Sqs 27, 26, 32, 33). Large sections of the Old City, especially in the Muslim Quarter and in part of the Christian Quarter, are slums—despite the historical buildings in them—because of long neglect. Great natural increase notwithstanding, the non-Jewish population of the Old City has kept within the narrow limits of 22,000–23,000 throughout the years 1967–1985. Thus, its proportional share among Jerusalem's total non-Jews has fallen from 33 to 18 percent. In contrast, the population of the non-Jewish subquarters outside the walls grew 2.3 times during the same years, and accounted in 1985 for 79 percent of Jerusalem's non-Jews.

As of 1983, the non-Jewish population of Jerusalem could be divided according to residential typology roughly as follows (in percentages):

	Total Non-Jews (%)	Muslims (%)	Christians (%)
Total	100.0	100.0	100.0
Old City (Sqs 1–4)	19.0	15.5	47.2
Other urban sections, first set up before 1948 (Sq 25, part of Sq 26)[a]	11.0	10.1	18.6
Other urban sections, set up after 1948 (most of Sq 27, part of Sq 32)[a]	24.7	24.5	26.3
Ex-villages (in a hemicyle around the Old City) with old nuclei and many new buildings	35.5	38.8	7.9
Ex-Bedouin (in part of Sq 33)	5.0	5.6	0.0
Refugee camp (in part of Sq 27)	4.8	5.5	0.0

[a]Including also non-Jews scattered in relevant Jewish subquarters.

Socioeconomically, according to a variety of indicators, the highest Muslim level was in the older urban neighborhoods outside the walls (Sq 25),

---

[30]The northern part of this subquarter—Musrara proper—is now being rehabilitated. The southern part has been virtually emptied of population because of large-scale rebuilding plans for the approaches to Jaffa Gate.

but lowest in the Old City (Sqs 1–4), among the ex-Bedouin (Sq 33), and in the refugee camp (Sq 27).

Jerusalem's Christians were concentrated in particular neighborhoods. A much larger proportion of Christians than Muslims lived in the Old City. The respective percentages in 1967, 1972, and 1983 were as follows: Christians—53, 56, 47 percent; Muslims—29, 23, 15.5 percent. Christians formed a majority of non-Jews and of the total population in the Christian and Armenian quarters of the Old City (Sqs 4 and 3), and were also numerous in those sections of the Muslim Quarter (Sq 2) that were contiguous with their own. They have two more concentrations in Jerusalem, in upper-level non-Jewish neighborhoods: as of 1983 they formed 18 percent in the older urban areas outside the walls (American Colony, etc., Sq 25) and altogether 9 percent in the northern Sq 27 (Beit Hanina, etc.), but as many as 22 percent in a particular tract thereof. There exist specific neighborhoods inhabited by adherents of certain Christian churches, particularly in the Old City. On the other hand, Christians are hardly represented in the south of Jerusalem (Sqs 32, 33). Socioeconomically, their upper class is found mainly in Sq 25; Sqs 27 and 3 (the latter is the Armenian Quarter) rank next; while the Christian population elsewhere in the Old City ranks lowest, on the whole.

The major changes in the spatial distribution of Jerusalem's total population between 1967 and 1985 can be seen in tables 22–23, which furnish evidence of a strong centrifugal tendency that has increased demographic dispersal over the large municipal territory. The share of the population residing in enlarged East Jerusalem among the entire municipal population increased from about a quarter to one-half—from 26 to 49 percent—during 1967–1985, because of the new residential neighborhoods established there. For the same reason, the proportion of Jews in enlarged East Jerusalem rose from nil to 43 percent of the total population there.

SURROUNDINGS OF THE CITY

Demographic dispersal did not stop at the city's boundaries, but went beyond them. The Jewish population in the corridor that links Jerusalem with the bulk of the state's territory grew from 28,000 to 44,000 during 1966–1985. The corridor now comprises 64 Jewish localities. In addition to the townlet of Beit Shemesh at its western end, there is another, Mevasseret Zion, at the eastern end, bordering on Jerusalem. The latter's recent rise of population, to 10,200 in 1985, is largely accounted for by Jerusalemites moving to one-family houses there.

At the end of 1985, Judea and Samaria had 105 Jewish settlements with 44,000 inhabitants. A large proportion of the settlers in Judea and in the southern part of Samaria came from Jerusalem, either for ideological and religious reasons or in quest of improved quality of life at comparatively low cost. Of several townlets that are being built, two lie quite close to Jerusalem: Ma'ale Adumim, with a population of only 3,500 at the time of the 1983 census, but with 9,300 inhabitants at the end of 1985; and Givat Ze'ev, which had not yet been settled in 1983, but which had 2,200 registered inhabitants at the end of 1985. These two and many other localities in Judea-Samaria fulfill a dormitory function for families whose earners work in Jerusalem. While these localities have put an end to the previous isolation of Jerusalem (from the Jewish point of view), they draw population away from the city's municipal territory. Moreover, those who leave are usually younger couples who are likely to have additional children, so that both the migration balance and the natural increase of the city's Jews are affected.

There has also been some out-movement of Jerusalem Arabs to dormitory neighborhoods beyond the municipal boundaries. In terms of building continuity, Arab Jerusalem is now increasingly linked with Arab towns and townlets on three sides: the triplet of Bethlehem, Beit Jala, and Beit Sahur in the south; Ezaria and Abu Dis in the east; and the twin towns of Ramallah and El Bira in the north. The functional links extend over a much wider area and are of a multifold character, since, as noted above, they bring into contact the Arab population of Judea-Samaria with the Arab sector, the Jewish sector, and public institutions in Jerusalem.

While it is evident that the city of Jerusalem exercises a powerful influence on its wider geographical surroundings, existing distinctions—legal, administrative, and political—between the state territory of Israel and Judea-Samaria, as well as between the Arab and Jewish localities in the latter region, make it difficult at present to speak in terms of an integrated Jerusalem metropolitan area.

Conclusion

Since 1967, substantial advances have taken place in Jerusalem, in terms of population growth, socioeconomic development, and modern town planning. However, the city's overall situation is highly complex. For one thing, its international status remains in dispute; for another, its demographic diversity is a source of considerable tension, actual or potential. Two people and three major religions have stakes in Jerusalem—and each of these, in turn, is divided and subdivided along a variety of lines. What these diverse groups have in common is a deep awareness of the city's place in history, its spiritual importance over the centuries. In their many different ways, the people of Jerusalem cherish the uniqueness of the city they share.

APPENDIX

TABLE 1. POPULATION OF ISRAEL, BY RELIGION, 1967–1985

Date	Total	Jews	Muslims	Christians	Druze[a]	% Jews	% Muslims Among Non-Jews
		Absolute Numbers (Thousands)					
Sept. 1967[b]	2,764.7	2,373.9	287.9	71.0	31.9	85.9	73.7
May 1972	3,147.7	2,686.7	352.0	72.1	36.9	85.4	76.4
June 1983	4,037.6	3,350.0	526.6	94.2	66.8	83.0	76.6
Dec. 1985	4,266.2	3,517.2	577.6	99.4	72.0	82.4	77.1
		Relative Growth (Sept. 1967=100)					
1985	154	148	201	140	226		
		Annual Percent of Growth					
1967–85	2.4	2.2	3.9	1.9	4.6		

Sources: For sources of data for all tables, see text pp. 44–45.
[a]Incl. some "others."
[b]My estimate.
Note: Details may not add to totals because of rounding.

TABLE 2.   POPULATION OF JERUSALEM, BY RELIGION, 1967–1985

Date	Total[a]	Jews	Muslims	Christians	% Jews	% Muslims Among Non-Jews
	Absolute Numbers (Thousands)					
Sept. 1967[b]	267.8	196.8	58.1	12.9	73.5	81.8
May 1972	313.9	230.3	71.8	11.7	73.4	85.9
June 1983	428.7	306.3	108.5	13.7	71.4	88.6
Dec. 1985	457.7	327.7	115.7	14.2	71.6	89.1
	Relative Growth (Sept. 1967=100)					
1985	171	167	199	110		
	Annual Percent of Growth					
1967–85	3.0	2.8	3.8	0.5		
1967–72	3.5	3.5	4.6	−2.0		
1972–83	2.9	2.6	3.8	1.4		
1983–85	2.6	2.6	2.5	1.4		

[a]Incl. some "Druze and others."
[b]My estimate.

TABLE 3. JEWS IN JERUSALEM AND OTHER LOCATIONS, 1967–1985

Location	Absolute Numbers (Thousands)				Relative Growth[a]	
	Jan. 1967	May 1972	June 1983	Dec. 1985	1967–83	1983–85
Jerusalem	193.0	230.3	306.3	327.7	159	107
Tel Aviv:						
City	383.2	357.4	317.8	312.6	83	98
Conurbation[b]	943.6	1,083.5	(1,300.0)	n.a.	138	n.a.
" [c]	n.a.	n.a.	1,530.1	1,579.7	n.a.	103
Haifa:						
City	195.8	207.2	208.4	205.8	106	99
Conurbation[b]	292.4	323.1	(364.5)	n.a.	125	n.a.
" [c]	n.a.	n.a.	369.1	372.8	n.a.	101
Israel	2,344.9	2,686.7	3,350.0	3,517.2	143	105

[a]Base year=100.
[b]As delimited for the 1972 census.
[c]As delimited for the 1983 census.
Note: "n.a." indicates data not available.

TABLE 4. COMPONENTS OF CHANGE IN POPULATION SIZE IN JERUSALEM AND OTHER LOCATIONS, BY RELIGION, 1967–1985 (RATES PER 1,000)

Components of Change	Jerusalem	Jews Tel Aviv Conurb.[a]	Haifa Conurb.[a]	Israel	Non-Jews, Jerusalem
		Jan. 1967[b]–Dec. 1976			
Total changes	32	23	18	25	38
Natural increase	21	14	12	17	34
Births	28	22	20	24	43
Deaths	7	8	8	7	9
Migratory movement	11	9	6	8	4
External migration[c]	7	2	7	8	n.a.
Internal migration	4	7	−1	0	n.a.
Entered	24	45	33	38	n.a.
Left	20	38	34	38	n.a.
		Jan. 1977–June 1983			
Total changes	21	14	6	18	32
Natural increase	21	12	8	15	34
Births	27	20	18	22	39
Deaths	6	8	10	7	5
Migratory movement	0	2	−2	3	−2
External migration[c]	2	0	0	3	−2
Internal migration	−2	2	−2	0	0
Entered	24	43	37	42	n.a.
Left	26	41	39	42	n.a.
		June 1983–Dec. 1985			
Total changes	22	10	1	16	24
Natural increase	22	11	7	14.5	28
Births	28	19	17	22	32
Deaths	6	8	10	7.5	4

Continued on the next page

TABLE 4.—*(Continued)*

Components of Change	Jerusalem	Jews Tel Aviv Conurb.[a]	Haifa Conurb.[a]	Israel	Non-Jews, Jerusalem
Migratory movement	0	−1	−6	1.5	−4
External migration[c]	3	−1	0	1.5	−4
Internal migration	−3	0	−6	0	0
Entered	28	44	36	45	2
Left	31	44	42	45	2

[a]1972 delimitation of conurbations for 1967–1976 and 1977–June 1983; 1983 delimitation for June 1983–1985.
[b]September 1967 for non-Jews in Jerusalem.
[c]Immigration minus emigration.
Note: "n.a." indicates data not available.

TABLE 5. TOTAL FERTILITY RATES[a] OF JEWISH WOMEN IN JERUSALEM AND OTHER LOCATIONS, BY REGION OF BIRTH, 1972 AND 1983

Region of Birth	Jerusalem	Tel Aviv-Yafo	Haifa	Israel
		1972		
Total	3.28	2.50	2.72	3.19
Israel	3.16	2.33	2.77	2.96
Asia-Africa	3.70	3.40	3.62	3.85
Europe-America	3.06	2.13	2.43	2.71
		1983		
Total	3.65	2.13	2.37	2.83
Israel	3.94	2.12	2.32	2.85
Asia-Africa	3.23	2.46	2.75	3.13
Europe-America	3.44	2.04	2.26	2.83

[a]"Total fertility rate" indicates the average number of children that a woman would bear during her lifetime if the age-specific fertility rates remained the same as in the year(s) under consideration. Under conditions of very low mortality the "replacement level" is 2.1 children per woman (regardless of marital status).

TABLE 6. AVERAGE BIRTH ORDER OF NEWBORN CHILDREN OF JEWISH WOMEN (AGED 30–34) IN JERUSALEM, BY ORIGIN AND RELIGIOSITY, 1974–1983[a]

Indicators of Religiosity	Total	Origin Israel	Origin Asia-Africa Born in Israel	Origin Asia-Africa Born Abroad	Origin Europe-America Born in Israel	Origin Europe-America Born Abroad
			1970–1974[b]			
Religiosity of residential region:						
Total	n.a.	4.4	n.a.	n.a.	3.3	3.2
Low	n.a.	3.6	n.a.	n.a.	3.0	2.9
High	n.a.	6.2	n.a.	n.a.	5.0	5.4
			1975–1976			
Total	3.7	4.2	3.3	4.1	3.3	3.2
Woman does not go to *mikveh*	3.0	2.9	3.0	3.6	2.6	2.4
Woman goes to *mikveh* and husband is:						
-not in yeshivah	4.3	4.4	3.8	4.5	3.8	4.0
-in yeshivah	5.2	5.5	(5.6)	4.7	4.9	5.3
			1983			
Religiosity of residential region:						
Total	3.8	4.4	3.3	3.5	3.9	3.9
Very low	3.0	3.1	3.2	3.3	2.7	3.0
Rather low	4.1	4.3	3.4	4.1	4.2	4.4
Rather high	5.4	5.8	4.7	5.2	5.5	5.6
Very high	5.9	5.8	4.9	4.9	5.9	6.5

[a]For sources, see footnote 12 to text.
[b]Both spouses of European or Israeli origin.
Note: "n.a." indicates data not available.

TABLE 7. JEWS IN JERUSALEM AND OTHER LOCATIONS, BY REGIONS OF BIRTH AND ORIGIN, 1972 AND 1983 (PERCENT)

	Jerusalem	Tel Aviv Conurb.[a]	Haifa Conurb.[a]	Israel
Region of Birth				
1972:				
Total	100.0	100.0	100.0	100.0
Israel	58.7	46.7	42.7	47.4
Asia	11.3	14.5	6.0	11.8
Africa	9.7	6.6	11.0	13.0
Europe-America	20.3	32.2	40.3	27.9
1983:				
Total	100.0	100.0	100.0	100.0
Israel	62.7	56.8	52.1	57.5
Asia	8.4	11.8	4.7	8.9
Africa	7.3	6.0	9.0	9.6
Europe-America	21.6	25.5	34.3	23.9
		Percentage Asian-African-Born Among Foreign-Born		
1972	50.8	39.5	29.7	47.0
1983	42.1	41.0	28.5	43.6
		Percentage Born in Central and Western Europe or America Among All European-American-Born		
1972	43.5	21.1	26.3	25.8
1983	53.5	23.5	20.7	27.7
Region of Origin[b]				
1972:				
Total	100.0	100.0	100.0	100.0
Israel	19.6	8.7	7.8	8.4
Asia	26.9	28.7	12.0	24.4

TABLE 7.—*(Continued)*

	Jerusalem	Tel Aviv Conurb.[a]	Haifa Conurb.[a]	Israel
Africa	17.8	11.7	19.1	23.0
Europe-Americas	35.7	50.9	61.1	44.2
1983:				
Total	100.0	100.0	100.0	100.0
Israel	23.9	16.2	14.5	15.9
Asia	23.7	27.7	11.4	22.1
Africa	16.5	13.4	19.7	21.9
Europe-Americas	35.9	42.8	54.5	40.1

[a]In this and the following tables, conurbations are as delimited for the 1972 and 1983 censuses, respectively.
[b]Birth country of foreign-born and father's birth country for Israeli-born.

TABLE 8. JEWS IN JERUSALEM AND ISRAEL, BY PRINCIPAL COUNTRY OF ORIGIN, 1983 (PERCENT)

Principal Country of Origin[a]	Jews in Jerusalem			Jews in Israel		
	Total	Born in Israel	Born Abroad	Total	Born in Israel	Born Abroad
Israel	23.9	38.2	—	15.9	27.7	—
Abroad, total	100.0	100.0	100.0	100.0	100.0	100.0
Asia, total	31.3	39.7	22.6	26.3	31.7	20.9
Turkey	3.0	3.8	2.2	3.3	3.5	3.1
Syria, Lebanon	1.7	2.1	1.2	1.4	1.6	1.1
Iraq	13.0	17.1	8.8	9.4	11.8	7.1
Yemen, South Yemen	3.3	4.8	1.8	5.8	8.1	3.6
Iran	8.7	10.1	7.2	4.3	4.6	4.0
India, Pakistan	0.4	0.5	0.5	1.3	1.3	1.4
Others in Asia	1.1	1.3	0.9	0.7	0.8	0.6
Africa, total	21.6	23.6	19.6	26.1	29.7	22.8
Morocco	16.1	18.0	14.2	16.2	18.2	14.3
Algeria, Tunisia	3.0	3.1	2.9	4.3	5.0	3.7
Libya	0.5	0.7	0.3	2.7	3.6	1.9
Egypt	1.3	1.4	1.2	2.5	2.7	2.3
Others in Africa	0.6	0.4	1.0	0.4	0.2	0.6
Europe-America, total	47.1	36.7	57.8	47.6	38.6	56.3
USSR	9.2	6.9	11.7	10.6	7.0	14.0
Poland	7.9	8.7	7.1	11.3	10.9	11.7
Rumania	5.8	4.3	7.3	10.0	7.4	12.6
Bulgaria, Greece	0.9	1.0	0.8	2.4	2.4	2.4
Germany, Austria	4.1	4.0	4.2	3.3	3.4	3.2
Czechoslovakia	1.7	1.6	1.7	1.5	1.5	1.6
Hungary	2.4	2.2	2.5	1.7	1.6	1.7
Others in Europe	6.3	4.2	8.5	3.2	2.4	3.9
North America, Oceania	6.6	2.7	10.5	1.7	0.8	2.6
Latin America	2.3	1.1	3.5	1.9	1.2	2.6

[a]See note b to table 7.

TABLE 9. FOREIGN-BORN JEWS IN JERUSALEM AND OTHER LOCATIONS, BY PERIOD OF IMMIGRATION AND REGION OF BIRTH, 1983 (PERCENT)

Period of Immigration	Total	Jerusalem Asia-Born	Jerusalem Africa-Born	Jerusalem Europe-America-Born	Tel Aviv Conurb.	Haifa Conurb.	Israel
Total	100.0	100.0	100.0	100.0	100.0	100.0	100.0
Up to 1947	16.0	18.3	3.5	19.3	19.1	18.9	15.4
1948–1954	27.8	58.0	30.7	15.1	57.5	56.3	34.1
1955–1964	17.8	10.4	43.3	12.0			23.5
1965–1971	10.8	5.7	11.4	12.5			9.2
1972–1974	8.7	1.5	3.4	13.2	23.4	24.8	7.2
1975–1979	10.8	4.1	4.3	15.6			7.0
1980–1983	8.2	1.9	3.4	12.2			3.6

TABLE 10. POPULATION OF JERUSALEM AND OTHER LOCATIONS, BY RELIGION AND AGE, 1972 AND 1983 (PERCENT AND MEDIAN)

Age	Jerusalem, total	Jews Jerusalem	Tel Aviv Conurb.	Haifa Conurb.	Israel	Non-Jews, Jerusalem Muslims	Christians
1972							
Total	100.0	100.0	100.0	100.0	100.0	100.0	100.0
0–14	35.1	31.0	26.3	25.0	29.6	49.3	29.2
15–64	58.2	61.6	64.5	65.2	62.6	46.6	61.1
65+	6.7	7.4	9.1	9.8	7.7	4.1	9.6
Median age	22.1	23.8	27.9	29.2	25.1	15.4	28.3
1983							
Total	100.0	100.0	100.0	100.0	100.0	100.0	100.0
0–14	35.1	31.7	28.2	25.9	30.0	45.9	26.7
15–64	57.4	59.6	60.2	60.7	59.9	50.5	62.6
65+	7.5	8.7	11.5	13.3	10.1	3.6	10.7
0–4	12.7	11.4	9.3	8.5	10.2	17.1	8.3
5–14	22.4	20.3	18.9	17.4	19.8	28.8	18.4
15–24	18.9	18.2	14.5	14.4	15.9	21.2	17.0
25–34	14.5	15.2	15.7	14.8	15.8	12.7	13.7
35–44	9.9	10.5	11.3	10.5	10.8	7.8	12.9
45–54	7.9	8.7	9.4	10.0	8.9	5.2	11.0
55–64	6.1	7.0	9.3	11.0	8.4	3.6	8.0
65–74	4.5	5.2	7.4	8.7	6.6	2.2	6.8
75+	2.9	3.5	4.1	4.6	3.5	1.4	3.9
Median age	22.8	25.1	29.9	31.7	27.6	16.9	29.4

TABLE 11. PERCENTAGE OF MALES IN JERUSALEM AND OTHER LOCATIONS, BY RELIGION AND AGE, 1972 AND 1983

Age	Jerusalem, total	Jews Jerusalem	Jews Tel Aviv Conurb.	Jews Haifa Conurb.	Jews Israel	Non-Jews, Jerusalem Muslims	Non-Jews, Jerusalem Christians
				1972			
Total	50.1	50.0	49.5	49.7	50.1	51.0	47.0
0–14	51.6	51.5	51.2	51.7	51.4	52.1	50.6
15–64	49.4	49.4	48.8	49.2	49.6	50.1	46.3
65+	48.1	48.6	49.6	47.7	49.1	48.1	40.2
				1983			
Total	49.9	49.8	49.0	49.0	49.6	50.5	45.6
0–14	51.5	51.7	51.1	51.3	51.3	51.0	50.5
15–64	51.8	49.5	48.4	48.6	49.3	50.1	45.1
65+	45.3	45.3	46.8	46.0	46.7	48.7	36.5

TABLE 12. POPULATION OF JERUSALEM AND ISRAEL, BY RELIGION, SEX, AND MARITAL STATUS,[a] 1972 AND 1983 (PERCENT)

Marital Status	Jerusalem, total 1983	Jews Jerusalem 1972	Jews Jerusalem 1983	Jews Israel 1972	Jews Israel 1983	Non-Jews, Jerusalem Muslims 1983	Non-Jews, Jerusalem Christians 1983
			Men				
Total	100.0	100.0	100.0	100.0	100.0	100.0	100.0
Single	36.6	35.4	34.6	31.5	28.9	41.8	46.9
Married	60.2	61.4	61.7	65.1	66.8	56.6	50.0
Divorced	1.4	1.0	1.7	0.9	1.6	0.5	0.9
Widowed	1.8	2.2	2.0	2.5	2.6	1.1	2.2
			Women				
Total	100.0	100.0	100.0	100.0	100.0	100.0	100.0
Single	27.6	28.3	26.6	22.9	20.8	28.4	42.4
Married	59.0	58.8	59.5	63.7	64.1	60.4	42.9
Divorced	3.0	2.1	3.5	1.9	3.2	1.5	1.7
Widowed	10.3	10.7	10.4	11.5	11.9	9.7	13.0

[a]Ages 15 and over.

TABLE 13. PERCENTAGE OF EVER-MARRIED PERSONS IN JERUSALEM AND ISRAEL, BY RELIGION, SEX, AND AGE, 1972 AND 1983

| | Jews | | | | Non-Jews, Jerusalem | |
| | Jerusalem | | Israel | | Muslims | Christians |
Age	1972	1983	1972	1983	1983	1983
			Men			
15–19	1.2	1.3	1.1	0.9	2.4	0.5
20–24	22.2	17.5	23.2	17.2	25.3	6.5
25–29	69.0	61.3	72.5	67.7	66.4	34.3
30–34	87.9	86.0	90.7	88.6	87.8	64.1
35–39	92.0	93.2	94.3	94.7	93.8	78.1
40–44	94.2	95.1	95.3	96.5	96.5	80.5
45–64	95.1	95.5	96.8	96.9	97.7	81.4
65+	97.0	96.7	97.7	97.7	96.4	74.7
			Women			
15–19	5.5	4.6	6.7	5.1	22.1	5.3
20–24	43.8	38.8	52.9	47.5	62.7	36.3
25–29	75.6	73.4	84.2	81.7	84.7	62.1
30–34	89.2	84.4	93.8	90.5	89.1	71.0
35–39	93.9	89.6	96.8	93.8	89.6	71.3
40–44	95.7	93.3	97.5	96.1	90.6	68.5
45–64	96.2	96.0	97.9	97.9	94.2	68.6
65+	96.3	96.6	97.4	97.7	95.9	61.0

TABLE 14. HOUSEHOLDS IN JERUSALEM AND OTHER LOCATIONS, BY RELIGION AND HOUSEHOLD SIZE, 1972 AND 1983

Number of Persons per Household	Jerusalem, total	Jews Jerusalem	Jews Tel Aviv Conurb.	Jews Haifa Conurb.	Jews Israel	Non-Jews, Jerusalem Muslims	Non-Jews, Jerusalem Christians
Percent Distribution, 1983							
Total	100.0	100.0	100.0	100.0	100.0	100.0	100.0
1	19.4	21.6	19.6	21.9	18.6	7.5	23.4
2–3	33.0	36.4	40.7	43.8	39.3	16.7	27.1
4–5	27.4	28.8	32.4	28.8	32.4	20.0	27.0
6–7	11.8	9.9	6.2	4.6	7.7	21.1	15.0
8–9	4.7	2.4	0.9	0.7	1.5	16.6	5.1
10+	3.6	0.9	0.3	0.2	0.5	18.2	2.3
Average Household Size							
1972	4.0	3.6	3.3	3.2	3.6	6.2	4.1
1983	3.8	3.3	3.1	2.9	3.2	6.3	3.8

TABLE 15. POPULATION IN JERUSALEM AND OTHER LOCATIONS, BY RELIGION, SEX, AND EDUCATIONAL LEVEL, 1972 AND 1983[a] (PERCENT)

Year and Sex	Jerusalem, total	Jews Jerusalem	Jews Tel Aviv Conurb.[b]	Jews Haifa Conurb.[b]	Israel	Non-Jews, Jerusalem Muslims	Non-Jews, Jerusalem Christians
			0–4 Years of Study				
1972:							
Total	18.3	11.4	10.9	11.4	13.7	44.3	25.6
Men	13.3	7.4	8.3	9.0	10.4	34.5	22.6
Women	23.1	15.1	13.6	13.9	16.8	54.1	28.1
1983:							
Total	11.6	7.4	8.1	7.6	9.0	26.8	11.0
Men	7.8	4.7	n.a.	n.a.	6.6	18.8	6.8
Women	15.3	9.9	n.a.	n.a.	11.3	34.9	14.4
			13+ Years of Study				
1972:							
Total	21.5	26.2	16.0	17.2	14.9	4.6	12.4
Men	23.5	28.2	17.1	20.1	15.9	6.6	16.4
Women	19.6	24.4	14.3	15.1	13.9	2.5	9.1
1983:							
Total	29.9	34.8	23.2	26.3	23.1	12.7	27.4
Men	31.6	35.7	n.a.	n.a.	23.9	16.7	33.1
Women	28.3	33.9	n.a.	n.a.	22.4	8.7	23.0

[a] In 1972, ages 14 and over; in 1983, ages 15 and over.
[b] In 1972, total population, i.e., including some non-Jews.
Note: "n.a." indicates data not available.

TABLE 15A. POPULATION IN JERUSALEM, BY RELIGION, ORIGIN, SEX, AND EDUCATIONAL LEVEL, 1983 (PERCENT)

Religion and Origin	0–4 Years of Study[a] Men	0–4 Years of Study[a] Women	13+ Years of Study[a] Men	13+ Years of Study[a] Women
Total	8.1	14.7	31.8	28.4
Jews, total	4.6	8.9	35.9	34.1
Origin Israel	1.9	4.3	33.0	27.5
Origin Asia				
Born in Israel	3.7	10.7	18.3	15.8
Born abroad	11.3	24.8	21.6	20.2
Origin Africa				
Born in Israel	4.2	7.9	15.9	18.9
Born abroad	9.0	18.4	27.2	24.5
Origin Europe-America				
Born in Israel	1.3	3.2	56.1	55.2
Born abroad	1.5	2.2	56.6	54.9
Non-Jews, total	21.4	35.2	18.1	10.5
Muslims	24.9	41.9	15.3	7.7
Christians	6.3	11.5	34.3	26.6

[a]Age-standardized data according to age distribution of Jerusalem's total population (ages 15 and over); my tabulations.

TABLE 16. POPULATION OF JERUSALEM, BY RELIGION AND SPOKEN LANGUAGES, DAILY[a] AND PRINCIPAL USE, 1983 (PERCENT)[b]

Language	Total Population[c] Daily Use	Total Population[c] Principal Use	Jews Daily Use	Jews Principal Use	Muslims Daily Use	Muslims Principal Use	Christians Daily Use	Christians Principal Use
Hebrew	72.2	62.8	93.9	84.2	8.9	0.5	12.5	3.4
Arabic	33.2	25.5	11.5	1.7	99.3	98.9	77.8	68.2
English	14.2	3.3	15.0	4.1	10.3	0.3	30.1	6.2
French	4.2	1.2	5.3	1.5	0.0	—	6.5	2.7
Yiddish	3.9	1.1	5.2	1.5	—	—	0.1	0.0
Spanish[d]	2.9	0.7	3.9	1.0	0.1	0.0	0.8	0.4
Russian	2.6	1.3	3.4	1.7	0.0	0.0	1.5	1.3
Persian	2.1	0.6	2.9	0.8	0.0	—	—	—
German	2.0	0.6	2.5	0.7	0.1	0.0	2.3	1.5
Rumanian	1.5	0.5	2.0	0.7	0.0	0.0	0.7	0.4
Hungarian	1.1	0.4	1.4	0.5	—	—	0.2	0.2
Kurdish	0.8	0.1	1.1	0.2	—	—	—	—
Polish	0.5	0.1	0.7	0.2	—	—	0.7	0.5
Grusinian[e]	0.5	0.3	0.7	0.4	0.1	0.1	0.0	0.0
Armenian	0.4	0.3	0.0	0.0	0.0	0.0	10.3	8.5
Bokharian	0.4	0.2	0.5	0.2	0.1	0.1	—	—
Italian	0.3	0.1	0.3	0.1	0.1	0.0	2.9	1.7
Greek	0.2	0.1	0.0	0.0	0.0	0.0	3.5	2.4

[a] Principal or second language in daily speech.
[b] My tabulations; the percentages in the "Daily Use" columns add up to more than 100.0, since two languages could be reported by a person.
[c] Aged 15 and over.
[d] Incl. Ladino.
[e] I.e., Georgian.

TABLE 17. PERCENTAGE IN LABOR FORCE[a] IN JERUSALEM AND OTHER LOCATIONS, BY RELIGION AND SEX, 1972 AND 1983[b]

Year and Sex	Jerusalem, total	Jews Jerusalem	Jews Tel Aviv Conurb.[c]	Jews Haifa Conurb.[c]	Jews Israel	Non-Jews, Jerusalem Muslims	Non-Jews, Jerusalem Christians
1972:							
Total	49.9	51.9	50.8	50.3	51.6	35.9	40.4
Men	66.5	66.7	69.9	69.3	68.4	66.1	63.7
Women	33.9	41.2	32.5	32.5	35.0	6.1	21.5
1983:							
Total	51.7	57.3	54.5	53.3	55.3	33.7	38.0
Men	63.3	64.6	68.0	66.2	67.1	59.8	54.8
Women	40.5	50.4	42.1	40.7	44.2	7.3	24.8

[a]Annual civilian labor force.
[b]In 1972, ages 14 and over; in 1983, ages 15 and over.
[c]In 1972, total population, i.e., including some non-Jews.

TABLE 17A. PERCENTAGE IN LABOR FORCE[a] IN JERUSALEM, BY RELIGION, ORIGIN, AND SEX, 1983

Religion and Origin	Men[b]	Women[b]
Total	64.0	40.5
Jews, total	64.7	50.7
Origin Israel	63.3	49.6
Origin Asia		
Born in Israel	65.7	48.1
Born abroad	65.3	44.9
Origin Africa		
Born in Israel	65.1	49.1
Born abroad	65.0	49.4
Origin Europe-America		
Born in Israel	66.1	57.0
Born abroad	65.8	56.2
Non-Jews, total	60.2	10.3
Muslims	60.8	7.3
Christians	53.9	25.7

[a] Annual civilian labor force.
[b] Age-standardized data according to age distribution of Jerusalem's total population (ages 15 and over); my tabulations.

TABLE 18. PERCENTAGE EMPLOYED IN PUBLIC AND COMMUNITY SERVICES[a] IN JERUSALEM AND OTHER LOCATIONS, BY RELIGION AND SEX, 1972 AND 1983[b]

Year and Sex	Jerusalem, total	Jews Jerusalem	Jews Tel Aviv Conurb.[c]	Jews Haifa Conurb.[c]	Israel	Non-Jews, Jerusalem Muslims	Non-Jews, Jerusalem Christians
1972:							
Total	45.3	49.0	25.5	31.0	28.2	22.2	38.0
Men	35.4	39.5	19.5	24.6	21.8	19.0	29.3
Women	64.5	64.5	38.6	45.3	41.4	69.7	58.3
1983:							
Total	45.9	48.8	27.6	34.8	31.5	26.6	47.3
Men	34.6	37.7	n.a.	n.a.	21.8	22.2	35.0
Women	62.6	62.1	n.a.	n.a.	45.7	75.0	68.1

[a] Among annual civilian labor force.
[b] In 1972, ages 14 and over; in 1983, ages 15 and over.
[c] In 1972, total population, i.e. including some non-Jews.
Note: "n.a." indicates data not available.

TABLE 18A. PERCENTAGE EMPLOYED IN PUBLIC AND COMMUNITY SERVICES[a] IN JERUSALEM, BY RELIGION, ORIGIN, AND SEX, 1983

Religion and Origin	Men[b]	Women[b]
Total	34.2	62.5
Jews, total	37.2	62.0
Origin Israel	34.3	61.5
Origin Asia		
Born in Israel	29.9	61.3
Born abroad	27.5	60.3
Origin Africa		
Born in Israel	36.9	55.8
Born abroad	35.6	61.5
Origin Europe-America		
Born in Israel	48.6	68.0
Born abroad	44.5	62.0
Non-Jews, total	25.1	71.2
Muslims	23.7	72.1
Christians	34.3	67.8

[a] Among annual civilian labor force.
[b] Age-standardized data according to age distribution of Jerusalem's total labor force; my tabulations.

TABLE 19. PERCENTAGE EMPLOYED IN ACADEMIC, OTHER PROFESSIONAL, MANAGERIAL, AND CLERICAL OCCUPATIONS[a] IN JERUSALEM AND OTHER LOCATIONS, BY RELIGION AND SEX, 1972 AND 1983[b]

Year and Sex	Jerusalem, total	Jews Jerusalem	Tel Aviv Conurb.[c]	Haifa Conurb.[c]	Israel	Non-Jews, Jerusalem Muslims	Christians
1972:							
Total	52.3	58.3	44.6	47.0	40.3	15.8	42.5
Men	41.9	49.2	35.6	38.3	32.2	12.3	34.2
Women	72.2	72.7	63.6	65.8	56.3	68.5	59.3
1983:							
Total	57.5	63.2	53.6	56.5	50.3	21.9	54.5
Men	45.8	53.5	n.a.	n.a.	37.3	16.5	44.9
Women	74.7	74.7	n.a.	n.a.	65.6	77.6	71.1

[a] Among annual civilian labor force.
[b] In 1972, ages 14 and over; in 1983, ages 15 and over.
[c] In 1972, total population, i.e., including some non-Jews.
Note: "n.a." indicates data not available.

TABLE 19A. PERCENTAGE EMPLOYED IN ACADEMIC, OTHER PROFESSIONAL, MANAGERIAL, AND CLERICAL OCCUPATIONS[a] IN JERUSALEM, BY RELIGION, ORIGIN, AND SEX

Religion and Origin	Men[b]	Women[b]
Total	45.3	73.5
Jews, total	52.7	73.8
Origin Israel	53.3	78.3
Origin Asia		
Born in Israel	38.8	70.9
Born abroad	35.1	57.6
Origin Africa		
Born in Israel	42.7	69.2
Born abroad	44.3	56.8
Origin Europe-America		
Born in Israel	69.5	87.2
Born abroad	67.6	78.0
Non-Jews, total	21.1	72.5
Muslims	17.3	74.0
Christians	45.2	70.8

[a] Among annual civilian labor force.
[b] Age-standardized data according to age distribution of Jerusalem's total labor force; my tabulations.

TABLE 20. SELECTED INDICATORS OF HOUSING CONDITIONS AND STANDARD OF LIVING IN JERUSALEM AND OTHER LOCATIONS, BY RELIGION, 1972[a] AND 1983

			Jews			Non-Jews, Jerusalem	
Selected Indicators	Jerusalem, total	Jerusalem	Tel Aviv Conurb.[a]	Haifa Conurb.[a]	Israel	Muslims	Christians

1972

% Apartments:							
With up to 2 rooms	45.1	39.9	42.0	40.0	39.8	67.2	4.4
With 4+ rooms	16.3	17.0	11.0	13.0	13.0		
Aver. no. of persons per room	1.6	1.4	1.3	1.3	1.4	2.7	
% Apartments owned by household	55.4	58.2	n.a.	n.a.	65.3[d]	45.0	
% Households possessing:							
Telephone	43.0	51.3	52.6	60.9	44.5	7.5	
Car	19.7	22.8	27.1	23.7	23.3	6.3	
Index of average income of employee-headed households (Jewish average for Israel = 100.0)[b]							
Per household	98.2	107.4	103.8	112.9	100.0	51.0	
Per person	89.6	108.1	122.4	128.7	100.0	31.4	

	1983					
% Apartments:						
Built 1975+	20.9	23.1	20.6	19.2	23.5	12.7
With up to 2 rooms	29.4	24.2	24.1	24.3	22.2	52.0
With 4+ rooms	22.6	23.3	20.0	21.2	23.6	19.3
Aver. no. of persons per room	1.3	1.1	1.0	1.0	1.1	2.3
% Apartments owned by household	63.0	64.7	78.0	73.2	71.8	63.7
% Households that moved into apartments 1975+	52.8	54.9	47.4	46.5	50.5[d]	41.6
% Households possessing:						
Telephone	75.0	87.8	77.6	86.0	75.8	18.4
Car	40.2	44.8	49.5	45.5	46.4	20.6
Index of average income of employee-headed households (Jewish average for Israel = 100.0)[b]						
Per household	92.3	101.2	102.5	104.5	100.0	53.6
Per standard person[c]	86.5	104.2	105.7	107.8	100.0	34.8

9.7	
18.7	
46.2	27.9
58.6	53.9

[a]In 1972, total households, i.e., including some non-Jewish ones.
[b]In 1972, gross annual income in urban localities only; in 1983, net monthly income.
[c]I.e., adjusted for number of persons in household.
[d]Urban localities only.
Note: "n.a." indicates data not available.

TABLE 21. POPULATION OF JERUSALEM, BY RELIGION AND SUBQUARTER, 1983

Subquarter[a] No./Designation	Total population (thousands)	Total	Jews	Muslims	Christians	% Jews	% Muslims Among Non-Jews
Total	428.7	100.0	100.0	100.0	100.0	95.7	88.7
Old Israeli zone, total	232.7	54.2	75.1	1.4	10.2	98.7	51.6
5,6 Town Center	8.1	1.9	2.5	0.1	2.1	95.1	34.0
7,8 Me'ah She'arim, Kerem Avraham	44.6	10.4	14.5	0.0	0.3	99.8	36.8
9 Nahla'ot	9.5	2.2	3.1	0.0	0.2	99.7	13.3
10 Rehaviah	8.3	1.9	2.7	0.0	0.6	99.0	2.4
11,12 Talbieh, Katamon	15.8	3.7	5.1	0.1	2.0	97.9	14.7
13,14 Bak'a, Talpiot	20.1	4.7	6.2	0.9	2.0	93.9	76.7
15 Rassco	13.5	3.1	4.4	0.0	0.3	99.6	10.7
16 Katamonim	24.0	5.6	7.8	0.1	0.2	99.6	77.8
17,18 Romemah, Givat Sha'ul	19.3	4.5	6.3	0.0	0.2	99.0	55.6
19–21 Kiryat Moshe, Bayit va-Gan	37.4	8.7	12.1	0.1	0.7	99.7	58.8
22–24 Kiryat ha-Yovel	32.1	7.5	10.4	0.1	1.6	98.8	40.0

Ex-Jordanian zone, total	196.0	45.8	24.9	98.6	89.8	39.1	89.6
1–4 Old City	25.5	6.0	0.7	15.5	47.2	8.8	72.1
25 American Colony	7.6	1.8	0.0	5.7	10.0	0.1	32.9
26,27 Et-Tur, Beit Hanina	50.1	11.7	0.0	42.7	26.3	0.3	92.8
28 Ramat Eshkol[b]	14.8	3.4	4.7	0.2	0.4	98.2	75.8
29–31 French Hill, Neveh Ya'akov, Ramot	34.1	8.0	10.7	0.9	2.2	96.3	74.2
32,33 Silwan, Sur Bahir	36.7	8.6	0.0	33.5	2.4	0.1	99.1
34,35 East Talpiot, Gilo	27.2	6.3	8.8	0.1	1.3	98.8	42.8

[a]For principal neighborhoods in the various subquarters see map 1.
[b]Until 1967 across the armistice line and unbuilt.

TABLE 22. CHANGES IN SPATIAL DISTRIBUTION OF JERUSALEM'S POPULATION, BY RELIGION AND SUBQUARTER, SEPT. 1967[a]–1985

Subquarter[b] No./Designation	Total Population 1967	Total Population 1985	Jews 1967	Jews 1983	Jews 1985	Non-Jews 1967	Non-Jews 1985
				Thousands			
Total	267.8	457.7[d]	196.5	306.3	327.7[d]	71.3	130.0[d]
Old Israeli zone	199.2	234.3	196.5	229.7	231.2	2.7	3.1
Ex-Jordanian zone	68.6	223.4	—	76.6	96.5	68.6	126.9
				Percent			
Total	100.0	100.0	100.0	100.0	100.0	100.0	100.0
Old Israeli zone, total	74.4	51.1	100.0	75.1	70.6	3.8	2.5
5,6 Town Center	6.0	1.5	7.9	2.5	2.1	0.9	0.3
7,8 Me'ah She'arim, Kerem Avraham	14.8	10.0	20.2	14.5	13.9	0.0	0.1
9 Nahla'ot	7.0	1.8	9.5	3.1	2.5	0.0	0.0
10 Rehaviah	3.9	1.7	5.3	2.7	2.3	0.0	0.1
11,12 Talbieh, Katamon	7.0	3.2	9.1	5.1	4.4	0.7	0.2
13,14 Bak'a, Talpiot	6.5	4.5	8.3	6.2	5.9	1.9	1.0
15 Rassco	2.1	3.0	2.8	4.4	4.1	0.0	0.1
16 Katamonim	7.5	5.3	10.2	7.8	7.3	0.1	0.1
17,18 Romemah, Givat Sha'ul	3.7	5.2	5.1	6.3	7.2	0.0	0.0
19–21 Kiryat Moshe, Bayit va-Gan	6.0	8.2	8.1	12.1	11.5	0.0	0.2
22–24 Kiryat ha-Yovel	9.9	6.8	13.5	10.4	9.4	0.2	0.4

Ex-Jordanian Zone, total	25.6	48.9	—	24.9	29.4	96.2	97.5
1–4 Old City	8.8	5.7	—	0.7	0.8	33.2	18.3
25 American Colony	2.3	1.7	—	0.0	0.0	8.7	5.9
26,27 Et-Tur, Beit Hanina	8.1	11.7	—	0.0	0.0	30.3	40.9
28 Ramat Eshkol[c]	—	3.3	—	4.7	4.5	—	0.2
29–31 French Hill, Neveh Ya'akov, Ramot	—	9.8	—	10.7	13.3	—	1.1
32,33 Silwan, Sur Bahir	6.4	8.8	—	0.0	0.0	24.0	30.7
34,35 East Talpiot, Gilo	—	7.9	—	8.8	10.8	—	0.4

[a] My estimates except for census figures of non-Jews in ex-Jordanian zone (East Jerusalem).

[b,c] See notes a and b to table 21.

[d] Including some persons whose domicile was not known.

TABLE 23. CHANGES IN SIZE AND DENSITY OF JERUSALEM'S POPULATION, BY SUBQUARTER, SEPT. 1967[a]–1985

Subquarter[b] No./Designation	Population Thousands 1967	Population Thousands 1985	% Change	Density[e] 1967	Density[e] 1985
Total	267.8	457.7[d]	+71	2.5	4.2
Old Israeli zone, total	199.0	234.0	+18	5.3	6.3
5,6 Town Center	16.1	7.1	−56	12.6	5.6
7,8 Me'ah She'arim, Kerem Avraham	39.6	45.5	+15	14.9	17.1
9 Nahla'ot	18.7	8.2	−56	30.4	13.3
10 Rehaviah	10.4	7.7	−26	16.2	12.0
11,12 Talbieh, Katamon	18.5	14.9	−19	10.5	8.5
13,14 Bak'a, Talpiot	17.5	20.5	+17	4.0	4.8
15 Rassco	5.6	13.5	+141	4.8	11.5
16 Katamonim	20.1	24.0	+19	9.8	11.7
17,18 Romemah, Givat Sha'ul	10.0	23.6	+136	1.5	3.7
19–21 Kiryat Moshe, Bayit va-Gan	16.0	37.7	+135	1.8	4.2
22–24 Kiryat ha-Yovel	26.5	31.3	+18	3.6	4.2

Ex-Jordanian zone, total	68.6	222.6	+224	1.0	3.2
1–4 Old City	23.7	26.2	+10	27.2	30.1
25 American Colony	6.2	7.6	+22	4.1	5.0
26,27 Et-Tur, Beit Hanina	21.6	53.2	+146	1.0	2.4
28 Ramat Eshkol[c]	—	15.0	great	—	10.5
29–31 French Hill, Neveh Ya'akov, Ramot	—	44.9	great	—	3.2
32,33 Silwan, Sur Bahir	17.1	39.8	+132	0.6	1.5
34,35 East Talpiot, Gilo	—	35.9	great	—	9.4

[a,d] See notes [a] and [d] to table 22.
[b,c] See notes [a] and [b] to table 21.
[e] Thousands of inhabitants per square kilometer.

Review of the Year

UNITED STATES

Civic and Political

Intergroup Relations

TWO EVENTS IN 1985 created particular tension for the Jewish community. One was President Ronald Reagan's decision to visit the military cemetery at Bitburg in West Germany, where 47 *Waffen* SS soldiers were buried. The second was the nationwide speaking tour of Black Muslim leader Louis Farrakhan, preaching his anti-Israel and anti-Jewish message to successively larger, and seemingly approving, black audiences. The first event stirred memories of a time when the Christian world had been indifferent, if not worse, to the tragedy of the Holocaust. The second was seen by many as proof that the decline in black-Jewish relations, which set in after the 1960s civil rights revolution, was in fact growing worse.

The Bitburg Controversy

The Bitburg episode began when Chancellor Helmut Kohl of West Germany invited U.S. president Ronald Reagan to add a visit to Germany to a scheduled economic summit meeting in Europe in May. At this time, the two leaders would commemorate the 40th anniversary of Nazi Germany's surrender to the Allies in World War II. Kohl, who had been upset by the refusal of the Western Allies to include him in the 1984 D-Day celebration in France, saw the V-E Day anniversary as an opportunity to demonstrate U.S.-German reconciliation. Although Chancellor Kohl had suggested that the ceremonies include visits to both a concentration camp and a military cemetery, President Reagan announced in February—without giving a reason—that he would not visit a camp. On March 21, responding to a question about this at a press conference, the president said that the German people have had "a guilt feeling that's imposed on them, and I think it's unnecessary." Further, he indicated, he did not want to "reawaken" painful memories of the past.

The announcement on April 11 that the president would visit a military cemetery at Bitburg and the subsequent discovery that among the 2,000 dead soldiers were 47 members of the notorious *Waffen* SS ignited a storm of protest. Jewish organizations, which, predictably, were sharply critical, were joined in their protest by a range of non-Jewish groups that included the American Legion, the National Council of Churches, the National Association for the Advancement of Colored People

(NAACP), and such eminent public figures as former president Jimmy Carter and Archbishop John J. O'Connor of New York.

In response to the outcry, and following an April 16 meeting with a delegation of the Conference of Presidents of Major Jewish Organizations, the president announced that he would visit a concentration camp. The change in plans did not, however, mollify the critics. Speaking at a Holocaust memorial service taking place in New York the very next day, Dr. Norman Lamm, president of Yeshiva University, told the audience of over 5,000: "A courtesy call at a conveniently located concentration camp cannot compensate for the callous and obscene scandal of honoring dead Nazis."

The U.S. Senate sent Reagan a letter "strongly urging" him not to visit the cemetery, and a similar request was made by the U.S. Holocaust Memorial Council, whose 55 members, presidential appointees, were prepared to consider mass resignation. The president managed to further inflame his critics when he said in a speech to newspaper editors and broadcasters on April 18 that the "young soldiers" buried in Bitburg were "victims of Nazism also," thus appearing to equate those who fought under Hitler with those whom Nazi soldiers burned in the crematoria.

The emotional climax of the controversy occurred the next day, at a White House ceremony in which Elie Wiesel, after receiving the Congressional Gold Medal of Achievement, implored President Reagan to cancel the Bitburg visit. "That place, Mr. President," Wiesel said—more in sadness than in anger—"is not your place. Your place is with the victims of the SS."

Unmoved by the protests and pleas, the president insisted, in remarks delivered just before his departure for Europe, that the cemetery visit was "morally right." His intention, he said, was not to honor anyone but to affirm the "miracle" of postwar reconciliation. In the final days before the president's departure, both houses of Congress passed resolutions (the Senate by a voice vote, the House by a vote of 390-26), calling on the president to change his plans.

Despite the uproar, the president's trip went forward essentially as planned. Both at Bergen-Belsen and at Bitburg Reagan delivered moving and sensitive remarks. At Bitburg, addressing himself to survivors of the Holocaust, he said, "Many of you are worried that reconciliation means forgetting. But I promise you, we will never forget."

On the president's return, some Jewish leaders sought to contain any potential damage in relations with the White House that might have been caused by the visit. Kenneth J. Bialkin, chairman of the Conference of Presidents of Major Jewish Organizations, told a press conference that while the Bitburg episode "was most regrettable," the president's words at Bitburg and at Bergen-Belsen "confirm our confidence in his compassion and understanding." He went on to acknowledge the president's support of Israel and his commitment to persecuted Jews in the USSR and elsewhere.

Jewish sensitivity to the repercussions of the episode grew out of awareness that Jews and non-Jews did not necessarily view the visit in the same light. A *Washington*

Post- ABC poll conducted at the height of the controversy, on April 22, revealed that Americans disapproved of the president's visit by only a slim margin: 51 percent considered it a bad idea; 39 percent approved. A *Newsweek* telephone poll published a week later yielded similar results.

A troubling finding in various surveys was the degree of hostility expressed toward Jewish critics. According to a *New York Times*/CBS News poll, 38 percent of respondents—including 60 percent of those who supported the cemetery visit and 18 percent of those who opposed it—agreed with the statement that "Jewish leaders in the U.S. protested too much over his visit." Reacting to such responses, Midge Decter suggested, in the August *Commentary,* that because the Holocaust "is no longer a living memory" for many people, in the course of a month "Jews had progressed from being seen as people whose overweening sensitivity sometimes got in the way of necessary policy to being seen as no more than a self-serving pressure group, like the oil or farm lobby." (See "The Bitburg Controversy," in this volume, for a more detailed treatment of the subject.)

Holocaust-Related Issues

The Bitburg episode took place against a background of rising interest in the role played by U.S. intelligence officials after World War II in helping Nazi war criminals and former enemy scientists to enter the country and to become citizens, presumably to give the United States an edge on the Soviets in the cold war. Evidence for such a conspiracy was presented in a number of recent books, including *Quiet Neighbors: Prosecuting Nazi War Criminals in America,* written by Alan A. Ryan, Jr., former director of the Office of Special Investigations of the Justice Department. Some doubt was cast on the conspiracy theory, however, by a report submitted to Congress by the General Accounting Office. According to the GAO study, while 12 percent of the 114 individuals investigated were considered to have questionable records, there was no evidence of a program "specifically developed to aid the immigration of these types of aliens into the U.S." By the end of the year there was a growing demand for the formation of a commission to investigate the role of U.S. intelligence agencies in bringing former Nazis to the United States after the war.

The issue of Nazi war criminals receiving safe haven in the United States continued to exacerbate the relations of various émigré organizations with both the Jewish community and the Justice Department. In April the World Jewish Congress issued a report charging more than 30 Baltic, Ukrainian, and other Eastern European groups with engaging in "an intensive and shocking campaign aimed at undermining the Justice Department's Nazi prosecution program." Specific activities cited in the report were: raising legal defense funds for accused Nazis, being openly anti-Semitic in their publications, and waging a campaign to set a statute of limitations on war crimes and to close down the Justice Department's Nazi-hunting unit. Officials of the Justice Department's Office of Special Investigations, which was responsible for pursuing Nazi war criminals, confirmed that émigré groups hampered the department's work. In response, leaders of these organizations attacked the World Jewish Congress for its "vicious defamation campaign." They also countercharged that U.S. prosecutors relied on evidence supplied by the KGB, which was obviously suspect, since the Soviets sought to defame the Eastern European groups.

In July the Superior Court of Los Angeles ruled that the Institute for Historical Review must pay Mel Mermelstein, a Holocaust survivor, the $50,000 reward it had offered for "proof" that the Nazis gassed Jews in concentration camps. The episode stemmed from 1980, when, in response to a challenge issued by the institute, Mermelstein submitted declarations by Auschwitz survivors who had witnessed friends and relatives being taken away to be gassed. In 1981, when the institute refused to pay the reward it had promised, Mermelstein brought suit. Even after agreeing to the settlement, the institute continued to publicize its contention that the Holocaust never happened, a position shared by a small number of so-called revisionist historians.

Black-Jewish Relations

LOUIS FARRAKHAN

The year saw the rising popularity of Louis Farrakhan, the Chicago-based leader of the Nation of Islam movement, who first gained public attention through his association with Jesse Jackson in the latter's bid to gain the Democratic presidential nomination in 1984. In the months following the election, Farrakhan embarked on a speaking tour of campuses and major cities around the country. During this period, the size of the crowds he attracted, the extremist and anti-Semitic tenor of his remarks, and the enthusiasm that greeted his statements made him a focus of attention and concern.

Whereas 300 had been a large crowd in Detroit a year earlier, some 6,000 now came to see him in that city. In Atlanta about 7,000 packed the hall and a large crowd stood outside. In Chicago there were 15,000 in the audience, in Philadelphia, 7,000, in Houston, 5,000. In July some 10,000 blacks jammed the Washington, D.C., Convention Center to hear Farrakhan's message. By the time he reached Los Angeles on September 15, where he spoke before 15,000 at the Felt Auditorium, he had become a major media event, appearing on "The Phil Donahue Show," the Cable News Network, and other news outlets.

Farrakhan's call for black self-determination and economic self-sufficiency was a primary source of his appeal. In May he announced the receipt of a $5-million interest-free loan from Libyan leader Muammar Qaddafi that would be used "to help blacks build economic enterprises in the U.S.," specifically, businesses to produce and sell toiletries, such as soap, deodorant, and toothpaste. (Qaddafi had addressed a Nation of Islam conference in Chicago, in February, by satellite, urging black soldiers to "leave the American army" and to join with other blacks to fight "your racist oppressors" and establish a separate nation.)

If Farrakhan's vision of economic independence for blacks had widespread appeal, so too, apparently, did his anti-Jewish and anti-Israel sentiments. In a report summarizing Farrakhan's activities, issued in June, the Anti-Defamation League (ADL) noted that he blended the preacher's call to self-respect and self-help with the demagogue's call to scapegoating and suspicion. At the State University of New York at Old Westbury, Long Island, Farrakhan charged Jews with threatening Jesse Jackson's life and with killing Jesus and declared they would be "punished and die" for these acts. In a speech at Northeastern University in Boston, Farrakhan was quoted as saying that Jews had "failed in their covenant." In October the *New York Times* reported that Farrakhan had been meeting with a former leader of the Ku Klux Klan in California, sharing intelligence about Jewish "extremist" organizations, and that the latter had attended the Farrakhan rally in Los Angeles as an invited guest. Of special concern was Farrakhan's apparent appeal to black college and high school students, who seemed to enjoy his general bashing of whites.

Early on, Jewish groups publicly and privately pressed black leaders to denounce Farrakhan's anti-Semitic remarks. While some did, the response was often timid or ambivalent. In some of Farrakhan's appearances, especially at the start of his nationwide tour, black city council members, state representatives, and prominent clergymen sat on the platform with him, and he was applauded by black intellectuals and professionals as well as the underprivileged. Only as Farrakhan's racism began drawing adverse comment from editorial writers in leading journals, as well as from civic and religious leaders, did black politicians show increasing discomfort. At the same time, they were reluctant to denounce Farrakhan publicly, for fear of dividing the black community and antagonizing their own base of support. Washington mayor Marion Barry, for example, delayed for two months in speaking out; then he offered a mild rebuke, not of Farrakhan but of specific remarks made by him. Los Angeles mayor Tom Bradley refused to denounce Farrakhan before his September West Coast appearance; afterward he criticized the "racism, hatred and bigotry" he said he found in the speech. Atlanta mayor Andrew Young declared in a newspaper interview, with obvious reference to Farrakhan's economic ideas, that he was "a legitimate player in the mainstream of black ideas." In November all 14 black members of the Chicago City Council voted against a resolution to condemn him.

A number of black political leaders expressed annoyance at appeals from Jews to speak out—to pass a litmus test, as it were, on where they stood on Farrakhan—on the grounds that this would make them appear to be bowing to Jewish pressure. Indeed, Farrakhan charged in September, in a Baltimore speech, that black politicians who criticized him were only seeking to "placate the Jews." In turn, Jewish leaders were attacked by Martin Peretz, publisher of the *New Republic,* for being "obsequious" in pressing for denunciations and then accepting responses that were, at best, grudging and weak.

When Farrakhan reached Madison Square Garden in New York in October, he addressed an overflow crowd of 25,000. Calling Jews "blood suckers whom Jesus condemned in the plainest of language," he warned that the "Jewish lobby has a stranglehold on government." Building on the experience of previous cities visited by the black leader, Jewish organizations in New York sought to maintain a low profile. They limited their protest to a single public statement that was issued by a coalition of Jews and non-Jews, including blacks and Hispanics, political and religious leaders. On the night of the event, the only protesters to be seen outside the Garden were 18 members of the Jewish Defense League.

In October Dr. Alvin Pouissant, a professor of psychiatry at the Harvard University School of Medicine and a respected observer of black affairs, presented a psychological and political appraisal of Farrakhan to a meeting of the National Jewish Community Relations Advisory Council (NJCRAC). Pouissant suggested that Farrakhan drew large audiences because he tapped the frustration and anger many blacks still felt over the unfulfilled promises of the civil rights revolution. Pouissant conceded that it was difficult to tell the degree to which Farrakhan's audiences absorbed or agreed with his anti-Semitic views; at the same time, he was optimistic that Farrakhan's continued anti-Semitic rhetoric would eventually alienate the black political leadership.

A few respected blacks did speak out forcefully against "Minister" Farrakhan, and not only for his anti-Semitism. Former civil rights leader Bayard Rustin, writing on October 11 in New York's *Daily News,* cited "three basic problems with the Farrakhan message: his anti-Semitism; the destructiveness of his black nationalism; and his insistence that black economic 'renewal' can be achieved only through a politically disastrous course for black America." Julius Lester, a black activist of the 1960s and 1970s who subsequently converted to Judaism, expressed his dismay that Farrakhan had become "America's preeminent black leader." In an essay in the October 28 *New Republic,* Lester wrote, "No people should make the journey from Martin Luther King, Jr., to Louis Farrakhan in fewer than 20 years." While acknowledging the "despair, poverty, deprivation . . . and the relentless heat of racism" that many blacks endured, Lester asserted that none of these "justified hatred, anti-Semitism, or the elevation of Louis Farrakhan to the position of spokesman and leader."

MAYOR EDWARD KOCH

An outspoken Jewish critic of Farrakhan was New York's mayor Edward Koch, who had many harsh words to say about the Black Muslim leader. Some observers attributed the strained relations between blacks and Jews in New York —at least in part—to the intemperate remarks made by Mayor Koch. As the year began, and on the eve of his reelection bid, the Union of American Hebrew Congregations (UAHC) called on Koch to proclaim "a moratorium on racial rhetoric and polarization, beginning with himself," a view reiterated a few days later by the executive head of the American Jewish Congress. In the mayor's defense, Nathan Perlmutter of the ADL suggested that Jewish leaders who accused Koch of irritating race relations in the city were themselves "contributing to black-Jewish abrasions." He maintained that while the mayor was sometimes impolitic, he was not antiblack.

The mayor's feisty tongue continued to get him into trouble, however. Before the mayoral election, he accused two respected columnists of trying to elect a black mayor rather than a good one. He also complained publicly that few blacks attended the May solidarity rally in support of Soviet Jewry. In a newly published book, *I, Koch: A Decidedly Unauthorized Biography of the Mayor of New York City,* by Arthur Browne et al., the mayor was quoted as referring to California black congressman Ronald Dellums as a "Zulu warrior and a Watusi from Berkeley." This last prompted *Philadelphia Daily News* columnist Chuck Stone, a black, to ask why the media and Jewish leaders were not as critical of Koch as they were of Farrakhan and Jesse Jackson. In as near to an apology as he ever came in such matters, Koch declared that he meant to be, and was actually, complimenting Mr. Dellums. During the election campaign Koch lowered the volume of his rhetoric; in the election—which political observers predicted he would (and did) win handily—he actually fared better among black and Hispanic voters than he had in the past.

JESSE JACKSON

In contrast to the previous year, when he had been a potential presidential candidate, Jesse Jackson appeared much less frequently in the public eye. Nevertheless, he continued to express views regarded by many Jews as pro-Third World and anti-Israel. In a speech delivered in April to a symposium sponsored by Arab groups, Jackson called Israeli settlements on the West Bank a violation of international law and an impediment to peace. He appeared to be cool, also, to Israel's spectacular rescue and absorption of starving black Jews from Ethiopia, labeling the operation "a military mission," even though it was clearly humanitarian in purpose.

At the same time, and undoubtedly with an eye to the 1988 presidential race, Jackson appeared to want to heal the breach with the Jewish community. On his return from a trip to West Germany and France, Jackson declared that the time had come to reaffirm the "community of suffering" shared by blacks and Jews and the "collective capacity" of the two groups when they operated as a coalition. In November Jackson made a dramatic appearance at the Reagan-Gorbachev summit conference in Geneva, where he held an impromptu public dialogue with the Soviet leader—in full view of the television cameras. Jackson pressed Gorbachev on the predicament of Soviet Jews, telling him that trust between the two countries would be improved if anxiety over Soviet Jews were eliminated. Jackson's action won him praise from the American Jewish Congress and other Jewish groups that had been critical of him in the past.

SOUTH AFRICA

The issue of apartheid in South Africa was one over which Jewish and black groups could lay aside their differences and, in a manner reminiscent of civil rights efforts in the 1960s, join together in protest. Beginning in November 1984, regular daily demonstrations were organized outside the South African embassy in Washington by the Free South Africa movement. By the end of 1985 more than 3,000 protesters had been arrested, including many Jews. The protest movement reached a peak on August 12 when some 5,500 persons marched from the Washington Monument to the State Department, to demand an end to racial segregation in South Africa and the imposition of U.S. government sanctions on that country. Leadership in these efforts in the Jewish community came primarily from the UAHC and the American Jewish Congress. The ADL, although often seen as the most conservative of the major national Jewish bodies, staged an antiapartheid protest outside the South African embassy, in the form of a menorah-lighting ceremony on the first day of Hanukkah.

Despite the spirit of unity expressed in public demonstrations, black-Jewish interests did not entirely coincide. While some Jewish bodies supported the strategy of divestment advocated by many black groups—as a means of pressing American businesses to pull out of South Africa—others opposed it. They argued that American-run companies often played a liberalizing role and that their departure might actually destabilize the South African government, thereby opening the door to revolutionary rather than reform forces. The appearance at the August 12 Washington demonstration of numerous marchers in the crowd carrying anti-Israel placards and leaflets prompted Rabbi Sidney H. Schwarz, executive director of the Jewish Community Council of Greater Washington, to warn—in an op-ed piece distributed by Washington Jewish Week Features—that unless Third World rhetoric was shunned by the Free South Africa movement, it risked condemnation for intolerance and bigotry.

Jewish leadership was concerned also—although the concern was muted—about the visits to a number of U.S. cities of Bishop Desmond Tutu, the South African leader who won the Nobel Prize for Peace in 1984. Writing in *Midstream,* in May, David Neiman reviewed Bishop Tutu's ambivalent record with regard to Jews and Israel. He noted particularly his speech at the Jewish Theological Seminary the year before, in which he praised the Jewish people as "a light unto the nations" but declared himself "sad that Israel . . . should make refugees" of Palestinian Arabs. Tutu also accused Jews of behaving with "the arrogance of power," because they "are a powerful lobby" in the United States.

REVIVING THE ALLIANCE

Various black and Jewish groups made efforts to demonstrate that a reservoir of goodwill existed despite the strains. In Philadelphia, for example, the local

American Jewish Committee chapter worked with a group of black leaders and Congressman William Gray, chairman of the House Budget Committee, and sent a group of black and Jewish high school seniors to visit Senegal and Israel during the summer. In May delegates of the UAHC and the NAACP met in Washington to consider programs of joint activity at both the grassroots and national levels. Existing community projects in the areas of economic development, health, and social welfare were reviewed and new activities proposed. The presidents of the two organizations, Rabbi Alexander Schindler and Benjamin Hooks, declared their belief that "the traumas which our communities sustained in recent years are in the process of being overcome."

A dissenting view on efforts at black-Jewish cooperation was expressed by Marvin Schick, writing in the *Long Island Jewish World* (October 18–24). He suggested that harmful side effects could result from "the perception by blacks that their destiny once more is being determined by . . . whites—and by whites who are Jewish." He urged both groups to lower their expectations of one another "on the grounds that the more we champion the idea of a special coalition, the more will Jews and blacks draw apart . . . [and] engage in conflict."

A survey of black members of Congress, released by the World Jewish Congress in August, found that most black legislators deeply resented the Jewish reaction to Jesse Jackson in the 1984 presidential campaign. The lawmakers also believed that the once strong alliance had deteriorated during the year as a result of some Jewish opposition to affirmative action and Israel's relations with South Africa. At the same time, according to the survey, the lawmakers saw enough "affinity of ideals and interests" to overcome obstacles to cooperation.

A pessimistic appraisal of black-Jewish relations was offered by Glenn C. Loury, a black political economist, writing on "Behind the Black-Jewish Split" in the January 1986 issue of *Commentary*. According to Loury, persistent feelings of inferiority in relation to Jews—"abetted by apartheid abroad and by poverty at home"—had combined to produce, among black intellectuals in particular, a broadly embraced, if somewhat nebulously defined, Pan-African political identity. This self-definition led blacks at all levels to see themselves as a "Third World people" whose relations with Americans of European descent were analogous "to the position of the nonwhite peoples of the developing countries vis-à-vis their former European colonizers." Loury concluded, "I fear that the conflict among blacks and Jews is not likely soon to abate, notwithstanding the earnest efforts of so many people of good will."

Urban Issues

New initiatives were taken by Jews in areas apart from traditional Jewish philanthropy. In February, spurred by the battle in Congress over the federal budget and threatened cuts to welfare programs, 36 leaders of major Protestant and Jewish denominations, religious agencies, and ecumenical organizations issued a call for a national commitment to end poverty in America. The statement, which was initiated by the Interfaith Action for Economic Justice in Washington, D.C., claimed that it was possible to "finance the programs necessary to end poverty in this country without exacerbating the deficit problem."

The formation of a new foundation, the Jewish Fund for Justice, was announced in August. While some financial aid would go to Jews, the fund's organizers said, its primary purpose was to contribute to nonsectarian causes and to do so as Jews. In discussing the decision to create the fund, Lois Roisman, its executive director, claimed that political and religious developments were causing Jews to reassess their position in American life. "The Moral Majority's call for the Christianization of America underlines the importance of a more active Jewish participation in efforts to create a just society," she said. Initial grants made by the fund were to Navajos in Arizona, homeless blacks in Boston, and low-income Mexican-Americans in Colorado.

Another new organization, Mazon, was launched this year as "a Jewish response to hunger," to serve non-Jews and Jews alike. Its novel approach to fund raising was to ask for a voluntary 3-percent surcharge on the cost of life-cycle events, such as weddings and bar/bat mitzvahs, as well as other festivities.

Quotas and Affirmative Action

A 1984 Supreme Court decision paved the way for the Justice Department to move this year to eliminate quotas and other "race conscious" measures currently in force. (The high court had upheld a Memphis fire fighters' union refusal to adhere to an affirmative-action plan requiring that white fire fighters with greater seniority be laid off before black fighters with less seniority.) In January the department wrote to 47 cities and states—by May the number was expanded to 56—requesting them to modify affirmative-action court decrees and to eliminate hiring quotas except where they were used to help victims of past discrimination. The move came under sharp attack by civil rights groups, including the American Jewish Committee, which accused the Justice Department of "blurring the important distinction" between goals and quotas. In his statement, the Committee's president, Howard I. Friedman, stressed that his group had always opposed the latter but favored the former.

Civil rights groups vigorously challenged the move to promote William Bradford Reynolds, the Justice Department's chief civil rights officer and signer of the letter to the cities and states, to associate attorney general, the number-three position in the department. In July some 100 pickets from the NAACP and UAHC marched outside the Senate Judiciary Committee hearings on Reynolds. The committee eventually voted against his confirmation.

Strong protests were voiced in August when the White House staff drafted an executive order to repeal requirements that federal contractors set numerical goals to remedy possible job discrimination. American Jewish Committee president Friedman stated that the answer to abuses in affirmative-action programs "must be vigorous supervision and correction, not the eradication of the programs themselves." The ADL's somewhat different view on the issue of goals and quotas had been expressed in testimony before the U.S. Civil Rights Commission in March by ADL director Nathan Perlmutter. Calling the distinction between quotas and goals "artificial," he asserted that "just as perniciously," a goal "can function as a ceiling for minorities." While ADL opposed affirmative action based on "racial proportionality," Perlmutter said, it favored practices that took into account an individual applicant's disadvantages and any "social, educational or economic barriers he or she may have overcome."

Anti-Semitism

In a major new work, *A Certain People: American Jews and Their Lives Today*, journalist-scholar Charles E. Silberman declared that anti-Semitism was no longer the significant factor in Jewish or American life that it had been a generation earlier. The new climate of acceptance, Silberman claimed, had dramatically altered the choices available to American Jews—choices about where to study, what occupation or profession to follow, and where to live.

This rosy view was not universally subscribed to. Basing himself on various community studies, Prof. Gary Tobin of the Brandeis University Center for Modern Jewish Studies claimed that most Jews in the United States believed they had experienced some form of anti-Semitism in their lifetime. Data from a Washington, D.C., study, for example, indicated that most personal experiences with anti-Semitism went unreported to the police, employers, or even Jewish agencies.

In the only index that is kept of reported anti-Semitic incidents, the ADL indicated that in 1985 acts of vandalism against Jews or their institutions or property were 11 percent lower than the previous year. The new findings reflected a five-year downward trend, interrupted only by a slight increase in 1984.

Anti-Israel Activity

American college campuses continued to be centers of anti-Israel propaganda. The Muslim Students Association at Wayne State University in Detroit, Michigan, distributed copies of the anti-Semitic czarist forgery *The Protocols of the Elders of Zion*, while the Stanford University *Daily* published an op-ed piece attacking Israel for "destroying Palestinian identity."

Arab-American groups became more aggressive and sophisticated in their campaign against Israel. In March the National Association of Arab Americans placed advertisements in the *Christian Science Monitor* and publications in Michigan and Ohio opposing aid to Israel. Similarly, the American-Arab Anti-Discrimination

Committee ran a series of full-page advertisements in the *Washington Post* in June, each ad headed "Should Congress give away almost $5 billion each year for one foreign country's military buildup?"

Federal legislation protecting American companies and individuals trading with Israel from the Arab League's boycott was restored in July—following its expiration the previous October—without change in the antiboycott provisions. In the five fiscal years beginning in 1979 and ending in 1984, penalties imposed under the law totaled $4,088,500. In an out-of-court settlement this year, the Lockheed Corporation agreed to pay a $10,000 fine and to be stripped of its export privileges to Saudi Arabia for one year as a result of charges that the company violated antidiscrimination provisions of the Export Administration Act. Late in the year, the House of Representatives passed a bill that would require colleges and universities receiving federal aid to disclose sizable gifts from foreign donors.

During the summer the Senate and House adopted a joint resolution condemning the 1975 UN General Assembly resolution that equated Zionism with racism and urging its repeal. The lawmakers declared that the UN resolution was "itself clearly a form of bigotry."

A new book, *The American House of Saud,* by Steven Emerson, documented the use of Arab "petrodollars," beginning with the 1973 oil shortage, to influence American public opinion and win behind-the-scenes support for the Arab cause.

Attitudes Toward Israel

American public opinion reacted against Israel when Arab-inspired terrorist incidents occurred abroad, especially when they involved Americans. The reactions, however, proved to be transitory. During the Beirut hostage crisis in June, in which 40 male passengers from a hijacked TWA airliner were held prisoner by members of the Shi'ite Amal militia, a series of ABC/*Washington Post* polls found increasing support (a high of 42 percent with 41 percent disagreeing) for the proposition that "the United States should reduce its ties to Israel in order to lessen the acts of terrorism against us in the Middle East." This result paralleled a poll taken after the massacre of Palestinians at the Sabra and Shatila refugee camps in Lebanon in 1982, when 42 percent said U.S.-Israeli ties should be reduced, and 47 percent disagreed.

That the anti-Israel sentiment was a temporary phenomenon became clear as soon as the hostages were released. A subsequent poll found that a majority of the public opposed reducing U.S. ties; indeed, a plurality (47 to 34 percent) believed that Israel had helped the United States to resolve the crisis to the extent of its ability. Writing in the October issue of *Commentary,* Mitchell Bard noted that while "the Arabs have made impressive strides in improving their standing with the public," as a result of sophisticated propaganda efforts, "greater support for their cause has not eroded support for Israel."

Church-State Relations

Reverberations of the election campaign of 1984, in which attempts were made to introduce religious doctrines into public life, continued into this year. In Denver, for example, the regional representative of the Department of Education distributed copies of a speech delivered to Christian educators that lamented the fact that "godlessness" had taken over a once "Christian" United States. Following a complaint by the American Jewish Congress, the department issued an official apology.

The Supreme Court ruled during the year on several major cases involving church-state relations. On March 27 the court divided 4-4 on whether the village of Scarsdale, New York, was required to permit the display of a privately sponsored Nativity scene on public land—a display opposed by the board of trustees of the heavily Jewish community. The effect of the split judgment was to automatically affirm a lower-court ruling allowing erection of a crèche as a free-speech right. The outcome of the Scarsdale case, taken together with a decision the year before in a Pawtucket, Rhode Island, case, seemed to indicate a trend toward an accommodation of religion in the public sphere.

In light of these decisions, a June 4 ruling by the high court appeared as a surprising about-face. By a vote of 6-3, and emphasizing that "government must pursue a course of complete neutrality toward religion," the court struck down an Alabama law that permitted a daily one-minute period of silent meditation or prayer in the public schools. Since "moment of silence" laws existed in varying versions in 25 states, the negative decision gave impetus to a renewed effort in Congress to pass a constitutional amendment permitting organized prayer in the public schools. In September Sen. Jesse Helms (R., N.C.) sponsored a proposal that would have removed the prayer issue from federal court jurisdiction and given state and local governments authority in this area. In what was regarded as a blow to the agenda of the Christian Right, the bill was defeated by a vote of 62-36. However, as the year drew to a close, the Senate Judiciary Committee, by a vote of 12-6, agreed to send to the floor of the Senate a proposed constitutional amendment that would permit silent prayer or meditation in the public schools.

On the issue of government aid to parochial schools, on July 1 the Supreme Court ruled unconstitutional the spending of millions of dollars in Michigan and New York to send public-school teachers into religious schools to conduct remedial programs. By a 5-4 vote, the justices invalidated a "shared time" program in Grand Rapids, Michigan, that placed 470 public-school teachers in 40 Roman Catholic and other religious schools, during regular hours, for special instruction. In the second case, the justices also divided 5-4 in finding constitutional flaws in a 19-year-old New York City public-school program that used Title I funds to provide remedial and other special education on religious-school premises to 40,000 children from low-income families. While these decisions were hailed by groups like the American Jewish Committee and the American Jewish Congress, they were decried by members of the Orthodox community. The National Jewish Commission on Law and Public Affairs (COLPA), which filed friend-of-the-court briefs in both cases in behalf of Orthodox Jewish bodies, called the decisions "devastating" to children attending Jewish religious schools.

The apparent move by the Supreme Court toward renewed adherence to the separation principle brought sharp attacks from the Reagan administration. Attorney General Edwin Meese III lashed out at the court, arguing that the principle that government must maintain a course of neutrality between religion and nonreligion "would have struck the founding generation as somewhat bizarre." The newly installed secretary of education, William J. Bennett, cautioned state superintendents against scaling back all forms of aid to parochial schools, on the grounds that the high court's rulings did not necessarily affect forms of federal aid other than remedial programs. In speeches around the country, Secretary Bennett sought to stimulate interest in a voucher system; this would circumvent the court's decisions barring the use of public funds by giving parents in disadvantaged areas government vouchers with which to pay for schools of their choice, public or parochial.

On February 19 the Supreme Court agreed to rule in a Williamsport, Pennsylvania, case on whether public high schools could allow religious clubs to meet for prayer and discussion on school grounds on the same basis as other student groups. In July 1984 a three-judge panel of the U.S. Court of Appeals for the Third Circuit had reversed a ruling of a U.S. District Court upholding the students' right to meet. A day before the Circuit Court opinion was handed down, however, Congress passed the Equal Access Act, requiring schools that provide a "limited open forum" for student activities to permit religious groups to meet also. The American Jewish Committee, the UAHC, and others opposed the act as a violation of the separation principle, and the UAHC issued a guide alerting parents and community leaders to its dangers. The Pennsylvania case was seen as providing an opportunity for the court to review the constitutionality of the act.

Mainstream Jewish groups viewed attempts to reverse "proseparation" court decisions with alarm. In June the American Jewish Congress announced the creation of a new body, the Fund for Religious Liberty, whose purpose would be to combat the "Christianizing of America" through support of relevant litigation. At the fund-raising dinner held to launch the fund, Congressman Stephen L. Solarz (D., N.Y.) warned, "You can see from Beirut to Belfast the consequences of sectarianism."

This view was challenged by Prof. Nathan Glazer of Harvard University in an article in *The New Republic* of October 21. Conceding that evangelicals and fundamentalists had to be opposed when they sought equal time for "creationism" and other improper intrusions of religion in the public arena, Glazer worried that in New York City 20,000 poor children in nonpublic and Catholic schools, who had been receiving remedial aid for years under a historic 1965 compromise on the church-state issue, were now barred from receiving such aid. Moreover, he maintained, since Christians were a majority in this country, the fact "that this should find some expression in public life seems not unreasonable." "It is impossible," Glazer concluded, "to draw too neat or sharp a line" between the public and private aspects of religion.

Writing from an entirely different perspective, author and political activist Arthur Waskow also challenged traditional Jewish-establishment assumptions about church-state relations. In an essay in the January-February issue of *Moment* magazine, he suggested that there is "a more 'Jewish' way to prevent Christianization than to take comfort in a bland, homogenized-secular culture." Waskow urged Jews to bring "the wisdom of Torah into the great public arena—rather than either withdrawing from the debate altogether, into a privatized religion, or relying on a frozen secular modernism as its way of thinking."

The Christian Right

There were indications this year that significant elements of the Christian Right were attempting to fashion a less hard-line identity for themselves. Writing in the *Philadelphia Inquirer* magazine on January 20, Larry Eichel reported, "They [the fundamentalists] have been smoothing away the rough and more controversial edges of their politics with hopes of expanding their potential base of support." In a debate with Judy Goldsmith of the National Organization for Women in February, Jerry Falwell, head of the Moral Majority, declared that he could support abortion, albeit reluctantly, to save the life of the mother. At the same time, he urged prolifers to create mechanisms to make "homes, beds, doctors, counselors and adoptive families" available at no expense to those who chose to forgo abortions. Appearing before the annual convention of the Rabbinical Assembly (Conservative) in March, he apologized for having advocated the "Christianization" of America. "We were wrong and we are sorry," he declared. Continuing with words of praise for Israel, he promised to mobilize Christians on behalf of the Jewish state and to fight anti-Semitism.

The most dramatic instance of the search for rapprochement with Jews was undoubtedly the turnabout of Jesse Helms. In March he led six other Republican senators in an attack on President Reagan's September 1982 Middle East peace initiative, urging the president to support continued Israeli occupation of the West Bank and Gaza Strip. The Helms attack, conveyed in a letter to the president, was a landmark of a sort in the conservative leader's evolving views with regard to Israel. Following the Israeli incursion into Lebanon in 1982, he had been sharply critical of the Jewish state, calling for a halt to U.S. assistance and for the resignation of Prime Minister Menachem Begin. Credit for Helms's shift was given, in part, to a small pro-Israel group, Americans for a Safe Israel, which had entered into discussions with the senator and arranged for him (and several others), later in the year, to visit Israel for the first time. In June, when the administration withdrew its request for the sale of sophisticated weapons to Jordan because of overwhelming opposition in both the House and Senate, the National Jewish Coalition, an arm of the Republican party, attributed this victory to a growing awareness on the part of Republicans like Helms of the real dangers to Israel's security.

The term "New Right" was often applied to the newest brand of conservatives within the Republican party—congressmen like Jack Kemp of New York, Newt Gingrich of Georgia, and other House members affiliated with a caucus known as the Conservative Opportunity Society—but it was not a wholly accurate label. Often called the "C-Span Boys," since they used broadcasts of House sessions by the cable television network of that name as a forum for transmitting their views, they preferred to describe themselves as "populists." While giving nominal support to the Christian Right social agenda—and more than nominal support to the issue of voluntary school prayer—they sought to deemphasize more disruptive issues like abortion. During the year, they shocked some conservatives by joining with blacks and liberals to protest the Reagan administration's policy in South Africa, which they viewed as acquiescence in "the unacceptable status quo" of racial apartheid.

These developments on the Right had repercussions in the Jewish community. In February Kenneth Bialkin, national chairman of the ADL and chairman of the Conference of Presidents of Major Jewish Organizations, proposed to an ADL audience that Jews should reach out to Christian evangelical leaders, at the same time keeping a watchful eye on the boundary between church and state. Similarly, Rabbi Irving Greenberg, president of CLAL—the National Jewish Center for Learning and Leadership, urged in his syndicated column in the Jewish press that Jews seek common ground with right-wing groups in return for their "resocialization to true pluralism."

One Jewish leader who was less sanguine about relationships with the Right was Henry Siegman of the American Jewish Congress. He accepted Falwell at his word as a friend of Israel and said, "I don't believe he is an anti-Semite." "But," he went on, in Falwell's new willingness to accept Jews as Americans, he "misses the point . . . it's that the government is not identified with any one group."

Even as Christian Right groups sought to broaden their appeal, there were indications that they were not abandoning their basic goals. People for the American Way—a group founded to combat the Moral Majority—reported in August that attempts by rightist groups to censor curriculum and books in public schools nationwide had increased by nearly 40 percent during the previous academic year. The *New York Times* noted that school systems throughout the country remained under pressure to restrict discussion on such topics as evolution, abortion, communism, and something labeled "valuing."

Jewish-Catholic Relations

A number of events were held throughout the year to mark the 20th anniversary of "Nostra Aetate" ("In Our Time"), the declaration by the Second Vatican Council that rejected the charge of deicide against the Jews and repudiated anti-Semitism. In February a delegation of top American Jewish Committee leaders met with Pope

John Paul II at the Vatican to discuss problems of mutual interest. Following the papal audience, at which the pope reconfirmed the Vatican's support of the declaration, Rabbi Marc Tanenbaum, the Committee's director of international relations, said that over the past two decades "there has been a 180-degree turnaround" in Catholic attitudes toward Judaism. Moreover, he said, Vatican II "has now made possible the emergence of a whole new theology in which Jews and Judaism are respected in their own right."

An international conference organized by the ADL, in cooperation with the Vatican Commission for Religious Relations with Judaism, took place in Rome in April. The following month the Reform movement's UAHC announced the inauguration of a program aimed at bringing together Jews and Catholics at the local level in an effort to foster better relations between the two groups.

To commemorate the anniversary, Cardinal John O'Connor of New York delivered an address on Catholic-Jewish relations at that city's Temple Emanu-El, in October. Other observances of the anniversary were arranged in cities around the country, sponsored by Catholic and Jewish groups.

The spirit of good relations was marred somewhat by the appearance in June of guidelines ("Notes") for teaching about Judaism in the Catholic church, issued by the Vatican. While the document contained many positive elements, it drew immediate criticism from the International Jewish Committee on Interreligious Consultations (IJCIC), which included the American Jewish Committee, the ADL, and the World Jewish Congress. The group faulted the Vatican publication for including only a "vague, passing and almost gratuitous reference" to the Nazi crimes against the Jews and for failing to deal adequately with the religious significance of the State of Israel. A month later, a meeting of Catholic and Jewish leaders agreed on the need for further dialogue to clarify the issues raised in the document.

In the fall, leaders of the IJCIC gathered at the Vatican to celebrate the exact anniversary of "Nostra Aetate." Rabbi Mordecai Waxman, chairman of the group, said that while the Vatican declaration had "encouraged Jews everywhere to feel that there was a new spirit in the Christian world," Jews were "conscious that much of its vision has yet to be translated into reality and universal acceptance." For Jews, there were still outstanding issues—theological questions relating to the Holocaust and Israel as well as the practical matter of the Vatican's relationship with Israel.

While many Jewish leaders expressed satisfaction with the progress being made on these matters, the feeling persisted in some quarters that the pace was too slow. This view came to public attention in November, when Edgar M. Bronfman, president of the World Jewish Congress, made a dramatic appeal to New York's Cardinal O'Connor—at a dinner honoring the prelate for interfaith work—to press the Vatican for diplomatic recognition of the State of Israel. Bronfman's public challenge reflected a division among Jewish leaders about the kinds of tactics—public or private—most likely to achieve this goal. While the cardinal made no comment on the issue at the dinner, he later told reporters that he had "no hesitancy at all" about raising the issue with the Vatican, recognizing that that was about all he could do.

Extremism

Extremist right-wing groups received considerable attention during the year, either because of stepped-up activity on their part or action by public authorities taken against them.

Computer technology was being used increasingly by the rightists to maintain contact among themselves and to spread their propaganda. In January the ADL released a report detailing the operations of two computer networks that were intended for "Aryan patriots" but were in fact accessible to anyone with a home computer and modem attachment. The more widely known of the two was run by the Idaho-based Aryan Nations, a group whose aim was to establish a "nationalist racist state." The second hate network was operated out of West Virginia by George Dietz, a German immigrant (and former Hitler Youth member) who was well known as a distributor of neo-Nazi literature.

In April state and federal officials took control of a paramilitary camp in Arkansas run by the Covenant. In addition to an extensive arsenal and munitions factory and a cache of neo-Nazi hate literature, searchers found a converted submachine gun virtually identical to the weapon used to kill Alan Berg, the Jewish talk-show host, in Denver in 1984, and also, two weeks prior to the raid, a Missouri state trooper. In the camp, officials discovered in hiding four members of a neo-Nazi group called the Silent Brotherhood, or the Order, a splinter group of the Aryan Nations, whose objective was the violent overthrow of the government. Two of those detained, along with 21 other members of the white supremacist group, went on trial in September in Seattle, on charges including the two murders, robberies and bank holdups that netted the Order more than $4 million, and counterfeiting. FBI director William H. Webster declared the Order to be more dangerous than the Ku Klux Klan. The trial lasted three and a half months, ending on December 30 with the conviction of the defendants under the federal racketeering act.

An ABC News "20/20" telecast in August, devoted to the economic crisis in the Midwest plains states, claimed that extremist right-wing groups, some of them anti-Semitic, were winning adherents among financially troubled farmers. Groups such as the Posse Comitatus, the new Populist party, and the Aryan Nations blamed the farmers' plight on the Federal Reserve System, the legal profession, and the banks, all of which, they charged, were controlled by Jews. Two leading Jewish organizations disagreed in their assessment of the danger posed by the extremists. On September 19 the ADL's research director, Irwin Suall, said, "Despite their intense efforts, they are not meeting with much success." He did indicate, however, that the ADL would continue to monitor the situation. The ADL view was disputed by Dixon Terry, chairman of the Iowa Farm Unity Coalition, and Rabbi James Rudin of the American Jewish Committee. At a news conference in New York City on September 20, Rabbi Rudin, who had just returned from a 10-day fact-finding tour of the Midwest, reported that the radical right was making "significant gains among some of the economically threatened farmers."

Jewish groups came under suspicion this year in five terrorist attacks that caused two deaths and four injuries. Among the groups suspected were the Jewish Defense League and the Jewish Defense Organization. The American-Arab Anti-Discrimination Committee was the target of numerous threats and three attacks, including a bombing in Santa Ana, California, in October, that killed Alex Odeh, the group's regional director. Mainstream Jewish groups were quick to denounce the violence.

Political Affairs

Two studies published this year by the American Jewish Congress shed additional light on the political behavior of Jews in the 1984 elections. The first, an analysis by Martin Hochbaum that surveyed some 2,900 Jewish voters in 14 regions across the country, concluded that fear of growing ties between government and religion and concern for social-justice issues were the factors that led American Jews to favor Democratic candidate Walter Mondale over President Reagan by a three-to-one margin. A definite denominational pattern characterized the vote, Hochbaum reported, with secular Jews giving Mondale 83 percent of their votes; Reform Jews, 72 percent; Conservative Jews, 71 percent; and Orthodox Jews, 49 percent. In the second study, *The Political Future of American Jews,* Earl Raab and Seymour Martin Lipset cited "overwhelming" journalistic and anecdotal evidence that on the national level more than a majority of the funds collected by the Democratic party, and as much as a quarter of Republican funds, came from Jewish sources.

Much of this money was contributed through Jewish political action committees (PACs) to support pro-Israel, or oppose anti-Israel, candidates. According to the *Wall Street Journal* of February 26, the network of these organizations had "multiplied its clout" in 1984, its contributions to candidates almost doubling since the 1982 elections to nearly $3.6 million. The number of Jewish PACs also doubled, to more than 70. Taken together, the paper said, Jewish PACs gave $1 million more during the 1984 campaign than the nation's largest single PAC, the Realtors PAC, which expended $2.5 million.

A sharp break in the contribution patterns of the pro-Israel PACs occurred in 1985, the *Washington Post* reported on November 4. In the first six months of the year the groups gave more money (55 percent) to Republicans than to Democrats (contrasted with 80 percent to Democrats in 1983–1984). The shift occurred, apparently, because of a decision to favor powerful Republican incumbents, such as Robert Dole of Kansas and Bob Packwood of Oregon, who had been firm in their support of Israel, over liberal Democratic challengers who might better represent Jewish views on other matters. "We are single-minded about being single-issue," said Thomas Dine, executive director of the American Israel Public Affairs Committee (AIPAC), a group that did not itself raise funds but advised many of the Jewish PACs.

This position was criticized by Earl Raab and Seymour Martin Lipset (in their above-mentioned study), who cautioned the Jewish community against narrowing its focus of interest to Israel. "American Jewish political effectiveness will depend not on . . . Israel-related activism," they declared, "but on general Jewish influence in the political process." In a debate on this subject at the 54th General Assembly of the Council of Jewish Federations, in November, Hyman Bookbinder, director of the American Jewish Committee's Washington office, argued that Jews should support a variety of issues that promoted the general good, not only because they were right but because by doing so the Jewish community gained sympathy and allies for its own causes, including Israel. Opposing Bookbinder, Marshall Breger, former White House liaison to the Jewish community, asserted that Jews diminished their political leverage by "not focusing on priorities." He urged Jews to concentrate on winning new friends, especially in the South and Southwest and among the Christian Right.

The whole question of the Jewish role in politics was examined in a new book by Murray Friedman, *The Utopian Dilemma: New Political Directions for American Jews*. Friedman argued that what seemed to be emerging in the Jewish community was "a better balance between universalism and particularism." "If this is a valid conclusion," he noted, "it cannot help being 'good for the Jews' and good for the broader society of which they are a part."

MURRAY FRIEDMAN

The United States, Israel, and the Middle East

FOR U.S. POLICY IN the Middle East, 1985 began with a convergence of developments that seemed to offer new hope for reviving the stalemated Arab-Israeli peace process. Although President Ronald Reagan's September 1982 peace initiative had been set aside because it aroused strong opposition in both Israel and the Arab world, the Reagan administration appeared optimistic that direct negotiations between Israel and a joint Jordanian-Palestinian delegation could conceivably begin by the end of the year. To this end, Assistant Secretary of State for Near Eastern and South Asian Affairs Richard W. Murphy and his aides met repeatedly with key figures in the area in an attempt to devise a diplomatic formula that would break the impasse.

As eager as the United States was to encourage progress toward peace in the region, President Reagan and Secretary of State George Shultz made it clear that the Arabs must first take the initiative by demonstrating a commitment to peace with Israel and a readiness for direct negotiations. The fact that the president not only had won reelection by a landslide but was a second-term president—not beholden to Jewish or any other voters—did not mean that he was prepared to pressure Israel into unilateral concessions, as some Arab leaders vainly hoped. In addition, the administration had learned from bitter experience in Lebanon that the United States could not impose peace in the Middle East. The terrorist bombings of the U.S. embassy in Beirut and heavy losses among U.S. Marines two years earlier had forced the administration, in the face of domestic pressures, to withdraw its military presence from Lebanon, thus dooming U.S. efforts to help end the Lebanese civil war.

Although the diplomatic activity that took place in 1985 did not result in any tangible accomplishment, it did open opportunities for future breakthroughs going beyond the bilateral peace treaty signed by Egypt and Israel in 1979. Hopes now centered on the possibility of negotiations between Israel and Jordan, with the participation of representative Palestinians.

Developments in Israel

Within Israel, a change in political leadership had taken place in July 1984, when Israel Labor party leader Shimon Peres became prime minister of a national unity government. Because of policy differences between the major Likud and Labor political blocs, as well as among the other political factions within the government, pundits in Israel and abroad did not expect the new government to survive. However, the unity coalition in fact worked cooperatively and effectively on a number of pressing issues. By January the government announced the decision to carry out a three-stage rapid withdrawal from Lebanon. In addition, working closely with Secretary of State Shultz, who took a personal interest in Israel's economy, the regime embarked on a stringent program of economic recovery. Indeed, a major rationale for the formation of the national unity government had been that unpopular and harsh economic measures could only be implemented if the onus was equally shared by the two major parties, thus taking the issue out of the realm of partisan politics and enabling the broad coalition to enlist the cooperation of labor and industry both.

Although Shimon Peres had never been one of the more popular figures in Israeli politics, after he assumed leadership of the government his ratings in public opinion polls soared. While some of the change could be attributed merely to incumbency, a major factor was his effort to reduce jarring confrontations between the two major political groupings and to create an atmosphere of joint responsibility for running the government. Peres's good personal working relations with Likud deputy prime minister and foreign minister Yitzhak Shamir were to a certain degree also based on political calculations. The government of national unity was formed on the basis of a personal agreement between Peres and Shamir to exchange ministerial roles after two years. Peres did not want to be seen by the voting public as responsible for violating the rotation agreement, and Shamir knew that if the coalition government collapsed and new elections were called before the scheduled changeover, his position as leader of the Likud was open to challenge.

Prime Minister Peres made it clear that he wanted to see real movement toward peace during his term in office. Unlike his Likud coalition partners, who rejected the idea of giving up any territory west of the Jordan River, Peres did not dismiss entirely the 1982 Reagan proposal that in exchange for formal Arab recognition, genuine peace, and security, Israel would relinquish much of Judea and Samaria to a Jordanian-Palestinian federation. If negotiations with Jordan were to produce a real prospect for peace, Peres would have a legitimate reason to call early elections and seek public approval of the agreement.

Israel began its phased withdrawal from Lebanon in January. It had paid a heavy price for its 1982 "Operation Peace for Galilee." Over 600 Israeli troops lost their lives and close to 3,500 were wounded, a far higher toll than most Israelis had anticipated. The war had also sapped Israeli morale and broken the national consensus; for the first time in Israeli history, a movement of conscientious objectors developed among recruits and reservists.

Israel had scaled back its objectives and decided not to link its pullback from Lebanon to a comparable withdrawal by Syrian forces, or even to a political agreement with the Lebanese government. Reflecting bitterly on Israel's experience in Lebanon, Defense Minister Yitzhak Rabin, in a February address to the Conference of Presidents of Major American Jewish Organizations in New York, declared: "If Syria wants to stay in Lebanon, let them. Whoever puts a foot in the Lebanese mud will sink in it." He was suggesting that while Syria might remain the dominant military and political force in Lebanon, it was unlikely to be able to establish an effective government in the strife-filled country.

The war in Lebanon, despite its tragic cost, had not been a total failure, however. While Defense Minister Ariel Sharon's ambitious geopolitical plans came to naught, the Israel Defense Forces achieved much of their initial objective of destroying the Palestine Liberation Organization's military infrastructure in southern Lebanon and in Beirut. For the first time in many years, the northern Galilee was relatively free from bombardment by terrorist rockets fired from Lebanon, and there was no longer an autonomous and independent PLO with a territorial base of its own on any of Israel's borders.

Developments in the Arab World

A number of factors helped to buttress Prime Minister Peres's confidence in his ability to engage in more active diplomacy. The knowledge that Shamir would replace Peres in two years, coupled with Peres's greater openness to compromise, were believed to provide Jordan's King Hussein with an incentive to negotiate a settlement with Israel. Another factor was Hussein's concern over the fate of the West Bank. The extent of Jewish settlement activity during the previous seven years of Likud rule and the consolidation of de facto Israeli rule over the area contributed to the king's sense that time was running out.

Deprived of its independent military base in Lebanon, the PLO had become increasingly fragmented, and inter-Arab politics were proving as deadly to its fortunes as its avowed enemy, Israel. Syria was a leading player, with Damascus actively backing the defectors from Yasir Arafat's al-Fatah organization who were headed by Col. Saeed Musa, as well as other dissident Palestinian groups united in the Syrian-created Palestine National Salvation Front. With the help of Syrian military power, these factions hounded Arafat loyalists out of Tripoli, the last bastion of Arafat's forces in northern Lebanon.

The continuing decline in the importance of Arab oil was matched by a parallel decline in Arab financial power. The Organization of Petroleum Exporting Countries (OPEC) was forced to accept three price cuts in 1985, while its share in international markets fell to less than one-third. In an attempt to stem the oil glut, Saudi Arabia cut its output from a peak of 9.6 million barrels a day in 1981 to 3 billion barrels a day in 1985. As a result of these developments, pressure from Arab oil-producing countries became less significant in Western political calculations.

The Peace Process

NEW U.S. APPROACH

After nearly a year of avoiding any high-level meetings with Arab leaders, the Reagan administration once again turned its attention to Middle East diplomacy. This time, however, the subject was approached with lower expectations and more caution than previously. In place of active American intervention and mediation, the administration tried quietly to encourage direct negotiations between the parties to the Arab-Israel conflict. The operating premise of U.S. Mideast policy, according to administration strategists, was that "direct negotiations were the only way to achieve a settlement." The United States would not attempt to mediate problems that the Arabs and Israelis were not ready to solve themselves.

The new approach was evident when King Fahd of Saudi Arabia met with President Reagan in February—the first visit to Washington by a Saudi monarch since the late King Faisal's trip in 1971—and also during Egyptian president Hosni Mubarak's visit to Washington in March. Both Arab leaders were expected to focus on nuts-and-bolts issues, including requests for more American arms, and, in the case of Egypt, an increase in military and economic aid.

Pointing to the continuing Iraq-Iran war as justification for requesting additional sophisticated U.S. arms, the Saudis presented a shopping list that included nearly $3 billion worth of F-15 fighter jets, Sidewinder missiles, M-1 tanks, and other advanced weapons systems. A week before the scheduled visit by King Fahd, the Reagan administration announced that it would postpone for several weeks a decision on new arms sales to Saudi Arabia or to any other Arab state. Assistant Secretary Murphy explained that before the administration proposed any new sales it would conduct "a comprehensive review of our security interests and our strategy in the area." The review, according to Murphy, would focus "on how our various programs in the security field will complement our efforts in the peace process and how it can help achieve a general stability in the region."

King Fahd's agenda was by no means confined to arms requests and oil-pricing policies. The Saudi ruler also urged the president to reactivate American involvement in Mideast diplomacy. In statements issued at the end of their meetings on February 13, Fahd and Reagan agreed that a stable peace in the Middle East must provide security "for all states in the area and for the exercise of the legitimate rights of the Palestinian people." However, the official communiqué underscored the differences between them on how to achieve these goals. The Saudi king continued to insist on the 8-point peace plan he had proposed—and which was accepted by Arab leaders at Fez, Morocco, on September 9, 1982—which called for the complete withdrawal by Israel from all territory captured in the June 1967 war, including East Jerusalem, the dismantling of all Jewish settlements on the West Bank and the Gaza Strip, and the establishment of a Palestinian state, with Jerusalem as its capital. The Fez plan did not call for direct negotiations but simply set out Arab conditions and vaguely suggested that the UN Security Council would guarantee peace among all states in the region.

The Fez plan was unacceptable to Israel for several reasons, among them the fact that it spoke of the Palestinian people's "right to self-determination and the exercise of inalienable national rights under the leadership of the Palestine Liberation Organization." This clause was also contrary to U.S. policy—as outlined in the 1982 Reagan plan—which rejected the creation of a separate Palestinian Arab state under PLO leadership. In the communiqué, President Reagan stated that he still stood by his own Middle East initiative of September 1982, emphasizing his view that "the security of Israel and other nations in the region and the legitimate rights of the Palestinian people can and should be addressed in direct negotiations." Elaborating on the president's statement, Secretary Shultz declared more bluntly: "After all, if we're going to get some place in the peace process, an Arab negotiator has to sit down with an Israeli negotiator and try to work out the answers."

THE HUSSEIN-ARAFAT AGREEMENT

Although the Fahd-Reagan talks did not break new ground, simultaneous developments in the Middle East provided the impetus for more active American involvement in the peace process. The new developments centered on a "framework for common action" between Jordan and the PLO, announced on February 11.

For several years, Jordan had been reluctant to launch any peace initiative on its own. In late 1984, however, King Hussein, with Egypt's encouragement, began to pursue a more active policy. (Jordan had resumed relations with Egypt in September 1984 after a five-year break over Cairo's peace treaty with Israel.) Although Jordan had rejected the 1982 Reagan plan's call for direct negotiations, Hussein now viewed the Reagan initiative as an approach that could serve his own needs. The chance of movement seemed more likely now that Shimon Peres had assumed the premiership in Israel, since Peres had voiced qualified support for the Reagan plan when it was proposed in 1982, despite its rejection by the Likud government headed by Menahem Begin. Peres had also used his inaugural address to the Knesset in September 1984 to invite Hussein to join him at the negotiating table, without insisting that the Camp David accords serve as the basis for a peace settlement with Jordan.

In the belief that he needed authoritative Palestinian support for any move toward negotiations with Israel, Hussein began a series of discussions with PLO chairman Yasir Arafat, hoping to forge a common policy. Arafat, concerned about his position within a badly fragmented PLO, having no independent base of operations, and relentlessly hounded by Syria's president, Hafez al-Assad, was rapidly running out of options. Thus, a weakened PLO presented King Hussein with the opportunity to pressure Arafat into accepting a peace formula that might also be acceptable to the United States.

The process of PLO-Jordanian reconciliation had actually begun with Hussein serving as host of a meeting of the Palestinian National Council (PNC) in Amman the previous November. The Jordanian king had sharply criticized the PLO, calling on it to abandon the fruitless policy of armed struggle, and had invited Arafat to join him in seeking a negotiated settlement with Israel on the basis of Security Council Resolution 242 in the framework of a UN-sponsored international conference. Since the November 1984 PNC meeting, Hussein and Arafat had met periodically to hammer out the terms of an agreement, which was made public by the Jordanian side on February 11, although the text was not released until February 23.

The accord outlined a framework for an approach to peace, based on five principles: (1) total Israeli withdrawal from the territories occupied in 1967; (2) right of self-determination for the Palestinian people . . . within the context of the formation of the proposed confederated Arab states of Jordan and Palestine; (3) resolution of the problem of Palestinian refugees in accordance with UN resolutions; (4) resolution of the Palestine question in all its aspects; and (5) peace negotiations to be conducted "under the auspices of an international conference in which the five permanent members of the Security Council and all the parties to the conflict will participate, including the Palestine Liberation Organization, the sole legitimate representative of the Palestine people, within a joint delegation [joint Jordanian-Palestinian delegation]."

Israel and the United States objected to the agreement on several grounds. For one thing, there was no explicit mention of PLO acceptance of UN Security Council Resolutions 242 and 338. In addition, Israel and the United States were opposed in general to an international conference and specifically to one that included the Soviet Union. Also, Israel had long opposed the concept of total withdrawal from all the territory it captured in the June 1967 war. And finally, although the agreement did not specifically call for the establishment of a Palestinian state, its insistence on the right of self-determination for the Palestinian people clearly left open such a possibility.

Initial cautious optimism in Washington gave way to increasing doubts as to whether the agreement represented a significant breakthrough. Although Hussein had been pressing Arafat for an unambiguous statement that might allow the United States to accept the PLO as a party to negotiations, he settled for less. Arafat himself would not be pinned down, in several interviews refusing explicitly to endorse Resolution 242, a *sine qua non* for the United States. The very fact that the announcement was made by Hussein alone, rather than jointly with Arafat, pointed to unresolved differences between the Jordanian and PLO positions. As noted, the actual text of the agreement was not released for nearly two weeks. The Jordanians had apparently publicized a draft accord, and Arafat had not cleared it with other PLO leaders.

Although the Jordanians claimed that the PLO had implicitly accepted UN Resolution 242, this assertion conflicted with a statement issued in Tunis on February 20 by the PLO executive committee, which repeated the organization's long-standing rejection of the UN resolution. PLO leader Hani al-Hassan was quoted as saying, "Frankly and clearly, I say that we reject Resolution 242. We rejected it in the past and we reject it in the future." The executive committee announced its approval of the general principles contained in the agreement, but with reservations, until certain amendments were made.

Perhaps the most significant aspect of the accord was the notion of a joint Palestinian-Jordanian delegation, rather than a separate PLO representation, at future peace talks. Since Israel had long rejected negotiations with the PLO, while the Arabs had insisted that only the PLO could represent the Palestinians, the

Jordanian concept was an attempt to finesse the issue of PLO representation at peace talks. The Jordanian text of the agreement in fact included both principles. The international conference would conduct peace negotiations in which "all parties to the conflict will participate, including the Palestine Liberation Organization, the sole legitimate representative of the Palestinian people, within a joint delegation [joint Jordanian-Palestinian delegation]." But this proved not satisfactory to the PLO executive committee, which demanded that the words "Jordanian-Palestinian" delegation be changed to "Arab delegation," presumably one consisting of all the Arab states and the PLO. In addition, top PLO leaders, including those loyal to Arafat, demanded an explicit commitment to the creation of an independent Palestinian Arab state on the West Bank *before* any arrangement for a "confederation" with Jordan could be agreed upon.

The changes demanded by the PLO executive would have made the agreement wholly unacceptable to the United States as a vehicle for serious negotiations. Even if Arafat had not equivocated over the original Jordanian text of the agreement, it was clear to the United States that the PLO chairman could not deliver his executive committee and was becoming increasingly irrelevant as a potential partner to negotiations.

For the Reagan administration, the short-lived Hussein-Arafat agreement indicated that there had not yet been sufficient movement for the United States to embark on a new Middle East peace effort. Some officials remained encouraged by what appeared to be a serious effort by Jordan and Egypt to revive the peace process. The Jordanian approach in particular sparked U.S. interest, and the concept of a joint Jordanian-Palestinian delegation was seen as worthy of further exploration, provided, of course, that senior PLO members were not part of that delegation.

To U.S. officials, the Arab states most friendly to the United States—Egypt, Jordan, and Saudi Arabia—seemed genuinely interested in promoting a serious peace effort with active U.S. involvement. As already noted, when King Fahd was in Washington in February he had called on the United States to play a more active role, meaning to press Israel for concessions. Egyptian president Hosni Mubarak was scheduled to begin talks in Washington in mid-March and was also expected to press the administration to involve itself in the peace process. Secretary of State Shultz indicated that the administration might soon be amenable to more active involvement. Testifying before the House Foreign Affairs Committee in late February, he stated that the United States "was prepared to work in a helpful and direct way whenever we see the timing of it appropriate. And it may be that that would occur sometime soon."

THE MUBARAK INITIATIVE

In a February 24 interview with the *New York Times,* in anticipation of his visit to Washington two weeks later, Mubarak urged the administration to invite Israel and members of a joint Jordanian-Palestinian delegation to the United States to lay the groundwork for direct peace talks. In an attempt to get around U.S. and Israeli opposition to dealing with the PLO, Mubarak suggested that a joint Jordanian-Palestinian delegation did not necessarily have to include known members of that organization. Although the Hussein-Arafat agreement had called for PLO participation in peace talks under UN auspices, Mubarak said he favored direct talks first between Israel and the joint Jordanian-Palestinian delegation, with an international conference to come after an agreement had been negotiated. "An international conference could be the last stage," he said, "as a blessing of the solution."

The timing of Mubarak's initiative, two weeks before his arrival in the United States, led some Israelis to wonder if the Egyptian president's proposals were simply part of an effort to gain a sympathetic ear in Washington for his request for more economic and military aid. Foreign Minister Yitzhak Shamir, leader of the Likud party, charged that the Mubarak initiative was a transparent attempt to draw the United States into talks with the PLO. But Prime Minister Peres reacted favorably, albeit cautiously, to the Egyptian president's call for direct negotiations. In a statement that some considered a deviation from the traditional Israeli position, Peres said that "if it is a Jordanian-Palestinian delegation without PLO members, that was always acceptable to us." Later, when asked by an ABC correspondent how closely Israel would check the credentials of Palestinian members of a joint delegation, Peres replied that it was "for them to do," and that Israel would not take part "in making" a Palestinian-Jordanian delegation.

As for the U.S. government, Assistant Secretary Murphy told a House foreign affairs subcommittee that while the administration was "ready to get more actively engaged" in the Middle East peace process, no one knew whether Mubarak's call for direct talks would be accepted by King Hussein. Despite the new flurry of diplomatic activity, therefore, State Department officials cautioned against the expectation of an imminent breakthrough.

Subsequent ambiguities in the Egyptian and Jordanian positions lent weight to administration concerns. President Mubarak began to downplay his initial call for direct talks. He suggested, instead, that the United States first hold talks with the proposed Jordanian-Palestinian delegation and only later bring in Israel, with the United States acting, in effect, as a mediator. Then, following discussions with King Hussein in early March to resolve differences with Jordan over the proposed peace negotiations, Mubarak appeared to backtrack on his earlier proposal that the joint delegation need not include known PLO members. In response to reporters' questions, he denied that he had ever suggested that non-PLO members be named to the delegation, adding that the United States could hold "discussions" or engage in "dialogue" with the PLO without formally recognizing it.

When President Mubarak arrived in Washington on March 11, President Reagan applauded his efforts to revive the peace process. At the same time, he rejected the Egyptian leader's proposal for a U.S. meeting with Jordanian and PLO representatives, reminding Mubarak that the United States had pledged not to talk to the PLO before it unequivocally accepted Security Council Resolutions 242 and 338 and publicly recognized Israel's right to exist. The administration was prepared to assist the parties in reaching a settlement, Reagan said, but only if they were engaged in direct negotiations. Administration officials stressed to Mubarak that they saw nothing to be gained by having the United States first act as a mediator in indirect talks, and only later having the parties enter into direct dialogue with Israel.

Mubarak also faced harsh criticism from members of Congress for failing to return an Egyptian ambassador to Tel Aviv and reneging on pledges to normalize relations with Israel. To add injury to insult, Mubarak failed to receive any commitments for the additional military and economic aid he had come to request. Perhaps to soften these rebuffs, Secretary of State Shultz announced that in order to sustain the momentum toward peace, Assistant Secretary Richard Murphy would tour the Middle East to explore various proposals in greater depth.

THE MURPHY MISSION

For the United States, the two major issues that had to be resolved before the peace process could move forward were the framework within which negotiations could take place and the nature of Palestinian representation. King Hussein had insisted that he needed the backing of Palestinians—specifically the Arafat wing of the PLO—before he could proceed, as well as the "cover" of an international conference—with the participation of the permanent members of the UN Security Council—to neutralize Syrian and Soviet opposition. The king contended that his February 11 agreement with PLO chairman Arafat represented PLO acceptance both of negotiations with Israel on the basis of UN Resolution 242 and the linkage of any Palestinian entity with Jordan, thus meeting two of the primary objectives of the 1982 Reagan plan. However, as we have seen, the PLO executive failed to endorse Resolution 242 explicitly and insisted on amending the February 11 accord so that it would include the goal of an independent Palestinian state.

During this same period, an escalation of Palestinian terrorist attacks, including some sponsored by Arafat's own Fatah group, raised serious doubts about Arafat's readiness for peace. In reality, PLO acceptance of UN Resolution 242 would not have been sufficient. The appropriations bill passed by Congress in October 1984 (PL 98-473) had put into law the existing policy of banning negotiations with the PLO "so long as [it] does not recognize Israel's right to exist, does not accept Security Council Resolutions 242 and 338, and does not renounce the use of terrorism." The administration's intent had been conveyed in March 1984 in a letter from national security adviser Robert McFarlane to Sen. Rudy Boschwitz (R., Minn.), chairman of the Subcommittee on Near Eastern and South Asian Affairs of the Senate Foreign Relations Committee, which assured Congress that the United States would not negotiate with the PLO "unless the organization formally recognizes Israel's right to exist and disavows terrorism." The United States and Israel also opposed a broad international conference that would bring in the Soviet Union and include the more radical Arab states.

In an effort to prevent another breakdown in the peace process over these seemingly intractable problems, Assistant Secretary Murphy began to explore the possibility of selecting a Jordanian-Palestinian delegation that would include Palestinian representatives acceptable to all sides. Murphy also quietly investigated whether the PLO might be willing, as Hussein continued to claim, to accept UN Resolutions 242 and 338 explicitly. King Hussein's concept of a joint delegation was appealing to U.S. policymakers because it also offered the possibility of moving negotiations forward, even without direct PLO participation.

The process led inevitably to policy differences between the United States and Israel. Shortly before Murphy was to launch his sounding-out effort, President Reagan seemed to indicate a shift in the American position when he said in a televised news conference on March 22 that the United States would be willing to meet with a Jordanian-Palestinian delegation so long as it did not include members of the PLO. Since the administration had previously opposed the concept of talks from which Israel would be excluded, the State Department, in an attempt to quell growing Israeli fears, quickly qualified the president's remarks. What Mr. Reagan meant, officials explained, was that he would be prepared to meet with such a delegation if the move showed promise of leading to direct talks with Israel.

The administration and Israel also differed over the wisdom of supplying additional arms to Jordan. The State Department contended that Hussein required the weapons in order to demonstrate that he had credible U.S. backing to defend himself against Syria, which was aggressively opposing the peace process. Selling additional arms to Jordan, in the administration's view, would provide encouragement to Hussein and give him the confidence to pursue his efforts to open negotiations with Israel. Israel and its supporters on Capitol Hill stressed that advanced weapons should be provided to Jordan only after it recognized and began negotiations with Israel, not before.

It was widely accepted that Syria constituted the major regional obstacle to progress toward peace with Israel. President Hafez al-Assad was personally opposed to Arafat's leadership of the PLO and to any effort that would challenge Syrian status and prestige in the region by bringing together his rivals for power—Egypt, Jordan, and Israel. At the end of March, six Palestinian factions allied to Syria announced in Damascus the formation of a new coalition, the National Palestinian Salvation Front, whose purposes were to "obtain abrogation" of the February 11 Hussein-Arafat accord and to thwart efforts by Jordan to revive peace negotiations with Israel. The Syrian-sponsored coalition included the PLO-affiliated Popular Front for the Liberation of Palestine–General Command, led by Ahmed Jibril; the Popular Struggle Front; the Syrian-controlled As-Saiqa; the Palestine Liberation Front; the breakaway Fatah faction led by Abu Musa; and George Habash's Popular Front for the Liberation of Palestine. (The last had previously broken official ties to the PLO.)

In an attempt to keep alive his options and to outmaneuver Syria, PLO chairman Arafat convened a meeting of the PLO executive committee in Baghdad, in April, coinciding with Murphy's visit to the Middle East. Arafat failed, however, to obtain sufficient backing for the assistant secretary's efforts to form a joint Jordanian-Palestinian delegation, and Murphy was unable to get a list of Palestinians who were acceptable to the United States and Israel and who were prepared to represent Palestinian interests in a joint delegation with Jordan. Indeed, when Murphy met with a group of Palestinian residents of the West Bank and Gaza, the majority were reported to have declared their allegiance to the PLO as their "sole legitimate representative."

THE SHULTZ MISSION

Despite the continuing deadlock over the composition of an Arab delegation, the State Department announced that Secretary of State Shultz would visit the Middle East in May. Department spokesman Bernard Kalb tried to minimize the failure of Murphy's mission by saying that while no dramatic breakthroughs had been made, neither had there been any setbacks.

The primary purpose of Shultz's trip was to take part in ceremonies honoring Holocaust victims at the Yad Vashem memorial in Jerusalem. (On May 5, President Reagan visited the Bitburg military cemetery in West Germany, which contained graves of Nazi SS troops, an episode that created wide opposition and protest both in Israel and in the United States.) Few observers expected the secretary to be any more successful than Murphy had been in promoting Arab-Israeli negotiations.

Just prior to Shultz's departure, the State Department announced that the United States would consider the possible participation of "independent" members of the Palestine National Council in a potential Jordanian-Palestinian delegation. This would allow the United States to maintain that it was not dealing with official members of the PLO and would also permit Arafat to claim that the PLO was sufficiently represented in negotiations. An official U.S. distinction between the PLO and the PNC that had been drawn up two years before and was now reiterated by the State Department declared that the United States did not oppose "direct contact with Palestinians, including PNC members, who, as independents, have no affiliation with the PLO's constituent political organizations."

On the heels of the State Department announcement, however, key PLO leaders in Tunis declared that the only acceptable Palestinian representation in a joint delegation with Jordan would be members of the PLO executive. Ahmed Abdel Rahman, the PLO's chief spokesman, Saleh Khalef (Abu Iyad), a leading member of al-Fatah, and Farouk Kaddoumi, the PLO's "foreign minister," ruled out any meeting between American officials and undeclared PLO members. They also voiced strong opposition to the February 11 Hussein-Arafat accord, thus indicating the PLO chairman's weakening position within his own organization. Moreover, Khalef bluntly declared that the PLO did not accept UN Resolution 242, further undermining Hussein's optimistic assertions.

Names of prospective members of a joint Jordanian-Palestinian delegation were reported to have been raised during Secretary Shultz's visit to Israel, Egypt, and Jordan, but apparently no real progress was made. PLO chairman Arafat's conditional response to a *Washington Post* reporter a day after Shultz's return from the Middle East that yes, he would accept Resolution 242 *if* Washington endorsed "self-determination" for the Palestinians, did not satisfy U.S. officials. Assistant Secretary Murphy, who stayed in the Middle East to brief Israeli officials, told them that Jordan still insisted on PLO participation in any joint delegation. As for the other key stumbling block, Jordan's foreign minister, Taher al-Masri, stated that "neither the PLO nor we speak of direct negotiations. We speak of direct talks between the PLO and the United States side only, within the Jordanian-Palestinian delegation." This backing away from direct Jordanian-Israeli talks seemed to confirm Israeli suspicions that Arab maneuvering over Palestinian representation was merely an effort to obtain prior U.S. consent to PLO participation in any future negotiations.

HUSSEIN'S PROPOSAL

Some in the State Department remained optimistic that movement could be achieved. King Hussein, who was scheduled to visit Washington at the end of May, had expressed a sense of urgency that his visit might be the "last opportunity" to revive the stalled peace process. In order to accommodate Hussein's concern for international support, the administration let it be known that some kind of international "umbrella" conference leading to direct negotiations would be discussed during the king's visit, although differences with Jordan over the nature of such a conference had not been resolved. U.S. policymakers were using the term to mean something less than a full-blown Geneva-style international conference, but enough to give Hussein the international sanction he believed he needed to talk with Israel. Some Israeli leaders expressed concern about Washington's apparent weakening on the issue of an international conference, and Defense Minister Yitzhak Rabin commented that "whenever anyone mentions 'umbrella' it reminds me of [Neville] Chamberlain and Munich."

When Hussein arrived in Washington he appeared to have moved significantly toward the U.S. position on the nature of an international conference. "It is our hope," he said, "that an international conference would enable the parties to the conflict to negotiate the establishment of a just and durable peace in the Middle East. We need the international umbrella to offer us the opportunity to negotiate, and when I speak of negotiations I obviously mean negotiations amongst the parties to the confict; in other words, negotiations between the Arab side, in this case a Jordanian-Palestinian delegation, with Israel on the other side." The Jordanian monarch proceeded to outline a complicated four-stage process, one that could eventually lead to direct negotiations with Israel, but that could also fall apart at many points along the way.

The first step in the Hussein plan envisioned preliminary discussions between the United States and a joint Jordanian-Palestinian delegation that would not include PLO representatives. In the second stage, the PLO would formally accept UN Resolution 242 and announce its willingness to recognize and negotiate with Israel, but only after the United States had declared publicly its support for the right of "self-determination" for the Palestinian people within the context of a Jordanian-Palestinian confederation. In stage three, the United States would hold another meeting with a joint Jordanian-Palestinian delegation, which would now include PLO officials, in order to discuss details for an international conference. The final stage would see the convening of the international conference, consisting of the five permanent members of the UN Security Council (China, France, the United Kingdom, the United States, and the USSR), the neighboring Arab states, and Israel, for the purpose of producing a comprehensive peace agreement.

The components of Hussein's proposal left many issues unresolved, and highlighted once again the differences between Israel, Jordan, and the United States over proper pathways toward negotiations. Among its shortcomings, the Hussein plan did not guarantee that the preliminary talks between the United States and the Arab delegation would actually lead to direct talks with Israel. Perhaps most significantly, critics of the Hussein proposal pointed out, Israel did not enter into the Jordanian scenario until the very last stage of an international conference, or, as Prime Minister Peres characterized it, Israel would be "left in some darkened anteroom while everything is settled without her." The plan, taken in its entirety, was in fact predicated on U.S. recognition of the PLO and of Palestinian self-determination (by which the PLO meant a Palestinian state) in advance of any direct negotiations between Israel and the Arab side.

On June 11, Prime Minister Peres responded to King Hussein's four-stage proposal with his own five-point plan. In a speech to the Knesset, he said that his proposal was a realistic alternative to the king's plan, which he described as doomed to failure. The five points of the Israeli plan were: (1) continuation of U.S. contacts with Israel, Jordan, Egypt, and Palestinians who were not PLO members; (2) the naming of a Jordanian-Palestinian team to prepare an agenda for a conference in which the United States would also participate; (3) the enlistment of the UN Security Council's support for direct talks between the Jordanian-Palestinian delegation and Israel; (4) the appointment of "authentic Palestinian representatives" from the West Bank and Gaza; and (5) the opening of a full-fledged peace conference within three months.

Despite the many serious differences between the two proposals, the administration believed that the gap dividing the Jordanians and Israelis had narrowed sufficiently to enable the United States to continue its efforts. To encourage King Hussein, who, it believed, was sincere in his desire to negotiate peace with Israel, the administration proposed additional economic and military aid to the Hashemite kingdom. The administration requested and obtained $250 million in economic support funds for Jordan, a substantial increase over the usual $50-million annual allocation. However, Israel's supporters in Congress continued to object to the sale of additional arms until such time as Jordan entered into direct negotiations with Israel.

The administration again pressed Jordan to recommend potential Palestinian participants in a joint delegation. In July PLO leader Arafat presented a list of names to King Hussein, who forwarded it to Washington, which relayed it to Prime Minister Peres. Peres's initial reaction, on July 17, was that the delegation, consisting almost entirely of top- and mid-level PLO leaders, was unacceptable. A few days later, however, Peres indicated that two of the seven Palestinian names proposed were acceptable. The two were Hanna Seniora, editor of the East Jerusalem pro-PLO newspaper *Al-Fajr,* and Faiz Abu Rahman, chairman of the Gaza lawyers' association. While both men were ardent Palestinian nationalists, they were not formally PLO leaders; they were also the only proposed delegates actually living in the administered territories. Despite—or perhaps because of—the positive Israeli reaction, the PLO later qualified the inclusion of the two, claiming that they were to participate only as "consultants."

OTHER DIPLOMATIC MOVES

Another visit by Secretary Murphy to the Middle East in August again failed to produce progress. He reportedly planned to meet with a joint Jordanian-Palestinian delegation during the six-day mission to Jordan, Israel, and Egypt, in order to lay the groundwork for direct talks with Israel. However, according to State Department sources, when Israel vehemently objected to such a meeting, fearing that it might lead to U.S. recognition of the PLO, Murphy cut short his trip and returned home.

In fact, the talks between Murphy and the joint delegation did not materialize because Jordan and the PLO again failed to meet U.S. conditions for such a meeting. On August 17, as Murphy prepared for his final meeting with King Hussein, Arafat told reporters in Amman that the American official had come with nothing to offer "except further demands for concessions according to Israeli conditions." The previous day, Jordan's prime minister, Zaid Rifai, had stated that Jordan remained committed both to U.S. recognition of the PLO and an international peace conference. Moreover, Murphy was still unable to win assurances that if the United States agreed to meet with an as yet undetermined Jordanian-Palestinian delegation, direct talks between Jordan and Israel would soon follow.

Although the administration continued to portray the Jordanians as having been cooperative in efforts to move the peace process forward, even letting it be known —while Murphy was still in Amman—that it would go ahead with plans for a major arms sale to the Hashemite kingdom, despite growing congressional opposition, it was difficult to mask U.S. disappointment over the slow pace of progress. King Hussein had hoped to win Arab endorsement for his accord with Arafat at the Arab League summit, convened by King Hassan of Morocco in Casablanca in early August. Yet even though the more radical states of Syria, Libya, Algeria, and South

Yemen boycotted the conference, Hussein failed to win formal approval from the ostensibly more moderate members—either for his peace initiative or for his bid to supersede the Rabat conference's designation of the PLO as sole representative of the Palestinians.

An episode involving Great Britain and the PLO proved instructive to U.S. policymakers as well as to King Hussein. London had agreed to meet with a joint Jordanian-Palestinian delegation that included two members of the PLO executive committee, counting on assurances that they would sign a statement disavowing terrorism and recognizing Israel's right to exist within its pre-1967 borders. The meeting between Britain and the Jordanian-Palestinian group was originally proposed by Prime Minister Margaret Thatcher on September 20, during a visit to Jordan, with Mrs. Thatcher making it clear that the two PLO members—Mohammed Milhem, a former mayor of Hebron on the West Bank, and Elias Khoury, an Anglican bishop from Jerusalem—would be invited to London as individuals, not as representatives of the PLO. According to British officials, Britain had received definite assurances from Jordan that the Palestinians would sign the required statement, presumably with the approval of Arafat. The meeting, scheduled for October 14, was canceled when the two PLO delegates reneged on the commitment to join in the statement renouncing violence and explicitly accepting Israel's right to exist. At this point King Hussein, embarrassed by the incident, began to distance himself from the PLO chairman.

One more serious effort toward reviving the peace process was made before the end of the year. Prime Minister Peres had already been moving toward endorsement of an international conference, if it served as an umbrella for direct negotiations, despite severe opposition from his Likud coalition partners and even from hard-line members within his own Labor party. On October 21, in his address to the UN General Assembly in New York, Peres offered a new seven-point peace plan. The major element in the plan was the suggestion that talks with Jordan could take place under international sponsorship. Peres reiterated Israeli insistence on direct negotiations, but added that the talks, "if deemed necessary, may be initiated with the support of an international forum agreed upon by the parties." The international forum, he stated, "while not being a substitute for direct negotiations, can offer support for them." The permanent members of the Security Council could be invited to support the initiation of these negotiations, he said. But, in a pointed allusion to the Soviet Union, he added, "It is our position that those who confine their diplomatic relations to one side of the conflict, exclude themselves from such a role."

Peres did not explicitly reject all members of the Palestine National Council as negotiating partners, but simply stated that Palestinians who "represent peace, not terror" would be welcome to participate in a joint delegation with Jordan. Although Peres's address was favorably received in Amman (there had been some reports that Peres had met secretly with King Hussein in Paris before formulating his plan) and in Cairo, other concerns, including a renewed spate of terrorist activity and American preoccupation with the upcoming summit between President Reagan and new Soviet leader Mikhail Gorbachev, meant that Middle East diplomacy would not likely progress for the balance of the year. Assistant Secretary of State Murphy did make one more visit to the Middle East in December, but nothing came of it. King Hussein had proclaimed 1985 "the year of opportunity" for forward movement in the peace process. As 1985 ended, however, there was no breakthrough in sight.

Terrorism

The U.S. government was trying to project a determined and tough stand against terrorists and their state supporters, especially in the aftermath of attacks on U.S. forces in Lebanon in 1983 and 1984. Israel, too, had a policy of acting tough with terrorists. The uncertainty underlying the policy of both countries became painfully apparent, however, during two episodes: Israel's release of over a thousand terrorists in May, and the hijacking to Beirut of a TWA airliner in June.

In what appears to have been a desire to close the final chapter in its involvement in Lebanon, the Israeli government decided in May to release 1,150 convicted Arab terrorists being held in prison in exchange for three Israeli soldiers held in Damascus by Ahmed Jibril's Popular Front for the Liberation of Palestine–General Command, which had captured them in Lebanon in July 1982. The decision was subjected to severe criticism in Israel and in the United States, with many commentators suggesting that the prisoner exchange was a blunder that would create long-lasting damage to Israel's counterterrorist strategy. It was not the numbers involved—such lopsided trades had been made in previous exchanges of prisoners of war after Arab-Israeli conflicts. Rather, the paramount concern was with the government's departure from the principle of not yielding to terrorist demands for the release of hostages. Public consternation about the prisoner swap was heightened by the knowledge that among the released terrorists were 167 convicted murderers, including Kozo Okamoto, the Japanese terrorist serving a life sentence for his part in the May 1972 Lod airport massacre, in which 27 persons were killed and 80 wounded. At least 380 of the terrorists were serving life sentences, and many others among the freed prisoners were directly responsible for killing Israelis.

TWA HIJACKING

On June 14, a month after the prisoner exchange, the United States and Israel together faced a challenge to the principle of refusing to negotiate with terrorists for the release of hostages. TWA Flight 847 was hijacked from Athens to Beirut, this time with 39 Americans on board. One of them, a U.S. serviceman, Robert Stethem, was shot and killed by the terrorists. The hijackers not only singled out American passengers but identified those passengers with "Jewish-sounding names," in a process reminiscent of the notorious "selections" practiced by the Nazis during the Holocaust.

Uli Dereckson, the German-born purser of the hijacked plane, was the focus of a brief controversy when it was reported that she had been involved in the selection, since she had collected the passengers' passports at the behest of the terrorists. It was made clear afterward, following investigations by the FBI and the American Jewish Committee, that she had actually tried to hide the passports and frustrate the terrorists' efforts. She was later praised for her role by a number of the hostages, who said that her actions had probably saved several lives.

The Shi'ite Muslim hijackers made it known that the hostages would be freed only upon the release of 766 Lebanese, mostly Shi'ites, who were being held in an Israeli detention camp in Atlit, near Haifa. Most of the prisoners were affiliated with the Shi'ite militia, Amal, and had been arrested for suspected involvement in attacks on Israeli army units in southern Lebanon.

The choices facing the United States and Israel were not easy ones. President Reagan had stressed several times before and during the hijacking and hostage crisis that the United States would not make concessions to terrorists, because to do so would only invite more attacks. Israel, too, had long been on record against negotiations with terrorists, yet the government's own recent departure from that principle made it difficult not to release the Lebanese being held in Israel when American lives were at stake. Ironically, Israel had already begun the gradual release of the Lebanese Shi'ites it was holding on suspicion of anti-Israel activity; however, officials became concerned that if they were suddenly to release the remainder of the detainees, it would appear that Israel was giving in to blackmail.

Israeli officials were also troubled by the seemingly contradictory signals coming from Washington. While President Reagan and Secretary of State Shultz were insisting that they opposed yielding to terrorist demands or asking Israel to do so, lower-ranking U.S. officials were suggesting that Israel's transfer of the Shi'ites from Lebanon and their detention at the Israeli prison in Atlit were violations of international law. Israel claimed that the prisoners had participated in acts of violence against the Israeli army in Lebanon, and that their detention was permitted under Article 78 of the Fourth Geneva Convention, which allowed for internment "if the occupying power considers it necessary for imperative reasons of security, to take safety measures." Their transfer to Israel, according to the Israelis, was permitted under Article 49 of the same convention, which prohibited the transfer of detainees "except when for material reasons it is impossible to avoid," and with the understanding that those evacuated would be transferred back to their homes when hostilities ceased. In fact, 500 such detainees had already been released and returned to Lebanon.

Israel was under the strong impression that American officials had been implying that Israel should quickly exchange the Shi'ite prisoners for the TWA hostages. This led Israel's defense minister, Yitzhak Rabin, in an interview on U.S. television, to call on the Reagan administration to "not play games," but to state clearly what it wanted Israel to do. Other officials made it known that Israel wanted a specific and public request from the United States before it would consider yielding to the hijackers' demands for the release of the Shi'ite prisoners still held in Israel.

When Reagan administration officials were angered by the Rabin remarks, Prime Minister Peres attempted to calm the waters. In a speech to the World Zionist Organization's General Council in Jerusalem on June 21, Peres stated that "as far as I know, there has been no change in the U.S. position, nor has the U.S. approached Israel with a request that it take any action. We are not indifferent to the fate of the hostages—irrespective of nationality or religion. But from our experience we know that an operation to free hijacked persons must be carried out in a unified fashion. There is no one method of dealing with hostages because hijackings themselves are not the result of one single method. It is for this reason that Israel is refraining from giving advice or making declarations."

The TWA hostage crisis was complicated by internal factional rivalries within Lebanon. The hijacking had been carried out by pro-Iranian Shi'ite fundamentalists, members of Hezbollah (the "party of God"), who turned most of the hostages over to Nabih Berri, leader of Amal, Lebanon's dominant Shi'ite group. The leader of the Amal militia, who also served as minister of justice in the largely impotent Lebanese government, represented the more secular, and presumably more pragmatic, elements within the Lebanese Shi'ite community. Berri, who was being challenged for leadership by the pro-Iranian fundamentalists, was allied with Syria. He had little interest in the Islamic revolution or in war with Israel, but relied on Syrian support against Amal rivals within Lebanon.

The 39 American hostages were released on June 30, ostensibly with the help of the Syrian government. Their departure was briefly delayed when their captors added a new demand, calling on the United States to pledge publicly not to retaliate militarily after the hostages were freed. The United States refused, but at Syria's suggestion it issued an old policy statement that seemed to satisfy the hijackers. The statement indicated that the United States reaffirmed "its long-standing support for the preservation of Lebanon, its Government, its stability and security, and for the mitigation of the suffering of its people."

Despite rumors that seven other Americans who had been abducted from the streets of Beirut over the previous 15 months might also be released, Berri indicated that he had no control over those holding the missing Americans. They were believed to have been kidnapped by another shadowy terrorist group, the Islamic Holy War, that was demanding the release of relatives held in Kuwaiti prisons for terrorist acts committed there.

Although Israel did not immediately free the Lebanese prisoners whose release had been demanded by the hijackers, it was understood that Israel would soon do so. Israel continued to claim that there was no formal linkage and that the release of the Lebanese who were being held temporarily at Atlit was a gesture toward Washington, not a direct result of the negotiations with the terrorists. Likewise, administration officials in Washington continued to assert that the freedom of the Americans had been achieved without concessions being made. They also maintained that they had never pressed Israel for a guarantee that the suspected Lebanese terrorists interned in Israel would be freed.

The TWA hijacking had little impact on the Arab-Israeli dispute. Although the United States applauded Syria's role in the release of the hostages, sharp disagreements continued between Washington and Damascus over Middle East peace efforts, with the United States still attempting to salvage what it could of the February 11 accord between Jordan's King Hussein and PLO chairman Yasir Arafat, which Syria strongly opposed.

PLO ROLE

The year 1985 saw the reemergence of the Arafat wing of the PLO as a political factor in the Middle East, after its ouster from Lebanon in 1982 and the dispersal of its terrorist forces throughout the region had effectively destroyed it as a conventional military force and crippled it as a guerrilla movement. Following the agreement between King Hussein and Arafat on February 11, there was some speculation that the PLO had finally opted for a peaceful solution to the Arab-Israeli conflict. Recent Palestinian terrorist actions, it was suggested, were no longer the work of Arafat's al-Fatah but of more radical Palestinian factions opposed to Arafat's diplomatic approach. While conceding that rival Palestinian groups had been responsible for many of the terrorist attacks—apparently seeking either to embarrass the PLO chairman or to sidetrack any peace initiatives he might have considered joining—Israeli officials maintained that Arafat himself was still involved. They pointed to his long record of publicly denying complicity in terrorist actions for which elements under his control or linked to his organization were responsible. In 1970, for example, when Arafat was driven out of Jordan, he had pursued this two-track approach: a public diplomatic offensive to win wider legitimacy and recognition for the PLO, and a secret terror campaign directed by his closest associates, but in the guise of the group known as "Black September." The Israelis suggested that Arafat might be using the same tactics in the mid-1980s.

As if to bear out this theory, the signing of the Hussein-Arafat accord was followed by a marked increase in PLO attacks against Israel and targets abroad. According to Israeli sources, many of these attacks were planned at the PLO's new headquarters and training camps in Tunisia. These were under the complete control of Arafat and his associates, although Tunisian police and army troops assisted in guarding the facilities. Since the beginning of 1984, al-Fatah had also gradually begun to build up its presence in Jordan.

In addition to regular Fatah guerrilla forces, a special elite group of terrorist commandos, dubbed "Force 17," had been established by Arafat in the early 1970s. While the original function of its members had been to serve as bodyguards for Arafat and other PLO leaders, it evolved into a larger force which, in addition to its security functions, carried out special assassinations and attacks, sometimes against Arafat's rivals within al-Fatah or opposing Palestinian factions. In addition to its headquarters in Tunisia, Force 17 established offices in Amman that took on responsibility for carrying out anti-Israel activity in the West Bank.

On September 25, 1985 (Yom Kippur), three PLO terrorists attacked an Israeli civilian yacht anchored in the marina at Larnaca, Cyprus, and murdered its three Israeli passengers—a woman and two men. Arafat's Force 17 was implicated, as it had also been in three separate attempts to infiltrate Israel by sea between April and the end of August. Before their capture, the Larnaca terrorists demanded the release of 20 PLO prisoners being held in Israeli prisons, including the deputy commander of Force 17, who had been caught a few weeks earlier by the Israel Navy off the Lebanese coast. After a nine-hour siege, the terrorists surrendered to Cypriot police. Although PLO officials disclaimed any connection with the Larnaca attack, two of the gunmen captured were identified as Arab members of Force 17; the third was a British mercenary who had joined al-Fatah in Lebanon several years earlier and subsequently been recruited by Arafat into the elite unit.

On October 1, in retaliation for the attack at Larnaca and other recent terrorist attacks by PLO units under Arafat's control, the Israel Air Force bombed the PLO headquarters and facilities belonging to Force 17 at Hamam ash-Shaat in Tunisia. To no one's surprise, the attack was denounced at the United Nations, on October 4, as a violation of international law and an infringement of Tunisian sovereignty.

U.S. administration pronouncements left some confusion about the American position. On October 1, immediately after the Israeli bombing, President Reagan stated that the air strike was "understandable as an expression of self-defense" and a "legitimate response to terrorist attacks." The following day, in the face of mounting Arab criticism of what appeared to be the president's endorsement of the Israeli action, the White House issued a statement that continued to characterize the air raid as "understandable," but added that the bombing could "not be condoned." Sensitive to the possible repercussions for the pro-American government of Tunisian president Habib Bourguiba, the United States did not veto the Security Council resolution of October 4, but abstained in the vote, noting the lack of reference to the terrorist actions that had provoked the bombing. On the same day, Secretary of State Shultz told the *New York Times* that while the United States had helped persuade President Bourguiba to offer refuge to some of the PLO units evacuated from Beirut in August 1982, it had not expected the establishment of a base "out of which terrorist operations would be conducted."

Events in October offered further evidence that Arafat was employing Force 17 and members of smaller, pro-Arafat PLO factions to carry out his ongoing campaign of terror. For example, on October 5, two Israeli seamen were found tortured and murdered in the Spanish port of Barcelona. An anonymous caller told Western news agencies that Force 17 was responsible.

ACHILLE LAURO

The most dramatic instance of PLO-linked terror occurred on October 7, when the Italian cruise ship *Achille Lauro,* bound for the Israeli port of Ashdod, was hijacked by four members of the Palestine Liberation Front (PLF), a group with close ties to Arafat. The original intention of the hijackers was reportedly to reach Israel, where they would take hostages and demand the release of convicted terrorists being held in Israeli prisons. The plan was foiled, however, when the weapons of the terrorists were discovered by crew members after the ship left the Egyptian port of Alexandria. The terrorists succeeded in taking control of the ship, holding some 97 passengers and 350 crew members as hostages. (Most of the 750 passengers had gotten off at Alexandria for an overland tour in Egypt.) They forced the *Achille Lauro* to sail toward Syria, and, to underscore their demands, threatened to kill passengers. Their threat was carried out when they shot and killed a 69-year-old disabled American Jewish tourist, Leon Klinghoffer, throwing his body and his wheelchair overboard.

The young men who perpetrated the hijacking and murder belonged to the Abu Abbas faction of the PLF. Its leader, Mohammed Abu al-Abbas, was an Arafat ally whose links to the PLO chairman became closer after al-Fatah broke up into pro-Syrian and pro-Arafat factions in 1983. In 1984 Arafat personally nominated Abbas and saw to it that he was elected to the PLO's ruling 11-member executive committee.

When the Syrian government refused to assist the *Achille Lauro* hijackers, they turned the ship back toward Egypt. PLF leader Abu Abbas, who had already flown to Cairo, was able to negotiate a deal for his terrorist cohort. If the ship and its passengers were released, the hijackers would be given safe passage out of Egypt. Over strenuous American objections, the Egyptian government allowed the four hijackers and Abu Abbas to leave the country on an Egyptian airliner, the hijackers under Egyptian police guard. The plane was initially bound for Tunisia, where, according to the Egyptians, Arafat had agreed to put the men on trial. This maneuver was undoubtedly intended to spare Egypt further embarrassment. At the same time, it would give Arafat a chance to demonstrate both that he was in control of his supporters and that he opposed unauthorized acts of violence against innocent civilians. Whether Arafat would really have punished the *Achille Lauro* hijackers was to remain a moot point because the Tunisian authorities refused to allow the plane to land.

While in flight over international waters in the Mediterranean, the plane was intercepted by U.S. Navy jets and forced to fly to an American base in Sicily. There the terrorists were seized by Italian guards who refused to permit American troops to take them into U.S. custody.

Throughout the episode, Arafat and the PLO observer at the UN denied that the American tourist had been murdered. Abu Abbas, too, denied that any of his group had killed Klinghoffer, and claimed that in fact he had died of a heart attack. A week after the hijacking, Syria announced that a body—which turned out to be that of the slain Leon Klinghoffer—had washed up on a beach near the Syrian city of Tartus. When the Syrians turned the body over to the U.S. embassy, it was clear that they were only too happy to add to the embarrassment of Arafat and his loyalists in the PLO—especially since an autopsy confirmed that Klinghoffer had died from bullet wounds and not of natural causes.

The Syrians clearly wanted to undermine Arafat's relationship with Egypt and Jordan; they further wanted to damage Arafat's credibility and any possibility that the PLO leader would be included in peace moves initiated by Jordan's King Hussein. Egyptian president Mubarak had been encouraging the Jordanian monarch in his efforts to portray Arafat as a legitimate partner in peace negotiations. Now, the PLO chairman's apparent involvement in the *Achille Lauro* affair was a major setback for those efforts. If Arafat had indeed authorized Abbas to carry out the hijacking, that proved that the PLO leader was still supporting indiscriminate terrorist actions. On the other hand, if Arafat could not be directly linked to the *Achille Lauro* attack, he would be seen as having lost control of the PLO and therefore unable to commit it to peaceful negotiations.

The *Achille Lauro* affair had other consequences, including a temporary rift in Egyptian-U.S. relations. President Mubarak had issued conflicting statements on the whereabouts of the hijackers when they left the ship after returning to Egypt. He was clearly indignant over the U.S. interception and diversion of the Egyptian airliner carrying the terrorists out of Egypt, which he considered an affront to Egyptian sovereignty (although there were reports that the U.S. interception was aided by elements within the Egyptian defense establishment).

The incident also created tensions between the United States and Italy. Prime Minister Bettino Craxi, in a statement on November 6 that appeared to justify PLO violence in principle, observed that the PLO could legitimately resort to armed struggle since it was a "movement wanting to liberate its own country from a foreign occupation." The Italian government was widely denounced when it allowed Abu Abbas to flee to Yugoslavia, this despite urgent requests that he be held until the United States was able to provide documentation showing his direct involvement in the hijacking. U.S. officials believed that evidence existed that would warrant either bringing Abbas to trial in Italy for the hijacking or extraditing him to the United States for the killing of Leon Klinghoffer. The Italian government's haste in helping to spirit Abbas out of the country was sharply criticized both within Italy and the United States as a cowardly act of expediency.

Sensitive to the negative repercussions of the *Achille Lauro* incident, Arafat announced in Cairo on November 7, following a meeting with President Mubarak, that henceforth the PLO would limit its attacks to targets inside Israel and the Israeli-occupied territories. He also said he would "take drastic measures" to punish those who violated the order. Israeli officials dismissed Arafat's statement as a public-relations gimmick designed to improve the PLO's image in the West and an effort to mend strained relations with Egypt and Jordan over the *Achille Lauro* affair. Simcha Dinitz, a Labor-party member of the Knesset and a former ambassador to the United States, remarked that Arafat's declaration meant that "stabbing Jews on their way to prayers at the Wailing Wall will be permitted, but killing Americans on a ship will be forbidden."

OTHER INCIDENTS

PLO and PLO-inspired terrorism continued in the wake of the *Achille Lauro* hijacking. The most dramatic of the attacks were apparently intended to further discredit Arafat, since they were perpetrated by rival terrorist factions allied with the PLO leader's main enemies in the Arab world—Libya and Syria.

On November 23, armed Palestinian terrorists, later described by Egyptian officials as members of a "dissident group" backed by Libya, but believed to be members of the faction led by dissident Abu Nidal, hijacked an Egyptian airliner bound from Athens to Cairo with 91 passengers and a crew of 6 on board. The plane was diverted to Malta, where the terrorists began methodically shooting passengers, including two Israeli women, one of whom was thrown from the plane and miraculously survived. During an ill-planned rescue operation by Egyptian commandos who stormed the plane, the terrorists hurled grenades at the passengers. In all, 60 people died, including two of the three hijackers. The presumed motive of the terrorists, who issued no demands, was to humiliate both Egypt and Arafat for having pledged not to use violence outside of Israel. The terrorists had said they were members of a group called "Egypt's Revolution" that had earlier claimed responsibility for the slaying of an Israeli diplomat in Cairo, Albert Atrakchi, in August. Abu Nidal was known to use various names for the groups under his banner.

Abu Nidal had been expelled from Arafat's Fatah organization in 1974, after he engaged in unapproved terrorist acts designed to prevent the PLO's entry into negotiations following the October 1973 war. Until the end of 1980, Abu Nidal was based in Baghdad, operating with the support of the Iraqi regime. When his group was expelled from Iraq, Abu Nidal relocated his headquarters to Syria, although he frequently visited Libya, where he apparently also maintained facilities. The Abu Nidal faction was responsible for killing PLO officials allied to Arafat as well as Israeli and European Jews. Three members of his group were held responsible for critically wounding Israel's ambassador to London, Shlomo Argov, in June 1982. That shooting triggered Israel's invasion of Lebanon.

The year ended with two more dramatic terrorist attacks, apparently coordinated, on December 27, at the Rome and Vienna airports. The assaults left 20 persons dead, including 5 Americans—one of them an 11-year-old girl—and over 100 wounded. Although the gunmen, wielding grenades and submachine guns, focused their attacks on the El Al Israel Airlines counters, they managed to wreak havoc in the areas where passengers of other airlines were waiting to check in. One of the three terrorists in Vienna and three of the four attackers in Rome were killed by security police. A surviving gunman in Vienna declared that they were all members of the Fatah Revolutionary Council, which was the official name of Abu Nidal's organization. Israel charged that Libya and Syria were also implicated.

American officials, too, accused Libya of aiding and abetting the airport terrorists, and said they would support any Israeli retaliation against the sources of the attacks.

Israeli officials welcomed U.S. approval of the principle of retaliation, but questioned why Israel alone should bear the burden of responding to international terrorism. MK Simcha Dinitz, reflecting the concern of many Israelis, remarked, "We greatly appreciate the decisions the U.S. has adopted against terrorism—in words and deeds. But we would like to feel that the battle against terrorism is an international concern and not the exclusive domain of Israel."

As the year ended, America seemed determined to fight back against international and state-supported terrorism. The successful military interception of the jetliner carrying the *Achille Lauro* terrorists out of Egypt provided a needed morale booster, helping to compensate for the frustration experienced over the failure of earlier American efforts to deal effectively with terrorists and hostage-takers in Iran and Lebanon.

U.S.-Israel Cooperation

The year 1985 witnessed increasingly close cooperation between the United States and Israel in strategic planning, intelligence, and other defense-related areas. Traditional bipartisan support for Israel in Congress reached new heights, with the 99th Congress proving more favorably disposed than any of its predecessors toward Israel's needs.

The House and Senate voted $1.8 billion in grant military aid and $1.2 billion in grant economic aid. (The previous year's aid package of $2.6 billion was the first to be given entirely in the form of grants rather than loans.) In April the administration topped the congressional aid package by announcing an additional two-year grant of $1.5 billion in emergency economic aid, after it was convinced that Israel was serious about implementing necessary economic reforms. (Secretary of State Shultz, an economist by training, had taken a close personal interest in working with a team of American and Israeli economists and officials to develop Israel's austerity measures.)

A Free Trade Agreement (FTA) was signed by U.S. and Israeli officials on April 22; implementing legislation was passed by a 422-0 vote in the House of Representatives two weeks later and by the Senate on May 23. The FTA legislation would benefit Israel by gradually eliminating tariffs on its exports to the United States and would similarly benefit U.S. firms. The FTA would also allow U.S. businesses to take advantage of Israel's preferential relationship with the European Common Market countries by establishing plants or subsidiaries in Israel and exporting to Europe from there.

Congressional opposition to U.S. arms sales to Jordan intensified amid growing evidence that King Hussein was not prepared to enter into direct negotiations with Israel. In November the House of Representatives gave final congressional approval to compromise legislation blocking the administration's proposed arms sale to Jordan until March 1, 1986, unless "direct and meaningful peace negotiations" between

Jordan and Israel began before that date. The Senate had adopted an identical measure in October.

Americans played an important role in a purely humanitarian effort: the airlift of over 7,000 Ethiopian Jews from the Sudan in late 1984 and early 1985. The United States had been cooperating quietly with Israel in the rescue operation, with much of the cost of the Israeli-sponsored airlift being paid for out of $15 million in resettlement aid and $5 million in transportation aid given to Israel in the fiscal 1985 budget. When the Israeli airlift ended suddenly on January 6, due in part to its premature disclosure by Israeli officials in the Jewish and general press, at least a thousand Ethiopian Jews, possibly more, were left stranded in refugee camps in the Sudan. On March 23, some 800 Jews were flown from the Sudan to Israel on U.S. Air Force C-130 Hercules transport planes. This secret operation, directed by the CIA with the cooperation of the State and Defense departments, had been approved by the president and the Senate. The details of the plan were worked out during a scheduled trip by Vice-President George Bush to the Sudan in early March, when Sudanese president Gaafar al-Nimeiry agreed to the evacuation of virtually all the remaining Jews in the camps, as long as Israeli planes were not involved. When President Nimeiry was ousted in a military coup on April 6, among the many charges brought against him by his opponents was his alleged cooperation with the United States and Israel in the airlift of Ethiopian Jews.

The United States supported Israel in its efforts to prevent the inclusion of anti-Zionist references in the official report of the UN conference marking the end of the Decade for Women, held in Nairobi, Kenya, in mid-July. The first UN conference of the Women's Decade, held in Mexico City in 1975, had issued a declaration equating Zionism with racism, which served as a precedent for the subsequent UN General Assembly Resolution 3379. The Mid-Decade Women's Conference in Copenhagen in 1980 had adopted a "Program of Action" that also contained the Zionism-racism equation. At the conference in Nairobi, Maureen Reagan, the president's daughter and head of the American delegation, played a key role in assuring that the final document would not include the anti-Zionist slur.

In January President Reagan asked Israel to allow the Voice of America to set up a relay station in the Negev desert, to enhance American radio transmitting ability to the USSR. The Israeli government informed the United States of its agreement in principle to installation of a transmitter.

In April Israel responded positively to Washington's invitation to participate in research for the Strategic Defense Initiative.

The Pollard Affair

The arrest on November 21 of a Jewish U.S. Navy intelligence analyst, Jonathan Jay Pollard, on charges of spying for Israel, threatened to upset the equilibrium that had been achieved in U.S.-Israeli relations. When the story broke, two low-level

Israeli diplomats—Pollard's alleged contacts in the Israel embassy in Washington —quickly returned to their country. The two, Ilan Ravid and Yosef Yagor, were employees of a little-known branch of the Israel Defense Ministry, the Scientific Liaison Bureau, ostensibly an office for the collection of scientific data. According to Israeli sources at the time, Pollard was not recruited by anyone, but on his own approached an unnamed Israeli in Washington in the spring of 1984, offering to cooperate in counterterrorist activity. He was put in contact with a senior counterterrorism official in Israel, identified as Rafi Eitan, adviser on terrorism to then prime minister Yitzhak Shamir, and also with a top official of the Scientific Liaison Bureau—known as *LEKEM,* its Hebrew acronym. Eitan reportedly encouraged Pollard in his offer to obtain for Israel secret American intelligence on Arab armies and on Soviet weapons supplied to the Arab states, but it appeared that he was acting independently. Israeli officials claimed that despite Eitan's connections with the Israeli intelligence community—he had been a former chief of operations for the Mossad—he engaged Pollard on his own initiative and without gaining clearance from senior intelligence officials or political leaders.

Israel quickly issued an apology, declaring that "spying on the United States is in total contradiction to our policy." The statement went on: "The relations with the United States are based on solid foundations of deep friendship, close affinity and mutual trust. . . . Such activity to the extent that it did take place was wrong and the government of Israel apologizes."

At a meeting in Jerusalem on December 31 with leaders of the Conference of Presidents of Major American Jewish Organizations, Prime Minister Peres announced that the United States and Israel "had cleared up a great deal of the misunderstanding and I am optimistic that we will resume the close relationship between our two countries which reached new heights recently." Secretary of State Shultz welcomed the Israeli statement and Peres's offer to cooperate with American investigators. Shultz's positive response was seen as part of an effort on both sides to prevent the Pollard affair from causing any permanent damage to relations between the two countries.

Yet the Pollard affair was not easily swept under the rug. The Justice Department and the FBI were determined to pursue the investigation vigorously and to enforce the law. The United States, for a time at least, reduced its customary sharing of intelligence information with Israel. Many Israelis feared that the affair would undermine the American people's confidence in Israel as a trusted ally. Fears were also expressed, in Israel and among American Jews, that the discovery of an American Jew spying for Israel could have a detrimental effect on the position of the American Jewish community, raising suspicions of dual loyalty. On the other hand, some Israelis attempted to minimize the incident, pointing out that Pollard had supplied intelligence material only on Arab military matters, and that in contrast to other American spies recently apprehended, Pollard had not handed over any information that could be considered harmful to the security of the United States.

Although the Pollard affair was viewed with utmost seriousness on both sides, it was too soon to tell what the ultimate consequences would be. Israel and her supporters hoped that it would ultimately be judged as a minor, isolated episode and that Israel would continue to enjoy favorable public opinion in the United States. As earlier swings in public opinion had shown, however, Israel could not be complacent but had to demonstrate continually that the interests of the two countries remained congruent.

Violations of American law obviously ran counter to this objective. Fortunately, senior officials in the White House and the State Department, as well as in the Israeli government, were determined to repair the damage caused by the Pollard affair and to prevent such actions in the future, hoping to maintain the traditional excellent relations between the United States and Israel.

GEORGE E. GRUEN
MARC BRANDRISS

Demographic

Jewish Population in the United States, 1986

THIS SECTION OF the AJYB, which is being presented in a revised format, is the work of a team of researchers associated with a new institution on the communal scene, the North American Jewish Data Bank. Created in 1986 as a joint endeavor of the Council of Jewish Federations and the Center for Jewish Studies of the Graduate School and University Center of the City University of New York, the data bank's main task is the collection and study of population and survey data on Jewish communities in the United States and Canada, using advanced information-retrieval techniques. Through its services to Jewish federations, other communal agencies, and the academic community, the research group aims both to assist the communal planning process and to further scholarly investigation of significant contemporary Jewish issues.

One justification for the foundation of the data bank was the completion over the previous decade of more than 40 local Jewish population surveys, carried out by Jewish communities across the country, mainly the largest, with most of the studies leading to major reassessments of Jewish population counts. The availability of a sizable body of up-to-date, reasonably reliable data now makes it possible to place the annual collection of population estimates into a wider geographical and sociohistorical context, thereby providing a broader perspective on the dynamics of social change among American Jews.

CHANGING PATTERNS IN GEOGRAPHIC DISTRIBUTION, 1930–1986

Among the many demographic characteristics of American Jews that are regularly studied and written about, one that has received less attention than it deserves is geographic distribution—the patterns of Jewish movement and settlement within the borders of the United States. Whether there has been a consistent pattern, or whether and how the pattern has changed, is a subject of more than academic interest. Apart from adding to our understanding of American Jewry generally, the matter of distribution has enormous practical implications for Jewish organizational life and for planning communal services.

This survey examines changes that have taken place in the last two generations, focusing specifically on the years 1930 and 1986. To help place these recent developments in perspective, a brief review of the period prior to 1930 is in order.

The first large migration of Jews to the United States, that of German Jews in the early to middle 19th century, settled primarily in the interior of the country, particularly in Pennsylvania, Ohio, and Wisconsin. While non-Jewish German immigrants tended to remain in the areas of their first settlement, many German Jews moved on to California, to other parts of the West, and to the pre-Civil War South, all areas that offered growing economic opportunities.

By contrast, the mass migration of East European Jews—over a million and a half between 1881 and 1914—tended to remain in the ports of entry, particularly in New York City and, to a somewhat lesser extent, Boston, Philadelphia, and Baltimore. In 1900, of the estimated 1,058,000 Jews in the United States, 57 percent lived in the Northeast. Close to half (46 percent) lived in New York City, and nearly a third (30 percent) resided in Manhattan, the majority on the Lower East Side. Over the next 30 years, as large-scale migration continued, Jewish concentration in the Northeast rose still higher: in 1930, 68 percent of American Jews were residents of the New England and Middle Atlantic states.[1]

The tables that follow document and illustrate the changes that have taken place since 1930. A word first, however, on the quality of the data. We are much more sure of the figures for the recent period, i.e., 1980–1986, then we are for those from the 1930s. Since the early data were often based upon "guesstimates" reported by key informants, in many instances our 1930–1936 numbers represent, at best, approximations or orders of magnitude.[2] For the recent period, the figures come from the large number of communal surveys that have been carried out, mostly by professional demographers.

---

[1]For an overview of East European Jewish migration, see Simon Kuznets, "Immigration of Russian Jews to the United States: Background and Structure," *Perspectives in American History*, vol. 9, 1975, pp. 35–124. On 19th-century German Jewish migration to and within the United States, see Avraham Barkai, "German-Jewish Migration in the Nineteenth Century, 1830–1910," in Ira A. Glazier and Luigi De Rosa (eds.), *Migration Across Time and Nations* (New York, 1986), pp. 202–215. Discussions of the changing geographic distribution of 20th-century American Jewry are presented in Sidney Goldstein, "Population Movement and Redistribution Among American Jews," in U.O. Schmelz, P. Glikson, and S. DellaPergola (eds.), *Papers in Jewish Demography, 1981* (Jerusalem, 1983), pp. 315–341, and Sidney Goldstein, "Jews in the United States: Perspectives from Demography," AJYB, vol. 81, 1981, pp. 3–59.

[2]An introduction to the issue of the Jewish population estimates of the 1930s may be found in Ira Rosenwaike, "A Synthetic Estimate of American Jewish Population Movement over the Last Three Decades," in U.O. Schmelz, P. Glikson, and S. DellaPergola (eds.), *Papers in Jewish Demography, 1977* (Jerusalem, 1980), pp. 83–102.

Although the U.S. Jewish population continued to increase during the past half century, its rate of growth slowed considerably. At the same time, because the growth of the Jewish population did not keep up with that of the general population (which almost doubled during this period), the relative size of the Jewish population of the United States fell by about 30 percent, from 3.6 percent of the total population to 2.5 percent.

Table 1 compares the Jewish population of the United States in 1930 and 1986, in absolute numbers and in the Jewish proportions of each state's overall population. The largest increase in absolute numbers occurred in California, where the Jewish population went up by 691,000 persons over the two-generation period. The next largest gain was Florida's, which increased by 506,000. If we look at change as a multiple, i.e., the 1986 figure as a multiple of the 1930 figure—in order to determine relative increases—then the greatest growth occurred in Hawaii, where the Jewish population increased 95 times, and in Nevada, where it went up 76 times. The greatest absolute decline occurred in Illinois, which went down by 86,000, with the next largest absolute decline occurring in Pennsylvania, which lost 63,000. The greatest relative losses were incurred by Wyoming at 77 percent and Iowa at 69 percent.

An increase or decrease in absolute size was frequently accompanied by a corresponding change in relative Jewish population size, but not in all cases. For example, Alabama's Jewish population declined in absolute numbers and also as a percent of the total population of the state. In Alaska, however, the number of Jews rose from 700 to 1,000, but since the total population of Alaska increased even more rapidly, the relative size of the Alaskan Jewish population was reduced. Arizona's Jewish population, which increased over 40-fold during the period, grew more rapidly than did the population of the state as a whole. As a result, whereas Jews were 0.3 percent of the population in 1930, they accounted for 2.1 percent in 1986.

Analysis of the figures reveals the dramatic changes that have taken place in the last 50 years. The much publicized shifting of Jewish population to the Sunbelt is reflected in the figures for California, Nevada, Arizona, New Mexico, and Florida and in the medium gains shown in Colorado, Texas, and some of the southern states (e.g., Georgia, North Carolina, and Virginia). Contrary to the common perception, the Northeast—with the exception of one state, Pennsylvania—has shown continual Jewish population growth, with several states, notably New Hampshire and Vermont, experiencing significant increases. The areas of greatest decline in Jewish population were in the high plains (Montana, Wyoming, the Dakotas), the Midwest, and the south-central states (Alabama, Mississippi, Arkansas).

Is there anything special about these Jewish population shifts, or have Jews simply followed in the footsteps of other Americans? For example, we know that the West Coast has grown enormously over the past 56 years. Did Jewish growth in that area parallel the general population growth, or did it differ in any significant way?

TABLE 1. DISTRIBUTION OF U.S. JEWISH POPULATION, BY STATE, 1930/1986

	1930		1986	
State	Estimated Jewish Population	Estimated Jewish % of Total	Estimated Jewish Population	Estimated Jewish % of Total
Total United States	4,228,000	3.6	5,814,000	2.5
Alabama	13,000	0.5	10,000	0.3
Alaska	700	1.2	1,000	0.2
Arizona	1,500	0.3	64,000	2.1
Arkansas	9,000	0.5	2,000	0.1
California	123,000	2.2	814,000	3.2
Colorado	20,000	1.9	48,000	1.5
Connecticut	92,000	5.6	107,000	3.4
Delaware	5,500	2.2	9,500	1.6
District of Columbia	16,000	3.3	24,000	3.9
Florida	13,000	1.0	519,000	4.7
Georgia	23,000	0.8	60,000	1.0
Hawaii	80	0.1	7,600	0.7
Idaho	1,000	0.2	500	0.1
Illinois	346,000	4.7	260,000	2.2
Indiana	27,000	0.9	20,000	0.4
Iowa	16,000	0.7	6,600	0.2
Kansas	8,000	0.4	15,000	0.6
Kentucky	20,000	0.8	12,000	0.3
Louisiana	16,000	0.9	17,000	0.4
Maine	8,500	1.1	9,000	0.8
Maryland	71,000	4.4	203,000	4.6
Massachusetts	226,000	5.3	273,000	4.7
Michigan	89,000	2.0	82,000	0.9
Minnesota	43,000	1.6	31,000	0.8
Mississippi	6,500	0.4	3,000	0.1
Missouri	81,000	2.3	65,000	1.3
Montana	1,500	0.2	500	0.1
Nebraska	14,000	1.0	7,000	0.4

TABLE 1.—*(Continued)*

State	1930 Estimated Jewish Population	1930 Estimated Jewish % of Total	1986 Estimated Jewish Population	1986 Estimated Jewish % of Total
Nevada	250	0.3	19,000	2.1
New Hampshire	3,000	0.6	7,000	0.7
New Jersey	225,000	5.6	421,000	5.6
New Mexico	1,000	0.3	5,500	0.4
New York	1,904,000	15.1	1,911,000	10.8
North Carolina	8,500	0.3	14,000	0.2
North Dakota	2,500	0.4	1,000	0.1
Ohio	174,000	2.6	138,000	1.3
Oklahoma	8,000	0.3	6,000	0.2
Oregon	13,000	1.5	11,000	0.4
Pennsylvania	405,000	4.2	342,000	2.9
Rhode Island	25,000	3.6	17,500	1.8
South Carolina	7,000	0.4	8,000	0.2
South Dakota	1,500	0.2	500	0.1
Tennessee	23,000	0.9	20,000	0.4
Texas	47,000	0.9	95,000	0.6
Utah	3,000	0.6	3,000	0.2
Vermont	2,000	0.6	3,600	0.7
Virginia	26,000	1.0	60,000	1.1
Washington	15,000	0.9	23,000	0.5
West Virginia	7,500	0.4	4,000	0.2
Wisconsin	36,000	1.2	31,000	0.7
Wyoming	1,300	0.6	400	0.1

Sources: 1930 estimates are from AJYB, vol. 33, 1931–1932, p. 276, and U.S. Census of Population, 1930. 1986 figures are from Appendix table A-1, below, but have been rounded for ease of comparison.

Table 2 enables us to compare Jewish and general population change, state by state, by means of a simple index. The number 1.0 indicates that the proportion of Jews in a state did not change over the 56 years, while numbers over 1.0 indicate an increase in the Jewish proportion and numbers less than 1.0 a decrease. We

TABLE 2. INDEX OF JEWISH POPULATION CHANGE RELATIVE TO GENERAL POPULATION CHANGE, BY STATE, 1930/1986

(1.00 = Equivalent Change)

1.	Hawaii	44.1	26.	Wisconsin	.71
2.	Nevada	10.1	27.	Oklahoma	.71
3.	Arizona	8.0	28.	Alabama	.69
4.	Florida	7.0	29.	Louisiana	.67
5.	New Mexico	2.1	30.	Rhode Island	.66
6.	California	1.9	31.	Illinois	.65
7.	Kansas	1.8	32.	Michigan	.65
8.	Georgia	1.7	33.	Ohio	.64
9.	Vermont	1.6	34.	Tennessee	.63
10.	Maryland	1.4	35.	Minnesota	.59
11.	New Hampshire	1.4	36.	West Virginia	.57
12.	Virginia	1.3	37.	Indiana	.57
13.	New Jersey	1.3	38.	Kentucky	.57
14.	Massachusetts	1.2	39.	Nebraska	.55
15.	North Carolina	1.1	40.	North Dakota	.50
16.	Colorado	1.0	41.	Mississippi	.49
17.	Texas	.96	42.	Iowa	.46
18.	Maine	.95	43.	South Dakota	.43
19.	New York	.93	44.	Oregon	.39
20.	Pennsylvania	.90	45.	Utah	.36
21.	Delaware	.88	46.	Arkansas	.26
22.	South Carolina	.81	47.	Idaho	.24
23.	Connecticut	.78	48.	Montana	.24
24.	Missouri	.76	49.	Alaska	.21
25.	Washington	.75	50.	Wyoming	.16

Washington, D.C. 1.6

arrived at the index numbers by dividing the proportion of the state's population that was Jewish in 1986 by the proportion that was Jewish in 1930. Then, to allow for the fact that the Jewish population nationwide grew only 69 percent as much as the general population, we further divided the total state increases by a constant of 0.69.

Looking now at table 2, we note that the Jewish populations of Arizona, Nevada, Hawaii, Florida, and New Mexico grew at a rate at least twice that of each state's population as a whole. California's Jewish population growth was significantly greater than that of the state, and the Georgia and Washington, D.C., Jewish populations also grew much more rapidly than did the general populations of those areas. The Northeast, which was thought to have been in decline, largely maintained its relative Jewish population size, with some states increasing a bit and others declining. The major East Coast increases were in Virginia and Maryland, reflecting the growth in the Washington, D.C., suburbs. The most significant declines were in the Midwest, the south-central states, and the northern plains.

What lies behind the differing rates of Jewish and general population growth? We suggest that the Jewish "overgrowth," that is, the rate of increase in the Jewish population beyond that of the general population, occurred precisely in those areas of the country that were experiencing the greatest economic development. A recent congressional study on patterns of economic growth in the United States reported annual growth rates of 4.0 percent for the two coasts but only 1.4 percent for the country's interior.[3] A closer examination of the data suggests that those parts of the country that were part of the postindustrial "high-tech" economy and that showed the greatest economic growth also had the highest increases in Jewish population. Those areas whose economies were based on extraction, agriculture, and heavy manufacturing showed the slowest rates of economic growth as well as the greatest absolute and relative losses in Jewish population. For the period 1981–1985, the ten states whose Jewish population increased significantly faster than the general population experienced average (unweighted) growth of wages and proprietorships of 20.3 percent. In the ten states showing the lowest Jewish population growth or even Jewish population decline, average economic growth for the five-year period was only 3.1 percent.

To test the thesis further, we have examined Jewish and general population shifts in the United States over the 50-year period 1935–1986. As the data summarized in table 3 demonstrate, there is a much clearer and stronger relationship between population distribution and economic growth for the Jewish population than for the nation as a whole.[4]

The high educational attainments of Jews and their changing occupational profile have been amply studied and documented.[5] The last 25 years have seen significant movement out of light manufacturing and merchandising and into high-tech occupations, management, and word, number, and paper functions generally, often in

---

[3]Democratic Staff of the Joint Economic Committee, Congress of the United States, *The Bi-Coastal Economy,* 1986, typescript.

[4]The Chi squares for the Jewish and general populations, respectively, are 61.6 and 55.6 with 4 degrees of freedom.

[5]See, for example, David L. Featherman, "The Socioeconomic Achievement of White Religio-Ethnic Subgroups," *American Sociological Review,* April 1971, pp. 207–222; Sidney Goldstein, "Jews in the United States: Perspectives from Demography," AJYB, vol. 81, 1981, pp. 3–59; and Barry R. Chiswick, "The Labor Market Status of American Jews: Patterns and Determinants," AJYB, vol. 85, 1985, pp. 131–153.

TABLE 3. PERCENTAGE OF STATES WITH HIGH POPULATION INCREASES, TOTAL AND JEWISH, BY ECONOMIC GROWTH OF STATES, 1930–1985

States Categorized by Economic Growth[a]	% of States with High Population Increase[b] Total	Jewish
High growth (14 states)	43	57
Med. growth (21 states)	52	29
Low growth (15 states)	27	7

[a]Based on per capita income, by state.
[b]Defined as significantly above-average proportional growth.

government and academic settings. The data on population and economic growth presented here suggest that Jews have been more responsive to opportunity and more willing to move to take advantage of opportunities offered than the population at large.

Further evidence in support of the proposition is seen in the growth of Jewish population in cities and metropolitan areas within states that otherwise showed declines in Jewish population. Such communities include Champaign-Urbana, Illinois; Carbondale, Illinois; Bloomington, Indiana; Ames, Iowa; Madison, Wisconsin; Ann Arbor, Michigan; and Lansing, Michigan. Some of these are college or university towns, others are state capitals. Still other instances are locales dominated by specific industries that attracted large numbers of Jewish employees. Two such examples are Rochester, Minnesota, the home of the Mayo Clinic, and Huntsville, Alabama, site of a major aerospace installation.

Given the propensity of Jews to move in search of jobs, it is not surprising to find that the Jewish population has become more diffused over the last 50 years. This is seen clearly in tables 4A and 4B, which compare the Jewish populations of metropolitan areas in the mid-1930s and mid-1980s.[6] The New York–Northern New Jersey–Lower Connecticut area has remained the largest Jewish population center, but its share of total U.S. Jewish population has been reduced from over one-half to a bit less than two-fifths. Chicago has been replaced by Los Angeles in second

---

[6]In order to provide a valid comparison, every effort has been made to use the same geographic units for the two time periods, basing them on the official designations in use in 1986. It should be borne in mind that in respect to Jewish distribution, the entities are not wholly comparable. In the 1930s, Jews were heavily concentrated in urban areas. By the 1980s, as a result of the tremendous growth of suburbs following World War II, metropolitan communities had become embedded in complex urban regions, in which Jews tended to be widely dispersed. However, while Jews in metropolitan areas are now physically widely dispersed, in various important ways they can still be viewed as discrete "communities."

TABLE 4A. RANK-ORDERED METROPOLITAN AREAS, 1936, BY JEWISH POPULATION

Metro Area	Estimated Jewish Population	Jewish % of Total Population	% Share of U.S. Jewish Population	Cumulative % Share of Jewish Population
1. New York-Northern N.J.	2,600,000	20.1	55.8	55.8
2. Chicago	378,000	7.8	7.9	63.7
3. Philadelphia-Camden	312,000	9.9	6.5	70.3
4. Boston	217,000	7.7	4.5	74.8
5. Cleveland	104,000	7.7	2.2	77.0
6. Los Angeles	96,000	3.3	2.0	79.0
7. Detroit	94,000	3.9	2.0	80.9
8. Pittsburgh-SW Pa.	75,000	3.0	1.6	82.5
9. Baltimore	74,000	6.7	1.6	84.1
10. St. Louis	56,000	4.0	1.2	85.2
11. San Francisco-Oakland-San Jose	52,000	3.2	1.1	86.3
12. Minneapolis-St. Paul	35,000	3.6	.7	87.1
13. New Haven	35,000	7.2	.7	87.8
14. Milwaukee	32,000	3.2	.7	88.5
15. Kansas City	29,000	3.9	.6	89.1
16. Hartford	28,000	6.4	.6	89.6
17. Providence	27,000	4.4	.6	90.2
18. Cincinnati	24,000	2.6	.5	90.7
19. Rochester	24,000	5.4	.5	91.2
20. Buffalo	23,000	2.5	.5	91.7
21. Scranton-Wilkes Barre	23,000	3.1	.5	92.2
22. Washington, D.C.	19,000	2.4	.4	92.6
23. Denver	19,000	4.5	.4	93.0
24. Albany	17,000	3.7	.4	93.3
25. Houston	16,000	2.4	.3	93.7
26. Seattle	15,000	1.9	.3	94.0
27. Worcester	15,000	3.1	.3	94.3

TABLE 4A.—*(Continued)*

Metro Area	Estimated Jewish Population	Jewish % of Total Population	% Share of U.S. Jewish Population	Cumulative % Share of Jewish Population
28. Springfield, Mass.	15,000	4.4	.3	94.6
29. Syracuse	15,000	5.0	.3	94.9
30. Atlantic City	14,000	11.4	.3	95.2

Source: AJYB, vol. 42, 1940–1941.

place and has dropped to fifth place. The decline of the industrial cities of Cleveland, Detroit, and Pittsburgh and the rapid rise of Miami and San Francisco reflect both Jewish occupational change and the emergence of new life-styles and social patterns. The university-government bias in Jewish employment has produced not only the slight increase of Jewish population in cities like Baltimore and Boston but most notably the rise of Washington, D.C., as a major Jewish center.

To appreciate fully the extent to which increased mobility has changed the face of the American Jewish community it is useful to examine the changing proportions of the total Jewish population residing in various locales. New York, for example, which was home to 56 percent of U.S. Jews in 1936, could claim only 38 percent in 1986. By contrast, two communities in Florida—Miami–Ft. Lauderdale and W. Palm Beach–Boca Raton—were not even among the "top 30" in 1935; in 1986, they ranked 3rd and 10th, respectively, in Jewish population size and jointly accounted for 8 percent of U.S. Jewry.

The cumulative totals (last columns of tables 4A and 4B) are the most telling. Whereas in the mid-1930s, 90 percent of the country's Jewish population was found in 17 metropolitan areas, in the 1980s, in order to reach 90 percent it was necessary to include over 30 metropolitan areas. (It is interesting to compare this with the situation in Canada, where two metropolitan regions, Toronto and Montreal, accounted for 74 percent of the country's Jewish population, and 90 percent of the country's Jewish population was to be found in only six metropolitan areas.)

In summary, this review of national geographical data has highlighted several key attributes of American Jewish population distribution and movement. First, even though it has experienced declining numbers, the Northeast still has a disproportionate share of Jewish population. Second, the U.S. Jewish population seems to be more mobile than the nation's population generally, apparently more willing to pull up stakes in search of occupational advancement. This has clear implications for communal planners, who should be keeping an eye on changes in local economic conditions. Finally, and this too has implications for communal organization, there are more Jewish population centers than in the past, but with fewer Jews in each center.

TABLE 4B. RANK-ORDERED METROPOLITAN STATISTICAL AREAS, 1986, BY JEWISH POPULATION

Metro Area	Estimated Jewish Population	Jewish % of Total Population	% Share of U.S. Jewish Population	Cumulative % Share of Jewish Population
1. New York-Northern N.J.*	2,216,000	12.4	38.1	38.1
2. Los Angeles*	604,000	4.7	10.4	48.5
3. Miami-Ft. Lauderdale*	367,000	12.8	6.3	54.8
4. Philadelphia-Wilmington-Trenton*	309,000	5.4	5.3	60.1
5. Chicago*	254,000	3.1	4.4	64.5
6. Boston*	235,000	5.8	4.0	68.6
7. Washington, D.C.	159,000	4.6	2.7	71.3
8. San Francisco-Oakland-San Jose*	136,000	2.3	2.3	73.6
9. Baltimore	101,000	4.5	1.7	75.3
10. W. Palm Beach-Boca Raton	95,000	13.1	1.6	77.0
11. Cleveland-Akron*	77,000	2.8	1.3	78.3
12. Detroit-Ann Arbor*	74,000	1.6	1.3	79.6
13. St. Louis	54,000	2.2	0.9	80.5
14. Atlanta	52,000	2.1	.9	81.4
15. Pittsburgh*	47,000	2.0	.8	82.2
16. Phoenix	45,000	2.4	.8	83.0
17. Denver-Boulder*	45,000	2.5	.8	83.7
18. Houston-Galveston*	43,000	1.2	.7	84.5

TABLE 4B.—*(Continued)*

Metro Area	Estimated Jewish Population	Jewish % of Total Population	% Share of U.S. Jewish Population	Cumulative % Share of Jewish Population
19. San Diego	37,000	1.2	.6	85.1
20. Minneapolis-St. Paul	30,000	1.3	.5	85.6
21. Hartford	28,000	2.7	.5	86.1
22. Dallas-Ft. Worth*	27,000	0.8	.5	86.6
23. Milwaukee*	24,000	1.6	.4	87.0
24. New Haven	24,000	4.7	.4	87.4
25. Cincinnati*	23,000	1.4	.4	87.8
26. Kansas City	22,000	1.5	.4	88.2
27. Seattle-Tacoma*	20,000	0.9	.3	88.6
28. Rochester	20,000	2.1	.3	88.9
29. Tampa-St. Petersburg	20,000	1.1	.3	89.2
30. Albany-Schenectady-Troy	20,000	2.3	.3	89.5

Sources: Boundaries and general population estimates, Bureau of the Census, June 1985. Areas marked * = CMSA (Consolidated Metropolitan Statistical Area); otherwise unit is PMSA (Primary Metropolitan Statistical Area). Jewish figures, Appendix table A-3, below.

1986 JEWISH POPULATION ESTIMATES

The Jewish population of the United States in 1986 was estimated to be 5.814 million. This figure is approximately the same order of magnitude as that reported for 1985.

The basic population units used in this analysis are the fund-raising areas of local Jewish federations. These geographic units vary in size and may represent several towns, one county, or an aggregate of several counties. Some estimates, from areas without federations, are from UJA field representatives. Still other estimates have been given by local rabbis and other informed Jewish community leaders.

The state and regional totals shown in Appendix tables A-1 and A-2 are derived by summing the individual estimates shown in table A-3 and then making three adjustments. First, communities of less than 100 are added. Second, duplicated counts within states are eliminated. Third, communities whose populations reside in two or more states (e.g., Kansas City and Washington, D.C.) are distributed accordingly.

The reader should be aware that population estimating is not an exact science, and that collection procedures can result in annual fluctuations in community or state totals. It is also important to note that the results of a completed local demographic study often change the previously reported Jewish population figure, even where there has been no actual demographic change. Thus, even though the 1986 totals for Florida, New Jersey, and Arizona show Jewish population losses over 1985, these new lower figures are solely the result of adjustments of previous data.

In determining Jewish population, communities count both affiliated and nonaffiliated residents. In most cases, counts are made by households, with that number multiplied by the average number of self-defined Jewish persons per household. In a few instances, the reported totals from local surveys include spouses and children who are declared to be non-Jewish by the responding household head. While every effort has been made to exclude non-Jews from the figures, this has not always been feasible. We calculate that non-Jews *not* excluded comprise under 2 percent of the national Jewish population. Some areas, such as in the Sunbelt region, often include part-time residents in their totals. In the interest of accuracy and consistency, adjustments have been made for such overcounts.

Among the communities reporting substantial Jewish population increases in 1986 were Birmingham, Alabama; Palm Springs, Orange County, and Sacramento, California; Palm Beach County, Florida; Honolulu, Hawaii; Howard County, Maryland; Atlantic County, New Jersey; Houston, Texas, and the Boston metropolitan region, Massachusetts.

As a result of our efforts to widen the coverage of the population counts in order to make them as comprehensive as possible, a number of college towns not previously included now appear in table A-3, e.g., Greenville, North Carolina; Lawrence, Kansas, and Hanover, New Hampshire. In all cases, their numbers report only permanent Jewish residents.

In order to better aid the reader in assessing the data in table A-3, several changes in notation have been introduced. The footnotes detailing the areas included in particular communities have been expanded and grouped by state. Also: one asterisk indicates that the population includes the entire county; two asterisks indicate a two-county area; three asterisks indicate that the Jewish population figure has not been updated for several years.

BARRY A. KOSMIN
PAUL RITTERBAND
JEFFREY SCHECKNER

APPENDIX

TABLE A-1. JEWISH POPULATION IN THE UNITED STATES, 1986

State	Estimated Jewish Population	Total Population*	Estimated Jewish % of Total
Alabama	10,240	3,990,000	0.3
Alaska	960	500,000	0.2
Arizona	63,930	3,053,000	2.1
Arkansas	2,300	2,349,000	0.1
California	813,525	25,622,000	3.2
Colorado	48,145	3,178,000	1.5
Connecticut	107,120	3,154,000	3.4
Delaware	9,500	613,000	1.6
District of Columbia	24,285	622,823	3.9
Florida	518,990	10,976,000	4.7
Georgia	60,040	5,837,000	1.0
Hawaii	7,600	1,039,000	0.7
Idaho	420	1,001,000	0.1
Illinois	260,390	11,511,000	2.2
Indiana	20,045	5,498,000	0.4
Iowa	6,615	2,910,000	0.2
Kansas	14,600	2,438,000	0.6
Kentucky	12,240	3,723,000	0.3
Louisiana	17,230	4,462,000	0.4
Maine	8,870	1,156,000	0.8
Maryland	203,340	4,439,000	4.6
Massachusetts	273,060	5,798,000	4.7
Michigan	82,260	9,075,000	0.9
Minnesota	31,285	4,162,000	0.8
Mississippi	3,005	2,598,000	0.1
Missouri	64,590	5,008,000	1.3
Montana	425	824,000	0.1
Nebraska	6,955	1,606,000	0.4
Nevada	19,300	911,000	2.1
New Hampshire	6,950	977,000	0.7
New Jersey	420,850	7,515,000	5.6
New Mexico	5,510	1,424,000	0.4
New York	1,911,300	17,735,000	10.8

State	Estimated Jewish Population	Total Population*	Estimated Jewish % of Total
North Carolina	14,400	6,165,000	0.2
North Dakota	970	686,000	0.1
Ohio	137,750	10,752,000	1.3
Oklahoma.........	5,820	3,298,000	0.2
Oregon	11,050	2,674,000	0.4
Pennsylvania	342,835	11,901,000	2.9
Rhode Island......	17,500	962,000	1.8
South Carolina.....	8,245	3,300,000	0.2
South Dakota......	525	706,000	0.1
Tennessee.........	19,635	4,717,000	0.4
Texas	94,655	15,989,000	0.6
Utah	2,700	1,652,000	0.2
Vermont..........	3,620	530,000	0.7
Virginia...........	60,375	5,636,000	1.1
Washington	22,815	4,149,000	0.5
West Virginia......	3,770	1,952,000	0.2
Wisconsin.........	31,425	4,766,000	0.7
Wyoming	355	511,000	0.1
U.S. TOTAL	**5,814,000	236,031,000	2.5

N.B. Details may not add to totals because of rounding.
*Resident population, July 1, 1984, provisional. (Source: *Provisional Estimates of the Population of Counties: July 1984,* Bureau of the Census, series P-26, No. 84-52-C, March 1985.)
**Exclusive of Puerto Rico and the Virgin Islands, which previously reported Jewish populations of 1,800 and 510, respectively.

TABLE A-2. DISTRIBUTION OF U.S. JEWISH POPULATION BY REGIONS, 1986

Region	Total Population	% Distribution	Jewish Population	% Distribution
Northeast:	49,728,000	21.1	3,092,105	53.2
New England	12,577,000	5.3	417,120	7.2
Middle Atlantic	37,151,000	15.7	2,674,985	46.0
North Central:	59,118,000	25.0	657,405	11.3
East North Central	41,602,000	17.6	531,870	9.1
West North Central	17,516,000	7.4	125,535	2.2
South:	80,667,000	34.2	1,068,070	18.4
South Atlantic	39,541,000	16.8	902,945	15.5
East South Central	15,028,000	6.4	45,120	0.8
West South Central	26,098,000	11.1	120,005	2.1
West:	46,538,000	19.7	996,735	17.1
Mountain	12,554,000	5.3	140,785	2.4
Pacific	33,984,000	14.4	855,950	14.7
TOTALS	236,031,000	100.0	5,814,000	100.0

N.B. Details may not add to totals because of rounding.

TABLE A-3. COMMUNITIES WITH JEWISH POPULATIONS OF 100 OR MORE, 1986 (ESTIMATED)

State and City	Jewish Population
ALABAMA	
Anniston	100
*Auburn	100
*Birmingham	5,100
Dothan	205
Florence (incl. in Sheffield total)	
Gadsden	180
Huntsville	550
Jasper	130
**Mobile	1,250
**Montgomery	1,650
Selma	210
Sheffield	150
Tuscaloosa	315
Tuscumbia (incl. in Sheffield total)	
ALASKA	
Anchorage	600
Fairbanks	210
ARIZONA	
*Flagstaff	250
*Phoenix	45,000
*Tucson	18,000
Yuma	100
ARKANSAS	
Fayetteville	120
Ft. Smith	160
Helena	100
Hot Springs (incl. in Little Rock)	
**Little Rock	1,250
Pine Bluff	100
Southeast Arkansas[N]	140
***Wynne-Forest City	110

State and City	Jewish Population
CALIFORNIA	
Alameda & Contra Costa counties	35,000
Antelope Valley	375
Bakersfield (incl. in Kern County)	
Berkeley (incl. in Alameda & Contra Costa total)	
***El Centro	125
***Elsinore	250
Eureka	250
***Fontana	165
*Fresno	2,000
Kern County	850
Lancaster (incl. in Antelope Valley)	
Long Beach (also incl. in Los Angeles total)[N]	13,500
Los Angeles Metro. Area	500,870
***Merced	100
Modesto	260
Monterey	1,500
Oakland (incl. in Alameda & Contra Costa counties)	
Ontario (incl. in Pomona Valley)	
Orange County	80,000
Palm Springs[N]	8,950
Pasadena (also incl. in L.A. Metro. Area)	2,000
Petaluma	800
Pomona Valley[N]	3,500
Riverside	1,325
Sacramento[N]	10,000
Salinas	350

State and City	Jewish Population
San Bernardino	2,065
*San Diego	37,000
San Francisco[N]	80,000
*San Jose (Palo Alto & Los Altos incl. in San Francisco total)	18,000
San Luis Obispo	450
***San Pedro	300
*Santa Barbara	3,800
Santa Cruz	1,000
Santa Maria	200
Santa Monica (also incl. in Los Angeles total)	8,000
Santa Rosa	750
*Stockton	1,500
***Sun City	800
Tulare & Kings County	500
Vallejo	400
*Ventura County	7,000
COLORADO	
Boulder (incl. in Denver total)	
Colorado Springs	1,000
Denver[N]	45,000
*Ft. Collins	1,000
Greely	100
Loveland (incl. in Ft. Collins total)	
Pueblo	375
CONNECTICUT	
Bridgeport[N]	18,000
Bristol	250
Colchester	525
Danbury[N]	3,500
Greenwich	4,950
Hartford[N]	26,000

State and City	Jewish Population	State and City	Jewish Population	State and City	Jewish Population
***Lebanon	175	**Daytona Beach	2,000	Kuaii	100
Lower Middlesex County (incl. in New London)		Fort Lauderdale^N	60,000	Maui	220
		Fort Pierce	270		
		Gainesville	1,000	IDAHO	
Manchester (incl. in Hartford)		Hollywood^N	60,000	Boise	120
		**Jacksonville	6,800	Lewiston	100
Meriden	1,400	Key West	170	Moscow (incl. in Lewiston total)	
Middletown	1,300	Lakeland	800		
***Moodus	150	Lee County (incl. Ft. Myers)	3,500		
New Haven^N	22,000			ILLINOIS	
New London^N	3,600	Lehigh Acres	125	Aurora	320
***New Milford	200	*Miami (incl.all of Dade County)	247,000	Bloomington	125
Newtown (incl. in Danbury)				*Champaign-Urbana	2,000
		**Orlando	9,000		
Norwalk^N	4,000	Palm Beach County (excl. Boca Raton-Delray)	50,000	Chicago Metro. Area	248,000
Norwich	2,500			Danville	240
Putnam	110			*Decatur	230
Rockville (incl. in Hartford)		Pensacola	400	East St. Louis (incl. in Southern Ill.)	
		Port Charlotte	150		
Shelton (incl. in Valley Area)		**Sarasota	8,500	Elgin^N	700
		***St. Augustine	100	Galesburg	120
Stamford/New Canaan	12,000	*St.Petersburg (incl. Clearwater)	9,500	*Joliet	850
Torrington	560	Tallahassee	1,000	Kankakee	260
Valley Area^N	700	*Tampa	10,500	*Peoria	1,200
***Wallingford	440			Quad Cities^N	1,700
Waterbury^N	2,700	GEORGIA		Quincy	200
Westport (also incl. in Norwalk)	2,800	Albany	525	Rock Island (incl. in Quad Cities)	
		Athens	250		
Willimantic	400	Atlanta Metro. Area	52,000	Rockford^N	975
***Winsted	110			Southern Illinois^N	900
		Augusta^N	1,400	*Springfield	1,100
DELAWARE		***Brunswick	120	***Sterling-Dixon	110
Wilmington (incl.rest of state)	9,500	**Columbus	1,000	Waukegan	1,200
		Dalton	235		
		Fitzgerald-Cordele	125	INDIANA	
DISTRICT OF COLUMBIA		Macon	900	Anderson	105
Greater Washington^N	157,335	*Savannah	2,600	Bloomington	300
		Valdosta	145	Elkart (incl. in South Bend)	
FLORIDA		HAWAII		***Evansville	1,200
Boca Raton-Delray	45,000	Hilo	280	Ft. Wayne	1,170
Brevard County	2,250	Honolulu (incl. all of Oahu)	7,000	Gary (incl. in Northwest Ind.-Calumet Region)	

State and City	Jewish Population	State and City	Jewish Population	State and City	Jewish Population
**Indianapolis... 10,000		LOUISIANA		MASSACHUSETTS	
Lafayette[N] 600		***Alexandria...... 700		Amherst.......... 750	
Marion........... 170		Baton Rouge[N] ... 1,400		Andover[N] 3,000	
*Michigan City..... 430		Lafayette 600		Athol 110	
Muncie........... 175		Lake Charles...... 250		***Attleboro....... 200	
Northwest Ind.-Calumet		Monroe 550		Beverly (also incl. in	
Region[N] 2,700		**New Orleans .. 12,000		Lynn total) 1,000	
Richmond 110		*Shreveport...... 1,200		Boston (Metro.Region)[N]	
***Shelbyville...... 240		South Central La.[N]		 228,000	
South Bend[N] 1,900		 720		Fall River 1,780	
Terre Haute....... 450				Fitchburg......... 300	
		MAINE		Framingham[N] .. 10,000	
IOWA		Augusta.......... 215		Gardner.......... 100	
Ames 200		Bangor.......... 1,300		Gloucester (also incl. in	
Cedar Rapids 300		Biddeford-Saco (incl. in		Lynn total) 400	
Council Bluffs (also incl.		So. Maine)		Great Barrington .. 105	
in Omaha total) .. 150		Brunswick-Bath (incl. in		Greenfield 250	
Davenport (incl. in Quad		Southern Maine)		Haverhill 1,500	
Cities, Ill.)		***Calais.......... 135		Holyoke......... 1,100	
*Des Moines..... 3,000		Lewiston-Auburn .. 500		*Hyannis........ 1,200	
***Dubuque 105		Portland......... 3,900		Lawrence (incl. in	
Iowa City 750		Rockland......... 100		Andover total)	
***Mason City 110		Southern Maine (incl.		Leominster........ 750	
***Muscatine 120		Portland)[N] 5,500		Lowell 2,000	
**Sioux City 700		Waterville 300		Lynn (incl.Beverly, Pea-	
Waterloo 450				body, and Salem)[N]	
		MARYLAND		 19,000	
KANSAS		*Annapolis 2,000		New Bedford[N] .. 2,700	
Kansas City (incl. in		**Baltimore..... 92,000		Newburyport...... 280	
K.C.,Mo.)		Cumberland....... 265		North Adams (incl. in	
Lawrence......... 175		Easton Park Area[N]. 100		North Berkshire total)	
Manhattan........ 100		Frederick......... 400		North Berkshire ... 675	
*Topeka........... 500		Hagerstown....... 275		Northampton 700	
Wichita[N] 1,000		Harford County ... 500		Peabody (also incl. in	
		Howard County . 7,200		Lynn total) 2,600	
KENTUCKY		Montgomery and Prince		Pittsfield (incl.all Berk-	
Covington/Newport		Georges County		shire County) .. 3,100	
(incl. in Cincinnati		 99,500		Plymouth......... 500	
total)		Salisbury 400		Salem (also incl. in Lynn	
Lexington[N] 2,000		Silver Spring (incl. in		total) 1,150	
*Louisville....... 9,200		Montgomery County		Southbridge....... 105	
***Paducah........ 175		total)		Springfield[N].... 11,000	
				Taunton 1,200	

State and City	Jewish Population	State and City	Jewish Population	State and City	Jewish Population
Webster	125	**MISSOURI**		Bayonne	4,500
Worcester[N]	10,000	Columbia	350	Bergen County[N]	100,000
		Joplin	115	Bridgeton	375
MICHIGAN		Kansas City Metro.		Camden (incl. in Cherry Hill total)	
*Ann Arbor	3,000	Area	22,100		
Battle Creek	245	***Kennett	110	Carteret	300
Bay City	300	Springfield	230	Cherry Hill[N]	28,000
***Benton Harbor	500	*St. Joseph	325	Edison (incl. in Middlesex County total)	
**Detroit	70,000	**St. Louis	53,500		
*Flint	2,240			Elizabeth (incl. in Union County)	
*Grand Rapids	1,500	**MONTANA**			
***Iron County	160	Billings	160	Englewood (incl. in Bergen County)	
***Iron Mountain	105	Butte	150		
Jackson	375			Essex County[N]	121,000
*Kalamazoo	1,000	**NEBRASKA**		Flemington	875
*Lansing	2,100	Grand Island-Hastings (incl. in Lincoln total)		Gloucester (incl. in Cherry Hill total)	
Marquette County	175				
Mt. Clemens	420	Lincoln	800	Hoboken	350
Mt. Pleasant	100	Omaha[N]	6,000	Jersey City	3,500
Muskegon	235			Lakewood (incl. in Ocean County total)	
*Saginaw	300	**NEVADA**			
***South Haven	100	*Las Vegas	18,000	Middlesex County[N]	39,350
		*Reno	1,200		
MINNESOTA				Millville	240
***Austin	125	**NEW HAMPSHIRE**		Monmouth County	33,600
**Duluth	1,100	Bethlehem	100		
***Hibbing	155	Claremont	200	Morris-Sussex counties (incl. in Essex County)	
*Minneapolis	22,000	Concord	350		
Rochester	240	***Dover	425	Morristown (incl. in Morris County)	
**St. Paul	7,500	Hanover-Lebanon	360		
***Virginia	100	***Keene	105	Mt. Holly (also incl. in Cherry Hill total)	300
		***Laconia	150		
MISSISSIPPI		Littleton (incl. in Bethlehem total)		Newark (incl. in Essex County)	
Biloxi-Gulfport	100				
Clarksdale	160	Manchester[N]	3,000	New Brunswick (incl. in Middlesex County)	
Cleveland	180	Nashua	450		
Greenville	500	Portsmouth	1,000	North Hudson County[N]	7,000
Greenwood	100	Salem (also incl. in Andover, Mass. total)	150		
Hattiesburg	180			North Jersey[N]	28,000
**Jackson	700			Ocean County	9,500
Meridian	135	**NEW JERSEY**		Passaic-Clifton	8,000
***Natchez	140	*Atlantic City (incl. Atlantic County)	15,800	Paterson (incl. in North Jersey)	
***Vicksburg	260				

State and City	Jewish Population
Perth Amboy (incl. in Middlesex County)	
Plainfield (incl. in Union County)	
Princeton	2,600
Salem	230
Somerset County[N]	4,500
Somerville (incl. in Somerset County)	
Toms River (incl. in Ocean County)	
Trenton[N]	8,500
Union County[N]	32,000
Vineland[N]	2,450
Wildwood	425
Willingboro (incl. in Cherry Hill total)	

NEW MEXICO
*Albuquerque	4,000
Las Cruces	100
Los Alamos	100
Santa Fe	450

NEW YORK
*Albany	12,000
Amenia	140
Amsterdam	595
Auburn	315
***Batavia	165
Beacon (also incl. in Dutchess County total)	315
Binghamton (incl. all Broome County)	3,000
Brewster (also incl. in Danbury, Conn.)	300
*Buffalo	18,500
Canandaigua	135
Catskill	200
***Corning	125
Cortland	440
Dunkirk	150
Ellenville	1,450
Elmira[N]	1,100
Geneva	300
Glens Falls[N]	800
Gloversville	535
Herkimer	185
Highland Falls (incl. in Newburgh total)	105
Hudson	470
Ithaca	1,000
Jamestown	185
Kingston[N]	4,000
Lake George (incl. in Glens Falls total)	
Liberty (also incl. in Sullivan County total)	2,100
***Massena	140
Monroe (incl. in Newburgh-Middletown total)	
Monticello (also incl. in Sullivan County total)	2,400
Mountaindale	150
New York City Metro. Area[N]	1,742,500
New Paltz	150
Newark	220
Newburgh-Middletown	8,950
Niagara Falls	550
Norwich	120
Olean	140
Oneonta	175
Oswego	100
Pawling	105
Plattsburgh	275
Port Jervis (also incl. in Newburgh total)	560
Potsdam	175
*Poughkeepsie	4,900
**Rochester	19,600
Rockland County	60,000
Rome	205
Saratoga Springs	500
**Schenectady	5,400
***Sharon Springs	165
South Fallsburg (also incl. in Sullivan County total)	1,100
Sullivan County	7,425
Syracuse[N]	9,000
Troy area	900
Utica[N]	2,000
Walden (incl. in Newburgh-Middletown)	
Watertown	250

NORTH CAROLINA
Asheville[N]	2,100
**Chapel Hill-Durham	2,400
Charlotte[N]	4,000
*Fayetteville	500
Gastonia	220
Goldsboro	120
*Greensboro	2,500
Greenville	300
Hendersonville	105
High Point (incl. in Greensboro)	
Raleigh	1,375
***Rocky Mount	110
Whiteville Zone[N]	160
Wilmington	500
Winston-Salem	300

NORTH DAKOTA
Fargo	500
Grand Forks	100

OHIO
**Akron	6,000
Athens	100
Bowling Green (also incl. in Toledo total)	120
**Canton	2,500

JEWISH POPULATION IN THE UNITED STATES / 185

State and City	Jewish Population
Cincinnati[N]	22,000
**Cleveland	70,000
*Columbus	15,000
**Dayton	6,000
East Liverpool	300
Elyria	275
Hamilton	560
Lima	165
Lorain	1,000
Mansfield	600
Marion	150
Middletown	140
***New Philadelphia	140
**Newark	105
Piqua	120
Portsmouth	120
Sandusky	150
Springfield	340
*Steubenville	200
Toledo[N]	6,300
Warren (also incl. in Youngstown total)	500
Wooster	200
Youngstown[N]	5,000
***Zanesville	350

OKLAHOMA

***Muskogee	120
**Oklahoma City	2,300
*Tulsa	2,900

OREGON

Corvallis	240
Eugene	1,500
Portland	8,950
***Salem	200

PENNSYLVANIA

Aliquippa (also incl. in Pittsburgh total)	400
Allentown	4,980
*Altoona	580
Ambridge (also incl. in Pittsburgh total)	250
Beaver Falls	350
Bethlehem	960
Brownsville	150
Butler	300
***Carbon County	125
Chambersburg	340
Chester (incl. in Phila. total)	
Chester County	3,400
Coatesville (also incl. in Chester County total)	305
Connellsville	110
Delaware Valley (Lower Bucks County)[N]	14,500
Donora (also incl. in Pittsburgh total)	100
Easton	1,300
Ellwood City	110
*Erie	800
Farrell (also incl. in Youngstown, Ohio total)	150
Greensburg (also incl. in Pittsburgh total)	300
**Harrisburg	6,500
Hazleton area	430
Homestead	300
Indiana	135
Johnstown	490
***Kittanning	175
*Lancaster	2,100
Lebanon	425
Lewisburg	125
Lock Haven	140
McKeesport (also incl. in Pittsburgh total)	2,000
Monessen (also incl. in Pittsburgh total)	100
Mt. Pleasant	120
New Castle	400
New Kensington	560
Norristown (incl. in Philadelphia total)	
North Penn	200
Oil City	165
Oxford-Kennett Square	180
Philadelphia area[N]	240,000
Phoenixville (also incl. in Phila. total)	340
Pittsburgh[N]	45,000
Pottstown	700
Pottsville	500
*Reading	2,800
***Sayre	100
*Scranton	3,300
Sharon (also incl. in Youngstown, Ohio total)	330
***Shenandoah	230
State College	450
Stroudsburgh	410
Tamaqua (incl. in Hazleton total)	
Uniontown	390
Upper Beaver County	500
Washington (incl. in Pittsburgh)	
Wayne County	210
West Chester (also incl. in Chester County)	300
Wilkes-Barre[N]	4,000
Williamsport	415
York	1,700

RHODE ISLAND

Providence (incl. rest of state)	17,500

SOUTH CAROLINA

Aiken	100
*Charleston	3,500
**Columbia	2,000

State and City	Jewish Population	State and City	Jewish Population	State and City	Jewish Population
Florence	350	Lufkin (incl. in Longview total)		Martinsville	135
Greenville	600			Newport News (incl. Hampton)[N]	2,575
***Orangeburg County	105	Marshall (incl. in Longview total)		Norfolk (incl. Virginia Beach)	12,100
Rock Hill (incl. in Charlotte total)		McAllen	295	Petersburg	740
Spartanburg	295	Odessa-Midland	150	Portsmouth-Suffolk (also incl. in Norfolk total)	1,100
Sumter	190	Port Arthur	260		
		*San Antonio	9,000	Radford (incl. in Blacksburg total)	
SOUTH DAKOTA		Texarkana	100		
Sioux Falls	125	Tyler	450	Richmond[N]	8,000
		Waco[N]	500	***Roanoke	710
TENNESSEE		Wharton	170	Williamsburg (incl. in Newport News total)	
Bristol (incl. in Johnson City total)		Wichita Falls	260		
Chattanooga	2,000	UTAH		Winchester	110
Jackson	120	Ogden	100		
Johnson City	210	*Salt Lake City	2,400	WASHINGTON	
Kingsport (incl. in Johnson City total)				Bellingham	120
		VERMONT		Longview-Kelso (incl. in Portland, Ore. total)	
Knoxville	1,350	Bennington	120		
Memphis	10,000	Brattleboro	150	***Olympia	145
Nashville	5,120	Burlington	1,800	Pullman (incl. in Moscow, Idaho total)	
Oak Ridge	240	Montpelier-Barre	500		
		Rutland	450	Seattle[N]	19,500
TEXAS		St. Johnsbury	100	Spokane	1,000
Amarillo	300			Tacoma	750
*Austin	4,000	VIRGINIA		Tri Cities[N]	240
Baytown	300	Alexandria (incl. Falls Church, Arlington County & Fairfax County)	33,550		
***Beaumont	400			WEST VIRGINIA	
Brownsville	160			Bluefield-Princeton	250
College Station	400			*Charleston	1,025
*Corpus Christi	1,400	Arlington (incl. in Alexandria)		Clarksburg	205
**Dallas	23,000			Fairmont	100
De Witt County[N]	150	Blacksburg	300	Huntington area[N]	380
El Paso	4,800	Charlottesville	800	Morgantown	200
*Ft. Worth	3,600	Chesapeake (incl. in Norfolk total)		Parkersburg	155
Galveston	800			Weirton	150
**Houston	42,000	Danville	180	Wheeling	650
Kilgore (incl. in Longview total)		Fredericksburg	140		
		Hampton (incl. in Newport News)		WISCONSIN	
Laredo	420	***Harrisonburg	115	Appleton	250
Longview	265	***Hopewell	140	Beloit	120
Lubbock	350	Lynchburg	275	Eau Clair	120

State and City	Jewish Population	State and City	Jewish Population	State and City	Jewish Population
Fond du Lac	100	Oshkosh	150	Waukesha (incl. in Milwaukee)	
***Green Bay	280	*Racine	375		
*Kenosha	200	Sheboygan	250	Wausau	155
*Madison	4,500	Superior (also incl. in Duluth, Minn. total)			
Manitowoc	115			WYOMING	
Milwaukee[N]	23,900		165	Cheyenne	255

[N]See Notes below
*Includes entire county
**Includes all of 2 counties
***Figure not updated

Notes

ARKANSAS

Southeast Arkansas–towns in Chicot, Desha, and Drew counties.

CALIFORNIA

Long Beach–includes in L.A. County, Long Beach, Signal Hill, Cerritos, Lakewood, Rosmoor, and Hawaiian Gardens. Includes in Orange County, Los Alamitos, Cypress, Seal Beach, and Huntington Harbor.

Palm Springs–includes Desert Hot Springs, Cathedral City, Palm Desert, and Rancho Mirage.

Pomona Valley–includes Alta Loma, Chino, Claremont, Cucamonga, La Verne, Montclair, Ontario, Pomona, San Dimas, and Upland.

Sacramento–includes Yolo, Placer, El Dorado, and Sacramento counties.

San Francisco–includes San Francisco, Sonoma, Marin, and San Mateo counties and towns of Palo Alto and Los Altos in Santa Clara County.

COLORADO

Denver–includes Adams, Arapahoe, Boulder, Denver, and Jefferson counties.

CONNECTICUT

Bridgeport–includes Monroe, Easton, Trumbull, Fairfield, Bridgeport, Stratford, and part of Milford.

Danbury–includes Danbury, Bethel, New Fairfield, Brookfield, Sherman, Newtown, Redding, Ridgefield, and part of Wilton. Also includes Brewster and Goldens Bridge in New York.

Hartford–includes most of Hartford County and Vernon, Rockville, Ellington, and Tolland in Tolland County.

New Haven–includes New Haven, East Haven, Guilford, Branford, Madison, North Haven, Hampden, West Haven, Milford, Orange, Woodbridge, Bethany, and Cheshire.

New London–includes Central and Southern New London County. Also includes Lower Middlesex County.

Norwalk–includes Norwalk, Weston, Westport, East Norwalk, part of Darien, part of New Canaan, and part of Wilton.

Valley Area–includes Ansonia, Derby-Shelton, Oxford, Seymour.

Waterbury–includes Middlebury, Southbury, Naugatuck, Watertown, Waterbury, Oakville, and Woodbury.

DISTRICT OF COLUMBIA

Greater Washington–includes Montgomery and Prince Georges counties in Maryland; Arlington County, Fairfax County, Falls Church, and Alexandria in Virginia.

FLORIDA

Ft. Lauderdale–includes Ft. Lauderdale, Pompano Beach, Deerfield Beach, Tamarac, Margate, and other towns in Northern Broward County.

Hollywood–includes Hollywood, Hallandale, Dania, Davie, Pembroke, and other towns in Lower Broward County.

GEORGIA

Augusta–includes Burke, Columbia, and Richmond counties and part of Aiken County, South Carolina.

ILLINOIS

Elgin–includes Northern Kane County, Southern McHenry County, and Western edge of Cook County.

Quad Cities–includes Rock Island, Moline (Illinois), Davenport, and Bettendorf (Iowa).

Rockford–includes Winnebago, Boone, and Stephenson counties.

Southern Illinois–includes lower portion of Illinois below Carlinville, adjacent western portion of Kentucky, and adjacent portion of Southeastern Missouri.

INDIANA

Lafayette–includes Clinton, Montgomery, and Tippecanoe counties.

Northwest Indiana–includes Crown Point, East Chicago, Gary, Hammond, Munster, Valparaiso, Whiting, and the Greater Calumet region.

South Bend–includes St. Joseph and Elkhart counties and part of Berrien County, Michigan.

KANSAS

Wichita–includes Sedgwick County and towns of Salina, Dodge City, Great Bend, Liberal, Russel, and Hays.

KENTUCKY
Lexington—includes Fayette, Bourbon, Scott, Clark, Woodford, Madison, Pulaski, and Jessamin counties.

LOUISIANA
Baton Rouge—includes E. Baton Rouge, Ascencion, Livingston, St. Landry, Iberville, Pt. Coupee, and W. Baton Rouge parishes.

South Central—includes Abbeville, Lafayette, New Iberia, Crowley, and Opelousas.

MAINE
Southern Maine—includes York, Cumberland, and Sagadahoc counties.

MARYLAND
Easton Park Area—includes towns in Caroline, Kent, Queen Annes, and Talbot counties.

MASSACHUSETTS
Andover—includes Andover, N. Andover, Boxford, Lawrence, Methuen, Tewksbury, Dracut, and town of Salem, New Hampshire. Portion also included in Boston total.

Boston Metropolitan Region—includes 14 towns in Essex County, 34 towns in Middlesex County, 23 towns in Norfolk County, 15 towns in Plymouth County, 1 town in Bristol County, and all of Suffolk County.

Framingham—includes Maynard, Stow, Hudson, Marlborough, Framingham, Southborough, Ashland, Hopkinton, Holliston, Milford, Medway, Millis, Medfield, Billingham, and Franklin. Portion also included in Boston total.

Lynn—includes Lynn, Saugus, Nahant, Swampscott, Lynnfield, Peabody, Salem, Marblehead, Beverly, Danvers, Middleton, Wenham, Topsfield; Hamilton, Manchester, Ipswich, Essex, Gloucester, and Rockport. Portion also included in Boston total.

New Bedford—includes New Bedford, Dartmouth, Fairhaven, and Mattapoisett.

Springfield—includes Springfield, Longmeadow, E. Longmeadow, Hampden, Wilbraham, Agwam, and W. Springfield.

Worcester—includes Worcester, Northborough, Westborough, Shrewsbury, Boylston, W. Boylston, Holden, Paxton, Leicester, Auburn, Millbury, and Sutton.

NEBRASKA
Omaha—includes Douglas and Sarpy counties; also Pottawatomie County, Iowa.

NEW HAMPSHIRE
Manchester—includes Manchester, Hookset, Merrimac, Amherst, Goffstown, Auburn, Derry, and Londonderry.

NEW JERSEY
Bergen County—Allendale, Elmwood Park, Fair Lawn, Franklin Lakes, Oakland, Midland Park, Rochelle Park, Saddle Brook, and Wykoff also included in North Jersey estimate.

Cherry Hill–includes Camden, Burlington, and Gloucester counties.

Essex County–includes all of Essex County, Western Hudson County, all of Morris County except those towns in North Jersey estimate, several towns in Sussex and Warren counties, and Springfield, Berkeley Hts., Summit, New Providence, and Hillside in Union County.

Middlesex County–includes in Somerset County, Kendall Park and Somerset; in Mercer County, Hightstown.

North Hudson County–includes Guttenberg, Hudson Heights, North Bergen, North Hudson, Secaucus, Union City, Weehawken, West New York, and Woodcliff.

North Jersey–includes all of Passaic County except Passaic and Clifton. Also includes in Morris County, Pequannock, Lincoln Pk., Butler, Kinnelon, Riverdale, and Smoke Rise. Also includes 9 towns in Bergen County.

Somerset County–includes most of Somerset County and a portion of Hunterdon County.

Trenton–includes most of Mercer County.

Union County–includes all of Union County except Springfield, Summit, Hillside, New Providence, Berkeley Hts. Also includes a few towns in adjacent areas of Somerset and Middlesex counties.

Vineland–includes most of Cumberland County and towns in neighboring counties adjacent to Vineland.

NEW YORK

Elmira–includes Chemung, Tioga, and Schuyler counties. Also includes Tioga and Bradford counties in Pa.

Glens Falls–includes Warren and Washington counties, Lower Essex County, and Upper Saratoga County.

Kingston–includes eastern half of Ulster County.

New York City Metropolitan Area–includes the 5 boroughs of New York City, Westchester, Nassau, and Suffolk counties. For a total Jewish population of the New York Metropolitan Region, include Southwestern Connecticut, Rockland County, and Northeastern/New Jersey.

Syracuse–includes Onandago County, Western Madison County, and most of Oswego County.

Utica–southeastern third of Oneida County.

NORTH CAROLINA

Asheville–includes Buncombe, Haywood, and Madison counties.

Charlotte–includes Mecklenberg County. Also includes Lancaster and York counties in South Carolina.

Whiteville Zone–includes Elizabethtown, Fairmont, Jacksonville, Lumberton, Tabor City, Wallace, Warsaw, and Loris, S.C.

OHIO
Cincinnati–includes Hamilton County. Also includes Boone, Campbell, and Kenton counties in Kentucky.
Toledo–includes Fulton, Lucas, and Wood counties. Also includes Monroe and Lenawee counties, Michigan.
Youngstown–includes Mahoning and Trumbull counties. Also includes Mercer County, Pa.

PENNSYLVANIA
Delaware Valley–includes Bensalem Township, Bristol, Langhorne, Levittown, New Hope, Newtown, Penndel, Warington, Yardley, Richboro, Feasterville, Middletown, Southampton, and Holland.
Philadelphia–includes Philadelphia City, Montgomery, Delaware, and Central and Upper Bucks counties. For a total Jewish population of the Philadelphia Metropolitan Region, include Lower Bucks County, Chester County, and Cherry Hill area of New Jersey.
Pittsburgh–includes all of Allegheny County and adjacent portions of Washington, Westmoreland, and Beaver counties.
Wilkes-Barre–includes all of Lucerne County except Southern portion, which is included in Hazleton totals.

TEXAS
De Witt County–includes communities also in Colorado, Fayette, Gonzales, and La Vaca counties.
Waco–includes McLennan, Coryell, Bell, Falls, Hamilton, and Hill counties.

VIRGINIA
Newport News–includes Newport News, Hampton, Williamsburg, James City, York County, and Poquosson County.
Richmond–includes Richmond City, Henrico County, and Chesterfield County.

WASHINGTON
Seattle–includes King County and adjacent portions of Snohomish and Kitsap counties.
Tri Cities–includes Pasco, Richland, Kennewic, and Yakima.

WEST VIRGINIA
Huntington–includes nearby towns in Ohio and Kentucky.

WISCONSIN
Milwaukee–includes Milwaukee County, Eastern Waukesha County, and Southern Ozaukee County.

Review of the Year

OTHER COUNTRIES

Canada

National Affairs

THE NEWLY ELECTED Progressive Conservative (PC) government, headed by Prime Minister Brian Mulroney, introduced a number of changes in 1985, chiefly in the area of economic policy. As expected, the Conservatives were more business- and free-market oriented than their Liberal predecessors. At the same time, they maintained a commitment to providing traditional welfare-state protection for all Canadians.

Despite the long-standing tendency of Jewish voters to vote Liberal, the Jewish community felt more comfortable with the Conservative government than it had with some earlier Liberal ones. Even though Jewish representation in the Conservative caucus was low, the government appeared to be sympathetic to Jewish concerns, particularly with regard to foreign policy. In general, Jews were actively involved in all three national parties, as well as in provincial politics.

Ontario politics underwent upheaval during the year, beginning with a leadership contest within the long-dominant Progressive Conservative party. Frank Miller won the top position by a narrow margin over Larry Grossman, amidst speculation that Grossman's Jewishness and urban background were viewed negatively by the small-town conservatives who formed the backbone of the party. Grossman continued in his post as provincial treasurer and was joined in the cabinet by David Rotenberg, also of Toronto. Early May elections to the provincial legislature produced an upset, with the Conservatives failing to win a majority, and the opposition Liberals and New Democrats working out an agreement for a Liberal minority government. Thus ended 43 years of Conservative control of the Onatrio government. Within a few months, Miller was forced out of the PC leadership and, at a second convention, Grossman emerged victorious, thereby becoming the first Jew to lead the party. The Liberals had three Jews in their new caucus, including two cabinet ministers, Monte Kwinter and Elinor Caplan.

In a change welcomed by Montreal's Jews, the ruling Parti Québécois (PQ) was defeated by the Liberals in the Quebec election in December. Since its first victory in 1976, the PQ's nationalist and secessionist politics had had a deleterious effect on the vitality of the English-language community in the province, including most of the Jews, an estimated 8,000 to 10,000 of whom moved away between 1976 and 1985. Even French-speaking Jews opposed the PQ, preferring that Quebec remain part of Canada and not seek independence. Montreal's Jews actively supported the Liberal party in the election and were therefore delighted with the party's sweeping victory. Herbert Marx, the only Jew in the National Assembly, was appointed minister of justice in the new government, the first Jew to hold that important position.

Relations with Israel

Although Canada was viewed as generally supportive of Israel, a potentially damaging development was the lengthy investigation of Canadian Middle East policy conducted by the Senate Foreign Affairs Committee. After many hearings, including testimony by the Palestine Liberation Organization's (PLO) UN representative, the committee produced a report that stopped short of supporting formal recognition of the PLO but showed considerable sympathy for its cause. At the same time, the report was highly critical of Israeli policies in the occupied territories, suggesting that those lands belonged to the Palestinian Arabs, though not explicitly endorsing establishment of a new state there. Two senators, both Jewish, dissented from the committee majority's support of the final report, and the Canada-Israel Committee (CIC) charged that the document downplayed Arab opposition to Israel and presented a distorted picture of the PLO. Shortly after the report was issued, Prime Minister Mulroney publicly reaffirmed his government's "unshakeable commitment to the integrity and the independence of the State of Israel," and made other remarks that were interpreted as a repudiation of the report. Since, in the Canadian system, the Senate has very little power, the committee's report was considered unlikely to have much impact on policy, though it did cause a stir in the media.

Government policy became an issue in the House of Commons after the Israeli raid on PLO headquarters in Tunis, in October. External Affairs Minister Joe Clark condemned it as a violation of the UN Charter, and supporters and opponents of Israel in the House clashed over what response the government should make to Israel's action.

Foreign Minister Yitzhak Shamir of Israel visited Canada in March to discuss trade and commercial as well as political matters. In meetings with his Canadian counterpart, Joe Clark, Shamir requested Canadian troops for the multinational peacekeeping unit in the Sinai. The two foreign ministers agreed on an exchange of trade missions to encourage commerce between the two nations and also to hold talks on El Al's request for landing rights in Toronto (in addition to Montreal). Following meetings with Prime Minister Mulroney in Ottawa, Shamir met with Ontario premier Miller to pursue his search for markets for Israeli exports. In addresses to Jewish community gatherings in Montreal and Toronto, Shamir called for increased *aliyah*. Later in the year, the El Al negotiations were concluded successfully, and further steps to expand Canadian-Israeli trade were undertaken.

A group of five MPs took part in a fact-finding tour of Israel sponsored by the CIC, one of a series of trips designed to foster greater understanding of Israel's situation among the country's political leadership. Some 120 MPs—42.5 percent of the House of Commons membership—belonged to the Canada-Israel Parliamentary Friendship Group, headed by Bill Attewell of Toronto, who joined the trip to Israel.

In a public-opinion survey conducted for the government, 82 percent of respondents preferred that Canada remain neutral in the Middle East conflict, reflecting an established Canadian tendency to avoid taking sides in foreign policy. Among those willing to take sides, 10 percent favored Israel and 5 percent, the moderate Arab states. Even those professing neutrality, when pressed, divided heavily in favor of Israel—though still urging government neutrality.

The UN Conference on Women, held in Nairobi, Kenya, provided a major challenge to Canadian supporters of Israel, since previous conferences had been forums for virulent attacks on Israel and Zionism. Twenty-two Canadian Jewish women, including several from Hadassah-WIZO, attended in various capacities, some as members of the official Canadian government delegation. A well-organized effort by supporters of Israel succeeded in eliminating a reference to "Zionism is racism" from the final conference document—a feat regarded by the delegates as a significant victory.

Anti-Semitism

The year saw a rise in the number of overt anti-Semitic incidents, including the firebombing of Vancouver's Temple Shalom, arson attacks against a Jewish funeral chapel and a kosher butcher in Vancouver, and vandalism incidents in Toronto. Despite the increase, Victor Goldbloom, president of the Canadian Council of Christians and Jews, maintained that anti-Semitism was a much smaller problem in Canada than in other Western nations. Moreover, he asserted, there had been significant improvement in the situation of Canadian Jews during the last 50 years.

The long-awaited trials of Ernest Zundel and James Keegstra for anti-Semitic activities took place during the year, both receiving extensive national media coverage.

Zundel, a German immigrant who had lived in Toronto for some time without obtaining Canadian citizenship, ran a publishing house that specialized in material denying the historicity of the Holocaust. The charge against him was that he willfully published "a statement, tale or news that he knows is false and causes or is likely to cause injury or mischief to a public interest." In order to substantiate the charge of spreading false news, the prosecution had to establish by eyewitness testimony that the Holocaust actually happened. Jewish community organizations actively aided the Crown in the preparation of its case, among other things helping to secure authoritative witnesses like Holocaust scholar Raul Hilberg, who spent over three days on the witness stand. The star prosecution witness was Rudolph Vrba, a survivor of Birkenau, whose detailed testimony about the workings of the extermination camps refuted Zundel's published assertion that no authentic eyewitness account of gassings was available.

Defense attorney Douglas Christie subjected prosecution witnesses to aggressive cross-examination, calling Vrba a liar after the latter testified that he had seen 1,765,000 people go into the camp and none come out. The defense also called witnesses who asserted that the Holocaust never happened, among them Prof. Robert Faurisson of France, a familiar figure in the Holocaust-denial camp. Other defense witnesses testified that Jews at Auschwitz-Birkenau enjoyed a swimming pool, a theater, and dancing, and claimed that it was scientifically impossible to use Zyklon B to gas millions of people. Zundel, testifying in his own defense, attacked the Nuremberg trials as "a travesty of justice" and presented his ideas about a world conspiracy of Jews and Freemasons.

On February 28, after an eight-week trial, Zundel was found guilty by the jury and sentenced to 15 months in jail and three years' probation. As a noncitizen, he faced possible deportation if his conviction were to be upheld on appeal.

The trial of James Keegstra, which began in April and ended in July, was similar to Zundel's in many respects, even though the charge was somewhat different: willfully promoting hatred against an identifiable group. Keegstra, a former high-school social-studies teacher in a small Alberta town which he also served as mayor, had used his classroom to promote anti-Semitic views. Much of the prosecution testimony was from former students who told the court what they had learned from Keegstra about Jewish control of the media and governments and the Jewish role in fomenting wars and revolutions and promoting communism. Some of the students withered under the tough cross-examination of defense attorney Douglas Christie, but others withstood the pressure. While the students' testimony, backed up by evidence from school notebooks, was very persuasive, probably the most damaging testimony was Keegstra's own. During the 26 days he spent on the witness stand in his own defense, the beliefs he expressed were so absurd as to subject him to ridicule. In addition to claiming that Jews were the dominant players on the world historical stage, responsible for all manner of evil, he denied that gas chambers had been used by the Germans and referred to innumerable public figures as Jews, ranging from Robespierre to David Rockefeller.

Even after hearing the prosecution summarize Keegstra's record as that of a hatemonger, the jury required 30 hours of deliberation before reaching a guilty verdict. The judge fined Keegstra $5,000 (Cdn.) but declined to impose the jail sentence demanded by the prosecution. Afterward, the jury foreman offered to contribute to a fund to help pay Keegstra's fine.

While many within the Jewish community expressed satisfaction over the convictions, others expressed doubts about the wisdom of prosecuting hatemongers. Debate centered on the opportunities afforded the defendants to disseminate their views through the media as well as on the justification for limiting freedom of expression.

As a result of the attention focused on the Zundel and Keegstra trials, and increased public sensitivity to the issue of hate literature, Parliament passed a bill banning the importation of material advocating or promoting genocide or hatred against an identifiable group. Earlier in the year, James Keegstra had successfully challenged a government attempt to prevent him from importing a Holocaust-denial book. The new law precluded a recurrence of such a situation.

Nazi War Criminals

The government finally took action on the long-simmering issue of Nazi war criminals living in Canada, appointing Justice Jules Deschenes a one-man commission to recommend procedures for handling allegations about such individuals. Several unresolved questions prevented Deschenes from reporting before the end of the year, among them the validity of evidence that might be gathered in Soviet-bloc countries. Doubts were also voiced about the legal basis for action, although briefs from the Canadian Jewish Congress (CJC) and B'nai B'rith's League for Human Rights suggested ways to deal with legal impediments.

The background to the appointment of Deschenes included an interdepartmental committee of the federal government that had met in 1981 to consider action against former Nazis. That body had concluded that there was insufficient evidence to prove that the accused lied about their wartime activities. In the course of his investigation, Deschenes discovered that the committee had been unaware of the existence of certain crucial immigration files, and that subsequently those files had been destroyed. The present justice minister, John Crosbie, claimed the destruction of the files as the reason for his government's inability to institute denaturalization proceedings against suspected war criminals.

The revelation of the missing documents was only one of the factors that prompted human rights attorney Irwin Cotler to charge that Canada's failure to act on Nazi war criminals who came to the country during the 40 years following the war was an obstruction of justice. Cotler also cited a secret agreement between Canada, Britain, and six other Commonwealth countries in 1948 to cease prosecuting Nazi war criminals and contended that Canada had provided sanctuary for a number of war criminals, including an associate of Klaus Barbie. Finally, he accused the government of quashing judicial deportation orders that had been issued against alleged Nazi collaborators some years earlier.

JEWISH COMMUNITY

Demography

The Jewish population of Canada was estimated to be 310,000. Trends that had been under way for some years continued, primarily the movement of Jews from smaller centers to large metropolitan areas, mainly Toronto, and the change in the balance of the Montreal and Toronto populations, also in favor of Toronto. Minor but noteworthy data confirming these general trends came from a report on the settlement of Soviet Jewish immigrants to Canada between 1977 and 1984, issued by Jewish Immigrant Aid Services. During that period, of the 3,345 Soviet Jewish families who arrived in the country, 2,129 settled in Toronto, with a few going to other Ontario cities. Only 452 went to Montreal, and the balance settled in Winnipeg, Edmonton, Calgary, and Vancouver.

A study comparing the social and demographic characteristics of young adults born to Holocaust survivors and those born to native-born Canadians or non-Holocaust immigrants was carried out by two Montreal researchers, Morton Weinfeld, a McGill University sociologist, and John Sigal, a psychologist at the Jewish General Hospital. In interviews with over 500 young Jewish adults in Montreal, the researchers found that the survivors' children had attained levels of educational and occupational achievement at least comparable to those of the other two groups.

Prof. Leo Davids of York University continued to conduct demographic research on various aspects of Canadian Jewish life. In a recent study, based on 1981 census data, Davids found that the younger age groups of Canadian Jews were characterized by a relatively high age at marriage and low fertility. The only conspicuous exceptions to this pattern were the ultra-Orthodox and Sephardic groups.

Community Relations

Educational policy was high on the community relations agenda, especially in Ontario, where the long fight to obtain public funding for Jewish day schools continued unsuccessfully. (In Montreal, 60 percent of Jewish children attended day elementary schools, 30 percent, day high schools; in Toronto, the percentages were 40 and 12, respectively.) A provincial government decision to extend government funding to the final three years of the Roman Catholic high schools (earlier grades were already subsidized), without some corresponding gesture toward the Jewish schools, caused great disappointment within the community.

In order to defuse some of the controversy over demands for public aid to Jewish private schools, the government appointed Dr. Bernard Shapiro, director of the Ontario Institute for Studies in Education, as a one-man commission to recommend policy on the issue. After studying the matter for over a year, Shapiro presented his report late in 1985. Disregarding the strong objections of the public school boards of metropolitan Toronto, all of which condemned expansion of public funding, Shapiro recommended that all private schools, including Jewish day schools, be entitled to government funds, if they affiliated with public school boards. (Such an arrangement would be similar to one operating in Alberta and British Columbia, but unlike the one in Quebec, where Jewish schools received direct government grants without school-board intervention.) Shapiro's plan would, however, prohibit schools that received aid from charging tuition; from restricting enrollment on the basis of race, ethnic background, or religion; and from employing any but certified teachers. As the year ended, with the government concentrating on the legislation for funding of the Catholic schools, the outlook was gloomy for Jewish schools in general and for the Shapiro report in particular.

In Quebec, the Jewish community fought another kind of political battle over education. In an inexplicable move that it contended was necessary to comply with a court decision, the Parti Québécois government passed a law barring anyone other than Catholics or Protestants from voting in school-board elections or serving on school boards. There were no "neutral" boards in Quebec, only Protestant and Catholic ones, and Jews had only obtained the right to vote for their members in the 1970s, after a long struggle. Since then, Jews had also been serving as commissioners on the Montreal Protestant board. Despite widespread opposition from non-Jews as well as Jews, the bill was initially passed; subsequently it was suspended by the courts and eventually repealed by the new Liberal government. Nevertheless, the fact that a government of the day could treat Jewish legal rights in such cavalier fashion was deeply disturbing to a Jewish community already feeling on the defensive as a result of nine years of nationalist rule.

Two cases involving religion arose in Ontario schools. A Jewish parent of a child in the Windsor Catholic school system charged that its religious teachings reinforced traditional views of Jewish complicity in the crucifixion. The board agreed to exempt non-Catholics from religious instruction but refused to change the content of the curriculum, which contained New Testament references to Jewish responsibility for killing Jesus. In Sudbury, a group of parents went to court to challenge the regular recitation of the Lord's Prayer in the public schools on the ground that it favored one religion and therefore violated the Charter of Rights and Freedoms. The parents lost the case on a split decision and entered an appeal.

The Supreme Court of Canada ruled that the federal Lord's Day Act, a Sunday-closing law, was an unconstitutional infringement on religious freedom. However, since the court's decision only invalidated the federal law, not the laws of individual provinces, the effect on Jewish business people who were Sabbath observers was problematic.

Another legal matter of some significance was raised in Montreal, when the city denied a property-tax exemption for the nonprofit YM-YWHA and assessed the organization $725,000, plus interest for three years' back taxes. The "Y" appealed the case to the Quebec municipal commission, which issued a largely unfavorable ruling, in effect classifying the "Y" as a private club. The Jewish group then took the matter to court, where the case was still pending at year's end. Meanwhile, the CJC ran into similar problems with its national headquarters' building in Montreal.

Communal Affairs

Because of the exodus of nearly 10,000 Jews from Montreal—beginning with the 1976 election of the separatist Parti Québécois—the very perpetuation of the community had become a matter of great concern. Carl Laxer, on taking office as the new president of Allied Jewish Community Services (AJCS)—the Montreal federation—asserted that community viability could no longer be taken for granted. He called for a greater commitment to educational, cultural, and religious matters, possibly implying a departure from the community's traditional emphasis on health and welfare.

A major study of the state of Jewish education in Montreal, conducted by Prof. Morton Weinfeld of McGill University for the Jewish Education Council, was completed this year. In addition to recommending greater community funding of the day schools, Weinfeld proposed a controversial two-tier system in which the lower tier would offer minimal Jewish content and a reduced emphasis on instruction in Hebrew. Weinfeld's plan was designed to meet the needs of students who had difficulty with the intensive multilingual curriculum or whose parents had a weak commitment to Judaism but sent their children to day schools for other reasons. Some Jewish educators, as well as many parents, feared that the two-tier system would harm the quality of the education, and that the values of less committed parents would carry too much weight in determining the curriculum.

Although the community's educational leadership was still considering the extensive report as the year ended, the day schools moved quickly to request substantial increases in funding from the federation. A strong case was made that the decline in real terms of government grants had put the schools in a financial squeeze that could be alleviated only by a substantial injection of community funds. It was also pointed out that Montreal had traditionally devoted a smaller portion of its communal resources to day-school education than other communities, because of its reliance on government grants.

The United Talmud Torahs of Montreal was one of four day schools in the world selected by Israel's Melton Center as testing sites for a pilot program in teaching Jewish values. The new curriculum, developed for schools whose student body was not necessarily Orthodox, related the teachings of Judaism to contemporary issues.

A number of unusual meetings and conferences were held in Canada during the year, among them the Congress of Secular Jewish Organizations, meeting in Toronto, and the Commonwealth Jewish Council Conference, which brought representatives from many parts of the world to Ottawa to discuss such matters as Jewish identity in small communities and human rights. At the inaugural meeting of the World Assembly of Moroccan Jewry, held in Montreal in October, over 150 delegates from several countries, including Israel and Morocco, were urged to "strengthen our attachment to Morocco" and to foster peace between Arabs and Jews. The conference, which was endorsed by both the Moroccan and Israeli governments, established a permanent organization, the Rassemblement Mondial du Judaïsme Marocain, with headquarters in Paris. Organizers of the conference received strong criticism afterward from some Moroccan Jews in Montreal who questioned the representativeness of the delegates, the political goals of the conference, and the praise expressed for Morocco and its monarch during the proceedings.

The major Holocaust observance of the year was a gathering of some 5,000 survivors and their children in Ottawa in April. The three-day conference, including ceremonies on Parliament Hill, focused on the importance of perpetuating the memory of the Holocaust and also of taking stands on current issues, such as Holocaust-denial activity and Nazi war criminals in Canada. Another observance was a march and rally that took place in Toronto shortly after Ernest Zundel's conviction. Some 3,700 people jammed the O'Keefe Center, where they heard speeches affirming the memory of the Nazi victims and denouncing those who denied the reality of the Holocaust.

The Holocaust Memorial Center opened in Toronto in September, situated in the complex of community offices in Willowdale. One purpose of the center was to serve as a permanent witness to the destruction of European Jewry.

Soviet and Ethiopian Jews

Canadian Jews continued to work actively in behalf of Soviet Jews. In addition to public demonstrations, such as a major rally in support of Anatoly Shcharansky held in Toronto in January, the community's efforts were directed at getting the Canadian government to put pressure on the Soviet Union to allow Jews to emigrate. The Parliamentary Group for Soviet Jewry, chaired by David Kilgour, in fact persuaded Secretary of State for External Affairs Joe Clark to raise the matter of Jewish emigration with the Soviet leadership during his trip to the Soviet Union in April.

A group of Canadian MPs, led by Kilgour, spent a week in the Soviet Union meeting with several dozen refuseniks. Upon their return, they publicized the plight of the refuseniks and their families and of those who were incarcerated. The International Conference of Parliamentary Spouses for Soviet Jews, held in London in June, attracted six wives of Canadian MPs, representing the three national political parties. The conference took forthright stands on both the issue of Jewish rights within the Soviet Union and the right to emigrate. Another active group was the Canadian Committee of Lawyers and Jurists for Soviet Jewry.

The Canadian Jewish Congress (CJC) found itself embroiled in a controversy with the Canadian Association for Ethiopian Jews (CAEJ) over the state of that community and the means to be used to help it. CAEJ president Jack Hope contended that the Jewish establishment had not shown sufficient commitment to the cause of Ethiopian Jewry and criticized Israel's handling of the matter as inadequate. In response, CJC leaders accused the CAEJ of distortions and errors in its charges and defended Israel's rescue efforts as being both appropriate and effective.

Religion

A proposal to deal with the problem of the recalcitrant husband who refuses to grant his wife a *get* (religious divorce) in conjunction with a civil divorce was presented to a parliamentary committee by representatives of B'nai B'rith Canada and the Vaad Harabonim of Toronto. Similar to plans already enacted in the United States, the proposal would bar a civil court from granting a divorce if barriers existed to the remarriage of either spouse. In their brief to the Justice and Legal Affairs Committee, the two organizations claimed that there had been "an alarming number of cases in which a couple was granted a divorce decree in civil court, but one of the parties refused to cooperate in the execution of a *get*," thus preventing the other from remarrying under Jewish law. Since Jewish religious authorities were unable to compel the issuance of a *get,* the proposal to utilize the power of the state was viewed as a promising approach. The plan would have to be implemented by amending Canada's divorce laws, which were under the authority of the federal Parliament.

In Montreal, the YM-YWHA experimented with opening its main building on Saturday afternoons for a limited range of activities. The "Y" had traditionally been closed on the Sabbath, but the leadership decided that there was a need to have some recreational facilities available. Guidelines for the program were designed to prevent Sabbath violations, but objections were voiced by the president of the Quebec region of the Rabbinical Council. After discussions with representatives of the Orthodox rabbinate, the "Y" decided to scale down the scope of the Sabbath activities.

In Saskatoon, the membership of Congregation Agudas Israel voted to allow women to be counted in the *minyan* and to be called to the Torah. However, about one-quarter of the congregation expressed disaffection with the decision and indicated that they would no longer attend services. In Toronto, female cantors chanted the High Holy Day liturgy in one Conservative and one Reform synagogue. They were Esther Ghan-Firestone and Katrina Rimler. Phyllis Cole became the first woman cantor of Montreal's leading Reform congregation, Temple Emanu-El–Beth Shalom.

Culture

Toronto experienced an upsurge of interest in Jewish theater, with several companies presenting works in Yiddish or English. Some of the productions staged during 1985 were *Di Narishe Moid,* a musical comedy; *Mein,* a new play by Richard Rose; Eric Blau's *Dori*—a musical based on the life of Theodor Herzl—which premiered in Toronto; and *Einstein* by Gabriel Emanuel. In Montreal, Lionel Rocheman presented his own one-character play, *Zaida Schlomo.*

Srul Irving Glick's new choral symphony, *The Hour Has Come,* had its premiere in Toronto. Glick was one of three composers who presented new liturgical works on the occasion of *Shabbat Shirah* at three Toronto synagogues. The others were Paul Kowarsky and Abraham Kaplan. In Winnipeg, a new *klezmer* band, Finjan, began making appearances.

Five Canadian films were screened at a Jewish film festival in San Francisco. Particularly noteworthy was *Spadina,* a documentary about the immigrant Jewish community in Toronto, directed by David Troster.

"The Precious Legacy," an exhibit commemorating the pre-Holocaust life of the Jews of Czechoslovakia, was shown at the Royal Ontario Museum in Toronto, where it drew large crowds. A major academic conference on Maimonides was held in Montreal on the occasion of the 850th anniversary of the philosopher-rabbi's birth. Scholars from a number of countries delivered papers on the theme "Maimonides: The Master as Exemplar."

Five Jews were elected to the executive of the Writer's Union of Canada: Matt Cohen, Frank Rasky, Michael Gilbert, Donn Kushner, and Sharon Drache.

Publications

David Bercuson and Douglas Wertheimer produced a timely book on the Keegstra affair, *A Trust Betrayed,* in which they lamented the opportunity that Keegstra had "to spew his garbage all over the media." An analysis of the reaction of the Jews of Alberta to the exposure of Keegstra's anti-Semitism is a particularly valuable section of the book. Bercuson also published *Canada and the Birth of Israel,* documenting the ambivalence of Canada's policymakers, between 1945 and 1948, over proposals for a Jewish state. (Although Canada did vote for partition, it was not without reluctance on the part of Prime Minister W.L. Mackenzie King. Lester Pearson, later to lead the country, was instrumental in formulating Canada's pro-partition policy.)

The Nazi period was the subject of several new works: Frances Henry's childhood memoir, *Victims and Neighbors: A Small Town in Germany Remembered;* Alan Abrams's *Special Treatment,* dealing with the fate of so-called *mischlinge* Jews, the products of mixed marriages, under Hitler; and Erna Paris's topical study, *Unhealed Wounds: France and the Klaus Barbie Affair,* an exploration of French ambivalence about the Nazi war criminal whose trial had been delayed for an extended period.

Rabbi Basil Herring confronted a number of vital religious issues in *Jewish Ethics and Halakhah for Our Time.* Rabbi Stuart Rosenberg produced *The New Jewish Identity in America* and *Christians and Jews: The Eternal Bond.* The growing differences between the three main religious groupings were analyzed by Rabbi Reuven Bulka in *The Coming Cataclysm,* which also suggested steps for resolving some of the conflicts. Rabbi Abraham Price's third volume of *Sefer Mitzvot Gadol* appeared this year, as did *Zichron Meir al Avelut* by Rabbi Aaron Levine. *You Can Be Your Own Rabbi—Most of the Time* by Rabbi Aron Horowitz combined memoir with an analysis of the state of Jewish life.

Other new works on Jewish subjects included an anthology of Canadian Jewish literature, *Mirror of a People,* coedited by Elaine Newton and Sheldon Oberman, and *Treasures of a People: The Synagogues of Canada,* a photographic study by three architecture students, S. Levitt, L. Milstone, and S.T. Tenenbaum.

A Canadian Jewish politician was the subject of a new biography, *Unlikely Tory: The Life and Times of Allan Grossman,* by Peter Oliver. Grossman, who served as a member of three Ontario cabinets, was the father of the present Progressive Conservative leader of Ontario. The poet Irving Layton was the subject of a biography by Elspeth Cameron, *Irving Layton: A Portrait.*

Personalia

Stanley Hartt was appointed to the position of deputy minister of finance in the federal government. Judge Rosalie Abella of Ontario Provincial Court, serving as a one-person Ontario Royal Commission, produced a report on equality in employment. Hershell Ezrin was appointed principal secretary to the premier of Ontario. Martin Chernin became a member of the Economic Council of Canada. Mark Resnick resigned his executive position at the CIC to become director of policy development for the federal Liberals. Mel Lastman was reelected to his seventh term as mayor of North York, part of metropolitan Toronto. Max Teitelbaum became the first Jew to serve on the Federal Court of Canada, Trial Division. Philip Cutler and Henry Steinberg were appointed judges of Quebec Superior Court. Lou Ronson and Mayer Levy were appointed to the Ontario and Quebec Human Rights Commissions, respectively. Michael Goldbloom became president of Alliance Quebec. David Cohen was elected president of the Winnipeg stock exchange.

In the educational and cultural fields, new appointments included Harry Arthurs as president of York University, where Joyce Zemans was appointed dean of fine arts; Gary Polonsky as president of Red River Community College; and John Hirsch as director of the Stratford Shakespeare Festival. Phil Gold won the Killam Prize for cancer research; the Order of Canada was conferred on Phyllis Lambert and Morris Saltzman; and Lambert and Phil Gold received the Order of Quebec.

Within the Jewish community, some of the major appointments included Harry Bick as president of B'nai B'rith Canada; Herb Abrams as executive director of Jewish Immigrant Aid Services; John Fishel as executive vice-president of AJCS in Montreal; Harriet Morton as president of Women's Canadian ORT; Phillip Leon as chairman of the League for Human Rights and Alan Shefman as its national director; Saul Zitzerman as president of the Jewish National Fund of Canada; Shira Herzog Bessin as national executive director, Robert Willmot as national director of government relations, and David Weinberg as director of research of the CIC. Three new appointments at the CJC were Ian Kagedan, national director of religious affairs; Janet Bendon, national director of communications; and Jeff Kushner, Quebec region executive director. Marvin Garfinkel was elected president of the Vaad Ha'ir of Winnipeg; Charles Bronfman and Allan Offman were reelected chairman and president, respectively, of the United Israel Appeal; while Morton Brownstein and Joe Ain were named to the board of the Jewish Agency. Glenna Uline became national program director of the Canadian Zionist Federation and Victor Goldbloom became chairman of the Community Relations Committee of

Congress, Quebec Region. George Kantrowitz retired as director of planning in the Montreal federation.

Among those who died in 1985 were the following: Leon Kronitz, community leader and executive vice-president of the Canadian Zionist Federation, aged 68; Shloime Wiseman, principal of Montreal's Jewish People's Schools for nearly 50 years, aged 86; Hy Hochberg, executive vice-president of the Ottawa Jewish Community Council, aged 62; Herbert Levy, longtime executive vice-president of B'nai B'rith Canada, aged 72; Rabbi Isaac Hechtman, executive vice-president of Montreal's Vaad Ha'ir for 30 years, aged 67; Ben Beutel, former president of United Talmud Torahs of Montreal and the man who negotiated the first school grants with the Quebec government in 1969, aged 83; Theodore Richmond, philanthropist and Toronto community leader, aged 67; Rabbi Phillip Sigal, a Toronto native who held a pulpit in Michigan and was a Conservative authority on Jewish law, aged 58; Louis Lockshin, community leader in Toronto, aged 69; Jack Steinberg, one of the five brothers who established a leading supermarket chain, aged 82; Harry Pullan, a founder of the United Jewish Appeal in Toronto, aged 92; Frank Goldblatt, Hamilton philanthropist, aged 88; Baroness Aileen Minda Bronfman de Gunzberg, an active worker on behalf of public causes, especially in the field of art, aged 60; actors Paul Kligman, aged 62, and Paul Mann, aged 71; Dr. Harry Paikin, Hamilton communal and civic leader, aged 79; Gershon Golan, national administrator of Canadian Friends of the Hebrew University, aged 56; Monty Raisman, a founder of Toronto's Congregation Beth Tzedec, aged 87; Hyman Share, a communal fundraiser, aged 65; Albert Cohen, World War II flying ace, aged 69; Rabbi Ephraim Carlebach, who revived and led the only congregation in Quebec's Laurentian Mountains, aged 73; Fred Lebensold, prominent Montreal architect, aged 67; and Dr. Abram Stilman, physician, community leader, and author, aged 82.

HAROLD M. WALLER

Western Europe

Great Britain

National Affairs

THE GOVERNMENT SHOWED surprising stability in 1985, despite the continuing economic slowdown, labor difficulties, and growing racial unrest.

The strike by the National Union of Mineworkers, which had begun in March 1984, ended a year later with the workers agreeing to accept reduced terms and the government going ahead with its program of pit closures. Another indicator of weakening trade-union strength was an abortive strike in August by the National Union of Railwaymen, whose protest failed to halt the introduction of driver-only trains. Elsewhere on the labor front, a breakdown in teachers' pay talks in February was followed in July by strikes, which continued with growing intensity during the autumn.

Unemployment in Britain remained at around 3.4 million during the year, some 14 percent of the labor force. On the economic front, the year began with the pound at a record low of $1.1587. When it plunged to below $1.10 in February, interest rates were raised from 12 to 14 percent, which helped stem the decline.

Racism and Anti-Semitism

Racial and social tensions in British society erupted in violence on several occasions during the year. In September police in riot gear battled black youths in Handsworth (Birmingham) and Brixton (London); in October a policeman was stabbed to death in an outbreak in Tottenham in which, for the first time, rioters fired shots at police. The number of police and civilians injured in riots during the year reached 254.

Right-wing National Front (NF) members were increasingly implicated in violence at soccer matches. In February some 40 MPs issued a statement expressing concern at the "scandalous and unacceptable behavior of a fascist minority" that shouted racial abuse at games. In June, following a major riot in Brussels between English and Italian fans, the European Parliament member for London Central,

Stan Newens, introduced a motion in that body calling for immediate action against those responsible for fomenting racial violence at international soccer matches. In July Mr. Justice Poppleworth's report on crowd and safety control recommended making it a criminal offense to chant obscene or racist abuse at sports grounds.

A government white paper in May advocated tighter laws against racism that would make even possession of racially inflammatory material potentially illegal and would give police new powers of search, seizure, and forfeiture. In November leading NF member Martin Wingfield was jailed for 90 days for refusal to pay fines and costs imposed when he was found guilty in April (under an existing law) of distributing leaflets deemed likely to stir up racial hatred.

Opinion on the incidence of anti-Semitism in Britain varied. While the Board of Deputies of British Jews reported in July that the frequency of anti-Semitic incidents had remained virtually static in the first half of 1985 (75 cases as compared with 74 in the previous six months), the Center for Contemporary Studies (CCS), an independent, privately sponsored body, claimed a sharp increase, citing 225 incidents between July 1, 1984, and June 30, 1985. The discrepancy probably reflected the different methods of reporting used by the two bodies, with the CCS making allowance for unreported incidents. Center director Eric Moonman warned that an intensified campaign of anti-Semitism would be launched by the NF in the coming year, focusing on the issue of ritual slaughter (see "Religion").

Relations with Israel

Britain threw its support behind a peace initiative put forward early in the year by Egyptian president Hosni Mubarak, calling for direct talks between Israel and a Jordanian delegation that would include agreed-upon Palestinians. To encourage movement in this direction, Prime Minister Margaret Thatcher held talks in London with President Mubarak in March and with King Hussein of Jordan in June; in April she met with King Fahd in Saudi Arabia and in September with President Mubarak in Cairo and King Hussein in Jordan (she was the first British prime minister to visit that country while in office). During a visit by a Foreign Office delegation to Tunis in April, Deputy Under Secretary of State Ewen Fergusson met with PLO officials.

Foreign Minister Yitzhak Shamir of Israel used the occasion of a London visit in June to reiterate Israel's objections to negotiating with the PLO and to protest Britain's continued embargo on oil and arms shipments to Israel. Israel also criticized Britain's agreement to sell military equipment to Saudi Arabia and Jordan.

Relations between the two countries were further strained when the government invited a Jordanian-Palestinian delegation for talks with Foreign Secretary Geoffrey Howe in October. Strong objections were raised in various quarters to the inclusion of two of the delegates, Bishop Elias Khoury and former West Bank mayor Mohammed Milhem. While Mrs. Thatcher described the two as "men of peace," others accused them of being terrorists. In the end, the meetings were canceled by the foreign secretary because of the last-minute refusal by the Palestinians to sign a previously agreed-upon statement renouncing terrorism. The incident, which was an embarrassment to the government, dampened hopes that peace talks could take place any time soon.

Conservative Friends of Israel (CFI), which celebrated its tenth anniversary in November, once again claimed to be the largest special-interest group in Parliament, with a membership comprising 156 MPs (including 9 cabinet ministers and 27 ministers outside the cabinet), 69 members of the European Parliament, and members of the House of Lords. CFI also had a growing youth section of about 1,000 members, including all the officers of the Federation of Conservative Students.

In October Ian Mikardo, deputy chairman of the Labor Friends of Israel (LFI), reported that eight unions were affiliated with Trade Union Friends of Israel—including the five million members of the Amalgamated Union of Engineering Workers and 4 of the 11 regions of the Transport and General Workers Union. Some elements in the labor movement continued to express anti-Zionist views, which they made efforts to distinguish from anti-Semitism. Brent East Labor party, for example, passed a motion in June condemning all forms of anti-Semitism in the Labor movement and demanding the resignation of South Yorkshire Labor councillor and police chief George Moore for alleged anti-Semitic remarks. In October, however, the group was willing to consider a resolution to expel Poale Zion from its ranks on the grounds that it was "racist and anti-working class." The motion was defeated by the group's general management committee in November.

A complaint against the *Jewish Chronicle* was upheld by the Press Council in May. The Jewish weekly was accused of denying the Palestine Solidarity Campaign (PSC) the right of reply to a September 1984 editorial that had criticized both the holding of a PSC conference in London and the Labor-led Greater London Council's (GLC) decision to fund it. Relations between London's Jewish community and the GLC, already strained, were exacerbated by an incident that took place in October. Chief Rabbi Immanuel Jakobovits was scheduled to be the guest of honor at a civic luncheon, but canceled his appearance when he learned that GLC leader Ken Livingstone would also be a guest.

Although the GLC had definite pro-Arab sympathies, its actions were not all one-sided. In November the council decided against awarding a proposed £27,000 grant to finance a British Friends of Palestine cultural festival. And locally, GLC made generous grants to London's Satmar community.

A spate of anti-Zionist activity on the campus began in January. A notable episode was the refusal of Sunderland Polytechnic's student union to ratify a Jewish society's constitution because it mentioned Israel. After debating and defeating a pro-Israel motion, and despite a demonstration by some 800 sympathizers from the national Union of Jewish Students (UJS), the student union imposed a three-year ban on the small society. The Sunderland Jewish Society did finally gain recognition in October, but only after the National Union of Students (NUS) threatened the Sunderland student union with disfranchisement unless the ban was lifted.

The organized Jewish community sought means to combat this type of discrimination. In February the Board of Deputies asked the Commission for Racial Equality to investigate Sunderland's action. In March the United Synagogue (US) announced a plan to develop strategies for use by Jewish students in countering anti-Zionism on the campus. Meanwhile, the Zionist Federation organized a series of conferences on the subject in a number of provincial cities.

The Board of Deputies, the Zionist Federation, and other major organizations arranged a conference at the House of Commons in October to mark the tenth anniversary of the adoption by the United Nations of Resolution 3379, which defined Zionism as a form of racism. The gathering urged Parliament to condemn the resolution, but no action was forthcoming.

JEWISH COMMUNITY

Demography

The Jewish population of Great Britain was estimated to be 330,000. Leading Jewish population centers were London, Manchester, Leeds, and Glasgow.

A study conducted by Dr. Barry A. Kosmin, head of the Statistical and Demographic Research Unit of the Board of Deputies, concluded that there had been large-scale defection of young Jews from the community, with no evidence of any religious revival to compensate for the losses. Kosmin's report, published in July, compared figures for synagogue marriages in the early 1980s with communal circumcision records of two and three decades earlier. This analysis suggested that of Jewish men born in the 1950s and 1960s, only half chose to be wed under synagogue auspices. The number of synagogue marriages in Britain had, in fact, been declining steadily, with the 1984 figure of 1,153 the second lowest in this century (only 1982, with 1,110 marriages, was lower). The 1984 total comprised 743 marriages performed under modern-Orthodox auspices; 110 under right-wing Orthodox; 49 under Sephardi; 179 under Reform; and 72 under Liberal.

According to the board's research unit, the number of burials and cremations under Jewish religious auspices rose by nearly 5 percent in 1985, from 4,715 the previous year to 4,945. This represented a death rate of 15 per 1,000, which, compared with the national rate of 11.8 per 1,000, showed the relative aging of the Jewish population.

A study by Barry Kosmin and Caren Levy found that emigration had been a more significant factor in the numerical decline of British Jewry than was generally recognized. Based on census statistics for Israel, the United States, Australia, Canada, South Africa, and Rhodesia, the researchers reported that as of 1971, over 44,000 British-born Jews lived in other countries, a number equivalent to 12 percent of the Anglo-Jewish population at that time. Since the early 1960s, more Jews had left Britain than had entered it; in view of the current economic climate and stringent immigration laws, it was generally agreed that the trend was unlikely to be reversed.

Communal Activities

A threatened boycott of the Board of Deputies' February meeting by Progressive members was averted by a compromise agreement. The Progressives were protesting a decision made two months earlier to increase the powers of the board's ecclesiastical authorities. After several months of meetings, Orthodox and Progressive leaders announced in June that they would cooperate "in a spirit of mutual respect" in areas where they could unite for the well-being of the community, and that negotiations would continue over the areas of controversy that frequently led to public acrimony.

The end of President Greville Janner's six-year term of office, in July, produced the first contested presidential election since 1967; Lionel Kopelowitz, a Newcastle physician, was chosen president. Progressive Eric Moonman defeated Victor Lucas, president of the United Synagogue (US), in a close contest for senior vice-president.

With a membership of 680 deputies—an all-time high—the board found its headquarters at US-owned Woburn House in London decidedly inadequate. Because of crowded conditions in that building—which housed, in addition to the Board of Deputies, the London Board of Jewish Religious Education, Office of the Chief Rabbi, Jewish Museum, and Beth Din—US officials spent a good part of the year considering whether to retain, modernize, or sell Woburn House, but without coming to any decision.

In June, for the first time ever, the US bought a retirement residence for Chief Rabbi Immanuel Jakobovits, who was due to retire in 1991. In the same month the chief rabbi reorganized his "cabinet" to include several new and younger men.

The Board of Deputies celebrated its 225th anniversary in March with a Festival of British Jewry, featuring lectures, exhibitions, concerts, and other activities.

Reduced government funding caused serious problems for welfare organizations, focusing attention on the inadequacy of communal support. Community donations provided less than 12 percent of the Jewish Welfare Board's (JWB) budget of over £5 million and only 20 percent of Norwood Childcare's annual income. In June the *Jewish Chronicle* reported that the Anglo-Jewish community needed an additional £4 million simply to maintain its welfare services.

All the major agencies experienced difficulties. In March the JWB was forced to close Fenton House, a 20-bed home for the elderly in Ealing, West London. The agency's drastic cutback program also involved staff and training-course reductions and a freeze on planned improvements to its 11 homes. In June the JWB announced that for the first time, the families of new residents in its homes would be asked to pay fees.

The Jewish Blind Society (JBS) made public in June its need for an additional £70,000 to care for residents in its new Finchley Road, North London, home, which had facilities for physically disabled as well as blind young people. In October chairman Sidney Bloch warned that Norwood would need to curtail operations unless its financial position improved. In the same month Asher Corren, executive director of Nightingale House, the Home for Aged Jews, where work had begun in June on a new £45,000 crafts center, reported a probable annual deficit of half a million pounds.

The Central Council for Jewish Social Services, under the chairmanship of Stuart Young, took steps to improve the situation. In September the council merged the Jewish Society for the Mentally Handicapped with the Ravenswood Foundation, transferring the former to the Golders Green, North London, building used by JBS, JWB, and Norwood. In October the council considered proposals aimed at improving its effectiveness, including centralized fund raising, staff sharing, and better coordination among agencies to prevent overlap. In November the council approved funds for expansion of JWB's training department to enable it to provide services to JBS and Norwood.

Soviet Jewry

The plight of Soviet Jews evoked concern and support across the political spectrum. In April Prime Minister Thatcher pledged to continue her fight on their behalf; Britain, she said, frequently raised the issue with Soviet leaders. In September she declared that no matter how much Britain desired improved relations with Moscow, the country would not "soft pedal" questions of human rights in the Soviet Union. Labor leader Neil Kinnock told his party's September conference that in "efforts to secure the release of refuseniks and so-called dissidents in the Soviet Union the value of freedom must know no bounds." In July Liberal-party leader David Steel joined Avital Shcharansky's newest campaign to win her husband's release. In November, prior to the U.S.-Soviet Geneva summit conference, an all-party group of MPs sponsored a motion in the House of Commons calling on the Soviet Union to permit Soviet Jews who wished to join their families abroad to leave the USSR.

Youth played an active part in the Soviet Jewry movement during the year. In July it was announced that eight leading members of the UJS would attend the World Festival of Youth and Students in Moscow, as part of the British Youth Council delegation. In November, under the auspices of the NUS, student leaders from all over the country took part in a lobbying effort at the House of Commons to draw MPs' attention to the problems of Soviet Jewry, specifically to the condition of Jewish students. In December over 250 students attended a Soviet Jewry solidarity meeting held during the NUS conference.

While London was the center of the movement, other communities were active as well. In April, for example, Brighton and Hove's Committee for Soviet Jewry appealed to visiting Russian musicians to intercede in behalf of singer Viktor Delganov and his pianist wife, Elena. In Manchester a lawyers' association for Soviet Jewry was established. In Leeds former refusenik Itzhak Shkolnik led a solidarity march in company with the lord mayor and lady mayoress of the city.

Religion

The Board of Deputies' research unit estimated overall male synagogue membership at over 78,000, of which 70.5 percent belonged to modern-Orthodox synagogues; 4.4 percent to right-wing Orthodox; 2.7 percent to Sephardi; 15.2 percent to Reform; and 7.2 percent to Liberal synagogues.

In March, following nearly 12 months of discussions, the Reform Synagogues of Great Britain (RSGB) and the Union of Liberal and Progressive Synagogues (ULPS) rejected a merger proposal on the grounds that "the existing diversity of attitudes and practices" was "too broad" to be contained within one organization. Subsequently, a standing committee was established to promote cooperation in such areas as education, Israel, Soviet Jewry, and social issues, and the ULPS council approved a resolution stating that a single Progressive movement was still its eventual aim. In July Rabbi John Rayner, senior rabbi at London's St. John's Wood Liberal Synagogue, reported that the Liberal movement in Britain, with some 12,500 members, was experiencing "zero growth."

In January Rabbi Jacqueline Tabbick, the first woman rabbi in Britain, became chairman of RSGB's Assembly of Rabbis. The RSGB's membership had grown by 4 percent over the previous year, to some 40,000, reported executive director Raymond Goldman in June. The normal annual increase had been 2 to 2½ percent.

The ongoing threat of a law against ritual slaughter (*shehitah*) was a source of concern throughout the year, although by December no bill had actually been put forward in Parliament. All sections of the community protested a report issued in July by the Farm Animal Council, a body appointed by the government to advise on legislation to prevent animal suffering. The council recommended that religious slaughter be banned, and that the Jewish and Muslim communities, the two groups concerned, be given three years in which to consider alternative methods for the prestunning of animals—a procedure not allowed under religious law. Although critics tended to link Jewish and Muslim slaughter together, Jewish spokesmen preferred to discuss *shehitah* on its own, pointing to the substantial differences between the two methods. In November the Royal Society for the Prevention of Cruelty to Animals published a pamphlet supporting the anti-*shehitah* view. In December an ad hoc committee of presidents of Jewish organizations was formed to present an official defense of *shehitah*.

S. S. Levin, president of the National Council of Shechita Boards, reported in July that kosher meat and poultry consumption was declining by 4 percent annually. In October the London Board for Shechita approved increased fees for cattle and poultry slaughter.

Jewish Education

Special efforts were made this year to improve the quality of Jewish teaching through pay incentives and intensified training. The London Board for Jewish

Education offered supplementary-school teachers raises based on performance and on completion of in-service training programs, in addition to across-the-board increases. In December, for example, the salaries of 350 London teachers, already nearly doubled in the previous two years, were increased by an additional 20 to 25 percent.

A £25,000 scholarship program, financed by the Jewish Educational Development Trust (JEDT) for the purpose of training senior teachers of Jewish studies in day schools, was launched in April. Under the program, three scholarships would be awarded annually, to cover two years of study at the Hebrew University, Jerusalem, and Jews' College, London. The latter's Institute of Jewish Education launched new courses for Jewish day-school teachers in July.

A new JEDT study reported that the majority of general studies teachers in Jewish secondary schools throughout the country were not Jewish, and that women outnumbered men, especially among Jewish teachers. The 55 secondary, primary, and nursery schools included in the survey had 66 full-time Jewish teachers in subjects other than Jewish studies and 145 non-Jewish teachers. Altogether, the schools had 944 full- and part-time teachers, 530 of them Jewish, including 41 Israelis on two-year contracts.

In April the Independent Jewish Day School, Hendon, with 150 pupils aged three to ten, became the first British school to receive a World Zionist Organization Jerusalem Prize for its contribution to Torah education in the Diaspora.

Jews' College had 55 students enrolled in 1985–1986, 20 percent more than the previous year. Of these, some 20 intended to teach after completing B.A., B.Ed., or postgraduate courses; 6 to 8 were registered in three-year rabbinic courses; and 6 were enrolled in the new M.A. course designed for general enrichment.

Rabbi Jonathan Magonet succeeded Prof. J. B. Segal as principal of Leo Baeck College, the rabbinical school for the Liberal and Reform movements. In September the school had 24 students enrolled in its five-year program.

Publications

The Jewish Socialist group launched a new magazine, *Jewish Socialist*. In July Colin Shindler was appointed editor of the *Jewish Quarterly*, succeeding Tony Lerman, who had taken the position following the death last year of founder-editor Jacob Sonntag.

Among the books on Jewish history published during the year were *The Jews of Islam* by Bernard Lewis; *The Last Arab Jews* by Abraham L. Udovitch and Lucette Valensi; *The Jews of Europe and the Inquisition of Venice, 1550–1670* by Brian Pullan; *The Road from Babylon: The Story of Sephardi and Oriental Jews* by Chaim Raphael; *The Carrière of Carpentras* by Marianne Calmann; *Memories: The Jewish East End* edited by Aumie and Michael Shapiro; *An Outstretched Arm: A History of the Jewish Colonization Association* by Theodore Norman; *Hitler and the Final Solution* by Gerald Fleming; *The German Jew: A Synthesis of Judaism and Western*

Civilization, 1730–1930 by H. I. Bach; *Leo Baeck Institute Year Book,* vol. 29, 1984; *Neither Your Honey Nor Your Sting: An Offbeat Story of the Jews* by Bernard Kops; and *The History of Anti-Semitism,* vol. 4: *Suicidal Europe, 1870–1933* by Léon Poliakov.

Books on Jewish religious themes included *Ages of Man: A Practical Guide to Jewish Practice and Belief* by Lucien Gubbay and Abraham Levy; *The Humanity of Jewish Law* by Dayan Dr. Meyer Lew; *Forms of Prayer: Days of Awe,* RSGB's new High Holy Day prayer book; and *The Essene Odyssey: The Mystery of the True Teacher and the Essene Impact on the Shaping of Human Destiny* by Hugh Schonfield.

Biographical and autobiographical works included two books to mark the Montefiore centenary year, *The Century of Moses Montefiore: A Collection of Essays* edited by Sonia and V. D. Lipman; and *Sir Moses Montefiore, 1784–1885* by Myrtle Franklin and Michael Bor; *Time and Time Again,* Dan Jacobson's autobiography; *Secrets: Boyhood in a Jewish Hotel 1932–54* by Ronald Hayman; *Grief Forgotten: The Tale of an East End Jewish Boyhood* by Ralph L. Finn; *Chaim Weizmann* by Yehuda Reinharz; *My Life on the Silver Screen* by politician Gerald Kaufman; and *Stage Struck: An Autobiography* by show-business personality Lionel Blair.

Books on Israel and Zionism included *A Land of Two Peoples: Martin Buber on Jews and Arabs* edited by Paul Mendes-Flohr; *Israel and South Africa—The Unnatural Alliance* by James Adams; *The Special Relationship Between West Germany and Israel* by Lily Gardner Feldman; *Jerusalem: Rebirth of a City* by Martin Gilbert; *Operation Moses* by Tudor Parfitt; and *From Time Immemorial: The Origins of the Arab-Jewish Conflict in Palestine* by Joan Peters.

New fictional works of Jewish interest included *Floating Down to Camelot* by David Benedictus; *Proofs of Affection* by Rosemary Friedman; *After Midnight* by Irmgard Keun; *The Price of Fame* by Maisie Mosco; *The Bread of Exile* by Karen Gershon; *Blood Libels* by Clive Sinclair; *Family and Friends* by Anita Brookner; *Mr. Wakefield's Crusade* by Bernice Rubens; *The Secret of Anna Katz,* a first novel by Steven Swift; *Beginning Again* by Ruth Adler; *Heaven and Earth* by Frederic Raphael; and two novels by Brian Glanville, *Kissing America* and *Love Is Not Love.* *Book of Mercy* contained poems by Leonard Cohen; Steven Berkoff published *Berkoff, West and Other Plays;* and Arnold Wesker was represented by *Distinctions,* a collection of essays, correspondence, and dissertations.

Among the new literary studies were *At the Handles of the Lock: Themes in the Fiction of S. Y. Agnon* by David Aberbach; *Kafka: Judaism, Politics and Literature* by Ritchie Robertson; *Images in Transition: The English Jew in English Literature, 1660–1830* by Abba Rubin; and *Short Digest of Jewish Literature in the Middle Ages (1000 CE to 1500 CE)* by Armin Krausz.

Other works of interest included *Hebrew Manuscript Painting* by David Goldstein; *I've Taken a Page in the Bible: A Book of Jewish Humor* by Alfred Marks; and *Jewish Commitment: A Study in London* by sociologist Julius Gould.

Personalia

Knighthoods were awarded to Jeffrey Sterling, chairman of the Peninsular and Oriental Steam Navigation Company, and Peter Lazarus, permanent secretary in the Department of Transport. Sam Silken, former Labor MP and attorney general, and Sir Leonard Wolfson, cochairman and managing director of Great Universal Stores, became life peers.

Among British Jews who died in 1985 were Sir Robert Mayer, founder of the Robert Mayer Children's Concerts, in January, aged 105; Col. James Grant, military man and schoolteacher, in February, aged 79; Olga Franklin, journalist, author, and broadcaster, in February, aged 72; Hyman Brody, for many years consultant senior physician, Sheffield Royal Infirmary, in March, aged 79; Arnold Daghani, artist, in April, aged 76; Reuben Louis Goodstein, emeritus professor of mathematics, Leicester University, in April, aged 72; Morris Harold Davis, president, Federation of Synagogues, 1928–1945, in April, aged 90; Ronald James D'Arcy Hart, leading professional genealogist, in April, aged 89; Fred Uhlman, artist and writer, whose novel *Between the Lightning and the Moon* was published this year, in April, aged 84; Oscar Nemon, sculptor, in April, aged 79; Minna Tym, secretary, Children and Youth Aliyah movement, in April, aged 76; David Clore, philanthropist, in May, in London, aged 78; Arthur Super, former mayor of Hackney and communal worker, in May, aged 75; Myer Berman, for 40 years rabbi of London's Wembley Synagogue, in May, aged 76; Lionel Schalit, leading figure in the Maccabi movement, in May, aged 78; Anne Stern, Nightingale House chairman, in June, aged 61; Samuel, Lord Segal of Wytham, Labor parliamentarian, Zionist, and communal personality, in June, aged 83; Donald Roodyn, emeritus reader in biochemistry, London University, in June, aged 54; Sir Charles Abrahams, business magnate and philanthropist, in June, aged 71; Judge Laurence Joseph Libbert, in June, aged 95; Leonard Lurie, ophthalmic surgeon, in July, aged 74; Annie Elboz, Stepney civic personality, in July, aged 84; Herbert Sulzbach, cultural officer at London's West German embassy, in July, aged 91; Ewen Edward Samuel Montagu, lawyer and community figure, in July, aged 84; Tosco Fyvel, writer, broadcaster, and *Jewish Chronicle* literary editor 1973–1983, in July, aged 78; Israel Preiskel, surgeon and communal figure, in July, aged 77; Asher Fishman, communal leader, in July, aged 66; Alexander Bernfes, Holocaust historian, in August, aged 76; Leslie Prince, civic leader and communal worker, in August, aged 84; Hermann Lehmann, Cambridge University biochemist, in August, aged 75; Gabriel Haus, communal personality, in August, aged 71; Rabbi Dr. Solomon Fisch, Hebraic scholar, in September, aged 96; Zygmunt Ratuszniak, Institute of Jewish Affairs archivist, in September, aged 76; Pinchas Shebson, rabbi, Southend and Westcliff Hebrew Congregation, in September, aged 76; Maxwell Shaw, actor, director, and drama teacher, in September, aged 56; Bernard Gore, founder of the Association of Jews of Polish Origin, in October, aged 79; Simon Frisner, honorary life president, Polish Jewish Ex-Servicemen's Association, aged 74; Hans Keller, music critic and musicologist, in

November, aged 66; Harry Kayne, bandleader, in November, aged 63; Elaine Blond, noted Zionist and chairman of British WIZO, in November, aged 83; Louis Questle, organizing secretary, Federation of Jewish Relief Organizations, in November, aged 68; Benjamin Jolles, cancer specialist and consultant radiotherapist, Northampton General Hospital, in November, aged 78; Stanley Chazan, London East End physician, in December, aged 82; Peter Stone, *Jewish Chronicle* art critic until 1977, in December, aged 85; John Cohen, emeritus professor of psychology, Manchester University, in December, aged 74; Joseph Neville, director, Jewish Colonization Association, 1971–1979, in December, aged 76.

LIONEL & MIRIAM KOCHAN

France

National Affairs

FRENCH POLITICAL LIFE in 1985 was characterized by an uneasy calm, a kind of waiting period prior to the legislative elections scheduled for March 1986. With a return to power by the Right a growing certainty, there was widespread concern about the prospect of a Socialist president, François Mitterrand, having to run the country together with a rightist prime minister and cabinet. The Socialists seemed resigned to their fate, however, and were in fact preparing to play an active opposition role in the interim period, with an eye to the 1988 presidential elections, which they expected to win.

The country's economy continued in the doldrums. Prime Minister Laurent Fabius's policy of modifying Socialist programs and reinstating incentives for business investment was a decision taken too late to remedy the situation. Unemployment rose to over 2 million. Inflation, although not unreasonably high, was nevertheless higher than in neighboring countries, notably Germany, and restricted the purchasing power of salaried workers and retired people.

The Socialists' slipping popularity was not helped by signs of discord among their leaders. In December Prime Minister Fabius publicly criticized President Mitterrand for receiving Poland's leader, Gen. Wojciech Jaruzelski. Subsequently, Mitterrand appeared to disassociate himself from Fabius, although he rejected the premier's resignation when it was offered. Fabius himself proved something of a disappointment to his supporters, and his popularity dropped considerably.

The long-term shifts that had been occurring in French political alignments came into sharper focus this year. The decline of the Communist party was confirmed in regional elections throughout the country, as was the rise of the extreme-right National Front (NF), the Communists losing almost the same proportion of votes as the NF won—about 10 percent.

The continuing decline of the once-powerful Communist party was, in large measure, a reflection of profound changes that had taken place in French society. The old "working class," composed largely of industrial workers, had been supplanted by a class of technological specialists, whose outlook and life-style were no longer proletarian. At the same time, the new proletariat, composed largely of migrant laborers, many of them strangers to French language and culture, was not welcomed by the nationalist, xenophobic even, membership of the Communist party. In addition, the sympathies and political loyalty of many of the immigrants tended toward Islamic fundamentalism and the various forms of Arab nationalism that were actually hostile to atheistic communism.

The government touched off a controversy in May when it banned a television program about a wartime resistance group, probably as a result of Communist pressure. The film told the story of a group of 21 non-French resistance fighters—mainly East European Jews—who were executed by the Gestapo. The film charged that the Communist party itself had betrayed the group, in part to prevent "foreigners" from getting credit for heroic exploits against the Nazis. Groups of former Jewish resistance fighters, who wanted public exposure of the role Jews had played in the French resistance, protested the ban.

Racism and Anti-Semitism

National Front leader Jean-Marie Le Pen, whose party had been an insignificant fringe group only a few years earlier, continued to display his skills as a demagogue, attributing the rise in unemployment and crime to immigrant workers, especially North Africans—an assertion, his opponents pointed out, never supported by the statistical record. A surprising and disturbing aspect of the Le Pen phenomenon was his growing influence among low-salaried workers in municipalities and localities traditionally loyal to the Left.

While Le Pen himself never openly expressed anti-Semitism, the atmosphere created by the anti-immigrant campaign opened the door to such expressions by his followers. On one occasion during the year, Le Pen did open himself to legitimate suspicion. In a venomous tirade against radio and television journalists who, he complained, had attacked him unfairly, he singled out four who happened to be Jews. While he did not mention this fact when he named them in his diatribe, there was no question but that the choice of names was deliberate and that he counted on the effect the names would produce.

Most individual Jews believed that Le Pen was anti-Semitic, even if it was hard to prove. The attitude of Jewish organizations seemed to be one of watchful caution. While opposing the NF for its racism, they did not want to be unduly alarmist about anti-Semitism.

Contrary to what one might have expected, Le Pen presented himself as pro-Israel, praising Israel's firm stand against terrorism and inviting France to follow her example.

Relations with Israel

France continued to show friendship for Israel; it also displayed strong support for the Arabs generally, and specifically for the PLO as the representative of the Palestinian people. Official speeches with a "warm" pro-Israel tone were almost always confined to matters that did not directly affect foreign policy; statements from the foreign ministry were decidedly cooler.

Following the Israeli air raid against PLO headquarters in Tunis on October 1, Foreign Minister Roland Dumas canceled a scheduled trip to Israel. The French government, which maintained close ties with Tunisia, denounced the Israeli action as one that aggravated tensions in the region.

The incident caused only temporary damage to French-Israeli relations, however. Later in October, Prime Minister Shimon Peres visited Paris, en route home to Israel from the UN General Assembly in New York, and was cordially received by President Mitterrand and other high officials. Peres even reported an offer by the French to help Soviet Jews emigrate by flying them directly to Israel from the USSR —should Moscow agree to expand emigration.

JEWISH COMMUNITY

Demography

The estimated Jewish population of France was 535,000, according to a major demographic study released in March. The study also reported an intermarriage rate of higher than 50 percent among French Jews, as well as a continuing rise in the average age of the community. The authors of the study—Professors Doris Bensimon of Caen University and Sergio DellaPergola of the Hebrew University of Jerusalem—warned that the high proportion of Jewish women intermarrying had especially serious implications for the future of the community, since in French society "it is the father who is the dominant note in the family's religious practices and cultural options." The study was carried out jointly by the French National Research Center and the Hebrew University's Institute of Contemporary Jewry.

The proportion of French Jews who were of North African origin, according to the study, was more than 50 percent. The proportion of French Jews in contact with any Jewish religious, political, or cultural group was about one-third of the total.

Communal Activities

Open conflict erupted this year between Chief Rabbi René Sirat and the Consistory, the central religious body of French Jewry, over the marriage of a member of the Rothschild family to a Christian woman who had been converted to Judaism in Morocco. The leaders of the Consistory, including its lay president, Emile Touati, had approved the conversion (historically their prerogative), thereby implicitly legitimating the marriage. When Rabbi Sirat challenged the validity of the conversion, therefore, he was not only questioning the rigor of the conversion procedure, he was asserting the primacy of the Paris Beth Din (rabbinical court) in such matters.

While the conflict was undeniably one of jurisdiction, it also reflected the current struggle between liberal and fundamentalist forces in the community. Rabbi Sirat accused the Consistory of encouraging a return to an earlier permissiveness in religious matters (although President Touati—like Sirat, of Algerian origin—was known to be strictly observant); members of the Consistory, in turn, charged the chief rabbi with seeking to impose fundamentalist practices on the community. An agreement satisfactory to both sides was reached after numerous meetings and discussions—reported widely in major newspapers—but the underlying tensions remained.

The Consistory faced another major problem this year, a challenge to its control over kosher slaughter. A group of dissident butchers, who had recruited their own *shohetim* and were operating in a provincial city, succeeded in attracting part of the kosher meat business. Since their unofficial slaughter was considered to be in strict conformity with *kashrut* laws, the issue was not religion but rather jurisdiction and also finances, because the Consistory normally levied a special tax on kosher meat.

Former chief rabbi Jacob Kaplan celebrated his 90th birthday at a large gathering attended by many friends and admirers. Although retired for some years, Rabbi Kaplan was still active in Jewish life, especially in Zionist and pro-Israel causes.

Education and Culture

Speaking at an international conference on education in Jerusalem, Chief Rabbi Sirat reported that while Jewish education had virtually been abandoned in provincial cities, Paris was witnessing considerable interest in the study of Hebrew. The chief rabbi himself continued to direct modern Hebrew studies at the National Institute of Oriental Languages, a prestigious university-affiliated institution. In the few years since Rabbi Sirat assumed the position, enrollment had risen from 40 to 800 students. Enrollment at the Centre Universitaire d'Etudes Juives (CUEJ, University Center for Jewish Studies) remained stable, with most students choosing courses in modern Hebrew and Talmud.

The Jefroykin Center (formerly the Federation of French Jewish Organizations) continued to be a lively, well-attended gathering place for both Sephardim and Ashkenazim. It offered, among other activities, a theater group and a "people's university." The Rashi Center, which was intended primarily for students and teachers, also served an important educational function in French Jewish life.

Due to the positive interest of Culture Minister Jack Lang (a Jew) in Jewish affairs, several government-supported projects were proposed this year, among them a museum (of as yet undetermined character) and an international symposium on Jewish literature, scheduled to take place early in 1986.

Publications

A novel by actress Simone Signoret, *Adieu Volodya* (Fayard), recreates the history of immigrant Jews in Paris during the 1920s, including the trial of Shalom Schwarzbard, the watchmaker who murdered Simon Petlyura, the Cossack leader responsible for pogroms in the Ukraine in 1919.

A biography, *Vie de Siegmund Warburg* ("Life of Siegmund Warburg," Fayard), by Jacques Attali, was praised for its depiction of the life and times of the international banker.

Nos illusions perdues ("Our Lost Illusions," Balland), by Adam Rayski, a former Communist leader, is the lucid and painful confession of a disillusioned revolutionary.

Personalia

Marc Chagall, the most famous contemporary Jewish artist, died in March at his home in Vence on the French Riviera. He was 97 years old.

Rahamim Naouri, former chief rabbi of Bône, Algeria, and, since his arrival in France, head of the rabbinical court in Paris, died in August.

Simone Signoret, the actress, died in September, aged 64.

ARNOLD MANDEL

The Netherlands

THE SITUATION OF THE Dutch Jewish community remained essentially what it had been for the previous decade. The Jewish population was relatively stable (a small emigration and immigration balancing each other out), and there was little evidence of anti-Semitism. Most Jews, especially younger ones, lived in comfortable circumstances, while those who needed assistance, primarily older people, benefited from welfare-state provisions and, in many instances, payments to victims of Nazism. Although the proportion of Jews affiliated with the organized community continued to show a slow decline, and an estimated 50 percent of all marriages of Jews were to non-Jews, the communal picture was not entirely bleak. A small but growing Orthodox group was making its influence felt; there was a significant number of conversions to Judaism, not all for purposes of marriage; and a new generation of young adults, born after World War II, was moving into positions of leadership in the community.

National Affairs

The Netherlands continued to be governed, as it had been since 1982, by a center-right coalition of Christian Democrats (CDA) and Liberals (VVD), with Ruud (Rudolph) Lubbers (CDA) as premier and Hans van den Broek (also CDA) as foreign minister. In the 150-member Second Chamber of Parliament—the lower house—the coalition commanded a majority of 81, of whom 45 were CDA and 36 VVD members. The opposition was spearheaded by the Labor party (Partij van de Arbeid, PvdA), whose 47 members made it the largest single party in the legislature. With regular quadrennial elections for both Parliament and the municipal councils scheduled for 1986, political activity increased considerably in 1985.

Economic recovery, which had started slowly in 1984, continued steadily in 1984 and 1985. The Dutch guilder remained stable; inflation amounted to only 1.5 percent (as against 2.8 percent in 1984); volume of production, investments—both of local and foreign capital—and profits, in particular of large industrial enterprises, all showed increases. Although unemployment remained high at 16 percent of the labor force, the number out of work actually dropped for the first time in several years, from over 850,000 at the beginning of 1985 to about 700,000 at year's end.

An issue that continued to trouble the country was the planned deployment of 48 American cruise missiles on Netherlands soil. Although, as a NATO partner, Holland was virtually obliged to house the missiles, the government had several times put off accepting them, in the hope that a significant arms-control agreement with the USSR could be reached. As the November 1 deadline for the government's final decision drew nearer, opposition intensified, with opponents staging demonstrations and sit-ins at Woensdrecht, the proposed missile site near the Belgian border. Some of the protests turned violent and had to be broken up by antiriot police. The government faced the possibility that a small number of CDA parliamentarians, most of them Protestants opposed to the missiles, might vote with the opposition and thereby rob the government of its majority. In the end, only one CDA member voted against the government, and the formal agreement with the United States was signed. Although opposition to the missiles continued, it appeared that a majority of the public had come to accept their presence.

Protests and demonstrations were also mounted during the year against the domestic use of nuclear energy, and were directed specifically against the two existing nuclear power stations: at Borssele, in the southwest of the country, and at Doodewaard, in central Holland. Because of widespread antinuclear sentiment, the previous government had agreed not to construct additional power stations. This did not satisfy the antinuclear elements, however, who wished to see the two existing plants closed down.

A parliamentary commission of inquiry—only the second such since 1945—completed its investigation of the so-called R.S.V. affair, involving government subsidies to the giant Rijn-Schelde-Verolme shipbuilding company. Although the company was poorly managed and stood no chance of surviving, successive governments had been pumping money into it in the hope of saving thousands of jobs. The commission's report, published in December, blamed a number of people for mishandling the situation. The news media singled out Gijsbert M. van Aardenne, minister of economic affairs in the present and previous governments, for his role in the affair, and the PvdA introduced a motion to unseat him. However, after he publicly apologized in Parliament, and after the VVD, to which Van Aardenne belonged, threatened to leave the government, the motion was rejected, 82–63, and he remained in office.

Racism, Extremism, and Terrorism

A continuing cause of concern was the activity of the extreme right-wing Centrum party (CP), generally regarded as fascist in character, which opposed the admission of immigrants, especially those from Surinam (former Dutch Guyana), Morocco, and Turkey. On the infrequent occasions when the party's one MP, Henk Janmaat, rose to speak in Parliament, most of the other members left the hall. Fears that the CP's influence might be growing mounted when two of its candidates won by-elections in two new satellite towns of Amsterdam.

The question of racism in Holland was a complex one. On the one hand, demonstrations were organized by Moroccans, Surinamese, Turks, Kurds, and other immigrant groups, as well as by antifascist groups, such as the Anne Frank Foundation and Affra (Anti-Fascist Front Amsterdam), to protest the alleged rise of racism and fascism in the Netherlands. In Amsterdam a statue was erected in memory of Kerwin Duynmeyer, a 15-year-old black youth from Curaçao who was stabbed to death in 1984 by a white 16-year-old. The killer gave as his motive the fact that he did not like Negroes.

On the other hand, the people and government of Holland were increasingly accepting of their society's growing pluralism, both cultural and racial. Considerable attention was paid by the government and others to the problems experienced by the so-called *allochtones* ("people who came from elsewhere"), the 600,000 or so persons from Turkey, Morocco, and other countries who had begun arriving in the Netherlands as guest workers in the mid-1960s and were later joined by their wives and children. Also included in this category were immigrants from Surinam who were allowed to take up residence in Holland during the five years following that country's independence in 1975. In addition to the members of these groups, who came to Holland primarily for economic betterment, there were others who came for political reasons, such as the 3,500 Tamils who fled from Sri Lanka to East Berlin, then to West Berlin, and subsequently claimed political asylum in the Netherlands.

The Ministry of the Interior had a special department for ethnic minorities, which made available some Dfl. 650 million ($260 million) solely for cultural and social programs. Although the government was interested in helping the newcomers integrate into Dutch society, it also encouraged them to maintain their own identities, offering, for example, clubs organized along nationality lines, foreign-language radio programs, and even lessons in Arabic, Turkish, etc., given by native teachers in elementary schools during school hours.

Not only was discrimination on the basis of race, religion, or sex a punishable offense, "positive discrimination," or affirmative action, was widely advocated and practiced, especially in the allocation of jobs in municipal services. In May 1985 a law was adopted that all aliens who had not become Dutch citizens but who had resided in the Netherlands for at least five years, and who were 18 years and older, could vote in municipal council elections, though not for Parliament. Some 320,000 persons were enfranchised by this measure, and among the newly elected officials were nine members of ethnic minorities.

The presence of some 400,000 Muslims—mostly from Morocco and Turkey but also from Surinam, Pakistan, and other countries—on the whole posed no problem to the Jewish community in the Netherlands. A few small radical groups did identify with the cause of the Palestinians, such as the left-wing Committee of Moroccan Workers in the Netherlands (KMAN). Certain Middle East regimes, such as Saudi Arabia, which had hardly any nationals in the Netherlands, were known to have made substantial donations for the construction of Muslim prayer halls. Other countries, such as Morocco and Turkey, with large numbers of nationals in Holland, exerted influence by appointing *imams* loyal to those governments, thereby maintaining control of the religious councils.

Crime and vandalism were on the rise, and there was some violence involving anarchist groups, in particular members of the squatters movement (*"krakers,"* in Dutch), who occupied vacant buildings and refused to obey court orders to leave, leading to serious battles with police.

Although politically inspired terrorism was not a problem for Holland as a whole, it was an ongoing concern in the Jewish community. As a precaution against possible terrorist attack, some 40 Jewish meeting places, such as synagogues and Jewish schools, continued to receive protection, either daily or on special occasions. For the most part these security arrangements were paid for by a Jewish foundation established for this purpose, but on the High Holy Days and for large gatherings the local police also stood guard.

War Criminals

According to a report issued by the office of the special public prosecutor charged with finding and prosecuting missing Dutch war criminals who had been sentenced in absentia or had escaped from prison, it was most unlikely that further trials would take place in the Netherlands. Of the 314 persons on the list, most had died during the previous 40 years, or the statute of limitations had run out, or they had become citizens of countries that were not willing to extradite them.

Appeals for the release of the last two war criminals still imprisoned in the Netherlands, both Germans—Ferdinand H. Aus der Fuenten and Franz Fischer—were again denied by authorities on the ground that setting them free would cause suffering to victims of Nazism.

Relations with Israel

As a member of the European Community (EC), the Netherlands continued to subscribe to that body's 1980 Declaration of Venice on the Middle East. (The policy outlined in that document included support for the rights of all states in the region, including Israel; "recognition of the legitimate right of the Palestinian people" to "self-determination"; renunciation of force or violence; and inclusion of the PLO in peace negotiations.) In February the Netherlands representative to the UN Human Rights Commission in Geneva appealed to Israel to respect human rights in the West Bank and Gaza and to adhere to the 1949 Geneva Convention. The government criticized Israel for its bombardment of PLO headquarters in Tunisia in October; however, it also condemned the Arab hijackings of a TWA passenger aircraft in June and of the *Achille Lauro* in October and expressed concern at the increase in terrorism and violence in the Middle East.

In the UN General Assembly, in December, the Netherlands was one of 16 countries voting against a resolution demanding Israel's unconditional withdrawal from territories occupied since 1967. (It had also voted against condemning Israel, in 1981, for extending its jurisdiction in the Golan Heights. On the other hand, also in 1981, the Netherlands had supported a resolution that labeled Israel's incorporation of East Jerusalem unlawful.) At the UN Conference on Women in Nairobi in July, the Dutch delegation opposed a resolution equating Zionism with racism.

The PLO office in The Hague, which had opened in July 1983, continued to operate with official approval, although without diplomatic status.

The Dutch UNIFIL force in South Lebanon, which began with 800 men in October 1979, was reduced to 150 members in October 1984, when the government decided they could no longer play a useful role in that volatile situation. Even this small contingent was withdrawn on October 19, 1985, as violence increased and the men's lives were increasingly endangered. In Sinai, however, where the Dutch had a contingent of over 100 men in the Multinational Force of Observers (MFO)—80 communications workers and 25 military police—the situation remained unchanged.

The Netherlands embassy in Moscow continued to represent Israel's interests in the USSR, including serving as the intermediary for Soviet Jews applying for visas to Israel.

Yaakov Nechushtan, who had been Israel's ambassador to The Hague since 1982, returned home in September. He was succeeded by Ze'ev Suffot, a career diplomat.

Israel received considerable attention in the Dutch media. Thirteen correspondents represented the Netherlands in Israel, all of them Dutch-born and most of them Jewish. This was the largest press corps Holland had in any country except the United States, where it had 16 members. The Arab world was covered by only two Dutch resident correspondents, both stationed in Cairo.

The Netherlands Palestine Committee's bimonthly newsletter, in 1985 in its 13th year of publication, focused heavily on the evils of the Israeli occupation of the West Bank and Gaza. The University of Amsterdam continued its relationship with the University of Bir Zeit, near Ramallah on the West Bank, under terms of an agreement signed in November 1984, which included, among other items, the exchange of students.

The Netherlands Council of Churches (representing most Protestant churches but not the Roman Catholic Church) came under fire from the Consultative Council of Jews and Christians (OJEC) and other groups when it became known that at the end of 1984 the group had received the unofficial PLO representative in The Hague, Ghazi Khoury, a Christian from Bethlehem, and had later issued a press communiqué on this meeting. It also came out that following the meeting with Khoury, the council asked Parliament to hold a public hearing on Israel's violation of human rights on the West Bank and in Gaza, a request that was rejected.

The Roman Catholic organization Pax Christi Nederland, which had always shown interest in the Palestinians, announced a symposium on the Middle East, with Israeli and Palestinian representatives, to take place July 1–3 in Amsterdam. The initiator of the conference was Pax Christi's Middle East specialist, Toine van Teeffelen, who was closely connected with the Netherlands Palestine Committee.

Three Labor members of the Knesset who had initially accepted invitations to participate subsequently withdrew, objecting to the preponderance in the Israeli delegation of extreme leftists and PLO supporters. Although the conference was then postponed, some of those invited, including several extreme-left Israelis, did take part in a substitute one-day symposium.

The Genootschap Nederland-Israel (Netherlands-Israel Friendship League) continued to offer lectures on cultural aspects of Israel to its various local branches. Most of the organization's members were older persons. Despite unexpected financial problems, the 6,000-member Israel Committee Nederland (ICN), composed mostly of orthodox Protestants, sent its customary shipment of flower bulbs to Israel as a token of friendship. The group celebrated its tenth anniversary in May.

40th Anniversary of Liberation

The 40th anniversary of the end of World War II and the liberation of the Netherlands from German occupation was celebrated on a much larger scale than had been the practice in recent years. One reason was the realization that many of those who had been adults in the war years would no longer be alive for the 50th anniversary. Another reason was the desire on the part of those concerned about the threat of fascism to use the Nazi period as an object lesson and warning.

Unlike the immediate postwar period, when the wartime suffering of the Jews was largely ignored, this year's commemorations emphasized the fate of Dutch Jews, 100,000 of whom—two-thirds of the community—perished as a result of the German occupation. (About special Jewish commemorations, or those devoted specifically to the Jews, see below.) The Dutch postal service issued four special stamps to commemorate the 40th anniversary, one of them showing the yellow badge that the Germans required all Jews to wear in public.

In addition to the many official observances, national and local, there was an outpouring of books dealing with almost every aspect of the German occupation of the Netherlands and the Japanese occupation of the Dutch East Indies. Of some 400 works that appeared during the year, 250 were original Dutch works published for the first time, the others reprints and translations. Books on local wartime history were in greatest demand, and considerable interest was shown in works dealing with Jewish wartime suffering—in contrast to the years right after the war, when such books found few readers. Films about the war were widely shown in cinemas and on television, and all the daily and weekly newspapers published special supplements commemorating the anniversary.

Dutch television presented a number of original documentaries dealing specifically with Jewish wartime experiences. A noteworthy one made by the NCRV Broadcasting Company and Belbo Films concerned a little-known episode in which German and British officials, the International Red Cross, and the Jewish Agency arranged the secret exchange of 222 Dutch Jews imprisoned in Bergen Belsen and 52 Jews from France for a group of German women and children who had been interned by the British in Palestine as enemy aliens. The liberated Jews arrived in Palestine in July 1944.

The Netherlands State Institute for War Documentation (RIOD), in Amsterdam, which itself had come into being immediately after liberation, observed its 40th anniversary on May 7 and 8 with a symposium on the theme "An Undigested Past?" Two of the participants, Jewish psychiatrists, presented papers on the trauma suffered by Jewish survivors and their children.

THE JEWISH COMMUNITY

Demography

The number of Jews in the Netherlands in 1985 was estimated at around 25,000, a figure essentially unchanged for some years. Of these, some 10 percent had settled in the country after 1948, coming from Eastern Europe, North Africa, and the Middle East. The total figure did not include 3,000 or so Israelis residing in Holland either temporarily or permanently.

Jewish population statistics had to be viewed with some caution because of the lack of any up-to-date, scientifically gathered data. The most recent survey, conducted in 1966 by the Commission for Jewish Demography of the Jewish Social Welfare Organization (Joods Maatschappelijk Werk, JMW) and published only in 1971, put the number of persons in the Netherlands who were "Jewish according to *halakhah*"—irrespective of self-identification—at 28,000. However, the study was criticized both for its methodology and its definition of Jewishness. As to general population surveys, the government itself had virtually halted its own census-taking activity since the early 1970s, because of widespread public opposition to any form of "registration."

In December 1983 the JMW appointed a commission to prepare a new demographic survey, primarily to assist in planning basic services, such as old-age homes. Two years later, in December 1985, an article about the proposed survey in the Dutch-Jewish weekly *Nieuw Israelietisch Weekblad* touched off such a wave of emotional opposition that the plan had to be shelved, at least temporarily. To one group of opponents, to whom the prospect of registering Jews raised the specter of deportations during the Nazi era, even assurances by those in charge that every precaution would be taken to guarantee anonymity were of no avail. Others objected to the criterion to be applied for determining Jewishness. This would no longer be *halakhic* norms, but a more subjective "feeling of attachment."

Holocaust Commemorations

A number of events commemorating the Jewish victims of Nazi persecution were arranged during the year, some initiated by Jews, some by non-Jews.

The annual community observance of Holocaust Memorial Day took place on the evening of April 17 at the site of the Hollandse Schouwburg in Amsterdam. This now largely demolished theater had been used by the Germans in 1942–1944 as a collecting station, where Jews were brought prior to their transfer to Westerbork concentration camp. One of the speakers at the ceremony, which drew a much larger attendance than usual, was Mayor Ed van Thijn of Amsterdam, himself of Jewish origin, who, as a child, had been interned for a time in Westerbork.

On April 18, which was the 40th anniversary of the liberation of Westerbork by the Canadian army, the non-Jewish foundation "Former Camp Westerbork" organized an impressive two-part commemoration. The first ceremony took place in a hall in Assen, near the site of Westerbork, in the presence of former Queen Juliana, the minister of social welfare and culture, the ambassador of Israel, and Lt. Col. B.H. Calway, DSO, commander of the Canadian regiment that had first entered Westerbork. Some 800 former inmates and their relatives also attended. Afterward, the participants made a pilgrimage to the site of the camp. Although the camp was completely demolished around 1970, a private committee had erected a monument there.

In the town of Vught, near Bois-le-Duc, in the province of North Brabant, where another camp was situated in 1943–1944, a memorial tablet was unveiled at the railway station, from which some 14,000 persons, mostly Jews, and including 1,800 children, had been deported. Other towns and villages that unveiled memorials to local Jews who perished in the war included Zwolle, the capital of the province of Overijssel, where the synagogue was being restored with funds collected from local inhabitants; Coevorden, Cuyk, Doesburg, Elburg, Raalte, Weesp, Zaandam, and Stadskanaal. All of these were small towns or villages in which no Jews or only a few remained; in many cases the majority of the local Jews had left for larger towns even before 1940.

Jewish-Christian Relations

The visit of Pope John Paul II to Holland in May caused turmoil in the country in general and in the Jewish community in particular. Among Holland's 6 million Catholics (out of a population of 14 million) were many militant liberals—among the most liberal Catholics in the world—who opposed the pope's stand on women's rights and sexual issues. Some groups boycotted the visit; others staged large protest demonstrations that often erupted in violence. In the Jewish community, controversy centered on an invitation to Jewish representatives to meet with the pope—a customary feature of papal visits. After first accepting the invitation, the Central Council of the majority Ashkenazi community decided on December 17, 1984, by 12 votes to 11, and with the support of Sephardi and Liberal leaders, that the council's officers would meet the pope only if three conditions were met: he would have to publicly recognize the State of Israel; admit the role of the Catholic Church and the Vatican in the persecution of the Jews, specifically the failure of the wartime pope, Pius XII, to condemn Nazi persecutions; and agree to publication of the exchange that occurred at the meeting. Several discussions took place between Jewish representatives and representatives of the Roman Catholic Church, but since the Vatican refused to accept the three conditions, no meeting was held.

The Consultative Council for Jews and Christians (OJEC), which had been established in December 1981 to promote better understanding and to take joint action on matters concerning both groups, had a Protestant minister, Simon Schoon, as chairman, and an Orthodox rabbi, Hans Rodrigues Pereira, as vice-chairman. Among other activities, the group published three pamphlets during the year: "The Image of the Other: Jews and Christians on Prejudice," containing four contributions by Jews and four by Christians; "Jerusalem in Judaism, Christianity and Islam"; and "Judaism in Catechistic Teaching: Directives for an Examination of Anti-Jewish Prejudice in Catechistic Material." OJEC continued to sponsor the so-called Houses of Learning, where Jews and Christians studied Bible together. Christian interest in this kind of activity remained strong, at least in certain circles, but on the Jewish side it was slight.

The Reverend Dr. Hans Jansen, a Protestant theologian (and former Roman Catholic), published the second part of his monumental *Christian Theology After Auschwitz,* in which he denounced the anti-Jewish teachings of Christianity from the Middle Ages onward. The work aroused great interest and much controversy as well.

Community Relations

Since 1973, when the government passed legislation granting allowances to war victims, the Jewish Social Welfare Organization (JMW) had been mainly engaged in processing applications for such assistance. By 1985, the majority of these applications had been dealt with, and the JMW found itself increasingly occupied with the matter of Jewish old-age homes. A number of these institutions, which were largely subsidized by the government, had become too large for existing Jewish needs and were now required to admit non-Jews as well. All the homes faced a growing shortage of Jewish staff; at the Beth Shalom in Amsterdam, for example, the staff had been almost entirely non-Jewish for several years.

A stormy controversy relating to ritual slaughter that began in 1984 was resolved in May of this year. Responding to pressure from the local Society for the Protection of Animals, Agriculture Under Secretary Adrian Ploeg announced in November 1984 that he intended to forbid ritual slaughter for export, though not for local consumption, by both Jews and Muslims, and to ban slaughter for local use within three years. The impact of the initial ban would have been considerable for the Jewish community, which used relatively little kosher meat itself but which exported large quantitites of it to countries where ritual slaughter was forbidden, such as Switzerland, or to those that did not raise much cattle, such as Israel. Opponents of the measure lobbied successfully, basing their claim on Article 6 of the Dutch constitution, which guaranteed freedom of religion. On May 14 Ploeg revoked the ban on ritual slaughter for export, provided that the kosher meat was exported only to a rabbinical body recognized by the Chief Rabbinate of Holland.

Another issue of contention between the Jewish community and the government was the proposal by Under Secretary for Social Welfare J.P. van der Reyden to stop monthly payments to children of Nazi victims who had been covered under the Law on Payments to Victims of Persecution 1940–1945 (WUV). Basing itself on the fact that children of resistance fighters and civilian war victims did not receive WUV payments, the government proposed limiting second-generation Jewish victims to payments for needed medical and psychiatric treatment. Jewish circles not only opposed the reduction, they asked that the present system be broadened to include children of Jews who had immigrated into the Netherlands after the war and up to January 1, 1973, when the WUV came into force.

Anti-Semitism

Although there was little evidence of anti-Semitism in Holland, at least three organizations were concerned with it and with discrimination in general. The Foundation for Combating Anti-Semitism in the Netherlands (STIBA), led by Chicago-born Richard Stein, specialized in legal matters. Established originally with the support of the American Anti-Defamation League of B'nai B'rith, STIBA celebrated its fifth anniversary on October 14 with a symposium attended by some 200 persons. The speakers included Nazi-hunter Simon Wiesenthal and Minister of Justice Frits Korthals Altes, who surveyed measures taken or planned by his ministry to combat racism and discrimination. *Forty Years After 1945,* a book of essays by various contributors, was published for the occasion.

The Center for Information and Documentation on Israel (CIDI), located in The Hague, which had been founded in 1973 to counter anti-Israel propaganda, was, under its present director, Ronny D. Naftaniel, increasingly involved in combating anti-Semitism and in other local issues. In 1984 and 1985 the CIDI issued reports on anti-Semitic incidents in the Netherlands; in both years they were negligible. The Anne Frank Foundation, which was not under Jewish auspices or management, directed most of its activities to countering discrimination against Turks, Moroccans, Surinamese, and other ethnic minorities. In addition to the three aforementioned organizations, a number of other groups claimed to be engaged in "the struggle against fascism, racism, and anti-Semitism."

A case of anti-Semitism, or at least of religious discrimination, that attracted much attention was that of a gospel-preaching couple, Lucas and Jenny Goeree, of Zwolle, who preached and also wrote in their periodical *Evan* that the Holocaust was caused by the Jews' rejection of Jesus as the messiah. Suit was brought against the Goerees by the Anne Frank Foundation, the CIDI, the OJEC, the Netherlands Auschwitz Committee, the Jewish congregations of Zwolle and Utrecht, and four private persons, charging the couple with religious discrimination, a criminal offense. On September 13 the Zwolle district court decided that the couple's allegations were indeed illegal and barred distribution of those issues of *Evan* containing the false charges, threatening a heavy fine for infringement. The Goerees appealed the decision on the ground that a secular judge had no right to interfere in matters of religious belief. Although many orthodox Christians joined the Goerees in charging interference with freedom of religion, the Protestant Council of Churches distanced itself from the couple. The case was still under review at the end of the year.

Communal Affairs

The Nederlands Israelietisch Kerkgenootschap (NIK), the central governing body of the Ashkenazi community, reported its official membership at 10,968. (In 1972 it had been 14,600.) Of this number, 81 percent resided in the three main metropolitan centers: Amsterdam (7,940), The Hague (431), and Rotterdam (500). Another 10 percent were in nine small communities, of which Bussum, some 25 kilometers east of Amsterdam, with 250 Jews, was by far the largest; 11 communities numbered between 75 and 40 members, and 19, fewer than 40. The Sephardi community had some 800 members, including a number of fairly recent immigrants from Morocco, Iraq, and other Middle Eastern countries. The country's 2,400 Liberal Jews were organized in six communities, in Amsterdam, Rotterdam, The Hague, Arnhem, the Twenthe area, and the North Brabant area.

The 350th anniversary of the establishment of an independent Ashkenazi congregation in Amsterdam in 1635 was observed on September 1 with various festive events. The highlight of the celebrations was a synagogue service held in the Sephardi synagogue, itself over 300 years old, which was chosen because existing Ashkenazi synagogues were not spacious enough to accommodate all who wanted to attend. Among the honored guests were Queen Beatrix and Prince-Consort Claus, a cabinet minister, the Israeli ambassador, and the mayor of Amsterdam. Former chief rabbi Aaron Schuster, who had moved to Jerusalem on his retirement, came to Holland to deliver the main address. The service was broadcast live on Dutch television, followed by a documentary on the history of the Jews of Amsterdam. A volume of photographs of Jewish life in Amsterdam, *En er was nog over* ("And a Remnant Remained"), by Joel Cahen, was published on the occasion of the anniversary, as was a special 96-page issue of *Hakehillah,* the monthly of the Amsterdam community.

A continuing problem for the Ashkenazi community—both the nationwide NIK and the Amsterdam congregation (NIHS)—was the five-year-old dispute with Rabbi Meir Just, who refused to relinquish his position as chief rabbi of Amsterdam, even though he had long since reached the age of retirement. The Slovakian-born rabbi, who before his arrival in Amsterdam had headed the yeshivah at Montreux, Switzerland, was appointed a communal rabbi of Amsterdam in 1963 and in 1975 head of the *bet din* (rabbinical court) as well. In 1976 he was appointed chief rabbi of Amsterdam for a five-year term. At the end of that period, Rabbi Just claimed that his earlier appointments as rabbi and head of the *bet din* had been for an unlimited duration, and that he was therefore entitled to continue in those posts. In June 1985, after attempts to reach a compromise failed, the matter was brought before the court of the Chief Rabbinate in Jerusalem. In the end, no court case was necessary. Through the mediation of the Israeli rabbinic authorities, at the end of 1985 an agreement was reached, according to which Rabbi Just would renounce all claims to the lesser, earlier appointments and sever his connection with the NIHS. At the same time, he would be allowed to remain as chairman of the Chief Rabbinate of the Netherlands for another three years—continuing to grant Jewish divorces, accept conversions, and supervise *kashrut* for export. (One of the complicating factors in the case was that Rabbi Just was an internationally recognized *kashrut* authority, whose granting of certificates—*hekhsherim*—brought in considerable revenue to the communal treasury, which would almost certainly suffer if he left.) While Rabbi Just would be permitted to represent the Chief Rabbinate of the Netherlands abroad during the three-year period, his rabbinical tasks within the country—other than those previously mentioned—were to be transferred to other rabbis.

The resolution of this problem made it possible to fill the existing Ashkenazi vacancies for which, during 1985, several candidates from Israel and elsewhere were interviewed. In one case a new chief rabbi of Amsterdam was actually appointed, but the man declined the appointment in view of the unclear status of Rabbi Just. The rabbinical situation was all the more pressing because Chief Rabbi Eliezer Berlinger of Utrecht (comprising all areas of the Netherlands outside the three main cities) passed away on October 31, at the age of 80, having remained active as a rabbi until shortly before his death. Rabbi Berlinger, who was born in Germany, where he studied at the Rabbinical Seminary in Berlin, served as rabbi in Malmö, Sweden, and as chief rabbi of Helsinki, Finland, before coming to the Netherlands as a communal rabbi of Amsterdam in 1954. Appointed chief rabbi of Utrecht the following year, he was greatly respected by all elements of the Jewish community.

The Liberal Jewish Congregation in Amsterdam, which had enjoyed a reputation for 30 years as a model of stability, faced a rebellion by a younger generation that accused the aging leadership of undemocratic and patronizing conduct. The congregation was also plagued by growing debt, one cause of which was the need to make extensive repairs to its beautiful but poorly constructed synagogue building, opened only in 1967.

Although the Liberal Jewish community was small in number—roughly 10 percent of Dutch Jews—its lay leaders and rabbis occupied key positions in Dutch Jewish affairs and in relations with the non-Jewish world. The Liberal rabbi of The Hague, Avraham Soetendorp, was frequently seen and heard on Dutch television, radio, and the press, often in his role as chairman of the Dutch Solidarity Committee with Soviet Jewry. (His late father, Jacob Soetendorp, who served as rabbi of the

Liberal Jewish congregation of Amsterdam from 1954 to 1972, had also been a well-known public figure.) The former and present directors of the CIDI, R.A. Levisson and R.D. Naftaniel, who also appeared frequently in the media, were Liberal Jews, as were prominent members of the JMW and the board of governors of the Jewish Historical Museum in Amsterdam.

Two of the country's leading synagogues made extensive changes in their housing, largely as a result of declining membership. In Amsterdam, the Ashkenazi Lekstreet Synagogue, which was inaugurated in 1937, only three years before the German invasion, officially opened its new, smaller sanctuary in July—a hall seating 100 men and 50 women, constructed in an annex to the main building. That structure, much too large for present-day needs, could not be sold because, as one of the few examples in Amsterdam of the "New Business" architecture, it had been designated a protected monument. The main synagogue was leased to the Dutch Resistance Museum, which opened its doors on November 1.

The Ashkenazi congregation in The Hague began construction on its third main synagogue in 140 years. In 1975 the congregation had sold its building in the Wagenstreet, in the center of the city, because most of its Orthodox members had moved away. The purchaser, The Hague municipality, in turn rented it for use as a Turkish mosque. The Ashkenazi congregation bought a former Protestant church building in the residential Bezuidenhout quarter and turned it into a synagogue and community center. When that structure proved, with the passing of time, to be unsuitable and too great a financial burden, the congregation decided to demolish it and to construct an apartment building on the site, with a smaller synagogue on the ground floor. Demolition of the building started in October.

Two synagogues in Gelderland, at Winterswijk and at Zutphen, were restored, largely with funds provided by local and provincial authorities. Although the congregations were tiny, the two buildings continued to be used for worship and also for cultural functions. Of the 100 or so synagogue buildings still in existence in Holland, only 30 were being used for worship, though in many of these no regular weekly services were held. The remaining buildings served other functions, some as cultural centers. (See "Culture," below.)

Several local and provincial authorities showed interest in preserving and cataloging the tombstones in the largely unused Jewish cemeteries in their areas. In the province of Groningen such a survey had been in progress for several years; in North Brabant a survey was completed in 1985 by a local Jewish resident, Max Cahen; for the province of Gelderland a survey was being started.

The Deborah Jewish women's group, established in 1978, continued to press for the right of women in Ashkenazi congregations to be elected to congregational councils and, in turn, to the executive of the NIK. Although women had been voting in the NIK since 1946, a more active role for them was opposed, in particular by the Chief Rabbinate of Amsterdam. In the Utrecht congregations, however, under the *halakhic* jurisdiction of Chief Rabbi Berlinger, women had been accepted as council members for several years.

With a membership of about 200, concentrated mainly in Amsterdam, Deborah groups held meetings about once a month, with smaller discussion groups or courses on specific issues taking place more frequently, and nationwide conclaves twice a year. The organization was found to fill a real need, as it dealt with aspects of life and problems of Jewish women that were outside the scope of WIZO—a longer-established, larger organization, involved primarily in fund raising for Israel.

The Dutch Jewish women's monthly *Kolenoe* ("Our Voice," in Hebrew), the first issue of which appeared in November 1981, continued publication, though now as a bimonthly. The volunteer-produced publication was independent of Deborah, but all the members of its editorial committee belonged to that group. Recent issues included articles on politics, anti-Semitism, women's news from Israel, biographies of prominent Jewish women in prewar Holland, and book reviews.

Activities in support of the Jews in the Soviet Union were most often organized by Dutch Solidarity with Jews of the USSR, a group headed by Rabbi Avraham Soetendorp. An interparliamentary conference on Soviet Jewry took place in The Hague on April 26, under the chairmanship of MP Dick Dolman, chairman of the Second Chamber of Parliament. On October 1, prior to a visit by Secretary Mikhail Gorbachev of the USSR to Paris, Dutch Solidarity organized its annual demonstration, this time with the participation of representatives of political parties, including the Communists, and of the Amsterdam Council of Churches. After the demonstration, a busload of demonstrators traveled to Paris, hoping to present a petition to Gorbachev. Prevented from doing so because of security measures, they met instead with leaders of the French Jewish community. Attention was focused on many occasions on the plight of Soviet prisoner of conscience Anatoly Shcharansky, whose wife, Avital, was received by Premier Lubbers.

Zionism and Israel

Leaders of the Netherlands Zionist Organization (NZB) claimed that a downward trend in membership had been halted by the appointment in 1984 of a full-time director, whose salary was paid by the World Zionist Organization. In fact, while the membership did remain stable at about 1,200, it did not increase significantly; nor did the establishment of a special group of Liberal Zionists (members of the Liberal Jewish community) lead to any significant increase, since most of its members already belonged to the NZB.

In general, the organization displayed a noticeable loss of vitality. There was little Zionist activity, and the NZB and its officers had virtually no impact on Jewish affairs or on public opinion, this in marked contrast to the earlier postwar period when Zionist leaders were also communal leaders.

Approximately 150 persons from Holland settled in Israel in 1985, many of them retired people receiving pensions and/or WUV allowances. A number of these emigrants had children living in Israel.

In fund raising for Israel, the United Israel Appeal (in the Netherlands, Collectieve Israel Actie, CIA) no longer occupied the central position it had for many years. Recently, societies of "friends" of various Israeli institutions had sprung up, each conducting its own fund raising, independent of the central body. Still, the CIA reported receipts in 1984 of some Dfl. 4.4 million in donations and Dfl. 3.7 million in bequests and legacies, or a total of approximately $25 million.

WIZO-Nederland, the Women's Zionist Organization, had 2,400 members in 20 local branches. Its chairman, Mrs. Freddy Markx, was a member of the official Dutch delegation to the UN Conference on Women in Nairobi, as she had been to the earlier Mexico City and Copenhagen conferences.

Culture

The 120th anniversary of the founding of the only remaining Jewish weekly, *Nieuw Israelietisch Weekblad,* was observed in mid-November with the publication of a special enlarged issue of the weekly and with several public events. A cantorial concert was presented in the Sephardi synagogue, with the participation of Chief Cantor Hans Bloemendaal of Amsterdam and cantors A. Lopez Cardozo of Congregation Shearith Israel in New York and Asher Hainowitz of the Yeshurun Synagogue in Jerusalem. The concert was later shown on television, as part of a 40-minute program about the Jewish publication. Also in honor of the anniversary, a symposium of Jewish journalists from Israel, the United States, and Great Britain took place on November 14, and the Jewish Historical Museum presented an exhibit about the Jewish press in the Netherlands from its beginnings.

Among several special exhibitions offered during the year, the Jewish Historical Museum in Amsterdam presented one entitled "After the Persecution: Portraits of a New Generation." It included videotaped interviews with young Jewish men and women who were born in Holland during or after the war and focused on the problems of the second generation. Seven of these interviews were shown on Dutch television.

Preparations were being made to move the Jewish Historical Museum—which had been taken over by the municipality in the late 1960s—from its premises in the Waag building to much more spacious quarters, scheduled for completion in 1987. The new structure encompassed a complex of four former synagogues, all adjoining, including the Great and New Ashkenazi synagogues, founded respectively in 1670 and 1730 and closed respectively in 1943 and 1938. The interior of the combined structures was being completely renovated at the expense of the Amsterdam municipality and the Netherlands government, both of which were expected to make annual grants for the building's maintenance, to supplement private donations. Although the museum's board members were predominantly Jews, the Jewish community as such had no official role in running the museum, and non-Jews as well as Jews served on its staff. (The chairman was a Jew.) The museum's purpose was to preserve the Jewish cultural heritage of the Netherlands.

Publications

Among new original Dutch books on the Jewish wartime experience the following were especially worthy of mention: *Strepen aan de Hemel* ("Stripes Along the Sky"), the autobiography of sociologist Gerhard Durlacher, describing his experiences as a teenager in Westerbork, Theresienstadt, and Auschwitz; *Aan het Goede Adres* ("At the Good Address"), a work by a non-Jew, Bert Kok, about the rescue in 1943–1944 of a group of Jewish children from Amsterdam by a group of young non-Jews, who placed the children with foster families in the southeastern province of Limburg; C. van Dam's *De Jodenvervolging in de stad Utrecht* ("The Persecution of the Jews in the City of Utrecht"); and Helene Weyel's *In Twee werelden* ("In Two Worlds"), ten interviews with Jewish members of the postwar generation.

A reprint—but for the vast majority who had never heard of it, a new work—was the facsimile edition of *Le'ezrath Ha'am*, the modest Dutch-Jewish periodical published between January and October 1945 in the already liberated southern part of the Netherlands by Abraham de Jong (later, in Israel, Avraham Yinnon). The editors, Tamarah Benima and Frits J. Hogewoud (librarian of the Bibliotheca Rosenthaliana), added articles to the facsimile about the general situation in the liberated south in that period, the attitudes of the general press, and the problems faced by the surviving Jews, including unexpected manifestations of anti-Semitism.

Among other new works of interest was the monumental *Pinkas Hakehilloth beHolland*, by J. Michman, H. Beem, and Dan Michman, published by the Institute for the History of Dutch Jewry in Jerusalem (in Hebrew), within the framework of the various *Pinkasei Hakehilloth* issued by Yad Vashem. The institute also published Volume IV of the *Studies on the History of Dutch Jewry*, containing most of the papers read at the symposium on the history of Dutch Jewry held in Israel at the end of 1982. The Jewish Historical Museum published *A Guide to Jewish Amsterdam* (in English and in Dutch), by Jan Stoutenbeek and Paul Vigeveno. The Netherlands Ashkenazi community published a Dutch adaptation and translation of Chaim Pearl and Reuben Brooke's *A Guide to Jewish Knowledge*, and a biography of the late Amsterdam chief rabbi, A.S. Onderwijzer (1862–1934), written by Dr. J. Michman and the rabbi's granddaughter, Judith Onderwijzer Ilan, who lived in Israel.

Personalia

On the occasion of the queen's birthday, Prof. F. Schwartz of the University of Utrecht and Prof. E.A. Noach of the University of Leyden were named Knights of the Order of the Netherlands Lion. Named an Officer of the Order of Orange-Nassau was Annie Fels-Kupferschmidt, of the Netherlands Auschwitz Committee. Named Knights of that order were Herman Natkiel, a wartime resistance leader; Dr. Julius Elzas, former chairman of the Netherlands Zionist Organization, now a resident of Jerusalem; and Maurits Kopuit, editor of the *Nieuw Israelietisch Weekblad.*

Ivo Samkalden, a former mayor of Amsterdam, became a minister of state.

Well-known Jews who died in 1985 included Louis J.F. Wijsenbeek, art historian, aged 73; and Sal van Gelder, wartime resistance fighter and postwar communal leader of Bussum.

HENRIETTE BOAS

Central Europe

Federal Republic of Germany

Domestic Affairs

ELECTION LOSSES AND internal government scandals in 1985 presented Chancellor Helmut Kohl with the biggest setbacks he had faced since taking office in 1982. Even his coveted "reconciliation" meeting with U.S. president Ronald Reagan at Bitburg in May, surrounded as it was by controversy, failed to bolster his sagging popularity.

In two important state elections, Kohl's conservative Christian Democratic Union (CDU) lost to the left-of-center Social Democratic party (SPD). In the Saarland on March 10 the SPD won 49.2 percent of the vote, followed by the CDU (37.3 percent), the Free Democratic party (FDP) (10 percent), and the Greens party (2.5 percent). State elections in North Rhine–Westphalia on May 12 were swept by the ruling SPD, which obtained an absolute majority (52.1 percent), followed by CDU (36.5 percent), FDP (6 percent), and the Greens (4.6 percent). The newly elected head of North Rhine–Westphalia, Johannes Rau, was nominated by the SPD to run against Kohl for the chancellorship in the 1987 general elections.

Kohl's prestige was further shaken by an espionage scandal and by continuing revelations of corruption and illegal tax deals involving both political parties and prominent individuals. Otto Graf Lambsdorff, the West German economic minister who was forced to resign in 1984, went on trial in Bonn, together with his predecessor, Hans Friderichs, and former Flick manager Eberhard von Brauchitsch, on charges of bribery and corruption. The trial continued into 1986.

The announcement in December by Friedrich Karl Flick that the industrial conglomerate he headed would be taken over by Deutsche Bank, the state's largest financial institution, for DM 5 billion, reopened the issue of Flick's failure to make good on his promise to pay 5 to 8 million marks as indemnification to former Jewish slave workers in Flick enterprises during World War II. The New York Conference on Jewish Material Claims Against Germany, in a letter to Deutsche Bank, voiced the hope that, following the takeover, payment would be forthcoming. The group's demand was supported by Werner Nachmann, chairman of the board of the Central

Council of Jews in Germany. (Early in 1986, Deutsche Bank announced payment of DM 5 million to the Claims Conference.)

The controversial bill to punish public denial or minimization of Nazi crimes was passed by the Bundestag (federal parliament) in April. Opponents had objected to the law because, in effect, it equated Holocaust victims with Germans uprooted by the war. They also maintained that existing legislation was sufficient to punish persons denying or belittling the Holocaust.

In January the federal parliament adopted a Social Democratic motion nullifying all decisions and sentences passed by the Nazi People's Court in the Hitler era. Widespread praise greeted this repudiation of the court which, according to an SPD speaker, had committed "state-sanctioned murder." At the same time, observers noted that the German judiciary had never really faced up to its Nazi past after the war, allowing judges of the People's Court not only to go unpunished but to reach the highest ranks in the system.

Former *Stern* reporter Gerd Heidemann and Nazi memorabilia dealer Konrad Kujau were convicted in Hamburg, in July, of fabricating bogus diaries of Adolf Hitler and selling them on the international media market in 1983. Heidemann was sentenced to four years and eight months in prison; Kujau to four years and six months.

40th Anniversary of Nazi Defeat

The 40th anniversary of the end of World War II was observed with a number of public events. Although the official anniversary fell on May 8, the event that drew the most public attention took place on May 5, when U.S. president Ronald Reagan participated with Chancellor Kohl in ceremonies that were intended to transcend issues of victory or defeat and to celebrate 40 years of reconciliation between the former enemies. Because of the hostility aroused in both Germany and the United States over the choice of the Bitburg military cemetery—which included *Waffen* SS graves—as the site for the ceremony, a visit to the Bergen-Belsen concentration camp was added to the itinerary.

In their speeches at Belsen and at Bitburg, the two principals attempted to strike what everyone agreed was a difficult balance. At the first site, Chancellor Kohl declared: "We have learned our lesson from history. The supreme target of all our efforts is to prevent a repetition of such a cruel attack on human life and dignity." President Reagan echoed the chancellor's words and then went on to sound the basic theme of the occasion, reconciliation: "Your nation and the German people have been strong and resolute in your willingness to confront and condemn the acts of a hated regime of the past. This reflects the courage of your people and their devotion to freedom and justice since the war." Speaking later at Bitburg, President Reagan assured victims of the Nazis that "reconciliation" did not mean "forgetting." To the Germans he was equally reassuring, saying that "we can honor the German war dead today as human beings crushed by a vicious ideology. . . . We do not believe in collective guilt. All these men have now met their supreme judge, and they have been judged by him, as we shall be judged."

The Bitburg visit aroused sharp public controversy in Germany. Most Germans supported it, seeing it as a long overdue gesture of reconciliation between former enemies. The political Left, however, sided with Jewish bodies and individuals, in Germany and abroad, and with groups of Nazi victims and anti-Nazi organizations in denouncing the Bitburg ceremony as an insult to the victims of Nazism and their descendants.

A group of Americans and Germans arranged a ceremony which they believed was a more suitable commemoration, on May 3, at the Perlacher Cemetery in Munich. There they paid tribute to the heroes of the White Rose movement, a small group of German Christian students who had organized resistance to Hitler in 1942, for which they paid with their lives. The Americans and Germans also visited the memorial site at the former Dachau concentration camp, where speakers emphasized that they were protesting the Reagan-Kohl visit to the German military cemetery.

Small protests were organized on the day of the Bitburg ceremony. Several hundred Jews, mostly students from various countries, demonstrated outside the cemetery gates.

The official anniversary of the Nazi surrender to the Allies was commemorated on May 8 with statements by political and other public leaders, special media programs and publications, as well as public meetings and debates throughout the country. The nation seemed to be evenly divided in its view of the historic defeat: some viewed the downfall of the Third Reich as a national disaster; others celebrated the liberation from Nazi tyranny as a chance for a new and better Germany to emerge.

In a widely publicized speech delivered to the federal parliament on the historic anniversary, President Richard von Weizsäcker was somewhat less forgiving of his own people than President Reagan had been a few days earlier. While acknowledging that "execution of the [Nazi] crimes lay in the hands of a few and was hidden from the eyes of the public," he asserted that "everyone who opened his ears and wanted to be informed could not fail to observe that the deportation trains were on their way." It may not have been possible to imagine the nature and extent of extermination, he said, but "there were many ways to have one's conscience diverted, to feel incompetent, look away and remain silent. . . ." And when "the entire unutterability of the Holocaust became evident" after the war, the president went on, "too many of us reacted by claiming to have neither known nor surmised anything." Von Weizsäcker refused to condemn the entire German people for the Holocaust, however. Certainly, he said, those who were either children or unborn "cannot confess guilt for crimes they did not commit." Nevertheless, he concluded, "their forefathers have left a heavy heritage. . . . We are all concerned by its consequences and are held responsible for them."

In November, on the 40th anniversary of the opening of the Allied military trials at Nuremberg, some 400 jurists from 13 countries met in that city to discuss the principles of international law that had been formulated by the tribunal and their implications for more recent political situations.

Extremism

Although the government maintained, as it had in the past, that political extremism was a marginal problem, and that left-wing extremism was more dangerous than that on the Right, terrorist acts on both sides posed an increasing security problem. A total of 1,604 acts of violence, including 221 terrorist attacks, were committed by left-wing extremists in 1985, resulting in seven people killed and many injured. Preliminary investigations pointed to the left-wing Rote Armee Fraktion (RAF, Red Army Faction) and the radical left-wing Revolutionäre Zellen (RZ, Revolutionary Cells) as the perpetrators of most of the attacks. Terrorist attacks were directed chiefly against "imperialist" and "capitalist" targets, including NATO installations, U.S. army bases and personnel, and nuclear, arms, and computer plants.

According to police sources, there was increased cooperation between terrorist groups. Thus, RAF was known to have established close operational contacts with the French Action Directe (AD). Following a bomb attack on the Frankfurt U.S. air base in August, in which 2 U.S. citizens were killed and 20 injured, both RAF and AD claimed responsibility.

Violence by foreign extremists—including Turks, Yugoslavs, and Arabs—also threatened public security in the Federal Republic and West Berlin. State agencies received warnings that Palestinian groups were under orders to attack American, Israeli, and Jewish institutions and persons in Europe. However, even stepped-up precautionary measures could not entirely forestall armed attacks, and the use of false identity papers by many Palestinians made it difficult to track down suspected terrorists. A Palestinian commando was responsible for the bombing of a U.S. shopping center in Frankfurt in November that caused numerous civilian injuries. A 25-year-old Palestinian was sentenced to a three-year prison term in Frankfurt on charges of transporting explosives, and several Turkish citizens were arrested in that city for engaging in drug traffic to finance the activities of their radical right-wing group, Graue Wölfe (Gray Wolves).

At year's end, there were 29 neo-Nazi groups in West Germany, with 1,270 members. Of the known neo-Nazis, 219 were classified as militant. Groups classified as "right-wing extremists," but not neo-Nazi, numbered 78, with a membership of over 22,000. Some 1,500 political offenses, including 5 terrorist acts and 64 acts of violence, were attributed to neo-Nazis, of which 355 had a clear anti-Semitic character. Officials recorded 35 acts of desecration of Jewish cemeteries and places of worship during the year.

Neo-Nazi groups, such as the National Democratic party (NPD), showed increasing belligerence and were involved in numerous clashes with police and anti-Nazi demonstrators. Neo-Nazi "skinheads" assaulted foreign citizens, killing a young

Turk in Hamburg in December. One of the assailants admitted affiliation with the militant Freiheitliche Deutsche Arbeiterpartei (FAP, Free German Labor party), the group that succeeded the outlawed ANS and that was reported to be concentrating its activities among youngsters of school and university age. After FAP organized a gathering in a Hameln cemetery, paying tribute to Nazi criminals who had been executed for atrocities at the Belsen camp, the Hameln city council decided to demolish the graves and erect a memorial to Nazi victims instead. Several West German political leaders and the teachers' union asked the federal interior ministry to outlaw the FAP, but no action had been taken by year's end.

Bavarian state agencies voiced concern over the growth of rightist groups formed by Gerhard Frey, whose primary organization, Deutsche Volksunion (DVU, German People's Union), with over 12,000 members, was the largest right-wing group in the country. The publication that Frey edited, *Deutsche National-Zeitung,* was among the country's biggest weeklies, with a circulation exceeding 100,000.

The federal parliament rejected an SPD motion to ban SS veterans' rallies. Such gatherings, which were held at various places during the year, were protested by politically middle-of-the-road organizations as well as the left, groups of Nazi victims, former resistance members, and Jewish circles. These groups tried unsuccessfully to obtain a government order barring a privately arranged reunion of members of Hitler's *Waffen*-SS 6th Mountain Division and veterans of the U.S. 70th Infantry Division. The American and German veterans, who had already been meeting informally for ten years, gathered at Bad Windsheim in Bavaria, where they laid wreaths at the World War II memorial.

West Berlin prohibited the use on car license plates of letter combinations associated with Nazi organizations and institutions, such as SS, SA, and the like. Similar regulations were already in force in other federal states.

Anti-Semitism

A marked rise in anti-Jewish attitudes and expressions among broad segments of the West German population was associated with three specific events, or types of events, that took place during the year: the Reagan-Kohl visit to Bitburg, the production of Rainer Werner Fassbinder's anti-Semitic play *Garbage, the City, and Death,* in Frankfurt, and the holding of SS veterans' rallies throughout the country. In all three instances, vocal Jewish protests triggered counterprotests and denunciations. Jews were accused of arrogant use of influence, of trying to impose censorship, of not really seeking reconciliation with Germans, of being insensitive to the Germans' need to honor their war dead. Many Germans also expressed resentment against what they regarded as the "privileged" treatment that had been accorded to Jews by the German government since the war.

The play by Fassbinder had been a focus of controversy since its first appearance in 1975, when protests succeeded in halting its presentation. Criticism of the work, which dealt with the destruction of a Frankfurt residential area to make way for commercial development, centered on the character of a real-estate speculator who was referred to only as "the rich Jew" and was depicted in blatantly stereotypical terms. Although the play's anti-Semitism was denounced by respected critics and public figures, the protests by the Jewish community that ultimately succeeded in preventing public presentation of the play evoked charges that Jews wielded too much power.

Interviews with young Jews revealed that anti-Semitism in West German schools was no rarity. Students referred, for example, to experiences with brutal "skinheads" who predicted new gas chambers for the Jews, and with "normal" fellow students who regarded Jews as "strangers" and said they did not want to hear about Auschwitz and other Nazi crimes anymore. As a result of the bias they experienced, Jewish students said they felt estranged from the non-Jewish environment and doubted if they could ever become fully integrated into German society.

Jewish circles were dismayed by the failure of West German political leaders to take a clear stand against anti-Jewish manifestations or to show understanding of Jewish sensitivities, especially with regard to the Bitburg and Fassbinder issues. Burkhard Hirsch, a spokesman for the FDP faction in the Bundestag (not a Jew), appealed to Germans to understand that Jewish criticism grew out of the "deep wounds that have not healed even 40 years after the Holocaust."

The year's anti-Jewish manifestations shocked and frightened Jews in the Federal Republic, especially the evidence of anti-Semitic bias among the young. The growth of Christian-Jewish and German-Israeli cooperative activities over the previous decades had lulled Jews into believing that German attitudes toward Jews had become positive.

The actual extent of anti-Semitism in Germany was difficult to assess, however. A study carried out in 1974 by Cologne sociologist Alphons Silbermann, published in 1982, found 20 percent of Germans expressing strong anti-Semitism and another 30 percent showing signs of latent bias. There was reason to believe that Silbermann's findings still held true in 1985, or even that anti-Jewish attitudes had increased, especially among the young. This development had begun in 1982 with the Israeli invasion of Lebanon, which produced anti-Jewish feeling in the guise of anti-Zionism and anti-Israelism, and was exacerbated by the Bitburg and Fassbinder episodes. Some observers suggested that the postwar generations, uninhibited by personal Nazi involvement, felt free to speak out on Jewish issues in ways never dared by their elders. Most young non-Jews, it was claimed, could not comprehend Jewish fears and insecurity; they were tired of public debate on the Nazi past, and they wanted Jews to stop exploiting their suffering to pressure the German people.

Nazi Trials

At the beginning of 1985, West German legal authorities were investigating some 1,400 persons suspected of involvement in Nazi crimes. The Central Agency for the Investigation of Nazi Crimes reported that since the end of World War II, West German public prosecutors had investigated a total of 90,196 persons, of whom

6,478 had been convicted and sentenced: 172 to life imprisonment, 6,191 to varying terms, 114 to fines, and one as a juvenile offender. In his annual report, Heinz Eyrich, justice minister in the state of Baden-Württemberg and responsible for the Central Agency, noted that 40 years after the fall of the Nazi regime, and 27 years after its own establishment, the agency's task had not yet been completed. Despite problems in obtaining convictions, such as the aging and ill health of suspects and a shortage of evidence, Eyrich said the agency was still receiving considerable documentary material on Nazi atrocities.

Legal actions during the year included the following:

Hagen: In October, at the conclusion of his retrial, former SS sergeant Karl Frenzel, 74, was again sentenced to life for his part in the mass murder of Jews at the Sobibor extermination camp.

Düsseldorf: In August, also after a retrial, former SS sergeant Heinz Wisner, 68, was sentenced to five years' imprisonment as an accomplice in the murder of two Jews at the Riga-Kaiserwald concentration camp.

Waldshut-Tiengen: In May former Nazi lieutenant Kurt Rahäuser was sentenced to three years in prison for complicity in the murder of eight Lithuanian slave workers in southwest Germany in April 1945.

Traunstein: In August Johann Hörner, 68, a former Russian auxiliary in the armed forces, was sentenced to three years for complicity in the murder of over a hundred Jews in the Ukraine in 1942.

Bochum: In January, after court proceedings lasting almost six years, former Gestapo official Helmut George Krizons, 68, was sentenced to three years in prison for complicity in the deportation and murder of over 15,000 inmates of the ghetto at Lodz.

Hamburg: In July former Gestapo official Harri Schulz, 70, was acquitted of the murder of seven Polish Jews. In October former Nazi police officer Otto Siemers, 70, was found guilty of complicity in the murder of about one thousand Jews at a concentration camp near Lublin in 1941. The jury withheld punishment, however, on the grounds that his personal part in the crime had been "minor": he left the camp after learning of the inmates' fate and openly declared that he felt ashamed to be a German.

Frankfurt: In September the court stopped the trial of former SS lieutenant Friedrich Paulus, 79, charged with complicity in a massacre in Poland, on the ground that the 20-year duration of the proceedings violated the international Human Rights Convention.

Bonn: In August the trial of former SS captain Modest Graf Korff, 76, was adjourned indefinitely on procedural grounds. Proceedings had opened in April against Korff and a codefendant, former SS sergeant Rudolf Bilarz, 75, both charged with complicity in the murder of over 70,000 French Jews. The trial of Bilarz had been dropped at the start on account of his ill health.

Lüneburg: In March the retrial opened of former SS sergeant Horst Czerwinsky, 62, charged with the murder of eight inmates of the Auschwitz subcamp at Lagischa.

Krefeld: In November former SS sergeant Wolfgang Otto, 74, went on trial for the murder of German communist leader Ernst Thälmann at the Buchenwald concentration camp in 1944.

The arrest of former SS lieutenant Walter Kutschmann, 72, in Buenos Aires, was reported in November. He had been sought for the murder of Jews and other civilians in Poland, and the Bonn government requested his extradition. The Syrian government failed to respond to an extradition request for former SS captain Alois Brunner, 73, reported to be living in Damascus, who, as a former aide to Adolf Eichmann, was sought for his part in the murder of over 100,000 Jews. The West Berlin public prosecutor was investigating 5 former judges and 12 prosecutors of the Nazi People's Court for their part in that body's proceedings.

In January, in the belief that former SS doctor Josef Mengele was still alive, the public prosecutor at Frankfurt increased the award offered by the state for information leading to his arrest from DM 50,000 to DM 1 million. In June the remains of a man believed to be Mengele were exhumed at Embu in Brazil, and a panel of Brazilian, West German, and American scientists confirmed the skeleton's identity. This appeared to end the 40-year hunt for the infamous Auschwitz experimenter.

Foreign Affairs

The visit to Bonn in the first week of May by U.S. president Ronald Reagan was the highlight of the diplomatic year. While the visit served to underscore the Federal Republic's firm alliance with the leading Western power, its success was marred by the controversy over Bitburg (see "40th Anniversary of Nazi Defeat") and by leftist demonstrations against U.S. policies in Nicaragua and Europe.

Seeking to defuse East European and Soviet opposition to West Germany's support for deployment of U.S. missiles, the Bonn government made efforts to strengthen its ties with the Communist states. In his "state of the nation" report to the federal parliament in February, Chancellor Kohl stressed his interest in cooperation with East Germany and emphasized that West Germany had no territorial claims against her eastern neighbors.

In March the chancellor attended the funeral in Moscow of Soviet state and party chief Konstantin Chernenko, at which time he met with Soviet representatives and East German state chief Erich Honecker. That same month, Foreign Minister Hans-Dietrich Genscher visited Moscow, Warsaw, and Sofia. A delegation of the Supreme Soviet paid a one-week visit to West Germany in April, at the invitation of the Bonn parliament, and a Bundestag delegation returned the visit in October. SPD opposition leader Willy Brandt met with Soviet leaders in Moscow in May.

Regarding the Middle East, the Bonn government expressed support for all initiatives aimed at bringing peace to that region, and hailed Israeli troop withdrawal from Lebanon as a major step in that direction.

The issue of arms sales to Arab states continued to be problematic, and the government seemed unable to follow a consistent policy. Following renewed requests for arms from Saudi Arabia, and against strong SPD opposition, the government declared that military support of Saudi Arabia would not be a threat to the region's security. However, talks with Saudi Arabia on the issue were not concluded. The government did grant permission to two West German companies, Thyssen and Rheinmetall, to engage in preliminary talks on plans to sell a multibillion-dollar plant to Saudi Arabia for manufacturing shells for tanks and artillery. Also, the Bonn government agreed not to oppose the sale of Tornado fighter jets —a joint British–West German–Italian development project—to Saudi Arabia by Great Britain. At the same time, a Bonn spokesman confirmed a previous decision, made in response to widespread demand, not to sell Leopard II tanks to the Arab kingdom.

President von Weizsäcker visited Jordan and Egypt in February and Israel in October (see below).

Relations with Israel

While the cordial relations that existed between the two countries were affirmed by their leaders on various occasions, there were also sharp exchanges over areas of difference. Bonn continued to maintain that no durable solution to the Middle East conflict was possible without Israeli recognition of the Palestinians' right to a national home and readiness to negotiate withdrawal from occupied Arab territories. In addition, Israel's policy of bombing Palestinian guerrilla targets in retaliation for terrorist attacks was condemned by both government and opposition parties, with the Greens, for example, charging that Jerusalem seemed more prepared to incite a new Middle East war than to seek peaceful coexistence.

In May, on the 20th anniversary of the establishment of diplomatic relations between the Federal Republic and Israel, Foreign Minister Genscher declared that his country was a reliable partner that would remain aware of its special commitment to the fate of the Jewish people. The SPD opposition leader in the Bundestag, Hans-Jochen Vogel, described ties with the Jewish state as "frank and friendly, but exposed to heavy strain," while Israel's ambassador to Bonn, Yitzhak Ben-Ari, said that mutual trust between the two countries had grown in the past years "in spite of all difficulties." Ben-Ari went on to say that "except with the United States of America, my country's relations with no other country are as important as those we have with the Federal Republic."

A high point in the year was the German president's visit to the Jewish state in October. President von Weizsäcker's crowded itinerary included a visit to the Museum of the Diaspora in Tel Aviv, where he presented a German state donation of DM 100,000 for various research projects. At the Weizmann Institute of Science he was awarded an honorary doctorate. Von Weizsäcker was praised by Israeli leaders for his clear stand on the Nazi past and Jewish suffering—as expressed in his Bundestag speech of May 8—as well as his friendship with Israel; commentators, however, pointed out that von Weizsäcker was not necessarily representative of the German people and could not influence his government's Middle East policy in any decisive way.

The Bonn government supported Israel's agricultural interests in the European Common Market. The government also contributed DM 921,000 for occupational training programs in Israel for Jews from Ethiopia. The two countries continued to cooperate in a wide range of economic, industrial, and agricultural endeavors, involving both the public and private sectors. These included West German participation in Israeli postal-modernization projects, cooperation in metal processing and technology, and joint agricultural projects in arid and semiarid countries. This year marked the tenth anniversary of the establishment of the German-Israeli Research and International Development Fund (GIFRID), which had carried out almost a hundred joint projects, with the Germans contributing about DM 3.5 million and the Israelis about DM 2 million.

West German and Israeli trade unionists observed the tenth anniversary of a friendship pact between the German trade-union federation Deutscher Gewerkschaftsbund and the Israeli Histadrut with a meeting in Israel in the spring. The German-Israeli Society (DIG) and its Israeli counterpart, the Israeli-German Society (IDG), held their ninth joint conference, attended by both Knesset and Bundestag members, in Tel Aviv in November. A conference held at Bonn in March brought together German, Israeli, and Palestinian representatives to discuss peace prospects in the Middle East. The meeting was sponsored by CDU's Konrad Adenauer Foundation and the Munich International Institute for Nationality Rights and Regionalism.

Germans and Israelis worked together in a variety of educational and cultural activities. A project begun in 1979, in which educators, authors, and historians studied the presentation of each country in the other's textbooks, culminated in September with the publication of the experts' findings and recommendations by the project sponsor, the Georg Eckert Institute for International School Book Research. Among a number of conferences arranged for teachers was a five-day seminar at Brunswick in October, which was the 11th of its kind arranged by the German Education and Science Union. Attended by Israelis and Germans, it dealt with methods for teaching about Jews and Judaism.

At the initiative of FDP's Friedrich Naumann Foundation, West German and Israeli authors met in Haifa in May for an exchange of information and views on cultural and political issues. The Haifa Municipal Theater, under the direction of Noam Semel, toured the Federal Republic with Joshua Sobol's plays *Ghetto* and *A Jewish Soul—Weininger's Night*.

According to an Israeli publication listing friendship and partnership agreements between Israeli and foreign townships and villages, 44 such agreements were with municipalities in the German Federal Republic. The municipalities participated in a variety of programs during the year, including social, cultural, political, youth, and sports exchanges. A new body, Haifa Foundation Germany, was incorporated in Düsseldorf in November; it planned to finance social and cultural projects in the Israeli city.

Jerusalem mayor Teddy Kollek was awarded the Peace Prize of the West German Booksellers Union at a ceremony held during the International Book Fair in

Frankfurt in October. Kollek was honored for his "untiring and committed support of Israeli-Arab reconciliation." Eighteen Israeli publishers were represented at the fair. The number of West German tourists to Israel climbed to 159,000, a 19-percent increase over the previous year.

The Service Cross of the Federal Order of Merit was awarded to the following Israeli citizens for noteworthy contributions to improved understanding between the two countries: Josef Tal, composer; Alexander Czerski, a blind author; Elchanan Scheftelowitz, rabbi and author; Fritz Joseph David, educator; Zvi Goldstein, Walter Gad Guggenheim, Karl Heinz Kornfeld, Sigmund Tittmann, and Erwin Wohl, leaders of the organization of Jews from Central Europe; Puah Menczel, pedagogue and author; Mordechai Surkis, former president of the Union of Israeli Local Authorities; and Naftali Sturm, trade unionist and Alignment representative. Israeli author Miriam Akiva received the year's Janusz Korczak Prize of the German Korczak Society at Giessen.

The Weizmann Institute of Science awarded an honorary doctorate to Hans-Hilger Haunschild, secretary of state at the federal Ministry of Research and Technology, for promoting German-Israeli scientific cooperation. His ministry had financed the establishment of a research center for computer science, Leibniz Center, at the Hebrew University. Ernst Gerhardt, the city of Frankfurt's treasurer, received an honorary doctorate from Tel Aviv University for his support of that institution's programs. The Volkswagenwerk Foundation contributed DM 1 million for the establishment of the Max Born Chair in Natural Philosophy at the Hebrew University.

In September Israel joined in mourning the death of West Berlin publisher Axel Springer, who had been a leader in the movement for German-Israeli reconciliation and had contributed generously to projects in the Jewish state.

A number of West German citizens who helped rescue Jews during the Nazi era were honored by Yad Vashem as "Righteous Gentiles," among them: Liselotte Flemming, Karl Stippler (posthumously), Elisabeth Stippler, Elly Hoffmann, and Fritz Strassmann (posthumously).

Bonn's ambassador to Israel for many years, Niels Hansen, retired in the fall; he was succeeded by foreign ministry official Wilhelm Haas.

JEWISH COMMUNITY

Demography

As of January 1, 1985, the 65 local Jewish communities in the Federal Republic and West Berlin numbered 27,561 members—14,024 males and 13,537 females. A year later, the communities registered 27,538 members—13,990 males and 13,548 females—with an average age of 44.3. There were estimated to be an additional 25,000 or so Jews who were not affiliated with any community.

In 1985 the Central Welfare Agency of Jews in Germany, located in Frankfurt, recorded 595 immigrants and 346 emigrants, 114 births, 519 deaths, and 52 conversions to Judaism. The largest Jewish communities, as of January 1, 1986, were those in West Berlin (6,101), Frankfurt (4,837), and Munich (4,030), followed by Düsseldorf (1,658), Hamburg (1,365), and Cologne (1,229).

Communal Activities

Commemorative events were held throughout the year to mark significant anniversaries related to the Holocaust.

The 40th anniversary of the liberation of the concentration camps was observed on April 21 with a ceremony at the Bergen-Belsen memorial site; the event was arranged by the Central Council of Jews in Germany, the community's representative body. Chancellor Helmut Kohl, Werner Nachmann, chairman of the Central Council's board, Arthur F. Burns, the U.S. ambassador to Bonn, and Mrs. Lola Fischel, a survivor of the camp, were the main speakers; President von Weizsäcker and other leading public figures were present at the ceremony. Kohl announced that his government would promote the establishment of an archive devoted to the history of German Jews and their contributions to German life.

Smaller ceremonies were held at Auschwitz in January and at Dachau in April, to mark the anniversaries of their liberation. At Dachau, some 5,000 people attended religious services and laid wreaths at the Jewish memorial. Speaking at the ceremony, Simone Veil of France, herself a survivor of Auschwitz, warned against trivializing the Nazi camps or treating them merely as artifacts of war.

Earth samples from Bergen-Belsen and Dachau were flown to Washington in October, as part of the ground-breaking ceremonies for the Holocaust Memorial Center there.

The Central Council dealt with a wide range of concerns, both external and internal. While anti-Jewish and neo-Nazi manifestations were troubling, the leadership of the community did not perceive any significant threat to its existence. Still, the Central Council stressed the need for vigilance and was vocal in its opposition to the holding of SS veterans' rallies and various neo-Nazi activities. Council representatives held talks with Israeli foreign minister Yitzhak Shamir on the occasion of his visit to Bonn in February, maintained contacts with international Jewish bodies on issues of common concern, and supported plans for visits to West Germany by Jewish youth groups from abroad.

Internally, the community was troubled by the issues of intermarriage, assimilation, and education. Council leaders appealed to community members to strengthen Jewish family life, emphasizing the importance of educating children in the Jewish tradition. The council also proposed that Jews who intermarried not be allowed to occupy leading positions in the community. Concerned about the alienation of young Jews, the council pleaded for intensified youth and educational activities in the local communities and urged Jewish students to enroll in the Academy for Jewish Studies in Heidelberg.

The cornerstone for a new synagogue was laid at Freiburg in the Black Forest in July, and the first phase in the erection of a new communal center in Frankfurt was completed in November. The Great Synagogue at Augsburg in Bavaria, which had been destroyed by fire during the pogroms of 1938, was reconsecrated in September. The Hamburg community celebrated the 25th anniversary of the opening of its New Synagogue.

WIZO Germany marked the 25th anniversary of its establishment. The Jüdischer Frauenbund (Jewish Women's League) continued its activities on behalf of women's interests and held its 15th Arbeitstagung (action meeting) at Cologne in November. Charlotte Knobloch was elected president of the Jewish community of Munich in November, succeeding Hans Lamm, who had died in March.

A new cooperation agreement was signed in Jerusalem in March between the Hebrew University of Jerusalem and the Academy for Jewish Studies in Heidelberg, which trained young Jews for leadership positions in the Jewish community and also offered courses in Judaism for non-Jews.

A contingent of 86 athletes and officials represented Makkabi Deutschland at the 12th Maccabiah in Israel in July. The team, which was accompanied by representatives of the West German sports organization Deutscher Sportbund, won four medals, among them one gold in the judo competition by Robert Spierer of Berlin.

The Bundesverband Jüdischer Studenten in Deutschland (BJSD, Union of Jewish Students in Germany) arranged seminars on political, cultural, and social issues in a number of West German towns. In an effort to fight apathy among young Jews, BJSD started publication of a new periodical, *Najes,* which covered politics, anti-Semitism on the campus, and problems of Jewish identity. Three issues were produced by the end of the year, with a circulation of 1,000 copies each.

The West German Jewish community was host to a number of Jewish visitors from abroad, including delegations from the American Jewish Committee, the Hebrew University, and Israeli trade unions. The president of B'nai B'rith International, Gerald Kraft, addressed the Foreign Affairs Association in Bonn on "The Jewish Community in the United States." Kraft and the group's executive vice-president, Daniel Thursz, met with representatives of the Central Council and were received by Chancellor Kohl and other West German political and public figures.

Culture

An event of special significance was the Leo Baeck Institute's fifth International Historical Conference, held in October in West Berlin. It was the first meeting of an international Jewish organization to take place on German soil since World War II. At the sessions, some 150 scholars from many countries considered various aspects of Jewish life in National Socialist Germany in the years 1933–1939.

Max Gruenewald, LBI president, spoke at the opening session about German Jewry's scholarly achievements and about the founding of the LBI 30 years earlier in order to preserve the historical past of German-speaking Jews. Addressing the same session, which was attended by leading political and intellectual figures, Chancellor Helmut Kohl thanked the organizers for meeting in Germany and thus affirming the possibility of German-Jewish coexistence. In an address that some observers saw as an attempt to repair the damage caused by Bitburg, the German leader said that past injustice and evil could not be undone, and that Germans had to examine why it all happened and what lessons could be drawn for the future. He also reaffirmed Germany's commitment to Israel; it remained firm, he declared, despite differences over specific political issues.

The gathering concluded with the ceremonial opening of an exhibit of German-Jewish art of the 18th to the 20th centuries that was organized jointly by the Berlinische Galerie and the LBI. The *Tagesspiegel* reviewer wrote, "This is doubtless the most important cultural-historical exhibit that Berlin has confronted since the war. It displays a major portion of that intellectual substance... cold-bloodedly murdered, while the city silently tolerated it.... One leaves the exhibit with a mixture of shame, shamefacedness, rage, and historical wonder."

Other exhibitions on Jewish subjects that opened during the year included "Jewish Publishing Houses in Germany 1933–1938," at the West Berlin State Library, in the fall; documents relating to the fate of Frankfurt-born Anne Frank, at the Frankfurt Paulskirche, during the summer; documents on Jewish emigration from Germany between 1933 and 1941, at the Frankfurt German Library, in November.

Georg Heuberger, 39-year-old Jewish jurist and sociologist, was appointed director of a Jewish museum in Frankfurt to be opened in 1987. The Volkswagenwerk Foundation allocated DM 300,000 for a research project on Jewish life in postwar Germany at Duisburg University.

The Warsaw Jewish Theater presented two plays about the Warsaw ghetto on West German stages in May: *Planet Ro,* by Ryszard Marek Gronski, and *Under Collapsing Walls,* by Szymon Szurmiej and Michael Szwejlich. The Traveling Jewish Theater from the United States performed in Hamburg in September.

Erwin Lichtenstein's *Report to My Family,* depicting the life of a German-Jewish emigrant, was chosen West German Book of the Month in May. The city of Dortmund's Nelly Sachs Literature Prize went to the South African author Nadine Gordimer. The Arts Prize of Darmstadt municipality was given to Roland Topor, artist and draftsman, in Paris, and the 1986 Book Prize of the German Union of Evangelical Libraries was awarded to Jewish poet Rose Ausländer, of Düsseldorf, for her collection of poems, *Mein Atem heisst jetzt* ("My Breath Means Now").

Christian-Jewish Relations

The German Coordinating Council of Associations for Christian-Jewish Cooperation took steps to develop closer cooperation with the Central Council of Jews in

Germany and with the German-Israeli Society. One issue of particular concern to all the groups was an increase in Christian missionary activity among Jews. The Coordinating Council's 1985 Buber and Rosenzweig Medal for outstanding contributions to Christian-Jewish relations was awarded to Catholic theologian Franz Mussner, professor at Regensburg University, a leading church official and author of numerous works on Christian-Jewish theological topics. The award was presented at the official opening of Brotherhood Week, at Augsburg, on March 3.

The International Council of Christians and Jews (ICCJ), with headquarters at the Martin Buber House in Heppenheim, observed the tenth anniversary of its establishment in February. Speakers at the anniversary celebration reviewed the group's efforts to eradicate racial and religious prejudice, citing as one noteworthy accomplishment the removal of biased descriptions of Judaism from many religious textbooks. In June, on the occasion of the 20th anniversary of Martin Buber's death, President von Weizsäcker visited ICCJ headquarters to take part in a discussion on "Martin Buber's Legacy for the Renewal of Christian-Jewish Relations Today."

West German government officials and political leaders held meetings throughout the year with Jewish representatives from the Federal Republic and abroad to exchange views and discuss affairs of mutual concern. In May, Alois Mertes, minister of state in the Bonn foreign ministry, addressed the 79th annual meeting of the American Jewish Committee in New York. He was the first West German official to appear before a national gathering of American Jews.

In New York in October, Chancellor Kohl met with representatives of major Jewish organizations to explain his perspective on the Bitburg episode. At the meeting, World Jewish Congress president Edgar M. Bronfman said that he had welcomed Kohl as "a good friend" and would say good-bye to him as "a better friend." He asked the German chancellor to support better education among young Germans about German-Jewish history.

Issues relating to the Nazi past and Jewish-Christian relations were on the agenda of the 21st German Evangelical Congress at Düsseldorf in June. In addition to an address by President von Weizsäcker, the group heard a number of Jewish speakers, including Michael Wyschogrod and Rabbi Marc Tanenbaum from the United States, Rabbi Ernst M. Stein of Berlin, and Rabbi Jakob Posen and Ernst L. Ehrlich from Switzerland.

Non-Jews who were honored by the government this year for the help they gave Jews during the Nazi period included Gertrud Luckner, 85, who received the Great Service Cross with Star of the German Order of Merit for her rescue activity and also for efforts in behalf of Christian-Jewish reconciliation following the war. Josef Engels, a 56-year-old chimney sweep, received the Service Cross for his support of Jews in the final phase of the war. Karl Ott received the Service Cross for tending the old Jewish cemetery at Buttenhausen and compiling a history of the village's former Jewish community.

The Frankfurt Jewish community's Honorary Seal in Silver was presented to the city's mayor, Walter Wallmann, in tribute to his endeavors in behalf of

Christian-Jewish understanding. Giessen municipality's Hedwig Burgheim Medal, named in memory of a local Jewish pedagogue, was given to Barbara Just-Dahlmann, German jurist and judge, for her contributions to Christian-Jewish and German-Israeli relations.

A number of West German towns and villages again invited former Jewish citizens who had emigrated to visit as guests of the municipalities. The town of Kitzingen welcomed the last prewar rabbi of its Jewish community, Isaiah Wohlgemuth, who resided in the United States.

Memorial stones and plaques to commemorate Jewish victims of Nazism were unveiled in the following towns: Trier, Hünfeld, Idar-Oberstein, Hennweiler, Bad Godesberg, Rendsburg, Berlichingen, and Elmshorn. A plaque was affixed to the building at Meinekestrasse 10 in the Charlottenburg district of West Berlin, showing that it had once housed the Palestine Office of the Jewish Agency, the Zionist Association in Germany, and other prewar Zionist groups.

Publications

New works relating to Jews and the Nazi era included: Marie-Luise Recker, *Nationalsozialistische Sozialpolitik im Zweiten Weltkrieg* ("National Socialist Social Policy in World War Two"; Oldenbourg); Gisela Bock, *Zwangssterilisation im Nationalsozialismus. Untersuchungen zur Rassenpolitik und Frauenpolitik* ("Compulsory Sterilization Under Nazism: Research on Policies on Race and Women"; Westdeutscher Verlag); Christian Zentner, ed., *Der Zweite Weltkrieg* ("The Second World War"; Delphin); Tomasz Szarota, *Warschau unter dem Hakenkreuz. Unterdrückung und Widerstand im Alltag* ("Warsaw Under the Swastika: Suppression and Resistance in Everyday Life"; Schöningh); Jürgen Schmädeke and Peter Steinbach, eds., *Der Widerstand gegen den Nationalsozialismus. Die deutsche Gesellschaft und Widerstand gegen Hitler* ("Opposition to Nazism: German Society and Opposition to Hitler"; Piper); Klaus Scholder, *Die Kirchen und das Dritte Reich. Bd.2: Das Jahr der Ernüchterung 1934. Klärungen und Scheidungen* ("The Churches and the Third Reich. Vol.2, The Year of Disenchantment 1934: Clarifications and Differentiations"; Siedler); Bedrich Fritta, *Für Tommy zum dritten Geburtstag. Ein Vater malt für sein Kind im KZ Theresienstadt 1944* ("For Tommy on His Third Birthday: A Father Paints for His Child at the Theresienstadt Concentration Camp in 1944"; Neske); Anton Maria Keim, ed., *Yad Vashem—Die Judenretter aus Deutschland* ("Yad Vashem—German Rescuers of Jews"; Grünewald/Kaiser); Joseph Walk, ed., *Als Jude in Breslau 1941. Aus den Tagebüchern von Studienrat a.D. Dr. Willy Israel Cohn* ("A Jew in Breslau 1941: From the Diaries of Former High School Teacher Dr. Willy Israel Cohn"; Bleicher); Heiner Lichtenstein, *Mit der Reichsbahn in den Tod. Massentransporte in den Holocaust 1941 bis 1945* ("To Death with the Railways of the Reich: Mass Transports in the Holocaust 1941– 1945"; Bund); Bernd Eichmann, *Versteinert, verharmlost, vergessen. KZ-Gedenkstätten in der Bundesrepublik* ("Petrified, Minimized, Forgotten: Concentration

Camp Memorial Sites in the Federal Republic"; Fischer); Werner T. Angress, *Generation zwischen Furcht und Hoffnung. Jüdische Jugend im Dritten Reich* ("Generation Between Fear and Hope: Jewish Youth in the Third Reich"; Christians); Dieter Rossmeisl, *Ganz Deutschland wird zum Führer halten . . . Zur politischen Erziehung in den Schulen des Dritten Reiches* ("All Germany Will Remain Loyal to the Führer: On Political Education in the Schools of the Third Reich"; Fischer); Matthias von Hellfeld and Arno Klönne, *Die betrogene Generation. Jugend im Faschismus. Quellen und Dokumente* ("The Deceived Generation: Youth Under Fascism. Sources and Documents"; Pahl-Rugenstein); Ludwig Eiber, ed., *Verfolgung, Ausbeutung, Vernichtung. Die Lebens- und Arbeitsbedingungen der Häftlinge in deutschen Konzentrationslagern 1933-1945* ("Persecution, Exploitation, Extermination; The Living and Working Conditions of Prisoners in German Concentration Camps 1933-1945"; Fackelträger); Herbert A. Strauss and Norbert Kampe, eds., *Antisemitismus. Von der Judenfeindschaft zum Holocaust* ("Antisemitism: From Hostility Toward Jews to the Holocaust"; Campus); Hans-Dieter Schmid/ Gerhard Schneider/Wilhelm Sommer, *Juden unterm Hakenkreuz. Dokumente und Berichte zur Verfolgung und Vernichtung der Juden durch die Nationalsozialisten 1933 bis 1945* ("Jews Under the Swastika: Documents and Reports on the Extermination of Jews by the Nazis 1933-1945," 2 vols.; Schwann-Bagel); Walter Schwarz, ed., *Die Wiedergutmachung nationalsozialistischen Unrechts durch die Bundesrepublik Deutschland* ("The Reparation of Nazi Injustice by the Federal Republic of Germany," 5 vols.; Beck).

New books on Judaism, Jewish history, culture, and religion included: Julius Guttmann, *Die Philosophie des Judentums* ("The Philosophy of Judaism"; Fourier); Heinz Kremers, Leonore Siegele-Wenschkewitz, and Bertold Klappert, eds., *Die Juden und Martin Luther—Martin Luther und die Juden. Geschichte, Wirkungsgeschichte, Herausforderung* ("The Jews and Martin Luther—Martin Luther and the Jews: History, Impact, Challenge"; Neukirchener); Herbert A. Strauss and Christhard Hoffmann, eds., *Juden und Judentum in der Literatur* ("Jews and Judaism in Literature"; Deutscher Taschenbuch-Verlag); Alphons Silbermann and Julius H. Schoeps, eds., *Antisemitismus nach dem Holocaust. Bestandsaufnahme und Erscheinungsformen in deutschsprachigen Ländern* ("Antisemitism After the Holocaust: Inventory and Manifestations in the German-speaking Countries"; Wissenschaft und Politik); Gottfried Schimanowski, *Weisheit und Messias. Die jüdischen Voraussetzungen der urchristlichen Präexistenzchristologie* ("Wisdom and Messiah: Jewish Preconditions of Early Christian Pre-Existential Christology"; Mohr); Heinrich Graetz, *Volkstümliche Geschichte der Juden. 6 Bände* ("Popular History of the Jews," 6 vols.; Deutscher Taschenbuch-Verlag); Nahum Goldmann, *Das jüdische Paradox. Zionismus und Judentum nach Hitler* ("The Jewish Paradox: Zionism and Judaism After Hitler"; Europäische Verlagsanstalt); Herbert Liedel and Helmut Dollhopf, *Haus des Lebens. Jüdische Friedhöfe* ("House of Life: Jewish Cemeteries"; Stürtz); Hans-Georg von Mutius, *Rechtsentscheide rheinischer Rabbinen vor dem Ersten Kreuzzug. Quellen über die sozialen und wirtschaftlichen*

Beziehungen zwischen Juden und Christen ("Legal Decisions by Rhenish Rabbis Before the First Crusade: Sources on Social and Economic Relations Between Jews and Christians"; Lang); Heinrich Pleticha, ed., *Das Bild des Juden in der deutschen Kinder- und Jugendliteratur 1800 bis heute* ("The Picture of Jews in German Child and Youth Literature from 1800 to This Day"; Königshausen und Neumann); Falk Wiesemann, ed., *Zur Geschichte und Kultur der Juden im Rheinland* ("History and Culture of Jews in the Rhineland"; Schwann-Bagel); Edmund Silberner, *Kommunisten zur Judenfrage. Zur Geschichte von Theorie und Praxis des Kommunismus* ("Communists on the Jewish Question: On the History of Theory and Reality of Communism"; Westdeutscher Verlag); Alfred Udo Theobald, ed., *Der Jüdische Friedhof. Zeuge der Geschichte—Zeugnis der Kultur* ("The Jewish Cemetery: Witness to History, Testimony to Culture"; Badenia); Gunter E. Grimm and Hans-Peter Bayerdörfer, eds., *Im Zeichen Hiobs. Jüdische Schriftsteller and deutsche Literatur im 20. Jahrhundert* ("Under the Sign of Job: Jewish Writers and German Literature during the 20th Century"; Athenäum); Ferdinand Seib, ed., *Die Juden in den böhmischen Ländern* ("Jews in the Bohemian Countries"; Oldenbourg); Klaus Meier-Ude and Valentin Senger, *Die jüdischen Friedhöfe in Frankfurt* ("Jewish Cemeteries in Frankfurt"; Kramer); Emmanuel Lévinas, *Wenn Gott ins Denken einfällt. Diskurse über die Betroffenheit von Transzendenz* ("When God Invades Our Thoughts: Discourses on the Perplexity of Transcendence"; Alber).

New biographical works and memoirs included: Friedrich Weinreb, *Das Wunder vom Ende der Kriege. Erlebnisse im letzten Krieg 1943–1945* ("The Miracle of the End of Wars: Experiences of the Last War 1943–1945"; Thauros); Schmuel Hugo Bergman, *Tagebücher und Briefe. Bd.1: 1901–1948. Bd.2: 1948–1975* ("Diaries and Letters," 2 vols.; Athenäum); Friedbert Aspetsberger and Gerald Stieg, eds., *Elias Canetti. Blendung als Lebensform* ("Elias Canetti: Delusion as a Form of Life"; Athenäum); Jacques le Rider, *Der Fall Otto Weininger. Wurzeln des Antifeminismus und Antisemitismus* ("The Otto Weininger Case: Roots of Anti-Feminism and Anti-Semitism"; Löckner); Dafna Mach and Tuvia Rübner, eds., *Martin Buber und Ludwig Strauss: Briefwechsel* ("Martin Buber and Ludwig Strauss: Correspondence"; Lambert Schneider); Jakob Hessing, *Else Lasker-Schüler. Biographie einer deutsch-jüdischen Dichterin* ("Else Lasker-Schüler: Biography of a German-Jewish Poet"; Loeper); Lotte Köhler and Hans Saner, eds., *Hannah Arendt–Karl Jaspers. Briefwechsel 1926–1969* ("Hannah Arendt–Karl Jaspers: Correspondence"; Piper); Friedrich Georg Friedemann, *Hannah Arendt. Eine deutsche Jüdin im Zeitalter des Totalitarismus* ("Hannah Arendt: A German Jewess in the Epoch of Totalitarianism"; Piper); Manès Sperber, *Ein politisches Leben. Gespräche mit Leonhard Reinisch* ("A Political Life: Conversations with Leonhard Reinisch"; Deutsche Verlags-Anstalt); Marcel Reich-Ranicki, ed., *Meine Schulzeit im Dritten Reich. Erinnerungen deutscher Schriftsteller* ("My School Time in the Third Reich: Memoirs by German Authors"; Deutscher Taschenbuch-Verlag); Paul Michael Lützeler, *Hermann Broch. Eine Biographie* ("Hermann Broch: A Biography"; Suhrkamp); Schlomo Krolik, ed., *Arthur Ruppin—Tagebücher, Briefe, Erinnerungen* ("Arthur

Ruppin—Diaries, Letters, Memoirs"; Athenäum); Jakob Katz, *Richard Wagner—Vorbote des Antisemitismus* ("Richard Wagner—Harbinger of Antisemitism"; Athenäum); Peter Sichrovsky, *Wir wissen nicht was morgen wird, Wir wissen wohl was gestern war—Junge Juden in Deutschland und Österreich.* ("We Do Not Know What Will Be Tomorrow, But We Know What Was Yesterday—Young Jews in Germany and Austria"; Kiepenheuer & Witsch); Elias Canetti, *Das Augenspiel. Lebensgeschichte 1931–1937* ("The Play of Eyes: Life Story 1931–1937"; Hanser); Marc Chagall, *Bonjour Paris* (Herder); Chagall and Mayer, *Wie schön ist deine Liebe* ("How Beautiful Is Your Love"; Echter).

New editions of collected works and translations included: Moses Mendelssohn, *Gesammelte Schriften. Jubiläumsausgabe. 20 Bände* ("Collected Writings: Jubilee Edition," 20 vols.; Fromman-Holzboog); Franz Kafka, *Amtliche Schriften. Mit einem Essay von Klaus Hermsdorf* ("Official Writings: With an Essay by Klaus Hermsdorf"; Akademie-Verlag, East Berlin). Vera Hacken edited a series of translations from Yiddish, including: Isaac Leib Perez: *Die Seelenwanderung einer Melodie* ("The Transmigration of a Melody"); Scholem Aleichem: *Das bessere Jenseits* ("The Better Beyond"); Mendele Moicher Sforim: *Die Mähre* ("The Mare"); Schalom Asch: *Mottke der Dieb* ("Mottke the Thief"); Josef Opatoschu: *Bar-Kochba* ("Bar Kochba") (Thienemanns).

Among new works of fiction published this year were Meir M. Faerber, *Drei mal drei Glieder einer Kette* ("Three Times Three Links of a Chain"; Bleicher); Esther Kreitmann, *Deborah—Narren tanzen im Getto* ("Deborah—Fools Dancing in the Ghetto"; Alibaba); David Markisch, *Narren des Zaren* ("The Czar's Fools"; Klett-Cotta); and Peter Härtling, *Felix Guttmann. Jüdisches Schicksal im Dritten Reich* ("Felix Guttmann: A Jewish Fate in the Third Reich"; Luchterhand).

Personalia

The Theodor Heuss Foundation in Bonn, named for the first president of the postwar German Federal Republic, announced in December that its 1986 Theodor Heuss Prize would be awarded to Werner Nachmann, chairman of the board of the Central Council of Jews in Germany, "out of deep-felt gratitude . . . for his contributions to reconciliation," to "the integration of Jewish returnees in postwar German society," and the "enhancement of relations between Germany and Israel." The Ruperto Carola University at Heidelberg appointed Nachmann an honorary senator the previous October.

Alexander Ginsburg, secretary-general of the Central Council, received the Great Service Cross with Star of the West German Federal Order of Merit on the occasion of his 70th birthday. The same honor was bestowed on Alphons Silbermann, noted professor of sociology at the University of Cologne. Leo Adlerstein, Düsseldorf attorney and Jewish community leader, received the Great Service Cross. The Service Cross was awarded to Jakob Altaras, physician and head of the Jewish community in Giessen; Jakob Fern, Jewish communal leader in Stuttgart; Julia

Aronowitsch, WIZO chairwoman in West Berlin; and Walter Lippmann, Hamburg attorney, on the occasion of his 90th birthday.

The Freedom of the City of Hamburg was awarded for the first time to a woman, Ida Ehre, 85, noted actress and theater director, for major contributions to the cultural and spiritual renewal of that city after World War II. Martha Blum, chairwoman of the Jewish community in the Saarland, received the Order of Merit of that federal state for her part in the building of Jewish communal life and her efforts in behalf of the blind in Germany and Israel. Wolf Weil, chairman of the Bavarian Jewish community of Hof for almost 40 years, received the Golden Citizens' Medal of that town.

SPD chairman and former chancellor Willy Brandt received the International Peace Prize of the Albert Einstein Peace Prize Foundation in Washington, D.C., for his continuing contributions to reconciliation and world peace. The Freedom of the City of Sarajevo, Yugoslavia, was conferred on Zwi-Hermann Wollach of Stuttgart, for helping Yugoslav prisoners of war, partisans, and Auschwitz inmates at the end of World War II.

Among German Jews who died in 1985 were Hans Lamm, president of the Jewish community of Munich, leading member of the Central Council of Jews in Germany, historian, journalist, and author of books on German-Jewish history, in March, aged 71; Wilhelm Unger, author and journalist, founder of the German Library in London during his emigration, cofounder of Germania Judaica—the noted library of German Jewry in Cologne—and a leader in Jewish-Christian dialogue, in December, aged 81; and Samuel Kessler, a prominent leader of the Cologne Jewish community, in March, aged 73.

FRIEDO SACHSER

German Democratic Republic

THE NUMBER OF registered Jews in the German Democratic Republic (GDR) dropped to about 400 in 1985, of whom approximately half were in East Berlin. The steady aging of the community (a quarter were reported to be over 80) was the main cause of the community's decline. The number of Jews not affiliated with the organized community was estimated at several thousand.

Representatives of the Jewish community attended various international Jewish meetings abroad, including those of the World Jewish Congress, in Vienna; the European Union of Jewish Students, in Cordoba, Spain; and the International Council of Christians and Jews, in Dublin, Ireland. In September Helmut Aris, president of the Union of Jewish Communities in the GDR, and Peter Kirchner, head of the East Berlin Jewish community, addressed a meeting at the East German Culture Center in Paris and met with representatives of French Jewish groups.

Among the growing number of Jewish visitors to the GDR from abroad were a delegation from the American Jewish Committee, headed by its president, Howard Friedman; Alan Rose, vice-president of the Canadian Jewish Congress; Gerhart Riegner, vice-president of the World Jewish Congress; several rabbis from the United States, including Ernst Lorge of Chicago, who conducted High Holy Day services in East Berlin; and Richard Yellin, of Boston, who addressed a Christian gathering at Leipzig.

Since there was no rabbi in East Berlin, Rabbi Ernst Stein and Cantor Estrongo Nachama came frequently from West Berlin to participate in communal functions. Leaders of the community reported that Jews continued to enjoy "full and equal rights" in the GDR and to receive regular subsidies from the state for communal institutions and activities. Jews were represented in the National Front, a body comprising delegates of the five East German political parties, public organizations, and religious groups; they also maintained contacts with Jewish communities and organizations abroad.

A number of special events marked the 40th anniversary of the defeat of the Third Reich and the liberation of Nazi prisoners and victims of persecution. Memorial services held at the former concentration camps of Buchenwald, Ravensbrück, and Sachsenhausen were attended by thousands of non-Jews, as well as Jews. On the anniversary of the Nazi surrender, Horst Sindermann, president of the East German People's Chamber (parliament), paid homage to the war dead, including the "six million Jews who died as a result of criminal Fascist policy." The Union of Evangelical Churches in the GDR arranged several memorial meetings, one of which paid tribute to the Jewish dead. Special memorial services held at the Marienkirche in East Berlin were attended by Rabbi Albert Friedlaender of London.

To mark the 50th anniversary of the passage of the Nuremberg racial laws, the Christian-Jewish committee "Kirche und Judentum" sponsored an international conference at Leipzig. A gathering arranged at the Dresden synagogue by the Jewish community to commemorate the November 1938 pogroms was attended by East German officials and guests from abroad, among them Gerhart Riegner, who delivered a message on behalf of the World Jewish Congress. A memorial plaque was unveiled at the site of the former synagogue in Mühlhausen in September.

On the cultural scene, the 50th anniversary of the death of painter Max Liebermann was observed at a gathering arranged by the Jewish community in conjunction with the East German Arts Academy. The Evangelical Academy at Berlin-Brandenburg organized a seminar in March on "Jews in Europe Between 1933 and 1945," which was addressed by Dr. Riegner. The East Berlin publisher Union Verlag issued a new work on Jewish philosophy by Prof. Heinrich Simon and Marie Simon.

Herbert Ringer, vice-president of the Union of Jewish Communities, was awarded the Fatherland's Order of Merit in Gold, on the occasion of his 80th birthday. Siegmund Rotstein, chairman of the Jewish community of Karl-Marx-Stadt, received the Fatherland's Order of Merit in Bronze, for his contributions to the upbuilding of the East German state and Jewish communal life. Elisabeth Bergner, 87, noted German-Jewish actress living in London, received GDR's Hans Otto Medal, for her achievements in the theater and films.

In July a court at Frankfurt on Oder convicted Otto Balke, former member of a Nazi police battalion, of war crimes against humanity in Poland and the Soviet Union and sentenced him to life imprisonment. Official sources reported that GDR courts had convicted almost 12,900 Nazi suspects since the war, of whom 127 were sentenced to death and 266 to life imprisonment.

In May the office of the East German attorney general announced that it had handed over extensive documentary evidence on crimes committed by members of the Nazi People's Court to the justice ministers of Belgium, France, Holland, and Austria. The office noted that not a single judge of this court had been tried and sentenced in West Germany so far, despite the fact that extensive evidence had been passed to West German authorities by GDR agencies as far back as the late 1950s.

East German state agencies and the press issued a steady stream of pro-Arab, anti-Israel, and anti-Zionist statements. Communist state and party chief Erich Honecker called for a Middle East conference to be attended by all interested parties, including the Palestine Liberation Organization (PLO), and confirmed his government's "unwavering solidarity with all patriotic Arab forces." East Germany continued to admit Palestinians to its military academies and signed an agreement with the PLO for increased cultural and scientific cooperation. The Germans undertook to provide fellowships for Palestinian students at East German universities and medical care for injured Palestinians at East German hospitals.

FRIEDO SACHSER

Eastern Europe

Soviet Union

Domestic Affairs

ON MARCH 11, 1985, Mikhail Gorbachev became the fourth Soviet Communist party leader of the 1980s, succeeding Konstantin Chernenko, who died after only a year in office. In contrast to his three elderly predecessors (Chernenko, Yuri Andropov, and Leonid Brezhnev), Gorbachev entered office at the relatively young age of 54, following a meteoric rise through the Stavropol-area Komsomol and party hierarchies. Gorbachev's rise to the general secretaryship of the party was widely interpreted, in and out of the USSR, as the definitive end of the "Brezhnev Era," which had begun in 1964. Soviet citizens and foreign observers alike looked to see how Gorbachev would deal with his country's mounting problems: a sluggish and increasingly corrupt economy and society; a stagnant political system that seemed to have lost some of its dynamism at home and much of its appeal abroad; and increased tensions between the superpowers.

In the first months of his regime, Gorbachev moved quickly in the area of personnel, more cautiously in the area of policy. In the month following his assumption of office he named three new members of the Politburo, including the head of the KGB. A number of government ministers were retired, and on lower levels many changes were made in both party and state hierarchies.

In September the chairman of the Council of Ministers ("prime minister"), Nikolai Tikhonov, retired at age 80 and was replaced by Politburo member and economics specialist Nikolai Ryzhkov, aged 56. Earlier, Foreign Minister and long-time diplomat Andrei Gromyko had been made chairman of the Presidium of the Supreme Soviet ("president" of the USSR) and been replaced by Eduard Shevardnadze, a younger man with no foreign-policy experience, whose career had been in the party apparatus of Georgia.

A major change instituted by Gorbachev was a widely publicized campaign against alcoholism, the country's most severe social problem. From the specific measures put into effect, it seemed clear that this was not going to be a repeat of previous half-hearted programs but a long-term effort to change deeply ingrained habits and behavioral patterns.

Another theme struck by the new leader was the need for more *glasnost,* openness and frankness, in Soviet society. Problems of red tape, venality, irrational behavior on the part of officials, *pro forma* fulfillment of official duties, and lack of enthusiastic participation in political activities were some of the subjects which began to be discussed more openly. Both the possibilities and the limitations of the new *glasnost* were illustrated by an episode involving Yevgeniy Yevtushenko, the well-known poet and writer. Addressing a closed session of the Writers Congress in December, he strongly criticized censorship, special privileges, cover-ups of Stalin's purges, the enormous human losses during the collectivization drives, and the rewriting of history to suit political needs. However, what was allowed in a speech to a closed group could not be revealed to a mass readership: the published version of the poet's address in *Literaturnaia gazeta* (December 18) omitted many critical references.

Gorbachev's approach to improving the Soviet economy leaned toward upgrading the quality of leadership, creating more effective policies, and eliminating corruption, rather than making major structural changes. Though proposals for such reforms were discussed openly, and officials made favorable comments about Hungarian economic reforms, no major structural changes were carried out in the Soviet economy in 1985. One small but noteworthy change was announced in November: five ministries and a state committee dealing with agriculture were abolished and their functions combined in a new "superagency," the State Committee for Agro-Industrial Complexes.

Human Rights

In December Elena Bonner, wife of Andrei Sakharov, the scientist and champion of human rights, arrived in Italy for medical treatment, following a long struggle for permission to go abroad. Although she had agreed not to make public statements concerning her husband's and her own exile in the city of Gorky, it became clear that Sakharov had gone on extended hunger strikes until she was allowed to leave.

In line with earlier commitments, at the end of the year the Soviets permitted two Soviet citizens to emigrate in order to join their American spouses. Although the problem of "divided families" had long been under discussion by the USSR and the United States, it was apparent that the issue would not be resolved quickly. For example, American-born Abe Stolar received permission for himself, his wife, and his sons to emigrate; however, since permission was refused for his son's wife, the entire family decided to remain in the USSR.

Foreign Affairs

Since neither Secretary Gorbachev nor Foreign Minister Shevardnadze had had any significant experience in international relations prior to his elevation to high office, the new regime proceeded cautiously in the international arena. Limited probes were made toward China and Japan, and in December it was announced that, for the first time in 20 years, Chinese and Soviet foreign ministers would exchange visits (in 1986). The Soviet leadership failed in its attempt to negotiate Euromissile agreements directly with France and Britain but succeeded in establishing diplomatic ties with Zimbabwe and the United Arab Emirates.

East-West relations proceeded unevenly. On the one hand, there were tensions around several cases of spying and defection. On the other hand, a summit meeting between Gorbachev and President Ronald Reagan of the United States took place in Geneva in November. Although the summit produced no major breakthroughs, the talks were generally described as cordial and useful. Agreements were reached on a number of lesser items, such as air safety, environmental protection, and the reestablishment of educational, scientific, cultural, and athletic exchanges between the two countries.

Two weeks after the summit meeting, a U.S.-Soviet agreement on academic cooperation was signed. The five-year agreement, covering more than a hundred joint research groups, included projects in Judaic studies, mainly the cataloging and publication of large collections of Judaic manuscripts in libraries in Moscow and Leningrad. No progress was made on the trade issue. Addressing 400 American business representatives in Moscow on December 10, Gorbachev said that "political obstacles" were preventing "normal" Soviet-American trade, among them the Jackson-Vanik Amendment, which linked most-favored-nation status to free emigration.

Relations with Israel

Hopes were raised on several occasions during the year that a change in Soviet attitude toward Israel might be in the offing. In July the Soviet ambassador to France, Yuli Vorontosov, met with the Israeli ambassador to that country, Ovadia Sofer. Early in October, on a visit to France, Gorbachev told a press conference that once the situation in the Middle East was "normalized," the Soviet Union could consider restoring diplomatic relations with Israel. According to the report in *Izvestiia,* the Soviet leader said, "There will be no obstacles for us then. We recognize the sovereignty of that state and its right to life and to security. But as to how security is understood, as to how Israel's ruling circles and we understand it—there are major differences here."

Toward the end of October, when world leaders gathered in New York to mark the 40th anniversary of the founding of the United Nations, Israeli prime minister Shimon Peres met with Soviet foreign minister Shevardnadze. A few days later, stopping off in Paris on his way home, Peres reported a French offer to fly Soviet Jews directly to Israel, in the event that the USSR agreed to expand emigration and permit such flights. According to the *New York Times* (October 26), Peres also "strongly suggested" that if the USSR were to permit mass emigration, Israel might consider Soviet participation in a Middle East peace conference.

In addition to increased diplomatic contacts, there were a few other indications of a slight thawing in the Soviet attitude toward Israel. For the first time since 1967, an Israeli television correspondent was permitted to work in the Soviet Union. Also, a Soviet delegation spent a week in Israel, commemorating the 40th anniversary of the defeat of Nazi Germany. Subsequently, an Israeli delegation that included past and present Knesset members visited Moscow, Leningrad, and Tashkent at the invitation of a Soviet peace committee.

Counterbalancing the hopeful signs, the USSR cast its customary vote against seating Israel in the General Assembly. Among the Soviet bloc countries, Rumania and Yugoslavia voted for seating Israel, as they had in the past. For the first time, however, Poland and Hungary, which had always voted with the opposition, abstained.

JEWISH COMMUNITY

Demography

The Jewish population of the USSR was estimated at 1.8 million, with the largest concentration in the Russian republic (700,651) and the second largest in the Ukraine (634,154), where Jews were the third-largest nationality.

Some direct figures on intermarriage among Jews became available, albeit limited to one Soviet republic. Boris Viner defended a dissertation at Leningrad State University on "Inter-Ethnic Marriages in the Ukraine, 1923–1982, Based on a Study of Vinnitsa." He found that in the early 1980s nearly 40 percent of marriages involving Jews were ethnically mixed. This proportion was about the same as among Ukrainians, but significantly lower than among Russians, and much lower than among Poles of the area. Previous estimates had placed Jewish intermarriage in the Ukraine at somewhat less than 40 percent, about one-third.

Emigration and Emigration Activists

In 1985, 1,139 Jews emigrated from the USSR, slightly more than the 869 who left in 1984 but far below the annual figures for the 1970s. The number of those who had requested *vyzovs* (invitations to emigrate) was estimated at about 400,000.

The government continued its persecution of Hebrew teachers and emigration activists. At least a dozen Jews were arrested and sentenced, usually to three-year sentences, mostly on charges of "hooliganism," "anti-Soviet slander," or "anti-Soviet propaganda." Thus, for example, when 53-year-old Mark Niepomniashchy appealed to the West on behalf of the arrested Yakov Levin, his daughter's fiancé, Niepomniashchy was sentenced to three years for "anti-Soviet slander." Leonid Volvovsky, arrested in Gorky, and Leonid Shrayer, of Chernovtsy, were given similar sentences. Among others jailed or sentenced to labor camps were Alexander Kholmiansky, Roald (Alex) Zelichonok, Yevgeniy Aizenberg, Vladimir Frenkel, and Vladimir Brodsky. Anatoly Virshuvsky of Moscow, a 24-year-old observant

Jew, was arrested in Kiev on charges of stealing books from the local synagogue. Yuri Fedorov, the last defendant in the 1970 Leningrad trials still behind bars, was released after serving his full term, but Alexei Murzhenko, the other non-Jewish defendant in those trials, was rearrested for alleged parole violations (he had served a 14-year term). Yevgeniy Koifman of Dnepropetrovsk was arrested on drug charges, as were others, all of whom claimed the police had planted the drugs. Dmitri (Dan) Shapiro was arrested and tried in June, receiving a suspended sentence because he had "repented" and "did not represent a social danger." He made a public recantation of his Zionist beliefs on television.

In November the *New York Times* reported a "senior Reagan administration official" as saying that if the Soviet Union would allow a "significant movement" of Jews and others from the USSR, the United States would move to ease trade restrictions. For their part, the Soviets continued to maintain that the Jackson-Vanik Amendment, "as is known, aims at making the development of trade-economic ties between the USSR and USA dependent on irrelevant issues" (*Moscow News*, October 29–November 1). Toward the end of the year, while there was no increase at all in the overall number of emigrants, some well-known and long-standing refuseniks were allowed to leave. In the early fall, Isaac Shkolnik of Vinnitsa and Mark Nashpits of Moscow received exit permits for Israel, both having been "in refusal" for more than a decade, and both having been imprisoned for Zionist activities. World Jewish Congress president Edgar Bronfman met with Eliahu (Ilya) Essas in September and urged his release when meeting with Soviet officials. In December, Essas, one of the leaders of the *ba'al t'shuvah* movement (newly observant Jews), was permitted to leave for Israel, where he and his family were reunited with his parents. Yakov Mesh of Odessa, a Zionist activist who had been severely injured in prison, was also allowed to emigrate.

Anti-Zionism and Anti-Semitism

Soviet media, books, mass media, and official spokesmen continued to condemn and attack Zionism as a major force for evil in the world. In November *Leningradskaia pravda* published a long article "exposing" Hebrew study groups as centers of Zionist activity. Based on statements by "Soviet citizens who had fallen under the influence of certain nationalistic and pro-Zionist elements," the writer concluded that the *ulpanim,* or Hebrew study groups, were used by foreign contacts sent by "Zionist centers" to deliver information which is "of a pronounced propagandistic, pro-Zionist nature." Further, the article charged, *ulpan* participants "vote for Komsomol decisions at meetings, but in the evenings they run to the synagogue and study literature supplied by Zionist emissaries, wittingly or unwittingly preparing themselves for a 'struggle against the Soviet regime on a narrow front.' No one is allowed to do this in our country, and they will not be allowed to."

The Anti-Zionist Committee of the Soviet Public, which thus far did not seem to have opened the local branches originally proposed, or even to be particularly active, sent a telegram to the U.S. Congress protesting the "715 anti-Semitic acts of vandalism, insults and attacks on Jews and Jewish organizations" reported to have taken place in the United States during the previous year. The committee, a body composed of well-known Jews, opposed "all forms of chauvinism, whether Zionism or anti-Semitism" and called on American lawmakers "to do all necessary to put an end to these acts" and to secure the human rights and personal safety of all American citizens.

Soviet officials continued to deny the existence of anti-Semitism in the USSR. *Pravda* and *Isvestiia* both published (October 2) Mikhail Gorbachev's press conference statement that "if there is any country in which Jews enjoy the political and other rights that they do in our country, I would like to hear about it." According to Gorbachev, "the Jewish population, which makes up 0.69 percent of the country's total population, is represented in its political and cultural life on the order of at least 10 to 20 percent."

Religion

There was no significant change in the religious life of Soviet Jewry in 1985, at least not in the numbers of synagogues (about 60) and rabbis (10–12). There was some evidence of a growing tendency among young people to adopt a religious way of life, especially in Moscow and Leningrad. It was estimated that in Moscow 300 persons, the great majority under the age of 30, were involved in systematic study of Bible, Talmud, and other religious works. Outside the two major cities, this phenomenon of *ba'alei t'shuva* was not as widespread.

Culture

Soviet sources reported considerable activity in Judaic scholarship. Early in the year, the Leningrad branch of the Russian-Palestine Society (founded in 1882 as the Russian Orthodox Palestine Society) honored the noted Hebraist Klavdia Borisovna Starkova, on her 70th birthday, with a special gathering. Ten of the twelve papers read at the event related to Hebrew, biblical studies, or the history of Palestine. Shimon Yakirson and Igor Voevutskii, both described as "young scholars," presented papers on early Hebrew books, on collections of religious books compiled in the 19th century by M. Fridland and D. Chwolson, and on Judaeo-Spanish. M. Zislin spoke about two medieval Hebrew grammarians, Ibn Janah and Abu Al-Faraj Harun Ibn Al-Faraj. The Leningrad branch of the society was reported by *Sovetish haimland* (No. 8, p. 162) to have about 50 members "of different generations."

The 850th birthday of Maimonides was commemorated in an article by Samuil Kliger and Efim Drutz in *Sovetish haimland* (No. 9), in which the authors assert that "Maimonides' philosophical heritage is relevant today. It is suffused with the spirit of optimism, rationalism, and belief in people's creative potential. In its content it is not a strictly Jewish heritage, but its ethical pathos, its call to peace in the world, express the international hopes of all peoples." The authors devote six pages to a biography of Maimonides, noting that his scientific work influenced Soviet medicine; they also refer to a Russian translation of his *Guide for the Perplexed* that appeared in 1969.

Papers on contemporary Hebrew language were delivered at meetings of the Institute of Slavistics and Balkan Studies of the Academy of Sciences. Candidates of Linguistic Sciences Alexander Barulin and Alexandra Eikhenvald were reportedly developing a computerized system for translating from Russian to Hebrew. In November TASS announced that the Nauka publishing house would publish a book entitled *Contemporary Hebrew* by Eikhenvald, to include essays on Hebrew syntax, morphology, and phonetics. Eikhenvald, who was born in 1957 into a long-assimilated Jewish family, was a graduate of the applied linguistics department at Moscow State University. Her senior thesis was on Hittite languages, her candidate's thesis on Berber languages. She studied Hebrew with Candidate of Historical Sciences Mikhail Chlenov, and had been employed since 1980 by the Oriental Institute of the Academy of Sciences, in Moscow.

One-third of the book *Lyrical Poetry of the Ancient East*, published this year by Nauka, is a translation into Russian of the biblical Song of Songs. The translator, the well-known Semitics specialist I. Diakonov, based his translation on a text of the Bible from the year 1008 that was found in the Leningrad Saltykov-Shchedrin Library.

The Leningrad Institute of Oriental Studies published a catalogue of Hebrew incunabula, arranged by Shimon Yakirson and Ilya Shifman. The State Ethnographic Museum of the Estonian Republic, located in Tartu, issued an annotated catalogue of its Jewish collection of about 110 items, prepared by the Estonian Yiddish-speaking scholar Paul Ariste.

The administrator of the Yiddish and Hebrew sections of the Lenin State Library in Moscow, Leib Angovich, estimated that there were 30,000 Hebrew and 25,000 Yiddish books and periodicals in the general holdings, among them the Ginzburg collection of mainly 16th- to 18th-century items, mostly of a religious nature, and the Poliakov collection of some 15,000 items, including Hebrew incunabula and books from the 16th and 17th centuries. In an interview with *Sovetish haimland* (No. 10, p. 149), Angovich related that he was born in Kaunas (Kovno), Lithuania, graduated from a secular Hebrew *gymnasium*, and served in the Soviet army from 1940 to 1973. He began working in the Lenin Library in 1978.

Announcement was made of a forthcoming anthology of Yiddish prose and poetry in Lithuania (19th century to 1941), to be published in two volumes in 1987 in Lithuanian translation. The editor, 28-year-old Emanuelis Zingeris, was writing a doctoral dissertation on "Lithuanian-Yiddish Literary Connections."

On August 18 the 10,000th issue of the newspaper *Birobidzhaner shtern* appeared. Writing on the publication's philosophy, the editor, Leonid Shkolnik, took pains to point out that the newspaper was not limited to Jewish subjects. "When we write about successes or shortcomings in this or that group we do not differentiate according to the nationalities involved. The newspaper is fully Soviet and Communist." Shkolnik mentioned eight "veteran" and seven "young" members of the staff. The latter, he said, learned Yiddish on their own and "develop their knowledge of the language in the course of their work."

Also in Birobidzhan, it was reported that Zinaida Belman was teaching Yiddish in "one of the groups of the Birobidzhan Pedagogic School." Some of her former students were employees of the *Birobidzhaner shtern* and some were actors in the local people's theater. As her texts, she was using the recently published Russian-Yiddish dictionary and a new primer, *Alefbais.*

The Jewish Musical Chamber Theater was included in the program of the Twelfth World Youth Festival in Moscow. The report in *Sovetish haimland* (No. 10, p. 142) stressed that Israeli participants in the festival were particularly impressed, because "in the Jewish state there is no Yiddish theater."

The Moscow Jewish Dramatic Ensemble, directed by Yakov Gubenko, gave performances in six cities in the RSFSR during the year. In Moscow it presented Arkady Stavitsky's *40 Sholem Aleichem Street,* a topical play about the emigration of a Jewish family from Odessa and the reactions of neighbors to their departure.

David Belkin, identified as a Candidate of Philological Sciences, published an article in *Sovetish haimland* (No. 4) about a critique of the Habimah Theater written by Maxim Gorky in 1918. (Habimah was a Hebrew-language company that originated in Russia, left the country in the 1920s, and settled in Palestine, where it became the leading repertory theater.) What is noteworthy about the Belkin piece is that the author nowhere mentions that Hebrew was the language of the theater, or the fact that the company left the USSR, or why.

In the area of popular culture, national television showed a Russian-language performance of Sholem Aleichem's *Tevye* during prime viewing time. Reviews in major newspapers, including *Pravda, Izvestiia, Literaturnaia gazeta,* and *Sovetskaia kultura,* were uniformly positive, especially in praise of the actors. Neither *Pravda* nor *Izvestiia* mentioned the words "Jew" or "Jewish" even once, and *Pravda* described Tevye merely as a "resident of Kasrilevke." All the reviews stressed the universality of the story, and some noted the vivid depiction of Tevye's "patriotism" and attachment to his homeland.

Personalia

USSR People's Artist Maia Plisetskaia, a ballerina with the Bolshoi Ballet, received the title of Hero of Socialist Labor with the Order of Lenin and the Hammer and Sickle Gold Award for contributions to Soviet choreography.

Among prominent Soviet Jews who died in 1985 were pianist Emil Gilels, aged 69; painter Vladimir Veisberg, aged 60; Rabbi Israel Shvartsblat, formerly of Odessa and most recently instructor in Talmud at the Moscow Choral Synagogue, in his 70s; and Genrikas Oshervich Zimanas, veteran Communist activist and former editor of the Lithuanian party newspaper, aged 76.

ZVI GITELMAN

Soviet Bloc Nations

THE SELECTION OF Mikhail Gorbachev as general secretary of the Soviet Communist party, in March, brought no sign of any loosening of the military, political, and economic ties within the Soviet bloc. Moreover, at a meeting in April of the Warsaw Treaty Organization (established 1955), the member nations renewed the pact, unchanged, for another 20 years, with an automatic extension of 10 additional years built into the agreement. On the economic front, except for the German Democratic Republic (GDR), whose economy seemed to be on an even keel, most of the countries of the area experienced serious problems in 1985.

Bulgaria

In Bulgaria the standard of living dropped markedly, as a harsh winter strained Bulgarian resources to an extent unknown since the 1950s. The major social and political issue of the year was the campaign to "Bulgarize" the Turkish minority —some 10–15 percent of the population—by discouraging Turkish-language use in public, closing mosques, restricting religious practices, and prohibiting emigration to Turkey.

JEWISH COMMUNITY

The Jewish population of Bulgaria was estimated at about 5,000. According to the local Jewish newspaper, during the previous five years, 420 Jews had been awarded highest national honors in science, culture, and politics. The community continued to publish its yearbook in Bulgarian and in English translation.

Czechoslovakia

The political leadership continued on its cautious, conservative path, reassuring new Soviet leader Gorbachev that there would be no Czech deviations from orthodoxy in either foreign or domestic policies. Church-state conflict flared up over the 1,100th anniversary of St. Methodius, a national as well as a religious hero. Despite efforts by the state to play down the religious significance of the occasion and to emphasize its cultural importance, about a quarter of a million people attended celebratory masses. The Czechoslovak government maintained its militantly anti-Zionist posture and, unlike Hungary and Poland, had few if any contacts with Israel. Still, 29 Israelis, former inmates of the Terezin camp, were invited for a two-week tour of the country, during which they participated in ceremonies marking the 40th anniversary of the camp's liberation by the Soviet army.

JEWISH COMMUNITY

The Jewish population of Czechoslovakia was estimated at 5,000. There were said to be 5 functioning Jewish communities in Bohemia and Moravia and 11 in Slovakia. The only rabbi in the country was the recently ordained Daniel Meyer, aged 27, a graduate of the Budapest Jewish Theological Seminary. His wedding in March was attended by official representatives of the Hungarian Jewish community and by other foreign visitors.

The North American and British tours of the "Precious Legacy" exhibit, composed of ritual and domestic objects from the State Jewish Historical Museum in Prague, focused Western attention on the history of Jews in Czechoslovakia. The success of the exhibit apparently resulted in some increase in Western Jewish tourism to that country.

Hungary

The Hungarian economy ran into difficulties in 1985, with declining exports to the West, energy shortfalls, and a foreign debt that rose to nearly $9 billion. Under its recently reformed system, which loosened government controls and allowed more free-market competition, wealth differentials were perhaps greater in Hungary than anywhere else in Eastern Europe. One result was an increase in social instability, with divorce and suicide rates among the highest in the world and a crime rate that seemed to be rising.

JEWISH COMMUNITY

With no firm data available on the size of the Hungarian Jewish population, estimates ranged from 35,000 to 100,000.

The community suffered the loss of two major personalities during the year. Professor Alexander Scheiber, rector of the Budapest Jewish Theological Seminary, the only such institution in Eastern Europe, passed away on March 3, at the age of 71. Professor Scheiber's scholarly interests encompassed several fields, including rabbinics, linguistics, and folklore. His Friday-evening lectures were popular among younger elements of the Jewish population, and his books reached a wide audience. In July Chief Rabbi Laszlo Salgo of Budapest died at the age of 75. In the months prior to his death, Dr. Salgo had taken over some of Professor Scheiber's functions at the seminary and had also been elected to the national parliament. In earlier years, Dr. Salgo officiated at the Dohanyi Street Temple, one of the largest in the world, but that building had been closed for some time, in need of major repairs to make it safe for public use. The adjacent Jewish Museum was closed during the winter months because the heating system, dating to the prewar era, had broken down.

For the first time in its history, Hungary issued a series of postage stamps depicting Jewish art in the country, primarily ritual objects.

Poland

With Poland's economy continuing to slip, General Wojciech Jaruzelski's military regime tried hard to improve its image abroad, at least partially in order to regain international confidence so as to obtain economic assistance. The elections to the national parliament (Sejm) in October were regarded as a crucial test of "normalization," that is, of a return to civilian rule. Since leaders of the now illegal Solidarity organization had called on the people to boycott the election, the government made the voting a test of its and Solidarity's relative strength. Not surprisingly, in the event, both sides claimed victory, with the authorities citing 21 percent nonparticipation and Solidarity, 34 percent. Even if one accepted the government figure, the turnout was the lowest by far of any national election since 1947.

JEWISH COMMUNITY

The Jewish population of Poland was estimated at 5,000, of whom nearly 2,000 were registered with the religious community.

The Eighth Congress of the Social and Cultural Society of Polish Jews (TSKZ) elected Szymon Szurmiej of the Warsaw Yiddish Theater as chairman of its Central Board, and A. Kwaterko as vice-chairman. Szurmiej was elected to parliament in the October national election.

The 40th anniversary of the liberation of Auschwitz was observed with special ceremonies at the camp site. Two members of the Knesset, eight "Mengele twins" —of whom five were from Israel—and a dozen or so other survivors, with relatives and friends, participated in the event, which included a symbolic reenactment of the two-mile death march from Auschwitz to Birkenau.

Israeli Stefan Grayek, president of the World Federation of Jewish Fighters, Partisans, and Camp Inmates, was awarded a medal by the central board of ZBoWiD, the Polish veterans' association. An Israeli delegation was present at the ceremony, held in Warsaw. Later in the year, Grayek and Yitshak Arad, of the Yad Vashem Institute in Jerusalem, decorated 50 Poles for acts of heroism during the war. The ceremony took place in the presence of Polish government, party, and military officials.

A number of gestures favorable to Jewish culture and Israel were made by the authorities during the year. The change in attitude may have stemmed from a desire to improve Poland's image among world Jewry—believed by some Poles to play a major role in world financial markets and international politics—or from a growing appreciation of the role Jews had played in Poland's history and culture. Either way, the result was small steps being taken to restore some semblance of a Jewish cultural presence in Poland and to improve cultural ties with the Jewish state.

A lectureship in Yiddish was established at the University of Warsaw in January, with Michal Frydman of the TSKZ named as lecturer. Roman Marcinkowski of the same university, which offered instruction in Hebrew, participated in a conference at the Hebrew University of Jerusalem on the teaching of Hebrew.

The Public Committee for the Preservation of Jewish Cemeteries and Cultural Monuments carried out a survey of Jewish cultural remains in 14 cities, compiling a list of the most important extant Jewish cemeteries. With the help of a donation of $50,000 received from a group of American rabbis, the committee was able to complete restoration work on the graves of Gerer, Belzer, Bobover, and other Hasidic rabbis. A plaque was affixed to the building that once housed the yeshivah Khachmei Lublin, one of the largest and most famous of the 1930s, forced to close after the Nazi invasion of 1939. The building had since become part of the Marie Curie-Sklodowska University.

The American musical *Fiddler on the Roof* was given six performances in April, in Warsaw, by the Gdynia Musical Theater. This company presented the first Polish version of the show in Lodz in 1983 and performed it in Poznan and Gdynia in 1984. Proceeds from all 120 performances to date were contributed to the above-mentioned committee to preserve Jewish monuments.

A Polish theater group was warmly received when it performed in Tel Aviv, and talks were held regarding a proposed visit by the Israel Philharmonic Orchestra to Poland. There was also a proposal to send the Cameri Theater of Tel Aviv and an Israeli dance company to Poland, and the Warsaw Philharmonic and the ballet of the Polish National Opera to Israel, in 1986.

Excerpts from the film *Shoah*, produced by Claude Lanzmann of France, were shown on Polish television, followed by a televised studio debate. The program stimulated a great deal of press commentary, particularly concerning the portrayal of Poles in the film. Typical of reaction in Poland was a long commentary by Jerzy Turowicz, editor-in-chief of *Tygodnik Powszechny*, an independent Catholic newspaper published in Krakow. Writing in the issue of November 10, 1985, Turowicz criticized Lanzmann's "anti-Polish, anti-Catholic and anti-peasant prejudices," asserting that "Polish anti-Semitism, which we do not mean to diminish or justify, had nothing to do with the extermination of the Jews." Turowicz also criticized Lanzmann for ignoring the Nazi persecution of Poles and for neglecting to show that "hundreds of thousands" of Poles had actively aided the Jews during the German occupation. Like some of Lanzmann's milder critics abroad, including Jan Karski, the courier who brought out news of the Warsaw ghetto to the West and who was featured in the film, Turowicz reprimanded the filmmaker for ignoring the fact that the Western allies "did nothing" to help the Jews, even after they learned of what was happening.

Rumania

Continuing efforts to reduce his country's huge foreign debt, President and Party Secretary Nicolae Ceausescu imposed drastic measures to cut energy consumption. These included a ban on heat in private dwellings and public places, electrical power stoppages, a three-month ban on private automobile traffic, and cuts in television programming. Industrial production was disrupted, and many foodstuffs were unavailable or in extremely short supply.

Several ambitious plans were announced by Ceausescu. One called for moving pensioners out of the cities and resettling them in the countryside. Another was the construction of a grandiose political-civic center in the heart of the older section of Bucharest. To make room for the structure, several historic churches and monasteries were taken down, and major portions of the traditional Jewish quarter were slated to be razed.

JEWISH COMMUNITY

The Rumanian Jewish population, standing at 26,000 in 1985, was declining rapidly as a result of emigration and the high mortality rate of an aged population. In each of the preceding few years about 1,000 Jews had died and between 1,000 and 1,500 had emigrated, most to Israel. Population figures for some individual communities, based on communal records, were: Timisoara—1,400, only 50 of whom were under age 20; Sibiu—121; Arad—900, with fewer than 20 children; Bacua—700; Dorohoi—366; Piatra Neamt—378; Botosani—411; and Iasi—around 1,800.

The central body of Rumanian Jewry, the Federation of Jewish Communities, headed by Chief Rabbi Moses Rosen, encompassed over 60 local communities. Religious schools *(talmudei torah)* functioned in 24 communities, with a total enrollment of between 500 and 800 students. The number of functioning synagogues was down to 105 (from 120 in 1983); there were 18 choirs and 4 amateur orchestras under Jewish auspices; 11 cities and towns had kosher restaurants. There were only three rabbis for the entire country and eight ritual slaughterers. In Bucharest, Iasi, and a few other communities, a total of nearly 600 people who were unable to go to the kosher restaurants were provided with "meals on wheels." There were about 450 beds in six old-age homes, three of them in Bucharest and the others in Timisoara, Arad, and Dorohoi. The communities in Bucharest, Botosani, and Iasi also ran day centers for the elderly. The largest old-age home, situated in Bucharest, and named in honor of Chief Rabbi Rosen and his wife, had 210 beds in a modern, well-equipped facility.

A major event of the year was the visit of Prime Minister Shimon Peres in February. During an official visit to Rumania, the Israeli leader paid his respects to the Bucharest Jewish community. He was greeted by a large audience in the Choral Synagogue, where he delivered an address.

Chief Rabbi Rosen was elected for the seventh time as a deputy to the Grand National Assembly.

Yugoslavia

Yugoslavia continued to experience social unrest caused by conflicting nationalist groups and severe economic difficulties. By November the cost of living was 100 percent higher than it had been the previous year, the inflation rate was the highest in Europe, and about 1.3 million persons were unemployed. Officials looked to sales of the Yugo automobile in the United States, which began during the year, to help reduce the country's $23-billion foreign debt.

JEWISH COMMUNITY

The Yugoslav Jewish community numbered only about 5,000 and included many intermarried families. According to a demographic study carried out by the Belgrade Jewish community at the end of 1983, 33 percent of the Jews in the capital were over 65 years old, 28 percent were aged 46–65, and only 11 percent were under 26.

Despite its small size, the Yugoslav Jewish community was well organized and active. The community-run Pirovac summer camp enrolled some 120 children, the majority Yugoslavs and the rest residents of other socialist countries. A "Little Maccabiah" athletic competition held on the island of Brac attracted about 400 participants.

At a ceremony held in the Federation of Jewish Communities building in Belgrade, the only rabbi in the country, former partisan fighter Tsadik Danon, was awarded the Order of Merit with Golden Wreath by the president of Yugoslavia. Professor Teodor Kovac, a medical scholar and vice-president of the Novi Sad Jewish community, was awarded the Order of Merit with Golden Rays, on the occasion of the 40th anniversary of the victory over Nazism and fascism.

The community continued to publish *Pregled,* a Jewish review, in 2,700 copies, and the *Zbornik,* a scholarly publication, in 1,000 copies. A functioning library and a museum were housed in the building of the federation in Belgrade. There was one professional Jewish communal worker in Belgrade and one in Zagreb. The latter city had the only Jewish old-age home.

ZVI GITELMAN

Israel

IF THE MOOD OF Israel at the beginning of 1985 was one of tremendous uncertainty—over the stalemated war in Lebanon, intolerable economic pressures, mounting Arab terrorism, and a rise in domestic extremism—by the end of the year it had become decidedly more confident. Under the leadership of Prime Minister Shimon Peres and the national unity government, the Israel Defense Forces (IDF) withdrew from Lebanon—thus effectively ending the war that had begun in 1982 —and a major economic recovery plan was introduced. These two events generated a rapid turnabout in the mood of the country.

The War in Lebanon

The new government was pledged to carry out a withdrawal from Lebanon, but without compromising security in the northern part of the country. To that end, it had begun talks in November 1984 with Lebanese military officials, meeting under UN auspices in the town of Nakoura in southern Lebanon. Even as the parties negotiated the crucial matter of who would take control of the areas to be evacuated by Israel—making little progress—the violence continued.

Within the first ten days of 1985, ten Israeli soldiers were wounded in various clashes, Israel Air Force (IAF) planes attacked a base of a Syrian-backed terrorist organization in the Beka'a Valley, and the crack Golani Brigade killed three terrorists in an ambush near the Awali River in southern Lebanon. On January 9 Israel informed UNIFIL (United Nations Interim Force in Lebanon) that it would not return to the stalled Nakoura talks, and four days later the cabinet began discussing a plan for the unilateral withdrawal of all Israeli troops.

Following two lengthy sessions, on January 14 the cabinet decided, by a 16–6 vote (all the nay votes were cast by Likud ministers, including Vice-Premier and Foreign Minister Yitzhak Shamir), on a three-stage withdrawal from Lebanon, to begin in February in the Sidon area. No specific time frame was set for the second and third stages, the intention being to examine the on-ground effects of each phase before proceeding with the next. However, the cabinet resolution did specify that a security zone immediately north of the Israel-Lebanon border would be "maintain[ed]" by the IDF in coordination with the South Lebanon Army (SLA). In a painful counterpoint to the withdrawal decision, two Israeli soldiers were killed and a third fatally wounded on the very day it was taken.

Seeking to prevent the emergence of a dangerous power vacuum in the Sidon area following the IDF's pullback and to enable the Lebanese government to assert its sovereignty there, on January 22 Israel returned to the Nakoura talks. However, under pressure from Syria, the Lebanese delegation refused to discuss the immediate postwithdrawal situation around Sidon until Israel presented a detailed plan for a total withdrawal from Lebanon. The upshot was that Israel declared the talks suspended, indicating that internal developments in Lebanon were now "Lebanon's responsibility and Lebanon's problem."

The new Israeli attitude was spelled out by Defense Minister Yitzhak Rabin in an early February speech to the Conference of Presidents of Major Jewish Organizations, meeting in New York. Pulling no punches, Rabin said that "Syria came out of the war in Lebanon with the upper hand vis-à-vis Israel in terms of deciding the political future of Lebanon. [Syria] won in that respect." Looking ahead, the defense minister—alluding to a declaration by Prime Minister Menachem Begin at the outset of the war in 1982—asserted: "We are not promising any more that not one Katyusha rocket will fall on an Israeli settlement. No one can prevent that."

Stage one of the Israeli withdrawal from Lebanon was completed on February 16, at which time the port city of Sidon and the surrounding area to the east and south reverted to local Lebanese authority.

On March 3, two weeks after the Sidon pullback, the cabinet gave the go-ahead for the second stage of the withdrawal, from the Beka'a Valley—opposite Syrian forces—and from part of the central sector. The period between the first and second stages of the withdrawal was marked by a major upsurge of terrorist attacks by fanatic Shi'ite elements on IDF troops in Lebanon, which took a fearful toll of Israeli lives. The worst episode occurred on March 10, when 12 soldiers were killed and 14 wounded, many seriously, when a suicide car-bomber detonated the vehicle he was driving as it passed an open military truck just north of Metullah. In response to such incidents the IDF adopted a so-called iron-fist policy, dispatching patrols to flush out hostile elements in villages throughout southern Lebanon.

As Israeli casualties mounted, on March 16 some 20,000 persons attended a demonstration in Tel Aviv, organized by the Peace Now movement to protest the pace of the withdrawal from Lebanon and the price it was exacting. Interviewed the following day on CBS-TV's "Face the Nation" program, Prime Minister Peres indicated that Israel was in fact accelerating the pace of the pullback, stating, "We are on our way out, not only from the land of Lebanon but also from the politics of Lebanon."

By the end of March, six weeks after the introduction of the iron-fist policy in southern Lebanon, the IDF had killed about 70 guerrillas, arrested over 500 persons suspected of affiliation with them, combed 23 villages, and demolished 84 buildings that either belonged to the detainees or in which combat matériel was found. On March 26, Defense Minister Rabin upped the ante in southern Lebanon when he told the Knesset's Defense and Foreign Affairs Committee that Israel would resort to a "scorched-earth" policy if Shi'ite terrorism did not cease.

On April 2–3, the IDF, "out of a desire to improve its relationship with the local population" in southern Lebanon (as an official IDF announcement put it), released 752 prisoners, mainly Shi'ites, from the Ansar detention facility near Tyre, which was dismantled prior to the second stage of the withdrawal. Another 1,200 detainees, deemed too dangerous for release at that juncture, were transferred to the Atlit detention facility in Israel. The IDF communiqué ended by noting that the detainees moved to Israel would be released "in accordance with developments in southern Lebanon, as IDF forces withdraw from Lebanon." (These prisoners were subsequently to become the focus of the demands of the hijackers of a TWA passenger plane; see "Terrorism.")

On April 11, two days after two Israeli soldiers were killed when a young Arab woman blew herself up together with the booby-trapped car she was driving, the IDF completed the second stage of its Lebanon withdrawal, this time pulling out of a 300-square-kilometer area in and around Nabatiyeh. This left the IDF in control of some 2,000 square kilometers, or 19 percent of the country's total area. (At the peak of its involvement, in September 1982, the IDF was in control of 3,400 square kilometers, or fully 33 percent of Lebanese territory.)

Ten days later the cabinet authorized the IDF to proceed with implementation of the third and final stage of its withdrawal "by the beginning of June." Speaking to reporters after the cabinet meeting, Defense Minister Rabin explained the three goals of the government's defense plans for the country's north: "the redeployment of the IDF along the international border, from where it will do whatever is necessary to defend Israel"; the establishment of "a security zone adjacent to the Lebanon-Israel border," based on local civil guards; and the use of its "right of self-defense" to thwart any incipient terrorist activity anywhere in Lebanon that could endanger Israeli security.

On April 24—as it happened, Memorial Day for those who fell in Israel's wars—the IDF withdrew from the Beka'a Valley on the eastern front, followed five days later by a pullback from the Tyre area. This left all the remaining Israeli troops in Lebanon within the actual security zone: an area 8–15 kilometers wide, comprising 11 percent of Lebanese territory, with a population of 235,000, including 135,000 Shi'ites. Although the intention had been to complete the pullback on the third anniversary of the war's outbreak, June 6, the final withdrawal from the security zone was delayed by a few days, due to a spate of attacks on the IDF and concomitant doubts within the defense establishment as to the effectiveness of General Antoine Lahad's South Lebanon Army. The IDF carried out several search-and-patrol missions in the area, demolishing a number of houses belonging to terrorists and seizing arms and ammunition. At the same time, in a gesture intended to show that a peaceful option was also available to the residents of southern Lebanon, on May 29 the IDF released 249 of the prisoners it had earlier transferred from the Ansar facility to Israel.

Finally, on June 10, three years and four days after it had begun, Israel's direct military involvement in Lebanon came to an end. Inauspiciously, within hours two

Katyusha rockets landed in Upper Galilee, and the following day two Israeli soldiers were wounded in a security-zone clash in which four Arab gunmen were killed. Despite these setbacks, the new three-pronged Israeli conception regarding defense of the northern border proved its worth for the remainder of 1985. While a number of soldiers were wounded over these six months, and about 20 Katyusha rockets hit various parts of Galilee sporadically, only two soldiers were killed (August 5) in Lebanon in the entire second half of 1985. (Their deaths brought to over 660 the number of soldiers and security personnel killed in Lebanon in the war's three years.)

On the credit side of the ledger, 13 car-bombs and two bombs attached to mules were detected and neutralized in the security zone, and not a single would-be infiltrator was able to reach Israeli territory. On September 10, the last of the Shi'ite detainees still being held in Israel were released. December 2–3 saw the deepest strike by Israeli ground forces into Lebanon since the June withdrawal, as an IDF infantry unit killed five terrorists from Ahmed Jibril's organization, captured several others, seized arms, and stymied preparations for raids against Israel. "We will act wherever and whenever operational needs dictate in our war against terrorism," military sources were quoted as saying.

Economic Developments

The second major achievement of the national unity government in its first full year in office was effecting a turnabout in the economy. This was not unrelated to the winding down of the war in Lebanon, with its prodigious cost, officially put at $1.3 billion prior to the expenditures entailed in the withdrawal itself. The most dramatic evidence of the change was a drop in the inflation rate from a dizzying 150 percent in the first seven months of the year to just 14 percent in the final five months, after the introduction of the economic recovery plan at the beginning of July.

Prior to the implementation of the plan, the government adopted a number of stopgap measures, notably an "Agreement on Stabilizing the Economy," entered into jointly with the Histadrut (General Federation of Labor) and private industry on January 24. The eight-month accord, which came into effect on February 2, was designed to replace the three-month "package deal" that had been signed in November 1984. (See AJYB, vol. 86, 1986, p. 312.) For the average Israeli, the immediate effect of the new agreement was deleterious: drastically slashed government subsidies on basic commodities resulted in huge price increases, notably, 55 percent in public transportation and 25 percent in basic foodstuffs. On top of this, salaried workers had to cope with a 7.5-percent shortfall in their wages over the following three months. In a further effort to curb spending and put a brake on the outflow of dollars, the travel tax was upped from $100 to $150 per person, and a 20-percent levy was imposed on the cost of tickets for foreign travel. The public was further disgruntled when the Treasury, ignoring calls from the Histadrut, decided to further raise prices of subsidized items by up to 20 percent just before the Passover holiday, when purchases of these goods were traditionally heavy.

Yet the net effect of these stringent measures was a jump in the April inflation rate of 19.4 percent. Announced May 15, this figure galvanized the government into action. A 12-hour cabinet session on May 19 produced additional tax increases and a three-month freeze on wages in the public sector. As a means of stimulating production, workers in industry and in the export-oriented sector were to receive incentive tax breaks; however, one week later the government decreed yet another 25-percent increase in the prices of subsidized goods, which were then to be frozen until the beginning of August. With no apparent end in sight to the economic instability, the country was rocked by a spate of strikes, industrial sanctions, slowdowns, and work stoppages. Employers, too, mounted protests, and a number of manufacturers simply stopped production until they were granted the price rises they sought.

Just as the economy seemed about to lurch totally out of control, the government took its most dramatic action yet. On July 1, after a record 24-hour cabinet meeting, Prime Minister Peres and Finance Minister Yitzhak Modai informed the nation of a drastic plan to save the Israeli economy from total breakdown. (The vote was 15–7 with one abstention, by Defense Minister Rabin, who objected to the size of the cut in the defense budget; as in the case of the Lebanon-withdrawal decision, all the nay votes were cast by Likud ministers.) Prime Minister Peres told the nation in a television interview that the primary reason for the new plan was "to prevent an actual collapse." "Time had run out," Peres said, "we had to adopt acute measures."

The main points of the plan were: a devaluation of the shekel by 18.8 percent and a freeze on the new rate of 1,500 shekels to the U.S. dollar; a $750-million reduction in the deficit of the state budget; ruthless slashes in subsidies to the point where prices in public transportation were doubled, water went up by 82 percent, electricity by 53 percent, and postal services by 40 percent; a 17-percent across-the-board price rise in most other goods and services, though some prices were upped a good deal more; a three-month freeze on wages; a 3-percent cut in staff, meaning about 10,000 jobs, throughout virtually the entire public sector (excluding defense, security, and education); and a lowering of VAT (value-added tax) to its former level of 15 percent just six weeks after it was upped to 17 percent.

Infuriated by the plan, especially by those elements directly affecting workers, the Histadrut called an unprecedented one-day general strike in the country on July 2. Violent demonstrations protesting the new measures erupted in one of Jerusalem's underprivileged neighborhoods. An unusual political convergence of views emerged when Histadrut secretary-general Israel Kessar was joined in his vehement attacks on the economic plan—and, by inference, on his own Labor party leadership—by Deputy Prime Minister David Levy from Herut. Levy's public denunciation of the plan and his failure to attend the Knesset vote on the measures (July 1) led to calls in Labor for his dismissal, but these were rebuffed by the Likud.

Despite sporadic protests, including an unruly demonstration by several thousand civil servants in front of the Knesset, on July 8 the government easily defeated four motions of no confidence on the economic plan. Replying on behalf of the government, Prime Minister Peres listed its three primary aims: to reduce inflation to a minimum without generating large-scale unemployment; to help the poorest section of the public cope; and to set the country on the road to economic growth. Subsequently, the government and the Histadrut reached agreement—under the latter's threat to call an indefinite general strike—on a series of wage supplements and on the dismissal of public-sector workers, with the government agreeing to act in this matter according to existing labor agreements and not to implement emergency regulations.

One indication that the recovery plan stood a good chance of achieving its aim was the decision by Histadrut-owned chain stores and supermarkets to reduce prices in order to offset the drastic reduction in the public's purchasing power. This trend grew during the remainder of the year, as Israelis began to rediscover what it was like to live in a relatively noninflationary world, after years of coping with annual price rises of hundreds of percent. Total inflation from August through December ran at just 14 percent, with the November rate of 0.5 percent the lowest for any month in 9 years and the lowest for a November in 15 years. December's 1.3-percent CPI increase was the lowest in a decade for that month.

In October the Knesset extended the emergency regulations for various parts of the economic recovery plan until June 1986. This came just after a government move that Israelis could hardly believe: an actual reduction, of 4 percent, in the prices of all fuels.

The state budget for fiscal 1985—in the amount of 20.2 trillion shekels, or approximately $23.3 billion—was passed by the Knesset at 1:40 A.M. on March 29, following a marathon special session and protracted delays caused by disagreements over allocations to religious institutions. A less publicized aspect of the budget, one with serious long-term implications, was the cabinet decision to slash the defense budget by some $600 million. Recognizing the gravity of its action, the entire cabinet, in a highly unusual move taken at the defense minister's request, agreed to accept ministerial responsibility for Israel's security preparedness. Concern about security and about the future of the country's aircraft industry may explain the decision taken on August 21 by the inner cabinet to proceed with the highly controversial and extremely costly Lavi jet fighter project. (The vote was 8–2; the dissenters were Finance Minister Modai and Minister Without Portfolio Ezer Weizman.)

The imposition of austerity measures produced a series of financial crises. These occurred not only in government corporations and public institutions—including the country's hospitals and universities, along with Israel Shipyards—but also in major private concerns, such as the country's largest construction company, Clarin, whose collapse left thousands of families without apartments and without funds, and the Kopel tourism concern. In addition, after a year of debates, delays, and deferments, the government decided not to rescue the veteran Haifa-based Ata textile firm, long one of the symbols of Israeli industrial proficiency. Not even the new pride of Israeli industry, the high-tech corporations, escaped the pinch. Elscint, a multinational concern manufacturing advanced medical-imaging equipment, was hit by losses, and in November Prime Minister Peres himself intervened to get banks to reschedule the company's debt repayments.

The country's banks were themselves in the spotlight during much of the year. Israeli economic life had focused heavily on the Tel Aviv stock exchange, where, until the bank-shares collapse of 1983, easy profits had seemed almost divinely ordained. On the final day of 1984 the state comptroller published his report on the collapse, in which he assailed the financial and banking establishment. Although the heads of Israel's four largest banks, all of whom were implicated in the comptroller's report—as were senior officials in the Bank of Israel and leading politicians responsible for economic policy at the time of the crisis—asserted that they would not resign, public pressure led to the establishment of a judicial commission of inquiry into the matter. In late January, Supreme Court Justice Moshe Beisky was named to head a five-man panel, whose other members were a district court judge and three university professors.

On March 17 the eighth judicial commission of inquiry in Israel's history began its public hearings, in Jerusalem. The first witness was the chairman of the Tel Aviv Stock Exchange, Meir Heth, who was followed during the rest of the year by a veritable "who's who" of the Israeli financial establishment. On June 19, 16 individuals and 11 commercial banks and government agencies received letters from the commission—as required by law—warning that they were liable to be "harmed" by its findings. The hearings continued throughout the year.

Inflation in 1985 was 185.8 percent, high by any criterion, but a major improvement over the almost 450 percent of 1984. From August through December, once the economic recovery plan took effect, the inflation rate was less than 10 percent of what it had been for the first seven months of the year.

Tourism was up by 14 percent from the previous year, and revenues from tourism were 7 percent higher than in 1984. Nevertheless, there was an ominous tapering off of tourism in the second half of the year, which most observers attributed to an upsurge in acts of terrorism in Israel and abroad.

The trade deficit showed a marked improvement in 1985, standing at $4 billion, or 17 percent lower than in 1984. If defense imports—which increased by 25 percent—were subtracted, the trade deficit decreased by no less than 35 percent. Israeli exports in 1985 stood at $10.7 billion, an overall increase of 2 percent over 1984.

Turning to the internal picture, 1985 saw a 3.6-percent rise in the GNP, a major improvement over 1984's 0.3 percent and the best performance since 1981. A 4-percent increase in public consumption stemmed largely from a growth in direct defense imports; indeed, if defense imports were deducted, public spending was actually down by 2 percent in 1985. Local defense consumption was down by 3 percent, following a 1-percent decline in 1984.

The dire predictions that mass unemployment would be generated by the economic recovery plan were not borne out in 1985, although total unemployment did increase over 1984, from 5.9 percent to 6.7 percent. Among non-Jews the situation was more acute, with unemployment up from 6.6 percent of the labor force in that sector in 1984 to 9.5 percent in 1985. Similarly, the plight of many of the "development towns" was exacerbated, with their share of the total number of unemployed increasing by a full percentage point over the year, to 10.2 percent. The government was more successful in its efforts to curb the public's buying power, at least in terms of salaries. Overall, in 1985, the average gross wage paid to salaried workers (in fixed prices) was 9 percent lower than in 1984.

On September 4 the Treasury introduced the new Israeli shekel, which was due to replace the old currency at the beginning of 1986. The change was largely a technical one, instituted because of difficulties—even for computers—in coping with the huge numbers produced by inflation. The equivalent of 1,000 old shekels, the new shekel was valued at 67 cents to the dollar.

Political Affairs

The first full year of the national unity government constituted a novel experience for Israel's politicians. With the overwhelming Knesset majority controlled by the coalition—indeed, by its two main components, Labor and Likud—there could be no meaningful opposition (with the potential, that is, to topple the government). In fact, the only significant "opposition" emanated from within the government itself —from the Likud, which in the latter part of the year voiced increasingly strident objections to regional peace moves initiated by Prime Minister Peres. However, because both sides were basically committed to the national unity formula—with a rotation of functions between Shimon Peres and Yitzhak Shamir slated to take place in October 1986—political crises tended to fizzle out almost as fast as they were generated.

The religious parties and their supporters were among the first in 1985 to find that the rules of the game had changed. Though the religious bloc was assiduously courted by both Labor and Likud—with an eye to future eventualities—it no longer held the balance of power in the coalition. This meant that the religious parties' continuing efforts to have the Law of Return amended, such that conversion to Judaism would have to take place "according to *halakhah*" (a maneuver whose underlying aim was to delegitimize Judaism's Conservative and Reform streams), were once more doomed to defeat. Indeed, on January 16 the bill was actually defeated by an absolute majority of the Knesset (62–51). At the very end of the year (December 28), the religious bloc, finding itself still unable to muster a majority in favor of the amendment, abruptly dropped its intention of putting the issue to another vote, even though it was already on the Knesset's agenda for that day.

It was not only the structural peculiarities of the national unity government that enabled Peres to have his way on the religious as well as other issues. The authority he wielded with mounting assurance in the course of the year was to no small degree a function of his own steady gains in the polls (another reason why he came under intensifying political attack by the Likud), which were, in turn, a reflection of his authoritative leadership on issues such as Lebanon and the economy. Additionally, although Peres was to some extent a beneficiary of the instant popularity enjoyed, to one degree or another, by all incumbent Israeli prime ministers, he also worked hard to cultivate his newfound image. Guided by a team of young American-style advisers, he took to the hustings, as it were, at least once a week, not hesitating to venture into locales where his name had been anathema while he was leader of the opposition. The upshot was that his popularity rating, already a solid 48 percent at the start of the year, was well over 60 percent at its end. Despite the power-sharing element of the national unity agreement, Peres was incontestably the head of the government and the dominant political figure in the country.

It appeared that Labor was riding high on Peres's coattails when the party gained a two-thirds majority in the elections to the governing body of the Histadrut on May 13, increasing its representation by 5 percent, while the Likud dropped by a similar amount. While the vote was considered by many as an indication of which way the political wind was blowing, other factors had to be taken into account. Among these were the personal popularity of Labor's candidate for Histadrut secretary-general, MK Israel Kessar, and the Likud's failure to run a front-rank candidate (Deputy Prime Minister Levy having refused to head the Likud list against Kessar, apparently feeling that even a minor setback would harm his prospects in the national political arena).

It was not long after the Histadrut elections that calls, at first muted but increasingly vocal, began to be heard in the Labor party for its unilateral abrogation of the rotation agreement. Fueled by a series of acrimonious disagreements between Labor and Likud over the Taba issue (see "Foreign Relations"), these calls grew more insistent following the vote of nearly all the Likud ministers against the economic recovery plan on July 1.

Open conflict between Prime Minister Peres and Industry and Trade Minister Ariel Sharon erupted several times during the year. The most serious episode involving Sharon occurred in mid-November, when Peres demanded that Sharon publicly retract a series of allegations he had made against the prime minister's foreign and defense policies, notably that Peres was "shaky and cowed" vis-à-vis Egypt, was conducting secret negotiations with Damascus for the return to Syria of the Golan Heights, and did not totally reject the PLO as a negotiating partner in peace talks. The prime minister had in fact prepared a letter of dismissal for Sharon, though his right to fire a minister from the Likud was challenged by that party, which asserted that it would be a violation of the coalition agreement. In the event, after three days of tension and intensive mediation by Interior Minister Rabbi Yitzhak Peretz of Shas, whose political stock rose sharply as a result, on November 14 Sharon sent a note to Peres which Sharon termed a "clarification," but which Peres accepted as a full apology, thus terminating the crisis.

It seemed evident that Sharon's moves were not directed against Prime Minister Peres and the Labor party alone. The conventional wisdom was that Sharon, who had his eye on the Herut party leadership, would not be averse to the breakdown of the national unity government and the cancellation of the rotation agreement, since if that agreement were to be implemented, it would prevent him from seeking his party's leadership at least until the next scheduled general election in 1988. Nor, according to this analysis, was Sharon particularly eager for the Herut convention, scheduled for February 1986, to take place, since the party would certainly not wish to rock the boat just eight months before rotation, and would therefore certainly reelect Yitzhak Shamir as party head.

Another wild card in this pack was David Levy, a populist of genuine working-class origins who regarded himself as the natural successor to Menachem Begin in Herut. In August, at a meeting of the Herut Central Committee called to ratify a merger of Herut with the splinter La'am faction, Levy entered the hall in the middle of a speech by Shamir. When Levy's supporters erupted in raucous cheers, the titular party head was forced to break off his remarks. Infuriated, Shamir called for an immediate vote and won a majority for the merger with La'am—a move not welcomed by Levy, who had few if any supporters in that group. Levy challenged this vote in the Herut party's supreme court, and another central committee meeting was subsequently scheduled for September 1, generating new tension in the party. Just before the meeting, however, Shamir and Levy met and agreed on the agenda for the meeting. An open vote was then taken which almost unanimously ratified the merger. Levy maintained that he had proven his point, which seemed to be that he held power of veto in Herut. It was clear that the disarray in the Likud was yet another factor enabling Shimon Peres, the uncontested head of his own party, to govern with a firm hand.

Peace Initiatives

Prime Minister Peres devoted considerable effort during 1985—notably in the latter part of the year, following the completion of the Israeli withdrawal from Lebanon—to attempts to bring about negotiations between Israel and Jordan, or between Israel and a joint Jordanian-Palestinian delegation. Unfortunately, beyond generating goodwill for Israel in the West and some ill will within the governing coalition in Jerusalem, by year's end these efforts had produced no perceptible concrete results.

Peres took a wait-and-see attitude toward the year's first innovative diplomatic move in the region—a February 11 agreement between Jordan's King Hussein and PLO chief Yasir Arafat to work for a peaceful Middle East settlement based on "land for peace," a Jordan–West Bank confederation, and an international peace conference. However, Peres did note that the accord represented something of a "departure" from the long-standing Arab rejectionist stance.

In an apparent effort to build on the Hussein-Arafat agreement, Egyptian president Hosni Mubarak, in a *New York Times* interview on February 25, called for direct talks between Israel and a Jordanian-Palestinian delegation. However, the Mubarak initiative ran into objections in Israel when it emerged that what the Egyptian president had in mind was an initial meeting between Washington and a Jordanian-Palestinian delegation, with Israel being brought into the picture only in a second stage. Both Peres and Vice-Premier Shamir expressed fears that this plan could lead to a situation in which Washington would find itself talking to the PLO and in which (as Peres told the cabinet on March 24) a solution would be imposed on Israel.

From the start, the makeup of the Palestinian component of a Jordanian-Palestinian delegation and the chronological sequence of the mooted peace talks proved major stumbling blocks to the various peace initiatives advanced during the year. Any possibility of progress in Middle East peacemaking came to hinge on the prior formation of a joint Jordanian-Palestinian delegation; however, the PLO was torn by internal conflict, and thus unable to sanction (or refuse to sanction) the possible makeup of a delegation, and the Israeli leadership was also divided over the issue. U.S. assistant secretary of state Richard Murphy discovered that this particular avenue was a dead end when he undertook a regional shuttle mission in late April, hoping to meet with members of the proposed Jordanian-Palestinian delegation. None of his meetings in Jordan, Egypt, and Israel—which included encounters with leading Palestinians from the territories—produced any progress.

Murphy's failure to make headway meant that an early May visit to the same three capitals by Secretary of State George Shultz would prove equally unproductive. In Jerusalem for three days (May 10–12), primarily to take part in a ceremony marking the 40th anniversary of the Nazi defeat, Shultz focused his political talks on the somewhat arcane but increasingly central topic of whether members of the Palestine National Council (the Palestinian "parliament in exile") would be acceptable to Israel as members of a Jordanian-Palestinian delegation.

On June 10, after having been notified by Shultz that King Hussein, during an end-of-May visit to Washington, had "taken some important initiatives that move in the direction of peace," Prime Minister Peres delivered a major policy statement in the Knesset in which he outlined an initiative that would eventuate in a peace conference within three months. Israel, he said, was proposing direct negotiations "between equals," with no prior conditions, to include only "the parties that are interested in peace." Peres then enunciated a five-stage plan which would enable such talks to begin:

1. Talks between representatives of the United States, Israel, Jordan, Egypt, and "Palestinian representatives who are not PLO members."
2. Formation of a "narrow Jordanian-Palestinian and Israeli team" to draft an agenda for a "Jordanian-Palestinian-Israeli conference," with U.S. participation.
3. "Enlistment of the support" of the permanent members of the UN Security Council for direct Jordanian-Palestinian-Israeli negotiations.
4. "Appointment of authentic Palestinian representatives from the territories who will represent the stands of the inhabitants, and will be acceptable to all parties."
5. The convening of "an opening conference within three months" at an agreed-upon site, in Europe, the United States, or the Middle East.

The initiative never got off the ground. Israel vetoed virtually every Palestinian name proposed, because of PLO connections, and a second shuttle by Assistant Secretary Murphy (August 13–18) proved to be a virtual replay of the first. As Defense Minister Rabin told the *Jerusalem Post,* while it was true that Israel opposed Washington's plan to launch the peace process by first meeting with a Jordanian-Palestinian delegation, the PLO, by refusing to meet Murphy halfway in his requests, had itself scuttled the U.S. plan.

Hussein, in whom Peres continued to rest his hopes—true to his party's concept of a "territorial compromise" with Jordan—employed terminology rarely heard from Arab leaders when he told the UN General Assembly on September 27 that his country was "prepared to negotiate, under appropriate auspices, with the government of Israel, promptly and directly, under the basic tenets of Security Council Resolutions 242 and 338." Apart from objections raised to such seemingly heretical remarks in the Arab world, Hussein's words called attention once more to the gulf dividing the two main components of Israel's national unity government. While the speech was welcomed by Prime Minister Peres and the Labor party, Vice-Premier Shamir dismissed it as containing "nothing new." Some commentators charged (as they had in February, with reference to Mubarak's peace initiative, which came on the eve of a visit to Washington by the Egyptian president) that Hussein's actual objective was to enhance his image in the United States in an effort to win congressional support for a proposed major arms deal. For his part, Defense Minister Rabin asserted that Hussein, by insisting that Yasir Arafat take part in any talks and that the Soviet Union cochair (with the United States) an international peace conference on the Middle East, had "imposed conditions that make progress impossible."

Prime Minister Peres seemed to be trying to sidestep at least the latter problem when he indicated during his mid-October visit to Washington that he was not unalterably opposed to Soviet or Chinese participation in a peace conference, provided those two countries first established diplomatic relations with Israel. A few days later (October 21), Peres seemed to take yet another bold step when he told the General Assembly that direct negotiations "between states" in the Middle East could, "if deemed necessary . . . be initiated with the support of an international forum, as agreed upon by the negotiating states." Such a "gathering" could take place "before the end of this year," Peres asserted, be it in Jordan, Israel, or any agreed-upon venue. Elaborating on the concept of an "international forum," Peres said that the permanent members of the Security Council "may be invited to support the initiation of these negotiations," though only such countries as did not "confine their diplomatic relations to one side of the conflict" would be acceptable. Peres called for small working teams to be set up and begin meeting within 30 days and urged the immediate termination of "the state of war between Israel and Jordan," adding: "Israel declares this readily in the hope that King Hussein is willing to reciprocate this step."

Hussein's reaction, devoid of any reciprocity, was mild in comparison with that of the prime minister's own coalition partners. In a specially convened meeting, the

Likud ministers sought to undercut Peres's moves by rejecting any sort of international auspices for Mideast negotiations. Following an at times acrimonious six-hour cabinet session on October 27, Peres replied the next day in the Knesset to a no-confidence motion based on his UN peace initiative, incorporating into his Knesset speech the operative elements of his General Assembly address. Peres won parliamentary endorsement for them when the House voted 68–10 (with 10 abstentions) to reject the no-confidence motion, and hence to approve his policy statement. Despite prior threats, only one Likud MK voted against the government. By early November Peres had coined a new phrase and was speaking of "international accompaniment" to peace negotiations. He explained that King Hussein required such "accompaniment" in the initial stage of talks in order to demonstrate to the Arab world that he was not isolated.

But isolation and disappointment continued to be the name of the game in 1985. On November 25, Morocco's King Hassan II made statements which were understood as expressing a desire to meet with Prime Minister Peres to discuss regional peace efforts. Peres immediately and effusively welcomed the Moroccan monarch's remarks, and the Israeli press ran banner headlines about a dramatic "breakthrough." Yet just one day later Rabat stated that Hassan had "neither directly nor indirectly" issued an invitation to Peres for talks. Hard on the heels of this fiasco came yet another visit to the region by the State Department's Richard Murphy. On December 3–4, the American official informed Peres and Shamir (separately) that a Jordanian-Syrian rapprochement was in the offing, although its ramifications were not yet clear, since Damascus remained unalterably opposed to any peace initiative. The reconciliation did, however, suggest a Jordanian break with the PLO, since Syria was an implacable foe of Yasir Arafat.

Israel's relations with its neighbor to the northeast, Syria, remained effectively unchanged in 1985. In a midyear assessment, the chief of Israeli military intelligence, Maj. Gen. Ehud Barak, predicted that Syria would make every effort to torpedo any possible peace talks. Speaking to military affairs correspondents, Barak said that Damascus was still pursuing its aim of achieving "strategic parity" with Israel, to which end it had acquired Soviet-made SS-21 surface-to-surface missiles capable of hitting targets deep inside Israel. General Barak thought it unlikely that Syria would launch a total war against Israel—certainly as long as Iraq was entangled in its war with Iran, and Jordan refused to take part in a new Mideast fray—though a lightning operation on the Golan could not be ruled out.

The only actual armed clash between Israel and Syria in 1985 occurred on November 19, when IAF planes, on what was termed a "routine reconnaissance patrol" over Lebanon, downed two Syrian MIG-23 interceptors in a dogfight that had its end over Syrian territory. Israel sustained no losses. On December 15, the Israeli army spokesman announced that the Syrians had moved up SA-2 surface-to-air missiles to just inside their own border with Lebanon. According to U.S. officials, the Syrian moves had been set in motion by Israel's downing of the two MIGs on November 19—a chain of events which could not but recall the developments that followed Syria's deployment of missile batteries in Lebanon in 1981 after Israel shot down two Syrian helicopters there. With this in mind, perhaps, a communiqué issued by the Israeli army spokesman noted that the November 19 clash had been an "isolated incident" and "did not reflect a change in Israel's policy," a fact which "the government of Israel [had] brought to the attention of the Syrians."

Reinforcing this stance, Defense Minister Rabin declared at year's end that press reports notwithstanding, there was no tension on the Israeli-Syrian front, that the Syrians had made no deployment changes opposite the Golan Heights, and that Damascus was continuing to adhere to its undertakings in the 1974 separation-of-forces agreement between the two countries. Nor, however, had there been any change in the Syrian attitude toward peace, as was evident from Prime Minister Peres's end-of-year comment that there was no prospect of Syria joining the peace process. Syrian president Hafez al-Assad was still bent on donning the mantle of Arab world leadership and realizing his dream of restoring "Greater Syria," a rubric that included Lebanon and Jordan, besides Israel.

The year's diplomatic activity was glumly appraised in a *Jerusalem Post* editorial on December 26 in these words: "The year that started with a distinct hope of an early resumption of Middle East peace negotiations is ending without a single step having been taken towards that end, and with the prospects for progress bleaker than they were a year ago."

Foreign Relations

THE UNITED STATES

With the United States out of Lebanon and Israel in the process of withdrawal from that country, and with the national unity government working to reform the economy, "improve the quality of life" in the territories, and revivify the peace process, all the elements existed for smooth and harmonious relations between Jerusalem and Washington—and such they were for almost the entire year.

On April 22, Israel signed a Free Trade Agreement (FTA) with the United States, its largest single trading partner. Under the terms of the agreement, which took effect on September 1, 1985, all trade barriers between the two countries would be eliminated in a four-stage process over the coming decade. In conjunction with the accord, the U.S. Department of Commerce was to open an Israel Information Center in Washington, which would inform U.S. businesses of the advantages available to them in Israel under the terms of the agreement.

While the FTA signaled Washington's long-term confidence in the resilience of the Israeli economy, in the short term the U.S. administration was concerned that Israel was not doing enough to resolve its economic problems. Although Congress approved a $4.5-billion economic–military aid package for Israel (all in the form of grants), Secretary of State Shultz demonstrated the administration's determination to intervene forcefully in Israeli economic decision making by dispatching two economists, professors Herbert Stein and Stanley Fischer, to Israel to study the situation. The ten-point plan proposed by the two experts, which covered, among other topics, inflation, the budget, monetary policy, and credit subsidization, became the basis for Washington's economic counsel to Jerusalem. When this degree of American involvement in the Israeli economy was assailed in some quarters as unacceptable intervention in the country's internal affairs, Prime Minister Peres depicted the American plan as constructive and inspired by benevolent motives. He placated domestic critics by noting that Israel had rejected American proposals which would have reduced inflation by generating unemployment. At the same time, it had adopted other American ideas, not under pressure, but because they were beneficial to Israel.

On May 2 Shultz informed Peres that Congress would be asked to approve an extra $1.5 billion in emergency economic aid requested by Israel. Setting this decision in a broader context, Shultz noted that the administration welcomed Israel's withdrawal from Lebanon and its efforts to promote the peace process in the region. However, it was only after the Israeli government's adoption on July 1 of a comprehensive economic recovery program—which Shultz termed a "courageous decision" that should be implemented "vigorously"—and after a second visit to Washington by Finance Minister Modai at the beginning of September, that the secretary of state announced the immediate transfer to Israel of $750 million, or half the requested emergency aid. In December, when Modai made the annual pilgrimage to the American embassy in Tel Aviv to present Israel's aid requests for the coming fiscal year (totaling $3.5 billion), he declared that Israel would not ask for any further emergency aid after receiving the outstanding $750 million scheduled for transfer in 1986.

Requests were by no means a one-way street in Israeli-U.S. relations in 1985. In April, in what some observers saw as a tacit American acknowledgment that Israel was a full-fledged ally in all but treaty, Israel was asked—along with the NATO countries, Japan, and Australia—to take part in research and development aspects of the administration's Strategic Defense Initiative, or "Star Wars" project. Although the proposal encountered some domestic political flak, at year's end Prime Minister Peres said that Israel's position on the topic was "unequivocally affirmative" and that Israeli firms could initiate contacts "with a view toward participating in this research."

That defense matters overall played a central role in relations between the countries could be gleaned from the fact that Defense Minister Rabin paid no fewer than three visits to Washington during the year, and that ranking American defense personnel also saw fit to visit Israel. In a January visit, Rabin was assured that the United States would continue to help Israel maintain its "qualitative edge" over the Arabs. He was further informed that "offset" arrangements, by which U.S. defense systems sold to Israel had to include a certain percentage of Israeli-made components, would be worth a hefty $200 million to Israel in the coming year.

On an April visit to Israel, Secretary of the Navy John Lehman announced that Israel and the United States would jointly build three submarines for the Israel Navy and that the two countries would undertake coproduction of a missile. It was also agreed that Israel would lease the U.S. Navy a second squadron of Israeli-manufactured Kfir jet fighters, which the Americans planned to use to simulate MIGs in maneuvers. Speaking at a ceremony held shortly afterward at the Naval Air Station at Oceana, Virginia, marking the introduction of the first three Kfirs into U.S. Navy service, Lehman said the event indicated "the new level of cooperation with our Israeli allies." A somewhat less harmonious visit was paid to Israel in May by U.S. under secretary of defense Fred Ikle, who—not for the first time—cast doubts on the feasibility of Israel's Lavi jet fighter project, though Defense Minister Rabin continued to back the costly endeavor.

The Lavi was also on the agenda in Rabin's June visit to Washington, as were two by now almost-ritual items: Israeli opposition to U.S. arms sales to Arab countries—in this case a mooted deal with Jordan involving advanced jet fighters and surface-to-air missiles (the deal was eventually deferred until 1986 due to Senate objections)—and the U.S. attitude toward PLO participation in possible peace negotiations. Washington's eagerness for peace talks to begin under its sponsorship —partly in order to reassert itself in the Middle East following the Lebanon debacle —led it, at least from Jerusalem's perspective, to inch toward a more flexible stance vis-à-vis PLO participation. Nevertheless, the administration continued to insist (as Shultz put it to newsmen during the visit to Washington of Finance Minister Modai in September) that "[its] conditions for talking with the PLO remain as they have been for many years"—meaning, PLO acceptance of Israel's right to exist and the organization's acceptance of UN Security Council Resolutions 242 and 338.

The ambivalence of the U.S. posture was manifested in the wake of Israel's October 1 attack on PLO headquarters in Tunisia (see below, "Terrorism"). Although President Ronald Reagan had stated, immediately following the operation, that it was "legitimate" and "an expression of self-defense," just three days later, when the Security Council was called on to condemn the attack, the United States abstained in the vote (effectively bringing about a condemnation).

Still, less than two weeks after the Security Council abstention, Prime Minister Peres found a highly receptive audience in Washington when he lashed out at the PLO. In his two days of talks (October 17–18), which came in the wake of a series of terrorist incidents, notably the *Achille Lauro* affair (see "Terrorism"), senior officials and leading members of Congress not only condemned the PLO, they expressed a desire to work more closely with Israel in combating international terrorism and in other defense-related areas. And following Peres's General Assembly address on October 21, the State Department was positively effusive, terming it "a statesmanlike, thoughtful, forward-looking exposition which underlined Prime Minister Peres's commitment to the peace process."

Several events during the year put U.S.–Israeli amity to the test, however. One was President Reagan's visit to the Bitburg military cemetery in Germany, on May

5, as part of the events marking the 40th anniversary of the defeat of Nazi Germany. Although reconciliation with former enemies was understandable, Prime Minister Peres said at a Holocaust Remembrance Day ceremony in Jerusalem on April 17, referring to the purpose cited by the White House for the Bitburg visit, "reconciliation with evil"—in the form of the SS officers buried in the cemetery—was incomprehensible. Israelis were equally critical of Reagan's same-day "balancing" visit to the site of the Bergen-Belsen concentration camp, which seemed to posit an "equality" between victims and victimizers.

In Israel on May 10 to take part in events commemorating Nazi Germany's defeat, Secretary of State Shultz sought to assuage the anger and hurt expressed by the Israelis. Speaking at Yad Vashem, he said: "Miraculously, here there is also hope. For who has erected this memorial? Not the perpetrators of evil but the conquerors of evil. Who preserves this memory? Not the enemies of the human spirit but its defenders." No words, however, could erase the act of moral insensitivity that had been committed. To the people of Israel, Bitburg revealed anew the fragility of Jewish existence, evoking that dark time when, as Prime Minister Peres recalled, "not the Allies, not the pope, not the Red Cross" offered the Jewish people a haven: "The world was silent and the destruction went on."

The second event that strained relations between the two countries had potentially more serious ramifications. On November 21, in Washington, just one month after Prime Minister Peres's visit to the U.S. capital and at the tail end of Defense Minister Rabin's third visit there in 1985, the FBI arrested a certain Jonathan Jay Pollard, 31, a civilian intelligence analyst for the U.S. Navy, on a charge of spying for Israel. Pollard was apprehended outside the Israeli embassy, where he was reportedly seeking political asylum under the Law of Return. Although the Foreign Ministry in Jerusalem issued a statement on November 24 expressing "shock and consternation" among the country's "political leadership" at the arrest, adding that a "thorough examination" into the matter was under way, the abrupt return home of two scientific attachés in the Israeli consulate in New York gave rise to speculation that they were involved in the affair.

It was not until December 1, a full ten days after Pollard's arrest, and after the media had played up the story for all it was worth, that the Israeli government reacted. The official statement asserted that Jerusalem was "determined to spare no effort in investigating this case thoroughly and completely," although the government was "not yet in possession of all the facts." If the charges proved true, the statement continued, "those responsible will be brought to account, the unit involved in this activity will be completely and permanently dismantled," and no recurrence of "such activities" would be countenanced. The statement concluded: "Such activity, to the extent that it did take place, was wrong, and the government of Israel apologizes."

While this belated exercise in damage control did have its intended placatory effect, on December 11 Washington dispatched a team, headed by the State Department's legal adviser, Abraham Sofaer, to investigate the matter further in Israel. On

December 20 the State Department released a communiqué, which had been hammered out jointly with Israel, noting that the Sofaer team had concluded its mission, that Israel had returned to the United States all the documents involved, and that it had disbanded the offending unit, about which few facts were made known. Reportedly called the Scientific Liaison Bureau, it was allegedly run by a Mossad man, Rafael Eitan, who had served as the prime minister's adviser on terrorism until early in 1985. Israel, the communiqué said, had assured Washington that those involved had acted "without authority and against [Israeli] policy," and that there would be no repetition "of such activities." These measures were regarded by the United States "as constituting the cooperation contemplated by the two governments," the statement concluded.

Yet even as Washington announced that regular intelligence cooperation with Israel was being resumed, another case, with similar overtones, was getting headline coverage. On December 13, U.S. customs agents, accompanied by an NBC News camera crew, raided the Napco company, alleging that it had illegally exported a new weapons technology to Israel. Israeli officials in Washington, still reeling from the Pollard affair, were quick to deny any wrongdoing, insisting that the Pentagon had given the necessary approval. Moreover, according to the Israeli spokesmen, the only plausible explanation for the presence of the TV crew at the raid—and the attendant publicity the case received—was that elements in the U.S. administration were bent on "punishing" Israel for its actions in the Pollard case. Although a State Department official confirmed that Israel had not acted improperly in the Napco case, this episode, coupled with the Pollard affair, threatened to cast a shadow over what had been, overall, an extraordinarily sunny year in relations between the two countries.

EGYPT

Despite the relatively upbeat note that was struck at the end of 1984, following Shimon Peres's accession to the premiership, relations between Israel and Egypt remained troubled. The main point of contention between the two countries was ownership of Taba, a tiny stretch of coast south of Eilat which was in Israeli hands but which had been in dispute since the signing of the peace treaty in 1979. Egypt continued to insist that until the Taba issue was settled, and until Israel withdrew from Lebanon (a move that was accomplished by mid-June), there could be no thaw in the "cold peace" that existed between the two countries, nor could its ambassador —recalled to Cairo in the wake of the Sabra-Shatilla massacre in September 1982 —return to Tel Aviv.

The year was studded with sudden "highs" followed by abrupt "downers." It opened on a hopeful note when talks on Taba in fact resumed in Beersheba on January 27—the first talks on bilateral issues between the two countries since April 1983. However, the three days of negotiations, in which U.S. representatives also participated, produced only a bland joint communiqué asserting that the differences between the sides had been "narrowed" and that the talks had been held "in a constructive and friendly spirit."

A surge of optimism followed one month later, in the wake of an interview in the *New York Times* with Egyptian president Mubarak on February 25. Speaking two weeks after Jordan's King Hussein and PLO chief Arafat had reached an agreement calling for an international peace conference on the Middle East, Mubarak proposed direct negotiations between Israel and a joint Jordanian-Palestinian delegation. On February 26, Mubarak dispatched his senior adviser, Osama al-Baz, and another ranking official, Abdul Halim Badawi, to Israel for two days of talks with Prime Minister Peres and other senior cabinet ministers; at the same time, the director-general of the Prime Minister's Office, Avraham Tamir, along with Energy Minister Moshe Shahal, went to Cairo for talks. The Mubarak initiative itself was welcomed by Peres but was given a frosty reception by Vice-Premier Yitzhak Shamir and other top Likud spokesmen, who feared that Mubarak was actually intent on bringing the PLO into negotiations, with Washington's help.

While nothing concrete came of the peace initiative itself, the intensive diplomatic activity between Jerusalem and Cairo helped to create a more forthcoming atmosphere between the two countries. Thus, in March, a 12-member delegation of Egyptian scientists, headed by Deputy Agriculture Minister Muhammad Dasouki, visited Israel to exchange ideas with Israeli counterparts on arid-zone development; in May experts from the two countries held talks near Jerusalem on another problem that afflicted both countries, insect-borne infections.

In between these two meetings, Minister Without Portfolio Weizman, one of the architects of the Camp David accords and a consistent proponent of better relations with Egypt, visited Cairo April 15–17 as the envoy of Prime Minister Peres. However, in a repeat of the Labor-Likud squabble over the Mubarak initiative, the Weizman mission came close to generating a government crisis in Jerusalem, with the Likud maintaining that Weizman would be encroaching on the turf of the Foreign Ministry. Although Weizman was accorded a warm reception in Cairo, and held talks with President Mubarak and Prime Minister Kamal Hassan Ali, the resultant headlines about an imminent Peres-Mubarak summit proved premature. One month after the Weizman visit, an Israeli delegation went to Cairo for talks on Taba and other bilateral issues. Inauspiciously, on the day the meeting opened, May 15, which happened to be the secular date of Israel's establishment, violent anti-Israel demonstrations were staged outside the main synagogue in Cairo. Still, on May 27, Oil Minister Abdel Hadi Kandil, reciprocating Energy Minister Shahal's February visit to Cairo, arrived in Israel for three days of talks. He was the first Egyptian minister to visit Israel in three years.

The visit to Jerusalem of Egyptian tourism minister Wahi Shindi on August 20 suggested that a level of normality had been achieved, especially as the Egyptian minister went ahead with his visit as scheduled, despite the murder of Israeli diplomat Albert Atrakchi by terrorists in Cairo on the very eve of the Egyptian's departure. Shindi in fact arrived bearing messages of condolence from Prime

Minister Ali and Foreign Minister Esmat Abdel Meguid for the attack, in which Atrakchi's wife and another Israeli embassy staffer were wounded. A group identified as "The Egyptian Revolution" claimed responsibility for the slaying—the same group that claimed to have shot and wounded another Israeli diplomat in Cairo one year earlier. On the day of Atrakchi's funeral, the Egyptian tourism minister announced that in the wake of Israel's final withdrawal from Lebanon restrictions on Egyptian tourism to Israel had been lifted, and that the two countries would seek ways to increase tourism between them.

Following Israel's attack on PLO headquarters in Tunis at the beginning of October, Egypt announced that it was suspending the Taba talks. The situation was further aggravated by Egypt's release of the hijackers of the *Achille Lauro* cruise ship. But it was an incident at Ras Burka, in Sinai, that put the greatest strain on relations between the two countries. On October 5 an Egyptian security man suddenly opened fire on a group of vacationing Israelis at Ras Burka, killing seven persons. It soon emerged that five of the seven victims of the attack—four of whom were children—had actually bled to death because Egyptian troops at the site had prevented them from receiving medical attention for some hours. Although Cairo initially sought to shrug off the incident, it soon changed course in the face of the anguished fury in Israel. President Mubarak, who had originally termed the incident "a small matter," subsequently called the killings "tragic" in an oral message to Prime Minister Peres (October 13), in which he also pledged that Egypt was proceeding "with urgency" to investigate the matter. In November Egyptian oil minister Kandil, paying his second visit of the year to Israel, met with the families of the Ras Burka victims, conveying to them President Mubarak's "personal regret for the tragedy." Finally, on December 28, the perpetrator of the crime was sentenced to life imprisonment with hard labor. However, a promised official Egyptian report on the case had not arrived by year's end, and the families of the victims declared themselves unsatisfied with the sentence. The entire affair left Israelis feeling bitter —besides, on the practical side, severely reducing the number of Israeli vacation trips to Sinai.

Following Kandil's meeting with the Ras Burka families, the Taba talks were resumed in Cairo from December 4 to 6, and were followed by another round, in Herzliyah, from December 10 to 12. Although Egypt continued to insist that the dispute be submitted to immediate international arbitration, the Israeli stance had by this time become ambivalent. The Likud continued to urge the path of "conciliation" (a prearbitration stage stipulated in the agreement between the two countries), and Labor was beginning to waver in the direction of the Egyptian position, in order to bring about what its leadership considered the more urgent goal of a Peres-Mubarak summit meeting. As tension in the national unity government flared again over the Taba issue, Defense Minister Rabin told a Labor party meeting at year's end that he regarded the improvement of relations with Egypt as Israel's top priority. He insisted, however, that both countries would have to make compromises to settle their differences, and that, with respect to the Taba question, what was needed was "arbitration with risks."

EUROPE

In 1985 Israel's relations with Western Europe attained the level of stability and normalcy that had characterized them prior to the Lebanon war, and relations with Eastern Europe, virtually frozen since the Six Day War in 1967, showed signs of incipient thaw.

In many ways the year's most notable diplomatic event was the visit to Israel by West German president Richard von Weizsäcker (October 8–11), the first ever by a German head of state while in office (in 1984 Helmut Kohl was the first German chancellor to visit Israel while in office) and made doubly momentous because it took place in the year marking the 40th anniversary of the defeat of Nazi Germany. The German president went straight to the heart of the matter when he declared on arrival, "We Germans will certainly not shun the remembrance of the past," and visited the Yad Vashem Holocaust Memorial on the very first day of his stay. Von Weizsäcker's itinerary included wreath-laying ceremonies at Mount Herzl in Jerusalem and at the tomb of David Ben-Gurion at Sde Boker in the Negev, a "private" tour of the holy places in the Old City of Jerusalem (since Bonn did not recognize East Jerusalem as Israeli territory), visits to three institutions of higher learning, and a stop in Haifa, where he announced that German-funded research centers were to be established at the two universities in that city. On the political side, the German president said his nation had a "deep understanding" of Israel's security needs and that Palestinian self-determination, which his country supported, must not conflict with those needs. Despite the general warm feelings expressed, Foreign Minister Hans-Dietrich Genscher, who headed a large contingent of senior German officials in the president's entourage, indicated that Bonn would not rescind its approval for a West German arms manufacturer to negotiate a major arms deal with Saudi Arabia.

In September Poul Schluter became the first Danish prime minister to visit Israel in 22 years. Greeting his guest at Ben-Gurion Airport, Prime Minister Peres called on Denmark and other friendly European countries to assume an active role in Middle East peace efforts. In a speech delivered during a dinner at the prime minister's residence in Jerusalem, Schluter gave expression to what seemed to be the prevailing tone vis-à-vis Israel in Western European capitals. He welcomed the Israeli withdrawal from Lebanon but added that his country also hoped for "new signals" regarding "some of your policies and practices in the occupied territories."

In a brief visit later in the year (December 9–10), Foreign Minister Roland Dumas of France declared that his country, while opposed to an imposed solution such as could result from an international peace conference on the Middle East, also continued to recognize the "legitimate rights" of the Palestinian people.

Prime Minister Peres discussed peace initiatives during brief visits to Italy (February 18–20) and Rumania (February 20–22). In the face of strong pro-Arafat inclinations in both Rome and Bucharest, Peres maintained that the organization's continued resort to terrorism and its refusal to recognize Israel's right to exist ruled it out as a potential participant in a Middle East peace process. On February 19, during his stay in Rome, Peres held a one-hour meeting with Pope John Paul II at the Vatican, afterward telling reporters that "His Holiness showed a keen interest in peace prospects."

Peace prospects and the PLO were at the center of a contretemps between Israel and England in the latter part of the year. In September British prime minister Margaret Thatcher took a bold leap into Middle East peacemaking when she told a press conference in Jordan, where she was concluding a week-long visit, that she had invited a Jordanian-Palestinian delegation to visit London for talks. The two Palestinians named as delegation members were Mohammed Milhem and Bishop Elias Khoury, both current PLO executive members who had been deported by Israel for suspected subversion and terrorism. Replying to a letter from Prime Minister Peres, in which he said that the invitation was "particularly puzzling" in view of Thatcher's "firm, consistent and courageous stand against international terrorism," the British leader described Milhem and Khoury as "moderates" who "accept Israel's right to exist within secure and recognized borders, and are opposed to terrorism and violence." Thatcher also informed Peres that the two "will reaffirm their position publicly during their stay in London."

In the end, a last-minute refusal by Milhem to sign a statement renouncing terrorism led to the cancellation of the scheduled October 14 meeting, deeply embarrassing Prime Minister Thatcher and infuriating King Hussein. The course of events appeared to confirm what Foreign Minister Shamir had said in a visit to London in June: that the PLO would never publicly recognize Israel, since this went "against their philosophy and their ideology."

Shamir's visits to Western Europe in 1985 were focused on protecting Israel's agricultural exports to the European Community—worth over $500 million annually and accounting for some 70 percent of all Israeli farm exports—in view of the fact that Spain and Portugal were scheduled to become members of the European Economic Community (EEC) at the beginning of 1986. Shamir's efforts in this direction, as well as those of Tunisia and Morocco, who also feared new competition, apparently succeeded: European Community leaders pledged in early April "to seek mutually acceptable solutions to all the concerns expressed by the Mediterranean countries" in view of the Iberian entry into the EEC. In October, when he visited Luxembourg to address the EEC-Israel Cooperation Council and to meet with foreign ministers of the EEC member states, Shamir professed himself "satisfied" with the EEC's response to Israel's requests regarding its agricultural exports.

President Chaim Herzog discussed his country's economic situation when he visited Luxembourg, Strasbourg, and Brussels in February. In June Herzog paid a nostalgia-laced state visit to Ireland, his birthplace, summing up the trip as having taken place "in a very good atmosphere [marked by] great cordiality"—words equally applicable to Israeli–Western European relations as a whole in 1985.

While relations between Israel and Eastern Europe could hardly be described in those terms, their improvement occupied a high position on the foreign-policy agenda of Prime Minister Peres. Peres began his search for what he termed "a window to the east" early in the year, when he visited Rumania, the only Eastern European country to maintain diplomatic relations with Israel. In September Peres conveyed a message to the new Soviet leader, Mikhail Gorbachev, by way of World Jewish Congress president Edgar Bronfman. The essence of the message was, as the prime minister subsequently revealed in a Knesset speech on October 28: "We in Israel see a need, and would welcome, an opportunity to hold a constructive dialogue with you." On October 23, Peres met informally with Foreign Minister Eduard Shevardnadze of the USSR when both men were in New York to address the UN General Assembly. Peres told the Knesset that he had found Shevardnadze's approach to be "substantive," though no concrete results could be expected until after the Reagan-Gorbachev summit in November. (See also "Israel and World Jewry.")

Foreign Minister Shamir utilized the General Assembly session to meet with ranking Eastern European officials, including the foreign ministers of Bulgaria and Poland. The latter, Stefan Olszowski, indicated that his country was ready to better relations with Israel in a number of areas, including tourism and culture. As a result of this encounter, in mid-December, Shamir, along with President Herzog and Prime Minister Peres, were among those in attendance when the Warsaw National Chamber Opera gave its premiere performance in Tel Aviv—the first such visit since Poland broke off relations with Israel in 1967.

OTHER FOREIGN RELATIONS

The very end of the year saw another breakthrough in Israel's growing rapprochement with black Africa when Prime Minister Peres flew secretly to Geneva for a meeting (December 18) with President Felix Houphouet-Boigny of the Ivory Coast. At a press conference convened by Israel after the meeting, it was announced that the two countries had decided to renew diplomatic relations; ambassadors would be exchanged once the new Ivory Coast government was sworn in. The Ivory Coast thus became the third of the African countries that had severed relations with Israel in the aftermath of the 1973 Yom Kippur War to resume those relations, following Zaire in 1982 and Liberia in 1983. Earlier in the year (May 12–17), President Mobutu Sese Seko of Zaire paid a state visit to Israel, during which the two countries signed a number of cooperation agreements in aviation, medicine, technology, and investments.

Israel's improved relations with black Africa placed it under growing pressure to distance itself from the regime in South Africa, especially in view of persistent press reports of Israeli–South African military and other cooperation. In August a ten-day visit by a leader of the South African black community, KwaZulu chief minister Gatsha Buthelezi, produced a spate of pronouncements from the Israeli political leadership deploring apartheid. Prime Minister Peres told a cabinet meeting on August 11, the day of Buthelezi's arrival, that any form of racial discrimination ran "contrary to the very foundations on which Jewish life is based." During his stay in Israel, Chief Buthelezi met with President Herzog, Prime Minister Peres (twice), and other ranking government officials, as well as holding talks with senior Histadrut (General Federation of Labor) personnel, academics, and industrialists. Buthelezi said he had been "very encouraged" by the prime minister's rejection of apartheid and expressed the hope that Israel would exert "optimum leverage" on Pretoria to dismantle the apartheid system. For its part, Jerusalem continued to tread a thin line between its long-standing relations with Pretoria—not losing sight of the large Jewish community in South Africa—and its growing ties with black Africa.

That Israel was still a long way from acceptance by most of black Africa and the rest of the Third World was brought home at the UN End of the Decade for Women Conference held in Nairobi, Kenya, in July. According to one of the Israeli delegates, former MK Tamar Eshel, the forces arrayed against Israel "came from five continents," seeking "to destroy and explode" the entire meeting. Overall, the conference demonstrated "the recurrence of UN double-standard practices," according to the prime minister's adviser on the status of women, Nitza Shapiro-Libai. However, with the help of the U.S. delegation, Israel was able to scuttle attempts to have a "Zionism equals racism" statement inserted into the final conference document.

A strong pro-Israel stance was taken by Costa Rican president Luis Albert Monge Alvarez, whose four-day state visit (October 13-17) was evidence of Israel's ongoing solid relations with the countries of Latin America. In an address delivered from the Knesset rostrum, Monge assailed the idea of internationalizing Jerusalem—Costa Rica had in fact returned its embassy to Jerusalem in 1982—and in a meeting with Foreign Minister Shamir he expressed his support for the Israeli attack on PLO headquarters in Tunis at the beginning of October.

Other ranking officials from Latin America to visit during the year included Mexican secretary of commerce and development Hernandez Cortes, whose six-day stay in May produced agreement on a joint Israel-Mexico energy project worth $120 million, and Honduran foreign minister Edgardo Paz Barnica, whose week-long visit in August—the first by a foreign minister from that country—led to a decision to establish full diplomatic representations in both countries "in the near future."

In August the Foreign Ministry officially denied that Israel was supplying military aid to the *contras* in Nicaragua; the occasion for the denial was an interview with Nicaraguan president Daniel Ortega, published in *Ha'aretz* on August 7, in which Ortega made this allegation.

In the wake of indications that Japan was reassessing its adherence to the Arab boycott, Foreign Minister Shamir paid a visit to Tokyo in September for high-level talks. Shamir, who was accompanied by several top executives from Israeli high-tech industries, said on his return home that "an important door has been opened for the Israeli economy" in Japan.

Economic and trade ties between Israel and Canada were also reinforced following talks in Ottawa between Shamir and senior Canadian officials, including Prime Minister Brian Mulroney. Relations with Oceania got a double boost in 1985: Papua New Guinea defense minister Boyamu Sali visited the country in February as the guest of Defense Minister Rabin, and Israel and Australia agreed to explore possibilities of scientific cooperation, in the wake of a visit in April by Australian science minister Barry Jones.

Terrorism

In 1985 Israel was confronted with terrorism at home, in the occupied territories, in the air, on the high seas, and at various locations across the seas.

ISRAEL AND THE TERRITORIES

Inside Israel and in the occupied territories, the "conventional" form of terrorism —explosive devices planted in public places, aimed at mass slaughter—gave way, to a large extent, to "private" terrorism directed against individuals, most often perpetrated with guns, knives, or even bare hands. Whether this brand of terrorism represented a new strategy on the part of the Arab terrorist organizations, or whether it resulted from the perpetrators' inability to produce sufficiently destructive bombs, it seemed to have an even more unsettling effect on the nation than the public form of terrorism. It also did much—and this may have been one of its intended results—to heighten anti-Arab feeling among certain sections of the country's Jewish population and to feed political extremism.

Hardly a month passed without one or more brutal killings. In January a flower grower from Petah Tikvah died of wounds sustained when a firebomb was thrown at his car as he was driving out of Kalkilya. In February a 29-year-old reserve soldier was gunned down in the Ramallah market. (His murderers, three young men from the Ramallah area, were subsequently apprehended and in December were sentenced to life imprisonment.) In March a 52-year-old Soviet immigrant, a West Bank settler, was shot through the head in Ramallah.

In April a Jewish Jerusalem cab driver was shot through the head. Three Arabs were soon arrested and charged with the murder, which evidently had a nationalist-terrorist background. In apparent revenge, an Arab taxi driver was shot through the head four days later. On May 17 police arrested three Israeli Jews, all in their 20s, one of them a woman university student, in connection with this murder. In June a 35-year-old reserve soldier from Eilat was murdered, evidently by terrorists, as he was hitchhiking to his base near Beersheba. In the same week, a bomb was thrown at an army jeep in Samaria and a gasoline bomb was thrown at an Israeli bus in

Nablus, but no one was hurt in either incident. The intensifying terrorism led to a mass demonstration in Tel Aviv on June 16, organized by Gush Emunim and other groups, at which speakers called for the death penalty or deportation for Arabs convicted of terrorism.

There was a spate of bomb explosions in Tel Aviv and Jerusalem in the latter part of June and early July. In a particularly ugly incident (July 19), a man from the village of Dura, near Hebron, slashed five Jewish children and their day-camp counselor with a razor as they waited for a bus in downtown Jerusalem. Although he was initially thought to be merely deranged, the assailant, it later emerged, belonged to the Fatah organization.

Two crimes that took place in June and July overshadowed all that had gone before, generating new heights of anti-Arab hysteria. On June 27 the bodies of a Jewish couple, Meir Ben-Yair and Michal Cohen, were found in a forest near Beit Shemesh, outside Jerusalem. Two Arabs, both aged 22, from the village of Tsurif, near the Etzion Bloc, were soon apprehended and confessed to the murder. Houses belonging to their families were demolished on July 9. (On November 21 the two killers, who were distant relatives, were sentenced by Lod military court to life imprisonment; they admitted to murdering the two Israelis after receiving orders from Fatah, to which they had been recruited earlier in the year, to kill some Jews. Subsequently, they laid an ambush at a spot in the woods which they knew to be frequented by hikers and shot Ben-Yair and Cohen even before the couple could leave their car.)

Just one month after the Beit Shemesh atrocity, on July 26 the dead bodies of two Afula teachers, Leah Elmakayis, 19, and Yosef Eliahu, 35, were found in a cave on Mount Gilboa. Three young Arabs, all under the age of 20, from the nearby West Bank village of Arrabuneh, close to Afula, were arrested the next day and soon confessed to the murders. When news of the discovery of the bodies reached Afula, a mob ran wild through the streets, stoning and beating Arabs and damaging Arab shops. There was further rioting during the funerals, on July 28. (On November 19, a 17-year-old minor received a seven-year prison sentence in Nazareth district court after being found guilty of being an accomplice in the murder of the two teachers. The trial of the two young men accused of the actual killing continued.)

For Afula there was more to come. On July 30, just two days after the funerals of the two teachers, with passions still intense, an Afula man, Albert Bukhris, 32, who ran a kiosk in Nablus, died after being shot in the back while shopping in the market there. At his funeral, 700 policemen were unable to prevent the mob from running wild and attacking media personnel, whom they held responsible for Bukhris's murder because his picture had been in the paper when he himself was detained as a rioter after the murder of the two teachers. Although MK Meir Kahane was barred from attending Bukhris's funeral, a large crowd gathered outside the Afula police station after the funeral, chanting "Kahane, king of Israel!"

Following a lengthy discussion of terrorism at its August 4 meeting, the cabinet appointed a committee to consider the possible imposition of a mandatory death penalty for terrorist acts. It also adopted a number of measures, notably administrative detention "for security reasons" and deportation of persons "who constitute a security risk."

A more far-reaching approach mooted by Industry and Trade Minister Sharon, that Israel should strike at what he termed the "new terrorist bases" of the PLO in Jordan, was rejected in early August by Prime Minister Peres; Israel did not wish "to create the impression that [it] has declared war on Jordan," Peres said. Later in the month, however, in an address to the graduating class of the army's Staff and Command College, Defense Minister Rabin cautioned Jordan to weigh its steps in this regard carefully, lest things reach a pass where "Israel could not sit idly by in view of what was liable to develop."

With or without Jordan's involvement, terrorist attacks continued, frequently directed against lone Jews who happened to be in Arab towns. On August 10, a Kiryat Arba resident was seriously wounded when he was stabbed in Hebron. Exactly two weeks later a Netanyah resident was shot in the back at point-blank range just as he entered a jewelry store in Tulkarm; he died en route to the hospital. On the same day, a Tiberias man was critically wounded when he was shot in the back while shopping in the Jenin market. Curfews and other restrictions were imposed on Tulkarm and Jenin, and by the end of August, 36 West Bank residents had been placed under administrative detention, while others had been deported or placed under town arrest.

A new wave of terrorism in September led to the reappearance of settlers' vigilante patrols and a heightened military presence in the West Bank. On September 3, two reservists doing guard duty in the Hebron market were the victims of a stabbing attack; one died of his wounds. Shortly after the attack, two local residents were wounded by soldiers' gunfire, and a ten-day curfew was imposed on the market. Two days after the Hebron attack a Beersheba man was wounded by two knife-wielding assailants in Gaza. They were arrested within hours and their rooms, in their families' homes, were destroyed. In an effort to counter the wave of terrorism, on September 15, 18 persons from among those released in the May prisoner exchange (see below) were deported to Jordan. In addition, some 70 persons throughout the West Bank were placed under administrative detention in the last week in August and first week in September. In a related move, the Knesset on September 9 passed in preliminary reading the amendment to the Prevention of Terrorism ordinance, which would all but ban private contacts between Israelis and members of terrorist organizations.

On September 22, on the eve of Sukkot, a probable catastrophe was averted when an alert passerby in Jerusalem's ultra-Orthodox Me'ah She'arim quarter reported a suspicious-looking van to police. The van, parked in a crowded shopping area, turned out to be booby-trapped and was quickly disarmed. A few days later, seven passengers (one of them an Arab) on a Jerusalem–Kiryat Arba bus were wounded when the bus was fired on as it entered the town of Halhoul. Curfew was imposed on Halhoul, and several hundred Jewish settlers seized the opportunity to carry out a reprisal raid on the town, damaging cars and a mosque before the security forces stepped in to impose order.

Arab residents were also victims of terrorist activity. A 13-year-old Hebron boy was killed and three other Arab residents of the city wounded, one seriously, when a grenade was thrown at an army patrol there on September 28. In Gaza, one local boy was killed and another wounded when soldiers opened fire at the vehicles they were traveling in, which had failed to stop at army roadblocks.

At the beginning of October, the year's third double murder of its kind occurred. The bodies of Edna Harari, 22, and Mordechai Suissa, 28, were found in the Judean Hills near Beit Shemesh on October 4, following an intensive search of several days after they were reported missing. The two, who came from religious families in Jerusalem, had met not long before and were said to have been on their first outing together without chaperones. Two days later a special antiterrorist unit of the border police flushed out a five-man terrorist gang that had been operating for over a year in a broad area stretching from Hebron to Beit Shemesh. Four of the gang's members were killed in the clash, which took place in the southern Hebron hills, and the fifth was wounded and captured.

According to the army spokesman, this gang was responsible for the latest double slaying as well as for the murder of another couple in the same area in June, and the slaying of a Jewish settler in the Ramallah market in March. Also attributed to them were four instances of firing on Israeli buses, including the September 26 incident in which seven persons were wounded. The homes of all five gang members were demolished by the security forces, who also arrested a number of persons in the Hebron area on suspicion of having aided the gang. Dozens of *mukhtars* in the area were warned that harsh punitive measures awaited them if residents of their villages were found to have aided terrorists.

One of the effects of the series of murders of persons hiking through woods was to cast a pall of danger and uncertainty over this favorite form of activity. Such fears were reinforced by the O/C Central Command, Maj. Gen. Amnon Shahak, who said in an interview following the elimination of the gang that while the area in question was now "clean," persons hiking in isolated areas should do so in groups and carry weapons.

There was no letup in the attacks, in Israel proper and in the territories, for the rest of the year. Among the more serious incidents were a series of knifings of Israelis in the Old City of Jerusalem in November, which effectively placed the Old City out of bounds as far as many Jewish Jerusalemites were concerned; the shooting of an Israeli Jew in Kalkilya on November 30 (the town's mayor, who visited the victim in hospital, offered a reward for information leading to the arrest of the perpetrator); the murder, in an apparent act of anti-Arab terrorism, of a well-known Ramallah lawyer, Aziz Shehadeh, 73, who was stabbed to death outside his home on December 2 (the Abu Nidal terrorist group claimed responsibility); and the murder of an 18-year-old soldier, Moshe Levy, while he was hitchhiking home from his base—his body, which was set afire after the killing, was found in a field off the Lod–Petah Tikvah highway on December 5.

Speaking to reporters in late November, Central Command's General Shahak said that half, if not more, of the recent terrorist acts in the West Bank had been perpetrated at what he termed the private initiative of local residents who were not affiliated with terrorist organizations. Because of this, and because the attacks were often spur-of-the-moment affairs, it was difficult to apprehend the assailants, he noted.

There were further developments in the case of the two terrorists killed in the aftermath of a bus hijacking on the Tel Aviv–Ashkelon route in April 1984. When security forces stormed the bus, which had been commandeered by four men, two of the terrorists were killed. The two others, it later emerged, had been taken off the bus alive but died shortly afterward as a result of blows to their heads. (See AJYB, vol. 86, 1986, pp. 333–334.) On August 13, 1985, an investigative commission headed by State Attorney Yona Blattman—which had been appointed a year earlier by the attorney general—made its conclusions public. The commission found prima facie evidence of the "use of violence toward the two terrorists (who had been taken alive), via blows with a pistol, by Brig. Gen. Yitzhak Mordechai." (The name of Mordechai, the chief infantry and paratroop officer, had been revealed in connection with the investigation, in violation of military censorship, by the weekly magazine *Koteret Rashit,* in February.) Similar evidence was found in connection with five members of the General Security Service (GSS) and three members of the Israel Police. Based on these conclusions, Attorney General Yitzhak Zamir decided to have the five GSS men tried before a GSS disciplinary court under the Civil Service Law, while the three policemen would face trial before a police disciplinary court. On August 18 the army exonerated General Mordechai of all charges against him, having concluded that his interrogation of the two terrorists was carried out "in order to obtain vital immediate information," and that his actions were "not unreasonable," since he sought to prevent danger to human life. In November the GSS personnel involved were also cleared in the deaths of the two terrorists.

FREEING OF TERRORISTS

In mid-May, even as pressure was being exerted by the Jewish settlers in the territories for tougher measures against terrorists, Israel announced that it was releasing 1,150 jailed terrorists—including some who were serving life sentences for having committed unspeakably heinous crimes—in exchange for three Israeli soldiers captured in Lebanon in 1982 and held by Ahmed Jibril's Popular Front for the Liberation of Palestine–General Command organization. Of the 1,150 released prisoners—over half of all the security detainees held by Israel—879 were serving sentences in jails in Israel and the territories, 150 were detainees from the Ansar detention facility in Lebanon who had been transferred to Israel during the army's withdrawal from that country (see "The War in Lebanon"), and the remaining 121 were members of the Jibril organization, among them Jibril's own nephew. About half of the released terrorists were to remain in the territories or Israel, with the rest either being flown, under International Red Cross auspices, to Geneva (from where they proceeded to Libya) or transferred to Syria at the Kuneitra checkpoint on the Golan Heights. The three Israeli soldiers were flown home via Geneva and arrived in Israel on May 21. (Four Israeli soldiers still remained unaccounted for in the wake of Operation Peace for Galilee.)

Among the terrorists released were Kozo Okamoto, who was serving multiple life sentences for his part in the 1972 Lod Airport massacre, in which 27 persons were killed; 2 Israeli Arabs serving life terms for their part in the 1969 bombing of the National Library cafeteria at the Hebrew University, which wounded 28 persons, some seriously; Ahmed Zmurid, from Jerusalem, who was responsible for the 1968 car-bomb attack that killed 15 persons and wounded about 50 in the capital's Mahaneh Yehudah market; and the 3 terrorists still in prison from the group that carried out the Beit Hadassah massacre in Hebron in May 1980, which took the lives of 6 settlers.

The exchange sparked a fierce public debate, especially when Israelis saw the released prisoners being greeted as heroes in their home villages in the territories. In response, Jewish settlers launched a campaign of intimidation aimed at forcing the newly freed convicts to leave the country. Motions of no confidence in the government over the issue of the prisoner exchange were heard in the Knesset and rejected, on May 29, by a vote of 65–6 and six abstentions. Speaking on behalf of the government, Defense Minister Rabin summed up the underlying conception of the exchange: "When there is no military option—and after a thorough examination of all the possibilities, there is no alternative but to enter into negotiations and pay a price . . . a government of Israel . . . cannot ignore the fate of its soldiers, who are sent into battle at its order, and who fall captive to terrorists, and say to them, 'We abandon you to your fate.' "

Soon after the May prisoner exchange, Israel found itself involved in the fate of captives who were not its citizens. On June 14, Shi'ite terrorists hijacked a TWA passenger plane en route from Athens to Rome, took it to Beirut (via Algiers), and demanded "the liberation of our brothers held in Israel" (referring to the inmates of the Ansar detention facility who had been brought to Israel from southern Lebanon during the Israeli withdrawal), in return for the release of the plane's passengers and crew. Although an official Israeli army statement issued at the time of the first exchange had noted that Israel would release the remaining prisoners in accordance with developments in Lebanon, it was clear that any such action taken while the hijackers still held the plane would be regarded as capitulation to terrorism. As the hijacking dragged on, suggestions began to be heard in certain American quarters that Israel should free the prisoners in question and thereby resolve the issue. In response, Defense Minister Rabin asserted that Israel would not yield to "unofficial pressure" and would not change its policy "unless the United States specifically asks us to do so. Then we will weigh what to do. . . ."

On June 24, Israel did release 31 Lebanese prisoners, following what was said to be routine procedure in the wake of a review of their case by an appeals board. Twenty other requests to the board were said to have been rejected. Prime Minister

Peres, while refuting claims that a deal had been struck with the hijackers, noted that once the TWA hostages were freed, Israel would be able to resume its policy of releasing the Shi'ite inmates still in custody without any "obstacle[s]" in the way. On July 3, three days after the hostages were finally flown to Frankfurt, Israel set free another 300 prisoners, denying that this step was in any way connected with the TWA hijacking.

ANTI-ISRAEL TERROR ABROAD

The final quarter of the year saw an upsurge in attacks against Israelis and Israeli targets abroad. At dawn on September 25, which happened to be Yom Kippur, three terrorists—two Palestinians and a British "skinhead"—stormed an Israeli-owned yacht that was docked at the marina in Larnaca, Cyprus, killing a Haifa couple, Esther and Reuven Paltzur, and Avraham Avneri, of Arad, all three in their 50s. Following nine hours of negotiations with the Cyprus authorities, the terrorists surrendered. Israel vowed that "the murderers would not go unpunished" and that it would use all the means at its disposal to protect its citizens wherever they were. Israeli requests for the extradition of the three perpetrators—believed to be operating as part of the Fatah organization's elite Force 17 unit—were rejected by Cyprus. (In late December a Nicosia court sentenced the three terrorists to life imprisonment.)

On the day following the Larnaca attack, the Israel Air Force struck at a PLO base in Lebanon. However, this turned out to be a mere prelude to a direct strike by the air force at the organization's nerve center in Tunisia on October 1 (see below).

A week later, the most dramatic terrorist action of the year took place, an action that became a major international incident. Four Arafat-affiliated terrorists hijacked an Italian cruise ship, the *Achille Lauro*, during a Mediterranean sailing. Their evident intention had been to make themselves known only when the ship docked at the Israeli port of Ashdod, and then to perpetrate a bargaining operation, holding the ship's passengers and crew hostage until Israel released imprisoned terrorists. However, their plan went awry when their presence was discovered by a ship's steward, at which point (October 7) they seized control of the vessel. The episode was to end tragically for one vacationer, Leon Klinghoffer, an elderly wheelchair-bound American Jew whom the terrorists shot and then threw overboard. The terrorists finally surrendered to Egyptian authorities in Port Said on October 9 and were released the following day (though not before President Mubarak had been caught out in an untruth: he maintained that the four had already left Egypt when in fact they were still on Egyptian soil). The plane carrying the hijackers was intercepted and forced to land in Sicily by U.S. aircraft. The squad's leader, Abul Abbas, a member of the PLO's executive and a confidant of Yasir Arafat, was, however, permitted to proceed to Yugoslavia by the Italian authorities—to the consternation of many throughout the world.

In an Israeli television interview on October 17, the chief of military intelligence, Maj. Gen. Ehud Barak, played a tape recording of a conversation between Abul Abbas and one of the hijackers aboard the *Achille Lauro,* monitored while the operation was still in progress. Although Arafat had dissociated himself from the hijacking of the ship and from the spate of terrorist attacks in Israel and abroad during the year, Barak maintained that Arafat was playing a "double game," posing as a moderate vis-à-vis the West while acting to maintain his credibility with the radical Palestinian groups.

Nitzan Mendelson, a young Israeli woman, lost her life and another woman was badly wounded during the hijacking of an Egyptian airliner en route from Athens to Cairo on November 23. In a subsequent Egyptian storming of the plane, the day following its hijacking, 59 other passengers were killed, as were four of the five terrorists.

Israel's national airline, El Al, was the victim of several attacks during the year. The first three attacks—in Milan (August 25), Istanbul (August 28), and Amsterdam (September 13)—caused little damage. However, on December 27, Arab terrorists, apparently from the anti-Arafat Abu Nidal organization, launched simultaneous attacks at the El Al counters in the Rome and Vienna airports, resulting in 20 persons killed and over 100 wounded. Among the dead was one Israeli citizen and one other El Al passenger. An El Al security guard in Rome showed particular courage as he returned fire at the terrorists, despite being wounded himself.

A call by Israel for a concerted international effort to eradicate the scourge of terrorism, specifically, for all countries to expel PLO representatives, noted that the attacks had "come against the background of declarations by the head of the PLO and those Arab states that support the PLO that these terrorists would cease terrorist operations outside Israel." The reference was to a declaration by PLO chief Arafat in Cairo on November 7, following the *Achille Lauro* affair, that the PLO "denounces and condemns all terrorist acts" and would cease such acts outside Israel, while reserving the right to perpetrate them in the territories.

COMBATING TERRORISM

Israel carried out its war against Arab terror in two main forms: by ongoing efforts to apprehend and bring to trial terrorists operating within Israel and the territories, and by direct military means utilizing chiefly the air force and the navy.

The pursuit of individual terrorists was carried out largely through undercover work by the General Security Service; indeed, some Israeli commentators suggested that terrorism inside the country had grown because the GSS and the army as a whole were preoccupied with Lebanon. During 1985 there were, nevertheless, some notable successes in the apprehension of individual terrorists and the uncovering of a number of terrorist cells. Among terrorists who were tried and convicted was a young resident of the Dehaishe refugee camp, sentenced to life imprisonment for the 1984 murder of two Jewish students in a wood near the camp.

Both the air force and the navy were heavily engaged in antiterrorist activity during the year. Naval patrolling of Israeli and Lebanese coastal waters resulted in the destruction, in the predawn hours of May 8, of a rubber dinghy in the Tyre area carrying five Fatah terrorists who planned to carry out an attack in northern Israel. Besides occasionally shelling terrorist bases in Lebanon from the sea, the navy also ventured onto the high seas with the aim of intercepting terrorist craft before they could approach Israel. These patrols scored three major successes in 1985. On April 21, the navy sank a vessel carrying 28 terrorists, of whom 8 were captured (the others presumably drowned), who were bound for Israel with the aim of disrupting Independence Day festivities. In the predawn hours of August 25, an Israel Navy patrol intercepted the yacht *Casselredit,* which was carrying eight Algerian-trained members of the Fatah organization. They were bound for Sidon, in southern Lebanon, there to be outfitted by Fatah agents before infiltrating into Israel by land in order to execute a large-scale attack in Galilee. Finally, on August 31, the yacht *Ganda,* belonging to Fatah's Force 17, was intercepted off the Lebanese coast. It was en route from Cyprus to Lebanon, carrying a terrorist squad that had orders to infiltrate into Israel to perpetrate a maximum-casualty operation.

The most daring antiterrorist action of the year, and the one with the most far-reaching implications, was carried out by the Israel Air Force on October 1. In response to the recent wave of terrorism, which was capped by the murder of the three Israelis in Larnaca, the IAF flew the longest mission in its history, a round trip of some 4,800 kilometers, to bomb PLO headquarters in Tunisia. In the strike, about 60 persons were killed and a number of buildings destroyed, including the headquarters of Yasir Arafat. (He himself was not at the site at the time of the attack, and Israel later denied that he had been a target of the operation. However, several senior members of Force 17 were reported to have been killed.)

In a government statement on terrorism delivered to the Knesset plenum on October 21, Defense Minister Rabin reported that 11 separate Arab terrorist organizations, comprising 17,000 terrorists, were currently active against Israel "in every possible arena." In the previous year, some 2,000 "Arafat terrorists" had returned to Lebanon, while some 6,000 members of other terrorist organizations had never left that country. According to Rabin, the attack on PLO headquarters in Tunis had been intended as a "clear signal to all the terrorist organizations that there will be no immunity for terrorists anywhere."

JEWISH TERRORIST ORGANIZATION

On July 22, just over a year after it had begun (June 27, 1984), the trial of the 25 members of the Jewish terrorist organization concluded. The members of the organization, activists from Jewish settlements in the West Bank and the Golan Heights, had been charged with a series of crimes, including an attack on the Islamic College of Hebron in 1983 and a conspiracy to blow up the Dome of the Rock shrine on the Temple Mount in Jerusalem. (See AJYB, vol. 86, 1986, pp. 336–339.)

What was probably the major turning point in the proceedings came in mid-May, when the Jerusalem district court panel of three judges trying the case ruled that evidence and testimony relating to the security situation in the West Bank in 1980 (when the group had been most active) were inadmissible. The court argued that the defendants had no right to take the law into their own hands, no matter what the situation, and that testimony about security in Judea-Samaria in 1980 was therefore irrelevant. Since the security situation was in fact the main argument of the defense, several of the defendants, including the leader of the underground, Menachem Livni, dismissed their lawyers, asserting that they no longer had need of counsel.

About a week after the release of 1,150 Arab terrorists in exchange for three Israeli soldiers (see above), Knesset members from the Likud, Tehiya, and the religious parties, joined by other public figures on the political right, called for the reciprocal release of the Jewish terrorist underground. Responding publicly to the growing calls for amnesty, which included a demonstration in front of the Knesset by about 3,000 persons, mainly from religious settlements in the territories, President Herzog, who was authorized by law "to pardon offenders," stated that he would not be a party to attempts to undermine the country's judicial system and would not be "pressured by any side" on this matter. In a ruling issued on June 3, Attorney General Zamir stated that no one can be pardoned "unless he has [first] been convicted in a court judgment, since until then he is held to be innocent."

On June 12 the state rested its case, with Assistant State Attorney Dorit Beinish asking for harsh sentences as a deterrent to others, because of the dangerous ideology underlying the defendants' deeds, and because "none of them expressed remorse or contrition for his actions."

The verdicts were handed down on July 10, and sentence was passed on July 22. Three of the 15 defendants (Menachem Livni, Uziahu Sharabaf, and Shaul Nir), who were convicted of murder in the attack on the Islamic College in Hebron, were sentenced to mandatory life imprisonment. Barak Nir (brother of Shaul Nir) received a 12-year sentence, half of it suspended, for manslaughter, attempted murder, conspiracy, and "membership in a terrorist organization"; Yehuda Etzion and Yitzhak Ganiram were given ten-year prison terms (three years of which were suspended), while the others received sentences ranging from five to seven years, with about 40 percent of the sentences suspended in each case. One defendant, Moshe Zar, was given a three-year sentence of which all but three months was suspended; he was then released because he had already served four months in prison and because of ill health.

The court's decisions were greeted with dissatisfaction by both supporters and opponents of the terrorist group. Renewed calls for a general amnesty were led by Vice-Premier Yitzhak Shamir, who reiterated to a meeting of Betar youth-movement alumni his view that the defendants were "excellent people who made a mistake"; he argued that a pardon for the group would virtually guarantee the end of a Jewish underground. By year's end, President Herzog had acted in three cases, reducing the sentences of Uri Maier, Yosef Zuria, and Dan Be'eri, all of whom had been convicted following plea bargaining.

On the other side, the state appealed to the Supreme Court for harsher sentences for five of those convicted, both because of the seriousness of their offenses and to correct imbalances in sentencing. The move drew the wrath of the country's right wing, which redoubled its calls for an amnesty and for the dismissal of Attorney General Zamir, who had made the decision to appeal.

In the course of the trial, ten of the defendants had concluded plea-bargaining agreements with the court and been duly sentenced. Several of these sentences were appealed to the Supreme Court by the defense, the prosecution (namely, the state), and sometimes both; in most of the appeals the court let the sentences stand as handed down, though in one case it stiffened the sentence (that of Noam Yinon, who had 10 months added on to his 18-month prison term), and in another it more than halved the original sentence (that of Gilad Peli, whose prison term was cut from 10 to 4½ years).

Several other Jews who had carried out acts of political violence, though acting as individuals, not as members of an organized group, also had sentence passed against them in 1985. On January 13, Yona Avrushmi, 27, who was convicted of the murder of Emil Grunzweig and of wounding nine other persons when he threw a grenade at a Peace Now demonstration in February 1983, was sentenced to life imprisonment. On April 17, David Ben-Shimol, 19, received a life sentence for murder resulting from two attacks he carried out in 1984: firing a rocket into an Arab bus in Jerusalem, killing one person and wounding ten, and throwing a bomb into a café in the Old City of Jerusalem, wounding four persons. Ben-Shimol's request to be imprisoned together with the members of the Jewish underground was rejected.

In September Shimon Barda, a member of the messianic Lifta gang, which, like the Jewish underground, had planned to blow up the Dome of the Rock, was sentenced to eight years in jail. (The two leaders of the bizarre group were found mentally incompetent to stand trial.) In October Yosef Harnoi from the settlement of Elon Moreh was sentenced to ten years in prison after being convicted of manslaughter in a 1983 incident in Nablus. Harnoi killed an 11-year-old girl and wounded her sister when he fired a submachine gun into a bakery, after his car was stoned while he was driving through the town and he leaped out to give chase.

In a follow-up to an earlier case of violence, the Supreme Court effectively reduced by as much as 20 years the prison term of Alan Goodman—the American who had run amok on the Temple Mount in April 1982, killing one Arab guard and wounding two others—by ruling that he could serve all his jail terms concurrently.

The Administered Areas

For various reasons, including the national unity government's limiting of new settlements to no more than six in its first year, little occurred to change the status quo in the territories, in terms either of Jewish expansion or in the situation of the Arab population. Work was, however, carried out to improve the infrastructure of existing Jewish settlements, and the larger, semiurban settlements continued to grow in population.

Regarding the local Arab population, it was the declared approach of Prime Minister Peres and Defense Minister Rabin—in response, *inter alia,* to American pressure—to work for what was termed "the improvement of the quality of life." Specific measures implemented, according to a "briefing paper" issued by the Foreign Ministry in June, included the lifting of restrictions on individual import of capital, provided the source of the funds was not the PLO or "other terrorist sources"; authorization for a group of local businessmen to open a bank (though no start was made on the actual establishment of such a bank, apparently due to a Jordanian veto); approval of plans for the construction of a fruit-processing plant in Gaza and for new hospitals in Hebron and Ramallah (again, there were no signs of implementation); and continued rehabilitation of refugees, with some 650 Gaza families having been allocated housing "last year alone." In a step taken to relieve a long-standing source of hostility, the government permitted a reduction in the number of books banned by the military censor from 1,500 to about 300. The government also extended direct overseas-dialing service to telephone users in the territories.

The first significant step was taken toward achieving another government objective—placing Arab leaders of moderate political outlook at the head of a number of West Bank towns that had been run by the Israeli military for several years, ever since the dismantling in 1980 of the PLO-linked National Guidance Committee. On November 26 the Judea-Samaria Civil Administration announced the appointment of the president of the Nablus chamber of commerce, Zafr al-Masri, 44, as mayor of that town. The appointment was consistent not only with the government's desire to improve the quality of life in the territories but also with Prime Minister Peres's "Jordanian option," as al-Masri was known to be well connected in Amman.

The gradualist approach taken by the government toward the Arab population extended to the Jewish settlers as well. In the absence of forceful support from the highest echelons of government—such as they had received under Likud governments for almost eight years, beginning in 1977—and in view of the national unity government's emphasis on reducing expenditures, the settlement movement focused its efforts on consolidating what had already been achieved.

The few demonstrations in support of intensified settlement that were held during the year centered mainly on Hebron. In April about 150 members of the Herut-affiliated Betar youth movement were turned back by border police when they marched into Hebron in an effort to reach the Tel Rumeida settlement site—where several Jewish families resided in trailers—and open an office there. Although allowing the original families to remain at the site, the government refused to permit other settlers to join them. In mid-June the Cave of Machpelah (Tomb of the Patriarchs) in Hebron once again became the focus of Jewish-Arab tensions when about 50 settlers, some of them armed, arrived at the site for morning prayers, knowing that the eastern entrance to the site had been closed to Jews temporarily because of a Muslim holiday. The would-be Jewish worshipers were denied access by three soldiers, but refused to move aside to allow Muslim worshipers to enter. A possibly serious incident was averted when officers of the military government convinced the Jewish group to pray outside the site and to depart before Muslims began arriving in large numbers.

In defiance of government policy, in early August a group of settlers from Kiryat Arba occupied an empty apartment in the center of Hebron. According to the settlers, the flat had been purchased from its Arab owners by the Committee for the Restoration of the Jewish Community in Hebron. This claim, however, was contested by the Israeli military authorities. Although the settlers were soon removed by the army, on August 15 three MKs from the ultranationalist Tehiya party moved in. Because of their parliamentary immunity, they could not be so easily dislodged, and a major political row quickly flared up. Likud leader Yitzhak Shamir contended that the seizure of the flat was consistent with prior cabinet decisions; Prime Minister Peres and Defense Minister Rabin countered that the move was in violation of the status quo and that the particular apartment at issue was in any case not included in any government decisions concerning Hebron.

In short order the original three MKs were joined by four others (from Tehiya, Likud, and Morasha) and soon received visits of support from ministers Ariel Sharon and Moshe Arens, both of Herut. With the situation threatening to get out of hand—demonstrations both supporting and opposing the occupation were staged at the site, and the settlers themselves were poised for militant action—Defense Minister Rabin met on August 19 with the seven MKs in the apartment and asked them to leave. When they refused, the building and its surroundings were declared a "closed military area," a formal eviction order was issued by the army at 3:15 A.M. August 20, and the MKs then left the flat under army escort and without resistance. The entire building was sealed off and a guard posted outside it. (One reservist doing such guard duty was killed and another seriously wounded in a knifing attack on September 3.)

At about the same time as the Hebron events, another aspect of West Bank settlement came under official and public scrutiny, one in which Arabs and Jews alike were victimized. The Tel Aviv district court began considering a case involving alleged illegal land sales in Judea-Samaria, with local Arabs claiming that they had been intimidated into selling or that land was sold without their knowledge. At the same time, Israeli Jews who bought land as future homesites were defrauded of their money because title to the land was not clear. The political ramifications of the case emerged when the Knesset's Public Audit Committee began looking into the matter, and when Vice-Premier Shamir accused the press of turning "isolated cases" into a "witch hunt" against land purchase in the territories, "with the aim of blocking this Zionist mission." In December two persons who had served as aides to Deputy Defense Minister Michael Dekel when he was deputy agriculture minister—and as such responsible for West Bank settlement activities—were arrested in connection with the case. On December 15, with a former top aide of his already having been charged with bribery and attempting to suborn witnesses in the case, Dekel himself was questioned by police.

This highly complex case—whose outcome was still unclear at year's end— brought into the open for public debate some of the means that had been employed to promote West Bank settlement, as well as highlighting the fact that "ideological" settlement was apparently declining. According to both Meron Benvenisti, director of the West Bank Data Base Project, and Arnon Sofer, a professor of geography and head of Haifa University's Jewish-Arab Center, Jewish settlement in the West Bank was being artificially sustained by the government. In a *Jerusalem Post* report published in November, Sofer pointed out that in the 18 years since the Six Day War, only about 50,000 Jews had settled in the West Bank, a figure that was equivalent to slightly more than two years' natural increase of the Arab population there.

According to Benvenisti, about two-thirds of the over 100 West Bank settlements consisted of fewer than 200 persons each, a level that could not guarantee natural growth. Moreover, nearly three-quarters of all the settlers resided in 15 semiurban settlements, with one-quarter of the total in one settlement alone—the Jerusalem suburb of Ma'aleh Adumim. At the same time, the potential for growth remained: Israel, according to the Benvenisti data, controlled over half (52 percent) of all the land in the West Bank, and while only 7 percent of this had been earmarked for housing, between 800,000 and a million persons could be settled in those areas. (About half of the land controlled by Israel—via seizure or administrative restrictions—was set aside for military purposes.)

The moves by Prime Minister Peres toward talks with Jordan evoked bitter response in the territories. A weekly published for and by settlers in Judea-Samaria, *Alef Yud* (Hebrew initials for *Eretz Yisrael*), ran an article on November 1 entitled "Judea and Samaria Shall Not Fall Again." In it the writer, M. Ben-Yisrael (a pseudonym), called on the settlers "to prepare to take up arms and fight brother against brother." Three days later the Council of Jewish Settlements in Judea-Samaria and Gaza adopted a resolution declaring that "the plans and proposals attributed to the prime minister [in connection with mooted negotiations with Jordan or a Jordanian-Palestinian delegation] are unlawful." The resolution went on to warn that "we will treat any government in Israel that commits one of these crimes [of yielding sovereignty in Jerusalem or the territories] as an unlawful government, just as de Gaulle did vis-à-vis Marshal Pétain's Vichy regime which betrayed the French people." Moreover, the council warned, in an echo of the *Alef Yud* article, if these plans, as published, were implemented, they would "necessarily cause a split in the nation."

With the specter of civil war brought so starkly into the public debate, condemnation of both the resolution and the article was swift, embracing virtually all political factions, including supporters of the settlement movement. Three days after passing its original resolution, the Council of Jewish Settlements adopted a new resolution asserting that it "takes a grave view of the prime minister's plans to hand over parts of *Eretz Yisrael* to strangers," and that "no body has the authority to hand over or yield sovereignty in [any part] of *Eretz Yisrael.*" On November 6, five days after the appearance of the inflammatory article in *Alef Yud,* the attorney general determined that the article in question constituted incitement to revolt, and the defense minister ordered the publication shut down. (A youth magazine, *Hamtzan* ["Oxygen"], distributed free in Israeli high schools, had one issue banned when its editor responded to the *Alef Yud* article by declaring in print that he was "ready to raise a hand against the opponents of peace. . . . I am willing also to take up the gun.")

On December 11, a small group of activists tried for the fourth time in 1985 to extend Israeli settlement in the territories to the town of Jericho, an oasis of quiet in the otherwise trouble-plagued areas. Although (as on previous attempts) Israeli troops prevented them from reaching their designated site—an ancient synagogue just north of Jericho—they pledged to continue their efforts until they had achieved their objective.

Political and Religious Extremism

Intensified Arab terrorism and the effects of the government's radical new economic measures, particularly on lower-income groups, provided fertile ground for the continued growth of "Kahanism," the anti-Arab, antisecular, antileftist activism propounded by MK Meir Kahane. Efforts to counterbalance this trend had gotten off to a bewildered and uncertain start, following the shock of Kahane's election to the Knesset in 1984. In 1985, however, the forces of moderation in the country launched a concerted drive to curb the American-born rabbi by legal and administrative means. They also sought ways to achieve what amounted to the virtual reeducation of large segments of the country's youth in the principles and practices of democracy.

On May 7 Justice Minister Moshe Nissim proposed two items for legislation by the Knesset. One, a bill to amend the Basic Law regulating the Knesset, would prohibit the election of any political party that incited to racism, negated the democratic character of the state, or denied Israel's existence "as the state of the Jewish people." This bill, which was also aimed at the left-wing, Arab-oriented, and nationalist Progressive List for Peace (PLP), was subsequently passed into law by a vote of 60–0.

Because the new amendment begged the question of what actually constituted "incitement to racism," the justice minister also introduced an amendment to the penal code to the effect that "anyone publishing something which incites to racism, or anyone publishing something with the intention of inciting to racism, shall be liable to two years' imprisonment." For several reasons, this bill appeared to be assured of speedy passage: an identical measure had been called for immediately after the 1984 elections by the attorney general; the justice minister viewed it as having important "educational" purposes; and, in its current formulation, it had been okayed by all the relevant government ministries, a special ministerial committee, and the entire cabinet. However, even though the bill appeared to have universal assent, after it was given its first reading, on July 9, and referred to the Constitution, Law, and Justice Committee for final formulation, objections suddenly began to be voiced.

The Likud, even though it was an equal partner in the government and held the justice portfolio to boot, now invoked the innovative notion of "symmetry," making its support conditional on passage of a parallel law that would bar unauthorized meetings between Israelis and members or representatives of the PLO. The ultranationalist Tehiya party took exception to certain elements in the bill which it thought likely to hamper its own activity, and the religious parties expressed concern that the bill could be utilized by secularist groups to have certain passages in the *halakhah* (Jewish religious law) itself declared as "incitement to racism." (Kahane himself consistently maintained that his actions and statements were all anchored in and cited from *halakhah*, though his detractors argued that he quoted such passages out of context.) The upshot was that the bill languished in committee for the rest of 1985.

With the Knesset unable to agree on the wording of an antiracism measure, the High Court of Justice ruled on October 31 that Kahane could present two private member's bills, even though the bills in question were blatantly antidemocratic and racist in nature. (They would have restricted the rights of non-Jews and banned sexual and other types of relations between Jews and non-Jews in Israel.) This was a virtual replay of a 1984 episode, when Kahane's candidacy was challenged and the court permitted him to stand for election to the Knesset. The essence of the court's reasoning on that question—made public only in May 1985—was that, abhorrent and distasteful as Kahane's platform might have been, there was no law on the books to prevent him from running, nor did he constitute a "clear and present" danger to the existence of the state. In the present instance, Kahane petitioned the High Court after the Knesset presidium rejected his proposed bills.

Despite the court ruling in his favor, in the end Kahane was prevented from submitting the legislation. The Knesset, spurred by Speaker Shlomo Hillel, voted on November 13 to amend the House rules (the recourse suggested by the High Court of Justice in its decision) so as to bar the submission of any private member's bill which in the opinion of the presidium was "racist in nature or negates the existence of the State of Israel as the state of the Jewish people." Kahane challenged the legality of this move in yet another petition to the High Court, but this time (November 18) the court ruled against him.

One Kahane-related action that was taken by the Knesset in 1985 undoubtedly delighted Kahane himself. In yet another instance of the tit-for-tat concept insisted on by the right-wing and religious parties, by which every action taken against Kahane had to be paralleled by a like move against the Progressive List for Peace, the Knesset plenum on October 15 voted 39–22 to partially lift the parliamentary immunity of PLP MK Muhammad Miarri, Kahane's own parliamentary immunity having been similarly reduced in 1984. Miarri petitioned the High Court of Justice to throw out this decision.

A more resolute, and more successful, anti-Kahanist stance was taken in July by the government and the attorney general following elections to the local council in Kiryat Arba, the Jewish settlement adjacent to Hebron. The new coalition there, which included Kahane's Kach party, inserted a clause in the coalition agreement under which all Arabs employed by the local council would be dismissed and joint Jewish-Arab economic enterprises in Kiryat Arba would be prohibited. Following a request from the prime minister for a legal opinion on the validity of this clause, on July 30 Attorney General Zamir ruled the clause in question to be "null and void," since it "stands in blatant contradiction to the principle of equality before the law, in that it discriminates on the basis of racist considerations of the sort which have served the enemies of the Jewish people for generations in their persecution of Jews."

There was some evidence that antiracist legislative and legal efforts, along with educational programs that brought Jews and Arabs together, were running against a strong tide of public opinion. A study by the Jerusalem Van Leer Institute, for example, found that fully 11 percent of the country's 18-year-olds, the generation born in the year of the Six Day War and about to be drafted into the army, would vote for Kahane, while a further 42 percent expressed agreement with his ideas. In religious high schools, support for Kahane ran to 60 percent, and in vocational schools it was 50 percent, the same figure as for families of Middle Eastern origin. Reinforcing these data were the results of a public-opinion poll conducted for the *Jerusalem Post* by the Smith Research Center among a representative sample of the country's Jewish population. According to the poll, in a new election, Kahane's Kach party would win no fewer than ten Knesset seats (9 percent of the popular vote), with the ultranationalist Tehiya taking another seven to eight seats.

Alarmed at these trends, the left-wing Mapam party and its affiliated kibbutz movement organized a mass Arab-Jewish antiracism rally on September 7 in Afula, which not long before had been the scene of anti-Arab rioting in the wake of terrorist murders (see "Terrorism"). Later that month, Kahane himself was shouted down when he tried to address an Afula meeting. Earlier, a group calling itself the Committee Against Racism had drowned out a Kahane rally in downtown Jerusalem. On the governmental plane, Education and Culture Minister Yitzhak Navon overturned a decision by the ministry's Council for State Religious Education that would have banned meetings between Jewish religious and Arab youth on the ground that such encounters might encourage intermarriage. In October the army radio station devoted an entire day's broadcasts to the theme of antiracism, this in conjunction with efforts by the army's educational apparatus to inculcate the values of democracy and human rights.

In November the Israel Football Association took an action that undoubtedly spoke far more forcefully to the nation's youth than court battles over legal principles or Ministry of Education pronouncements. The IFA ousted a member of the Israeli national soccer team for having made racist slurs against the two Arab players on the team. Backing the move, the chairman of the Israel Olympic Committee, Yitzhak Opek, asserted that his group would not tolerate racist behavior, as it was totally alien to the underlying philosophy of sport.

RELIGIOUS EXTREMISM

Another social problem, the ongoing conflict between Orthodox Jews and the nonobservant, while relatively quiescent during 1985, nonetheless continued to trouble the country. A midyear poll commissioned by the Gesher ("Bridge") movement—whose aim was to draw religious and secular Jews closer together—found that 35 percent of religious Jews and 55 percent of nonobservant Jews regarded the religious-secular problem as more serious than it had been five years earlier. Both groups also viewed religious-secular conflict as a graver long-term problem than Sephardi-Ashkenazi tension.

Interior Minister Peretz (Shas) outraged the secular public when he asserted, in June, that the deaths in a road accident of 17 schoolchildren and four adults were divine retribution for Sabbath violations in their hometown of Petah Tikvah. (The city's bylaw had been amended to permit Friday-evening film screenings.) The minister's subsequent attempts to explain himself by asserting that "nothing accidental happens to the Jewish people," and that the tragedy should be seen as a "sacrifice" meant "to arouse us to be better Jews," only served to highlight the enormous gulf dividing the Orthodox and secular outlooks on life.

The view of some observers that the future of Jewish Jerusalem belonged to the *haredi,* or ultra-Orthodox, population received some support from a survey conducted by the Jerusalem Institute for Israel Studies. The study found that the capital's ultra-Orthodox population at the end of 1985 already constituted fully 27 percent of the city's Jewish population and that it was increasing far more rapidly than any other section of that population.

Although Jerusalem's ultra-Orthodox residents seemed to have reconciled themselves to the use on the Sabbath of the Ramot road—scene of violent demonstrations in past years—some 3,000 of them tried to prevent Mayor Teddy Kollek from inaugurating a community swimming pool in Ramot, which they claimed would allow mixed bathing and be open on the Sabbath. About 1,500 persons took part in a counterdemonstration at the ceremony opening the pool in August, but in the end, some Sabbath restrictions on bathing were imposed.

The growing antipathy between secular and Orthodox Jews surfaced in November in French Hill, not far from Ramot, where residents demonstrated against a plan to build a synagogue-yeshiva complex in the largely secular neighborhood, many of whose residents were former Americans. Basing themselves on the experience of other Jerusalem neighborhoods, the protesters claimed that the infusion of ultra-Orthodox elements would disrupt the prevailing good relations between secular and moderate religious residents, as well as bring about the closure of the neighborhood's main road—where the complex was to be built—on the Sabbath. (In the event, the project failed to get off the ground when it was found that the builders had not obtained all the required permits.)

Toward the end of the year, ultra-Orthodox activists found a new target: bus-stop shelters in Jerusalem. Over 20 such shelters—a blessing to Jerusalemites both in the winter rains and the summer heat—were vandalized in the final weeks of the year throughout the capital, ostensibly because of objections to sexually immodest advertising posters on them. There were also instances of public buses being stoned in the Orthodox Me'ah She'arim quarter.

The Orthodox public turned its attention in 1985 to another religious community, the Church of Jesus Christ of Latter-day Saints, or Mormons. In July a mass "prayer of mourning" was held at the Western Wall to protest the ongoing construction, on Mount Scopus, of the Jerusalem Center for Near Eastern Studies, a branch of Brigham Young University in Salt Lake City, Utah. Spurred by a group called *Yad L'Achim,* or Israel Torah Activists, the Orthodox community, joined by ultranationalist elements, called on the government to halt construction on the huge project, which, they contended, would be used for missionary activity. This was denied by the Mormons, who pointed to the fact that they had been running extension programs at three centers in Israel for the past 16 years, without complaint.

With the issue threatening to assume not only national but international proportions, as a number of U.S. senators made known their support for the project at the highest levels in Jerusalem, Prime Minister Peres assured representatives of the religious parties that he would look into the matter. On December 22 the cabinet decided to set up a special ministerial committee to examine the entire matter afresh and to apprise the cabinet plenum of its "findings." Two days later the Knesset defeated by a large majority a no-confidence motion presented by the ultra-Orthodox Agudat Israel party (even though it was itself a member of the coalition), focusing on Sabbath violations and on the construction of the Mormon center on Mount Scopus.

Israel and World Jewry

"OPERATION MOSES"

On January 3 the Israel Government Press Office held a "press briefing on the absorption of Ethiopian immigrants" for both local and foreign correspondents, who turned out in droves for the event. At the briefing, government officials and Jewish Agency treasurer Akiva Levinsky confirmed what had suddenly become the country's worst-kept secret, the fact that (according to Levinsky) "a little over 10,000" Ethiopian Jews had arrived in Israel "in recent years." At the same time, the government refused to disclose details of how the operation was organized and what other countries were involved.

"Operation Moses," as the rescue of Ethiopian Jews was called, had been launched by the Begin government in the late 1970s, but involved relatively small numbers. The period immediately preceding the early January disclosures had seen an intensive airlift of thousands of Ethiopian Jews, because of worsening conditions in Ethiopia, reportedly via Sudan. Since the airlift was only made possible through secret diplomatic arrangements, the Israeli government had imposed censorship on stories about the rescue. Public acknowledgment became necessary as news of the Ethiopian immigration spread unofficially by way of leaks from high officials and inconsistencies in the censorship process. One unfortunate effect of the sudden spotlight turned on the operation was to cause Sudan to bring a halt to the airlift, leaving an estimated 4,000 Jews in camps in the Sudan—the exact numbers were never known—and 6,000-8,000 still in Ethiopia.

Another effect was an outpouring of recriminations within the Israeli establishment about the unauthorized leaks. The responsibility, to the extent that it could be pinpointed, seemed to lie partly with Jewish Agency executive chairman Arye Dulzin, who had let the cat out of the bag during a visit to New York in December 1984, but more directly with the director-general of the Jewish Agency's immigration department, Yehuda Dominitz, who referred to the operation in an interview published just before the press conference in the official organ of the Judea-Samaria-Gaza Council of Settlements, *Nekuda*. The weekly had not submitted the text of the interview for prior censorship, and from the time of its publication, the way was short to banner headlines in Israel's mass-circulation afternoon dailies. The government's press conference sought to apply damage control by focusing attention on the absorption process rather than on the Ethiopians' manner of arrival, but this approach was obviously naive.

As the political storm over the disclosures died down, attention shifted to problems attendant on the absorption process itself, in particular the religious status of the Ethiopians. In 1973 the then Sephardi chief rabbi, Ovadia Yosef, had ruled that the Beta Yisrael (as the Ethiopians called themselves, rather than the derogatory name "Falashas") were descendants of the biblical tribe of Dan. The current rabbinate, however, questioned their religious status on the ground that, having been cut off from the mainstream of Jewish religious development, they had not followed the same divorce and marriage practices as other Jews. A previous demand by the rabbinate that the males undergo symbolic circumcision was regarded as such an affront by the deeply religious Ethiopians that it was withdrawn. The rabbis now insisted, however, that the newcomers should undergo the processes of ritual immersion and formal acceptance of Jewish law.

This, too, was viewed as degrading. "We suffered for thousands of years for the sake of the Torah, and we never dreamed that one day we would come to Israel only to be told that we are not Jews," Ethiopian spiritual leaders were quoted as saying at a meeting in early February between elders of their community and Israel's chief rabbis. In June, even as rabbis were overseeing a mass bar-mitzvah ceremony and celebration at the Western Wall for 90 Ethiopian boys from 20 absorption centers throughout the country, the rabbinate was refusing to marry some 20 Ethiopian couples unless they first underwent ritual immersion. By July the rabbinate's unbending stance led several hundred Ethiopians from absorption centers in Safed and Carmiel to embark on a 150-kilometer "march of pain" to Ben-Gurion Airport, to symbolize their desire to return to Ethiopia, where "at least we knew who we were," as one of the marchers put it.

A July 23 meeting between Prime Minister Peres and the chief rabbis had inconclusive results. According to a joint communiqué, "the Chief Rabbis stressed that the Ethiopian Jews are indeed Jewish and an integral part of the Jewish people," but that "as with any Jew immigrating to Israel, their personal status in matters of matrimony must be clarified by the rabbinate's institutions."

Although the prime minister maintained that the problem had been solved to universal satisfaction, not all the Ethiopians agreed. In September several hundred Ethiopian immigrants began a sit-in across the road from Heichal Shlomo in Jerusalem, seat of the Chief Rabbinate, to protest the requirement of ritual immersion for couples who wished to marry. Compounding the issue was the refusal of the Chief Rabbinate to allow Ethiopian community elders to serve as marriage registrars for members of their own community, lest this set a precedent applicable to Conservative and Reform rabbis. The upshot was that the sit-in became a month-long camp-out of hundreds of Ethiopian families, who were encouraged by various public figures and by passersby, who also donated food.

The demonstration was called off after an intricate agreement was reached by which an "Institute for the Heritage of Ethiopian Jewry," whose members would include the Ethiopians' *kessim*, or priests, would be created to present evidence to marriage registrars about Ethiopian couples wishing to marry. However, since this evidence would not be considered definitive by the rabbinate—which refused to budge on this matter—a special rabbinical court to deal with all aspects of the marriage process for Ethiopians was also to be formed. Finally, Ethiopians whose Jewish lineage was not in doubt would be able to marry without any special immersion ritual.

Among the many problems involved in the physical and cultural absorption of this immigration, that of housing the Ethiopians was being resolved relatively satisfactorily. In early December, Immigration Absorption Minister Ya'akov Tzur was able to report that all the Ethiopians who had been temporarily housed in hotels would be settled in apartments by year's end. (A good many hotels had been leased for the operation, both because the country's absorption centers were quickly filled to overflowing by the mass influx, and because the idea was to keep the Ethiopians together in the initial stage, for mutual support.) According to Tzur, the plan was to settle the Ethiopians throughout the country in relatively small groups of no more than 250 families in any one existing community. One all-Ethiopian settlement was, however, planned—near the northern Negev town of Kiryat Gat—which would become the national center for the community, housing institutions designed to preserve its ancient culture.

SOVIET JEWRY

Although the year was rife with reports about an imminent reopening of the gates by the Soviet authorities to Jews wishing to leave the USSR, 1985 actually proved to be one of the worst years for Jewish emigration in recent times. Only 1,140 Jews were permitted to leave, and of those just 342 found their way to Israel.

The rumors about a major Soviet policy shift on Jewish emigration hit the headlines in Israel in late October, when Immigration Absorption Minister Tzur told the daily *Hadashot* that plans existed for the absorption of "thousands" of Soviet Jews who were likely to be allowed to leave the USSR shortly. The reports were in part self-generated, based on hopeful readings of the attitudes of the new Soviet leader, Mikhail Gorbachev, and in part evidently disseminated by Moscow for its own purposes, notably, the approaching summit meeting between Secretary Gorbachev and U.S. president Reagan. Hopes were also raised by reports of Prime Minister Peres's meeting with Soviet Foreign Minister Shevardnadze at UN headquarters in New York on October 23 (see also "Foreign Relations"), and his talks with French president François Mitterrand in Paris on October 25, at which—as Peres told the Knesset on October 28—Mitterrand pledged that his country "would supply the means of transportation required in order to bring [Soviet Jews] directly from the Soviet Union to Israel." Peres revealed that he had asked Mitterrand to raise the issue of Soviet Jewry with Gorbachev, and that he had made this topic one of the focal points of his mid-October talks in Washington with President Reagan and Secretary of State Shultz.

Prime Minister Peres told the cabinet on November 17, two days before the opening of the Geneva summit, that the struggle on behalf of Soviet Jewry should be conducted by both public action and quiet diplomacy, and that he saw "no contradiction between the two" methods. Nevertheless, the international movement for Soviet Jewry was deeply split on this issue. Even as the executive of the World Conference on Soviet Jewry told a press conference in Geneva on the eve of the summit that they had been assured that President Reagan would bring up the Soviet Jewry issue "forcefully" in his talks with Gorbachev, and urged that no pressure be brought on Washington to link Soviet Jewish emigration to other areas in which Moscow had an interest, a group of activists, including former refuseniks, was asserting publicly that such linkage was vital.

Although Prime Minister Peres's statement at the end of November that he could "all but assure" former Russians in Israel that the USSR would soon permit family reunification seemed unlikely to be realized in the foreseeable future, several Soviet Jewish activists did arrive during the year. Included among them were Dr. Eliahu Pushkin, a Moscow gynecologist, and his family, who were allowed to emigrate after a five-year wait; Leonid Zelkind, a computer programmer from

Leningrad; Mordechai Yudborovsky and his family, also from Leningrad; prisoner of Zion Yitzhak Shkolnik, who was reunited in August with his wife and daughter, now 18, after an imposed 13-year separation; and another veteran refusenik and former prisoner of Zion, Mark Nashpitz, who arrived in October with his wife and son.

HOLOCAUST-RELATED EVENTS

A unique and harrowing event that took place in February was the First International Convention of Twins. During the three-day conference, some 30 survivors of the notorious medical experiments of Josef Mengele at Auschwitz—perpetrated chiefly on sets of twins—testified before an international panel. A major goal of the conference was to focus world attention on the Nazi war criminal, who was thought to be living in South America. The conference led to an agreement between Israel and the United States to intensify their cooperation in the search for the doctor. On May 7, Justice Minister Nissim informed the Knesset that as a material incentive the Israel government and the World Zionist Organization would give $1 million to anyone who could supply information leading to the trial of Josef Mengele.

Shortly thereafter, in a surprising and unrelated development, the remains of a man who had drowned in 1979 while swimming in the sea near São Paulo, Brazil, were exhumed from a cemetery not far from that city and tentatively identified as those of Josef Mengele. According to Brazilian federal police, Mengele had lived in São Paulo for about 15 years, at the home of an elderly German couple, under an assumed Austrian identity. An autopsy on the body and comparisons with dental and other records supplied by West Germany were carried out in the presence of U.S. and West German forensic specialists, all of whom declared that the body was almost certainly that of Mengele. The U.S. Justice Department also expressed itself satisfied with the identification. However, in September the Israeli Foreign Ministry's World Jewish Affairs section informed Israeli embassies abroad that Israel was still examining the evidence and could not yet make a definitive pronouncement.

AMERICAN JEWS

Relations between Israel and American Jews were subjected to some strain when, in September, a delegation of the American Jewish Congress met with King Hussein in Amman, the first time a group of American Jews had ever been received by the Jordanian monarch. The delegation sought (according to a Congress press release of September 11) "to learn first-hand about prospects for progress in furthering the peace process," so that the organization could "play an informed and constructive role in encouraging that process." The group also met with other ranking Jordanian officials and was received in Cairo by President Mubarak and his top aides. In Jerusalem, however, Vice-Premier and Foreign Minister Shamir refused to meet with the delegation, maintaining (in an interview with the *Jerusalem Post*) that such missions "serve as instruments in the hands of the Arabs to score points against [Israel]." Shamir, who also raised objections to a visit to Moscow by World Jewish Congress president Edgar Bronfman that took place around the same time, maintained that "Israel [alone] represents the Jewish people on Jewish problems"—a position evidently not accepted by Prime Minister Peres, who did receive the American Jewish Congress delegation to hear its report.

Although Shamir's criticisms undoubtedly stemmed in part from ideological antipathy between the Herut party he headed and the two organizations he assailed, they also reflected differing views of Israel-Diaspora relations. As American Jewish Congress executive director Henry Siegman, who was one of the delegation members, summed up the matter in an article he wrote for the *Jerusalem Post* after the contretemps, "[Yitzhak Shamir] assumes that Diaspora Jewish communities and organizations are not independent. It should go without saying that Jewish communities throughout the world, especially in the U.S., categorically reject this proposition."

For Israeli leaders, the matter of Israel-Diaspora relations was sensitive on other grounds as well. President Herzog, speaking on Aliyah (immigration) Day, held in conjunction with the anniversary of the Balfour Declaration (November 2, 1917), stated that the failure of American Jews to settle in Israel in significant numbers would surely be regarded by history as "one of Zionism's major failures," adding his hope that "it is not too late to change that verdict."

Culture

While on a day-to-day basis Tel Aviv maintained its position as Israel's cultural capital, in 1985, Jerusalem, the country's political and spiritual center, was on its way to becoming its "festival capital" as well.

In May the 12th Jerusalem International Book Fair, held biannually, attracted some 1,000 publishers from 40 countries, who displayed over 100,000 volumes to an eager Israeli public. The Jerusalem Prize for the Freedom of Man in Society, presented in conjunction with the five-day fair, was awarded to the Czech émigré novelist Milan Kundera.

Later in May, the three-week annual Israel Festival/Jerusalem offered over 160 performances of 85 different productions from Israel and 11 other countries. The festival was devoted to four major themes or individuals: works by Nobel Prize laureate Samuel Beckett, to mark the playwright's 80th birthday; 50 works by Johann Sebastian Bach, including a five-hour Bach marathon, in honor of the 300th anniversary of the composer's birth; Jewish mysticism, as expressed in three different productions of S. Ansky's *The Dybbuk;* and the music of Kurt Weill and his circle. Complementing the festival were some 60 free street performances sponsored by the Jerusalem municipality, given downtown and in outlying neighborhoods. Held in conjunction with the festival was the Second Jerusalem Film Festival, a week-long affair in which some 50 films from 18 countries were screened in the capital's Cinematheque. Many of the films had their only Israeli showings at the festival.

Yet another international event that took place in May in Jerusalem, Jewish Art Week, featured the first-ever auction held in Israel by Sotheby's of London, at which bidders paid over $1 million for about 250 Judaica items, including rare books and art works. The highest single price, $82,500, was paid by a private South American collector for an oil painting by Isidore Kaufmann, *Portrait of a Rabbi Before the Curtain of the Ark.* Coinciding with Jewish Art Week was the International Jewish Art Seminar, which drew about 170 participants from 15 countries, including Hungary, Rumania, and Yugoslavia. Among the highlights of this first-time conference was a symposium on the meaning and essence of Jewish art.

Mid-May also saw a week-long celebration marking the 20th anniversary of the opening of the Israel Museum in Jerusalem. No fewer than three new galleries were officially opened during the week: one housing a permanent display entitled "Israel Communities: Tradition and Heritage"; a gallery of Asian art; and a gallery of old masters of the 15th–19th centuries. (Later in the year a two-floor pavilion devoted entirely to Israeli art was also opened.) Now over three times as large as it was when it opened its doors on May 12, 1965, the Israel Museum had presented some 600 special exhibitions since that day, including 44 devoted to archaeology and 24 featuring Jewish art, as well as nearly 100 one-man shows and exhibits. The single most popular exhibition was that of the Armand Hammer art collection, which attracted 350,000 viewers in 1985.

On the stage, two of the year's most important works dealt with sensitive and controversial historical-political issues. *Kastner,* by Motti Lerner, a major Cameri Theater production that opened in August, was a docudrama based on the so-called trucks-for-blood negotiations between Dr. Israel Kastner, a Hungarian journalist, and the Nazi occupiers of Hungary, notably Adolf Eichmann, in 1944. Two-and-a-half hours long, *Kastner* used 21 actors to play 30 parts in an effort—which the critics found largely successful—to shed light on the personal motivations of the figures involved in this tragic historical episode. The year's most controversial play was undoubtedly *The Palestinian Woman,* by one of Israel's most prolific—and most politically oriented—playwrights, Yehoshua Sobol. This Haifa Municipal Theater production, which premiered in November, dealt with racism and fanaticism among Jews and Arabs alike, against the backdrop of the ongoing Israeli military control of the territories. Hanoch Levin, generally considered Israel's leading playwright, was represented in 1985 by *Everyone Wants to Live,* a philosophical black comedy, produced by the Cameri Theater.

Musically, Israelis showed eclectic taste. In May the British rock group Dire Straits launched a world tour with three concerts in Israel, for which nearly 50,000 tickets were sold. In Jerusalem the group performed at the Sultan's Pool amphitheater, under the stars and just below the illuminated walls of the Old City. A highlight of the classical-music year was a joint concert in June by the Israel and New York philharmonic orchestras at Tel Aviv's Mann Auditorium, under the baton of Zubin

Mehta. The concert was a benefit for the Israel Philharmonic Foundation. In August a highly successful international jazz festival was held in Jerusalem.

Two of the country's institutions of higher learning celebrated anniversaries in 1985. To mark the 60th anniversary of its founding, the Hebrew University of Jerusalem held a week of festive events for some 800 members of its international board of governors and its alumni, leading off the ceremonies with the dedication of the Vidal Sassoon Center for the Study of Anti-Semitism. Bar-Ilan University, Israel's only religious institution of higher learning, celebrated its 30th anniversary by dedicating the Raoul Wallenberg Chair in Holocaust Research, named for the Swedish diplomat who saved thousands of Jews in Hungary and later disappeared while in Russian captivity.

The 12th Maccabiah Games—the so-called Jewish Olympics—were held July 15–25 with the participation of some 4,000 athletes from 39 countries. Because the event was viewed as a gathering of Jewish athletes from around the world, not a series of individual competitions, no official count was kept of medals won by each contingent. However, the unofficial tally showed the United States in first place with 246 medals, including 109 gold; Israel second, with 214 medals, among them 62 gold; and Canada third, with 51 medals, 12 of them gold.

ARCHAEOLOGY

Objects from one of the most important neolithic finds ever made anywhere in the world went on exhibit at the Israel Museum in May. The 9,000-year-old decorated human skulls and artifacts, some of them unique, were excavated on behalf of the Israel Department of Antiquities and Museums in a cave in the Judean Desert, not far from the site where the Dead Sea Scrolls were discovered. Like the scrolls, these objects had been preserved by a combination of climate and cave darkness.

Earlier in the year, the Israel National Parks Authority opened an archaeological park at Jericho, thought to be the oldest continuously inhabited city in the world, its deepest stratum dating back nearly 10,000 years. In May another major archaeological park was opened to the public at a site dating back a mere five millennia, though far more significant in Jewish history: the City of David in Jerusalem. Excavated in the course of six years by a team under the direction of Hebrew University professor Yigal Shilo (often in the face of fierce resistance by ultra-Orthodox groups, who claimed that the site was a Jewish burial ground), the new park contained the remains of a room burned when the First Temple was destroyed by the Babylonians in 586 B.C.E.

That the ocean could be as effective a preservative as the desert was demonstrated in an exhibition entitled "From the Depths of the Sea," which opened in July at the Rockefeller Museum in East Jerusalem. Among the items on display, all of them from the cargoes of three ships which sank nearly 3,000 years earlier in the waters off Mount Carmel, was an almost perfectly preserved Canaanite sword from the 14th century B.C.E. On Mount Carmel itself the remains of a major Jewish settlement dating to the 2nd–4th centuries C.E. were being excavated by a Bar-Ilan University team directed by Shimon Dar. Further north, workers in the 19th season of digs at Tel Dan, sponsored by Hebrew Union College, found an Israelite altar apparently dating back to the 8th century B.C.E.

The year's richest (literally) find was undoubtedly a synagogue collection box containing about 500 coins, half of them gold, unearthed at the site of the ancient Jewish settlement of Merot, in eastern Galilee. Apart from it being the largest such collection ever found, the fact that the coins covered a time span from the 4th century B.C.E. to 150 years after the Arab conquest pointed to the exceptional longevity of the community.

Other Domestic Matters

Israel's population at the end of 1985 stood at 4.25 million, of whom approximately 3.5 million were Jews and nearly 750,000 non-Jews. The country's Jewish population increased by about 1.2 percent as compared with 1984, about half the rate of the non-Jewish increase. Although nearly one-quarter of the country's population resided in the Tel Aviv area, the flight from Tel Aviv proper continued. The city's population declined by .5 percent, as did that of Haifa. By contrast, the population of Jerusalem grew by 2.3 percent, to stand at 458,000 (328,000 Jews, 130,000 non-Jews). According to the Central Bureau of Statistics, the Jewish population in Judea-Samaria totaled 41,000 persons, and that of the Gaza Strip 2,000, at the end of the year.

Immigration figures for 1985 were bleak indeed: the 11,283 new immigrants who arrived during the year constituted the lowest number for a single year since the establishment of the state. Although the large proportional decrease from 1984 (40 percent) was due largely to the cessation of Ethiopian immigration, the bulk of which had come in 1984, immigration from other countries was also down by 14–30 percent. Thus, for example, only about 2,375 immigrants arrived from North America in 1985, down 14 percent from the previous year. Immigration from Western Europe was down 20 percent, from Eastern Europe, 27 percent, and from South America, 15 percent.

Israel was no longer the polyglot society it had once been, according to data gleaned from the 1983 census. Among the country's Jewish population aged 15 and over, 83 percent reported Hebrew as their main or sole language, up from 67 percent in the 1961 census; another 9 percent cited Hebrew as their second language. Arabic was the main language of 95 percent of the non-Jewish population.

Road accidents with fatalities were the lowest since 1967, according to Transport Minister Haim Corfu. In 1985 there were 12,761 accidents (13,174 in 1984) in which 387 persons were killed, down from 436 in 1984. In the year's most horrendous accident, on June 11, a train plowed into a bus at a railway crossing, killing 21 persons, including 17 schoolchildren who were on an outing.

In January Minister Without Portfolio Weizman initiated a new policy toward the country's Arab citizens when he fired the prime minister's adviser on Arab affairs, Binyamin Gur-Arye, and abolished the position altogether. Explaining his move in a Knesset debate on January 29, Weizman, who was charged by the prime minister with coordinating government activities in the Arab sector, said the idea was to treat all Israeli citizens on an equal basis, through the normal machinery available in the various ministries. Two days later, the government-sponsored Arabic-language paper, *Al Anba,* was closed down, also on Weizman's orders, on the ground that its small circulation and sectarian reporting rendered it impractical under the new approach.

Due at least in part to Weizman's efforts, the annual Land Day (March 30), commemorating a violent general strike by the country's Arabs in 1976 to protest land expropriations, passed peacefully within Israel, although there was some unrest in the territories. On July 11, Umm al-Faham became the country's first Arab "village"—it had a population of 25,000—to be accorded the status of a town; the ceremony was boycotted by Interior Minister Peretz because the local council issued a leaflet vilifying the Israeli army.

In a gesture of friendship toward Israel's Arabs (as well as toward the Soviet Union), on December 4, President Herzog became the first Israeli head of state to attend a convention of the Israel Communist party, which drew most of its electoral support from the country's Arab population. Herzog, who was criticized in various quarters for his decision to appear at the festive opening session of the convention, was greeted with chants of "Arab-Jewish brotherhood" and received a standing ovation after his remarks. At year's end the cabinet voted overwhelmingly to grant Arab and Druze local authorities $6 million to help offset their accumulated debt of $8.5 million, this following a meeting between Prime Minister Peres and a delegation of heads of Arab local authorities.

Udi Adiv, a kibbutznik who had been convicted of spying for Syria in a sensational 1972 trial, when he was 27, was released from prison on parole on May 14, after serving 13 years of his 17-year term. The release was conditional on his not becoming involved in political activity or leaving the country until the full 17 years were up.

On June 4 the judicial commission of inquiry into the murder of Chaim Arlosoroff (appointed in March 1982 at the initiative of Prime Minister Menachem Begin to determine who murdered the Labor Zionist leader on June 16, 1933) issued its judgment, one that was welcomed by the former prime minister. The three-man commission, chaired by retired Supreme Court justice David Bechor, concluded unanimously that neither Avraham Stavsky nor Zvi Rosenblatt, both members of the Revisionist movement who had been linked to the crime, had any connection with the murder. According to the commission, "The evidence and material brought before us do not enable us to determine (a) who the murderers were; (b) whether it was a political murder on behalf of any party, or not."

The results of a poll conducted by the Dahaf Institute, released in August, showed that Israelis were essentially no different from people elsewhere. Asked to choose "the most important thing" from among money, social status, career, a comfortable life, good friends, and a happy family life, nearly two-thirds (65.7 percent) selected a happy family life. Money and its attendant comforts were well behind in second and third place at 8.6 and 8.2 percent, respectively.

Personalia

New government appointments included Amiram Nir, replacing Rafael Eitan, as the prime minister's adviser on terrorism, and Tel Aviv district police commander David Kraus as chief of the Israel Police, with the rank of inspector-general. In the military, Maj. Gen. Dan Shomron took over from Maj. Gen. David Ivri as deputy chief of staff, and Commodore Avraham Ben-Shushan was promoted to the rank of rear admiral, taking over from Rear Adm. Ze'ev Almog as commander of the Israel Navy. MK Michael Dekel (Herut) was approved by the Knesset as deputy defense minister and Rafael Pinhasi (Shas), as deputy labor and social welfare minister. Pinhasi succeeded MK Menahem Porush (Agudat Israel), who had resigned due to differences with Labor and Social Welfare Minister Moshe Katzav. MK Elazar Granot was elected by the Mapam Central Committee as the party's new secretary-general on February 10, succeeding Victor Shemtov.

On October 13, Jerusalem mayor Teddy Kollek was awarded the German Book Publishers Association's 1985 Peace Prize, in a Frankfurt ceremony. (In December Kollek marked the 20th anniversary of his initial election as mayor.)

Personalities who died during the year included Mordechai Ben-Tov, Zionist pioneer and former cabinet minister, in January, aged 84; MK Yitzhak Zaiger (Likud-Liberals), in February, aged 49 (he was replaced in the Knesset by Ya'akov Shamai of Herut); Shraga Netzer, longtime Labor party leader, in April, aged 87; Prof. Benjamin Akzin, a leading intellectual of Revisionist Zionism and an Israel Prize recipient for jurisprudence (1967), in April, aged 80; Justice Yitzhak Kahan, retired Supreme Court president who chaired the 1982 commission of inquiry into the Sabra and Shatilla massacre, in April, aged 72; Moshe Ron, leading Yiddish-language journalist and longtime secretary of the Editors Committee, in July, aged 81; Rabbi Ya'acov Israel Kanievsky, known as the "Steipeller," a leading *halakhic* authority, in August, aged 87; Pinhas Litvinovsky, an Israel Prize-winning artist, in September, aged 92; Yona Wallach, influential poetess, in September, aged 41; Noah Mozes, editor-in-chief and board chairman of the daily *Yediot Ahronot,* in October, of wounds sustained when he was struck by a car, aged 73; Dr. Moshe Rachmilewitz, a founder of the Hadassah–Hebrew University Medical School, in October, aged 86; Yosef Zaritsky, the doyen of Israeli art and an Israel Prize laureate

(1959), in November, aged 94; Arye Zimouki, a leading political journalist and chairman of the World Federation of Jewish Journalists, in December, aged 65; Arye El-Hanani, noted architect and Israel Prize recipient, in December, aged 87; Shlomo Rosen, former Mapam MK and cabinet minister, in December, aged 80; and Rachel Marcus, leading actress with the Cameri Theater company for 30 years, in December, aged 72.

RALPH MANDEL

World Jewish Population, 1984

THE 1986 AMERICAN JEWISH YEAR BOOK (AJYB) contained new estimates of the Jewish population in the various countries of the world at the end of 1984, as well as background information and analysis. The statistical tables are reprinted here, without the accompanying text. Changes have been made in one respect only. While the estimates for the Jews in the 1986 AJYB related to the end of 1984, the data for the general population of the respective countries reproduced the United Nations estimates as of midyear 1983. This time the updated United Nations estimates as of midyear 1984 have been used for the total population,[1] and the proportion of Jews per 1,000 of the respective country's total population has been adjusted accordingly.

The 1988 AJYB will present updated and, where necessary, revised Jewish population estimates for the countries of the world at the end of 1986.

The three main elements which affect the accuracy of each estimate are the nature of the base data, the recency of the base data, and the method of updating. A simple code combining these elements is used to provide a general evaluation of the reliability of the Jewish population figures reported in the detailed tables below. The code indicates different quality levels of the reported estimates: (A) base figure derived from countrywide census or relatively reliable Jewish population survey; updated on the basis of full or partial information on Jewish population movements in the intervening period; (B) base figure derived from less accurate but recent countrywide Jewish population investigation; partial information on population movements in the intervening period; (C) base figure derived from less recent sources, and/or unsatisfactory or partial coverage of Jewish population in country; updating according to demographic information illustrative of regional demographic trends; and (D) base figure essentially conjectural; no reliable updating procedure. In categories (A), (B), and (C), the years in which the base figures or important partial updates were obtained are also provided.

---

[1]United Nations, Department of International Economic and Social Affairs, Statistical Office, *Population and Vital Statistics Report: Data Available as of January 1, 1986.* Statistical Papers, Series A, Vol. 38, No. 1, 1986.

For a country whose Jewish population estimate of 1984 was not only updated but also revised in the light of improved information, the sign "X" is appended to the accuracy rating.

U.O. SCHMELZ
SERGIO DELLAPERGOLA

TABLE 1. ESTIMATED JEWISH POPULATION, BY CONTINENTS AND MAJOR GEOGRAPHICAL REGIONS, 1982 AND 1984

Region	1982 Original	1982 Revised Abs. Nos.	1982 Revised %	1984 Abs. Nos.	1984 %	% Change 1982–84
Diaspora	9,614,300	9,594,300	74.1	9,491,600	73.2	−1.1
Israel	3,374,300	3,349,600	25.9	3,471,700	26.8	+3.6
World	12,988,600	12,943,900	100.0	12,963,300	100.0	+0.2
America, Total	6,477,700	6,477,600	50.1	6,469,000	49.9	−1.3
North[a]	6,013,000	6,015,000	46.5	6,015,000	46.4	—
Central	46,800	46,800	0.4	47,300	0.4	+1.1
South	417,900	415,800	3.2	406,700	3.1	−2.2
Europe, Total	2,842,700	2,825,100	21.8	2,758,600	21.3	−2.6
West	1,070,900	1,053,300	8.1	1,048,900	8.1	−1.0
East & Balkans[b]	1,771,800	1,771,800	13.7	1,709,700	13.2	−3.5
Asia, Total	3,417,200	3,392,500	26.2	3,509,300	27.1	+3.4
Israel	3,374,300	3,349,600	25.9	3,471,700	26.8	+3.6
Rest[b]	42,900	42,900	0.3	37,600	0.3	−12.4
Africa, Total	172,000	169,700	1.3	147,400	1.1	−13.3
North	21,250	19,950	0.2	16,700	0.1	−17.5
South	120,250	119,250	0.9	119,100	0.9	−0.1
Rest[c]	30,500	30,500	0.2	11,600	0.1	−62.0
Oceania	79,000	79,000	0.6	79,000	0.6	—

a U.S.A. and Canada.
b The Asian territories of USSR and Turkey are included in "East Europe and Balkans."
c Including Ethiopia.

TABLE 2. ESTIMATED JEWISH POPULATION DISTRIBUTION IN THE AMERICAS, 1984

Country	Total Population	Jewish Population	Jews per 1,000 Population	Accuracy Rating	
Canada	25,150,000	310,000	12.3	A	1981 X
United States	236,681,000	5,705,000	24.1	B	1971–83
Total Northern America		6,015,000			
Bahamas	226,000	500	2.2	C	1970
Costa Rica	2,534,000	2,500	1.0	C	1984
Cuba	9,992,000	700	0.1	D	
Dominican Republic	6,102,000	100	0.0	D	
Guatemala	7,740,000	800	0.1	A	1983
Haiti	5,185,000	100	0.0	D	
Jamaica	2,301,000	300	0.1	B	1982
Mexico	76,792,000	35,000	0.4	C	1980
Netherlands Antilles	261,000	700	2.7	D	
Panama	2,134,000	3,800	1.8	D	
Puerto Rico	3,398,000	2,000	0.6	D	X
Virgin Islands	103,000	500	4.9	D	X
Other		300		D	
Total Central America		47,300			
Argentina	30,097,000	228,000	7.6	C	1960–75
Bolivia	6,253,000	600	0.1	C	1984 X
Brazil	132,580,000	100,000	0.8	B	1980
Chile	11,878,000	17,000	1.4	C	1982 X
Colombia	28,217,000	7,000	0.2	C	1977
Ecuador	9,115,000	1,000	0.1	C	1982
Paraguay	3,278,000	900	0.3	C	1984 X
Peru	19,198,000	5,000	0.3	C	1982
Surinam	370,000	200	0.5	B	1984
Uruguay	2,990,000	27,000	9.0	D	
Venezuela	16,851,000	20,000	1.2	D	
Total Southern America		406,700			
Total		6,469,000			

TABLE 3. ESTIMATED JEWISH POPULATION DISTRIBUTION IN EUROPE, 1984

Country	Total Population	Jewish Population	Jews per 1,000 Population	Accuracy Rating	
Austria	7,552,000	6,500	0.9	A	1981
Belgium	9,853,000	32,200	3.3	D	
Bulgaria	8,961,000	3,300	0.4	C	1965
Czechoslovakia	15,459,000	8,500	0.5	D	
Denmark	5,112,000	6,800	1.3	C	1984
Finland	4,882,000	1,000	0.2	A	1984
France	54,947,000	530,000	9.6	B	1972-78
Germany, East	16,671,000	800	0.0	D	
Germany, West	61,181,000	33,000	0.5	B	1984
Gibraltar	28,000	600	21.4	A	1981
Great Britain	56,488,000	330,000	5.8	B	1984 X
Greece	9,896,000	5,000	0.5	B	1984
Hungary	10,665,000	61,500	5.8	D	
Ireland	3,535,000	2,300	0.6	A	1984 X
Italy	56,983,000	32,000	0.6	B	1982
Luxembourg	363,000	700	1.9	C	1970
Netherlands	14,420,000	26,200	1.8	C	1984
Norway	4,140,000	1,000	0.2	A	1982
Poland	36,914,000	4,600	0.1	D	
Portugal	10,164,000	600	0.1	D	
Rumania	22,897,000	26,000	0.1	B	1984
Spain	38,333,000	12,000	0.3	D	
Sweden	8,337,000	15,000	1.8	C	1982
Switzerland	6,442,000	19,000	2.9	A	1980
Turkey[a]	48,265,000	20,000	0.4	C	1984
USSR[a]	275,000,000	1,575,000	5.7	B	1979
Yugoslavia	22,963,000	5,000	0.2	B	1980
Total		2,758,600			

[a] Including Asian regions.

TABLE 4. ESTIMATED JEWISH POPULATION DISTRIBUTION IN ASIA, 1984

Country	Total Population	Jewish Population	Jews per 1,000 Population	Accuracy Rating	
Hong Kong	5,364,000	1,000	0.2	C	1980
India	745,012,000	4,300	0.0	C	1971
Iran	43,414,000	25,000	0.6	D	X
Iraq	15,356,000	200	0.0	D	
Israel	4,200,000[a]	3,471,700	826.6	A	1984
Japan	120,018,000	1,000	0.0	C	1984
Lebanon	2,644,000	100	0.0	D	
Philippines	53,351,000	100	0.0	C	1982
Singapore	2,529,000	300	0.1	C	1984
Syria	9,934,000	4,000	0.4	D	
Thailand	50,396,000	300	0.0	C	1980
Yemen	6,660,000	1,000	0.2	D	X
Other		300		D	
Total		3,509,300			

[a]End 1984.

TABLE 5. ESTIMATED JEWISH POPULATION DISTRIBUTION IN AFRICA, 1984

Country	Total Population	Jewish Population	Jews per 1,000 Population	Accuracy Rating	
Egypt	45,817,000	200	0.0	D	
Ethiopia	42,441,000	10,000	0.2	D	
Kenya	19,536,000	100	0.0	B	1984 X
Morocco	21,408,000	13,000	0.6	D	X
South Africa	31,586,000	118,000	3.7	B	1980
Tunisia	6,937,000	3,500	0.5	C	1982
Zaire	29,671,000	200	0.0	D	
Zambia	6,445,000	300	0.0	D	
Zimbabwe	7,980,000	1,100	0.1	D	
Other		1,000		D	
Total		147,400			

WORLD JEWISH POPULATION / 337

TABLE 6. ESTIMATED JEWISH POPULATION DISTRIBUTION IN OCEANIA, 1984

Country	Total Population	Jewish Population	Jews per 1,000 Population	Accuracy Rating
Australia	15,544,000	75,000	4.8	B 1981
New Zealand	3,233,000	4,000	1.2	B 1981
Total		79,000		

TABLE 7. COUNTRIES WITH LARGEST JEWISH POPULATIONS (100,000 JEWS AND ABOVE), 1984

| | | | \% of Total Jewish Population ||||
| | | | In the Diaspora || In the World ||
Rank	Country	Jewish Population	%	Cumulative %	%	Cumulative %
1	United States	5,705,000	60.1	60.1	44.0	44.0
2	Israel	3,471,700	—	—	26.8	70.8
3	Soviet Union	1,575,000	16.6	76.7	12.1	82.9
4	France	530,000	5.6	82.3	4.1	87.0
5	Great Britain	330,000	3.5	85.8	2.5	89.5
6	Canada	310,000	3.3	89.1	2.4	91.9
7	Argentina	228,000	2.4	91.5	1.8	93.7
8	South Africa	118,000	1.2	92.7	0.9	94.6
9	Brazil	100,000	1.0	93.7	0.8	95.4

TABLE 8. DISTRIBUTION OF THE WORLD'S JEWS, BY NUMBER AND PROPORTION (PER 1,000 POPULATION) IN VARIOUS COUNTRIES, 1984

Number of Jews in Country	Jews per 1,000 Population					
	Total	Below 1	1–5	5–10	10–25	25 and over
Number of Countries						
Total	75[a]	50	15	6	3	1
Below 1,000	24	19	4	—	1	—
1,000–5,000	17	14	3	—	—	—
5,000–10,000	7	6	1	—	—	—
10,000–50,000	16	10	5	1	—	—
50,000–100,000	2	—	1	1	—	—
100,000–1,000,000	6	1	1	3	1	—
1,000,000 and over	3	—	—	1	1	1
Jewish Population Distribution (Absolute Numbers)						
Total	12,963,000	391,100	333,400	2,751,500	6,015,600	3,471,700
Below 1,000	11,500	8,500	2,400	—	600	—
1,000–5,000	41,400	31,600	9,800	—	—	—
5,000–10,000	43,800	37,000	6,800	—	—	—
10,000–50,000	362,400	214,000	121,400	27,000	—	—
50,000–100,000	136,500	—	75,000	61,500	—	—
100,000–1,000,000	1,616,000	100,000	118,000	1,088,000	310,000	—
1,000,000 and over	10,751,700	—	—	1,575,000	5,705,000	3,471,700
Jewish Population Distribution (Percent of World's Jews)						
Total	100.0	3.0	2.6	21.2	46.4	26.8
Below 1,000	0.1	0.0	0.0	—	0.0	—
1,000–5,000	0.3	0.2	0.1	—	—	—
5,000–10,000	0.3	0.3	0.0	—	—	—
10,000–50,000	2.8	1.6	0.9	0.2	—	—
50,000–100,000	1.1	—	0.6	0.5	—	—
100,000–1,000,000	12.5	0.8	0.9	8.4	2.4	—
1,000,000 and over	82.9	—	—	12.1	44.0	26.8

[a]Excluding countries with fewer than 100 Jews.

Special Supplement

The American Jewish Committee 80th Anniversary

In 1906, an outbreak of pogroms in czarist Russia impelled a small group of distinguished American Jews to create the American Jewish Committee, dedicated to the protection of civil and religious rights of Jews the world over. Over the ensuing eight decades, the organization's agenda came to reflect the growing range of concerns of American Jews. On the occasion of its 80th anniversary, the American Jewish Committee celebrated its past and turned, with renewed dedication, to the challenges of the future.

In Appreciation

THE American Jewish Committee observed its 80th anniversary with a series of events held throughout the year, in different parts of the country. Thanks to the generosity of the following men and women, the anniversary year—including the annual meeting and celebration in Washington, D.C., May 14–18, 1986—will long be remembered as an inspiring landmark in the Committee's history.

FOUNDERS

Mr. and Mrs. Norman E. Alexander
Mimi and Barry Alperin
Alan Batkin
The Blaustein Family
Barbara and David Burstin
Wilma and Howard I. Friedman
Mr. and Mrs. Reuben M. Ginsberg
E. Robert and Barbara Goodkind
Sally and Bob Gries
Mr. and Mrs. Robert S. Jacobs
Mort Lowenthal
Charles and Elaine Petschek
Robert and Arleen Rifkind
Walter H. Solomon
Shirley and George Szabad

PATRONS

Judith and Stanton Brody
Lois and Theodore Ellenoff
Eleanor Freed
Barbara and Howard Gilbert
Bee and Philip Hoffman
Mr. and Mrs. Joseph Lelewer
Libby and Leo Nevas
Mr. and Mrs. James Marshall
Mr. and Mrs. Norman S. Rabb
Valerie Richter
Henry Sherman

SPONSORS

Paul R. and Lenore Aronson
Meta and Ronald Berger
Mr. and Mrs. William Bransten
Mr. and Mrs. Matthew Brown
David B. Fleeman
Ginnie and George Grumbach
Robert L. and Frances A. Hess
Charlotte and Alexander Holstein
Arlyne and Jacob Imberman
Mr. and Mrs. Gerald S. Jeremias
Manette and Richard Kaufmann
Barbara Kest
Mrs. Harold L. Rosenthal
Dr. and Mrs. John Slawson
Mrs. Howard L. Tiger
Mrs. Elise D. Waterman
Ruth and Bernard Weinflash

The Continued Vitality of the American Jewish Committee at 80

by HENRY L. FEINGOLD

WHEN THE NEED FOR change is greatest, we are most prone to reenact the stratagems that have been successful in the past. This holds true for organizations, no less so than for individuals. The plethora of Jewish organizations that clutters the American Jewish scene is specific to time and place, yet we rarely acknowledge that some of these groups have become obsolete. Instead, we allow them to continue, watching with amazement as they become things they were never meant to be.

The test of the continued viability of particular Jewish organizations must come from within. Ultimately the judgment should be based on how well the founding principles of the organization have stood the test of time. From that perspective, the American Jewish Committee (AJC) is more fortunate than other Jewish community-relations and defense organizations, whose missions were less broadly conceived. When the threat to American Jewish survival stems more from acceptance than from raging anti-Semitism, agencies whose agendas rest solely on a defense function are threatened with a loss of function. Success, no less so than failure, it needs to be pointed out, can be a cause of obsolescence. What role can Zionist organizations play when the principal goal of Zionist ideology, the establishment of a Jewish state, has been realized? Zionism, in its American Jewish version, has become so much a part of Jewish consciousness in the United States that it is difficult today to find any Jewish organization that does not lay claim to being Zionist, at least in the functional sense of being a staunch supporter of Israel. The mission that was once the sole preserve of Zionist organizations is today shared by all.

Sometimes history simply bypasses an organization. The founders of the Jewish "congress" movement prior to World War I railed against the "court Jews" of the AJC, preaching endlessly about the right of the "Jewish masses." Today it is the descendants of those masses who constitute the membership of the AJC. The Jewish masses have gone on to become individuated members of the middle class, seeking desperately to differentiate themselves from the masses.

The AJC, of course, has no special exemption from the ravages of time, and we will presently note those areas where it has been compelled to reshape its mission to take account of new realities. Still, the agency continues to be remarkably vital. Indeed, the AJC's organizational culture and persona have grown more relevant to American Jewry as the descendants of the East European immigrants have become more like the German Jews they once held simultaneously in awe and contempt. Not all the reasons why the AJC continues to thrive are readily retrievable, but a fortunate confluence of heritage and present circumstance certainly has something to do with it.

The AJC never allowed its vision of the future to be colored by any blinding ideology. Such ideologies, of course, have inspired Jews in the past and continue to do so today, releasing enormous energy and talent. But there is another side to the coin; ideologies are highly perishable, and the debris of organizations that embraced them in the past litter the Jewish historical scene. The *halutz,* that product of Socialist-Zionist ideology, who once sang of the beauty of the soil, is hardly heard from at present. Today beauty is produced in the kibbutz beauty parlor, and salvation comes from calculating the profits generated by the kibbutz factory. All people eventually discover what the AJC's founders learned naturally from functioning in an American environment: life precedes ideology and, when necessary, breaks through the confines that the latter seeks to impose.

Of the 59 prominent Jews who were invited to convene on November 11, 1906, to establish the AJC, over a third were native born, and a high percentage of the remainder had arrived in the United States when they were quite young. Their American experience shaped the AJC founders into operationalists, men who were drawn more to common sense than to ideological fervor. To the newly arrived East European immigrants, who were likely to identify Jewishness with ideological heat, such types must have seemed alien. But it was precisely the penchant for pragmatism of the AJC founders that was crucial for long-range policy planning. This is one of the keys to the ongoing relevance of the AJC.

Clear evidence of the insight of the AJC founders into how a free society operates can be seen in the two areas where the organization has always been a pacesetter: information strategy and political tactics. Louis Marshall, the second president of the AJC, seemed to understand intuitively—there were no college courses in "communication arts" in his day—that the production and dissemination of information as building blocks for the perception of reality were crucial elements in modern society. Marshall grasped the fact that American society permitted all groups, including Jews, to have input in shaping—Marshall preferred the term "educating"—public opinion. Great care was thus taken by the AJC to build a capacity for the production and dissemination of information into the organization. Over the years, AJC-sponsored research, its use of the media, and its official publications have given the organization an influence which belies its comparatively small membership. Works like the five-volume *Studies in Prejudice,* the two-volume Lakeville study, and the various National Surveys of American Jews have not only produced important data but are in themselves historical data.

A clear sense of how a free society operates also shaped the political tactics of the AJC founders, which were based on a combination of "education" and coalition building. The latter has today become a commonplace in Jewish community-relations work, since without it a group that constitutes only 2.5 percent of the American population would easily be overshadowed by groups with greater numbers and more urgent agendas. Still, it was the AJC that pioneered efforts in this area.

The AJC founders were fearful that the East European immigrants arriving on these shores would, as a result of centuries of physical and spiritual ghettoization, revert to separatism in the United States and thereby become as vulnerable here as they had been in Europe. The problem, as the AJC leaders defined it, was to change their perceptions, which had been shaped by an experience with government and politics at their most malignant. Men like Louis Marshall could not understand how political action outside normal channels could have an impact on public policy. Why go on strike or talk about revolution, if the legal instruments for change were available to Jews? Why agitate in the streets if the education process could be used to build public opinion to support Jewish interests? If conflicting interests did indeed exist, Marshall maintained, they could be reconciled within the system. What was important to him was that in the United States there was no prohibition against Jews projecting influence. Indeed, Marshall dreamed of Jews educating the entire world with their "civilizing ideas."

Young, affluent, and often well educated, the early leaders of the AJC matched the mold of Progressive reformers. It was the Progressives, represented by "Teddy" Roosevelt in the White House and Charles E. Hughes and Woodrow Wilson in their respective state capitols, who had instilled a new sense of buoyancy in the American people. A confident feeling was about in the nation that despite failures, especially in the governance of cities, the American experiment would again be set aright. For their part, the AJC leaders' optimism about American society led naturally to a confidence regarding the future of American Jewry. And this confidence, in turn, was buttressed by a firm belief, which they shared with their relatives in Germany, that the full emancipation of Jews was assured. This optimism may seem naive in a post-Holocaust world, but many of the founding generation of the AJC did in fact live to see the granting of full civil and political rights under the Weimar constitution—which was written by a Jew. Were they alive today, the early AJC leaders might well argue that it was not their assumptions that were unreasonable, but rather the course of history.

Proud of the remarkable economic achievement of their group, which they attributed to the unprecedented freedom and opportunity provided by American society, the early AJC leaders could not imagine anything but a happy outcome to the American Jewish experience. Many of them no doubt believed that how Jews fared in the larger society was related more to the continued growth of the gross national product than to the abstract principles of ideology. It seemed inconceivable to them that over the long run a group like the Jews, which demonstrated the entrepreneurial energy and civic virtue so esteemed by the host culture, could long be excluded on the basis of religious prejudice. A thriving market economy, the AJC leaders reasoned, could not long abide measurements of value which did not relate to utility. And American Jews quite clearly possessed such utility.

The early AJC leaders were fully aware that the American system was not yet perfect from a Jewish standpoint. There was, for example, discrimination in some resort areas and social clubs. Moreover, some distressing stereotypes appeared in the press, and occasionally the charge was put forward that Jews were malingerers when it came to fulfilling their military obligations. In addition, there were the vexing activities of Christian missionaries and such shocking incidents as the lynching of Leo Frank in Georgia. Still, the AJC leaders took it for granted that things would improve, and especially so if Jews took care to appear like everyone else and to be good, loyal Americans. What they could not foresee was that the very freedom and openness of American society, which they had come to cherish, would bring in their wake a new set of problems for American Jews, problems that were no less threatening than exclusion.

Such leading AJC figures as Jacob Schiff, Louis Marshall, Oscar Straus, and Cyrus Adler were genuinely convinced that a confluence existed between American and Jewish values. Indeed, to them it seemed almost as if the American experiment were based on a Judaic idea. After all, Judaism, or at least the "Old Testament" Hebraic ethos, was cherished by the Puritans. That gave Jews an extra measure of legitimacy, and it was legitimation, most certainly, that was of primary interest to the founders of the AJC. When Oscar Straus established the American Jewish Historical Society in 1892, he commissioned Meyer Kayserling to write a book about the Jewish involvement in the discovery of America. The result was the still useful *Christopher Columbus and the Participation of the Jews in the Spanish and Portuguese Discoveries.* Straus must have been gratified with the volume, since Kayserling not only maintained that Columbus may have been a Marrano but also demonstrated that Marranos had financed several other voyages of discovery. Jews, it appeared, had not only been "present at the creation," but were, at least in some sense, the actual creators of the Republic.

Small wonder, then, that the AJC leaders viewed themselves as being as fully American as Jewish, looking upon American society as something of a derivative Jewish culture. It must have warmed the hearts of the surviving founders of the AJC when, in 1923, Robert Park, the distinguished non-Jewish social theorist, earnestly suggested that Jewish ethics be taught in high schools as the model of the American ethos. That was what the AJC leaders had felt all along. They saw no problem in being at once Jewish and American, no such thing as the "two-cultures" problem later identified by sociologists, but only confluence and harmony.

Even on the matter of Zionism, the original AJC approach falls remarkably close to where most American Jews locate themselves today. That may come as a surprise to those who believe that the AJC was founded by adamant anti-Zionists. There were, of course, some such individuals among the AJC founders. But there were also men like Julian Mack and Judah Magnes, who were outspoken political Zionists, and others, like Jacob Schiff and Louis Marshall, who considered themselves cultural Zionists. Jacob Schiff was joined by a number of other prominent AJC figures in extending generous financial support to the budding educational and cultural institutions of the *Yishuv*. During World War I, AJC leaders played an important role in providing sustenance to the hard-pressed Jewish community in Palestine. In 1918 the AJC officially endorsed the Balfour Declaration. In 1929 Louis Marshall and several other prominent individuals associated with the AJC were coopted as members of the expanded Jewish Agency, the political and administrative body created by the British government to help administer the Palestine Mandate.

Since the creation of the State of Israel, the AJC has come fully to terms with the aspirations and program of political Zionism. The very idea of a Jewish state struck terror in the hearts of some early AJC leaders, who dreaded the specter of "dual loyalty." That great fear, which was a reflection of their own insecurity, was needless. American Jewry has not negated its loyalty to the United States. Rather, it has followed the prescription of Louis Brandeis, when he wrote: "Practical experience and observation convince me that to be good Americans, we must be better Jews, and to be better Jews we must be Zionists." Brandeis's formulation, including its sequence of loyalties—American, Jewish, Zionist—has proved over time to be eminently acceptable to most American Jews. Support of Israel ranks near the top of what has been identified as the "civil religion" of American Jewry. At the same time, the number of American Jews choosing to settle in Israel remains low, the phenomenon being largely confined to the Orthodox sector of the community. American Jewry as a whole has come to view

Israel as an invaluable source of Jewish energy that can be enlisted in the cause of American Jewish survival.

In recent years the AJC's links to Israel have been strengthened in a number of significant ways. An Institute on American Jewish–Israeli Relations has been established, which in typical AJC fashion seeks to correct misperceptions on both sides by providing accurate information through research. The AJC has also founded the Matthew and Edna Brown Young Israeli Leadership Program to transfer important political skills to emerging leaders in Israeli society and to familiarize them with the workings of religious and political pluralism in the United States. A Hebrew-language journal, *Tefutsot Israel,* informs Israeli readers about events and problems relating to American Jewry.

II

Time has been relatively kind to the AJC, but it has not left the organization totally untouched. Thus, some problems that were once thought to be critical have either been solved or have taken on less menacing proportions. On the other hand, a number of victories that were once proudly tolled seem insignificant in retrospect. Most importantly, various problems that were only dimly foreseen in the past now loom large, while some solutions implemented in an earlier period appear inappropriate in present circumstances.

Anti-Semitism was a core problem for the AJC prior to World War II. In 1929, Cyrus Sulzberger sounded the alarm about an impending wave of anti-Semitism, which did in fact materialize during the troubled 1930s. Today, however, when American Jewry seems more threatened by absorption into a benevolent society, such concerns have lost their edge. No student of Jewish history would ever counsel a relaxing of defenses against the dreaded malady of anti-Semitism; it is too enduring a phenomenon for that. But surely the sounding of an alarm about a sustained loss of American Jewish particularity deserves a higher priority.

Similarly, the struggle waged by the AJC to assure Jewish students access to the nation's best colleges and professional schools has much less relevance today. The motivating factor in this situation was not merely the awareness that schools like Harvard offered a superior education but also the recognition that certification from such schools yielded access to the inner citadels of power in American society. With a little help from Sputnik and the courts, the education battle has been won. There is no Ivy League college today with a Jewish enrollment of less than ten percent, and in the prestigious professional schools the figures often climb to three times that.

A strong Jewish presence on campus, among both students and faculty, as well as a proliferation of Jewish studies programs, seems so natural today that it is difficult to imagine that the situation could ever have been otherwise. That is why the recent spate of research about the formal and informal quotas that once obtained at schools like Wellesley, Sarah Lawrence, and Yale produces gasps of disbelief among the Jewish students attending those institutions today. There are even some Jewish survivalists who have begun to ask if the victory is not an empty one. They see the prestige colleges, with their beautiful campuses, talented students, and liberal arts programs, as seductive traps, leading students away from a strong commitment to the Jewish community.

The struggle—ultimately unsuccessful—against immigration restriction was a key priority of the AJC in the 1920s. In 1965, too late for the Jewish victims of the Holocaust who might have found a haven here, a new immigration law went into effect, making a crucial distinction between normal immigrants and people in dire need of a place of refuge. Today there are fewer Jews in the refugee stream. Moreover, a haven for Jews exists in Israel. At present the problem is not where to put refugee Jews, but rather how to get them out of places like the Soviet Union and Syria.

There is one major instance in the history of the AJC in which the strategies that worked well in the past simply proved ineffective in a new context. That was during the 1930s and 1940s, when the AJC, despite its talent for coalition building, its political influence, and its skills in communication and education, could not convince officials of the Roosevelt administration to open the nation's doors to Jewish refugees and to forcefully impress upon the Nazis that the mass murder of Jews would not be tolerated. In retrospect it is clear that the quiet behind-the-scenes approach that the AJC preferred was inappropriate in the context of the Holocaust. The AJC leaders remained loyal to the Roosevelt administration even after it became clear that the U.S. State Department was undermining all attempts at rescue. What Rheinhold Niebuhr once observed about Jews generally seems particularly true of the AJC's wartime leadership. Niebuhr felt that Jews were theologically unable to fully imagine evil, especially the satanic evil represented by the Nazi regime in Berlin. Instead the AJC leaders were convinced that what worked before would work again. Still, it is difficult to say if a more vocal approach would have made much difference with regard to the outcome. Even if American officials had been willing to act, it seems impossible that they could have convinced the Nazi leaders to abandon their plans for a "final solution" after the invasion of the Soviet Union in June 1941. Regimes which dream up programs of mass murder are probably closed off to moral suasion, and until mid-1943 that was the only weapon Washington had available in combating Nazism.

A key concern of the AJC in the past was the welfare of Jewish communities abroad. Threats to far-flung Jewish communities still exist today, but now a sovereign Jewish state seems best able to cope with such situations. Indeed, Israel even has the capacity to bring to justice individuals whose hands are stained with Jewish blood. Moreover, new organizations have been established whose exclusive concern is aiding Jews in Russia, Iran, Ethiopia, or wherever. The defense function has long since ceased being the exclusive preserve of the AJC.

On the American scene, as we have noted, the need to protect the civil and religious rights of Jews has grown somewhat less urgent. The key problem today is restoring the inner vitality of American Jewry. What does it avail to safeguard the rights and interests of American Jews if they voluntarily choose to consign themselves to oblivion? This, indeed, is a new page in the American Jewish experience, and one that remains largely untouched by the AJC's formal legacy.

III

There are many American Jews who have no sense of an inner Jewish crisis. Why assume that things are bad, they ask, when things appear to be so good? Indeed, things are good, and it is the very success of American Jewry that makes the challenge to its survival so difficult to perceive. Forgotten is the fact that the remarkable success story is written primarily in terms of achievement in the secular society—the highest per capita income of any group; the highest level of formal education of any group; and so on. Jews are justifiably proud of the disproportionate role they play in the elites that assure the smooth functioning of American society. Still, despite their success, and, indeed, in some sense because of it, Jewish survival has become more problematic than ever before.

The sad truth is that individual achievement does not necessarily translate into communal well-being, and the full cost of the "making it" ethos to Jewish life has yet to be calculated. The statistics of success—scientized artifacts from beginning to end—measure only what is countable: so many lawyers; so many physicians; so high a per capita income; and so on. They tell us nothing about the inner spirit required for Jewish survival in a free society. Even if every American Jewish child attends an Ivy League college and becomes a skilled professional, it cannot be assumed that the collective Jewish enterprise will thereby be strengthened. The generation that founded the AJC linked its achievement and its good fortune to serving the Jewish community. Today, in contrast, only a small percentage of those who possess the financial and intellectual resources needed to play a leadership role in Jewish life choose to become involved. Ties to the Jewish community are voluntary and, in a growing number of cases, they have become extremely tenuous. What has clearly happened is that there has been an erosion in the Jewish cultural nexus which, in the past, produced the values that made Jews want to give, serve, and belong.

The secular mind-set, which a few generations ago was still tempered by traditional Jewish values, has taken an increasingly strong hold in American Jewish life. The impact of this on Jewish culture is hardly neutral, since the kind of intense Calvinist secularism that dominates American culture is highly fragmentizing; it insists on separating things which in other cultures continue to remain bound together. Thus, in the United States, it is not only church that is separated from state, but also ethics from etiquette, art from religion, theory from practice, health from happiness, and so on. The consequence of this fragmentizing process is particularly problematic for the Jewish enterprise: it has led to the separation of the religious component—Judaism—from the ethnic-peoplehood component—Jewishness.

A secular Jew is a person who is convinced that it is possible to be Jewish without being Judaic. Such a person considers himself or herself free to choose the degree of adherence to the tenets of the faith, to reshape those tenets, or to abandon them altogether. For many generations, secular Jews —Bundists, Yiddishists, Labor Zionists, and all shades of universalists— were able to share the same Jewish world as "observant" Jews. In recent years, however, several controversial matters, including the "who is a Jew" issue as embodied in the question of patrilineal descent, have led to a widening of the gulf between the various groups in Jewish life. If not narrowed, this gulf may prove more threatening to Jewish survival than the demographic decline which is also linked to modern secular assumptions. "Pluralism," "unity in diversity," and the other traditional assumptions that once helped to bridge the divisions that have existed among Jews since the Emancipation appear to have lost their healing properties.

In a sense the American Jewish life equation itself has grown larger since the founding of the AJC. The good things have become better and the bad things have become worse. Poverty and its attendant ills have almost vanished from the Jewish scene. A once marginal immigrant group now occupies a central place in American society. But the sense of belonging to a distinct people with its own worthwhile culture has also waned: American Jewry is becoming more American and less Jewish. Without a common base in experience and some shared values, the idea that affluent, professional Jews should act together for the greater good of all Jews—the essence of the AJC sensibility—may prove insufficient for Jewish survival.

IV

Where do the profound alterations in the American Jewish condition leave the AJC? Clearly the organization is located at the flashpoint of change. Moreover, it would appear that key elements of the AJC's organizational culture and persona have taken on increased importance for American Jews. The German-Jewish founders of the AJC were in approximately the same situation in their society that most American Jews find themselves in today. The former also needed to balance the claims of secular and Jewish culture, of individual and community needs, of freedom and responsibility. Perhaps sensing this, thousands of contemporary Jewish professionals, both male and female—gifted lawyers, skilled surgeons, successful managers in the public and private sectors—have in recent years entered the ranks of the AJC. By dint of its tradition, the AJC is the likeliest conduit to enlist such Jews for a greater Jewish purpose.

As early as 1962, John Slawson, then executive vice-president of the AJC, determined to turn the agency's programming in a more survivalist direction. But the question of how to change an organization whose sensibility is basically secular into a vehicle for Judaic enrichment is not easily answered. AJC members, to be sure, have been culturally enriched by participating in the summer seminar programs of the Academy for Jewish Studies. Similarly, telecourses in basic Judaism and the radio series "Jewish Viewpoints" have been well received by the membership. These and other programs have helped to make the AJC "less a committee and more Jewish." Still unanswered, however, is the question of how to reach out to a wider Jewish audience. And, most importantly of all, with what kind of message? Indeed, what kind of Judaism should a secular organization seek to project?

We need not search far for the answer. The AJC's propensity for generating information and research may be construed as a transmuted element of traditional Judaic culture. Whatever the matter under examination, be it the nature of anti-Semitism, the impact of intermarriage, and so on, the approach to the subject is related to the tradition of *lernen,* of close study of text, which is at the core of the Jewish tradition. True, the methods used are scientific, but the passion to be at the juncture where information and abstraction converge stems from a classical Jewish outlook. That does not mean people who are drawn to the AJC are talmudists dressed in modern garb. Rather, it places the talent for information strategy, which the AJC has cultivated since its very inception, within the Jewish fold. It is a contemporary way in which the AJC fulfills a Judaizing role.

Rather than focusing on texts, the AJC concentrates on Jewish life itself. In one way or another what American Jews are talking about is usually linked to an AJC study. Time and again Jewish agencies discover that the requisite research that defines a particular problem has already been undertaken by the AJC. And the tradition continues. In "Project 2000" the AJC seeks to open a window into the future, anticipating the emerging trends in Jewish life at the end of the 20th century and beyond, and developing policy recommendations around them. Soon a series of pamphlets will be available reporting the findings of a conference on "New Perspectives in American Jewish Sociology." While certainly not Talmud, the role such information plays in keeping the Jewish enterprise vital should be evident.

In keeping with its desire to project information to the widest possible audience, the AJC maintains the most extensive and diverse publications program of any Jewish organization. Appearing under AJC auspices are the *American Jewish Year Book, Commentary, Present Tense, AJC Journal, Washington Report,* and a number of issue-oriented newsletters, occasional studies, and position papers. Future plans call for making broad use of the electronic media to supplement printed materials.

The AJC did not expand its membership until 1944. Before that time, the organization was composed of a handful of influential laymen and a small professional staff. AJC leaders were convinced that people of weight and influence, individuals who were already well connected in the general community, could best represent the Jewish interest. The broadening of the AJC membership was based less on the sudden conviction that democracy should prevail than on the fact that over the years the "select few" had become the "select many." The number of American Jews who qualify for leadership at present has increased dramatically. At the same time, there has been a noticeable decline in the number of such Jews who manifest a compelling desire to use their wealth and position to serve the interests of the Jewish community. It is difficult to conceive of the survival of American Jewry without the resources of this elite element.

The need of the hour, then, is to persuade free Jews to make a commitment for a greater Jewish purpose. "Free Jews" is the key term here, going to the very heart of the matter. There is no force in post-Emancipation Jewish life that can compel Jews to be Jewish. Beyond that, the habit of linking freedom to responsibility, which stands at the center of the Jewish tradition, has been largely forgotten. Freedom, properly understood, should encompass not only civil and political rights, but also the freedom bestowed by individual estate and talent. At present, only a small percentage of the increasing number of American Jews who are blessed with the latter form of freedom—that based on personal resources, whether intellectual, spiritual, or financial—have been mobilized for Jewish survival. Many of them, unfortunately, are content to use their freedom to feed the cult of "self-fulfillment" that is yet another fruit of the modern secular ethos.

In the Jewish tradition, self-fulfillment is possible only in a familial and communal context, one in which freedom is always linked to responsibility. Classically, Jews live through community, rather than outside or against it. Today, free modern Jews need to be persuaded to behave in a fashion that came naturally to most Jews in the past: to participate in the work of Jewish communal organizations and to generally discharge vital Jewish communal functions. The founders of the AJC were keenly aware that history and kinship had assigned them special responsibility. It is that sense of responsibility which needs to be communicated to the American Jewish elite of today. Without it, the hope for Jewish survival under conditions of freedom is greatly diminished.

V

It would be easiest, of course, for the AJC to go on as before, to continue doing what it has always done so well. "If it ain't broke," the American maxim has it, "don't fix it." However, given the realities of American Jewish life at present, sticking with the stratagems and agendas of the past would be a prescription for disaster. Let us be clear about it: the signs of Jewish well-being in the United States are external, more like the flush on the cheeks of a consumptive patient than a symptom of good health. The statistics of success do not address the primary threat to American Jewish survival, which is internal, a matter of the spirit. That is the real meaning of the perceptible decline in Jewish commitment that we are witnessing today.

Is there a role that the AJC can play in helping to meet this new challenge? A great deal depends on how well the AJC understands its own organizational culture. Over the years, it has been an effective intergroup-relations and defense agency, guarding against a palpable external threat. Can the AJC now shift gears and face a threat that emanates largely from within? The foregoing discussion has pointed up several aspects of the AJC character that ideally suit it to play such a role.

The founders of the AJC were modern and urbane, firmly entrenched in the upper middle class, and proudly American. Yet, at the same time, they found a way to be Jewishly committed. Over the years, the AJC has brought thousands of free modern Jews into the arena of Jewish life, making them activists in the Jewish community. It is indeed possible to motivate such Jews to serve a larger Jewish purpose. The history of the AJC bears witness to that fact. The AJC has served American Jewry well for these past 80 years. May it continue to flourish to the traditional 120th year of life—and beyond.

Looking Ahead: The American Jewish Committee at 80

by David M. Gordis

Anniversaries are appropriate times for reflection—not only for individuals, but for organizations as well. And it is particularly appropriate for the American Jewish Committee, for which thoughtful reflection is a defining characteristic. In the most significant ethical treatise our people has produced, *The Ethics of the Fathers,* one of our sages set down for us, almost two millennia ago, the underlying motivation for the reflective process. He wrote:

> Consider three things and you will not go astray:
> Know from where you have come;
> And where you are going;
> And before whom you are destined to give an accounting.

Throughout its 80-year existence, the American Jewish Committee has sought to understand the past. We have sought to uncover the underlying causes of society's major problems and challenges. Our research regarding the roots of prejudice, the nature of ethnicity, and the ramifications of pluralism has enriched our understanding, both of the social pathology of our age and of how people behave within their own groups and with others. We have examined our Jewish values and explored their pertinence to contemporary realities. We have sought to anticipate events and to help plan for, guide, and shape the world in which we live. And our memories have constantly been harnessed to serve the future.

In that spirit we have pioneered in the struggle for human rights, on behalf of Jews and all others who have suffered physical abuse, prejudice and discrimination, hunger, poverty, and tyranny over mind and spirit, anywhere in the world. Our work on the international scene through the Jacob Blaustein Institute for the Advancement of Human Rights has broken new ground and set a high standard for all who labor in this field. In

---

Note: Text of address by David M. Gordis, executive vice-president of the American Jewish Committee, at the Committee's 80th-anniversary celebration, May 15, 1986, in Washington, D.C.

our own country, we have taken strong policy positions on issues involving civil rights, public education, immigration, law enforcement, and electoral reform. We have stood, and will continue to stand, in the front ranks in the battle to protect the constitutional separation of church and state.

At the same time we have been concerned about the apparent decline in values in our land—the general sense that such concepts as honesty, patriotism, and mutual respect and dignity do not command the importance they once did in the marketplace of ideas. Therefore we have helped spur the search for ways to teach common-core values in our society. Not Christian values, not even Judeo-Christian values, but values shared by all. And that transition is important. For while the values of many of us are shaped by our particular religious and ideological positions, those values must become nonparochial when they enter the public arena. In this country of diversity, Jews and Christians and Muslims and Buddhists and nonbelievers all share the responsibility for shaping the discourse on values, public ethics, and morality. And so we are concerned about inculcating beliefs that we can hold in common, not those determined by the outlook of one or another religious group. And in all of our efforts, we have been aware of our accountability—to the Jewish community, to the general community, and, perhaps most meaningfully, to our own traditions of excellence in whatever we undertake.

From its very beginning, this agency undertook to serve the needs of our people by advancing the freedoms of all people, and to do so responsibly and effectively, retaining our allegiance to the ethical principles of Judaism, to American democratic values, and to the humanistic insights of enlightened Western tradition. Over the years, we have held steadfastly to the conviction that these three sources of our character, far from being incompatible, are mutually reinforcing—are, indeed, the foundation upon which a creative Jewish life in America can and will continue to be built. We have always seen American Jews as full partners in the forging of the American character, and we are convinced that our Jewish community's creative vitality is enhanced by its interaction with American values. We reject assimilation. We seek, rather, acculturation and integration. And by word and deed we declare that this goal is both attainable and desirable.

It is this conviction—or, more precisely, the recent challenges to this conviction—that I should like to address here today. As we reflect on the past and seek to define the American Jewish Committee's role in Jewish and American public life in the years ahead, I think it is vital that we reaffirm our world view and understand the challenges to it, so that we ourselves are absolutely clear about our position and can promote it effectively in the Jewish and general communities.

II

The validity of our traditional AJC agenda has been challenged recently by powerful and prominent voices urging a sharp narrowing of Jewish concerns. More and more frequently in Jewish organizational life we hear the assertion that the only issue for Jews is Israel—that statements and positions on Israel are the sole criterion by which political candidates should be judged or supported, financially or otherwise. To a considerable extent, the creation of single-issue PACs is an expression of this phenomenon.

In that narrow framework, political and religious leaders whose views on the separation of church and state, on matters of social policy and other public concerns run counter to the views of most American Jews—and may even threaten vital Jewish interests here and abroad—are transformed overnight into Jewish heroes on the basis of a carefully crafted statement or two in support of Israel. Alliances are urged and political alignments pressed upon the Jewish community on the basis of this single issue. The separation of church and state, we are told, is not that important; Israel needs all the friends she can get, whatever the price paid for this friendship. Is the nation weighing policy alternatives regarding the levels of military appropriations and the funding of social programs? We are assured by some that we need not concern ourselves with determining a proper balance among national priorities or make painful choices. There is just a single principle to be applied: It is inconsistent for those who advocate support for Israel to oppose any military program at any time. How easy—and how tempting! With one stroke we are relieved of the need to consider vital issues carefully and to advocate what we feel is best for our country, for Israel, and for the world.

True to its past, and concerned about tomorrow, the American Jewish Committee rejects this single-issue agenda. Our commitment to Israel's strength, security, and vitality is unshakable. Our efforts to promote understanding of, and support for, Israel's needs are wide and deep, as is our determination to strengthen Israel-Diaspora relations and increase intergroup understanding inside Israel. Israel is a prime focus of our coalition building and our international diplomatic and cultural activities. But our credibility is rooted in the breadth of our concerns as Americans *and* as Jews. Our support of Israel derives both from our Jewish consciousness and from our commitment to America and its democratic values. It gains in effectiveness because we are recognized not as narrow advocates of self-interest, but as fully involved participants in the entire range of American and international issues. We reject out of hand the notion that our Jewish and general loyalties conflict with one another.

Let me stress that our rejection of the single-issue agenda goes deeper than the matter of effectiveness and credibility. We have no quarrel with organizations that focus exclusively on pro-Israel advocacy. We support AIPAC and participate in its work. What we reject is the confusion of that portion of the Jewish agenda, important as it is, with the whole. Israel is the critical center of Jewish life, and we are in awe of its accomplishments and its significance for all Jews everywhere. Israel is a threshold issue for us. We cannot and will not support candidates for public office who are unsympathetic to our concerns for Israel's security and future. But we are a world people. From thousands of years of living on the margins of often-hostile societies, Jews have distilled a sensitivity for the disadvantaged and the oppressed which we have put to good use in this free American climate.

American Jews have pursued justice and compassion in line with the authentic spirit and teachings of our heritage. This pursuit wears no label, either conservative or liberal. It is what defines us as a Jewish community living in the spirit of prophetic values. As participants and leaders in the movements to protect and extend human rights and improve intergroup relations, we have made an indelible contribution to the growth and enhancement of American life. I am convinced that the overwhelming majority of American Jews remains committed to that participation—even though some influential leaders, who have grown disheartened because these efforts are sometimes painful and never easy, urge us to turn away from our traditional social concerns and to formulate our positions in the narrowest self-interest.

III

Besides propounding a myopic view of Jewish concerns, some advocates of a narrow communal agenda also criticize the American Jewish Committee's traditional nonpartisanship. Technically and legally, of course, all Jewish communal agencies are nonpartisan—and no one is suggesting that this be changed. But a pattern of political alignment by national Jewish agencies has developed over the past few years, and there are pressures for the AJC to conform. Indeed, some American Jewish leaders have found it expedient to indicate broad Jewish support for one or another policy of the current administration, even when there is little evidence of such support.

Advocates of partisanship in Jewish public life argue that a political party or administration will support Jewish interests only if American Jews articulate their support for that party or administration's goals and ideology. We challenge that assertion. In recent days, for example, the suggestion has been made that the Jewish community actively support the sale of arms to

Saudi Arabia. It is a suggestion that a number of us have characterized as unrealistic. For strategic considerations, as well as a concern to be as helpful and supportive as we possibly can to an administration which has been a remarkable friend to Israel and to many Jewish needs, we have said we would not go to battle against this sale. The feeling has been conveyed that, in fact, the strategic balance will not be substantially altered by the reduced package proposed. But to expect anyone in the American Jewish community to actively support a proposal to supply arms to a government which is at war with the State of Israel—a government which has sought in every way possible to obstruct the peace process, and has supported and bankrolled international terrorism through Syria—is naive and unrealistic.

This is not a partisan matter. American Jews are not homogeneous in their political views and it is a distortion to portray them as such. The membership and leadership of the American Jewish Committee reflect a broad range of political views, and we feel strongly that Jews should be represented all across the American political spectrum. We do not believe that any political party or ideology has a monopoly on virtue, principle, or morality. But we believe with equal firmness that Jewish organizations must stand apart from, and above, partisan politics. Our policy positions must be determined through careful analysis of the issues, and in light of our broad interests, values, and objectives, not by the need to conform to any party line. To trade away the opportunity to bring a Jewish perspective to bear on the shaping of American society for some real or imagined *quid pro quo* would betray our vision of American pluralism and of Jews as full participants in this society. For both ethical and practical reasons, the American Jewish Committee has rejected partisanship *de facto* as well as *de jure*. I hope that we will continue to do so.

Another AJC approach that periodically comes under pressure is our disinclination to join umbrella organizations. The most significant case in point is our long-standing decision to participate as observers, rather than members, of the Conference of Presidents of Major American Jewish Organizations. We do not deny that it is important, in some instances, for the Jewish community to coordinate its policies and sometimes even to speak with a single voice. Umbrella organizations such as the Presidents' Conference, the National Jewish Community Relations Advisory Council, and such special-purpose umbrella groups as the National Conference on Soviet Jewry were created to foster such communication and coordination—and we work closely with them. We participate in their deliberations and make our wide-ranging expertise available to them. Our commitment to cooperation and coordination explains our membership in NJCRAC and the National Conference, and our active observer role in the Presidents' Conference. Recently, however, the leaders of some umbrella organizations, and some of the organizations themselves, have moved beyond coordination and presumed to speak for the total Jewish community—and even, in a sense, to govern it. But the AJC delegates to no other organization the right to speak on its behalf, except when an explicit decision to that effect has been taken by our Board of Governors.

The positions of the American Jewish Committee are respected and influential because they are thoughtful, richly nuanced, and informed by our own style and our own perspectives. They are not aimed at attaining a common denominator among all Jewish organizations, because we do not feel that is either realistic or desirable. Our positions are formulated carefully and represent our own views and perceptions. Through our national office, our offices in Washington and throughout the United States, and in Israel, Europe, and Latin America, we will continue to make our individual voice heard. We reaffirm the value of pluralism, not only for the larger society but for the Jewish community as well. While Jews are united in our commitment to creative Jewish continuity, we are enriched and strengthened by our diversity within that unity, and it is the American Jewish Committee's goal to maintain that diversity.

Our commitment to Jewish pluralism is one reason for our serious concern about the exacerbation of tensions among the religious ideological groups in Jewish life. Political realities in Israel have exacerbated these tensions in the United States, and we are working hard to bring together individuals from the different groups, both here and in Israel, who seek to restore civility to Jewish interrelationships. The very existence of a single Jewish people is at stake here. Unless we can close the fissures that have developed, we face the possible bifurcation of the Jewish people and the emergence of two separate Jewish communities that will not intermarry and will barely interact except in conflict. It is vital that we apply our human-relations and bridge-building skills to this most ominous challenge now facing us.

IV

In order to appreciate the central thrust and particular timeliness of the AJC's outlook and message, some historical perspective is necessary. Modern Jewish life began with the Emancipation's promise to the Jews of Western Europe that they could have full social and political acceptance if they divested themselves of that which made them Jewish. This offer was met both by individual Jews and the Jewish community with ambivalence, and their responses ranged from assimilation at one extreme to rejection of the offer and self-imposed isolation at the other. Though a range of responses continues to exist, even today, two great epochal events of the modern Jewish experience—the Holocaust and the establishment of the State of Israel—have transformed the picture.

The Holocaust demonstrated the limitless capacity of so-called "enlightened" people for the most extreme degenerate behavior and proved there were limits to the possibility of Jewish assimilation, even for those who found that goal desirable and attractive. It also challenged Jews to defy a hostile world and seize the responsibility for continued Jewish existence. Then, from the ashes of Jewish destruction, came the national rebirth of Israel, quickening the pulse of every Jew and exhilarating the Jewish community the world over. In the United States, a vigorous and creative reconstruction of Jewish community life began. New institutions were created; a resurgence of interest and affiliation, particularly within the liberal movements in Jewish religious life, became apparent; and the seeds of communal organizational structure began to sprout.

Post-World War II Jewry has been shaped by these two extraordinary events in contemporary Jewish history. Until now, however, American Jews have not succeeded in integrating our responses to these events and developing a balanced view of ourselves and our relationship with the world. Our behavior as a community continues to swing between two psychological extremes: an exaggerated self-confidence bordering on triumphalism on the one hand, and a sense of vulnerability bordering on paranoia on the other. We have not yet found our equilibrium—and this is precisely the challenge the American Jewish Committee offers the Jewish community as we look toward the 21st century. We assert that America must be seen as the third major experience of modern Jewish life. It offers Jews full participation as Jews and invites us to contribute a Jewish perspective to the building of this nation without sacrificing our character as Jews. Developing a coherent vision of contemporary life from a uniquely American Jewish viewpoint has been the AJC's hallmark for the past 80 years, and it is the principal task to which we must address ourselves.

This is why, on our 80th anniversary, we celebrate American life and commit ourselves anew to American and Jewish pluralism. This is why we reject the dangerous and unwise single-issue agenda which, by stressing Israel as the sole determinant of our political behavior, suggests to the larger community that we are less than fully loyal Americans, and are not concerned with the broad range of issues confronting American life. America is a new phenomenon in Jewish history. The AJC is not Pollyanna enough to think that Jews have no problems here. There continues to be anti-Semitism in this country, and we continue to be vigilant to manifestations of it when they occur. But if we are to take America seriously, we must overcome the mentality of an embattled minority in a hostile world.

This nation is not hostile to us; and we must not make defensiveness our fundamental mode of interaction with the larger society. We share the responsibility of shaping this society, and we must do so out of loyalty to Jewish values and commitments, not a narrowing of focus, not a defensiveness, not a new, self-imposed ghettoization. We must finally accept the notion that we are influential insiders, not tolerated outsiders in this land; and we must learn to use our influence wisely. At the same time, we must not delude ourselves into an exaggerated view of our power. America is responsive to Israel's needs, not because of the wealth and influence of American Jews, but because Americans resonate to Israel's struggles and ideals and view Israel as an ally, strategically and ideologically. Jewish influence should be used to articulate that reality in the political system, not with triumphalism and arrogance, but with intelligence and wisdom.

The complexity of American Jewish life requires a degree of coordination and communication, but it does not require a King of the Jews. The era of *shtadlanut* is over. Politically, philosophically, and ideologically, Jews properly approach the complex issues of this society in all of our diversity. We must welcome this pluralism and find ways to communicate with one another without hostility and recrimination. Except for those limited areas where we choose to speak as one, we must make clear to the larger society that there is no single voice that speaks for all American Jews.

Only if we come to terms with both American pluralism and Jewish pluralism can we engage the many serious issues of Jewish life that we have hardly touched upon. What should be the relationship between world Jewry and Israel? Beyond political and economic support, how do we internalize the reality of Israel in our experience and in the experience of those who will follow us? Can a nonfundamentalist Jewish religious ideology move us, engage us, have relevance for the decisions that we make? Do traditional Jewish values still command our loyalty, and if so, how do we apply them to our public lives—as Jews, and as citizens of the larger society? How do we transmit them to future generations? In all our diversity, how do we maintain the integrity of the Jewish community and exercise full partnership in determining the contours of American public policy?

The American Jewish Committee has pointed the way. Not by narrowing our concerns or by a meanness of spirit. Not by a rigid partisanship in Jewish communal organization. Rather, through a new integration of Jewish life, characterized by vigilance, but not fear; confidence, but not triumphalism; consolidation of our gains without turning away from the needs of others; attention to our particular concerns without overlooking the breadth and universal dimensions of our tradition—and allegiance to our ideological commitments without vilification of those who differ.

The threshold of a new and extraordinary period of Jewish life is before us here in America. As we begin our second 80 years, the American Jewish Committee stands poised to lead the way with enthusiasm, with skill, with informed commitment to principle, and with faith in what the future will bring.

Honors and Awards

DURING ITS 80th-anniversary year, the American Jewish Committee honored a number of individuals for outstanding contributions to the betterment of the human condition in this country and abroad.

The American Liberties Medallion

The medallion is the highest honor AJC has to bestow. It is given in recognition of a lifetime of exceptional service in the cause of human liberty and human rights.

In May 1986 the American Liberties Medallion was presented by AJC president Howard I. Friedman to U.S. Secretary of State *George P. Shultz,* "a statesman and humanitarian dedicated to both his country's national interests and the conscience and hopes of all mankind."

The Mass Media Award

This award is given to an individual and/or institution for a distinguished record of journalistic excellence, dedication to public enlightenment, and commitment to freedom of the press.

In May 1986 the Mass Media Award was presented by AJC honorary vice-president Ruth R. Goddard to *Norman Lear,* innovative television writer, producer, and director, "for exceptional contributions to the preservation of core American values through television."

The Akiba Award

This award honors an individual and/or institution for outstanding contributions to the enrichment of Jewish life through scholarship, leadership, literature, and communal activity.

In May 1986 the Akiba Award was presented by Howard Gilbert, chair of the Jewish Communal Affairs Commission, to *Abram L. Sachar,* first president and chancellor emeritus of Brandeis University, for "his innovative educational leadership, which has made the single Jewish-sponsored university in the United States one of the outstanding institutions of higher learning in the nation."

The Distinguished Leadership Award

This award honors men and women in the American Jewish Committee who have provided special inspiration and leadership in fulfilling the organization's goals both nationally and in their own communities.

In November 1985 the Distinguished Leadership Award was presented by AJC honorary president Maynard I. Wishner to *David B. Fleeman,* AJC national vice-president and past president of the Committee's Greater Miami chapter, for his decades of service to a host of social and philanthropic causes, Jewish and non-Jewish, in the local community and on the national scene.

In May 1986 the Distinguished Leadership Award was presented by AJC honorary president Maynard I. Wishner to outgoing president *Howard I. Friedman,* in recognition of his "special contribution to improving Vatican-Jewish relations and in appreciation of his outstanding leadership, insightful intelligence, and dedication that have served the American Jewish Committee to its everlasting gain."

Special Awards

In November 1985 the AJC conferred special awards on two individuals who had labored to make the closing conference of the United Nations Decade for Women in Nairobi a success.

Mimi Alperin, chair of AJC's Interreligious Affairs Commission and coleader of AJC's delegation to the NGO Forum in Nairobi, presented a special citation to *Dame Nita Barrow,* convener of the Forum of Non-Governmental Organizations at Nairobi, "in grateful recognition of [her] successful stewardship of the NGO Forum at the United Nations Decade for Women Conference, which helped make it a vehicle of positive dialogue and constructive cooperation."

Suzanne Elson, chair of the AJC's Women's Issues Committee and coleader of the AJC's delegation to the NGO Forum in Nairobi, presented a special citation to U.S. Undersecretary of State Designate *Alan L. Keyes,* "in grateful recognition of [his] vigorous and eloquent articulation of America's commitment to the ideals of universality, tolerance, and peace, expounded in the United Nations Charter, at the UN Decade for Women Conference."

In May 1986, on the occasion of Israel's 38th anniversary, Howard I. Friedman, the AJC's outgoing president, presented a special citation to Israel's ambassador to the United States, *Meir Rosenne,* "in celebration of the inseparable bonds between American Jews and Israel."

80th-Anniversary Planning Committee

CHAIR
Norman E. Alexander
Westchester

Mimi Alperin
New York

Meta S. Berger
Chicago

Sholom D. Comay
Pittsburgh

Theodore Ellenoff
New York

Edward E. Elson
Atlanta

Suzanne Elson
Atlanta

Arnold B. Gardner
Buffalo

Howard A. Gilbert
Chicago

Jerome R. Goldstein
New York

E. Robert Goodkind
New York

Leonard Greenberg
West Hartford

Rita E. Hauser
New York

Charlotte G. Holstein
Syracuse

Robert S. Jacobs
Chicago

Martin Kellner
Los Angeles

Jack Lapin
Houston

Michael Lapin
Orange County

Marcia E. Lazar
Chicago

Melvin L. Merians
Westchester

Leo Nevas
Westport

David H. Peirez
Long Island

Robert L. Pelz
New York

Robert S. Rifkind
New York

Ruth Septee
Philadelphia

R. Peter Straus
New York

Emily W. Sunstein
Philadelphia

Steven L. Swig
San Francisco

Directories
Lists
Obituaries

National Jewish Organizations[1]

UNITED STATES

Organizations are listed according to functions as follows:
- Community Relations 367
- Cultural 371
- Overseas Aid 376
- Religious, Educational 378
- Social, Mutual Benefit 396
- Social Welfare 398
- Zionist and Pro-Israel 401

Note also cross-references under these headings:
- Professional Associations 409
- Women's Organizations 410
- Youth and Student Organizations 411

COMMUNITY RELATIONS

AMERICAN COUNCIL FOR JUDAISM (1943). 298 Fifth Ave., NYC 10001. (212)947-8878. Bd. Chmn. Clarence L. Coleman, Jr.; Pres. Alan V. Stone. Seeks to advance the universal principles of a Judaism free of nationalism, and the national, civic, cultural, and social integration into American institutions of Americans of Jewish faith. *Issues of the American Council for Judaism; Special Interest Report.*

AMERICAN JEWISH ALTERNATIVES TO ZIONISM, INC. (1968). 501 Fifth Ave., Suite 1600, NYC 10017. (212)557-5410. Pres. Elmer Berger; V.-Pres. Mrs. Arthur Gutman. Applies Jewish values of justice and humanity to the Arab-Israel conflict in the Middle East; rejects nationality attachment of Jews, particularly American Jews, to the State of Israel as self-segregating, inconsistent with American constitutional concepts of individual citizenship and separation of church and state, and as being a principal obstacle to Middle East peace. *Report.*

AMERICAN JEWISH COMMITTEE (1906). Institute of Human Relations, 165 E. 56 St., NYC 10022. (212)751-4000. Pres. Theodore Ellenoff; Exec. V.-Pres. David M. Gordis. Seeks to prevent infraction of civil and religious rights of Jews in any part of the world; to advance the cause of human rights for people of all races, creeds, and nationalities; to interpret the position of Israel to the American public; and to help American Jews maintain and enrich their Jewish identity and, at the same time, achieve full integration in American life;

---

[1] The information in this directory is based on replies to questionnaires circulated by the editors.

includes Jacob and Hilda Blaustein Center for Human Relations, William E. Wiener Oral History Library, Leonard and Rose Sperry International Center for the Resolution of Group Conflict. AMERICAN JEWISH YEAR BOOK (with Jewish Publication Society); *Commentary; Present Tense; AJC Journal; The Washington Report.* Published in Israel: *Tefutsot Yisrael,* a quarterly, and *Alon Yedi'ot,* a monthly bulletin of the Institute on American Jewish-Israeli Relations.

AMERICAN JEWISH CONGRESS (1918). Stephen Wise Congress House, 15 E. 84 St., NYC 10028. (212)879-4500. Pres. Theodore R. Mann; Exec. Dir. Henry Siegman. Works to foster the creative cultural survival of the Jewish people; to help Israel develop in peace, freedom, and security; to eliminate all forms of racial and religious bigotry; to advance civil rights, protect civil liberties, defend religious freedom, and safeguard the separation of church and state. *Congress Monthly; Judaism; Boycott Report; National Report.*

ANTI-DEFAMATION LEAGUE OF B'NAI B'RITH (1913). 823 United Nations Plaza, NYC 10017. (212)490-2525. Chmn. Burton S. Levinson; Dir. Nathan Perlmutter. Seeks to combat anti-Semitism and to secure justice and fair treatment for all citizens through law, education, and community relations. *ADL Bulletin; Face to Face; Fact Finding Report; International Reports; Law Notes; Rights; Law; Research and Evaluation Report; Discriminations Report; Litigation Docket; Dimensions; Middle East Notebook; Nuestro Encuentro.*

ASSOCIATION OF JEWISH CENTER WORKERS (1918). 15 E. 26 St., Suite 1302, NYC 10010. (212)532-4949. Pres. Allan Just; Admin. Dir. Lois Carol Schlar. Seeks to enhance the standards, techniques, practices, scope, and public understanding of Jewish Community Center and kindred agency work. *Kesher; Viewpoints.*

ASSOCIATION OF JEWISH COMMUNITY RELATIONS WORKERS (1950). 155 Fifth Ave., NYC 10010. (212)533-7800. Pres. Muriel Berman; Exec. Dir. Ann Plutzer. Aims to stimulate higher standards of professional practice in Jewish community relations; encourages research and training toward that end; conducts educational programs and seminars; aims to encourage cooperation between community relations workers and those working in other areas of Jewish communal service. *Quarterly newsletter.*

CENTER FOR JEWISH COMMUNITY STUDIES (1970). 1017 Gladfelter Hall, Temple University, Philadelphia, PA 19122. (215)787-1459. Jerusalem office: Jerusalem Center for Public Affairs. Pres. Daniel J. Elazar. Worldwide policy-studies institute devoted to the study of Jewish community organization, political thought, and public affairs, past and present, in Israel and throughout the world. Publishes original articles, essays, and monographs; maintains library, archives, and reprint series. *Jerusalem Letter/Viewpoints; Survey of Arab Affairs; Iggeret.*

COMMISSION ON SOCIAL ACTION OF REFORM JUDAISM (1953, under the auspices of the Union of American Hebrew Congregations). 838 Fifth Ave., NYC 10021. (212)249-0100. Chmn. Harris Gilbert; Dir. Albert Vorspan; Assoc. Dir. David Saperstein. Develops materials to assist Reform synagogues in setting up social-action programs relating the principles of Judaism to contemporary social problems; assists congregations in studying the moral and religious implications in social issues such as civil rights, civil liberties, church-state relations; guides congregational social-action committees. *Briefings.*

COMMITTEE TO BRING NAZI WAR CRIMINALS TO JUSTICE IN U.S.A., INC. (1973). 135 W. 106 St., NYC 10025. (212)866-0692. Pres. Charles H. Kremer; Treas. Albert Sigal; Sec. Paul Schwarzbaum. Compiles and publicizes records of Nazi atrocities and labors to bring to justice the perpetrators of those crimes. Remains committed to preserving the memory of all victims of the Holocaust, and actively opposes anti-Semitism wherever and however it is found.

CONFERENCE OF PRESIDENTS OF MAJOR AMERICAN JEWISH ORGANIZATIONS (1955). 515 Park Ave., NYC 10022. (212)-752-1616. Chmn. Morris B. Abram; Exec. Dir. Malcolm Hoenlein. Coordinates the activities of 40 major American Jewish organizations as they relate to American-Israeli affairs and problems affecting Jews in other lands. *Annual report; Middle East Memo.*

CONSULTATIVE COUNCIL OF JEWISH ORGANIZATIONS-CCJO (1946). 135 William

St., NYC 10038. (212)349-0537. Cochmn. Clemens Nathan, Joseph Nuss, Adolphe Steg; V.-Chmn. Arnold Franco; Sec.-Gen. Moses Moskowitz. A nongovernmental organization in consultative status with the UN, UNESCO, ILO, UNICEF, and the Council of Europe; cooperates and consults with, advises and renders assistance to the Economic and Social Council of the UN on all problems relating to human rights and economic, social, cultural, educational, and related matters pertaining to Jews.

COORDINATING BOARD OF JEWISH ORGANIZATIONS (1947). 1640 Rhode Island Ave., NW, Washington, DC 20036. (202)857-6545. Pres. Gerald Kraft (B'nai B'rith), Leonard Kopelowitz (Board of Deputies of British Jews), David K. Mann (South African Jewish Board of Deputies); Exec. V.-Pres. Daniel Thursz (U.S.); Dir. Internat'l. Council Warren Eisenberg. As an organization in consultative status with the Economic and Social Council of the UN, represents the three constituents (B'nai B'rith, the Board of Deputies of British Jews, and the South African Jewish Board of Deputies) in the appropriate UN bodies for the purpose of promoting human rights, with special attention to combating persecution or discrimination on grounds of race, religion, or origin.

COUNCIL OF JEWISH ORGANIZATIONS IN CIVIL SERVICE, INC. (1948). 45 E. 33 St., NYC 10016. (212)689-2015. Pres. Louis Weiser. Supports merit system; encourages recruitment of Jewish youth to government service; member of Coalition to Free Soviet Jews, NY Jewish Community Relations Council, NY Metropolitan Coordinating Council on Jewish Poverty, Jewish Labor Committee, America-Israel Friendship League. *Council Digest.*

INSTITUTE FOR JEWISH POLICY PLANNING AND RESEARCH (*see* Synagogue Council of America)

INTERNATIONAL CONFERENCE OF JEWISH COMMUNAL SERVICE (*see* World Conference of Jewish Communal Service)

JEWISH LABOR COMMITTEE (1934). Atran Center for Jewish Culture, 25 E. 21 St., NYC 10010. (212)477-0707. Pres. Herb Magidson; Exec. Dir. Martin Lapan. Serves as a link between the Jewish community and the trade union movement; works with the AFL-CIO and others to combat all forms of racial and religious discrimination in the United States and abroad; furthers labor support for Israel's security and Soviet Jewry, and Jewish communal support for labor's social and economic programs; supports Yiddish cultural institutions. *JLC Review.*

———, NATIONAL TRADE UNION COUNCIL FOR HUMAN RIGHTS (1956). Atran Center for Jewish Culture, 25 E. 21 St., NYC 10010. (212)477-0707. Chmn. Sol Hoffman; Exec. Sec. Martin Lapan. Works with trade unions on programs and issues affecting both labor and the Jewish community.

———, WOMEN'S DIVISION OF (1947). Atran Center for Jewish Culture, 25 E. 21 St., NYC 10010. (212)477-0707. Natl. Chmn. Eleanor Schachner. Supports the general activities of the Jewish Labor Committee; provides secondary-school and college scholarships for needy Israeli students; participates in educational and cultural activities.

———, WORKMEN'S CIRCLE DIVISION OF (1939). Atran Center for Jewish Culture, 25 E. 21 St., NYC 10010. (212)477-0707. Promotes aims of, and raises funds for, the Jewish Labor Committee among the Workmen's Circle branches; conducts Yiddish educational and cultural activities.

JEWISH PEACE FELLOWSHIP (1941). Box 271, Nyack, NY 10960. (914)358-4601. Pres. Naomi Goodman. Unites those who believe that Jewish ideals and experience provide inspiration for a nonviolent philosophy and way of life; offers draft counseling, especially for conscientious objection based on Jewish "religious training and belief"; encourages Jewish community to become more knowledgeable, concerned, and active in regard to the war/peace problem. *Shalom/Jewish Peace Letter.*

JEWISH WAR VETERANS OF THE UNITED STATES OF AMERICA (1896). 1811 R St., NW, Washington, DC 20009. (202)265-6280. Natl. Comdr. Harvey S. Friedman; Natl. Exec. Dir. Steven Shaw. Seeks to foster true allegiance to the United States; to combat bigotry and prevent defamation of Jews; to encourage the doctrine of universal liberty, equal rights, and full justice for all; to cooperate with and support existing educational institutions and establish new ones; to foster the education of ex-servicemen, ex-servicewomen, and members in the ideals and principles of Americanism. *Jewish Veteran.*

———, NATIONAL MEMORIAL, INC; NATIONAL SHRINE TO THE JEWISH WAR DEAD (1958). 1811 R St., NW, Washington, DC 20009. (202)265-6280. Pres. Ainslee R. Ferdie. Maintains a national archives and museum commemorating the wartime service of American Jews in the armed forces of the U.S.; maintains *Golden Book* of names of the war dead; *Routes to Roots.*

NATIONAL CONFERENCE ON SOVIET JEWRY (formerly AMERICAN JEWISH CONFERENCE ON SOVIET JEWRY) (1964; reorg. 1971). 10 E. 40 St., Suite 907, NYC 10016. (212)679-6122. Chmn. Morris B. Abram; Exec. Dir. Jerry Goodman. Coordinating agency for major national Jewish organizations and local community groups in the U.S., acting on behalf of Soviet Jewry through public education and social action; stimulates all segments of the community to maintain an interest in the problems of Soviet Jews by publishing reports and special pamphlets, sponsoring special programs and projects, organizing public meetings and forums. *Newsbreak; annual report; Action and Program Kits; Wrap-Up Leadership Report.*

———, SOVIET JEWRY RESEARCH BUREAU. Chmn. Charlotte Jacobson. Organized by NCSJ to monitor emigration trends. Primary task is the accumulation, evaluation, and processing of information regarding Soviet Jews, especially those who apply for emigration.

NATIONAL JEWISH COMMISSION ON LAW AND PUBLIC AFFAIRS (COLPA) (1965). 450 Seventh Ave., Suite 2203, NYC 10001. (212)563-0100. Pres. Allen L. Rothenberg; Exec. Dir. Dennis Rapps. Voluntary association of attorneys whose purpose is to represent the observant Jewish community on legal, legislative, and public affairs matters.

NATIONAL JEWISH COMMUNITY RELATIONS ADVISORY COUNCIL (1944). 443 Park Ave. S., 11th fl., NYC 10016. (212)-684-6950. Chmn. Michael A. Pelavin; Sec. Barry Ungar; Exec. V.-Chmn. Albert D. Chernin. National coordinating body for the field of Jewish community relations, comprising 11 national and 113 local Jewish community relations agencies. Promotes understanding of Israel and the Middle East; freedom for Soviet Jews; equal status for Jews and other groups in American society. Through the NJCRAC's work, its constituent organizations seek agreement on policies, strategies, and programs for effective utilization of their resources for common ends. *Joint Program Plan for Jewish Community Relations.*

NEW JEWISH AGENDA (1980). 64 Fulton St., #1100, NYC 10038. (212)227-5885. Cochmn. Bria Chakofsky, Rabbi Gerry Serotta; Exec. Dir. Reena Bernards. Founded as "a progressive voice in the Jewish community and a Jewish voice among progressives." Works for nuclear disarmament, peace in Central America, Arab-Jewish reconciliation, feminism, and economic justice, and against anti-Semitism and racism. *Quarterly newsletter.*

NORTH AMERICAN JEWISH YOUTH COUNCIL (1965). 515 Park Ave., NYC 10022. (212)751-6070. Exec. Dir. Donald Adelman. Provides a framework for coordination and exchange of programs and information among national Jewish youth organizations to help them deepen the concern of American Jewish youth for world Jewry; represents Jewish youth in the Conference of Presidents, United States Youth Council, etc.

STUDENT STRUGGLE FOR SOVIET JEWRY, INC. (1964). 210 W. 91 St., NYC 10024. (212)799-8900. Natl. Dir. Jacob Birnbaum; Natl. Coord. Glenn Richter; Chmn. Avraham Weiss. Provides information and action guidance to adult and student organizations, communities, and schools throughout the U.S. and Canada; assists Soviet Jews by publicity campaigns; helps Soviet Jews in the U.S.; aids Rumanian Jews seeking emigration; maintains speakers bureau and research documents. *Soviet Jewry Action Newsletter.*

UNION OF COUNCILS FOR SOVIET JEWS (1970). 1411 K St., NW, Suite 402, Washington, DC 20005. (202)393-4117. Pres. Morey Schapira; Exec. Dir. Mark A. Epstein. A confederation of 38 grass-roots organizations established in support of Soviet Jewry. Works on behalf of Soviet Jews through public education, representations to the administration and Congress, letter-writing assistance, tourist briefing, speakers bureau, Adopt-A-Family, Adopt-A-Prisoner, Bar/Bat Mitzvah twinning, Tarbut, congressional vigil, congressional briefings, and publications programming; affiliations include Soviet Jewry Legal Advocacy Center and Medical Mobilization for Soviet Jewry. *Alert; UCSJ Quarterly Report.*

WORLD CONFERENCE OF JEWISH COMMUNAL SERVICE (1966). 15 E. 26 St., NYC 10010. (212)532-2526. Pres. Irving Kessler; Sec.-Gen. Solomon H. Green. Established by worldwide Jewish communal workers to strengthen their understanding of each other's programs and to communicate with colleagues in order to enrich the quality of their work. Conducts quadrennial international conferences in Jerusalem and periodic regional meetings. *Proceedings of international conferences; newsletter.*

WORLD JEWISH CONGRESS (1936; org. in U.S. 1939). 1 Park Ave., Suite 418, NYC 10016. (212)679-0600. Pres. Edgar M. Bronfman; Chmn. N. Amer. Branch Leo Kolber (Montreal); Chmn. Amer. Sect. Frieda S. Lewis; Sec.-Gen. Israel Singer; Exec. Dir. Elan Steinberg. Seeks to intensify bonds of world Jewry with Israel as central force in Jewish life; to strengthen solidarity among Jews everywhere and secure their rights, status, and interests as individuals and communities; to encourage development of Jewish social, religious, and cultural life throughout the world and coordinate efforts by Jewish communities and organizations to cope with any Jewish problem; to work for human rights generally. Represents its affiliated organizations —most representative bodies of Jewish communities in more than 70 countries and 32 national organizations in Amer. section—at UN, OAS, UNESCO, Council of Europe, ILO, UNICEF, and other governmental, intergovernmental, and international authorities. Publications (including those by Institute of Jewish Affairs, London): *Christian Jewish Relations; Coloquio; News and Views; Boletín Informativo OJI; Batfutsot; Gesher; Patterns of Prejudice; Soviet Jewish Affairs.*

CULTURAL

AMERICAN ACADEMY FOR JEWISH RESEARCH (1920). 3080 Broadway, NYC 10027. Pres. Isaac Barzilay; V.-Pres. Franz Rosenthal, David Weiss Halivni; Treas. Arthur Hyman. Encourages Jewish learning and research; holds annual or semiannual meeting; awards grants for the publication of scholarly works. *Proceedings of the American Academy for Jewish Research; Texts and Studies; monograph series.*

AMERICAN BIBLICAL ENCYCLOPEDIA SOCIETY (1930). 24 W. Maple Ave., Monsey, NY 10952. (914)352-4609. Pres. Leo Jung; Exec. V.-Pres. Irving Fredman; Author-Ed. Menachem M. Kasher. Fosters biblical-talmudical research; sponsors and publishes *Torah Shelemah* (Heb., 39 vols.), *Encyclopedia of Biblical Interpretation* (Eng., 9 vols.), *Divrei Menachem* (Heb., 4 vols.), and related publications. *Noam.*

AMERICAN FEDERATION OF JEWISH FIGHTERS, CAMP INMATES AND NAZI VICTIMS, INC. (1971). 823 United Nations Plaza, NYC 10017. (212)697-5670. Pres. Solomon Zynstein; Exec. Dir. Ernest Honig. Seeks to perpetuate the memory of victims of the Holocaust and make Jewish and non-Jewish youth aware of the Holocaust and resistance period. *Martyrdom and Resistance.*

AMERICAN JEWISH HISTORICAL SOCIETY (1892). 2 Thornton Rd., Waltham, MA 02154. (617)891-8110. Pres. Morris Soble; Dir. Bernard Wax. Collects, catalogues, publishes, and displays material on the history of the Jews in America; serves as an information center for inquiries on American Jewish history; maintains archives of original source material on American Jewish history; sponsors lectures and exhibitions; makes available historic Yiddish films and audiovisual material. *American Jewish History; Heritage.*

AMERICAN JEWISH PRESS ASSOCIATION (1943). c/o St. Louis Jewish Light, 12 Millstone Campus Dr., St. Louis, MO 63146. (314)432-3353. Pres. Robert A. Cohn. Seeks the advancement of Jewish journalism, the attainment of the highest editorial and business standards for members, and the maintenance of a strong Jewish press in the U.S. and Canada. *Membership bulletin.*

AMERICAN SOCIETY FOR JEWISH MUSIC (1974). 155 Fifth Ave., NYC 10010. (212)-533-2601. Pres. Paul Kavon; V.-Pres. David Lefkowitz; Sec. Hadássah B. Markson. Seeks to raise standards of composition and performance in Jewish liturgical and secular music; encourages research in all areas of Jewish music; publishes scholarly journal; presents programs and sponsors performances of new and rarely heard works and encourages their recording; commissions new works of Jewish interest. *Musica Judaica.*

ASSOCIATED AMERICAN JEWISH MUSEUMS, INC. (1971). 303 LeRoi Rd. Pittsburgh, PA 15208. Pres. Walter Jacob; V.-Pres. William Rosenthall; Sec. Robert H. Lehman; Treas. Jason Z. Edelstein. Maintains regional collections of Jewish art, historical and ritual objects, as well as a central catalogue of such objects in the collections of Jewish museums throughout the U.S.; helps Jewish museums acquire, identify, and classify objects; arranges exchanges of collections, exhibits, and individual objects among Jewish museums; encourages the creation of Jewish art, ceremonial and ritual objects.

ASSOCIATION FOR THE SOCIOLOGICAL STUDY OF JEWRY (1971). Dept. of Sociology, Brooklyn College, Brooklyn, NY 11210. (718)780-5315. Pres. Egon Mayer; V.-Pres. Morton Weinfeld; Sec.-Treas. Esther Fleishman. Arranges academic sessions and facilitates communication among social scientists studying Jewry through meetings, newsletter, and related materials. *Contemporary Jewry; ASSJ Newsletter.*

ASSOCIATION OF JEWISH BOOK PUBLISHERS (1962). 838 Fifth Ave., NYC 10021. (212)-249-0100. Pres. Bernard I. Levinson. As a nonprofit group, provides a forum for discussion of mutual problems by publishers, authors, and other individuals and institutions concerned with books of Jewish interest. Provides national and international exhibit opportunities for Jewish books. *Combined Jewish Book Catalogue.*

ASSOCIATION OF JEWISH LIBRARIES (1965). c/o National Foundation for Jewish Culture, 122 E. 42 St., NYC 10168. (212)-427-1000. Pres. Edith Lubetski; V.-Pres. Marcia Posner. Seeks to promote and improve services and professional standards in Jewish libraries; serves as a center for the dissemination of Jewish library information and guidance; promotes publication of literature in the field; encourages the establishment of Jewish libraries and collections of Judaica and the choice of Judaica librarianship as a profession. *AJL Newsletter; Judaica Librarianship.*

B'NAI B'RITH KLUTZNICK MUSEUM (1956). 1640 Rhode Island Ave., NW, Washington, DC 20036. (202)857-6583. Cochmn. Museum & Art Comm., David and Jane Greene; Dir. Linda Altshuler. A center of Jewish art and history in nation's capital, maintains exhibition galleries, permanent collection of Jewish ceremonial and folk art, B'nai B'rith International reference archive, outdoor sculpture garden, and museum shop. Provides exhibitions, tours, educational programs, research assistance, and tourist information. *Semiannual newsletter; exhibition brochures.*

CENTER FOR HOLOCAUST STUDIES, DOCUMENTATION & RESEARCH. (1974). 1610 Ave. J, Brooklyn, NY 11230. (718)338-6494. Dir. Yaffa Eliach. Collects and preserves documents and memorabilia, oral histories, and literary works on the Holocaust period for purposes of documentation and research; arranges lectures, exhibits, drama and music performances, and exhibitions of Holocaust art; conducts outreach programs to schools; maintains speakers bureau, oral history publication series, and audiovisual department. *Newsletter.*

CENTRAL YIDDISH CULTURE ORGANIZATION (CYCO), INC. (1943). 25 E. 21 St., 3rd fl., NYC 10010. (212)505-8305. Mgr. Jacob Schneidman. Promotes, publishes, and distributes Yiddish books; publishes catalogues.

CONFERENCE ON JEWISH SOCIAL STUDIES, INC. (formerly CONFERENCE ON JEWISH RELATIONS, INC.) (1939). 2112 Broadway, Rm. 206, NYC 10023. (212)724-5336. Hon. Pres. Salo W. Baron. Publishes scientific studies on Jews in the modern world, dealing with such aspects as anti-Semitism, demography, economic stratification, history, philosophy, and political developments. *Jewish Social Studies.*

CONGREGATION BINA (1981). 600 W. End Ave., Suite 1-C, NYC 10024. (212)873-4261. Pres. Elijah E. Jhirad; Exec. V.-Pres. Joseph Moses. Serves the religious, cultural, charitable, and philanthropic needs of the Children of Israel who originated in India and now reside in the U.S. Works to foster and preserve the ancient traditions, customs, liturgy, music, and folklore of Indian Jewry and to maintain needed institutions. *Kol Bina.*

HEBREW ARTS SCHOOL (1952). 129 W. 67 St., NYC 10023. (212)362-8060. Chmn.

Leonard P. Shaykin; Pres. Morris Talansky; Dir. Lydia Kontos; Founder Tzipora H. Jochsberger. Chartered by the Board of Regents, University of the State of New York. Offers instruction in music, dance, art, and theater to children and adults, combining Western culture with Jewish heritage. Classes for preschool children; Arts After School Program; workshops for teachers. Sponsors Hebrew Arts Chorale. Presents in its Merkin Concert Hall and Ann Goodman Recital Hall the Heritage Concerts, Tuesday Matinees, Music Today, On Original Instruments, Twilight Concerts of Jewish Music, Boston Camerata, and others; also the American Jewish Choral Festival and Young Musicians' Concerts. Sponsors resident ensemble, Mendelssohn String Quartet and Hebrew Arts Concert Choir. *Newsletter.*

HEBREW CULTURE FOUNDATION (1955). 515 Park Ave., NYC 10022. (212)752-0600. Chmn. Milton R. Konvitz; Sec. Herman L. Sainer. Sponsors the introduction and strengthening of Hebrew language and literature courses in institutions of higher learning in the United States.

HISTADRUTH IVRITH OF AMERICA (1916; reorg. 1922). 1841 Broadway, NYC 10023. (212)581-5151. Presidium: Boris Shteinshleifer, Matthew Mosenkis, Rabbi Joseph P. Sternstein; Exec. V.-Pres. Aviva Barzel. Emphasizes the primacy of Hebrew in Jewish life, culture, and education; aims to disseminate knowledge of written and spoken Hebrew in the Diaspora, thus building a cultural bridge between the State of Israel and Jewish communities throughout the world. *Hadoar; Lamishpaha.*

HOLOCAUST CENTER OF GREATER PITTSBURGH (1980). 242 McKee Pl., Pittsburgh, PA 15213. (412)682-7111. Dir. Edie Naveh; Chmn. Sidney N. Busis. Develops programs and provides resources to further understanding of the Holocaust and its impact on civilization. Maintains a library, archive; provides speakers, educational materials; organizes community programs.

JEWISH ACADEMY OF ARTS AND SCIENCES, INC. (1926). 888 Seventh Ave., Suite 403, NYC 10106. (212)757-1628. Hon. Pres. Leo Jung; Pres. Abraham I. Katsh; Sec. Bernard B. Cohen. An honor society of Jews who have attained distinction in the arts, sciences, professions, and communal endeavors. Encourages the advancement of knowledge; stimulates scholarship, with particular reference to Jewish life and thought; recognition by election to membership and/or fellowship; publishes papers delivered at annual convocations.

JEWISH INFORMATION BUREAU, INC. (1932). 250 W. 57 St., NYC 10019. (212)-582-5318. Dir. Steven Wise; V.-Chmn. Ruth Eisenstein. Serves as clearinghouse of information for inquiries regarding Jews, Judaism, Israel, and Jewish affairs; refers inquiries to communal agencies. *Index.*

JEWISH MEDIA SERVICE. JWB, 15 E. 26 St., NYC 10010. (212)532-4949. Pres. Harriet L. Rosenthal; Dir. Eric A. Goldman. National clearinghouse for evaluation and creative use of audiovisual media in Jewish programming and teaching. Provides consultation on use of film, video, TV programming, and acquisition. Publishes listings, filmographies, and evaluative reviews. Advises Jewish communities and organizations on establishment of local media centers. Cosponsored by JWB, CJF, UJA. *Medium; TV in Review; TV Memo.*

JEWISH MUSEUM (1904, under auspices of Jewish Theological Seminary of America). 1109 Fifth Ave., NYC 10028. (212)860-1888. Chmn. Bd. of Trustees James Weinberg; Dir. Joan H. Rosenbaum. Repository of the largest collection of Judaica—paintings, prints, photographs, sculpture, coins, medals, antiquities, textiles, and other decorative arts—in the Western Hemisphere. Includes the National Jewish Archive of Broadcasting and the Tobe Pascher Workshop for the design and creation of ritual and ceremonial art objects. Conducts tours of special exhibitions and permanent installations; gives lectures, film showings, and concerts. Special programs for children are conducted by the education department. *Special exhibition catalogues.*

JEWISH PUBLICATION SOCIETY (1888). 1930 Chestnut St., Philadelphia, PA 19103. (215)564-5925. Pres. Charles R. Weiner; Exec. V.-Pres. Nathan Barnett; Editor Sheila Segal. Publishes and disseminates books of Jewish interest for adults and children; titles include contemporary literature, classics, art, religion, biographies, poetry, and history. AMERICAN JEWISH YEAR BOOK (with American Jewish Committee).

JUDAH L. MAGNES MUSEUM—JEWISH MUSEUM OF THE WEST (1962). 2911 Russell St., Berkeley, CA 94705. (415)849-2710.

Pres. Jacques Reutlinger; Exec. Dir. Seymour Fromer. Serves as museum and library, combining historical and literary materials illustrating Jewish life in the Bay Area, the Western states, and around the world; provides archives of world Jewish history and Jewish art; repository of historical documents intended for scholarly use; changing exhibits; facilities open to the general public. *Magnes News; special exhibition catalogues.*

JUDAICA CAPTIONED FILM CENTER, INC. (1983). P.O. Box 21439, Baltimore, MD 21208-0439. Voice (301)922-4642; TDD (301)655-6767. Pres. Lois Lilienfeld Weiner. Developing a comprehensive library of captioned and subtitled films and tapes on Jewish subjects; distributes them to organizations serving the hearing-impaired, including mainstream classes and senior adult groups, on a free-loan, handling/shipping-charge-only basis. *Quarterly newsletter.*

JWB JEWISH BOOK COUNCIL (1942). 15 E. 26 St., NYC 10010. (212)532-4949. Pres. Blu Greenberg; Dir. Paula Gribetz Gottlieb. Promotes knowledge of Jewish books through dissemination of booklists, program materials; sponsors Jewish Book Month; presents literary awards and library citations; cooperates with publishers of Jewish books. *Jewish Book Annual; Jewish Books in Review; Jewish Book World.*

JWB JEWISH MUSIC COUNCIL (1944). 15 E. 26 St., NYC 10010. (212)532-4949. Chmn. Leonard Kaplan; Coord. Paula Gribetz Gottlieb. Promotes Jewish music activities nationally; annually sponsors and promotes the Jewish Music season; encourages participation on a community basis. *Jewish Music Notes* and numerous music resource publications for national distribution.

JWB LECTURE BUREAU. 15 E. 26 St., NYC 11369. (212)532-4949. Chmn. Irving Ruderman; Dir. Stephen L. Bayer. Provides, and assists in the selection of, lecturers, performing artists, artists, and exhibits for local Jewish communal organizations; advises on program design; makes booking arrangements. *The Jewish Arts; Learning for Jewish Living.*

LEAGUE FOR YIDDISH, INC. (1935). 200 W. 72 St., Suite 40, NYC 10023. (212)-787-6675. Pres. Sadie Turak; Exec. Dir. Mordkhe Schaechter. Promotes the development and use of Yiddish as a living language. *Afn Shvel.*

LEO BAECK INSTITUTE, INC. (1955). 129 E. 73 St., NYC 10021. (212)744-6400. Pres. Yosef Haim Yerushalmi; Sec. Fred Grubel. A library, archive, and research center for the history of German-speaking Jewry. Offers lectures, exhibits, faculty seminars; publishes a series of monographs, yearbooks, and journals. *LBI Bulletin; LBI News; LBI Year Book.*

MARTYRS MEMORIAL & MUSEUM OF THE HOLOCAUST (1963; reorg. 1978). 6505 Wilshire Blvd., Los Angeles, CA 90048. (213)651-3175. Chmn. Jack I. Salzberg; Dir. Michael Nutkiewicz. Seeks to commemorate the events and victims of the Holocaust and to educate against future reoccurrences; maintains permanent and traveling exhibits, sponsors public lectures, offers school curricula and teacher training. West Coast representative of Israel's Yad Vashem; affiliated with the Jewish Federation Council of Greater Los Angeles.

MEMORIAL FOUNDATION FOR JEWISH CULTURE, INC. (1964). 15 E. 26 St., NYC 10010. (212)679-4074. Pres. Philip M. Klutznick; Exec. Dir. Jerry Hochbaum. Through the grants that it awards, encourages Jewish scholarship and Jewish education, supports communities that are struggling to maintain their Jewish identity, makes possible the training of Jewish men and women for professional careers in communal service in Jewishly deprived communities, and stimulates the documentation, commemoration, and teaching of the Holocaust.

NATIONAL FOUNDATION FOR JEWISH CULTURE (1960). 1512 Chanin Bldg., 122 E. 42 St., NYC 10168. (212)490-2280. Pres. George M. Zeltzer; Exec. V.-Pres. Abraham Atik. Provides consultation and support to Jewish community organizations, educational and cultural institutions, and individuals for Jewish cultural activities; awards fellowships and publication grants to individuals preparing for careers in Jewish scholarship; presents awards for creative efforts in Jewish cultural arts and for Jewish programming in small and intermediate communities; publishes guides to national Jewish cultural resources, traveling exhibitions, and plays; serves as clearinghouse of information on American Jewish culture; administers Joint Cultural Appeal on behalf of nine national cultural organizations; administers Council for Archives and Research Libraries in Jewish Studies and Council of American Jewish Museums.

NATIONAL HEBREW CULTURE COUNCIL (1952). 1776 Broadway, NYC 10019. (212)247-0741. Pres. Frances K. Thau. Cultivates the study of Hebrew as a modern language in American public high schools and colleges, providing guidance to community groups and public educational authorities; annually administers National Voluntary Examination in Hebrew Culture and Knowledge of Israel in the public high schools, and conducts summer seminar and tour of Israel for teachers and other educational personnel of the public school system, in cooperation with Hebrew University and WZO. *Hebrew in Colleges and Universities.*

NATIONAL YIDDISH BOOK CENTER (1980). P.O. Box 969, East Street School, Amherst, MA 01004. (413)256-1241. Pres. Penina Glazer; Exec. Dir. Aaron Lansky. Collects used and out-of-print Yiddish books to distribute to individuals and libraries; offers courses in Yiddish language, literature, and cultural activities; publishes bimonthly *Catalogue of Rare and Out-of-Print Yiddish Books*, listing over 100,000 volumes for sale; *Der Pakn-treger/The Book Peddler.*

NEW YORK HOLOCAUST MEMORIAL COMMISSION (1981). 342 Madison Ave., Suite 717, NYC 10017. (212)221-1574. Cochmn. George Klein, Hon. Robert M. Morgenthau; Exec. Dir. David L. Blumenfeld. Seeks to create a major "living memorial" center in New York City, consisting of a museum, library, archives, and lecture/conference facilities which will commemorate the lives of the Jewish victims of Nazi Germany by creating a record of their cultural and societal lives in Europe, restoring to memory the close affinity between the Jews of Europe and the large Jewish immigrant population of New York City, educating future generations on the history and lessons of the Holocaust, and providing appropriate commemoration honoring the memory of those who died in the Holocaust.

RESEARCH FOUNDATION FOR JEWISH IMMIGRATION, INC. (1971). 570 Seventh Ave., NYC 10018. (212)921-3871. Pres. Curt C. Silberman; Sec. Herbert A. Strauss. Studies and records the history of the migration and acculturation of Jewish Nazi persecutees in the various resettlement countries. *International Biographical Dictionary of Central European Emigrés, 1933–1945; Jewish Immigrants of the Nazi Period in the USA.*

ST. LOUIS CENTER FOR HOLOCAUST STUDIES (1977). 12 Millstone Campus Dr., St. Louis, MO 63146. (314)432-0020. Chmn. Lois Gould-Rafaeli; Dir. Rabbi Robert Sternberg. Develops programs and provides resources and educational materials to further an understanding of the Holocaust and its impact on civilization. *Audio Visual Guide.*

SEPHARDIC HOUSE (1978). 8 W. 70 St., NYC 10023. (212)873-0300. Dir. Rabbi Marc D. Angel. Works to foster the history and culture of Sephardic Jewry by offering classes, programs, publications, and resource people; works to integrate Sephardic studies into the curriculum of Jewish schools and adult education programs; offers advice and guidance to individuals involved in Sephardic research. *The Sephardic House Newsletter.*

SKIRBALL MUSEUM, Los Angeles, CA (*see* Hebrew Union College-Jewish Institute of Religion)

SOCIETY FOR THE HISTORY OF CZECHOSLOVAK JEWS, INC. (1961). 87-08 Santiago St., Holliswood, NY 11423. (718)468-6844. Pres. Lewis Weiner; Sec. Joseph Abeles. Studies the history of Czechoslovak Jews, collects material and disseminates information through the publication of books and pamphlets.

YESHIVA UNIVERSITY MUSEUM (1973). 2520 Amsterdam Ave., NYC 10033. (212)-960-5390. Chmn. Bd. of Govs. Erica Jesselson; Dir. Sylvia A. Herskowitz. Collects, preserves, interprets, and displays ceremonial objects, rare books and scrolls, models, paintings, and decorative arts expressing the Jewish religious experience historically, to the present. Changing exhibits of contemporary artists, ceremonial objects, and historical subjects; programs for adults and children. *Special exhibition catalogues.*

YIDDISHER KULTUR FARBAND—YKUF (1938). 1123 Broadway, Rm. 305, NYC

10010. (212)691-0708. Pres. Itche Goldberg. Publishes a monthly magazine and books by contemporary and classical Jewish writers; conducts cultural forums; exhibits works by contemporary Jewish artists and materials of Jewish historical value; organizes reading circles. *Yiddishe Kultur.*

YIVO INSTITUTE FOR JEWISH RESEARCH, INC. (1925). 1048 Fifth Ave., NYC 10028. (212)535-6700. Cochmn. Mendl Hoffman, Joseph Greenberger. Exec. Dir. Samuel Norich. Engages in social and humanistic research pertaining to East European Jewish life; maintains library and archives which provide a major international, national, and New York resource used by institutions, individual scholars, and laymen; trains graduate students in Yiddish, East European, and American Jewish studies; offers exhibits, conferences, public programs; publishes books. *Yedies fun Yivo—News of the Yivo; Yidishe Shprakh; Yivo Annual of Jewish Social Science; Yivo Bleter.*

———, MAX WEINREICH CENTER FOR ADVANCED JEWISH STUDIES (1968). 1048 Fifth Ave., NYC 10028. (212)535-6700. Act. Dean Marvin I. Herzog; Assoc. Dean Jack Kugelmass. Provides advanced-level training in Yiddish language and literature, ethnography, folklore, linguistics, and history; offers guidance on dissertation or independent research. *YIVO Annual; The Field of Yiddish; Yidishe Shprakh; Jewish Folklore & Ethnology Newsletter.*

OVERSEAS AID

AMERICAN ASSOCIATION FOR ETHIOPIAN JEWS (1974). 2789 Oak St., Highland Park, IL 60035. (312)433-8150. Pres. Nathan Shapiro; Natl. Coord. LaDena Schnapper. Informs world Jewry about the plight of Ethiopian Jews; advocates rescue of Ethiopian Jewry as a major priority; provides relief in refugee areas and Ethiopia; and helps resettlement in Israel. *Release; Newsline.*

AMERICAN FRIENDS OF THE ALLIANCE ISRAÉLITE UNIVERSELLE, INC. (1946). 135 William St., NYC 10038. (212)349-0537. Pres. Henriette Beilis; Exec. Dir. Jack Kantrowitz. Participates in educational and human rights activities of the AIU and supports the Alliance System of Jewish schools, remedial programs, and teacher training in Israel, North Africa, the Middle East, and Europe. *Alliance Review; AF Notes.*

AMERICAN JEWISH JOINT DISTRIBUTION COMMITTEE, INC.—JDC (1914). 711 Third Ave., NYC 10017. (212)687-6200. Pres. Heinz Eppler; Exec. V.-Pres. Ralph I. Goldman. Organizes and finances rescue, relief, and rehabilitation programs for imperiled and needy Jews overseas; conducts wide range of health, welfare, rehabilitation, education programs and aid to cultural and religious institutions; programs benefiting 500,000 Jews in over 30 countries overseas. Major areas of operation are Israel, North Africa, and Europe. *JDC Annual Report; JDC World.*

AMERICAN JEWISH PHILANTHROPIC FUND (1955). 386 Park Ave. S., NYC 10016. (212)684-1525. Pres. Charles J. Tanenbaum. Provides resettlement and retraining assistance to Jewish refugees primarily through programs administered by the International Rescue Committee at its offices in Western Europe and the U.S.

AMERICAN ORT FEDERATION, INC.—ORGANIZATION FOR REHABILITATION THROUGH TRAINING (1924). 817 Broadway, NYC 10003. (212)677-4400. Pres. Alvin L. Gray; Exec. V.-Pres. Donald H. Klein. Teaches vocational skills in 30 countries around the world, maintaining 800 schools for over 158,000 students annually, with the largest program of 87,000 trainees in Israel. The teaching staff numbers 4,000. Annual cost of program is about $99 million. *ORT Bulletin; ORT Yearbook.*

———, AMERICAN AND EUROPEAN FRIENDS OF ORT (1941). 817 Broadway, NYC 10003. (212)677-4400. Pres. Simon Jaglom; Chmn. Exec. Com. Jacques Zwibak. Promotes the ORT idea among Americans of European extraction; supports the Litton ORT Auto-Mechanics School in Jerusalem and the ORT School of Engineering in Jerusalem. Promotes the work of the American ORT Federation.

———, AMERICAN LABOR ORT (1937). 817 Broadway, NYC 10003. (212)677-4400. Chmn. Sam Fine. Promotes ORT program of vocational training among Jews through activities of the ILGWU and the Amalgamated Clothing & Textile Workers Union. Promotes the work of the American ORT Federation.

———, BUSINESS AND PROFESSIONAL ORT (formerly YOUNG MEN'S AND WOMEN'S ORT) (1937). 817 Broadway, NYC 10003. (212)677-4770. Pres. Rose Seidel Kalich; Exec. Sec. Helen S. Kreisler. Promotes work of American ORT Federation.

———, NATIONAL ORT LEAGUE (1914). 817 Broadway, NYC 10003. (212)677-4400. Pres. Judah Wattenberg; First V.-Pres. Tibor Waldman. Promotes ORT idea among Jewish fraternal *landsmanshaften* and individuals. Promotes the work of the American ORT Federation.

———, WOMEN'S AMERICAN ORT (1927). 315 Park Ave. S., NYC 10010. (212)505-7700. Pres. Gertrude S. White; Exec. V.-Pres. Nathan Gould. Represents and advances the program and philosophy of ORT among the women of the American Jewish community through membership and educational activities; materially supports the vocational training operations of World ORT; contributes to the American Jewish community by encouraging participation in ORT campaigns and through general education to help raise the level of Jewish consciousness among American Jewish women; through its American Affairs program, cooperates in efforts to improve the quality of education and vocational training in the U.S. *Facts and Findings; Highlights; Insights; The Merchandiser; Women's American ORT Reporter.*

A.R.I.F.—ASSOCIATION POUR LE RÉTABLISSEMENT DES INSTITUTIONS ET OEUVRES ISRAÉLITES EN FRANCE, INC. (1944). 119 E. 95 St., NYC 10028. (212)-876-1448. Pres. Baroness Robert de Gunzburg; Sec.-Treas. Simon Langer. Helps Jewish religious and cultural institutions in France.

CONFERENCE ON JEWISH MATERIAL CLAIMS AGAINST GERMANY, INC. (1951). 15 E. 26 St., Rm. 1355, NYC 10010. (212)-696-4944. Pres. Israel Miller; Sec. and Exec. Dir. Saul Kagan. Monitors the implementation of restitution and indemnification programs of the German Federal Republic (FRG) arising from its agreements with FRG. Administers Hardship Fund, which distributes DM 400,000,000 appropriated by FRG for Jewish Nazi victims unable to file timely claims under original indemnification laws. Also assists needy non-Jews who risked their lives to help Jewish survivors. *Periodic reports.*

HIAS, INC. (HEBREW IMMIGRANT AID SOCIETY) (1880; reorg. 1954). 200 Park Ave. S., NYC 10003. (212)674-6800. Pres. Robert L. Israeloff; Exec. V.-Pres. Karl D. Zukerman. International Jewish migration agency with headquarters in the U.S. and offices, affiliates, and representatives in Europe, Latin America, Canada, Australia, New Zealand, and Israel. Assists Jewish migrants and refugees from Eastern Europe, the Middle East, North Africa, and Latin America. Via U.S. government-funded programs, assists in the resettlement of Indo-Chinese and other refugees. *HIAS Annual Report; HIAS Reporter; Quarterly Statistical Abstract.*

JEWISH RESTITUTION SUCCESSOR ORGANIZATION (1947). 15 E. 26 St., NYC 10010. (212)696-4944. Sec. and Exec. Dir. Saul Kagan. Acts to discover, claim, receive, and assist in the recovery of Jewish heirless or unclaimed property; to utilize such assets or to provide for their utilization for the relief, rehabilitation, and resettlement of surviving victims of Nazi persecution.

THANKS TO SCANDINAVIA, INC. (1963). 745 Fifth Ave., Rm. 603, NYC 10151. (212)-486-8600. Natl. Chmn. Victor Borge; Pres. and Exec. Off. Richard Netter. Provides scholarships and fellowships at American universities and medical centers to students and doctors from Denmark, Finland, Norway, and Sweden in appreciation of the rescue of Jews from the Holocaust. Informs current and future generations of Americans and Scandinavians of these singular examples of humanity and bravery; funds books about this chapter of history. *Annual report.*

UNITED JEWISH APPEAL, INC. (1939). 99 Park Ave., NYC 10016. (212)818-9100. Pres. Stanley Horowitz; Chmn. Bd. of Trustees Alexander Grass; Natl. Chmn. Martin F. Stein. Channels funds for overseas humanitarian aid, supports immigration, Youth Aliyah, and rural settlements in Israel, through the Jewish Agency; provides additional humanitarian assistance in 30 countries around the world through the American Jewish Joint Distribution Committee. *Newsbrief.*

———, RABBINIC CABINET (1972). 99 Park Ave., NYC 10016. (212)818-9100. Chmn. Rabbi Haskel Lookstein; Dir. Rabbi Oscar Groner. Promotes rabbinic leadership support for local and national UJA campaigns through education and personal commitment; uses rabbinic resources on behalf of UJA and Israel.

———, UNIVERSITY PROGRAMS DEPT. (1970). 99 Park Ave., NYC 10016. (212)818-9100. Student Advisory Bd. Chmn. Andrew Hochberg. Promotes Jewish commitment and active involvement on the campus through an educational fund-raising campaign including various programs, leadership training, a student winter mission to Israel, and participation in community functions. *HaKesher Newsletter.*

———, WOMEN'S DIVISION OF (1946). 99 Park Ave., NYC 10016. (212)818-9100. Pres. Harriet Zimmerman; Chmn. Judith A. Levy; Dir. Nan Goldberg. Strengthens communities to raise funds for Israel and Jews worldwide. *Campaign Network Newsletter.*

———, YOUNG LEADERSHIP CABINET (1977). 99 Park Ave., NYC 10016. (212)818-9100. Dir. Rabbi Daniel Allen; Chmn. Daniel Rubin. Committed to the creative survival of Jews, Judaism, and Israel through dialogues with leading scholars and writers, and through peer exchanges at retreats, conferences, missions to Israel, and special programs. *In Process; Judaica series.*

———, YOUNG WOMEN'S LEADERSHIP CABINET (1977). 99 Park Ave., NYC 10016 (212)818-9100. Chmn. Sandy Neuman. Attracts and recruits young women —both career women and professional volunteers—from around the country who have demonstrated proven leadership ability to serve the UJA as speakers, trainers, solicitors, and consultants. The women receive specialized training on a national level and return to their local communities prepared to assume major leadership roles in the future with strong ties to the UJA and its philosophies. *Directory.*

WOMEN'S SOCIAL SERVICE FOR ISRAEL, INC. (1937). 240 W. 98 St., NYC 10025. (212)666-7880. Pres. Ursula Merkin; Sec. Dory Gordon. Maintains in Israel subsidized housing for self-reliant older people, old-age homes for more dependent elderly, Lichtenstadter Hospital for chronically ill, subsidized meals, distribution of clothing collected in U.S. All-volunteer group in New York. *Annual journal.*

RELIGIOUS AND EDUCATIONAL

AGUDATH ISRAEL OF AMERICA (1922). 84 William St., NYC 10038. (212)797-9000. Pres. Rabbi Moshe Sherer; Exec. Dir. Rabbi Boruch B. Borchardt. Mobilizes Orthodox Jews to cope with Jewish problems in the spirit of the Torah; sponsors a broad range of projects aimed at enhancing religious living, education, children's welfare, protection of Jewish religious rights, outreach to the assimilated, and social services. *Jewish Observer; Dos Yiddishe Vort, Coalition.*

———, CHILDREN'S DIVISION—PIRCHEI AGUDATH ISRAEL (1925). 84 William St., NYC 10038 (212)797-9000. Pres. Yosef Simha; Dir. Rabbi Joshua Silbermintz. Educates Orthodox Jewish children in Torah; encourages sense of communal responsibility. Branches sponsor weekly youth groups and Jewish welfare projects. National Mishnah contests, rallies, and conventions foster unity on a national level. *Darkeinu; Leaders Guides.*

———, GIRLS' DIVISION—BNOS AGUDATH ISRAEL (1921). 84 William St., NYC 10038. (212)797-9000. Coord. Sara Zimmerman. Educates Jewish girls to the historic nature of the Jewish people as the people of the Torah. Branches throughout country sponsor weekly youth groups and welfare projects, with interregional conferences and conventions on national level. *Kol Bnos.*

———, WOMEN'S DIVISION—N'SHEI AGUDATH ISRAEL OF AMERICA (1940). 84 William St., NYC 10038. (212)363-8940. Presidium Esther Bohensky, Aliza Grund. Organizes Jewish women for philanthropic work in the U.S. and Israel and for intensive Torah education. Seeks to train Torah-guided Jewish mothers.

———, YOUNG MEN'S DIVISION—ZEIREI AGUDATH ISRAEL (1921). 84 William St., NYC 10038. (212)797-9000. Pres. Avrohom Biderman; Dir. Rabbi Labish Becker. Educates youth to see Torah as source of guidance for all issues facing Jews as individuals and as a people. Inculcates a spirit of activism through projects in religious, Torah-educational, and community-welfare fields. *Zeirei Forum; Am Hatorah; Daf Chizuk; Yom Tov Publications.*

AGUDATH ISRAEL WORLD ORGANIZATION (1912). 84 William St., NYC 10038. (212)-797-9000. Cochmn. Rabbi Moshe Sherer, Rabbi Yehudah Meir Abramowitz. Represents the interests of Orthodox Jewry on the national and international scenes. Sponsors projects to strengthen Torah life worldwide.

AMERICAN ASSOCIATION OF RABBIS (1978). 350 Fifth Ave., Suite 3308, NYC 10001. (212)244-3350. Pres. Rabbi Jacob Friedman; Sec. Rabbi Robert Chernoff. An organization of rabbis serving in pulpits, in areas of education, and in social work. Provides rabbinical fraternity. *Bimonthly newsletter; quarterly journal.*

ANNENBERG RESEARCH INSTITUTE (formerly DROPSIE COLLEGE FOR HEBREW AND COGNATE LEARNING) (1907; reorg. 1986). 250 N. Highland Ave., Merion, PA 19066. (215)667-1830. Dir. Bernard Lewis; Assoc. Dir. David M. Goldenberg. A center for advanced research in Judaic and Near Eastern studies at the postdoctoral level. *Jewish Quarterly Review.*

ASSOCIATION FOR JEWISH STUDIES (1969). Widener Library M., Harvard University, Cambridge, MA 02138. Pres. Ruth R. Wisse; Exec. Sec. Charles Berlin. Seeks to promote, maintain, and improve the teaching of Jewish studies in American colleges and universities by sponsoring meetings and conferences, publishing a newsletter and other scholarly materials, setting standards for programs in Jewish studies, aiding in the placement of teachers, coordinating research, and cooperating with other scholarly organizations. *AJS Review; newsletter.*

ASSOCIATION OF HILLEL/JEWISH CAMPUS PROFESSIONALS (1949). 2615 Clifton Ave., Cincinnati, OH 45220. (513)221-6728. Pres. Rabbi Abie I. Ingber; Exec. Off. Judith Schwartz. Seeks to promote professional relationships and exchanges of experience, develop personnel standards and qualifications, safeguard integrity of Hillel profession; represents and advocates before National Hillel Staff, National Hillel Commission, B'nai B'rith International, Council of Jewish Federations. *AHJCP Bulletin.*

ASSOCIATION OF JEWISH CHAPLAINS OF THE ARMED FORCES (1946). 15 E. 26 St., NYC 10010. (212)532-4949. Pres. Rabbi Selig Salkowitz; Sec. Rabbi Myron Geller. An organization of former and current chaplains of the U.S. armed forces which seeks to enhance the religious program of Jewish chaplains in the armed forces and in Veterans Administration hospitals.

ASSOCIATION OF ORTHODOX JEWISH SCIENTISTS (1948). 1373 Coney Island Ave., Brooklyn, NY 11219. (718)338-8592. Pres. Sheldon Kornbluth; Bd. Chmn. Nora Smith. Seeks to contribute to the development of science within the framework of Orthodox Jewish tradition; to obtain and disseminate information relating to the interaction between the Jewish traditional way of life and scientific developments—on both an ideological and practical level; to assist in the solution of problems pertaining to Orthodox Jews engaged in scientific teaching or research. Two main conventions are held each year. *Intercom; Proceedings; Halacha Bulletin; newsletter.*

BETH MEDROSH ELYON (ACADEMY OF HIGHER LEARNING AND RESEARCH) (1943). 73 Main St., Monsey, NY 10952. (914)356-7065. Bd. Chmn. Emanuel Weldler; Treas. Arnold Jacobs; Sec. Yerachmiel Censor. Provides postgraduate courses and research work in higher Jewish studies; offers scholarships and fellowships. *Annual journal.*

B'NAI B'RITH HILLEL FOUNDATIONS, INC. (1923). 1640 Rhode Island Ave., NW, Washington, DC 20036. (202)857-6560. Chmn. B'nai B'rith Hillel Comm. Edwin Shapiro; Internatl. Dir. Larry S. Moses. Provides a program of cultural, religious, educational, social, and counseling content to Jewish college and university students on more than 400 campuses in the U.S., Australia, Canada, England, Israel, Europe, and S. America. Also sponsors Academic Associates, National Jewish Law Students Network, and Student Secretariat. *Jewish Life on Campus; Igeret; NJLSN Newsletter.*

B'NAI B'RITH YOUTH ORGANIZATION (1924). 1640 Rhode Island Ave., NW, Washington, DC 20036. (202)857-6633. Chmn. Youth Comm. Aaron Grossman; Internatl. Dir. Sidney Clearfield. Helps Jewish teenagers achieve self-fulfillment and make a maximum contribution to the Jewish community and their country's culture; helps members acquire a greater knowledge and appreciation of Jewish religion and culture. *BBYO Advisor; Monday Morning; Shofar; Hakol; Kesher.*

BRAMSON ORT (1977). 304 Park Ave. S., NYC 10010. (212)677-7420. Dir. Ira L. Jaskoll. A two-year Jewish technical college offering certificates and associate degrees in high technology and business fields, including computer programming and technology, electronics technology, business management, word processing, and ophthalmic technology. Houses the Center for Computers in Jewish Education.

BRANDEIS-BARDIN INSTITUTE (1941). 1101 Peppertree Lane, Brandeis, CA 93064. (818)348-7201. Pres. Ira Weiner; Dir. Deborah E. Lipstadt. Maintains Brandeis Camp Institute (BCI), a Jewish student leadership program for college-age adults; Camp Alonim for children 8–16; introductory and membership House of the Book weekends for adults 25+, in an effort to instill an appreciation of Jewish cultural and spiritual heritage and to create a desire for active participation in Jewish communities. *BBI News.*

CANTORS ASSEMBLY (1947). 150 Fifth Ave., NYC 10011. (212)691-8020. Pres. Saul Z. Hammerman; Exec. V.-Pres. Samuel Rosenbaum. Seeks to unite all cantors who adhere to traditional Judaism and who serve as full-time cantors in bona fide congregations, to conserve and promote the musical traditions of the Jews and to elevate the status of the cantorial profession. *Annual Proceedings; Journal of Synagogue Music.*

CENTRAL CONFERENCE OF AMERICAN RABBIS (1889). 21 E. 40 St., NYC 10016. (212)684-4990. Pres. Rabbi Jack Stern; Exec. V.-Pres. Rabbi Joseph B. Glaser. Seeks to conserve and promote Judaism and to disseminate its teachings in a liberal spirit. *Journal of Reform Judaism; CCAR Yearbook.*

CENTRAL YESHIVA BETH JOSEPH RABBINICAL SEMINARY (in Europe 1891; in U.S. 1941). 1427 49 St., Brooklyn, NY 11219. Pres. and Dean Jacob Jofen. Maintains a school for teaching Orthodox rabbis and teachers, and promoting the cause of higher Torah learning.

CLAL (*see* National Jewish Center for Learning and Leadership)

CLEVELAND COLLEGE OF JEWISH STUDIES (1964). 26500 Shaker Blvd., Beachwood, OH 44122. (216)464-4050. Pres. David Ariel; Bd. Chmn. Dan Polster. Provides courses in all areas of Judaic and Hebrew studies to adults and college-age students; offers continuing education for Jewish educators and administrators; serves as a center for Jewish life and culture; expands the availability of courses in Judaic studies by exchanging faculty, students, and credits with neighboring academic institutions; grants bachelor's and master's degrees.

COALITION FOR ALTERNATIVES IN JEWISH EDUCATION (CAJE) (1976). 468 Park Ave. S., Rm. 904, NYC 10016. (212)696-0740. Chmn. Betsy Katz; Dir. Eliot G. Spack. Brings together Jews from all ideologies who are involved in every facet of Jewish education, and are committed to transmitting Jewish knowledge, culture, and experience; serves as a channel of communication for its membership to share resources and methods, and as a forum for exchange of philosophical and theoretical approaches to Jewish education. Sponsors programs and projects. *Bikurim; Crisis Curricula; Mekasher; CAJE Jewish Education News.*

COUNCIL FOR JEWISH EDUCATION (1926). 426 W. 58 St., NYC 10019. (212)713-0290. Pres. Rabbi Irwin E. Witty; Exec. Dir. Philip Gorodetzer. Fellowship of Jewish education professionals, comprising administrators and supervisors of national and local Jewish educational institutions and agencies, and teachers in Hebrew high schools and Jewish teachers colleges, of all ideological groupings; conducts annual national and regional conferences in all areas of Jewish education; represents the Jewish education profession before the Jewish community; cosponsors, with the Jewish Education Service of North America, a personnel committee and other projects; cooperates with Jewish Agency Department of Education and Culture in promoting Hebrew culture and studies; conducts lectureship at Hebrew University. *Jewish Education; Sheviley Hahinnuch.*

DROPSIE COLLEGE FOR HEBREW AND COGNATE LEARNING (*see* Annenberg Research Institute)

FEDERATION OF JEWISH MEN'S CLUBS, INC. (1929). 475 Riverside Dr., Suite 244, NYC 10115. (212)749-8100. Pres. Jules Porter;

Exec. Dir. Rabbi Charles Simon. Promotes principles and objectives of Conservative Judaism by organizing, sponsoring, and developing men's clubs or brotherhoods; supports OMETZ Center for Conservative Judaism on campus; promotes Home Library of Conservative Judaism and the Art of Jewish Living series; sponsors Hebrew literacy adult education program; presents awards for service to American Jewry. *Torchlight.*

GRATZ COLLEGE (1895). 10th St. and Tabor Rd., Philadelphia, PA 19141. (215)329-3363. Bd. Chmn. Stephen Sussman; Pres. Gary S. Schiff. Offers a wide variety of bachelor's, master's, teacher-training, continuing-education, and high-school-level programs in Judaic, Hebraic, and Middle Eastern studies. Grants BA and MA in Jewish studies, Bachelor and Master of Hebrew Literature, MA in Jewish education, MA in Jewish music, certificates in Judaica librarianship, Sephardic studies, Jewish chaplaincy, and other credentials. Joint bachelor's programs with Temple University and Beaver College. Gratz College's Division of Community Services serves as the central agency for Jewish education in Greater Philadelphia, providing consultation and resources to Jewish schools, organizations, and individuals. *Various newsletters, a yearbook, and scholarly publications.*

HEBREW COLLEGE (1921). 43 Hawes St., Brookline, MA 02146. (617)232-8710. Act. Pres. Michael Libenson; Bd. Chmn. Leon Brock. Provides intensive programs of study in all areas of Jewish culture from high school through college and graduate school levels, also at branch in Hartford; maintains ongoing programs with most major local universities; offers the degrees of Master of Jewish Studies, Bachelor and Master of Hebrew Literature, and Bachelor and Master of Jewish Education, with teaching certification; trains men and women to teach, conduct, and supervise Jewish schools; operates Hebrew-speaking Camp Yavneh in Northwood, NH; offers extensive Ulpan program and courses for community. *Hebrew College Bulletin.*

HEBREW THEOLOGICAL COLLEGE (1922). 7135 N. Carpenter Rd., Skokie, IL 60077. (312)267-9800. Pres. Rabbi Don Well; Bd. Chmn. Colman Ginsparg. An institution of higher Jewish learning which includes a division of advanced Hebrew studies, a school of liberal arts and sciences, a rabbinical ordination program, a graduate school in Judaic studies and pastoral counseling; the Fasman Yeshiva High School; a high school summer program combining Torah studies and computer science courses; and a Jewish studies program. *Or Shmuel Torah Journal; quarterly newsletter.*

HEBREW UNION COLLEGE–JEWISH INSTITUTE OF RELIGION (1875). 3101 Clifton Ave., Cincinnati, OH 45220. (513)221-1875. Pres. Alfred Gottschalk; Exec. Dean Eugene Mihaly; Exec. V.-Pres. Uri D. Herscher; Chmn. Bd. of Govs. Richard J. Scheuer. Academic centers: 3101 Clifton Ave., Cincinnati, OH 45220 (1875), Samuel Greengus, Dean; 1 W. 4 St., NYC 10012 (1922), Paul M. Steinberg, Dean; 3077 University Ave., Los Angeles, CA 90007 (1954), Uri D. Herscher, Chief Admin. Off.; 13 King David St., Jerusalem, Israel 94101 (1963), Michael Klein, Dean. Prepares students for Reform rabbinate, cantorate, religious-school teaching and administration, community service, academic careers; promotes Jewish studies; maintains libraries and a museum; offers bachelor's, master's, and doctoral degrees; engages in archaeological excavations; publishes scholarly works through Hebrew Union College Press. *American Jewish Archives; Bibliographica Judaica; HUC–JIR Catalogue; Hebrew Union College Annual; Studies in Bibliography and Booklore; The Chronicle.*

———, AMERICAN JEWISH ARCHIVES (1947). 3101 Clifton Ave., Cincinnati, OH 45220. (513)221-1875. Dir. Jacob R. Marcus; Admin. Dir. Abraham Peck. Promotes the study and preservation of the Western Hemisphere Jewish experience through research, publications, collection of important source materials, and a vigorous public-outreach program. *American Jewish Archives; monographs, publications, and pamphlets.*

———, AMERICAN JEWISH PERIODICAL CENTER (1957). 3101 Clifton Ave., Cincinnati, OH 45220. (513)221-1875. Dir. Jacob R. Marcus; Codir. Herbert C. Zafren. Maintains microfilms of all American Jewish periodicals 1823–1925, selected periodicals since 1925. *Jewish Periodicals and Newspapers on Microfilm (1957); First Supplement (1960); Augmented Edition (1984).*

———, EDGAR F. MAGNIN SCHOOL OF GRADUATE STUDIES (1956). 3077 University Ave., Los Angeles, CA 90007. (213)-749-3424. Dir. Stanley Chyet. Supervises programs leading to PhD (Education), DHS, DHL, and MA degrees; participates in cooperative PhD programs with the University of Southern California.

———, JEROME H. LOUCHHEIM SCHOOL OF JUDAIC STUDIES (1969). 3077 University Ave. Los Angeles, CA 90007. (213)749-3424. Dir. David Ellenson. Offers programs leading to MA, BS, BA, and AA degrees; offers courses as part of the undergraduate program of the University of Southern California.

———, NELSON GLUECK SCHOOL OF BIBLICAL ARCHAEOLOGY (1963). 13 King David St., Jerusalem, Israel 94101. Dir. Avraham Biran. Offers graduate-level research programs in Bible and archaeology. Summer excavations are carried out by scholars and students. University credit may be earned by participants in excavations. Consortium of colleges, universities, and seminaries is affiliated with the school.

———, RHEA HIRSCH SCHOOL OF EDUCATION (1967). 3077 University Ave., Los Angeles, CA 90007. (213)749-3424. Dir. Sara S. Lee. Offers PhD and MA programs in Jewish and Hebrew education; conducts joint degree programs with University of Southern California; offers courses for Jewish teachers, librarians, and early educators on a nonmatriculating basis; conducts summer institutes for professional Jewish educators.

———, SCHOOL OF EDUCATION (1947). 1 W. 4 St., NYC 10012. (212)674-5300. V.-Pres. and Dean Paul M. Steinberg; Dir. Kerry Olitzky. Trains teachers and principals for Reform religious schools; offers MA degree with specialization in religious education; offers extension programs in various suburban centers.

———, SCHOOL OF GRADUATE STUDIES (1949). 3101 Clifton Ave., Cincinnati, OH 45220 (513)221-1875. Dean Samuel Greengus. Offers programs leading to MA and PhD degrees; offers program leading to DHL degree for rabbinic graduates of the college.

———, SCHOOL OF JEWISH COMMUNAL SERVICE (1968). 3077 University Ave., Los Angeles, CA 90007. (213)749-3424. Dir. Gerald B. Bubis. Offers certificate and master's degree to those employed in Jewish communal services, or preparing for such work; offers joint MA in Jewish education and communal service with Rhea Hirsch School; offers MA and MSW in conjunction with the University of Southern California School of Social Work, with the George Warren Brown School of Social Work of Washington University, and with the University of Pittsburgh School of Social Work; offers joint master's degrees in conjunction with USC in public administration or gerontology.

———, SCHOOL OF JEWISH STUDIES (1963). 13 King David St., Jerusalem, Israel, 94101. Pres. Alfred Gottschalk; Dean Michael Klein. Offers first year of graduate rabbinic, cantorial, and Jewish education studies; program in biblical archaeology; program leading to ordination for Israeli students; undergraduate semester in Jerusalem and one-year work/study program on a kibbutz in cooperation with Union of American Hebrew Congregations.

———, SCHOOL OF SACRED MUSIC (1947). 1 W. 4 St., NYC 10012. (212)674-5300. V.-Pres. and Dean Paul M. Steinberg; Dir. Lawrence A. Hoffman. Trains cantors and music personnel for congregations; offers MSM degree. *Sacred Music Press.*

———, SKIRBALL MUSEUM (1913; 1972 in Calif.). 3077 University Ave., Los Angeles, CA 90007. (213)749-3424. Dir. Nancy Berman; Curator Grace Grossman. Collects, preserves, researches, and exhibits art and artifacts made by or for Jews, or otherwise associated with Jews and Judaism. Provides opportunity to faculty and students to do research in the field of Jewish art. *Catalogues of exhibits and collections.*

HERZLIAH–JEWISH TEACHERS SEMINARY (1967). Division of Touro College. 30 W. 44 St., NYC 10036. (212)575-1819. Pres. Bernard Lander; Dir. Jacob Katzman.

———, GRADUATE SCHOOL OF JEWISH STUDIES (1981). Pres. Bernard Lander; Dir. Michael Shmidman. Offers programs leading to MA in Jewish studies, including Hebrew language and literature, Jewish education, history, philosophy, and sociology. Admits men and women who have bachelor's degrees and backgrounds in Hebrew, Yiddish, and Jewish studies.

———, JEWISH PEOPLE'S UNIVERSITY OF THE AIR. (212)575-1819. Dir. Jacob Katzman; Coord. Marie Alderman. The educational outreach arm of Touro College, it produces and disseminates Jewish educational and cultural programming for radio broadcast and audio-cassettes.

INSTITUTE FOR COMPUTERS IN JEWISH LIFE (1978). 845 N. Michigan Ave., Suite 843, Chicago, IL 60611. (312)787-7856. Pres. Thomas Klutznick; Exec. V.-Pres. Irving J. Rosenbaum. Explores, develops, and disseminates applications of computer technology to appropriate areas of Jewish life, with special emphasis on Jewish education; provides access to the Bar-Ilan University Responsa Project; creates educational software for use in Jewish schools; provides consulting service and assistance for national Jewish organizations, seminaries, and synagogues. *Monitor.*

JEWISH CHAUTAUQUA SOCIETY, INC. (sponsored by NATIONAL FEDERATION OF TEMPLE BROTHERHOODS) (1893). 838 Fifth Ave., NYC 10021. (212)570-0707. Pres. Marshall Blair; Chancellor Carl J. Burkons; Exec. Dir. Av Bondarin. Disseminates authoritative information on Jews and Judaism; assigns rabbis to lecture at colleges and secondary schools; endows courses in Judaism for college credit at universities; donates Jewish reference books to college libraries; sends rabbis to serve as counselor-teachers at Christian church summer camps and as chaplains at Boy Scout camps; sponsors institutes on Judaism for Christian clergy; produces motion pictures for public-service television and group showings. *Brotherhood.*

JEWISH EDUCATION IN MEDIA, INC. (1978). PO Box 180, Riverdale Sta., NYC 10471. (212)362-7633. Exec. Dir. Rabbi Mark S. Golub. Seeks to promote Jewish identity and commitment through the creation of innovative and entertaining media materials, including radio and television programming, film, and audio and video cassettes for synagogue and institutional use.

JEWISH EDUCATION SERVICE OF NORTH AMERICA, INC. (JESNA) (1981). 730 Broadway, NYC 10003. (212)529-2000. Pres. Mark Schlussel; Exec. V.-Pres. Jonathan Woocher. Coordinates, promotes, and services Jewish education in federated communities of North America. Coordinating center for Jewish education bureaus; offers curricular advisement and maintains a National Educational Resource Center; runs regional pedagogic conferences; conducts evaluative surveys on Jewish education; engages in statistical and other educational research; provides community consultations; sponsors the National Board of License; administers Fellowships in Jewish Educational Leadership training program (FIJEL); provides placement of upper-level bureau and communal school personnel and educators. *Pedagogic Reporter; TRENDS; Information Research Bulletins; Jewish Education Directory;* annual report; *NISE Newsletter.*

JEWISH MINISTERS CANTORS ASSOCIATION OF AMERICA, INC. (1896). 3 W. 16 St., NYC 10011. (212)675-6601. Pres. Cantor Chaskele Ritter. Furthers and propagates traditional liturgy; places cantors in synagogues throughout the U.S. and Canada; develops the cantors of the future. *Kol Lakol.*

JEWISH RECONSTRUCTIONIST FOUNDATION (1940). 270 W. 89 St., NYC 10024. (212)-496-2960. Bd. Chmn, Rabbi Lee Friedlander; Exec. Dir. Rabbi Mordechai Liebling. Dedicated to the advancement of Judaism as the evolving religious civilization of the Jewish people. Coordinates the Federation of Reconstructionist Congregations and Havurot, Reconstructionist Rabbinical Association, and Reconstructionist Rabbinical College.

———, FEDERATION OF RECONSTRUCTIONIST CONGREGATIONS AND HAVUROT (1954). 270 W. 89 St., NYC 10024. (212)-496-2960. Pres. Lillian Kaplan; Exec. Dir. Rabbi Mordechai Liebling. Services affiliated congregations and havurot educationally and administratively; fosters the establishment of new Reconstructionist congregations and fellowship groups. Runs the Reconstructionist Press and provides programmatic materials. *Newsletter; Reconstructionist.*

———, RECONSTRUCTIONIST RABBINICAL ASSOCIATION (1975). Greenwood Ave. and Church Rd., Wyncote, PA 19095. (215)576-0800. Pres. Rabbi Ira J. Schiffer; Exec. Dir. Rabbi Lewis J. Eron. Professional organization for graduates of the Reconstructionist Rabbinical College and other rabbis who identify with Reconstructionist Judaism; cooperates with Federation of Reconstructionist Congregations and Havurot in furthering Reconstructionism in N. America. *Raayanot.*

———, RECONSTRUCTIONIST RABBINICAL COLLEGE (see p. 387)

JEWISH TEACHERS ASSOCIATION–MORIM (1931). 45 E. 33 St., NYC 10016. (212)-684-0556. Pres. Phyllis L. Pullman; V.-Pres. Eli Nieman. Protects teachers from abuse of seniority rights; fights the encroachment of anti-Semitism in education; provides legal counsel to protect teachers from discrimination; offers scholarships to qualified students; encourages teachers to assume active roles in Jewish communal and religious affairs. *Morim Jewish Teachers Association Newsletter.*

JEWISH THEOLOGICAL SEMINARY OF AMERICA (1886; reorg. 1902). 3080 Broadway, NYC 10027. (212)678-8000. Chancellor Ismar Schorsch; Chmn. Bd. of Directors and Exec. Com. Stephen M. Peck. Operates undergraduate and graduate programs in Judaica, professional schools for training Conservative rabbis and cantors, a pastoral psychiatry center, Melton Center for Jewish Education, the Jewish Museum, and such youth programs as the Ramah Camps, the OMETZ–Center for Conservative Judaism on Campus, and the Prozdor high-school division. Produces the "Eternal Light" radio and TV programs. *Academic Bulletin; JTS Bulletin; Seminary Progress.*

———, ALBERT A. LIST COLLEGE OF JEWISH STUDIES (formerly SEMINARY COLLEGE OF JEWISH STUDIES-TEACHERS INSTITUTE) (1909). 3080 Broadway, NYC 10027. (212)678-8826. Dean Anne Lapidus Lerner. Offers complete undergraduate program in Judaica leading to BA degree; conducts joint programs with Columbia University and Barnard enabling students to receive two BA degrees after four years.

———, AMERICAN STUDENT CENTER IN JERUSALEM (1962). PO Box 196, Neve Schechter, Jerusalem, Israel 91001. Dean Reuven Hammer; Dir. Midreshet Yerushalayim, Baruch Feldstern. Offers year-in-Israel programs for college students, graduate students—including rabbinical and cantorial students—and a program of intensive Jewish studies for undergraduates at the Hebrew University. A new two-year program in the art of translating in Jewish subjects leads to certification in translation. Headquarters also for the Saul Lieberman Institute for Talmudic Studies, Dr. Shamma Friedman, Director.

———, CANTORS INSTITUTE AND SEMINARY COLLEGE OF JEWISH MUSIC (1952). 3080 Broadway, NYC 10027. (212)678-8038. Dean Morton M. Leifman. Trains cantors, music teachers, and choral directors for congregations. Offers full-time programs in sacred music leading to degrees of BSM, MSM, and DSM, and diploma of *Hazzan.*

———, DEPARTMENT OF RADIO AND TELEVISION (1944). 3080 Broadway, NYC 10027. (212)678-8020. Exec. Prod. Milton E. Krents. Produces radio and TV programs expressing the Jewish tradition in its broadest sense, with emphasis on the universal human situation: "Eternal Light," a weekly radio program; 3 special "Eternal Light" TV programs, produced in cooperation with NBC. Distributes program scripts and related reading lists.

———, GRADUATE SCHOOL (formerly INSTITUTE FOR ADVANCED STUDY IN THE HUMANITIES) (1968). 3080 Broadway, NYC 10027. (212)678-8024. Dean Mayer Rabinowitz. Graduate programs leading to MA, DHL, and PhD degrees in Jewish studies, Bible, Jewish education, history, literature, philosophy, rabbinics, and medieval studies; dual degree with Columbia University School of Social Work.

———, JEWISH MUSEUM (see p. 373)

———, LOUIS FINKELSTEIN INSTITUTE FOR RELIGIOUS AND SOCIAL STUDIES (1938). 3080 Broadway, NYC 10027. (212)678-8815. Dir. Gordon Tucker. A scholarly and scientific fellowship of clergymen and other religious teachers who desire authoritative information regarding some of the basic issues now confronting spiritually minded individuals.

———, MELTON RESEARCH CENTER FOR JEWISH EDUCATION (1960). 3080 Broadway, NYC 10027. (212)678-8031. Dirs. Eduardo Rauch, Barry W. Holtz. Develops new curricula and materials for Jewish education; recruits, trains, and retrains educators through seminars and in-service programs; maintains consultant and supervisory relationships with a limited number of pilot schools; sponsors yearly "renewal" retreat for teachers. *Melton Journal.*

———, NATIONAL RAMAH COMMISSION (1947). 3080 Broadway, NYC 10027. (212)678-8881. Dir. Burton I. Cohen. Sponsors summer camps conducted in Hebrew; offers opportunities for students in Seminary schools to serve as teachers in formal classroom settings, discussion leaders, and counselors. Offers 4 special high-school and college programs: Bert B. Weinstein National Ramah Staff Training Institute, the Ramah Israel Seminar, the Ramah Kibbutz-Ulpan Program, and Tichon Ramah Yerushalayim.

———, PROZDOR (1951). 3080 Broadway, NYC 10027. (212)678-8824. Principal Aryeh Davidson. The high-school department of JTS, it provides a supplementary Jewish education for students who attend a secular (public or private) full-time high school. Classes in classical Jewish studies, with emphasis on Hebrew language, meet twice a week.

———, RABBINICAL SCHOOL (1886). 3080 Broadway, NYC 10027. (212)678-8816. Dean Gordon Tucker. Offers a program of graduate and professional studies leading to the degree of Master of Arts and ordination; includes one year of study at the American Student Center in Jerusalem and pastoral psychiatry training.

———, SCHOCKEN INSTITUTE FOR JEWISH RESEARCH (1961). 6 Balfour St., Jerusalem, Israel. Librarian Yaakov Katzenstein. Incorporates Schocken library and its related research institutes in medieval Hebrew poetry and Jewish mysticism. *Schocken Institute Yearbook (P'raqim).*

———, UNIVERSITY OF JUDAISM (1947). 15600 Mulholland Dr., Los Angeles, CA 90024. (213)879-4114. Pres. David L. Lieber; Sr. V.-Pres. Max Vorspan. West Coast school of JTS. Serves as center of undergraduate and graduate study of Judaica; offers preprofessional and professional programs in Jewish education and allied fields, including a prerabbinic program and joint program enabling students to receive BA from UCLA and BHL from U. of J. after four years, and an experimental undergraduate program in the humanities, Lee College, as well as a broad range of adult education and Jewish activities. *Direction; Bulletin of General Information.*

MACHNE ISRAEL, INC. (1940). 770 Eastern Pkwy., Brooklyn, NY 11213. (718)493-9250. Pres. Menachem M. Schneerson (Lubavitcher Rebbe); Dir., Treas. M.A. Hodakov; Sec. Nissan Mindel. The Lubavitcher movement's organ dedicated to the social, spiritual, and material welfare of Jews throughout the world.

MERKOS L'INYONEI CHINUCH, INC. (THE CENTRAL ORGANIZATION FOR JEWISH EDUCATION) (1940). 770 Eastern Pkwy., Brooklyn, NY 11213. (718)493-9250. Pres. Menachem M. Schneerson (Lubavitcher Rebbe); Dir., Treas. M.A. Hodakov; Sec. Nissan Mindel. The educational arm of the Lubavitcher movement. Seeks to promote Jewish education among Jews, regardless of their background, in the spirit of Torah-true Judaism; to establish contact with alienated Jewish youth; to stimulate concern and active interest in Jewish education on all levels; and to promote religious observance as a daily experience among all Jews; maintains worldwide network of regional offices, schools, summer camps, and Chabad-Lubavitch Houses; publishes Jewish educational literature in numerous languages and monthly journal in five languages: *Conversaciones con la juventud; Conversations avec les jeunes; Schmuessen mit Kinder un Yugent; Sihot la-No-ar; Talks and Tales.*

MESIVTA YESHIVA RABBI CHAIM BERLIN RABBINICAL ACADEMY (1905). 1593 Coney Island Ave., Brooklyn, NY 11230. (718)377-0777. Pres. Sol Eiger; Admin. Yerachmiel Stuppler. Maintains fully accredited elementary and high schools; collegiate and postgraduate school for advanced Jewish studies, both in America and Israel; Camp Morris, a summer study retreat; Prof. Nathan Isaacs Memorial Library; Gur Aryeh Publications.

MIRRER YESHIVA CENTRAL INSTITUTE (in Poland 1817; in U.S. 1947). 1791–5 Ocean Pkwy., Brooklyn, NY 11223. Pres. and Dean Rabbi Shrage Moshe Klamanowitz; Exec. Dir. and Sec. Manfred Handelsman. Maintains rabbinical college, postgraduate school for Talmudic research, accredited high school, and Kollel and Sephardic divisions; dedicated to the dissemination of Torah scholarship in the community and abroad; engages in rescue and rehabilitation of scholars overseas.

NATIONAL COMMITTEE FOR FURTHERANCE OF JEWISH EDUCATION (1941). 824 Eastern Pkwy., Brooklyn, NY 11213. (718)735-0200. Pres. J. James Plesser; Bd.

Chmn. Martin Domansky; Exec. V.-Pres. Jacob J. Hecht. Seeks to disseminate the ideals of Torah-true education among the youth of America; aids poor, sick, and needy in U.S. and Israel; provides aid to hundreds of Iranian Jewish youth through the Iranian Children's Fund; maintains camp for underprivileged children; sponsors Hadar HaTorah, Machon Chana, and Ivy League Torah Study Program, seeking to win back college youth and others to the fold of Judaism; maintains schools and dormitory facilities. *Panorama; Passover Handbook; Seder Guide; Spiritual Suicide; Focus.*

NATIONAL COUNCIL OF BETH JACOB SCHOOLS, INC. (1945). 1415 E. 7 St., Brooklyn, NY 11230. (718)979-7400. Bd. Chmn. Shimon Newhouse; Sec. David Rosenberg. Operates Orthodox all-day schools from kindergarten through high school for girls, a residence high school in Ferndale, NY, a national institute for master instructors, and a summer camp for girls. *Bais Yaakov Digest; Pnimia Call.*

NATIONAL COUNCIL OF YOUNG ISRAEL (1912). 3 W. 16 St., NYC 10011. (212)-929-1525. Pres. Harold M. Jacobs; Exec. V.-Pres. Rabbi Ephraim H. Sturm. Maintains a program of spiritual, cultural, social, and communal activity aimed at the advancement and perpetuation of traditional, Torah-true Judaism; seeks to instill in American youth an understanding and appreciation of the ethical and spiritual values of Judaism. Sponsors kosher dining clubs and fraternity houses and an Israel program. *Viewpoint; Hashkafa series; Masorah newspaper.*

———, AMERICAN FRIENDS OF YOUNG ISRAEL SYNAGOGUES IN ISRAEL (1926). 3 W. 16 St., NYC 10011. (212)929-1525. Chmn. Jack Forgash; Dir. Israel Programs Isaac Hagler; Exec. V.-Pres. Rabbi Ephraim H. Sturm. Promotes Young Israel synagogues and youth work in synagogues in Israel.

———, ARMED FORCES BUREAU (1912). 3 W. 16 St., NYC 10011. (212)929-1525. Advises and guides the inductees into the armed forces with regard to Sabbath observance, *kashrut,* and Orthodox behavior. *Guide for the Orthodox Serviceman.*

———, EMPLOYMENT BUREAU (1912). 3 W. 16 St., NYC 10011. (212)929-1525. Exec. V.-Pres. Rabbi Ephraim H. Sturm; Employment Dir. Dorothy Stein. Operates an on-the-job training program under federal contract; helps secure employment, particularly for Sabbath observers and Russian immigrants; offers vocational guidance. *Viewpoint.*

———, INSTITUTE FOR JEWISH STUDIES (1947). 3 W. 16 St., NYC 10011. (212)-929-1525. Pres. Harold M. Jacobs; Exec. V.-Pres. Rabbi Ephraim H. Sturm. Introduces students to Jewish learning and knowledge; helps form adult branch schools; aids Young Israel synagogues in their adult education programs. *Bulletin.*

———, YOUNG ISRAEL COLLEGIATES AND YOUNG ADULTS (1951; reorg. 1982). 3 W. 16 St., NYC 10011. (212)929-1525. Chmn. Kenneth Block; Dir. Richard Stareshefsky. Organizes and operates kosher dining clubs on college and university campuses; provides information and counseling on *kashrut* observance at college; gives college-age youth understanding and appreciation of Judaism and information on issues important to Jewish community; arranges seminars and meetings; publishes pamphlets and monographs. *Hashkafa.*

———, YOUNG ISRAEL YOUTH (reorg. 1968). 3 W. 16 St., NYC 10011. (212)929-1525. Chmn. Eugene Wilk; Dir. Richard Stareshefsky. Fosters a program of spiritual, cultural, social, and communal activities for the advancement and perpetuation of traditional Torah-true Judaism; strives to instill an understanding and appreciation of the high ethical and spiritual values and to demonstrate compatibility of ancient faith of Israel with good Americanism. Operates Achva Summer Mission study program in Israel. *Monthly newsletter.*

NATIONAL JEWISH CENTER FOR LEARNING AND LEADERSHIP—CLAL (1974). 421 Seventh Ave., NYC 10001. (212)714-9500. Chmn Herschel Blumberg; Pres. Irving Greenberg; Exec. V.-Pres. Paul Jeser. Devoted to leadership education and policy guidance for the American Jewish community. Conducts weekend retreats and community gatherings as well as conferences on various topics. *Perspectives.*

NATIONAL JEWISH HOSPITALITY COMMITTEE (1973). 201 S. 18 St., Rm. 1519, Philadelphia, PA 19103. (215)546-8293.

Pres. Allen S. Maller; Exec. Dir. Steven S. Jacobs. Assists converts and prospective converts to Judaism, persons involved in intermarriages, and the parents of Jewish youth under the influence of cults and missionaries, as well as the youths themselves. *Our Choice.*

NATIONAL JEWISH INFORMATION SERVICE FOR THE PROPAGATION OF JUDAISM, INC. (1960). 5174 W. 8 St., Los Angeles, CA 90036. (213)936-6033. Pres. Rabbi Moshe M. Maggal; V.-Pres. Lawrence J. Epstein; Sec. Rachel D. Maggal. Seeks to convert non-Jews to Judaism and revert Jews to Judaism; maintains College for Jewish Ambassadors for the training of Jewish missionaries and the Correspondence Academy of Judaism for instruction on Judaism through the mail. *Voice of Judaism.*

NER ISRAEL RABBINICAL COLLEGE (1933). 400 Mt. Wilson Ln., Baltimore, MD 21208. (301)484-7200. Pres. Rabbi Jacob I. Ruderman; V.-Pres. Rabbi Herman N. Neuberger. Trains rabbis and educators for Jewish communities in America and worldwide. Offers bachelor's, master's, and doctoral degrees in Talmudic law, as well as teacher's diploma. College has four divisions: Mechina High School, Rabbinical College, Teachers Training Institute, Graduate School. Maintains an active community-service division. Operates special program for Iranian Jewish students. *Ner Israel Bulletin; Alumni Bulletin; Ohr Hanair Talmudic Journal; Iranian B'nei Torah Bulletin.*

OZAR HATORAH, INC. (1946). 1 E. 33 St., NYC 10016. (212)689-3508. Pres. Joseph Shalom; Pres., France, Rabbi JP Amoyelle; Exec. Dir. Rabbi H. Augenbaum. Establishes, maintains, and expands schools for Jewish youth, providing religious and secular studies, worldwide.

P'EYLIM—AMERICAN YESHIVA STUDENT UNION (1951). 3 W. 16 St., NYC 10011. (212)989-2500. Pres. Jacob Y. Weisberg; Dir. Avraham Hirsch. Aids and sponsors pioneer work by American graduate teachers and rabbis in new villages and towns in Israel; does religious, organizational, and educational work and counseling among new immigrant youth; maintains summer camps for poor immigrant youth in Israel; belongs to worldwide P'eylim movement which has groups in Argentina, Brazil, Canada, England, Belgium, the Netherlands, Switzerland, France, and Israel; engages in relief and educational work among North African immigrants in France and Canada, assisting them to relocate and reestablish a strong Jewish community life. *P'eylim Reporter; News from P'eylim; N'shei P'eylim News.*

RABBINICAL ALLIANCE OF AMERICA (IGUD HARABONIM) (1944). 156 Fifth Ave., Suite 807, NYC 10010. (212)242-6420. Pres. Rabbi Abraham B. Hecht; Menahel Rabbinical Court Rabbi Herschel Kurzrock. Seeks to promulgate the cause of Torah-true Judaism through an organized rabbinate that is consistently Orthodox; seeks to elevate the position of Orthodox rabbis nationally, and to defend the welfare of Jews the world over. Also has Beth Din Rabbinical Court and marriage and family counseling. *Perspective; Nahalim.*

RABBINICAL ASSEMBLY (1900). 3080 Broadway, NYC 10027. (212)678-8060. Pres. Rabbi Kassel Abelson; Exec. V.-Pres. Rabbi Wolfe Kelman. Seeks to promote Conservative Judaism, and to foster the spirit of fellowship and cooperation among rabbis and other Jewish scholars; cooperates with the Jewish Theological Seminary of America and the United Synagogue of America. *Conservative Judaism; Proceedings of the Rabbinical Assembly.*

RABBINICAL COLLEGE OF TELSHE, INC. (1941). 28400 Euclid Ave., Wickliffe, OH 44092. (216)943-5300. Pres. Rabbi Mordecai Gifter; V.-Pres. Rabbi Abba Zalka Gewirtz. College for higher Jewish learning specializing in Talmudic studies and rabbinics; maintains a preparatory academy including a secular high school, postgraduate department, teacher-training school, and teachers seminary for women. *Pri Etz Chaim; Peer Mordechai; Alumni Bulletin.*

RABBINICAL COUNCIL OF AMERICA, INC. (1923; reorg. 1936). 275 Seventh Ave., NYC 10001. (212)807-7888. Pres. Rabbi Milton H. Polin; Exec. V.-Pres. Rabbi Binyamin Walfish. Promotes Orthodox Judaism in the community; supports institutions for study of Torah; stimulates creation of new traditional agencies. *Hadorom; Record; Sermon Manual; Tradition.*

RECONSTRUCTIONIST RABBINICAL COLLEGE (1968). Church Rd. and Greenwood

Ave., Wyncote, PA 19095. (215)576-0800. Bd. Chmn. Samuel Blumenthal; Gen'l. Chmn. Aaron Ziegelman; Act. Pres./Dean Arthur Green. Coeducational. Trains rabbis for all areas of Jewish communal life: synagogues, academic and educational positions, Hillel centers, Federation agencies; requires students to pursue outside graduate studies in religion and related subjects; confers title of rabbi and grants degrees of Master and Doctor of Hebrew Letters. *RRC Report.*

RESEARCH INSTITUTE OF RELIGIOUS JEWRY, INC. (1941; reorg. 1954). 471 W. End Ave., NYC 10024. (212)874-7979. Chmn. Rabbi Oswald Besser; Treas. Joseph Friedenson; Sec. Marcus Levine. Engages in research and publishes studies concerning the situation of religious Jewry and its problems all over the world.

SHOLEM ALEICHEM FOLK INSTITUTE, INC. (1918). 3301 Bainbridge Ave., Bronx, NY 10467. Pres. Burt Levey; Sec. Noah Zingman. Aims to imbue children with Jewish values through teaching Yiddish language and literature, Hebrew and the Bible, Jewish history, the significance of Jewish holidays, folk and choral singing, and facts about Jewish life in America and Israel. *Kinder Journal* (Yiddish).

SOCIETY FOR HUMANISTIC JUDAISM (1969). 28611 W. Twelve Mile Rd., Farmington Hills, MI 48018. (313)478-7610. Founder Rabbi Sherwin Wine; Exec. Dir. Miriam Jerris; Pres. Leonard Cherlin. Serves as a voice for Jews who value their Jewish identity and who seek an alternative to conventional Judaism, who reject supernatural authority and affirm the right of individuals to be the masters of their own lives. Publishes educational and ceremonial materials; organizes congregations and groups. *Humanistic Judaism.*

SOCIETY OF FRIENDS OF THE TOURO SYNAGOGUE, NATIONAL HISTORIC SHRINE, INC. (1948). 85 Touro St., Newport, RI 02840. (401)847-4794. Pres. Aaron Slom; Exec. Sec. Theodore Lewis. Assists in the maintenance of the Touro Synagogue as a national historic site. *History of Touro Synagogue.*

SPERTUS COLLEGE OF JUDAICA (1925). 618 S. Michigan Ave., Chicago, IL 60605. (312)922-9012. Pres. Howard A. Sulkin; Bd. Chmn. Stuart Taussig; V.-Pres. for Academic Affairs Byron L. Sherwin. Provides Chicago-area colleges and universities with specialized undergraduate and graduate programs in Judaica and serves as a department of Judaic studies to these colleges and universities; serves as Midwest Jewish information center, through its Asher Library, Maurice Spertus Museum of Judaica, Katzin Memorial Rare Book Room, and Chicago Jewish Archives. Grants degrees of MA in Jewish education, Jewish studies, and Jewish communal service; BA and Bachelor of Judaic Studies. Has community outreach/extension studies program for adults.

SYNAGOGUE COUNCIL OF AMERICA (1926). 327 Lexington Ave., NYC 10016. (212)-686-8670. Pres. Rabbi Herbert M. Baumgard; Exec. V.-Pres. Rabbi Henry D. Michelman. Serves as spokesman for, and coordinates policies of, national rabbinical and lay synagogal organizations of Conservative, Orthodox, and Reform branches of American Judaism.

TORAH SCHOOLS FOR ISRAEL—CHINUCH ATZMAI (1953). 167 Madison Ave., NYC 10016. (212)889-0606. Pres. Abraham Pam; Exec. Dir. Henach Cohen. Conducts information programs for the American Jewish community on activities of the independent Torah schools educational network in Israel; coordinates role of American members of international board of governors; funds special programs of Mercaz Hachinuch Ha-Atzmai B'Eretz Yisroel. *Israel Education Reporter.*

TORAH UMESORAH—NATIONAL SOCIETY FOR HEBREW DAY SCHOOLS (1944). 160 Broadway, NYC 10038. (212)227-1000. Pres. Sheldon Beren; Chmn. Exec. Com. David Singer; Exec. V.-Pres. Joshua Fishman. Establishes Hebrew day schools throughout U.S. and Canada and services them in all areas, including placement and curriculum guidance; conducts teacher-training institutes on campuses of major yeshivahs and seminars and workshops for in-service training of teachers; publishes textbooks and supplementary reading material; conducts research in ethics and character education; supervises federal aid programs for Hebrew day schools throughout the U.S. *Olomeinu–Our World; Torah Umesorah Report; Machberet Hamenahel.*

———, INSTITUTE FOR PROFESSIONAL ENRICHMENT (1973). 22 E. 28 St., NYC

10016. (212)683-3216. Dir. Bernard Dov Milians. Provides enriched training and upgraded credentials for administrative, guidance, and classroom personnel of Hebrew day schools and for Torah-community leaders; offers graduate and undergraduate programs, in affiliation with accredited universities which award full degrees: MA in early childhood and elementary education; MS in family counseling; MBA in management; MS in special education, reading; BS in education; BA in human relations, social sciences, education, gerontology. *Professional Enrichment News (PEN).*

———, NATIONAL ASSOCIATION OF HEBREW DAY SCHOOL ADMINISTRATORS (1960). 1114 Ave. J, Brooklyn, NY 11230. Pres. David H. Schwartz. Coordinates the work of the fiscal directors of Hebrew day schools throughout the country. *NAHDSA Review.*

———, NATIONAL ASSOCIATION OF HEBREW DAY SCHOOL PARENT-TEACHER ASSOCIATIONS (1948). 160 Broadway, NYC 10038. (212)406-4190. Pres. Mrs. Henry C. Rhein; Exec. Sec. Mrs. Samuel Brand; Bd. Chmn. Mrs. Clarence Horwitz. Acts as a clearinghouse and service agency to PTAs of Hebrew day schools; organizes parent-education courses and sets up programs for individual PTAs. *National Program Notes; PTA Bulletin; Fundraising with a Flair; PTA with a Purpose for the Hebrew Day School.*

———, NATIONAL CONFERENCE OF YESHIVA PRINCIPALS (1956). 160 Broadway, NYC 10038. (212)406-4190. Pres. Rabbi Kalman Rosenbaum; Bd. Chmn. Rabbi Yitzchock Merkin; Exec. V.-Pres. Rabbi A. Moshe Possick. A professional organization of primary and secondary yeshivah day-school principals which seeks to make yeshivah day-school education more effective. *Machberet Hamenahel.*

———, NATIONAL YESHIVA TEACHERS BOARD OF LICENSE (1953). 160 Broadway, NYC 10038. (212)406-4190. Bd. Chmn. Rabbi Elias Schwartz; Exec. Consult. Rabbi Zvi H. Shurin. Issues licenses to qualified instructors for all grades of the Hebrew day school and the general field of Torah education.

TOURO COLLEGE (1970). 30 W. 44 St., NYC 10036. (212)575-0190. Pres. Bernard Lander; Bd. Chmn. Max Karl. Chartered by NY State Board of Regents as a nonprofit four-year college with liberal arts programs leading to BA, BS, and MA degrees, emphasizing relevance of Jewish heritage to general culture of Western civilization. Offers JD degree and a biomedical program leading to the MD from Technion-Israel Institute of Technology, Haifa, and the University of Groningen, Holland.

———, COLLEGE OF LIBERAL ARTS AND SCIENCES. 30 W. 44 St., NYC 10036. Dean Stanley Boylan. Offers comprehensive Jewish studies along with studies in the arts, sciences, humanities, and preprofessional studies in health sciences, law, accounting, business, computer science, and finance. Coordinate and extension programs at Women's Division (221 W. 51 St., NYC) and Flatbush Center in Brooklyn.

———, DIVISION OF HEALTH SCIENCES. 30 W. 44 St., NYC 10036, and the Long Island campus in Huntington. Offers three programs: (1) Five-year program leading to MD degree from the Faculty of Medicine of Technion-Israel Institute of Technology, Haifa; includes one year of advanced clinical rotations in Israel; (2) Physician Assistant program; (3) Physical Therapist program.

———, FLATBUSH PROGRAM. 1277 E. 14 St., Brooklyn, NY 11230. Offers evening classes to students attending a yeshiva or seminary during the day; nine majors include accounting, business management, education, and computer science.

———, GRADUATE SCHOOL OF JEWISH STUDIES. 30 W. 44 St., NYC 10036. Offered in conjunction with Herzliah-Jewish Teachers Seminary Division.

———, INSTITUTE OF JEWISH LAW. Based at Fuchsberg Law Center, serves as a center and clearinghouse for study and teaching of Jewish law.

———, JACOB D. FUCHSBERG LAW CENTER. Long Island Campus, 300 Nassau Rd., Huntington, NY 11743. Dean Howard A. Glickstein. Offers studies leading to JD degree.

———, JEWISH PEOPLE'S UNIVERSITY OF THE AIR. Presents Sunday radio courses on New York stations WEVD and WNYC, carried by satellite to NPR's 320 affiliated stations nationwide; covers all aspects of Jewish culture and offers course outlines and cassettes.

———, SCHOOL OF GENERAL STUDIES. 240 E. 123 St., NYC 10021. Dean Alfredo Matthew. Offers educational opportunities to minority groups and older people; courses in the arts, sciences, humanities, and special programs of career studies.

———, YESHIVA OHR HACHAYIM. 141–61 71 Ave., Kew Garden Hills, NY 11367. A higher academy of Jewish learning, offers classes in Talmud, Bible, Jewish philosophy, education, and community services.

UNION OF AMERICAN HEBREW CONGREGATIONS (1873). 838 Fifth Ave., NYC 10021. (212)249-0100. Pres. Rabbi Alexander M. Schindler; Bd. Chmn. Charles J. Rothschild, Jr. Serves as the central congregational body of Reform Judaism in the Western Hemisphere; serves its approximately 850 affiliated temples and membership with religious, educational, cultural, and administrative programs. *Keeping Posted; Reform Judaism.*

———, AMERICAN CONFERENCE OF CANTORS (1956). 838 Fifth Ave., NYC 10021. (212)737-5020. Pres. Jay I. Frailich; Exec. Dir. Raymond Smolover. Members receive investiture and commissioning as cantors at ordination-investiture ceremonies at Hebrew Union College–Jewish Institute of Religion, Sacred School of Music. Through Joint Placement Commission, serves congregations seeking cantors and music directors. Dedicated to creative Judaism, preserving the best of the past, and encouraging new and vital approaches to religious ritual, music and ceremonies. *Koleinu.*

———, COMMISSION ON SOCIAL ACTION OF REFORM JUDAISM (*see* p. 368)

———, NATIONAL ASSOCIATION OF TEMPLE ADMINISTRATORS (NATA) (1941). 838 Fifth Ave., NYC 10021. (212)249-0100. Pres. Harold Press; Admin. Sec. Dennis Rice. Fosters Reform Judaism; prepares and disseminates administrative information and procedures to member synagogues of UAHC; provides and encourages proper and adequate training of professional synagogue executives; formulates and establishes professional ideals and standards for the synagogue executive; provides placement services. *NATA Journal.*

———, NATIONAL ASSOCIATION OF TEMPLE EDUCATORS (NATE) (1955). 707 Summerly Dr., Nashville, TN 37209. (615)352-0322. Pres. Robert E. Tornberg; Exec. Sec. Richard M. Morin. Represents the temple educator within the general body of Reform Judaism; fosters the full-time profession of the temple educator; encourages the growth and development of Jewish religious education consistent with the aims of Reform Judaism; stimulates communal interest in and responsibility for Jewish religious education. *NATE News; Compass magazine.*

———, NATIONAL FEDERATION OF TEMPLE BROTHERHOODS (1923). 838 Fifth Ave., NYC 10021. (212)570-0707. Pres. Carl J. Burkons; Exec. Dir. Av Bondarin. Promotes Jewish education among its members, along with participation in temple, brotherhood, and interfaith activities; sponsors the Jewish Chautauqua Society. *Brotherhood.*

———, NATIONAL FEDERATION OF TEMPLE SISTERHOODS (1913). 838 Fifth Ave., NYC 10021. (212)249-0100. Pres. Dolores Wilkenfeld; Exec. Dir. Eleanor R. Schwartz. Serves more than 640 sisterhoods of Reform Judaism; promotes interreligious understanding and social justice; awards scholarships and grants to rabbinic students; provides braille and large-type Judaic materials for Jewish blind; supports projects for Israel, Soviet Jewry, and the aging; is an affiliate of UAHC and is the women's agency of Reform Judaism; works on behalf of the Hebrew Union College–Jewish Institute of Religion; cooperates with World Union for Progressive Judaism. *Leaders Line; Notes for Now.*

———, NORTH AMERICAN FEDERATION OF TEMPLE YOUTH (NFTY; formerly NATIONAL FEDERATION OF TEMPLE YOUTH) (1939). 838 Fifth Ave., NYC 10021. (212)249-0100. Dir. Ramie Arian; Pres. Leon Morris. Seeks to train Reform Jewish youth in the values of the synagogue and their application to daily life through service to the community and congregation; runs department of summer camps and national leadership training institute; arranges overseas academic tours, work programs, international student exchange programs, and college student programs in the U.S. and Israel, including accredited study programs in Israel. *Ani V'Atah; The Jewish Connection.*

———, AND CENTRAL CONFERENCE OF AMERICAN RABBIS: COMMISSION ON JEWISH EDUCATION (1923). 838 Fifth Ave., NYC 10021. (212)249-0100. Chmn. Murray Blackman; Dir. Rabbi Daniel B. Syme. Develops curricula and teachers' manuals; conducts pilot projects and offers educational guidance and consultation at all age levels to member congregations and affiliates and associate bodies. *What's Happening; Compass; E³.*

———, AND CENTRAL CONFERENCE OF AMERICAN RABBIS: JOINT COMMISSION ON SYNAGOGUE ADMINISTRATION (1962). 838 Fifth Ave., NYC 10021. (212)-249-0100. Chmn. Harold J. Tragash; Dir. Myron E. Schoen. Assists congregations in management, finance, building maintenance, design, construction, and art aspects of synagogues; maintains the Synagogue Architectural Library, consisting of photos, slides, and plans of contemporary and older synagogue buildings. *Synagogue Service.*

UNION OF ORTHODOX JEWISH CONGREGATIONS OF AMERICA (1898). 45 W. 36 St., NYC 10018. (212)563-4000. Pres. Sidney Kwestel; Exec. V.-Pres. Pinchas Stolper. Serves as the national central body of Orthodox synagogues; sponsors National Conference of Synagogue Youth, Our Way program for the Jewish deaf, Yachad program for developmentally disabled youth, Israel Center in Jerusalem, *aliyah* department, national OU *kashrut* supervision and certification service; provides educational, religious, and organizational guidance to synagogues and groups; represents the Orthodox Jewish community in relation to governmental and civic bodies and the general Jewish community. Publishes synagogue programming publications and books of Jewish interest. *Jewish Action; OU Kosher Directory; OU Passover Directory; OU News Reporter; Synagogue Spotlight; Our Way magazine; Yachad magazine.*

———, NATIONAL CONFERENCE OF SYNAGOGUE YOUTH (1954). 45 W. 36 St., NYC 10018. (212)563-4000. Pres. Howie Siegel; Dir. Rabbi Raphael Butler. Serves as central body for youth groups of Orthodox congregations; provides such national activities and services as educational guidance, Torah study groups, community service, programs consultation, Torah library, Torah fund scholarships, Ben Zakkai Honor Society, Friends of NCSY; conducts national and regional events including week-long seminars, summer Torah tours in over 200 communities, Israel summer seminar for teens and collegiates, cross-country tours, and Camp NCSY East. Divisions include Senior NCSY in 18 regions and 465 chapters, Junior NCSY for preteens, Our Way for the Jewish deaf, Yachad for the developmentally disabled, and NCSY in Israel. *Keeping Posted with NCSY; Face the Nation—President's Newsletter; Oreich Yomeinu—Education Newsletter.*

———, WOMEN'S BRANCH (1923). 156 Fifth Ave., NYC 10010. (212)929-8857. Pres. Gitti Needleman; UN-NGO Rep. Fanny Wald. Seeks to spread the understanding and practice of Orthodox Judaism, and to unite all Orthodox women and their synagogal organizations; services affiliates with educational and programming materials, leadership and organizational guidance, and has an NGO representative at the UN. *Hachodesh; Hakol.*

UNION OF ORTHODOX RABBIS OF THE UNITED STATES AND CANADA (1900). 235 E. Broadway, NYC 10002. (212)964-6337. Dir. Rabbi Hersh M. Ginsberg. Seeks to foster and promote Torah-true Judaism in the U.S. and Canada; assists in the establishment and maintenance of *yeshivot* in the U.S.; maintains committee on marriage and divorce and aids individuals with marital difficulties; disseminates knowledge of traditional Jewish rites and practices and publishes regulations on synagogal structure; maintains rabbinical court for resolving individual and communal conflicts. *HaPardes.*

UNION OF SEPHARDIC CONGREGATIONS, INC. (1929). 8 W. 70 St., NYC 10023. (212)873-0300. Pres. The Haham Solomon Gaon; Exec. Sec. Joseph Tarica; Bd. Chmn. Victor Tarry. Promotes the religious interests of Sephardic Jews; prepares and distributes Sephardic prayer books; provides religious leaders for Sephardic congregations.

UNITED LUBAVITCHER YESHIVOTH (1940). 841–853 Ocean Pkwy., Brooklyn, NY 11230. (718)859-7600. Pres. Eli N. Sklar; Chmn. Exec. Com. Rabbi S. Gourary. Supports and organizes Jewish day schools and rabbinical seminaries in the U.S. and abroad.

UNITED SYNAGOGUE OF AMERICA (1913). 155 Fifth Ave., NYC 10010. (212)533-7800. Pres. Franklin D. Kreutzer; Exec. V.-Pres. Benjamin Z. Kreitman; Sr. V.-Pres./Chief Exec. Off. Jerome M. Epstein. International organization of 850 Conservative congregations. Maintains 12 departments and 20 regional offices to assist its affiliates with religious, educational, youth, community, and administrative programming and guidance; aims to enhance the cause of Conservative Judaism, further religious observance, encourage establishment of Jewish religious schools, draw youth closer to Jewish tradition. Extensive Israel programs. *Program Suggestions; United Synagogue Review; Yearbook Directory and Buyers' Guide; Book Service Catalogue of Publications.*

———, COMMISSION ON JEWISH COMMUNITY AND PUBLIC POLICY (1958). 155 Fifth Ave., NYC 10010. Cochmn. Burton Citak, Rabbi Zachary Heller; Dir. Rabbi Benjamin Z. Kreitman. Consists of representatives of United Synagogue of America, Women's League for Conservative Judaism, Rabbinical Assembly, and Federation of Jewish Men's Clubs; reviews public issues and cooperates with civic and Jewish community organizations to achieve social-action goals. *Today: Hayom.*

———, COMMISSION ON JEWISH EDUCATION (1930). 155 Fifth Ave., NYC 10010. (212)260-8450. Chmn. Rabbi Joel H. Zaiman; Cochmn. Harry Katz; Dir. Morton K. Siegel. Promotes higher educational standards in Conservative congregational schools and Solomon Schechter Day Schools and publishes material for the advancement of their educational programs. Provides guidance and information on resources, courses, and other projects in adult Jewish education; prepares and publishes pamphlets, study guides, tracts, and texts for use in adult-education programs; publishes the *Jewish Tract* series and distributes El-Am edition of Talmud. Distributes black-and-white and color films of "Eternal Light" TV programs on Jewish subjects, produced by Jewish Theological Seminary in cooperation with NBC. *Briefs; Impact; In Your Hands; Your Child; Kol Bana'yikh.*

———, JEWISH EDUCATORS ASSEMBLY (1951). 15 E. 26 St., NYC 10010. (212)532-4949. Pres. Michael Korman; Exec. Dir. Benjamin Margolis. Advances the development of Jewish education on all levels in consonance with the philosophy of the Conservative movement. Promotes Jewish education as a basis for the creative continuity of the Jewish people. Serves as a forum for the exchange of ideas, programs, and educational media. *The Observer; bulletins; newsletters; Tamtzit.*

———, KADIMA (formerly PRE-USY; reorg. 1968). 155 Fifth Ave., NYC 10010. (212)-533-7800. Dir. Enid L. Miller. Involves Jewish preteens in a meaningful religious, educational, and social environment; fosters a sense of identity and commitment to the Jewish community and Conservative movement; conducts synagogue-based chapter programs and regional Kadima days and weekends. *Mitzvah of the Month; Kadima Kesher; Chagim; Advisors Aid; Games; quarterly Kadima magazine.*

———, NATIONAL ASSOCIATION OF SYNAGOGUE ADMINISTRATORS (1948). 155 Fifth Ave., NYC 10010. (212)533-7800. Pres. Harvey L. Brown. Aids congregations affiliated with the United Synagogue of America to further aims of Conservative Judaism through more effective administration (PALS Program); advances professional standards and promotes new methods in administration; cooperates in United Synagogue placement services and administrative surveys. *NASA Newsletter; NASA Journal.*

———, UNITED SYNAGOGUE YOUTH OF (1951). 155 Fifth Ave., NYC 10010. (212)-533-7800. Pres. David Kaye; Exec. Dir. Paul Freedman. Seeks to strengthen identification with Conservative Judaism, based on the personality development, needs, and interests of the adolescent, in a Mitzvah framework. *Achshav; Tikun Olam; A.J. Heschel Honor Society Newsletter; USY Alumni Assn. Newsletter; USY Program Bank.*

VAAD MISHMERETH STAM (1976). 4902 16 Ave., Brooklyn, NY 11204. (718)438-4963. Exec. Dir. Rabbi Yakov Basch. A nonprofit consumer-protection agency dedicated to preserving and protecting the halachic integrity of Torah scrolls, phylacteries, and *mezuzot*. Makes presentations and conducts examination campaigns in schools and synagogues. *A Guide to Mezuzah; The Halachic Encyclopedia of the Sacred Alphabet; Yalkut Tzurat Haotiyot.*

WEST COAST TALMUDICAL SEMINARY (Yeshiva Ohr Elchonon Chabad) (1953). 7215 Warring St., Los Angeles, CA 90046. (213)-937-3763. Pres. Meilech DuBrow; Dean Rabbi Ezra Schochet. Provides facilities for intensive Torah education as well as Orthodox rabbinical training on the West Coast; conducts an accredited college preparatory high school combined with a full program of Torah-Talmudic training and a graduate Talmudic division on the college level. *Torah Quiz; Kobetz Migdal Ohr.*

WOMEN'S LEAGUE FOR CONSERVATIVE JUDAISM (1918). 48 E. 74 St., NYC 10021. (212)628-1600. Pres. Selma Weintraub; Exec. Bernice Balter. Constitutes parent body of Conservative women's groups in U.S., Canada, Puerto Rico, Mexico, and Israel; provides them with programs in religion, education, social action, Israel affairs, leadership training, services to the disabled, and community affairs; publishes books of Jewish interest; contributes to support of Jewish Theological Seminary and its residence halls. *Women's League Outlook; Ba'Olam.*

WORLD COUNCIL OF SYNAGOGUES (1957). 155 Fifth Ave., NYC 10010 (212)533-7693. Pres. Marshall Wolke; Exec. Dir. Barbara Kessel. International representative of Conservative organizations and congregations; promotes the growth and development of the Conservative movement in Israel and throughout the world; supports educational institutions overseas; holds biennial international conventions; represents the world Conservative movement on the Executive of the World Zionist Organization. *Jerusalem Newsletter; Spectrum.*

WORLD UNION FOR PROGRESSIVE JUDAISM, LTD. (1926). 838 Fifth Ave., NYC 10021. (212)249-0100. Pres. Gerard Daniel; Exec. Dir. Richard G. Hirsch; N. Amer. Dir. Martin Strelzer. International umbrella organization of Liberal Jewish organizations; promotes and coordinates efforts of Liberal congregations throughout the world; starts new congregations, recruits rabbis and rabbinical students for all countries; organizes international conferences of Liberal Jews. *International Conference Reports; News and Views; Shalhevet* (Israel); *Teshuva* (Argentina); *Ammi.*

YAVNE HEBREW THEOLOGICAL SEMINARY (1924). PO Box 185, Brooklyn, NY 11218.
(718)436-5610. Pres. Nathan Shapiro; Exec. Dir. Rabbi Solomon K. Shapiro. School for higher Jewish learning; maintains Machon Maharshal branch in Jerusalem for higher Jewish education and for an exchange student program. *Otzar Hashe'elot Vehateshuvot; Yavne Newsletter.*

YESHIVA UNIVERSITY (1886). 500 W. 185 St., NYC 10033. (212)960-5400. Pres. Norman Lamm; Chmn. Bd. of Trustees, Herbert Tenzer. The nation's oldest and largest independent university founded under Jewish auspices, with a broad range of undergraduate, graduate, and professional schools, a network of affiliates, publications, a widespread program of research and community outreach, and a museum. Curricula lead to bachelor's, master's, doctoral, and professional degrees. Undergraduate schools provide general studies curricula supplemented by courses in Jewish learning; graduate schools prepare for careers in medicine, law, social work, Jewish education, psychology, Semitic languages, literatures, and cultures, and other fields. It has five undergraduate schools, seven graduate and professional schools, and three affiliates, with its four main centers located in Manhattan and the Bronx. *Alumni Review/Inside; Yeshiva University Report.*

Undergraduate schools for men at Main Center: Yeshiva College (Dean Norman Rosenfeld) provides liberal arts and sciences curricula; grants BA and BS degrees. Isaac Breuer College of Hebraic Studies (Dean Rabbi Jacob M. Rabinowitz) awards Hebraic Studies and Hebrew teacher's diploma, AA, BA, and BS. James Striar School of General Jewish Studies (Dir. Rabbi Benjamin Yudin) grants AA degree. Yeshiva Program/Mazer School of Talmudic Studies (Dir. Rabbi Zevulun Charlop) offers advanced course of study in Talmudic texts and commentaries.

Undergraduate school for women at Midtown Center, 245 Lexington Ave., NYC 10016: Stern College for Women (Dean Karen Bacon) includes Teachers Institute for Women; offers liberal arts and sciences curricula supplemented by Jewish studies courses; awards BA, BS, BS in education, AA, Jewish Studies certificate, Hebrew teacher's diploma.

Sponsors one high school for boys and one for girls (Manhattan).

Universitywide services include Center for Continuing Education, Holocaust

Studies Program, Interdisciplinary Educational Conference on Bereavement and Grief, and Jacob E. Safra Institute of Sephardic Studies.

———, ALBERT EINSTEIN COLLEGE OF MEDICINE (1955). Eastchester Rd. and Morris Pk. Ave., Bronx, NY 10461. (212)-430-2000. Pres. Norman Lamm; Chmn. Bd. of Overseers Burton P. Resnick; Dean Dr. Dominick P. Purpura. Prepares physicians, conducts research in the health sciences, and provides patient care; awards MD degree; includes Sue Golding Graduate Division of Medical Sciences (Dir. Dr. Susan Henry), which grants PhD degree. Einstein College's clinical facilities and affiliates encompass Jack D. Weiler Hospital of Albert Einstein College of Medicine, Bronx Municipal Hospital Center, Montefiore Hospital and Medical Center, and the Rose F. Kennedy Center for Research in Mental Retardation and Human Development. *AECOM News; AECOM Today; Einstein Quarterly Journal of Biology and Medicine.*

———, ALUMNI OFFICE, 500 W. 185 Street, NYC 10033. Dir. E. Yechiel Simon. Seeks to foster a close allegiance of alumni to their alma mater by maintaining ties with all alumni and servicing the following associations: Yeshiva College Alumni (Pres. Henry Rothman); Stern College Alumnae (Pres. Rachel E. Oppenheim); Albert Einstein College of Medicine Alumni (Pres. Dr. Marvin Kirschner); Ferkauf Graduate School Alumni (Pres. Alvin I. Schiff); Wurzweiler School of Social Work Alumni (Pres. Eileen Stein Himber); Bernard Revel Graduate School—Harry Fischel School Alumni (Pres. Bernard Rosensweig); Rabbinic Alumni (Pres. Rabbi Steven Dworken); Benjamin N. Cardozo School of Law Alumni (Pres. Rosemary C. Byrne). Alumni Council (Chmn. Abraham S. Guterman) offers guidance to Pres. and Bd. of Trustees on university's academic development and service activities. *Alumni Review/Inside; AECOM Alumni News; Jewish Social Work Forum.*

———, BELFER INSTITUTE FOR ADVANCED BIOMEDICAL STUDIES (1978). Eastchester Rd. and Morris Pk. Ave., Bronx, NY 10461. Dir. Dr. Ernest R. Jaffé. Integrates and coordinates the Medical College's postdoctoral research and training programs in the biomedical sciences; awards certificate at term's completion.

———, BENJAMIN N. CARDOZO SCHOOL OF LAW (1976). 55 Fifth Ave., NYC 10003. Pres. Norman Lamm; Bd. Chmn. Jacob Burns; Dean Monroe E. Price. Provides innovative courses of study within a traditional legal framework; program includes judicial internships; grants Doctor of Law (JD) degree. Center for Professional Development assists students in obtaining employment. Leonard and Bea Diener Institute of Jewish Law explores American and Jewish jurisprudence. Bet Tzedek Legal Services Clinic provides services in cases involving public benefits to low-income individuals. *Cardozo Law Review; Arts and Entertainment Law Journal; Women's Annotated Legal Bibliography; Cardozo Law Forum.*

———, BERNARD REVEL GRADUATE SCHOOL (1937). 500 W. 185 St., NYC 10033. Dean Leo Landman. Offers graduate work in Judaic studies and Semitic languages, literatures, and cultures; confers MS, MA, and PhD degrees.

———, BROOKDALE INSTITUTE FOR THE STUDY OF GERONTOLOGY (YESHIVA UNIVERSITY GERONTOLOGICAL INSTITUTE) (1976). 500 W. 185 St., NYC 10033. Dir. Celia B. Weisman. Offers an interdisciplinary program for professionals holding master's degrees in such fields as social work, psychology, counseling, or nursing, or having ordination; fosters and coordinates universitywide research, study, and activities related to the process and problems of aging; grants postmaster's certificate.

———, DAVID J. AZRIELI GRADUATE INSTITUTE OF JEWISH EDUCATION AND ADMINISTRATION (1945). 245 Lexington Ave., NYC 10016. Dir. Yitzchak Handel. Offers MS degree in Jewish elementary and secondary education; Specialist's Certificate and EdD programs in administration and supervision of Jewish education. Block Education Program, under a grant from the Jewish Agency's L.A. Pincus Fund for the Diaspora, prepares administrators in Jewish education for positions throughout the U.S.; grants EdD degree.

———, FERKAUF GRADUATE SCHOOL OF PSYCHOLOGY (1957). 1165 Morris Pk. Ave., NYC 10461. Dean Morton Berger. Offers MA in general psychology; PsyD in clinical and school psychology; and PhD in clinical, developmental-experimental psychology, and in school, social, health, and bilingual educational-developmental psychology. Center for Psychological and Psychoeducational Services offers counseling, diagnostic evaluation, and psychotherapy.

———, HARRY FISCHEL SCHOOL FOR HIGHER JEWISH STUDIES (1945). 500 W. 185 St., NYC 10033. Dean Leo Landman. Offers summer graduate programs in Judaic studies and Semitic languages, literatures, and cultures; confers MS, MA, and PhD degrees.

———, (affiliate) RABBI ISAAC ELCHANAN THEOLOGICAL SEMINARY (1896). 2540 Amsterdam Ave., NYC 10033. Chmn. Bd. of Trustees Judah Feinerman; Dir. Rabbi Zevulun Charlop. Offers comprehensive program for preparing Orthodox rabbis; grants *semikhah* (ordination) and the degrees of Master of Religious Education, Master of Hebrew Literature, Doctor of Religious Education, and Doctor of Hebrew Literature. Includes Rabbi Joseph B. Soloveitchik Center of Rabbinic Studies, Marcos and Adina Katz Kollel (Institute for Advanced Research in Rabbinics, Dir. Rabbi Hershel Schachter), Kollel L'Horaah (Yadin Yadin), Caroline and Joseph S. Gruss Kollel Elyon (Dir. Rabbi Aharon Kahn), Chaver Program (Dir. Rabbi J. David Bleich), Caroline and Joseph S. Gruss Institute in Jerusalem (Dir. Rabbi Aharon Lichtenstein). Brookdale Chaplaincy Internship Program trains prospective rabbis to work effectively with the elderly. Maybaum Sephardic Fellowship Program trains rabbis for service in Sephardic communities here and abroad. Morris and Nellie L. Kawaler Rabbinic Training Program emphasizes professional aspects of the rabbinate. Philip and Sarah Belz School of Jewish Music (Dir. Cantor Bernard Beer) provides professional training of cantors and other musical personnel; awards Associate Cantor's certificate and cantorial diploma. Max Stern Division of Communal Services (Assoc. Dir. Rabbi Kenneth Hain) provides personal and professional service to the rabbinate and related fields, as well as educational, consultative, organizational, and placement services to congregations, schools, and communal organizations throughout North America and abroad. Dr. Joseph and Rachel Ades Sephardic Community Outreach Program provides educational, religious, and cultural programs and personnel to Sephardic communities. Stone-Sapirstein Center for Jewish Education identifies and trains future educators through programs of learning, service, and internship; works with schools in the community and across the country; sponsors academic programs, lectures, and special projects throughout the university. National Commission on Torah Education and Educators Council of America formulate uniform educational standards, provide guidance to professional staffs, rabbis, and lay leaders with regard to curriculum, and promote Jewish education. Camp Morasha (Dir. Zvi Reich) offers Jewish studies program.

———, WOMEN'S ORGANIZATION (1928). 500 W. 185 St., NYC 10033. Pres. Ann Arbesfeld; Dir. Deborah Steinhorn. Supports Yeshiva University's national scholarship program for students training in education, community service, law, medicine, and other professions, and its development program. *YUWO News Briefs*.

———, WURZWEILER SCHOOL OF SOCIAL WORK (1957). 500 W. 185 St., NYC 10033. Pres. Norman Lamm.; Chmn. Bd. of Governors Herbert H. Schiff; Interim Dean Samuel Goldstein. Offers graduate programs in social casework, social group work, community social work; grants MSW and DSW degrees; two-year, full-time Concurrent Plan combines classroom study and supervised field instruction; the Extended Plan permits a period of up to five years to complete requirements for some master's degree candidates. Block Education Plan (Dir. Samuel M. Goldstein) provides field instruction in Jewish communities in the U.S., Canada, Europe, and Israel. Clergy Plan (Dir. Irving N. Levitz) provides training in counseling for clergymen of all denominations. Plan for Employed Persons (Dir. Harriet Katz) is specifically designed for people working in social agencies.

———, (affiliate) YESHIVA UNIVERSITY OF LOS ANGELES (1977). 9760 W. Pico Blvd., Los Angeles, CA 90035. (213)553-4478. Dean Rabbi Marvin Hier; Bd. Chmn. Samuel Belzberg; Dir. Academic Programs Rabbi Sholom Tendler. Grants BA degree in Jewish studies. Has university program and graduate studies department. Also provides Jewish studies program for beginners. Affiliates are Yeshiva University of

Los Angeles High School and the Jewish Studies Institute.

———, SIMON WIESENTHAL CENTER (1977). 9760 W. Pico Blvd., Los Angeles, CA 90035. (213)553-9036. On campus of Yeshiva University of Los Angeles. Dean Rabbi Marvin Hier; Assoc. Dean Rabbi Abraham Cooper; Dir. Dr. Gerald Margolis. Branch Offices: 5715 N. Lincoln Ave., Suite #16, Chicago, IL 60659, (312)989-0022; 342 Madison Ave., Suite #437, NYC, 10017, (212)370-0320. Legal Counsel Martin Mendelsohn, Washington, DC. Programs include: Wiesenthal Holocaust Museum; library; archives; "Testimony to the Truth" Oral History Program; photo archive; educational outreach; Scholars' Forum; International Social Action Agenda. *Simon Wiesenthal Center Annual; Response magazine; Social Action Update; Page One,* a syndicated weekly radio news magazine presenting contemporary Jewish issues.

YESHIVATH TORAH VODAATH AND MESIVTA RABBINICAL SEMINARY (1918). 425 E. 9 St., Brooklyn, NY 11218. (718)-941-8000. Pres. Henry Hirsch; Bd. Chmn. Fred F. Weiss; Sec. Earl H. Spero. Offers Hebrew and secular education from elementary level through rabbinical ordination and postgraduate work; maintains a teachers institute and community-service bureau; maintains a dormitory and a nonprofit camp program for boys. *Chronicle; Mesivta Vanguard; Thought of the Week; Torah Vodaath News.*

———, ALUMNI ASSOCIATION (1941). 425 E. 9 St., Brooklyn, NY 11218. (718)941-8000. Pres. Marcus Saffer; Bd. Chmn. Seymour Pluchenik. Promotes social and cultural ties between the alumni and the schools through fund raising; offers vocational guidance to students; operates Camp Torah Vodaath; sponsors research fellowship program for boys. *Annual Journal; Hamesivta Torah periodical.*

SOCIAL, MUTUAL BENEFIT

AMERICAN FEDERATION OF JEWS FROM CENTRAL EUROPE, INC. (1942). 570 Seventh Ave., NYC 10018. (212)921-3871. Pres. K. Peter Lekisch; Bd. Chmn. Curt C. Silberman; Exec. Asst. Katherine Rosenthal. Seeks to safeguard the rights and interests of American Jews of Central European descent, especially in reference to restitution and indemnification; through its Research Foundation for Jewish Immigration, sponsors research and publications on the history of Central European Jewry and the history of its immigration and acculturation in the U.S.; sponsors a social program for needy Nazi victims in the U.S. in cooperation with United Help, Inc. and other specialized social agencies; undertakes cultural activities, annual conferences, publications, and lecture programs; member, Council of Jews from Germany.

AMERICAN SEPHARDI FEDERATION (1972). 8 W. 40 St., Suite 1601, NYC 10018. (212)-730-1210. Pres. Leon Levy; Exec. V.-Pres. Joshua Toledano; Exec. Dir. Joseph Tarica. Seeks to preserve the Sephardi heritage in the U.S., Israel, and throughout the world by fostering and supporting religious and cultural activities of Sephardi congregations, organizations, and communities, and uniting them in one overall organization; supports Jewish institutions of higher learning and those that train Sephardi lay and religious leaders to serve their communities everywhere; assists Sephardi charitable, cultural, religious, and educational institutions everywhere; disseminates information by the publication, or assistance in the publication, of books and other literature dealing with Sephardi culture and tradition in the U.S.; organizes youth and young-adult activities throughout the U.S.; supports efforts of the World Sephardi Federation to alleviate social disparities in Israel. *Sephardic Connection; ASF Newsbulletin.*

AMERICAN VETERANS OF ISRAEL (1949). c/o Samuel E. Alexander, 548 E. Walnut St., Long Beach, NY 11561. (516)431-8316. Pres. Louis Brettler; Sec. Samuel E. Alexander. Maintains contact with American and Canadian volunteers who served in Aliyah Bet and/or Israel's War of Independence; promotes Israel's welfare; holds memorial services at grave of Col. David Marcus; is affiliated with World Mahal. *Newsletter.*

ASSOCIATION OF YUGOSLAV JEWS IN THE UNITED STATES, INC. (1941). 247 W. 99 St., NYC 10025. (212)865-2211. Pres. Sal Musafia; Sec.-Treas. Mile Weiss. Assists all Jews originally from Yugoslavia; raises funds for Israeli agencies and institutions. *Bulletin.*

BNAI ZION—THE AMERICAN FRATERNAL ZIONIST ORGANIZATION (1908). 136 E. 39 St., NYC 10016. (212)725-1211. Pres. Ernest Zelig; Exec. V.-Pres. Mel Parness. Fosters principles of Americanism, fraternalism, and Zionism; offers life insurance, Blue Cross and Blue Shield and other benefits to its members. Sponsors various projects in Israel: settlements, youth centers, medical clinics, Beit Halochem Rehabilitation Centers for Israeli Disabled War Veterans, Bnai Zion Home for Retarded Children (in Rosh Ha'ayin), the Haifa Medical Center, and the Herman Z. Quittman Center in Hakfar Hashwedi in Jerusalem. Has Young Leadership Division—TAMID. *Beit Halochem Newsletter; Bnai Zion Voice; Bnai Zion Foundation Newsletter.*

BRITH ABRAHAM (1887). 136 E. 39 St., NYC 10016. (212)725-1211. Grand Master Robert Freeman. Protects Jewish rights and combats anti-Semitism; supports Soviet and Ethiopian emigration and the safety and dignity of Jews worldwide; furnishes regular financial assistance to Beit Halochem for the Israeli war disabled, Haifa Medical Center, Rosh Ha'ayin Home for Retarded Children, Kupat Cholim diagnostic centers, libraries, educational facilities, and other institutions to relieve the social burdens on the Israeli economy; aids and supports various programs and projects in the U.S.: Hebrew Excellence Program—Gold Medal presentation in high schools and colleges; Camp Loyaltown; Brith Abraham and Bnai Zion Foundations. *Voice.*

BRITH SHOLOM (1905). 3939 Conshohocken Ave., Philadelphia, PA 19131. (215)878-5696. Pres. Albert Bernbaum; Exec. Dir. Mervin L. Krimins. Fraternal organization devoted to community welfare, protection of rights of Jewish people, and activities which foster Jewish identity and provide support for Israel; sponsors Brith Sholom House for senior citizens in Philadelphia and Brith Sholom Beit Halochem in Haifa, a rehabilitation center for Israel's permanently war-wounded. *Brith Sholom Presents;* monthly news bulletin.

CENTRAL SEPHARDIC JEWISH COMMUNITY OF AMERICA (1940). 8 W. 70 St., NYC 10023. (212)787-2850. Pres. Morris Halfon; Sec. Isaac Molho. Seeks to foster Sephardic culture, education, and communal institutions. Sponsors wide range of activities; raises funds for Sephardic causes in U.S. and Israel.

FREE SONS OF ISRAEL (1849). 180 Varick St., 14th fl., NYC 10014. (212)924-6566. Grand Master Robert Grant; Grand Sec. Stanley Siflinger. Promotes fraternalism; supports State of Israel, UJA, Soviet Jewry, Israel Bonds, and other Jewish charities; fights anti-Semitism; awards scholarships. *National Reporter; Digest.*

JEWISH LABOR BUND (Directed by WORLD COORDINATING COMMITTEE OF THE BUND) (1897; reorg. 1947). 25 E. 21 St., NYC 10010. (212)475-0059. Exec. Sec. Joel Litewka. Coordinates activities of Bund organizations throughout the world and represents them in the Socialist International; spreads the ideas of socialism as formulated by the Jewish Labor Bund; publishes books and periodicals on world problems, Jewish life, socialist theory and policy, and on the history, activities, and ideology of the Jewish Labor Bund. *Unser Tsait* (U.S.); *Lebns-Fragn* (Israel); *Unser Gedank* (Australia); *Unser Shtimme* (France).

JEWISH SOCIALIST VERBAND OF AMERICA (1921). 45 E. 33 St., NYC 10016. (212)-686-1536. Pres. Meyer Miller; Natl. Sec. Herman Yonish. Promotes ideals of democratic socialism and Yiddish culture; affiliated with Social Democrats, USA. *Der Wecker.*

ROUMANIAN JEWISH FEDERATION OF AMERICA, INC. (1956). 135 W. 106 St., #2M, NYC 10025. (212)866-0692. Pres. Charles H. Kremer; Sec. Treas. Marian Marcu. Interested in protecting the welfare, preserving the culture, and easing the plight of Jews of Rumanian descent throughout the world. Works to influence the Rumanian government to grant freedom of worship to Jews and permission for their emigration to Israel.

SEPHARDIC JEWISH BROTHERHOOD OF AMERICA, INC. (1915). 97-29 64 Rd., Rego Park, NY 11374. (718)459-1600. Pres. Nick Levi; Sec. Jack Ezratty. Promotes the industrial, social, educational, and religious welfare of its members; offers funeral and burial benefits, scholarships, and aid to the needy. *Sephardic Brother.*

UNITED ORDER TRUE SISTERS, INC. (1846). 212 Fifth Ave., NYC 10010. (212)679-6790. Pres. Sylvia Fishgall; Exec. Off.

Dorothy B. Giuriceo. Philanthropic, community service; Natl. Project Cancer Service. *Echo.*

WORKMEN'S CIRCLE (1900). 45 E. 33 St., NYC 10016. (212)889-6800. Pres. Barnett Zumoff; Exec. Dir. Jack Noskowitz. Provides fraternal benefits and activities, Jewish educational programs, secularist Yiddish schools for children, and community activities; supports institutions in Israel and promotes public-affairs activities in the U.S. on international and national issues. Underwrites "Folksbiene," worldwide Yiddish cultural, music, and theatrical festivals. Allied to *Jewish Forward* and WEVD. *Workmen's Circle Call; Kultur un Leben.*

———, DIVISION OF JEWISH LABOR COMMITTEE (*see* p. 369)

SOCIAL WELFARE

AMC CANCER RESEARCH CENTER (formerly JEWISH CONSUMPTIVES' RELIEF SOCIETY, 1904; incorporated as AMERICAN MEDICAL CENTER AT DENVER, 1954). 1600 Pierce, Denver, CO 80214. (303)233-6501. Pres. Dr. Marvin A. Rich. Dedicated to advancing knowledge of cancer prevention, detection, diagnosis, and treatment through programs of laboratory, clinical, and community cancer control research. *Quarterly bulletin; annual report.*

AMERICAN JEWISH CORRECTIONAL CHAPLAINS ASSOCIATION, INC. (formerly NATIONAL COUNCIL OF JEWISH PRISON CHAPLAINS) (1937). 10 E. 73 St., NYC 10021-4194. (212)879-8415. (Cooperates with the New York Board of Rabbis and Jewish Family Service.) Pres. Rabbi Irving Koslowe; Exec. Dir. Rabbi Paul L. Hait; Assoc. Dir. Rabbi Moses A. Birnbaum. Provides religious services and guidance to Jewish men and women in penal and correctional institutions; serves as a liaison between inmates and their families; upgrades the quality of correctional ministrations through conferences, professional workshops, and conventions. *Bulletin.*

AMERICAN JEWISH SOCIETY FOR SERVICE, INC. (1949). 15 E. 26 St., Rm. 1302, NYC 10010. (212)683-6178. Pres. E. Kenneth Marx; Exec. Dir. Elly Saltzman. Conducts voluntary work-service camps each summer to enable high school juniors and seniors to perform humanitarian service.

ASSOCIATION OF JEWISH COMMUNITY ORGANIZATION PERSONNEL (1969). 1175 College Ave., Columbus, OH 43209. (614)-237-7686. Pres. Darrell Friedman; Exec. Dir. Ben Mandelkorn. An organization of professionals engaged in areas of fund raising, endowments, budgeting, social planning, financing, administration and coordination of services. Objectives are to develop and enhance professional practices in Jewish communal work; to maintain and improve standards, practices, scope and public understanding of the field of community organization, as practiced through local federations, national agencies, and by private practitioners serving as consultants.

ASSOCIATION OF JEWISH FAMILY AND CHILDREN'S AGENCIES (1972). 40 Worth St., Rm. 800, NYC 10013-2904. (212)608-6660. Pres. Cynthia B. Kane; Exec. Dir. Bert J. Goldberg. The national service organization for Jewish family and children's agencies in Canada and the U.S. Reinforces member agencies in their efforts to sustain and enhance the quality of Jewish family and communal life. *In-Box; Bimonthly Bulletin; Directory; Job Openings Memo.*

ASSOCIATION OF JEWISH FAMILY AND CHILDREN'S AGENCY PROFESSIONALS (1965). c/o NYANA, 225 Park Ave. S., NYC 10003. (212)674-7400. Pres. Arnold Marks; Exec. Dir. Solomon H. Green. Brings together Jewish caseworkers and related professionals in Jewish family, children's, and health services. Seeks to improve personnel standards, further Jewish continuity and identity, and strengthen Jewish family life; provides forums for professional discussion at national conference of Jewish communal service and regional meetings; takes action on social-policy issues. *Newsletter.*

BARON DE HIRSCH FUND (1891). 130 E. 59 St., NYC 10022. (212)980-1000, ext. 184. Pres. Ezra Pascal Mager; Mng. Dir. Robert B. Goldmann. Aids Jewish immigrants and their children in the U.S. and Israel by giving grants to agencies active in educational and vocational fields; has limited program for study tours in U.S. by Israeli agriculturists.

B'NAI B'RITH INTERNATIONAL (1843). 1640 Rhode Island Ave., NW, Washington, DC 20036. (202)857-6600. Pres. Gerald Kraft;

Exec. V.-Pres. Daniel Thursz. International Jewish organization with affiliates in 48 countries. Programs include communal service, social action, and public affairs, with emphasis on preserving Judaism through projects in and for Israel and for Soviet Jewry; teen and college-age movements; adult Jewish education. *The International Jewish Monthly; Shofar.*

———, ANTI-DEFAMATION LEAGUE OF (*see* p. 368)

———, CAREER AND COUNSELING SERVICES (1938). 1640 Rhode Island Ave. NW, Washington, DC 20036. (202)857-6532. Chmn. Burton M. Wanetik; Natl. Dir. Max F. Baer. Offers educational and career counseling to Jewish youth and adults on a group and individual basis through professionally staffed centers in New York, North Jersey, and Philadelphia.

———, HILLEL FOUNDATIONS, INC. (*see* p. 379)

———, KLUTZNICK MUSEUM (*see* p. 372)

———, YOUTH ORGANIZATION (*see* p. 379)

B'NAI B'RITH WOMEN (1897). 1640 Rhode Island Ave., NW, Washington, DC 20036. (202)857-6689. Pres. Irma Gertler; Exec. Dir. Elaine Binder. Promotes the principles of social advancement through education, action, and service. *Women's World; Leadership Letter; Public Affairs Update.*

CITY OF HOPE NATIONAL MEDICAL CENTER AND BECKMAN RESEARCH INSTITUTE (1913). 208 W. 8 St., Los Angeles, CA 90014. (213)626-4611. Pres. Abraham S. Bolsky; Chief Exec. Off. Dr. Sanford M. Shapero. Offers care to those with cancer and major diseases, medical consultation service for second opinions, and pilot research programs in genetics, immunology, and the basic life process. *Pilot; President's Newsletter; City of Hope Quarterly.*

CONFERENCE OF JEWISH COMMUNAL SERVICE (1899). 111 Prospect St., E. Orange, NJ 07017. (201)676-6070. Pres. Ethel Taft; Exec. Dir. Joel Ollander. Serves as forum for all professional philosophies in community service, for testing new experiences, proposing new ideas, and questioning or reaffirming old concepts; umbrella organization for eight major Jewish communal service groups. Concerned with advancement of professional personnel practices and standards. *Concurrents; Journal of Jewish Communal Service.*

COUNCIL OF JEWISH FEDERATIONS, INC. (1932). 730 Broadway, NYC 10003. (212)-475-5000. Pres. Shoshana S. Cardin; Exec. V.-Pres. Carmi Schwartz. Provides national and regional services to 200 associated federations embracing 800 communities in the U.S. and Canada, aiding in fund raising, community organization, health and welfare planning, personnel recruitment, and public relations. *Directory of Jewish Federations, Welfare Funds and Community Councils; Directory of Jewish Health and Welfare Agencies* (triennial); *Jewish Communal Services: Programs and Finances (1977); Yearbook of Jewish Social Services;* annual report.

HOPE CENTER FOR THE RETARDED (1965). 3601 Martin L. King Blvd., Denver, CO 80205. (303)388-4801. Pres. Lester Goldstein; Exec. Dir. George E. Brantley; Sec. Helen Fonda. Provides services to developmentally disabled of community: preschool training, day training and work activities center, speech and language pathology, occupational arts and crafts, recreational therapy, and social services.

INTERNATIONAL COUNCIL ON JEWISH SOCIAL AND WELFARE SERVICES (1961). 60 E. 42 St., NYC 10165. (NY liaison office with UN headquarters.) (212)687-6200. Chmn. Kenneth Rubin; Exec. Sec. Theodore D. Feder. Provides for exchange of views and information among member agencies on problems of Jewish social and welfare services, including medical care, old age, welfare, child care, rehabilitation, technical assistance, vocational training, agricultural and other resettlement, economic assistance, refugees, migration, integration and related problems, representation of views to governments and international organizations. Members: six national and international organizations.

JEWISH BRAILLE INSTITUTE OF AMERICA, INC. (1931). 110 E. 30 St., NYC 10016. (212)889-2525. Pres. Jane Evans; Exec. V.-Pres. Gerald M. Kass. Serves the religious, cultural, and educational needs of the Jewish blind, visually impaired, and reading-disabled by producing books of Judaica, including prayer books in Hebrew and English braille, large print, and on audio cassettes. Maintains free lending library of

Hebrew, English, Yiddish, and other-language cassettes for the Jewish blind, visually impaired, and reading-disabled in 40 countries. *Jewish Braille Review; JBI Voice; Or Chadash.*

JEWISH CONCILIATION BOARD OF AMERICA, INC. (1930). 235 Park Ave. S., NYC 10003. (212)777-9034. Pres. Milton J. Schubin; Exec. Dir. Beatrice Lampert. Offers dispute-resolution services to families, individuals, and organizations. Social-work, rabbinic, and legal expertise are available for family and divorce mediation and arbitration. Fee—sliding scale.

JEWISH FUND FOR JUSTICE (1984). 1334 G St., NW, Suite 601, Washington, DC 20005. (202)638-0550. Pres. Si Kahn; Exec. Dir. Lois Roisman. A national grant-making institution supporting efforts to combat poverty in the U.S. Acts as a catalyst to increase Jewish communal and individual involvement in social-justice issues; participates in grant-making coalitions with other religious and ethnic groups. *Newsletter.*

JWB (1917). 15 E. 26 St., NYC 10010. (212)-532-4949. Pres. Leonard Rochwarger; Exec. V.-Pres. Arthur Rotman. Major service agency for Jewish community centers, YM-YWHAs, and camps serving a million Jews in the U.S. and Canada; key source of Jewish educational and cultural programming; U.S.-government-accredited agency for providing services and programs to Jewish military families and hospitalized VA patients. *JWB Circle; Zarkor; JWB Personnel Reporter.*

———, JEWISH BOOK COUNCIL (see p. 374)

———, JEWISH CHAPLAINS COUNCIL (formerly COMMISSION ON JEWISH CHAPLAINCY) (1940). 15 E. 26 St., NYC 10010. Chmn. Rabbi Barry H. Greene; Dir. Rabbi David Lapp. Recruits, endorses, and serves Jewish military and Veterans Administration chaplains on behalf of the American Jewish community and the three major rabbinic bodies; trains and assists Jewish lay leaders where there are no chaplains, for service to Jewish military personnel, their families, and hospitalized veterans.

———, JEWISH MEDIA SERVICE (see p. 373)

———, JEWISH MUSIC COUNCIL (see p. 374)

———, LECTURE BUREAU (see p. 374)

LEVI ARTHRITIS HOSPITAL (sponsored by B'nai B'rith) (1914). 300 Prospect Ave., Hot Springs, AR 71901. (501)624-1281. Pres. Harry Levitch; Exec. Dir. D. E. Wagoner. Maintains a nonprofit, nonsectarian hospital for treatment of sufferers from arthritis; offers postoperative bone and joint surgery rehabilitation; stroke rehabilitation; and posttrauma rehabilitation. *Levi Letter; Levi Voice; Update.*

NATIONAL ASSOCIATION OF JEWISH FAMILY, CHILDREN'S AND HEALTH PROFESSIONALS (see Association of Jewish Family and Children's Agency Professionals)

NATIONAL ASSOCIATION OF JEWISH VOCATIONAL SERVICES (formerly JEWISH OCCUPATIONAL COUNCIL) (1940). 386 Park Ave. S., NYC 10016. (212)685-8355. Pres. Harold Friedman; Exec. Dir. Harvey P. Goldman. Acts as coordinating body for all Jewish agencies in U.S., Canada, and Israel, having programs in educational-vocational guidance, job placement, vocational rehabilitation, skills-training, sheltered workshops, and occupational research. *Newsletter; NAJVS Reports.*

NATIONAL CONGRESS OF JEWISH DEAF (1956; inc. 1961). 9102 Edmonston Court, Greenbelt, MD 20770. TTY (301)345-8612. Exec. Dir. Alexander Fleischman. Congress of Jewish congregations, service organizations, and associations located throughout the U.S. and Canada, advocating religious and cultural ideals and fellowship for the Jewish deaf. Publishes *Signs of Judaism,* a guide to American Sign Language.

NATIONAL COUNCIL OF JEWISH PRISON CHAPLAINS, INC. (see American Jewish Correctional Chaplains Association, Inc.)

NATIONAL COUNCIL OF JEWISH WOMEN (1893). 15 E. 26 St., NYC 10010. (212)-532-1740. Pres. Barbara A. Mandel; Exec. Dir. Dadie Perlov. Operates programs in community service, education and advocacy in women's issues, children and youth, aging, Jewish life, constitutional rights and Israel. Promotes education for the disadvantaged in Israel through the NCJW Research Institute for Innovation in Education at Hebrew University, Jerusalem. Promotes welfare of children through Center for the Child. *NCJW Journal; Washington Newsletter.*

NATIONAL JEWISH CENTER FOR IMMUNOLOGY AND RESPIRATORY MEDICINE (formerly NATIONAL JEWISH HOSPITAL/NATIONAL ASTHMA CENTER) (1899). 1400 Jackson St., Denver, CO 80206. (303)388-4461; 1-800-222-5864; Pres. Michael K. Schonbrun; V.-Pres. Public Affairs, Jerry L. Colness. Leading medical center for study and treatment of respiratory diseases, allergies, and immune system disorders. Clinical emphasis on asthma, emphysema, tuberculosis, chronic bronchitis, and interstitial lung diseases; immune system disorders such as juvenile rheumatoid arthritis and immune deficiency disorders. *New Directions; Update; annual report; Lung Line Letter.*

NATIONAL JEWISH COMMITTEE ON SCOUTING (Boy Scouts of America) (1926). 1325 Walnut Hill La., Irving, TX 75038-3096. (214)580-2059. Chmn. Murray L. Cole; Dir. Fred Tichauer. Seeks to bring Jewish youth and adults closer to Judaism through Scouting programs. Works through local Jewish committees on Scouting to establish Tiger Cub groups (1st grade), Cub Scout packs, Boy Scout troops, and coed Explorer posts in synagogues, Jewish community centers, day schools, and other Jewish organizations wishing to draw Jewish youth. Support materials and resources on request. *Hatsofe.*

NATIONAL JEWISH GIRL SCOUT COMMITTEE (1972). Synagogue Council of America, 327 Lexington Ave., NYC 10016. (212)686-8670. Chmn. Rabbi Herbert W. Bomzer; Field Chmn. Shirley W. Parker. Under the auspices of the Synagogue Council of America, serves to further Jewish education by promoting Jewish award programs, encouraging religious services, promoting cultural exchanges with Israeli Boy & Girl Scouts Federation, and extending membership in the Jewish community by assisting councils in organizing Girl Scout troops and local Jewish Girl Scout committees. *Newsletter.*

NORTH AMERICAN ASSOCIATION OF JEWISH HOMES AND HOUSING FOR THE AGING (1960). 2525 Centerville Rd., Dallas, TX 75228. (214)327-4503. Pres. Charles S. Wolfe; Exec. V.-Pres. Herbert Shore. Serves as a national representative of voluntary Jewish homes and housing for the aged; conducts annual meetings, conferences, workshops, and institutes; provides for sharing information, studies, and clearinghouse functions. *Directory; Perspectives.*

WORLD CONFEDERATION OF JEWISH COMMUNITY CENTERS (1947). 15 E. 26 St., NYC 10010. (212)532-4949. Pres. Ralph Goldman; Exec. Dir. Don Scher. Serves as a council of national and continental federations of Jewish community centers; fosters development of the JCC movement worldwide; provides a forum for exchange of information among centers. *Newsletter.*

ZIONIST AND PRO-ISRAEL

ALYN—AMERICAN SOCIETY FOR HANDICAPPED CHILDREN IN ISRAEL (1954). 19 W. 44 St., NYC 10036. (212)869-8085. Chmn. Simone P. Blum; Exec. Dir. Nathan N. Schorr. Supports the work of ALYN Orthopaedic Hospital and Rehabilitation Center for Physically Handicapped Children, located in Jerusalem, which encompasses a 100-bed hospital and outpatient clinics, and houses the Helena Rubinstein Foundation Research Institute for research in neuromuscular diseases. *ALYN News.*

AMERICA-ISRAEL CULTURAL FOUNDATION, INC. (1939). 485 Madison Ave., NYC 10022. (212)751-2700. Bd. Chmn. Isaac Stern; Pres. Carl Glick. Membership organization supporting Israeli cultural institutions, such as Israel Philharmonic and Israel Chamber Orchestra, Tel Aviv Museum, Rubin Academies, Bat Sheva Dance Co., Omanut La'am, and Tzlil Am; sponsors cultural exchange between U.S. and Israel; awards scholarships in all arts to young Israelis for study in Israel. *Hadashot.*

AMERICA-ISRAEL FRIENDSHIP LEAGUE, INC. (1971). 134 E. 39 St., NYC 10016. (212)213-8630. Pres. Herbert Tenzer; Exec. V.-Pres. Ilana Artman. A nonsectarian, nonpartisan organization which seeks to broaden the base of support for Israel among all Americans. Activities include cultural and educational exchanges, study tours to Israel, national speaking tours of prominent Americans and Israelis, and the dissemination of printed information. *Quarterly newsletter.*

AMERICAN ASSOCIATES, BEN-GURION UNIVERSITY OF THE NEGEV (1973). 342 Madison Ave., Suite 1924, NYC 10173. (212)687-7721. Pres. Arnold Forster; Bd.

Chmn. Irwin H. Goldenberg; Exec. V.-Pres. Donald L. Gartner. Serves as the university's publicity and fund-raising link to the U.S. The Associates are committed to publicizing university activities and curricula, securing student scholarships, transferring contributions, and encouraging American interest in the university. *AABGU Reporter; BGU Bulletin; Negev.*

AMERICAN COMMITTEE FOR SHAARE ZEDEK HOSPITAL IN JERUSALEM, INC. (1949). 49 W. 45 St., NYC 10036. (212)-354-8801. Pres. Charles Bendheim; Bd. Chmn. Ludwig Jesselson; Sr. Exec. V.-Pres. Morris Talansky. Raises funds for the various needs of the Shaare Zedek Medical Center, Jerusalem, such as equipment and medical supplies, nurse training, and research; supports exchange program between Shaare Zedek Medical Center and Albert Einstein College of Medicine, NY. *Heartbeat magazine.*

AMERICAN COMMITTEE FOR THE WEIZMANN INSTITUTE OF SCIENCE (1944). 515 Park Ave., NYC 10022. (212)752-1300. Pres. Maurice M. Weiss; Bd. Chmn. Norman D. Cohen; Exec. V.-Pres. Bernard N. Samers. Through 12 regional offices in the U.S., raises funds for the Weizmann Institute in Rehovot, Israel, and disseminates information about the scientific research under way there. *Interface; Rehovot; Research.*

AMERICAN FRIENDS OF HAIFA UNIVERSITY (1967). 41 E. 42 St., NYC 10162. (212)-818-9050. Pres. Edith Everett; Exec. V.-Pres. Edward Alcosser. Promotes, encourages, and aids higher and secondary education, research, and training in all branches of knowledge in Israel and elsewhere; aids in the maintenance and development of Haifa University; raises and allocates funds for the above purposes; provides scholarships; promotes exchanges of teachers and students. *Quarterly newsletter.*

AMERICAN FRIENDS OF THE HAIFA MARITIME MUSEUM, INC. (1977). PO Box 616, 217 E. 70 St., NYC 10021. (212)776-4509. Chmn. and Treas. Bernard Weissman; Pres. Stephen K. Haber. Supports National Maritime Museum in Haifa. Promotes interest in maritime life among American Jews. *Quarterly bulletin.*

AMERICAN FRIENDS OF THE HEBREW UNIVERSITY (1925; inc. 1931). 11 E. 69 St., NYC 10021. (212)472-9800. Pres. Fred S. Lafer; Exec. V.-Pres. Robert A. Pearlman; Bd. Chmn. Harvey L. Silbert. Fosters the growth, development, and maintenance of the Hebrew University of Jerusalem; collects funds and conducts programs of information throughout the U.S., interpreting the work of the university and its significance; administers American student programs and arranges exchange professorships in the U.S. and Israel. *News from the Hebrew University of Jerusalem; Scopus magazine.*

AMERICAN FRIENDS OF THE ISRAEL MUSEUM (1968). 10 E. 40 St., Rm. 1208, NYC 10016. (212)683-5190. Pres. Romie Shapiro; Exec. Dir. Michele Cohn Tocci. Raises funds for special projects of the Israel Museum in Jerusalem; solicits contributions of works of art for exhibition and educational purposes. *Newsletter.*

AMERICAN FRIENDS OF THE JERUSALEM MENTAL HEALTH CENTER—EZRATH NASHIM, INC. (1895). 10 E. 40 St., NYC 10016. (212)725-8175. Pres. Anita Blum; Exec. Dir. Sylvia Hilton. Supports research, education, and patient care at the Jerusalem Mental Health Center, which includes a 250-bed hospital, comprehensive outpatient clinic, drug abuse clinic, geriatric center, and the Jacob Herzog Psychiatric Research Center; Israel's only nonprofit, voluntary psychiatric hospital; used as a teaching facility by Israel's major medical schools. *Friend to Friend; To Open the Gates of Healing.*

AMERICAN FRIENDS OF THE SHALOM HARTMAN INSTITUTE (1976). 1735 Jefferson Davis Hwy., Crystal City, Arlington, VA 22202. (703)769-1240. Chmn. Robert P. Kogod; Dir. Ruth S. Frank. Supports the Shalom Hartman Institute, Jerusalem, an institute of higher education and research center, devoted to applying the teachings of classical Judaism to modernity. Founded in 1976 by David Hartman, the institute includes Beit Midrash and centers for philosophy, theology, *halakhah*, political thought, and medical science, and is developing model education programs and programs for lay leadership. *A Word from Jerusalem.*

AMERICAN FRIENDS OF THE TEL AVIV MUSEUM (1974). 133 E. 58 St., Suite 704, NYC 10022. (212)319-0555. Pres. Roy V. Titus; Chmn. Milton J. Shubin. Solicits contributions of works of art to enrich the Tel Aviv Museum collection; raises funds to support development, maintenance, and expansion of the educational work of the museum. *Exhibition catalogues.*

AMERICAN FRIENDS OF THE TEL AVIV UNIVERSITY, INC. (1955). 360 Lexington Ave., NYC 10017. (212)687-5651. Bd. Chmn. Lally Weymouth; Exec. V.-Pres. Jules Love. Promotes, encourages, aids, and advances higher education at Tel Aviv University and elsewhere. Among the many projects in the university's more than 50 research institutes are: the Moshe Dayan Center for Middle Eastern & African Studies, the Jaffe Center for Strategic Studies; 25 institutes in different fields of medicine; and the Institute for Cereal Crops Improvement. *Tel Aviv University Report; AFTAU Newsletter.*

AMERICAN ISRAEL PUBLIC AFFAIRS COMMITTEE (AIPAC) (1954). 500 N. Capitol St., NW, Washington, DC 20001. (202)-638-2256. Pres. Robert Asher; Exec. Dir. Thomas A. Dine. Registered to lobby on behalf of legislation affecting U.S.-Israel relations; represents Americans who believe support for a secure Israel is in U.S. interest. Works for a strong U.S.-Israel relationship. *AIPAC Papers on U.S.-Israel Relations.*

AMERICAN-ISRAELI LIGHTHOUSE, INC. (1928; reorg. 1955). 30 E. 60 St., NYC 10022. (212)838-5322. Pres. Mrs. Leonard F. Dank; Sec. Frances Lentz. Provides education and rehabilitation for the blind and physically handicapped in Israel to effect their social and vocational integration into the seeing community; built and maintains Rehabilitation Center for the Blind (Migdal Or) in Haifa. *Tower.*

AMERICAN JEWISH LEAGUE FOR ISRAEL (1957). 30 E. 60 St., NYC 10022. (212)-371-1583. Pres. Rabbi Reuben M. Katz; Bd. Chmn. Rabbi Aaron Decter. Seeks to unite all those who, notwithstanding differing philosophies of Jewish life, are committed to the historical ideals of Zionism; works, independently of class or party, for the welfare of Israel as a whole. Not identified with any political parties in Israel. *Bulletin of the American Jewish League for Israel.*

AMERICAN PHYSICIANS FELLOWSHIP, INC. FOR MEDICINE IN ISRAEL (1950). 2001 Beacon St., Brookline, MA 02146. (617)-232-5382. Pres. Dr. Edward H. Kass; Sec. Dr. Manuel M. Glazier. Helps Israel become a major world medical center; secures fellowships for selected Israeli physicians and arranges lectureships in Israel by prominent American physicians; supports Jerusalem Academy of Medicine; coordinates U.S. and Canadian medical and paramedical emergency volunteers to Israel; maintains Israel Institute of the History of Medicine; contributes medical books, periodicals, instruments, and drugs. *APF News.*

AMERICAN RED MAGEN DAVID FOR ISRAEL, INC. (1940). 888 Seventh Ave., NYC 10106. (212)757-1627. Natl. Chmn. Joseph Handlem; Pres. Louis Rosenberg; Exec. V.-Pres. Benjamin Saxe. An authorized tax-exempt organization; the sole support arm in the U.S. of Magen David Adom in Israel with a national membership and chapter program; educates and involves its members in activities of Magen David Adom, Israel's Red Cross Service; raises funds for MDA's emergency medical services, including collection and distribution of blood and blood products for Israel's military and civilian population; supplies ambulances, bloodmobiles, and mobile cardiac rescue units serving all hospitals and communities throughout Israel; supports MDA's 73 emergency medical clinics and helps provide training and equipment for volunteer emergency paramedical corps. *Lifeline.*

AMERICAN SOCIETY FOR TECHNION–ISRAEL INSTITUTE OF TECHNOLOGY (1940). 271 Madison Ave., NYC 10016. (212)889-2050. Pres. Martin Kellner; Exec. V.-Pres. Melvyn H. Bloom. Supports the work of the Technion–Israel Institute of Technology, Haifa, which trains nearly 10,000 students in 20 departments and a medical school, and conducts research across a broad spectrum of science and technology. *ATS Newsletter; ATS Women's Division Newsletter; Technion magazine; Technion USA; UPDATE: News for ATS Insiders.*

AMERICAN ZIONIST FEDERATION (1939; reorg. 1949 and 1970). 515 Park Ave., NYC 10022. (212)371-7750. Pres. Benjamin Cohen; Exec. Dir. Karen Rubinstein. Coordinates the work of the Zionist constituency in the areas of education, *aliyah,* youth and young leadership and public and communal affairs. Seeks to involve the Zionist and broader Jewish community in programs and events focused on Israel and Zionism (e.g., Zionist Shabbat, Scholars-in-Residence, Yom Yerushalayim) and through these programs to develop a greater appreciation for the Zionist idea among American Jewry. Composed of 16 national Zionist organizations, 10 Zionist youth movements, and affiliated organizations. Offices in Boston, Chicago, Los Angeles, New York. Groups in Baltimore, Detroit, Philadelphia, Pittsburgh, Rochester, Washington, DC. *Issue Analysis, Spectrum.*

AMERICAN ZIONIST YOUTH FOUNDATION, INC. (1963). 515 Park Ave., NYC 10022. (212)751-6070. Bd. Chmn. Eli Zborowski; Exec. Dir. Donald Adelman. Sponsors educational programs and services for American Jewish youth, including tours to Israel, programs of volunteer service or study in leading institutions of science, scholarship, and the arts; sponsors field workers who promote Jewish and Zionist programming on campus; prepares and provides specialists who present and interpret the Israeli experience for community centers and federations throughout the country. *Activist Newsletter; Guide to Education and Programming Material; Programs in Israel.*

———, AMERICAN ZIONIST YOUTH COUNCIL (1951). 515 Park Ave., NYC 10022. (212)751-6070. Chmn. Marc Sussman. Acts as spokesman and representative of Zionist youth in interpreting Israel to the youth of America; represents, coordinates, and implements activities of the Zionist youth movements in the U.S.

AMERICANS FOR A SAFE ISRAEL (1971). 147 E. 76 St., NYC 10021. (212)988-2122. Chmn. Herbert Zweibon; Dir. Peter Goldman. Seeks to educate the public to the necessity of a militarily strong Israel within defensible borders, viz., those which include Judea, Samaria, Gaza, and the Golan. Holds that a strong Israel is essential for the security of the free world. Produces pamphlets, magazines, video tapes, and radio shows and provides speakers; promotes college-campus activity and provides a congressional resource center. *Outpost.*

AMERICANS FOR PROGRESSIVE ISRAEL (1949). 150 Fifth Ave., Suite 911, NYC 10011. (212)255-8760. Pres. Harry Movchine. A socialist Zionist movement that calls for a just and durable peace between Israel and its Arab neighbors; works for the liberation of all Jews; seeks the democratization of Jewish communal and organizational life; promotes dignity of labor, social justice, and a deeper understanding of Jewish heritage. Affiliate of American Zionist Federation, World Union of Mapam, Hashomer Hatzair, and Kibbutz Artzi Fed. of Israel. *Israel Horizons; Progressive Israel; API Newsletter.*

AMIT WOMEN (formerly AMERICAN MIZRACHI WOMEN) (1925). 817 Broadway, NYC 10003. (212)477-4720. Pres. Frieda C. Kufeld; Exec. Dir. Marvin Leff. Conducts social service, child care, Youth Aliyah villages, and vocational-educational programs in Israel in an environment of traditional Judaism; promotes cultural activities for the purpose of disseminating Zionist ideals and strengthening traditional Judaism in America. *AMIT Woman.*

AMPAL—AMERICAN ISRAEL CORPORATION (1942). 10 Rockefeller Plaza, NYC 10020. (212)586-3232. Pres. Michael Arnon. Finances and invests in Israeli economic enterprises; mobilizes finance and investment capital in the U.S. through sale of own debenture issues and utilization of bank credit lines. *Annual Report; Prospectuses.*

ARZA—ASSOCIATION OF REFORM ZIONISTS OF AMERICA (1977). 838 Fifth Ave., NYC 10021. (212)249-0100. Pres. Rabbi Charles Kroloff; Exec. Dir. Rabbi Eric Yoffie. Individual Zionist membership organization devoted to achieving Jewish pluralism in Israel and strengthening the Israeli Reform movement. Chapter activities in the U.S. concentrate on these issues, and on strengthening American public support for Israel. *ARZA Newsletter.*

BAR-ILAN UNIVERSITY IN ISRAEL (1955). 853 Seventh Ave., NYC 10019. (212)315-1990. Chancellor Emanuel Rackman; Pres. Michael Albeck; Chmn. Bd. of Trustees Ludwig Jesselson; Pres. Amer. Bd. of Overseers Jane Stern. Supports Bar-Ilan University, a liberal arts and sciences institution, located in Ramat-Gan, Israel, and chartered by Board of Regents of State of NY. *Update; Bar-Ilan News; Academic Research; Philosophia.*

BETAR ZIONIST YOUTH MOVEMENT, INC. (1935). 41 E. 42 St., Suite 617, NYC 10017.

(212)687-4502. Pres. Mitch Chupak. Teaches Jewish youth love of the Jewish people and prepares them for *aliyah;* emphasizes learning Hebrew; keeps its members ready for mobilization in times of crisis; stresses Jewish pride and self-respect; seeks to aid and protect Jewish communities everywhere. *Herut; Etgar.*

COUNCIL FOR A BEAUTIFUL ISRAEL ENVIRONMENTAL EDUCATION FOUNDATION (1973). 350 Fifth Ave., 19th fl., NYC 10118. (212)947-5709. Pres. Dina Wald; Admin. Dir. Donna Lindemann. A support group for the Israeli body, whose activities include education, town planning, lobbying for legislation to protect and enhance the environment, preservation of historical sites, and the improvement and beautification of industrial and commercial areas. *Quarterly newsletter.*

DROR—YOUNG KIBBUTZ MOVEMENT—HABONIM (1948). 27 W. 20 St., NYC 10011. (212)675-1168. Exec. Dir. Shlomo Ravid. Provides an opportunity for individuals who have spent time in Israel, on a kibbutz program, to continue their contact with the kibbutz movement through regional and national activities and seminars; sponsors two *garinim* to kibbutz each year and a teenage summer program. *New Horizons.*

———, CHAVURAT HAGALIL (1978). Exec. Dir. Shlomo Ravid. Aids those aged 27-35 in making *aliyah* to a kibbutz. Affiliated with TAKAM kibbutz association.

———, GARIN YARDEN, THE YOUNG KIBBUTZ MOVEMENT (1976). Exec. Dir. Shlomo Ravid. Aids those aged 19-26 interested in making *aliyah* to a kibbutz; affiliated with TAKAM kibbutz association.

EMUNAH WOMEN OF AMERICA (formerly HAPOEL HAMIZRACHI WOMEN'S ORGANIZATION) (1948). 370 Seventh Ave., NYC 10001. (212)564-9045. Pres. Beverly Segal; Exec. Dir. Shirley Singer. Maintains and supports 200 educational and social-welfare institutions in Israel within a religious framework, including nurseries, day-care centers, vocational and teacher-training schools for the underprivileged. Also involved in absorption of Ethiopian immigrants. *The Emunah Woman; Lest We Forget; Emunah Connection.*

FEDERATED COUNCIL OF ISRAEL INSTITUTIONS—FCII (1940). 1475 47 St., Brooklyn, NY 11219. (718)853-6920. Bd. Chmn. Z. Shapiro; Exec. V.-Pres. Rabbi Julius Novack. Central fund-raising organization for over 100 affiliated institutions; handles and executes estates, wills, and bequests for the traditional institutions in Israel; clearinghouse for information on budget, size, functions, etc. of traditional educational, welfare, and philanthropic institutions in Israel, working cooperatively with the Israeli government and the overseas department of the Council of Jewish Federations. *Annual financial reports and statistics on affiliates.*

FUND FOR HIGHER EDUCATION (1970). 1500 Broadway, Suite 800, NYC 10036. (212)354-4660. V.-Pres. Sondra G. Kolker. Supports, on a project-by-project basis, institutions of higher learning in the U.S. and Israel. *In Response II; annual report; FHE brochure.*

GIVAT HAVIVA EDUCATIONAL FOUNDATION, INC. (1966). 150 Fifth Ave., Suite 911, NYC 10011. (212)255-2992. Chmn. Sydney A. Luria. Supports programs in Israel to further Jewish-Arab rapprochement, narrow economic and educational gaps within Israeli society, and improve educational opportunities for various disadvantaged youth. Affiliated with the Givat Haviva Center of the Kibbutz Artzi Federation, the Menachem Bader Fund, and other projects. In the U.S., GHEF, Inc. sponsors educational seminars, public lectures and parlor meetings with Israeli speakers, as well as individual and group trips to Israel. *News from Givat Haviva; special reports.*

HABONIM-DROR NORTH AMERICA (1934). 27 W. 20 St., 9th fl., NYC 10011. (212)-255-1796. Sec.-Gen. Mark Raider; Exec. Off. Ron Brawler. Fosters identification with pioneering in Israel; stimulates study of Jewish life, history, and culture; sponsors community-action projects, seven summer camps in North America, programs in Israel, and *garinei aliyah* to Kibbutz Lavon. *Batnua; Progressive Zionist Journal; Bimat Hamaapilim.*

HADASSAH, THE WOMEN'S ZIONIST ORGANIZATION OF AMERICA, INC. (1912). 50 W. 58 St., NYC 10019. (212)355-7900. Pres. Ruth Popkin; Exec. Dir. Zmira Goodman. In America helps interpret Israel to the American people; provides basic Jewish education as a background for intelligent and creative Jewish living; sponsors

Hashachar, largest Zionist youth movement in U.S., which has four divisions: Young Judaea, Intermediate Judaea, Senior Judaea, and Hamagshimim; operates six Zionist youth camps in this country; supports summer and all-year courses in Israel. Maintains in Israel Hadassah–Hebrew University Medical Center for healing, teaching, and research; Hadassah Community College; Seligsberg/Brandeis Comprehensive High School; and Hadassah Vocational Guidance Institute. Is largest organizational contributor to Youth Aliyah and to Jewish National Fund for land purchase and reclamation. *Update; Headlines; Hadassah Magazine.*

———, HASHACHAR (formerly YOUNG JUDAEA and JUNIOR HADASSAH) (1909; reorg. 1967). 50 W. 58 St., NYC 10019. (212)355-7900. Pres. of Senior Judaea (high-school level) Kenneth Kirschner; Coordinator of Hamagshimim (college level) Rachel Feit; Dir. Paul Goldberg. Seeks to educate Jewish youth from the ages of 9–27 toward Jewish and Zionist values, active commitment to and participation in the American and Israeli Jewish communities; maintains summer camps and year programs in Israel. *Hamagshimim Journal; Kol Hat'nua; The Young Judaean.*

HASHOMER HATZAIR, SOCIALIST ZIONIST YOUTH MOVEMENT (1923). 150 Fifth Ave., Suite 911, NYC 10011. (212)929-4955. Sec. Tzvi Fleisher; Central Rep. Avraham Israeli. Seeks to educate Jewish youth to an understanding of Zionism as the national liberation movement of the Jewish people. Promotes *aliyah* to kibbutzim. Affiliated with AZYC and Kibbutz Artzi Federation. Espouses socialist ideals of peace, justice, democracy, and brotherhood. *Young Guard.*

HERUT-U.S.A., INC. (UNITED ZIONISTS-REVISIONISTS OF AMERICA) (1925). 9 E. 38 St., Suite 1000, NYC 10016. (212)696-0900. Chmn. Hart N. Hasten; Exec. Dir. Hagai Lev. Supports Jabotinskean Herut policy in Israel for peace with security; seeks Jewish unity for Israel's defense; preaches Zionist commitment, *aliyah*, Jewish education, and mobilization of Jewish resources; advocates historic right to Eretz Israel and to Jewish residency throughout the land. Subsidiaries: Betar Zionist Youth; Young Herut; Tagar Zionist Student Activist Movement; Tel-Hai Fund, Inc. *The Herut Letter.*

JEWISH NATIONAL FUND OF AMERICA (1901). 42 E. 69 St., NYC 10021. (212)-879-9300. Pres. Joseph P. Sternstein; Exec. V.-Pres. Samuel I. Cohen. Exclusive fund-raising agency of the world Zionist movement for the afforestation, reclamation, and development of the land of Israel, including construction of roads, parks, and recreational areas, preparation of land for new communities and industrial facilities; helps emphasize the importance of Israel in schools and synagogues throughout the U.S. *JNF Almanac; Land and Life.*

KEREN OR, INC. (1956). 1133 Broadway, NYC 10010. (212)255-1180. Bd. Chmn. Edward Steinberg; Pres. N. Arnold Levin; Exec. V.-Pres. Jacob Igra. Funds the Keren Or Center for Multihandicapped Blind Children, in Jerusalem, providing long-term basic training, therapy, rehabilitative, and early childhood education to the optimum level of the individual; with major hospitals, conducts outpatient clinics in Haifa and Be'er Sheva; involved in research into causes of multihandicapped blind birth; campaign under way for new multipurpose building on government land-grant in Ramot.

LABOR ZIONIST ALLIANCE (formerly FARBAND LABOR ZIONIST ORDER; now uniting membership and branches of POALE ZION—UNITED LABOR ZIONIST ORGANIZATION OF AMERICA and AMERICAN HABONIM ASSOCIATION) (1913). 275 Seventh Ave., NYC 10001. (212)989-0300. Pres. Ezra Spicehandler; Exec. Dir. Menahem Jacobi. Seeks to enhance Jewish life, culture, and education in U.S. and Canada; aids in building State of Israel as a cooperative commonwealth, and its Labor movement organized in the Histadrut; supports efforts toward a more democratic society throughout the world; furthers the democratization of the Jewish community in America and the welfare of Jews everywhere; works with labor and liberal forces in America. *Jewish Frontier; Yiddisher Kempfer.*

LEAGUE FOR LABOR ISRAEL (1938; reorg. 1961). 275 Seventh Ave., NYC 10001. (212)989-0300. Pres. Ezra Spicehandler; Exec. Dir. Menahem Jacobi. Conducts Labor Zionist educational and cultural activities, for youth and adults, in the American Jewish community. Promotes educational travel to Israel.

NA'AMAT USA, THE WOMEN'S LABOR ZIONIST ORGANIZATION OF AMERICA,

INC. (formerly PIONEER WOMEN/ NA'AMAT) (1925; reorg. 1985). 200 Madison Ave., Suite 1808, NYC 10016. (212)-725-8010. Pres. Gloria Elbling; Exec. Dir. Shoshonna Ebstein. Part of a world movement of working women and volunteers, NA'AMAT USA helps provide social, educational, and legal services for women, teenagers, and children in Israel. It also advocates legislation for women's rights and child welfare in the U.S., furthers Jewish education, and supports Habonim-Dror, the Labor Zionist youth movement. *Na'amat Woman* magazine.

NATIONAL COMMITTEE FOR LABOR ISRAEL —HISTADRUT (1923). 33 E. 67 St., NYC 10021. (212)628-1000. Pres. Aaron L. Solomon; Exec. V.-Pres. Eliezer Rafaeli. Represents the Histadrut—Israel's General Federation of Labor; raises funds for Histadrut's network of social and welfare services in Israel, including Kupat Holim —the comprehensive health care organization which takes care of 80% of Israel's population—a vocational-school network, senior-citizen homes, and others. *Backdrop Histadrut; Amal Newsletter.*

———, AMERICAN TRADE UNION COUNCIL FOR HISTADRUT (1947). 33 E. 67 St., NYC 10021. (212)628-1000. Chmn. Matthew Schoenwald; Dir. Herbert A. Levine. Carries on educational activities among American and Canadian trade unions for health, educational, and welfare activities of the Histadrut in Israel. *Shalom.*

NEW ISRAEL FUND (1979). 111 W. 40 St., NYC 10018. (212)302-0066. Pres. David Arnow; Exec. Dir. Jonathan Jacoby. Supports the citizens'-action efforts of Israelis working to achieve social justice and to protect and strengthen the democratic process in Israel. Also seeks to enrich the quality of the relationships between Israelis and North American Jews through deepened mutual understanding. *A Guide to Arab-Jewish Peacemaking in Israel; quarterly bulletin; annual report.*

PEC ISRAEL ECONOMIC CORPORATION (formerly PALESTINE ECONOMIC CORPORATION) (1926). 511 Fifth Ave., NYC 10017. (212)687-2400. Pres. Joseph Ciechanover; Exec. V.-Pres. Frank J. Klein; Sec.-Asst. Treas. William Gold. Primarily engaged in the business of organizing, financing, and administering business enterprises located in or affiliated with enterprises in the State of Israel, through holdings of equity securities and loans. *Annual report.*

PEF ISRAEL ENDOWMENT FUNDS, INC. (1922). 342 Madison Ave., NYC 10173. (212)599-1260. Chmn. Sidney Musher; Sec. Harvey Brecher. Uses funds for Israeli educational and philanthropic institutions and for constructive relief, modern education, and scientific research in Israel. *Annual report.*

PIONEER WOMEN/NA'AMAT (see Na'amat USA)

POALE AGUDATH ISRAEL OF AMERICA, INC. (1948). 3190 Bedford Ave., Brooklyn, NY 11210. (718)377-4111. Pres. Rabbi Fabian Schonfeld; Exec. V.-Pres. Rabbi Moshe Malinowitz. Aims to educate American Jews to the values of Orthodoxy and *aliyah;* supports *kibbutzim,* trade schools, *yeshivot, moshavim, kollelim,* research centers, and children's homes in Israel. *PAI Views; PAI Bulletin.*

———, WOMEN'S DIVISION OF (1948). Pres. Aliza Widawsky; Presidium: Sarah Ivanisky, Miriam Lubling, Bertl Rittenberg. Assists Poale Agudath Israel to build and support children's homes, kindergartens, and trade schools in Israel. *Yediot PAI.*

PROGRESSIVE ZIONIST CAUCUS (1982). 27 W. 20 St., NYC 10011. (212)675-1168. Pres. Shlomo Ravid; Admin. Dir. Robert Fields; Educ. Dir. Rebecca Rowe. A campus-based grassroots organization committed to a progressive Zionist political agenda. Students organize local educational and political activities, such as speakers, *Kabbalot Shabbat,* and Arab-Jewish dialogue groups. The PZC Kvutzat Aliyah is a support framework for individuals interested in *aliyah* to a city or town. *La'Inyan.*

RELIGIOUS ZIONISTS OF AMERICA 25 W. 26 St., NYC 10010. (212)689-1414.

———, BNEI AKIVA OF NORTH AMERICA (1934). 25 W. 26 St., NYC 10010. (212)-889-5260. Exec. Pres. Danny Mayerfield; V.-Pres. Alan Silverman; Sec. Yitzchak Fuchs. Seeks to interest youth in *aliyah* to Israel and social justice through pioneering *(halutziut)* as an integral part of their religious observance; sponsors five summer camps, a leadership training camp for eleventh graders, a work-study program on a religious kibbutz for high school graduates, summer tours to Israel; establishes nuclei of college students for kibbutz or other settlement. *Akivon; Hamvaser;*

Pinkas Lamadrich; Daf Rayonot; Ma'Ohalai Torah; Zraim.

———, MIZRACHI-HAPOEL HAMIZRACHI (1909; merged 1957). 25 W. 26 St., NYC 10010. (212)689-1414. Pres. Hermann Merkin; Exec. V.-Pres. Israel Friedman. Disseminates ideals of religious Zionism; conducts cultural work, educational program, public relations; raises funds for religious educational institutions in Israel, including *yeshivot hesder* and Bnei Akiva. *Newsletters; Kolenu.*

———, MIZRACHI PALESTINE FUND (1928). 25 W. 26 St., NYC 10010. Chmn. Joseph Wilon; Sec. Israel Friedman. Fundraising arm of Mizrachi movement.

———, NATIONAL COUNCIL FOR TORAH EDUCATION OF MIZRACHI-HAPOEL HAMIZRACHI (1939). 25 W. 26 St., NYC 10010. Pres. Israel Shorr; Dir. Meyer Golombek. Organizes and supervises *yeshivot* and Talmud Torahs; prepares and trains teachers; publishes textbooks and educational materials; conducts a placement agency for Hebrew schools; organizes summer seminars for Hebrew educators in cooperation with Torah Department of Jewish Agency; conducts *ulpan.*

———, NOAM-MIZRACHI NEW LEADERSHIP COUNCIL (formerly NOAM-HAMISHMERET HATZEIRA) (1970). 25 W. 26 St., NYC 10010. (212)684-6091. Pres. Rabbi Marc Schneier; Dir. Moshe Bagaon. Develops new religious Zionist leadership in the U.S. and Canada; presents young religious people with various alternatives for settling in Israel through *garinei aliyah* (core groups); meets the religious, educational, and social needs of Jewish young adults and young couples. *Forum.*

SOCIETY OF ISRAEL PHILATELISTS (1948). 27436 Aberdeen, Southfield, MI 48076. (313)557-0887. Pres. Stanley H. Raffel; Exec. Sec. Irvin Girer. Promotes interest in, and knowledge of, all phases of Israel philately through sponsorship of chapters and research groups, maintenance of a philatelic library, and support of public and private exhibitions. *Israel Philatelist; monographs; books.*

STATE OF ISRAEL BONDS (1951). 730 Broadway, NYC 10003. (212)677-9650. Intnl. Chmn. David B. Hermelin; Pres. Yehudah Halevy; Exec. V.-Pres. Morris Sipser. Seeks to provide large-scale investment funds for the economic development of the State of Israel through the sale of State of Israel bonds in the U.S., Canada, Western Europe, and other parts of the free world.

THEODOR HERZL FOUNDATION (1954). 515 Park Ave., NYC 10022. (212)752-0600. Chmn. Kalman Sultanik; Sec. Isadore Hamlin. Cultural activities, lectures, conferences, courses in modern Hebrew and Jewish subjects, Israel, Zionism, and Jewish history. *Midstream.*

———, HERZL PRESS. Chmn. Kalman Sultanik; Editor Mordecai S. Chertoff. Publishes books and pamphlets on Israel, Zionism, and general Jewish subjects.

———, THEODOR HERZL INSTITUTE. Chmn. Jacques Torczyner; Dir. Sidney Rosenfeld. Program geared to review of contemporary problems on Jewish scene here and abroad, presentation of Jewish heritage values in light of Zionist experience of the ages, study of modern Israel, and Jewish social research with particular consideration of history and impact of Zionism. Lectures, forums, Encounter with Creativity; musicales, recitals, concerts; holiday celebrations; visual art programs, Nouveau Artist Introductions. *Annual Program Preview; Herzl Institute Bulletin.*

UNITED CHARITY INSTITUTIONS OF JERUSALEM, INC. (1903). 1141 Broadway, NYC 10001. (212)683-3221. Pres. Zevulun Charlop; Sec. Sam Gabel. Raises funds for the maintenance of schools, kitchens, clinics, and dispensaries in Israel; free loan foundations in Israel.

UNITED ISRAEL APPEAL, INC. (1925). 515 Park Ave., NYC 10022. (212)688-0800. Chmn. Henry Taub; Exec. V.-Chmn. Irving Kessler. As principal beneficiary of the United Jewish Appeal, serves as link between American Jewish community and Jewish Agency for Israel, its operating agent; assists in resettlement and absorption of refugees in Israel, and supervises flow of funds and expenditures for this purpose.

UNITED STATES COMMITTEE SPORTS FOR ISRAEL, INC. (1948). 275 S. 19 St., Philadelphia, PA 19103. (215)546-4700. Pres. Robert E. Spivak; Exec. Dir. Barbara G. Lissy. Sponsors U.S. participation in, and fields and selects U.S. team for, World

Maccabiah Games in Israel every four years; promotes education and sports programs in Israel; provides funds and technical and material assistance to Wingate Institute for Physical Education and Sport in Israel; sponsors coaching programs in Israel. *USCSFI Newsletter; commemorative Maccabiah Games journal.*

WOMEN'S LEAGUE FOR ISRAEL, INC. (1928). 515 Park Ave., NYC 10022. (212)838-1997. Pres. Muriel Lunden; Sr. V.-Pres. Linda Anopolsky; Exec. Dir. Bernice Backon. Promotes the welfare of young people in Israel; built and maintains homes in Jerusalem, Haifa, Tel Aviv, and Natanya; in cooperation with Ministry of Labor and Social Affairs, operates live-in vocational training center for girls, including handicapped, in Natanya, and weaving workshop for the blind. *In League.*

WORLD CONFEDERATION OF UNITED ZIONISTS (1946; reorg. 1958). 30 E. 60 St., NYC 10022. (212)371-1452. Copres. Bernice S. Tannenbaum, Kalman Sultanik, Melech Topiol. Promotes Zionist education, sponsors nonparty youth movements in the Diaspora, and strives for an Israel-oriented creative Jewish survival in the Diaspora. *Zionist Information Views.*

WORLD ZIONIST ORGANIZATION—AMERICAN SECTION (1971). 515 Park Ave., NYC 10022. (212)752-0600. Chmn. Bernice S. Tannenbaum; Exec. V.-Chmn. Isadore Hamlin. As the American section of the overall Zionist body throughout the world, it operates primarily in the field of *aliyah* from the free countries, education in the Diaspora, youth and *hechalutz*, organization and information, cultural institutions, publications; conducts a worldwide Hebrew cultural program including special seminars and pedagogic manuals; disperses information and assists in research projects concerning Israel; promotes, publishes, and distributes books, periodicals, and pamphlets concerning developments in Israel, Zionism, and Jewish history. *Israel Scene; Five Fifteen.*

——, DEPARTMENT OF EDUCATION AND CULTURE (1948). 515 Park Ave., NYC 10022. (212)752-0600. Exec. Counselor Arthur Levine; Exec. Dir. Mordechai Peled. Seeks to foster a wider and deeper knowledge of the Hebrew language and literature and a better understanding and fuller appreciation of the role of Israel in the destiny of Jewry and Judaism, to introduce the study of Israel as an integral part of the Jewish school curriculum, and to initiate and sponsor educational projects designed to implement these objectives.

——, NORTH AMERICAN ALIYAH MOVEMENT (1968). 515 Park Ave., NYC 10022. (212)752-0600. Pres. Susan Friedman Becker. Promotes and facilitates *aliyah* and *klitah* from the U.S. and Canada to Israel; serves as a social framework for North American immigrants to Israel. *Aliyon.*

——, ZIONIST ARCHIVES AND LIBRARY OF THE (1939). 515 Park Ave., NYC 10022. (212)752-0600. Acting Librarian Esther Togman. Serves as an archives and information service for material on Israel, Palestine, the Middle East, Zionism, and all aspects of Jewish life.

ZIONIST ORGANIZATION OF AMERICA (1897). ZOA House, 4 E. 34 St., NYC 10016. (212)481-1500. Pres. Alleck A. Resnick; Exec. V.-Pres. Paul Flacks. Public affairs programming to foster the unity of the Jewish people through General Zionism; parent organization of four institutes which promote the understanding of Zionism within the Jewish and non-Jewish world; sponsors of Masada Youth summer programs in Israel, ZOA House in Tel Aviv, and international high school programs at Kfar Silver, Ashkelon.

PROFESSIONAL ASSOCIATIONS*

AMERICAN CONFERENCE OF CANTORS, UNION OF AMERICAN HEBREW CONGREGATIONS (Religious, Educational)

AMERICAN JEWISH CORRECTIONAL CHAPLAINS ASSOCIATION, INC. (Social Welfare)

AMERICAN JEWISH PRESS ASSOCIATION (Cultural)

AMERICAN JEWISH PUBLIC RELATIONS SOCIETY (1957). 234 Fifth Ave., NYC 10001. (212)697-5895. Pres. Martin J. Warmbrand; Treas. Hyman Brickman. Advances professional status of workers in the public-relations field in Jewish communal service; upholds a professional code of ethics

---

*For fuller listing see under categories in parentheses.

and standards; serves as a clearinghouse for employment opportunities; exchanges professional information and ideas; presents awards for excellence in professional attainments, including the "Maggid Award" for outstanding literary or artistic achievement which enhances Jewish life. *The Handout.*

ASSOCIATION OF HILLEL/JEWISH CAMPUS PROFESSIONALS (Religious, Educational)

ASSOCIATION OF JEWISH CENTER WORKERS (Community Relations)

ASSOCIATION OF JEWISH CHAPLAINS OF THE ARMED FORCES (Religious, Educational)

ASSOCIATION OF JEWISH COMMUNITY ORGANIZATION PERSONNEL (Social Welfare)

ASSOCIATION OF JEWISH COMMUNITY RELATIONS WORKERS (Community Relations)

CANTORS ASSEMBLY (Religious, Educational)

CENTRAL CONFERENCE OF AMERICAN RABBIS (Religious, Educational)

CONFERENCE OF JEWISH COMMUNAL SERVICE (Social Welfare)

COUNCIL OF JEWISH ORGANIZATIONS IN CIVIL SERVICE (Community Relations)

JEWISH EDUCATORS ASSEMBLY, UNITED SYNAGOGUE OF AMERICA (Religious, Educational)

JEWISH MINISTERS CANTORS ASSOCIATION OF AMERICA, INC. (Religious, Educational)

JEWISH TEACHERS ASSOCIATION—MORIM (Religious, Educational)

JWB JEWISH CHAPLAINS COUNCIL (Social Welfare)

NATIONAL ASSOCIATION OF HEBREW DAY SCHOOL ADMINISTRATORS, TORAH UMESORAH (Religious, Educational)

NATIONAL ASSOCIATION OF SYNAGOGUE ADMINISTRATORS, UNITED SYNAGOGUE OF AMERICA (Religious, Educational)

NATIONAL ASSOCIATION OF TEMPLE ADMINISTRATORS, UNION OF AMERICAN HEBREW CONGREGATIONS (Religious, Educational)

NATIONAL ASSOCIATION OF TEMPLE EDUCATORS, UNION OF AMERICAN HEBREW CONGREGATIONS (Religious, Educational)

NATIONAL CONFERENCE OF YESHIVA PRINCIPALS, TORAH UMESORAH (Religious, Educational)

RABBINICAL ASSEMBLY (Religious, Educational)

RABBINICAL COUNCIL OF AMERICA (Religious, Educational)

RECONSTRUCTIONIST RABBINICAL ASSOCIATION, JEWISH RECONSTRUCTIONIST FOUNDATION (Religious, Educational)

UNION OF ORTHODOX RABBIS OF THE U.S. AND CANADA (Religious, Educational)

WORLD CONFERENCE OF JEWISH COMMUNAL SERVICE (Community Relations)

WOMEN'S ORGANIZATIONS*

AMIT WOMEN (Zionist and Pro-Israel)

B'NAI B'RITH WOMEN (Social Welfare)

BRANDEIS UNIVERSITY NATIONAL WOMEN'S COMMITTEE (1948). 415 South St., Waltham, MA 02254. (617)647-2194. Pres. Barbara J. Ehrlich; Exec. Dir. Carol S. Rabinovitz. Responsible for support and maintenance of Brandeis University libraries; sponsors University on Wheels and, through its chapters, study-group programs based on faculty-prepared syllabi, volunteer work in educational services, and a program of New Books for Old sales; constitutes largest "Friends of a Library" group in U.S. *Imprint.*

HADASSAH, THE WOMEN'S ZIONIST ORGANIZATION OF AMERICA, INC. (Zionist and Pro-Israel)

NA'AMAT USA, THE WOMEN'S LABOR ZIONIST ORGANIZATION OF AMERICA (Zionist and Pro-Israel)

NATIONAL COUNCIL OF JEWISH WOMEN (Social Welfare)

NATIONAL FEDERATION OF TEMPLE SISTERHOODS, UNION OF AMERICAN

---

*For fuller listing see under categories in parentheses.

HEBREW CONGREGATIONS (Religious, Educational)

UNITED ORDER TRUE SISTERS (Social, Mutual Benefit)

WOMEN'S AMERICAN ORT, AMERICAN ORT FEDERATION, INC. (Overseas Aid)

WOMEN'S BRANCH OF THE UNION OF ORTHODOX JEWISH CONGREGATIONS OF AMERICA (Religious, Educational)

WOMEN'S DIVISION OF POALE AGUDATH ISRAEL OF AMERICA (Zionist and Pro-Israel)

WOMEN'S DIVISION OF THE JEWISH LABOR COMMITTEE (Community Relations)

WOMEN'S DIVISION OF THE UNITED JEWISH APPEAL (Overseas Aid)

WOMEN'S LEAGUE FOR CONSERVATIVE JUDAISM (Religious, Educational)

WOMEN'S LEAGUE FOR ISRAEL, INC. (Zionist and Pro-Israel)

YESHIVA UNIVERSITY WOMEN'S ORGANIZATION (Religious, Educational)

YOUTH AND STUDENT ORGANIZATIONS*

AMERICAN ZIONIST YOUTH FOUNDATION, INC. (Zionist and Pro-Israel)

———, AMERICAN ZIONIST YOUTH COUNCIL

B'NAI B'RITH HILLEL FOUNDATIONS, INC. (Religious, Educational)

B'NAI B'RITH YOUTH ORGANIZATION (Religious, Educational)

BNEI AKIVA OF NORTH AMERICA, RELIGIOUS ZIONISTS OF AMERICA (Zionist and Pro-Israel)

BNOS AGUDATH ISRAEL, AGUDATH ISRAEL OF AMERICA, GIRLS' DIVISION (Religious, Educational)

DROR—YOUNG KIBBUTZ MOVEMENT—HABONIM (Zionist and Pro-Israel)

HABONIM-DROR NORTH AMERICA (Zionist and Pro-Israel)

HASHACHAR, HADASSAH (Zionist and Pro-Israel)

HASHOMER HATZAIR, SOCIALIST ZIONIST YOUTH MOVEMENT (Zionist and Pro-Israel)

JEWISH STUDENT PRESS SERVICE (1970)—JEWISH STUDENT EDITORIAL PROJECTS, JEWISH PRESS FEATURES. 15 E. 26 St., Suite 1350, NYC 10010. (212)679-1411. Dir. Suzanne Dashman; Editor Larry Yudelson. Serves all Jewish student and young adult publications, as well as many Anglo-Jewish newspapers, in North America, through monthly feature packets of articles and graphics. Holds annual national and local editors' conference for member publications. Provides technical and editorial assistance; maintains Israel Bureau. *Jewish Press Features.*

KADIMA, UNITED SYNAGOGUE OF AMERICA (Religious, Educational)

NATIONAL CONFERENCE OF SYNAGOGUE YOUTH, UNION OF ORTHODOX JEWISH CONGREGATIONS OF AMERICA (Religious, Educational)

NOAM-MIZRACHI NEW LEADERSHIP COUNCIL, RELIGIOUS ZIONISTS OF AMERICA (Zionist and Pro-Israel)

NORTH AMERICAN FEDERATION OF TEMPLE YOUTH, UNION OF AMERICAN HEBREW CONGREGATIONS (Religious, Educational)

NORTH AMERICAN JEWISH STUDENTS APPEAL (1971). 15 E. 26 St., Suite 1350, NYC, 10010. (212)679-2293. Pres. Adam Whiteman; Exec. Dir. Brenda Gevertz. Serves as central fund-raising mechanism for four national, independent Jewish student organizations; insures accountability of public Jewish communal funds used by these agencies; assists Jewish students undertaking projects of concern to Jewish communities; advises and assists Jewish organizations in determining student project feasibility and impact; fosters development of Jewish student leadership in the Jewish community. Beneficiaries include local and regional Jewish student projects on campuses throughout North America; current constituents include Jewish Student Press Service, Student Struggle for Soviet Jewry, *Response,* and *Yugntruf.*

NORTH AMERICAN JEWISH STUDENTS' NETWORK (1969). 1 Park Ave., #418,

---

*For fuller listing see under categories in parentheses.

NYC 10016. (212)679-0600. Pres. Moshe Ronen; Natl. Chmn. Ayall Schanzer. Coordinates information and programs among all Jewish student organizations in North America; promotes development of student-controlled Jewish student organizations; maintains contacts and coordinates programs with Jewish students throughout the world through the World Union of Jewish Students; runs the Jewish Student Speakers Bureau; sponsors regional, national, and North American conferences. *Network Spectrum; Jewish Students of America.*

NORTH AMERICAN JEWISH YOUTH COUNCIL (Community Relations)

STUDENT STRUGGLE FOR SOVIET JEWRY, INC. (Community Relations)

UNITED SYNAGOGUE YOUTH, UNITED SYNAGOGUE OF AMERICA (Religious, Educational)

YOUNG ISRAEL COLLEGIATES AND YOUNG ADULTS, NATIONAL COUNCIL OF YOUNG ISRAEL (Religious, Educational)

YUGNTRUF YOUTH FOR YIDDISH (1964). 3328 Bainbridge Ave., Bronx, NY 10467. (212)654-8540. Chmn. Itzek Gottesman; Editor Paul Glasser. A worldwide, nonpolitical organization for high school and college students with a knowledge of, or interest in, Yiddish. Spreads the love and use of the Yiddish language; organizes artistic and social activities, including annual conference for young adults; sponsors Yiddish-speaking preschool for non-Orthodox children. Offers services of full-time field worker to assist in forming Yiddish courses and clubs throughout the U.S. *Yugntruf.*

ZEIREI AGUDATH ISRAEL, AGUDATH ISRAEL OF AMERICA, YOUNG MEN'S DIVISION (Religious, Educational)

CANADA

CANADA-ISRAEL SECURITIES, LTD., STATE OF ISRAEL BONDS (1953). 1255 University St., Montreal, PQ H3B 3B2. (514)878-1871. Pres. Thomas O. Hecht; Exec. V.-Pres. Julius Briskin. Sells financial instruments to strengthen economic foundations of Israel. *Israel Bonds Digest.*

CANADIAN ASSOCIATION FOR LABOR ISRAEL (HISTADRUT) (1944). 4770 Kent Ave., Suite 301, Montreal, PQ H3W 1H2. Pres. Harry J. F. Bloomfield; Exec. Dir. Michael E. Meyer. Raises funds for Histadrut medical, cultural, and educational programs for the workers and families of Israel. Public relations work with trade unions to inform and educate them about the State of Israel.

CANADIAN B'NAI BRITH (1964). 15 Hove St., Suite 200, Downsview, ONT M3H 4Y8. (416)633-6224. Pres. Harry Bick; Exec. V.-Pres. Frank Dimant. Canadian Jewry's largest service organization; makes representations to all levels of government on matters of Jewish concern; promotes humanitarian causes and educational programs, community volunteer projects, adult Jewish education and leadership development; dedicated to human rights; sponsors youth programs of B'nai Brith Youth Org. and Hillel. *Covenant; Communiqué; Hillel Voice.*

——, LEAGUE FOR HUMAN RIGHTS (1970). Chmn. Phillip A. Leon. Dedicated to monitoring human rights, combating racism and racial discrimination, and preventing bigotry and anti-Semitism, through education and community relations. Sponsors Holocaust Education Programs, the R. Lou Ronson Research Institute on Anti-Semitism; distributor of Anti-Defamation League materials in Canada. *Review of Anti-Semitism.*

CANADIAN FOUNDATION FOR JEWISH CULTURE (1965). 4600 Bathurst St., Willowdale, ONT M2R 3V2. (416)635-2883. Pres. Mira Koschitzky; Exec. Sec. Edmond Y. Lipsitz. Promotes Jewish studies at university level and encourages original research and scholarship in Jewish subjects; awards annual scholarships and grants-in-aid to scholars in Canada.

CANADIAN FRIENDS OF THE ALLIANCE ISRAÉLITE UNIVERSELLE (1958). PO Box 578 Victoria Station, Montreal, PQ H3Z 2Y6. (514)481-3552. Pres. Joseph Nuss. Supports the educational work of the Alliance.

CANADIAN FRIENDS OF THE HEBREW UNIVERSITY (1944). 208-1 Yorkdale Rd., Toronto, ONT M6A 3A1. (416)789-2633. Pres. Gerald Halbert; Exec. V.-Pres. Joel Alpert. Represents and publicizes the Hebrew University in Canada; serves as fundraising arm for the university in Canada; processes Canadians for study at the university. *Scopus; Ha-Universita.*

CANADIAN JEWISH CONGRESS (1919; reorg. 1934). 1590 Dr. Penfield Ave., Montreal, PQ H3G 1C5. (514)931-7531. Pres. Dorothy Reitman; Exec. V.-Pres. Alan Rose. The official voice of Canadian Jewish communities at home and abroad; acts on all matters affecting the status, rights, concerns and welfare of Canadian Jewry; internationally active on behalf of Soviet Jewry, Jews in Arab lands, Holocaust remembrance and restitution; largest Jewish archives in Canada. *National Small Communities Newsletter; Community Relations Newsletter; Intercom; National Archives Newsletter; Bulletin du Congrès Juif Canadien.*

CANADIAN ORT ORGANIZATION (Organization of Rehabilitation Through Training) (1942). 5165 Sherbrooke St. W., Suite 208, Montreal, PQ H4A 1T6. (514)481-2787. Pres. J.A. Lyone Heppner; Exec. Dir. Mac Silver. Carries on fund-raising projects in support of the worldwide vocational-training-school network of ORT. *Canadian ORT Reporter.*

———, WOMEN'S CANADIAN ORT (1948). 3101 Bathurst St., Suite 604, Toronto, ONT M6A 2A6. (416)787-0339. Pres. Harriet Morton; Exec. Dir. Diane Uslaner. *Focus.*

CANADIAN SEPHARDI FEDERATION (1973). 345 Wilson Ave., Suite 303, Downsview, ONT M3H 5W1. (416)630-7136. Pres. Leon Oziel; Sec. Laeticia Benabou. Preserves and promotes Sephardic identity, particularly among youth; works for the unity of the Jewish people; emphasizes relations between Sephardi communities all over the world; seeks better situation for Sephardim in Israel; supports Israel by all means. Participates in *La Voix Sépharade, Le Monde Sépharade,* and *Sephardi World.*

CANADIAN YOUNG JUDAEA (1917). 788 Marlee Ave., Toronto, ONT M6B 3K1. (416)787-5350. Pres. Michael Goldbach; Exec. Dir. Alon Szpindel. Strives to attract Jewish youth to Zionism, with goal of *aliyah;* operates six summer camps in Canada and one in Israel; is sponsored by Canadian Hadassah–WIZO and Zionist Federation of Canada, and affiliated with Hanoar Hatzioni in Israel. *Judaean; The Young Judaean.*

CANADIAN ZIONIST FEDERATION (1967). 1310 Greene Ave., Montreal, PQ H3Z 2B8. (514)934-0804. Pres. Neri J. Bloomfield; Exec. V.-Pres. Rabbi Meyer Krentzman. Umbrella organization of all Zionist and Israel-related groups in Canada; carries on major activities in all areas of Jewish life through its departments of education and culture, *aliyah,* youth and students, public affairs, and fund raising for the purpose of strengthening the State of Israel and the Canadian Jewish community. *Canadian Zionist magazine.*

———, BUREAU OF EDUCATION AND CULTURE (1972). Pres. Neri J. Bloomfield; Exec. V.-Pres. Rabbi Meyer Krentzman. Provides counseling by pedagogic experts, in-service teacher-training courses and seminars in Canada and Israel; national pedagogic council and research center; distributes educational material and teaching aids; conducts annual Bible contest and Hebrew-language courses for adults. *Al Mitzpe Hachinuch.*

FRIENDS OF PIONEERING ISRAEL (1950s). 1111 Finch Ave. W., Suite 154, Downsview, ONT M35 2E5 (416)736-0977. Exec. Dir. Yigal Gilboa. Acts as a progressive voice within the Jewish community on Israeli and Canadian issues; expresses socialist and Zionist viewpoints; serves as a focal point for work of the progressive Zionist elements in Canada; acts as Canadian representative of Mapam and as the Canadian distributor of *New Outlook—Mideast Monthly.* Activities include lectures on political and Jewish topics open to the public; Jewish holiday celebrations.

HADASSAH–WIZO ORGANIZATION OF CANADA (1916). 1310 Greene Ave., 9th fl., Montreal, PQ H3Z 2B8. (514)937-9431. Pres. Cecily Peters; Exec. V.-Pres. Lily Frank. Extends material and moral support to the people of Israel requiring such assistance; strengthens and fosters Jewish ideals; encourages Hebrew culture in Canada and promotes Canadian ideals of democracy. *Orah magazine.*

JEWISH IMMIGRANT AID SERVICES OF CANADA (JIAS) (1919). 5151 Cote Ste. Catherine Rd., Montreal, PQ H3W 1M6. (514)-342-9351. Pres. Harold Ashley; Exec. V.-Pres. Herb Abrams. Serves as a national agency for immigration and immigrant welfare. *JIAS Bulletin.*

JEWISH NATIONAL FUND OF CANADA (KEREN KAYEMETH LE'ISRAEL, INC.)

(1902). 1980 Sherbrooke St. W., Suite 500, Montreal, PQ H3H 2M7. (514)934-0313. Pres. Saul B. Zitzerman; Exec. V.-Pres. Michael Goldstein. Fund-raising organization affiliated with the World Zionist Organization; involved in afforestation, soil reclamation, and development of the land of Israel, including the construction of roads and preparation of sites for new settlements; provides educational materials and programs to Jewish schools across Canada.

LABOR ZIONIST MOVEMENT OF CANADA (1939). 4770 Kent Ave., Montreal, PQ H3W 1H2. (514)342-9710. Chmn. Natl. Exec. Abraham Shurem. Disseminates information and publications on Israel and Jewish life; arranges special events, lectures, and seminars; coordinates communal and political activities of its constituent bodies (Pioneer Women/Na'amat, Labor Zionist Alliance, Poale Zion party, Habonim-Dror Youth, Israel Histadrut, affiliated Hebrew elementary and high schools in Montreal and Toronto).

MIZRACHI-HAPOEL HAMIZRACHI ORGANIZATION OF CANADA (1941). 159 Almore Ave., Downsview, ONT M3H 2H9. (416)-630-7575. Pres. Kurt Rothschild; Exec. Dir. Rabbi Menachem Gopin. Promotes religious Zionism, aimed at making Israel a state based on Torah; maintains Bnei Akiva, a summer camp, adult education program, and touring department; supports Mizrachi-Hapoel Hamizrachi and other religious Zionist institutions in Israel which strengthen traditional Judaism. *Mizrachi Newsletter; Or Hamizrach Torah Quarterly.*

NATIONAL COUNCIL OF JEWISH WOMEN OF CANADA (1947). 1111 Finch Ave. W., Suite 401, Downsview, ONT M3J 2E5. (416)665-8251. Pres. Sheila Freeman; Exec. Dir. Eleanor Appleby. Dedicated to furthering human welfare in Jewish and non-Jewish communities, locally, nationally, and internationally; provides essential services, and stimulates and educates the individual and the community through an integrated program of education, service, and social action. *New Edition.*

NATIONAL JOINT COMMUNITY RELATIONS COMMITTEE OF CANADIAN JEWISH CONGRESS (1936). 4600 Bathurst St., Willowdale, ONT M2R 3V2 (416)635-2883. Cochmn. Victor Goldbloom, Joseph J. Wilder; Exec. Dir. Manuel Prutschi. Seeks to safeguard the status, rights, and welfare of Jews in Canada; to combat anti-Semitism and promote understanding and goodwill among all ethnic and religious groups. *Community Relations Report.*

UNITED JEWISH TEACHERS' SEMINARY (1946). 5237 Clanranald Ave., Montreal, PQ H3X 2S5. (514)489-4401. Dir. A. Aisenbach. Trains teachers for Yiddish and Hebrew schools under auspices of Canadian Jewish Congress. *Yitonenu.*

ZIONIST ORGANIZATION OF CANADA (1892; reorg. 1919). 788 Marlee Ave., Toronto, ONT M6B 3K1. (416)781-3571. Pres. Max Goody; Exec. V.-Pres. George Liban. Furthers general Zionist aims by operating six youth camps in Canada and one in Israel; maintains Zionist book club; arranges programs, lectures; sponsors Young Judaea, Youth Centre Project in Jerusalem Forest, Israel.

Jewish Federations, Welfare Funds, Community Councils[1]

UNITED STATES

ALABAMA

BIRMINGHAM

BIRMINGHAM JEWISH FEDERATION (1936; reorg. 1971); PO Box 9157 (35213); (205)-879-0416. Pres. Phyllis Weinstein; Exec. Dir. Richard Friedman.

MOBILE

MOBILE JEWISH WELFARE FUND, INC. (inc. 1966; 1 Office Park, Suite 219 (36609); (205)-343-7197. Pres. Gerald A. Friedlander; Admin. Barbara V. Paper.

MONTGOMERY

JEWISH FEDERATION OF MONTGOMERY, INC. (1930); PO Box 20058 (36120); (205)-277-5820. Pres. Joy Blondheim.

ARIZONA

PHOENIX

JEWISH FEDERATION OF GREATER PHOENIX (incl. surrounding communities) (1940); 1718 W. Maryland Ave. (85015); (602)249-1845. Pres. Seymour Sacks.

TUCSON

JEWISH FEDERATION OF SOUTHERN ARIZONA (1942); 102 N. Plumer (85719); (602)-884-8921. Pres. Jerry Sonenblick; Exec. V. Pres. Charles Plotkin.

ARKANSAS

LITTLE ROCK

JEWISH FEDERATION OF LITTLE ROCK (1911); 4942 West Markham, Suite 5 (72205); (501)663-3571. Pres. Philip E. Kaplan; Exec. Dir. Nanci Goldman.

CALIFORNIA

FRESNO

JEWISH FEDERATION OF FRESNO (inc. 1978); 5094 N. West Ave. (93711); (209)432-2162. Pres. Robert Boro; Exec. Dir. Lisa M. Goldman.

LONG BEACH

JEWISH FEDERATION OF GREATER LONG BEACH AND WEST ORANGE COUNTY (1937); (sponsors UNITED JEWISH WELFARE FUND); 3801 E. Willow St. (90815); (213)-426-7601. Pres. Robert Blakey; Exec. Dir. Sandi Goldstein.

LOS ANGELES

JEWISH FEDERATION COUNCIL OF GREATER LOS ANGELES (1912; reorg. 1959); (sponsors UNITED JEWISH FUND); 6505 Wilshire Blvd. (90048); (213)852-1234. Pres. Stanley Hirsh; Exec. V. Pres. Wayne Feinstein.

OAKLAND

JEWISH FEDERATION OF THE GREATER EAST BAY (1918); 3245 Sheffield Ave.

---

[1]This directory is based on information supplied by the Council of Jewish Federations.

(94602); (415)533-7462. Pres. Herbert Friedman; Exec. V. Pres. Ami Nahshon.

ORANGE COUNTY

JEWISH FEDERATION OF ORANGE COUNTY (1964; inc. 1965); (sponsors UNITED JEWISH WELFARE FUND); 12181 Buaro, Garden Grove (92640); (714)530-6636. Pres. Eleanor Burg; Interim CEO Merv Lemmerman.

PALM SPRINGS

JEWISH FEDERATION OF PALM SPRINGS-DESERT AREA (1971); 611 S. Palm Canyon Dr. (92264); (619)325-7281. Pres. Harry Tarler; Exec. Dir. Nat Bent.

SACRAMENTO

JEWISH FEDERATION OF SACRAMENTO (1948); PO Box 254589 (95865); (916)486-0906. Pres. Arlene Pearl; Exec. Dir. Arnold Feder.

SAN DIEGO

UNITED JEWISH FEDERATION OF SAN DIEGO COUNTY (1936); 4797 Mercury St. (92111); (619)571-3444. Pres. Howard Brotman; Exec. Dir. Stephen M. Abramson.

SAN FRANCISCO

JEWISH COMMUNITY FEDERATION OF SAN FRANCISCO, THE PENINSULA, MARIN, AND SONOMA COUNTIES (1910; reorg. 1955); 121 Steuart St. (94105); (415)777-0411. Pres. Laurence E. Myers; Exec. Dir. Rabbi Brian Lurie.

SAN JOSE

JEWISH FEDERATION OF GREATER SAN JOSE (incl. Santa Clara County except Palo Alto and Los Altos) (1930; reorg. 1950); 14855 Oka Rd., Los Gatos (95030); (408)-358-3033. Pres. Sherman Naymark; Exec. Dir. Michael Papo.

COLORADO

DENVER

ALLIED JEWISH FEDERATION OF DENVER (1936); (sponsors ALLIED JEWISH CAMPAIGN); 300 S. Dahlia St. (80222); (303)321-3399. Pres. Jerry Carr; Exec. Dir. Sheldon Steinhauser.

CONNECTICUT

BRIDGEPORT

JEWISH FEDERATION OF GREATER BRIDGEPORT, INC. (1936; reorg. 1981); (sponsors UNITED JEWISH CAMPAIGN); 4200 Park Ave. (06604); (203)372-6504. Pres. Joel Lichtenstein; Exec. Dir. Gerald A. Kleinman.

DANBURY

JEWISH FEDERATION OF GREATER DANBURY (1945); 54 Main St., Suite E (06810); (203)792-6353. Pres. Melvin Pollack.

EASTERN CONNECTICUT

JEWISH FEDERATION OF EASTERN CONNECTICUT, INC. (1950; inc. 1970); 1 Bulkeley Place, New London (06320); (203)442-8062. Pres. Harold Weiner; Exec. Dir. Jerome Fischer.

GREENWICH

GREENWICH JEWISH FEDERATION (1956); 22 W. Putnam Ave., Suite 18 (06830); (203)-622-1434. Pres.'s Robert Mann, Joan Mann; Exec. Dir. Jay Yoskowitz.

HARTFORD

GREATER HARTFORD JEWISH FEDERATION (1945); 333 Bloomfield Ave., W. Hartford (06117); (203)232-2483. Pres. Philip D. Feltman; Exec. Dir. Don Cooper.

NEW HAVEN

NEW HAVEN JEWISH FEDERATION (1928); 419 Whalley Ave. (06511); (203)562-2137. Pres. Dr. Milton Wallack; Exec. Dir. Susan Shimelman.

NORWALK

JEWISH FEDERATION OF GREATER NORWALK, INC. (1946; reorg. 1964); Shorehaven Rd., E. Norwalk (06855); (203)853-3440. Pres. Nancy Oberst.

STAMFORD

UNITED JEWISH FEDERATION (inc. 1973); 1035 Newfield Ave., PO Box 3038 (06905); (203)322-6935. Pres. Melvin Goldstein; Exec. Dir. Debra Stein.

WATERBURY

JEWISH FEDERATION OF WATERBURY, INC. (1938); 1020 Country Club Rd. (06708); (203)758-2441. Pres. Dr. Jerome Sugar; Exec. Dir. Eli J. Skora.

DELAWARE

WILMINGTON

JEWISH FEDERATION OF DELAWARE, INC. (1934); 101 Garden of Eden Rd. (19803); (302)478-6200. Pres. Martin Mand; Exec. V. Pres. Robert Kerbel.

DISTRICT OF COLUMBIA

WASHINGTON

UNITED JEWISH APPEAL–FEDERATION OF GREATER WASHINGTON, INC. (1935); 7900

Wisconsin Ave., Bethesda, MD (20814-3698); (301)652-6480. Pres. Paul S. Berger; Exec. V. Pres. Ted Farber.

FLORIDA

DAYTONA BEACH
JEWISH FEDERATION OF VOLUSIA & FLAGLER COUNTIES, INC.; 533 Seabreeze Blvd. (32018-3916); (904)255-6260. Pres. Dr. Leonard Indianer; Exec. Dir. Iris Gardener.

FT. LAUDERDALE
JEWISH FEDERATION OF GREATER FT. LAUDERDALE (1968); 8358 W. Oakland Pk. Blvd. (33321); (305)748-8400. Pres. Brian Sherr; Exec. Dir. Kenneth Bierman.

JACKSONVILLE
JACKSONVILLE JEWISH FEDERATION (1935); 10829 Old St. Augustine Rd. (32223); (904)262-2800. Pres. Aaron M. Scharf.

LEE COUNTY
JEWISH FEDERATION OF LEE COUNTY (1974); 3628 Evans Ave., Ft. Myers (33901); (813)275-3554. Pres. Sheila Laboda.

MIAMI
GREATER MIAMI JEWISH FEDERATION, INC. (1938); 4200 Biscayne Blvd. (33137); (305)576-4000. Pres. Aaron Podhurst; Exec. V. Pres. Myron J. Brodie.

ORLANDO
JEWISH FEDERATION OF GREATER ORLANDO (1949); 851 N. Maitland Ave., PO Box 1508, Maitland (32751); (305)645-5933. Pres. Susan Bierman.

PALM BEACH COUNTY
JEWISH FEDERATION OF PALM BEACH COUNTY, INC. (1938); 501 S. Flagler Dr., Suite 305, W. Palm Beach (33401); (305)-832-2120. Pres. Erwin Blonder; Exec. Dir. Jeffrey L. Klein.

PINELLAS COUNTY (incl. Clearwater and St. Petersburg)
JEWISH FEDERATION OF PINELLAS COUNTY, INC. (1950; reincorp. 1974); 301 S. Jupiter Ave., Clearwater (33515); (813)446-1033. Pres. Stanley Newmark; Exec. Dir. Paul Levine.

SARASOTA
SARASOTA-MANATEE JEWISH FEDERATION (1959); 580 S. McIntosh Rd. (33582); (813)-371-4546. Pres. Adolph Shapiro; Exec. Dir. Jack Weintraub.

SOUTH BROWARD
JEWISH FEDERATION OF SOUTH BROWARD, INC. (1943); 2719 Hollywood Blvd., Hollywood (33020); (305)921-8810. Pres. Dr. Saul Singer; Exec. Dir. Sumner G. Kaye.

SOUTH COUNTY
SOUTH COUNTY JEWISH FEDERATION (inc. 1979); 336 NW Spanish River Blvd., Boca Raton (33431); (305)368-2737. Pres. James Nobil; Exec. Dir. Rabbi Bruce S. Warshal.

TAMPA
TAMPA JEWISH FEDERATION (1941); 2808 Horatio (33609); (813)875-1618. Pres. Douglas Cohn; Exec. Dir. Gary S. Alter.

GEORGIA

ATLANTA
ATLANTA JEWISH FEDERATION, INC. (1905; reorg. 1967); 1753 Peachtree Rd. NE (30309); (404)873-1661. Pres. Betty R. Jacobson; Exec. Dir. David I. Sarnat.

AUGUSTA
AUGUSTA JEWISH FEDERATION (1937); PO Box 3251, Sibley Rd. (30904); (404)736-1818. Pres. Dr. Michael Cohen; Exec. Dir. Louis Goldman.

COLUMBUS
JEWISH WELFARE FEDERATION OF COLUMBUS, INC. (1941); PO Box 6313 (31907); (404)568-6668. Pres. Charles Levy; Sec. Irene Rainbow.

SAVANNAH
SAVANNAH JEWISH COUNCIL (1943); (sponsors UJA-FEDERATION CAMPAIGN); PO Box 23527 (31403); (912)355-8111. Pres. Millie Melaver; Exec. Dir. Stan Ramati.

ILLINOIS

CHAMPAIGN-URBANA
CHAMPAIGN-URBANA JEWISH FEDERATION (member Central Illinois Jewish Federation) (1929); 503 E. John St., Champaign (61820); (217)367-9872. Pres. Daniel Bloomfield; Exec. Sec. Annette Glaser.

CHICAGO
JEWISH FEDERATION OF METROPOLITAN CHICAGO (1900); 1 S. Franklin St. (60606); (312)346-6700. Pres. Richard L. Wexler; Exec. Dir. Dr. Steven B. Nasatir.

JEWISH UNITED FUND OF METROPOLITAN CHICAGO (1968); 1 S. Franklin St. (60606);

(312)346-6700. Pres. Richard L. Wexler; Exec. Dir. Dr. Steven B. Nasatir.

DECATUR

DECATUR JEWISH FEDERATION (member Central Illinois Jewish Federation) (1942); c/o Temple B'nai Abraham, 1326 W. Eldorado (62522); (217)429-5740. Pres. Cheri Kalvort; Treas. Marvin Tick.

ELGIN

ELGIN AREA JEWISH WELFARE CHEST (1938); 330 Division St. (60120); (312)741-5656. Pres. Charles Zimmerman; Treas. Stuart Hanfling.

PEORIA

JEWISH FEDERATION OF PEORIA (1933; inc. 1947); 3100 N. Knoxville, Suite 17 (61603); (309)686-0611. Pres. Dr. Charles Enda; Exec. Dir. Marilyn Weigensberg.

QUAD CITIES

JEWISH FEDERATION OF THE QUAD CITIES (incl. Rock Island, Moline, Davenport, Bettendorf) (1938; comb. 1973); 224 18 St., Suite 511, Rock Island (61201); (309)793-1300. Pres. Sam Gilman; Exec. Dir. Ida Kramer.

ROCKFORD

ROCKFORD JEWISH COMMUNITY COUNCIL (1937); 1500 Parkview Ave. (61107); (815)-399-5497. Pres. Murray Monosoff; Exec. Dir. Tony Toback.

SOUTHERN ILLINOIS

JEWISH FEDERATION SERVING SOUTHERN ILLINOIS, SOUTHEASTERN MISSOURI AND WESTERN KENTUCKY (1941); 6464 W. Main, Suite 7A, Belleville (62223); (618)398-6100. Pres. Carol Korein; Exec. Dir. Jordan Harburger.

SPRINGFIELD

SPRINGFIELD JEWISH FEDERATION (1941); 730 E. Vine St. (62703); (217)528-3446. Pres. Gloria Schwartz; Exec. Dir. Lenore Loeb.

INDIANA

EVANSVILLE

EVANSVILLE JEWISH COMMUNITY COUNCIL, INC. (1936; inc. 1964); PO Box 5026 (47715); (812)477-7050. Pres. Alan Shovers; Exec. Sec. Maxine P. Fink.

FORT WAYNE

FORT WAYNE JEWISH FEDERATION (1921); 227 E. Washington Blvd. (46802); (219)422-8566. Pres. Lawrence Adelman; Acting Exec. Dir. Janet Latz.

INDIANAPOLIS

JEWISH WELFARE FEDERATION, INC. (1905); 615 N. Alabama St., Suite 412 (46204); (317)637-2473. Pres. Jerry Litwack; Exec. V. Pres. Harry Nadler.

LAFAYETTE

FEDERATED JEWISH CHARITIES (1924); PO Box 708 (47902); (317)742-9081. Pres. Arnold Cohen; Finan. Sec. Louis Pearlman, Jr.

MICHIGAN CITY

MICHIGAN CITY UNITED JEWISH WELFARE FUND; 2800 Franklin St. (46360); (219)874-4477. Treas. Harold Leinwand.

NORTHWEST INDIANA

THE JEWISH FEDERATION, INC. (1941; reorg. 1959); 2939 Jewett St., Highland (46322); (219)972-2251. Pres. Warren Yalowitz; Exec. Dir. Barnett Labowitz.

SOUTH BEND

JEWISH FEDERATION OF ST. JOSEPH VALLEY (1946); 804 Sherland Bldg. (46601); (219)233-1164. Pres. Dr. Joseph Wind; Exec. V. Pres. Bernard Natkow.

IOWA

DES MOINES

JEWISH FEDERATION OF GREATER DES MOINES (1914); 910 Polk Blvd. (50312); (515)277-6321. Pres. Dorothy Bucksbaum; Exec. Dir. Allan Eytan.

SIOUX CITY

JEWISH FEDERATION (1921); 525 14 St. (51105); (712)258-0618. Pres. Jack Bernstein; Exec. Dir. Doris Rosenthal.

KANSAS

WICHITA

MID-KANSAS JEWISH FEDERATION, INC. (1935); 400 N. Woodlawn, Suite 8 (67208); (316)686-4741. Pres. Hilary Zarnow; Exec. Dir. Nancy Matassarin.

KENTUCKY

LEXINGTON

CENTRAL KENTUCKY JEWISH FEDERATION (1976); 333 Waller, Suite 5 (40504); (606)-252-7622. Pres. Gail Cohen; Admin. Linda Ravvin.

LOUISVILLE

JEWISH COMMUNITY FEDERATION OF LOUISVILLE, INC. (1934); (sponsors UNITED JEWISH CAMPAIGN); PO Box 33035, 3630

Dutchman's Lane (40232); (502)451-8840. Pres. Michael Shaikun; Exec. Dir. Dr. Franklin Fogelson.

LOUISIANA

ALEXANDRIA
THE JEWISH WELFARE FEDERATION AND COMMUNITY COUNCIL OF CENTRAL LOUISIANA (1938); 1227 Southhampton (71303); (318)445-4785. Pres. Alvin Mykoff; Sec.-Treas. Roeve Weill.

BATON ROUGE
JEWISH FEDERATION OF GREATER BATON ROUGE (1971); 11744 Haymarket Ave., Suite B; P.O. Box 80827 (70898); (504)291-5895. Pres. Eleanor Fraenkel; Exec. Dir. Yigal Bander.

NEW ORLEANS
JEWISH FEDERATION OF GREATER NEW ORLEANS (1913; reorg. 1977); 1539 Jackson Ave. (70130); (504)525-0673. Pres. Donald Mintz; Exec. Dir. Jane Buchsbaum.

SHREVEPORT
SHREVEPORT JEWISH FEDERATION (1941; inc. 1967); 2030 Line Ave. (71104); (318)-221-4129. Pres. Melvin Goldberg; Exec. Dir. Monty Pomm.

MAINE

LEWISTON-AUBURN
LEWISTON-AUBURN JEWISH FEDERATION (1947); (sponsors UNITED JEWISH APPEAL); 74 Bradman St., Auburn (04210); (207)786-4201. Pres. Joel Goodman.

PORTLAND
JEWISH FEDERATION COMMUNITY COUNCIL OF SOUTHERN MAINE (1942); (sponsors UNITED JEWISH APPEAL); 57 Ashmont St. (04103); (207)773-7254. Pres. Harvey Berman; Admin. Cecelia Levine.

MARYLAND

BALTIMORE
ASSOCIATED JEWISH CHARITIES & WELFARE FUND, INC. (a merger of the Associated Jewish Charities & Jewish Welfare Fund) (1920; reorg. 1969); 101 W. Mt. Royal Ave. (21201); (301)727-4828. Chmn. Jonathan Kolker; Pres. Darrell D. Friedman.

MASSACHUSETTS

BERKSHIRE COUNTY
JEWISH FEDERATION OF THE BERKSHIRES (1940); 235 East St., Pittsfield (01201); (413)-442-4360. Pres. Dr. Stuart Masters; Exec. Dir. Rhoda Kaminstein.

BOSTON
COMBINED JEWISH PHILANTHROPIES OF GREATER BOSTON, INC. (1895; reorg. 1961); 72 Franklin St. (02110); (617)542-8080. Pres. Arthur Katzenberg, Jr.; Exec. V. Pres. David H. Rosen.

FRAMINGHAM
GREATER FRAMINGHAM JEWISH FEDERATION (1968; inc. 1969); 76 Salem End Rd., Framingham Centre (01701); (617)879-3301. Pres. Beverly Nesson; Exec. Dir. Lawrence Lowenthal.

LEOMINSTER
LEOMINSTER JEWISH COMMUNITY COUNCIL, INC. (1939); 268 Washington St. (01453); (617)534-6121. Pres. Martin Shaeval; Sec.-Treas. Howard J. Rome.

NEW BEDFORD
JEWISH FEDERATION OF GREATER NEW BEDFORD, INC. (1938; inc. 1954); 467 Hawthorn St., N. Dartmouth (02747); (617)997-7471. Pres. Lilian Shwartz; Exec. Dir. Larry Katz.

NORTH SHORE
JEWISH FEDERATION OF THE NORTH SHORE, INC. (1938); 4 Community Rd., Marblehead (01945); (617)598-1810. Pres. Neil Cooper; Exec. Dir. Bruce Yudewitz.

SPRINGFIELD
JEWISH FEDERATION OF GREATER SPRINGFIELD, INC. (1925); (sponsors SJF/UJA CAMPAIGN); 1160 Dickinson (01108); (413)-737-4313. Pres. Jay Loevy; Exec. Dir. Joel Weiss.

WORCESTER
WORCESTER JEWISH FEDERATION, INC. (1947; inc. 1957); (sponsors JEWISH WELFARE FUND); 633 Salisbury St. (01609); (617)756-1543. Pres. Nancy Leavitt; Exec. Dir. Joseph Huber.

MICHIGAN

DETROIT
JEWISH WELFARE FEDERATION OF DETROIT (1899); (sponsors ALLIED JEWISH CAMPAIGN); Fred M. Butzel Memorial Bldg., 163 Madison (48226); (313)965-3939. Pres. Dr. Conrad L. Giles; Exec. V. Pres. Martin Kraar.

FLINT
FLINT JEWISH FEDERATION (1936); 619 Clifford St. (48502); (313)767-5922; Pres. Peter Goodstein; Exec. Dir. David Nussbaum.

GRAND RAPIDS
JEWISH COMMUNITY FUND OF GRAND RAPIDS (1930); 1410 Pontiac SE (49506); (616)452-6619. Pres. Joseph N. Schwartz; Admin. Dir. Barbara Kravitz.

MINNESOTA

DULUTH-SUPERIOR
JEWISH FEDERATION & COMMUNITY COUNCIL (1937); 1602 E. 2 St. (55812); (218)724-8857. Pres. Selma Goldish; Sec. Admin. Gloria Vitullo.

MINNEAPOLIS
MINNEAPOLIS FEDERATION FOR JEWISH SERVICE (1929; inc. 1930); 7600 Wayzata Blvd. (55426); (612)593-2600. Pres. Sheldon Levin; Exec. Dir. Herman Markowitz.

ST. PAUL
UNITED JEWISH FUND AND COUNCIL (1935); 790 S. Cleveland, Suite 201 (55116); (612)690-1707. Pres. Rhoda Mains; Exec. Dir. Robert M. Hyfler.

MISSISSIPPI

JACKSON
JACKSON JEWISH WELFARE FUND, INC. (1945); Beth Israel Cong., 5315 Old Canton Rd. (39211); (601)956-5215. Pres. Jonathan Larkin; V. Pres. Ruth Friedman.

MISSOURI

KANSAS CITY
JEWISH FEDERATION OF GREATER KANSAS CITY (1933); 25 E. 12 St., 10th fl. (64106); (816)421-5808. Pres. Suzanne Parelman; Exec. Dir. Sol Koenigsberg.

ST. JOSEPH
UNITED JEWISH FUND OF ST. JOSEPH (1915); 509 Woodcrest Dr. (64506); (816)-279-7154. Pres. Lou Silverglat; Exec. Sec. Martha Rothstein.

ST. LOUIS
JEWISH FEDERATION OF ST. LOUIS (incl. St. Louis County) (1901); 12 Millstone Campus Dr. (63146); (314)432-0020. Pres. Thomas Green; Exec. V. Pres. William Kahn.

NEBRASKA

LINCOLN
LINCOLN JEWISH WELFARE FEDERATION, INC. (1931; inc. 1961); PO Box 80014 (68501); (402)423-5695. Pres. Charles H. Coren; Exec. Dir. Robert Pitlor.

OMAHA
JEWISH FEDERATION OF OMAHA (1903); 333 S. 132 St. (68154-2198); (402)334-8200. Pres. Mort Trachtenbarg; Exec. V. Pres. Steven Rod.

NEVADA

LAS VEGAS
JEWISH FEDERATION OF LAS VEGAS (1973); 1030 E. Twain Ave. (89109); (702)732-0556. Pres. Arne Rosencrantz; Exec. Dir. Norman Kaufman.

NEW HAMPSHIRE

MANCHESTER
JEWISH FEDERATION OF GREATER MANCHESTER (1974); 698 Beech St. (03104); (603)627-7679. Pres. Gary Wallin; Exec. Dir. Earnest Siegel.

NEW JERSEY

ATLANTIC COUNTY
FEDERATION OF JEWISH AGENCIES OF ATLANTIC COUNTY (1924); 5321 Atlantic Ave., Ventnor City (08406); (609)822-7122. Pres. Irwin Yeagle; Exec. Dir. Bernard Cohen.

BERGEN COUNTY
UNITED JEWISH COMMUNITY OF BERGEN COUNTY (inc. 1978); 111 Kinderkamack Rd., PO Box 4176, N. Hackensack Station, River Edge (07661); (201)488-6800. Pres. Eli Warach; Exec. V. Pres. Dr. James Young.

CENTRAL NEW JERSEY
JEWISH FEDERATION OF CENTRAL NEW JERSEY (1940; merged 1973); (sponsors UNITED JEWISH CAMPAIGN); Green Lane, Union (07083); (201)351-5060. Pres. Richard Goldberger; Exec. V. Pres. Burton Lazarow.

CLIFTON-PASSAIC
JEWISH FEDERATION OF GREATER CLIFTON-PASSAIC (1933); (sponsors UNITED JEWISH CAMPAIGN); 199 Scoles Ave., Clifton (07012). (201)777-7031. Pres. Seymour Bitterman; Exec. Dir. Yosef Muskin.

JEWISH FEDERATIONS, FUNDS, COUNCILS / 421

CUMBERLAND COUNTY
JEWISH FEDERATION OF CUMBERLAND COUNTY (inc. 1971); (incl. JEWISH COMMUNITY COUNCIL and ALLIED JEWISH APPEAL); 629 Wood St., Suite 204, Vineland (08360); (609)696-4445. Pres. Ronald Macon; Exec. Dir. Gail Milgram Beitman.

ENGLEWOOD
(Merged with Bergen County)

JERSEY CITY
UNITED JEWISH APPEAL (1939); 71 Bentley Ave. (07304); (201)332-6644. Chmn. Mel Blum; Exec. Sec. Madeline Mazer.

MERCER COUNTY
JEWISH FEDERATION OF MERCER AND BUCKS COUNTIES NJ/PA (formerly Delaware Valley); (1929; reorg. 1982); 999 Lower Ferry Rd., Trenton (08628); (609)883-5000. Pres. Lionel A. Kaplan; Exec. Dir. Charles P. Epstein. (Also see listing under Pennsylvania.)

METROWEST NEW JERSEY
UNITED JEWISH FEDERATION OF METROWEST (1923); (sponsors UNITED JEWISH APPEAL); 60 Glenwood Ave., E. Orange (07017); (201)673-6800; (212)943-0570. Pres. James Schwarz; Exec. V. Pres. Howard Charish.

MIDDLESEX COUNTY
JEWISH FEDERATION OF GREATER MIDDLESEX COUNTY (formerly Northern Middlesex County and Raritan Valley) (org. 1948; reorg. 1985); (sponsors UNITED JEWISH APPEAL); 100 Metroplex Dr., Suite 101, Edison (08817); (201)985-1234. Pres. Alvin Rockoff; Exec. Dir. Michael Shapiro.

MONMOUTH COUNTY
JEWISH FEDERATION OF GREATER MONMOUTH COUNTY (formerly Shore Area) (1971); 100 Grant Ave., PO Box 210, Deal (07723-0210); (201)531-6200-1. Pres. Dr. Lawrence Karasic; Exec. Dir. Marvin Relkin.

MORRIS-SUSSEX COUNTY
(Merged with MetroWest NJ)

NORTH JERSEY
JEWISH FEDERATION OF NORTH JERSEY (formerly Jewish Community Council) (1933); (sponsors UNITED JEWISH APPEAL DRIVE); 1 Pike Dr., Wayne (07470); (201)-595-0555. Pres. Alvin Reisbaum; Exec. Dir. Barry Rosenberg.

NORTHERN MIDDLESEX COUNTY
(See Middlesex County)

OCEAN COUNTY
OCEAN COUNTY JEWISH FEDERATION (1977); 301 Madison Ave., Lakewood (08701); (201)363-0530. Pres. Marlene Perlmutter; Exec. Dir. Michael Ruvel.

RARITAN VALLEY
(See Middlesex County)

SOMERSET COUNTY
JEWISH FEDERATION OF SOMERSET COUNTY (1960); 120 Finderne Ave., Bridgewater (08807); (201)725-6994. Pres. Dr. Daniel Frimmer; Exec. Dir. Elaine Auerbach.

SOUTHERN NEW JERSEY
JEWISH FEDERATION OF SOUTHERN NEW JERSEY (incl. Camden, Burlington, and Gloucester Counties) (1922); (sponsors ALLIED JEWISH APPEAL); 2393 W. Marlton Pike, Cherry Hill (08002); (609)665-6100. Pres. Dr. Eugene Bass; Exec. V. Pres. Stuart Alperin.

NEW MEXICO

ALBUQUERQUE
JEWISH FEDERATION OF GREATER ALBUQUERQUE, INC. (1938); 12800 Lomas NE, Suite F (87112); (505)292-1061. Pres. Arthur Gardenswartz; Exec. Dir. Elisa M. Simon.

NEW YORK

ALBANY
(Merged with Schenectady; see Northeastern New York)

BROOME COUNTY
JEWISH FEDERATION OF BROOME COUNTY (1937; inc. 1958); 500 Clubhouse Rd., Binghamton (13903); (607)724-2332. Pres. Victoria Rouff; Exec. Dir. Mark Steiner.

BUFFALO
JEWISH FEDERATION OF GREATER BUFFALO, INC. (1903); (sponsors UNITED JEWISH FUND CAMPAIGN); 787 Delaware Ave. (14209); (716)886-7750. Pres. Joel Lippman; Exec. Dir. Harry Kosansky.

422 / AMERICAN JEWISH YEAR BOOK, 1987

ELMIRA

ELMIRA JEWISH WELFARE FUND, INC. (1942); PO Box 3087 (14905); (607)734-8122. Pres. Kurt Wohl; Exec. Dir. Cy Leveen.

KINGSTON

JEWISH FEDERATION OF GREATER KINGSTON, INC. (inc. 1951); 159 Green St. (12401); (914)338-8131. Pres. Jay A. Kaplan.

NEW YORK

UJA-FEDERATION OF JEWISH PHILANTHROPIES OF NEW YORK, INC. (incl. Greater NY; Westchester, Nassau, and Suffolk Counties) (Fed. org. 1917; UJA 1939; merged 1986); 130 E. 59 St. (10022); (212)980-1000. Pres. Peggy Tishman; Bd. Chmn. Morton A. Kornreich; Exec. V. Pres.'s Ernest W. Michel, Stephen D. Solender.

NIAGARA FALLS

JEWISH FEDERATION OF NIAGARA FALLS, NY, INC. (1935); Temple Beth Israel, Rm. #5, College & Madison Ave. (14305); (716)-284-4575. Pres. Howard Kushner; Exec. Dir. Linda Boxer.

NORTHEASTERN NEW YORK

UNITED JEWISH FEDERATION OF NORTHEASTERN NEW YORK (formerly Albany and Schenectady) (1986); Latham Circle Mall, 800 New Loudon Rd., Latham (12110); (518)783-7800. Pres. Malka Evans; Exec. Dir. Norman J. Schimelman.

ORANGE COUNTY

JEWISH FEDERATION OF GREATER ORANGE COUNTY (1977); 360 Powell Ave., Newburgh (12550); (914)562-7860. Pres. Harold Levine; Exec. Dir. Marilyn Chandler.

ROCHESTER

JEWISH COMMUNITY FEDERATION OF ROCHESTER, NY, INC. (1939); 441 East Ave. (14607); (716)461-0490. Pres. Paul Goldberg; Exec. Dir. Avrom Fox.

ROCKLAND COUNTY

UNITED JEWISH COMMUNITY OF ROCKLAND COUNTY (1985); 300 N. Main St., Suite 311, Spring Valley (10977); (914)352-7100. Pres. Dr. William Schwartz; Exec. Dir. Robert Posner.

SCHENECTADY

(Merged with Albany; see Northeastern New York)

SYRACUSE

SYRACUSE JEWISH FEDERATION, INC. (1918); 2223 E. Genesee St., PO Box 510, DeWitt (13214); (315)422-4104. Pres. Gerald Meyer; Exec. V. Pres. Barry Silverberg.

TROY

TROY JEWISH COMMUNITY COUNCIL, INC. (1936); 2430 21 St. (12180); (518)274-0700. Pres. Oscar Wax.

UTICA

JEWISH FEDERATION OF UTICA, NY, INC. (1933; inc. 1950); (sponsors UNITED JEWISH APPEAL OF UTICA); 2310 Oneida St. (13501); (315)733-2343. Pres. R. Robert Sossen; Exec. Dir. Meyer L. Bodoff.

NORTH CAROLINA

ASHEVILLE

WESTERN NORTH CAROLINA JEWISH FEDERATION (1935); 236 Charlotte St. (28801); (704)253-0701. Pres. Abe Freedman; Admin. Ellen Sandweiss-Hodges.

CHARLOTTE

CHARLOTTE JEWISH FEDERATION (1938); PO Box 13369 (28211); (704)366-5007. Pres. Ron Katz.

DURHAM-CHAPEL HILL

DURHAM-CHAPEL HILL JEWISH FEDERATION & COMMUNITY COUNCIL (1979); 205 Mt. Bolus Rd., Chapel Hill (27514); (919)-967-6916. Pres. Lee M. Marcus.

GREENSBORO

GREENSBORO JEWISH FEDERATION (1940); 713A N. Greene St. (27401); (919)272-3189. Pres. Joel Liebling; Exec. Dir. Sherman Harris.

OHIO

AKRON

AKRON JEWISH COMMUNITY FEDERATION (1935); 750 White Pond Dr. (44320); (216)-867-7850. Pres. Martin Spector; Exec. Dir. Stanley H. Bard.

CANTON

CANTON JEWISH COMMUNITY FEDERATION (1935; reorg. 1955); 2631 Harvard Ave., NW (44709); (216)452-6444. Pres. Stanley Greenwald; Exec. Dir. Jay Rubin.

CINCINNATI

JEWISH FEDERATION OF CINCINNATI (merger of the Associated Jewish Agencies and Jewish Welfare Fund) (1896; reorg. 1967); 1811 Losantiville, Suite 320 (45237); (513)351-3800. Pres. Robert M. Blatt; Exec. V. Pres. Aubrey Herman.

CLEVELAND

JEWISH COMMUNITY FEDERATION OF CLEVELAND (1903); 1750 Euclid Ave. (44115); (216)566-9200. Pres. Amb. Milton A. Wolf; Exec. Dir. Stephen H. Hoffman.

COLUMBUS

COLUMBUS JEWISH FEDERATION (1926); 1175 College Ave. (43209); (614)237-7686. Pres. Miriam Yenkin; Exec. Dir. Alan Gill.

DAYTON

JEWISH FEDERATION OF GREATER DAYTON (1910); 4501 Denlinger Rd. (45426); (513)854-4150. Pres. Charles Abramovitz; Exec. V. Pres. Peter Wells.

STEUBENVILLE

JEWISH COMMUNITY COUNCIL (1938); PO Box 472 (43952); (614)282-9031. Pres. Morris Denmark; Exec. Sec. Mrs. Joseph Freedman.

TOLEDO

JEWISH FEDERATION OF GREATER TOLEDO (1907; reorg. 1960); 6505 Sylvania Ave., PO Box 587, Sylvania (43560); (419)885-4461. Pres. Robert Gersten; Exec. Dir. Steven J. Edelstein.

YOUNGSTOWN

YOUNGSTOWN AREA JEWISH FEDERATION (1935); PO Box 449, 505 Gypsy Lane (44501); (216)746-3251. Pres. Lawrence Heselov; Exec. V. Pres. Sam Kooperman.

OKLAHOMA

OKLAHOMA CITY

JEWISH FEDERATION OF GREATER OKLAHOMA CITY (1941); 3022 NW Expressway #116 (73112); (405)949-0111. Pres. Robert Heiman; Exec. Dir. Garth Potts.

TULSA

JEWISH FEDERATION OF TULSA (1938); (sponsors UNITED JEWISH CAMPAIGN); 2021 E. 71 St. (74136); (918)495-1100. Pres. Susan Fenster; Exec. Dir. David Bernstein.

OREGON

PORTLAND

JEWISH FEDERATION OF PORTLAND (incl. state of Oregon and adjacent Washington communities) (1920; reorg. 1956); 6651 SW Capitol Highway (97219); (503)245-6219. Pres. Harold Pollin; Acting Exec. Dir. Laurie Rogoway.

PENNSYLVANIA

ALTOONA

FEDERATION OF JEWISH PHILANTHROPIES (1920; reorg. 1940; inc. 1944); 1308 17 St. (16601); (814)944-4072. Pres. Morley Cohn.

BUCKS COUNTY

JEWISH FEDERATION OF MERCER AND BUCKS COUNTIES NJ/PA (formerly Delaware Valley); (1929; reorg. 1982); 999 Lower Ferry Rd., Trenton, NJ (08628); (609)883-5000. Pres. Lionel A. Kaplan; Exec. Dir. Charles P. Epstein. (Also see listing under New Jersey.)

ERIE

JEWISH COMMUNITY COUNCIL OF ERIE (1946); 701 G. Daniel Baldwin Bldg., 1001 State St. (16501); (814)455-4474. Pres. Joan Harf.

HARRISBURG

UNITED JEWISH FEDERATION OF GREATER HARRISBURG (1941); 100 Vaughn St. (17110); (717)236-9555. Pres. Harris Freedman; Exec. Dir. Elliot Gershenson.

JOHNSTOWN

UNITED JEWISH FEDERATION OF JOHNSTOWN (1938); 922 Windan Lane (15905); (814)535-6756. Pres. I. Samuel Kaminsky.

PHILADELPHIA

FEDERATION OF JEWISH AGENCIES OF GREATER PHILADELPHIA (1901; reorg. 1956); 226 S. 16 St. (19102); (215)893-5600. Pres. Bennett Aaron; Exec. V. Pres. Robert Forman.

PITTSBURGH

UNITED JEWISH FEDERATION OF GREATER PITTSBURGH (1912; reorg. 1955); 234 McKee Pl. (15213); (412)681-8000. Pres. Leon L. Netzer; Exec. V. Pres. Howard Rieger.

READING

JEWISH FEDERATION OF READING, PA., INC. (1935; reorg. 1972); (sponsors UNITED JEWISH CAMPAIGN); 1700 City Line St. (19604); (215)921-2766. Pres. George Viener; Exec. Dir. Daniel Tannenbaum.

SCRANTON

SCRANTON-LACKAWANNA JEWISH FEDERATION (incl. Lackawanna County) (1945);

601 Jefferson Ave. (18510); (717)961-2300. Pres. Dr. Alvin Greenwald; Exec. Dir. Seymour Brotman.

WILKES-BARRE
JEWISH FEDERATION OF GREATER WILKES-BARRE (1935); (sponsors UNITED JEWISH CAMPAIGN); 60 S. River St. (18702); (717)-822-4146. Pres. Dr. David Greenwald.

RHODE ISLAND

PROVIDENCE
JEWISH FEDERATION OF RHODE ISLAND (1945); 130 Sessions St. (02906); (401)421-4111. Pres. Charles Samdperil; Exec. V. Pres. Elliot Cohan.

SOUTH CAROLINA

CHARLESTON
CHARLESTON JEWISH FEDERATION (1949); 1645 Raoul Wallenberg Blvd., PO Box 31298 (29407); (803)571-6565. Pres. Herb Rosner; Exec. Dir. Michael Wise.

COLUMBIA
COLUMBIA UNITED JEWISH WELFARE FEDERATION (1960); 4540 Trenholm Rd., PO Box 6968 (29206); (803)787-2023. Pres. Samuel Jay Tenenbaum; Exec. Dir. Alex Grossberg.

SOUTH DAKOTA

SIOUX FALLS
JEWISH WELFARE FUND (1938); National Reserve Bldg., 513 S. Main Ave. (57102); (605)336-2880. Pres. Laurence Bierman; Exec. Sec. Louis R. Hurwitz.

TENNESSEE

CHATTANOOGA
CHATTANOOGA JEWISH FEDERATION (1931); 5326 Lynnland Terrace, PO Box 8947 (37411); (615)894-1317. Pres. Robert Siskin; Exec. Dir. Morris Rombro.

KNOXVILLE
KNOXVILLE JEWISH FEDERATION (1939); 6800 Deane Hill Dr., PO Box 10882 (37919); (615)693-5837. Pres. Mitchell Robinson.

MEMPHIS
MEMPHIS JEWISH FEDERATION (incl. Shelby County) (1935); 6560 Poplar Ave., PO Box 38268 (38138); (901)767-7100. Pres. Arthur Malkin, Jr.; Exec. Dir. Leslie Gottlieb.

NASHVILLE
JEWISH FEDERATION OF NASHVILLE & MIDDLE TENNESSEE (1936); 801 Perry Warner Blvd. (37205); (615)356-3242. Pres. David Steine, Jr.; Exec. Dir. Dr. Jay M. Pilzer.

TEXAS

AUSTIN
JEWISH COMMUNITY COUNCIL OF AUSTIN (1939; reorg. 1956); 11713 Jollyville Rd. (78759); (512)331-1144. Pres. Alan Sager; Exec. Dir. Marilyn Stahl.

CORPUS CHRISTI
COMBINED JEWISH APPEAL OF CORPUS CHRISTI (1962); 750 Everhart Rd. (78411); (512)855-6239. Pres. Jack Solka; Exec. Dir. Andrew Lipman.

CORPUS CHRISTI JEWISH COMMUNITY COUNCIL (1953); 750 Everhart Rd. (78411); (512)855-6239. Pres. Rona Train; Exec. Dir. Andrew Lipman.

DALLAS
JEWISH FEDERATION OF GREATER DALLAS (1911); 7800 Northaven Rd., Suite A (75230); (214)369-3313. Pres. Harold Kleinman; Exec. Dir. Morris A. Stein.

EL PASO
JEWISH FEDERATION OF EL PASO, INC. (incl. surrounding communities) (1937); 405 Mardi Gras, PO Box 12097 (79913-0097); (915)584-4437. Pres. Beth Lipson; Exec. Dir. Abraham Wasserberger.

FORT WORTH
JEWISH FEDERATION OF FORT WORTH AND TARRANT COUNTY (1936); 6801 Dan Danciger Rd. (76133); (817)292-3081. Pres. Bernard Appel; Exec. Dir. Harvey Freiman.

GALVESTON
GALVESTON COUNTY JEWISH WELFARE ASSOCIATION (1936); PO Box 146 (77553); (409)763-5241. Pres. Dr. Sidney Kay; Treas. Harold Levine.

HOUSTON
JEWISH FEDERATION OF GREATER HOUSTON (1936); 5603 S. Braeswood Blvd. (77096); (713)729-7000. Pres. Harold Raizes; Exec. Dir. Hans Mayer.

SAN ANTONIO
JEWISH FEDERATION OF SAN ANTONIO (incl. Bexar County) (1922); 8434 Ahern Dr.

(78216); (512)341-8234. Pres. Russell Davis; Exec. Dir. Alan Bayer.

WACO
JEWISH FEDERATION OF WACO AND CENTRAL TEXAS (1949); PO Box 8031 (76714-8031); (817)776-3740. Pres. Simone Bauer; Exec. Sec. Martha Bauer.

UTAH

SALT LAKE CITY
UNITED JEWISH COUNCIL AND SALT LAKE JEWISH WELFARE FUND (1936); 2416 E. 1700 S. (84108); (801)581-0098. Pres. Richard Rappaport; Exec. Dir. Bernard Solomon.

VIRGINIA

NEWPORT NEWS—HAMPTON—WILLIAMSBURG
UNITED JEWISH COMMUNITY OF THE VIRGINIA PENINSULA, INC. (1942); 2700 Spring Rd., Newport News (23606); (804)595-5544. Pres. Rhoda Mazur; Exec. Dir. Norman Olshansky.

RICHMOND
JEWISH COMMUNITY FEDERATION OF RICHMOND (1935); 5403 Monument Ave., PO Box 8237 (23226); (804)288-0045. Pres. Jay Weinberg; Exec. Dir. Robert Hyman.

ROANOKE
JEWISH COMMUNITY COUNCIL (1974); PO Box 1074 (24005). Chmn. Albert Lippmann.

TIDEWATER
UNITED JEWISH FEDERATION OF TIDEWATER (incl. Norfolk, Portsmouth, and Virginia Beach) (1937); 7300 Newport Ave., PO Box 9776, Norfolk (23505); (804)489-8040. Pres. Dr. Sanford Lefcoe; Exec. Dir. A. Robert Gast.

WASHINGTON

SEATTLE
JEWISH FEDERATION OF GREATER SEATTLE (incl. King County, Everett, and Bremerton) (1926); 510 Securities Bldg., 1904 Third Ave. (98101); (206)622-8211. Pres. Herman Sarkowsky; Exec. Dir. Rabbi Melvin Libman.

WEST VIRGINIA

CHARLESTON
FEDERATED JEWISH CHARITIES OF CHARLESTON, INC. (1937); PO Box 1613 (25326); (304)346-7500. Pres. Alvin Preiser; Exec. Sec. William H. Thalheimer.

WISCONSIN

KENOSHA
KENOSHA JEWISH WELFARE FUND (1938); 6537 Seventh Ave. (53140); (414)658-8635. Pres. Nathaniel S. Lepp; Sec.-Treas. Mrs. S. M. Lapp.

MADISON
MADISON JEWISH COMMUNITY COUNCIL, INC. (1940); 310 N. Midvale Blvd., Suite 325 (53705); (608)231-3426. Pres. Louis Swedarsky; Exec. Dir. Steven Morrison.

MILWAUKEE
MILWAUKEE JEWISH FEDERATION, INC. (1902); 1360 N. Prospect Ave. (53202); (414)-271-8338. Pres. Alan Crawford; Exec. Dir. Robert Aronson.

RACINE
RACINE JEWISH WELFARE COUNCIL (1946); 944 S. Main St. (53403); (414)633-7093. Chmn. Arthur Schaefer.

CANADA

ALBERTA

CALGARY
CALGARY JEWISH COMMUNITY COUNCIL (1962); 1607 90th Ave. SW (T2V 4V7); (403)-253-8600. Pres. Morris Dancyger; Exec. Dir. Drew Staffenberg.

EDMONTON
JEWISH FEDERATION OF EDMONTON (1954; reorg. 1982); 7200 156 St. (T5R 1X3); (403)-487-5120. Pres. Judith Goldsand; Exec. Dir. Howard Bloom.

BRITISH COLUMBIA

VANCOUVER
JEWISH FEDERATION OF GREATER VANCOUVER (1932); 950 W. 41 Ave. (V5Z 2N7); (604)266-8371. Pres. Ronald Coleman; Exec. Dir. Steve Drysdale.

MANITOBA

WINNIPEG
WINNIPEG JEWISH COMMUNITY COUNCIL (1938; reorg. 1973); (sponsors COMBINED JEWISH APPEAL OF WINNIPEG); 370 Har-

grave St. (R3B 2K1); (204)943-0406. Pres. Evelyn Katz; Exec. Dir. Robert Freedman.

ONTARIO

HAMILTON

HAMILTON JEWISH FEDERATION (1932; merged 1971); (sponsors UNITED JEWISH WELFARE FUND); 57 Delaware Ave. (L8M 1T6); (416)528-8570. Pres. Andrea Stringer; Exec. Dir. Sid Brail.

LONDON

LONDON JEWISH COMMUNITY COUNCIL (1932); 536 Huron St. (N5Y 4J5); (519)673-3310. Pres. Allan Richman; Exec. Dir. Gerald Enchin.

OTTAWA

JEWISH COMMUNITY COUNCIL OF OTTAWA (1934); 151 Chapel St. (K1N 7Y2); (613)-232-7306. Pres. Gerald Berger; Exec. Dir. Gittel Tatz.

TORONTO

TORONTO JEWISH CONGRESS (1937); 4600 Bathurst St.; Willowdale (M2R 3V2); (416)-635-2883. Pres. Ronald Appleby; Exec. Dir. Steven Ain.

WINDSOR

JEWISH COMMUNITY COUNCIL (1938); 1641 Ouellette Ave. (N8X 1K9); (519)973-1772. Pres. Richard Rosenthal; Exec. Dir. Joseph Eisenberg.

QUEBEC

MONTREAL

ALLIED JEWISH COMMUNITY SERVICES (1965); 5151 Cote St. Catherine Rd. (H3W 1M6); (514)735-3541. Pres. Carl Laxer; Exec. Dir. John Fishel.

Jewish Periodicals[1]

UNITED STATES

ARIZONA

ARIZONA POST (1946). 102 N. Plumer Ave., Tucson, 85719. (602)791-9962. Sandra R. Heiman. Fortnightly. Jewish Federation of S. Arizona.

GREATER PHOENIX JEWISH NEWS (1947). PO Box 26590. Phoenix, 85068. (602)870-9470. Flo Eckstein. Weekly.

CALIFORNIA

B'NAI B'RITH MESSENGER (1897). 2510 W. 7 St., Los Angeles, 90057. (213)380-5000. Rabbi Yale Butler. Weekly.

B'NAI B'RITH MESSENGER-Bay Area Edition (1986). 904 Irving St., Suite 236, San Francisco, 94122. (415)387-1744. Janet Gallin. Monthly.

HERITAGE-SOUTHWEST JEWISH PRESS (1914). 2130 S. Vermont Ave., Los Angeles, 90007. Dan Brin. Weekly. (Also SAN DIEGO JEWISH PRESS-HERITAGE, San Diego [weekly]; CENTRAL CALIFORNIA JEWISH HERITAGE, Sacramento and Fresno area [monthly]; ORANGE COUNTY JEWISH HERITAGE, Orange County area [weekly].)

JEWISH JOURNAL (1986). 3660 Wilshire Blvd., Suite 204, Los Angeles, 90010. (213)738-7778. Gene Lichtenstein. Weekly.

JEWISH SPECTATOR (1935). PO Box 2016, Santa Monica, 90406. (213)393-9063. Trude Weiss-Rosmarin. Quarterly.

JEWISH STAR (1956). 109 Minna St., Suite 323, San Francisco, 94105. (415)421-4874. Nevon Stuckey. Bimonthly.

NATIONAL JEWISH DAILY AND ISRAEL TODAY (1973). 6742 Van Nuys Blvd., Van Nuys, 91405. (818)786-4000. Phil Blazer. Daily.

NORTHERN CALIFORNIA JEWISH BULLETIN (1946). 121 Steuart St., Suite 302, San Francisco, 94105. (415)957-9340. Marc Klein. Weekly. San Francisco Jewish Community Publications.

SAN DIEGO JEWISH TIMES (1979). 2592 Fletcher Pkwy., El Cajon, 92020. (619)-463-5515. Carol Rosenberg. Biweekly.

WESTERN STATES JEWISH HISTORY (1968). 2429 23 St., Santa Monica, 90405. (213)-450-2946. Norton B. Stern. Quarterly. Western States Jewish History Association.

COLORADO

INTERMOUNTAIN JEWISH NEWS (1913). 1275 Sherman St., Suite 215–217, Denver, 80203. (303)861-2234. Miriam H. Goldberg. Weekly.

CONNECTICUT

CONNECTICUT JEWISH LEDGER (1929). PO Box 1688, Hartford, 06101. (203)233-2148. Berthold Gaster. Weekly.

DISTRICT OF COLUMBIA

ALERT (1970). 1411 K St., NW, Suite 402, Washington, 20005. (202)393-4117. Nurit Erger. Monthly. Union of Councils for Soviet Jews.

B'NAI B'RITH INTERNATIONAL JEWISH MONTHLY (1886 under the name MENORAH). 1640 Rhode Island Ave., NW,

---

[1] The information in this directory is based on replies to questionnaires circulated by the editors. For organization bulletins, see the directory of Jewish organizations.

Washington, 20036. (202)857-6645. Marc Silver. Ten times a year. B'nai B'rith.

JEWISH VETERAN (1896). 1811 R St., NW, Washington, 20009. (202)265-6280. Pearl Laufer. Irregularly. Jewish War Veterans of the U.S.A.

NEAR EAST REPORT (1957). 500 N. Capitol St., NW, Suite 307, Washington, 20001. (202)638-1225. Eric Rozenman. Weekly. Near East Research, Inc.

WASHINGTON JEWISH WEEK (1965). 1317 F St., NW, Washington, 20004. (202)783-7200. Lisa S. Lenkiewicz, Judith S. Deutsch. Weekly.

FLORIDA

JEWISH FLORIDIAN GROUP (1927). PO Box 012973, Miami, 33101. (305)373-4605. Fred K. Shochet. Weekly.

JEWISH JOURNAL (1977). PO Box 23909, Ft. Lauderdale, 33307. (305)563-3200. Dorothy P. Rubin. Weekly.

PALM BEACH JEWISH WORLD (1982). 2405 Mercer Ave., W. Palm Beach, 33401. (305)833-8331. Martin Pomerance. Weekly.

SOUTHERN JEWISH WEEKLY (1924). PO Box 3297, Jacksonville, 32206. (904)634-1812. Ronald A. Miller. Weekly.

GEORGIA

ATLANTA JEWISH TIMES (formerly SOUTHERN ISRAELITE). PO Box 250287, Atlanta, 30325. (404)355-6139. Vida Goldgar. Weekly.

JEWISH CIVIC PRESS (1965). 3179 Maple Dr. NE, Atlanta, 30305. (404)262-6786. Abner Tritt. Monthly.

ILLINOIS

CHICAGO JUF NEWS (1972). 1 S. Franklin St., Chicago, 60606. (312)444-2853. Joseph Aaron. Monthly. Jewish Federation of Metropolitan Chicago.

JEWISH COMMUNITY NEWS (1945). 6464 W. Main, Suite 7A, Belleville, 62223. (618)-398-6100. Jordan Harburger. Bimonthly. Jewish Federation of Southern Illinois.

SENTINEL (1911). 323 S. Franklin St., Chicago, 60606. (312)663-1101. J. I. Fishbein. Weekly.

INDIANA

ILLIANA NEWS (1975). 2939 Jewett St., Highland, 46307. (219)972-2250. Barnett Labowitz. Ten times a year. Jewish Federation, Inc. of Northwest Indiana.

INDIANA JEWISH POST AND OPINION (1935). PO Box 449097, Indianapolis, 46202. (317)927-7800. Gabriel Cohen. Weekly.

NATIONAL JEWISH POST AND OPINION. PO Box 449097, Indianapolis, 46202. (317)-927-7800. Gabriel Cohen. Weekly.

KENTUCKY

KENTUCKY JEWISH POST AND OPINION (1931). 1551 Bardstown Rd., Louisville, 40205. (502)459-1914. Lisa Shaikun. Weekly.

LOUISIANA

JEWISH CIVIC PRESS (1965). PO Box 15500, 924 Valmont St., New Orleans, 70115. (504)895-8784. Abner Tritt. Monthly.

JEWISH TIMES (1974). 1539 Jackson Ave., Suite 323, New Orleans, 70130. (504)524-3147. Fred Shochet, Leah Paller. Biweekly.

MARYLAND

BALTIMORE JEWISH TIMES (1919). 2104 N. Charles St., Baltimore, 21218. (301)752-3504. Gary Rosenblatt. Weekly.

MASSACHUSETTS

AMERICAN JEWISH HISTORY (1893). 2 Thornton Rd., Waltham, 02154. (617)891-8110. Marc Lee Raphael. Quarterly. American Jewish Historical Society.

BOSTON JEWISH TIMES (1945). Box 18427, Boston, 02118. (617)357-8635. Sten Lukin. Weekly.

JEWISH ADVOCATE (1902). 1168-70 Commonwealth Ave., Boston, 02134. (617)277-8988. Bernard M. Hyatt. Weekly.

JEWISH REPORTER (1970). 76 Salem End Rd., Framingham, 01701. (617)879-3300. Harvey S. Stone. Monthly. Greater Framingham Jewish Federation.

JEWISH WEEKLY NEWS (1945). PO Box 1569, Springfield, 01101. (413)739-4771. Leslie B. Kahn. Weekly.

JOURNAL OF THE NORTH SHORE JEWISH COMMUNITY. 564 Loring Ave., Salem, 01940. (617)741-1558. Barbara Wolf. Biweekly. North Shore Jewish Press Ltd.

MOMENT (1975). 462 Boylston St., Boston, 02116. (617)879-2936. Leonard Fein. Monthly (except Jan.–Feb. and July–Aug.). Jewish Educational Ventures.

MICHIGAN

DETROIT JEWISH NEWS (1942). 20300 Civic Center Dr., Suite 240, Southfield, 48076. (313)354-6060. Gary Rosenblatt. Weekly.

HUMANISTIC JUDAISM (1968). 28611 W. Twelve Mile Rd., Southfield, 48076. (313)-478-7610. M. Bonnie Cousens, Ruth D. Feldman. Quarterly. Society for Humanistic Judaism.

MICHIGAN JEWISH HISTORY (1960). 6600 W. Maple Rd., W. Bloomfield, 48033. (313)661-1000. Phillip Applebaum. Semiannually. Jewish Historical Society of Michigan.

MINNESOTA

AMERICAN JEWISH WORLD (1912). 4509 Minnetonka Blvd., Minneapolis, 55416. (612)920-7000. Stacey R. Bush. Weekly.

MISSOURI

KANSAS CITY JEWISH CHRONICLE (1920). 7373 W. 107 St., Suite 250, Overland Park, 66212. (913)648-4620. Stan Rose. Weekly.

MISSOURI JEWISH POST (1948). 9531 Lackland, Suite 207, St. Louis, 63114. (314)-423-3088. Kathie Sutin. Weekly.

ST. LOUIS JEWISH LIGHT (1947). 12 Millstone Campus Dr., St. Louis, 63146. (314)-432-3353. Robert A. Cohn. Weekly. Jewish Federation of St. Louis.

NEBRASKA

JEWISH PRESS (1921). 333 S. 132 St., Omaha, 68154. (402)334-8200. Morris Maline. Weekly. Jewish Federation of Omaha.

NEVADA

JEWISH REPORTER (1976). 1030 E. Twain Ave., Las Vegas, 89109. (702)732-0556. Jerry Countess. Monthly. Jewish Federation of Las Vegas.

LAS VEGAS ISRAELITE (1965). PO Box 14096, Las Vegas, 89114. (702)876-1255. Michael Tell. Biweekly.

NEW JERSEY

JEWISH COMMUNITY VOICE (1941). 2393 W. Marlton Pike, Cherry Hill, 08002. (609)-665-6100. Fredda Sacharow. Biweekly. Jewish Federation of Southern NJ.

JEWISH HORIZON (1981). 1391 Martine Ave., Scotch Plains, 07076. (201)889-9200. Fran Gold. Weekly. Jewish Federation of Central NJ.

JEWISH NEWS (1947). 60 Glenwood Ave., E. Orange, 07017. (201)678-3900. Charles Baumohl. Weekly. United Jewish Federation of MetroWest.

JEWISH RECORD (1939). 1537 Atlantic Ave., Atlantic City, 08401. (609)344-5119. Martin Korik. Weekly.

JEWISH STANDARD (1931). 385 Prospect Ave. Hackensack, 07601. (201)342-1115. Lois Goldrich. Weekly.

JEWISH STAR (1985). 100 Metroplex Dr., Edison, 08817. (201)985-1234. Rhea Basroon. Bimonthly. Jewish Federation of Greater Middlesex County.

JOURNAL OF JEWISH COMMUNAL SERVICE (1899). 111 Prospect St., E. Orange, 07017. (201)676-6070. Sanford N. Sherman. Quarterly. Conference of Jewish Communal Service.

NEW YORK

AFN SHVEL (1941). 200 W. 72 St., Suite 40, NYC, 10023. (212)787-6675. Mordkhe Schaechter. Quarterly. Yiddish. League for Yiddish, Inc.

ALBANY JEWISH WORLD (1965). 1104 Central Ave., Albany, 12205. (518)459-8455. Sam S. Clevenson. Weekly.

ALGEMEINER JOURNAL (1972). 404 Park Ave. S., NYC, 10016. (212)689-3390. Gershon Jacobson. Weekly. Yiddish.

AMERICAN JEWISH YEAR BOOK (1899). 165 E. 56 St., NYC, 10022. (212)751-4000. David Singer. Annually. American Jewish Committee and Jewish Publication Society.

AMERICAN ZIONIST (1910). 4 E. 34 St., NYC, 10016. (212)481-1500. Carol Binen. Quarterly. Zionist Organization of America.

AMIT WOMAN (1925). 817 Broadway, NYC, 10003. (212)477-4720. Micheline Ratzersdorfer. Six times a year. AMIT Women (formerly American Mizrachi Women).

AUFBAU (1934). 2121 Broadway, NYC, 10023. (212)873-7400. Gert Niers, Henry Marx. Fortnightly. German. New World Club, Inc.

BITZARON (1939). PO Box 623, Cooper Station, NYC, 10003. (212)598-3958. Hayim Leaf. Bimonthly. Hebrew. Hebrew Literary Foundation.

BUFFALO JEWISH REVIEW (1918). 15 E. Mohawk St., Buffalo, 14203. (716)854-2192. Harlan C. Abbey. Weekly. Kahaal Nahalot Israel.

COMMENTARY (1945). 165 E. 56 St., NYC, 10022. (212)751-4000. Norman Podhoretz. Monthly. American Jewish Committee.

CONGRESS MONTHLY (1933). 15 E. 84 St., NYC, 10028. (212)879-4500. Maier Deshell. Seven times a year. American Jewish Congress.

CONSERVATIVE JUDAISM (1945). 3080 Broadway, NYC, 10027. (212)678-8863. Rabbi David Silverman. Quarterly. Rabbinical Assembly.

CONTEMPORARY JEWRY (1974 under the name JEWISH SOCIOLOGY AND SOCIAL RESEARCH). Center for Jewish Studies, CUNY Graduate School and University Center, 33 W. 42 St., NYC, 10036. (212)-790-4404. Paul Ritterband. Annually.

ECONOMIC HORIZONS (1953). 500 Fifth Ave., NYC, 10110. (212)354-6510. Laurie Tarlowe. Quarterly. American-Israel Chamber of Commerce and Industry, Inc.

HADAROM (1957). 275 Seventh Ave. NYC, 10001. (212)807-7888. Rabbi Gedalia Schwartz. Annually. Hebrew. Rabbinical Council of America.

HADASSAH MAGAZINE (1921). 50 W. 58 St., NYC, 10019. (212)355-7900. Alan M. Tigay. Monthly (except for combined issues of June–July and Aug.–Sept.). Hadassah, Women's Zionist Organization of America.

HADOAR (1921). 1841 Broadway, Rm. 510, NYC, 10023. (212)581-5151. Shlomo Shamir, Yael Feldman. Weekly. Hebrew. Histadruth Ivrith of America.

ISRAEL HORIZONS (1952). 150 Fifth Ave., Suite 911, NYC, 10011. (212)255-8760. Arieh Lebowitz. Bimonthly. Americans for Progressive Israel.

ISRAEL QUALITY (1976). 500 Fifth Ave., Suite 5416, NYC, 10110. (212)354-6510. Beth Belkin, Laurie Tarlowe. Quarterly. American-Israel Chamber of Commerce and Industry, Inc. and Government of Israel Trade Center.

JEWISH ACTION (1950). 45 W. 36 St., NYC, 10018. (212)563-4000. Heidi Tenzer. Quarterly. Union of Orthodox Jewish Congregations of America.

JEWISH BOOK ANNUAL (1942). 15 E. 26 St., NYC, 10010. (212)532-4949. Jacob Kabakoff. Annually. English-Hebrew-Yiddish. JWB Jewish Book Council.

JEWISH BOOK WORLD (1945). 15 E. 26 St., NYC, 10010. (212)532-4949. William Wollheim. Quarterly. JWB Jewish Book Council.

JEWISH BRAILLE INSTITUTE VOICE (1978). 110 E. 30 St., NYC, 10016. (212)889-2525. Jacob Freid. Ten times a year (sound cassettes). Jewish Braille Institute of America, Inc.

JEWISH BRAILLE REVIEW (1931). 110 E. 30 St., NYC, 10016. (212)889-2525. Jacob Freid. Ten times a year. English-Braille. Jewish Braille Institute of America, Inc.

JEWISH CURRENT EVENTS (1959). 430 Keller Ave., Elmont, 11003. Samuel Deutsch. Biweekly.

JEWISH CURRENTS (1946). 22 E. 17 St., Suite 601, NYC, 10003. (212)924-5740. Morris U. Schappes. Monthly. Association for Promotion of Jewish Secularism, Inc.

JEWISH EDUCATION (1929). 426 W. 58 St., NYC, 10019. (212)245-8200. Alvin I. Schiff. Quarterly. Council for Jewish Education.

JEWISH FORWARD (1897). 45 E. 33 St., NYC, 10016. (212)889-8200. Simon Weber. Weekly. Yiddish. Forward Association, Inc.

JEWISH FRONTIER (1934). 15 E. 26 St., 13th fl., NYC, 10010. (212)683-3530. Jonathan Goldberg. Monthly. Labor Zionist Letters, Inc.

JEWISH GUARDIAN (1974). GPO Box 2143, Brooklyn, 11202. (718)384-4661. Pinchus David. Irregularly. English-Hebrew. Neturei Karta of U.S.A.

JEWISH JOURNAL (1969). 8723 Third Ave., Brooklyn, 11209. (718)238-6635. Daniel Santacruz. Weekly.

JEWISH LEDGER (1924). 148 S. Fitzhugh St., Rochester, 14608. (716)232-1802. Donald Wolin. Weekly.

JEWISH MUSIC NOTES (1945). 15 E. 26 St., NYC, 10010. (212)532-4949. Laura Leon-Cohen. Quarterly. JWB Jewish Music Council.

JEWISH OBSERVER (1963). 5 Beekman St., NYC, 10038. (212)791-1800. Nisson Wolpin. Monthly (except July and Aug.). Agudath Israel of America.

JEWISH OBSERVER (1978). 2223 E. Genesee St., PO Box 510, DeWitt, 13214-0510. (315)422-4104. Judith Rubenstein. Fortnightly. Syracuse Jewish Federation.

JEWISH POST AND RENAISSANCE (1977). 57 E. 11 St., NYC, 10003. (212)420-0042. Charles Roth. Monthly.

JEWISH PRESS (1950). 338 Third Ave., Brooklyn, 11215. (718)858-3300. Sholom Klass. Weekly.

JEWISH SOCIAL STUDIES (1939). 2112 Broadway, Rm. 206, NYC, 10023. (212)724-5336. Tobey B. Gitelle. Quarterly. Conference on Jewish Social Studies, Inc.

JEWISH TELEGRAPHIC AGENCY COMMUNITY NEWS REPORTER (1962). 165 W. 46 St., Suite 511, NYC, 10036. (212)575-9370. Murray Zuckoff. Weekly.

JEWISH TELEGRAPHIC AGENCY DAILY NEWS BULLETIN (1917). 165 W. 46 St., Suite 511, NYC, 10036. (212)575-9370. Murray Zuckoff. Daily.

JEWISH TELEGRAPHIC AGENCY WEEKLY NEWS DIGEST (1933). 165 W. 46 St., Suite 511, NYC, 10036. (212)575-9370. Murray Zuckoff. Weekly.

JEWISH WEEK (1876; reorg. 1970). 1 Park Ave., NYC, 10016. (212)686-2320. Phillip Ritzenberg. Weekly.

JOURNAL OF REFORM JUDAISM (1953). 21 E. 40 St., NYC, 10016. (212)684-4990. Samuel Stahl. Quarterly. Central Conference of American Rabbis.

JUDAISM (1952). 15 E. 84 St., NYC, 10028. (212)879-4500. Robert Gordis. Quarterly. American Jewish Congress.

JWB CIRCLE (1946). 15 E. 26 St., NYC, 10010. (212)532-4949. Lionel Koppman. Bimonthly. JWB.

KIBBUTZ JOURNAL (1984). 27 W. 20 St., 9th fl., NYC, 10011. (212)255-1338. Theodora Saal. Three times a year. Kibbutz Aliya Desk.

KOL HAT'NUA (1943). 50 W. 58 St., NYC, 10019. (212)355-7900. Heather Paskoff. Irregularly. Young Judaea.

KOSHER DIRECTORY (1925). 45 W. 36 St., NYC, 10018. (212)563-4000. Tziporah Spear. Annually. Union of Orthodox Jewish Congregations of America.

KOSHER DIRECTORY, PASSOVER EDITION (1923). 45 W. 36 St., NYC, 10018. (212)-563-4000. Tziporah Spear. Annually. Union of Orthodox Jewish Congregations of America.

KULTUR UN LEBN—CULTURE AND LIFE (1967). 45 E. 33 St., NYC, 10016. (212)-889-6800. Joseph Mlotek. Quarterly. Yiddish. Workmen's Circle.

LAMISHPAHAH. 1841 Broadway, Rm. 510, NYC, 10025. (212)581-5151. Yuval Shem-Ur, Hanita Brand. Ten times a year. Hebrew. Histadruth Ivrith of America.

LILITH—THE JEWISH WOMEN'S MAGAZINE (1976). 250 W. 57 St., NYC, 10019. (212)-757-0818. Susan Weidman Schneider. Quarterly.

LONG ISLAND JEWISH WORLD (1971). 115 Middle Neck Rd., Great Neck, 11021. (516)829-4000. Jerome W. Lippman. Weekly.

MIDSTREAM (1954). 515 Park Ave., NYC, 10022. (212)752-0600. Joel Carmichael. Monthly (bimonthly June–Sept.). Theodor Herzl Foundation, Inc.

MODERN JEWISH STUDIES ANNUAL (1977). Queens College, Kiely 802, 65-30 Kissena Blvd., Flushing, 11367. (718)520-7067. Joseph C. Landis. Annually. American Association of Professors of Yiddish.

MORNING FREIHEIT (1922). 43 W. 24 St., NYC, 10010. (212)255-7661. Paul Novick. Weekly. Yiddish-English.

NA'AMAT WOMAN (1926). 200 Madison Ave., Suite 1808, NYC, 10016. (212)725-8010. Judith A. Sokoloff. Five times a year. English-Yiddish-Hebrew. NA'AMAT USA, the Women's Labor Zionist Organization of America

OLOMEINU–OUR WORLD (1945). 160 Broadway, NYC, 10038. (212)227-1000. Rabbi Yaakov Fruchter, Nosson Scherman. Monthly. English-Hebrew. Torah Umesorah–National Society for Hebrew Day Schools.

OR CHADASH (1981). 110 E. 30 St., NYC, 10016. (212)889-2525. Gerald M. Kass. Two to four times a year (sound cassettes). Hebrew. Jewish Braille Institute of America, Inc.

PEDAGOGIC REPORTER (1949). 730 Broadway, NYC, 10003. (212)529-2000. Mordecai H. Lewittes. Quarterly. Jewish Education Service of North America, Inc.

PRESENT TENSE (1973). 165 E. 56 St., NYC, 10022. (212)751-4000. Murray Polner. Bimonthly. American Jewish Committee.

PROCEEDINGS OF THE AMERICAN ACADEMY FOR JEWISH RESEARCH (1920). 3080 Broadway, NYC, 10027. (212)678-8864. Isaac E. Barzilay. Annually. Hebrew-Arabic-English. American Academy for Jewish Research.

RABBINICAL COUNCIL RECORD (1953). 275 Seventh Ave. NYC, 10001. (212)807-7888. Rabbi Louis Bernstein. Quarterly. Rabbinical Council of America.

RECONSTRUCTIONIST (1935). 270 W. 89 St., NYC, 10024. (212)496-2960. Jacob J. Staub. Eight times a year. Federation of Reconstructionist Congregations and Havurot.

REFORM JUDAISM (1972; formerly DIMENSIONS IN AMERICAN JUDAISM). 838 Fifth Ave., NYC, 10021. (212)249-0100. Aron Hirt-Manheimer. Quarterly. Union of American Hebrew Congregations.

REPORTER. 500 Clubhouse Rd., Binghamton, 13903. (607)724-2360. Marc Goldberg. Weekly. Jewish Federation of Broome County.

RESPONSE (1967). 15 E. 26 St., Suite 1350, NYC, 10010. (212)679-1412. Cindy Rubin. Quarterly. Jewish Educational Ventures, Inc.

SEVEN ARTS FEATURE SYNDICATE (see News Syndicates, p. 434)

SHEVILEY HA-HINNUKH (1939). 426 W. 58 St., NYC, 10019. (212)713-0290. Zvulun Ravid. Quarterly. Hebrew. Council for Jewish Education.

SH'MA (1970). Box 567, Port Washington, 11050. (516)944-9791. Eugene B. Borowitz. Biweekly (except June, July, Aug.).

SHMUESSEN MIT KINDER UN YUGENT (1942). 770 Eastern Pkwy., Brooklyn, 11213. (718)493-9250. Nissan Mindel. Monthly. Yiddish. Merkos L'Inyonei Chinuch, Inc.

SPECTRUM (1982). 515 Park Ave., NYC, 10022. (212)371-7750. Karen Rubinstein. Quarterly. American Zionist Federation.

SYNAGOGUE LIGHT (1933). 47 Beekman St., NYC, 10038. (212)227-7800. Rabbi Meyer Hager. Quarterly. Union of Chassidic Rabbis.

TALKS AND TALES (1942). 770 Eastern Pkwy., Brooklyn, 11213. (718)493-9250. Nissan Mindel. Monthly (also Hebrew, French, and Spanish editions). Merkos L'Inyonei Chinuch, Inc.

TRADITION (1958). 275 Seventh Ave., NYC, 10001. (212)807-7888. Walter Wurzburger. Quarterly. Rabbinical Council of America.

TRENDS (1982). 730 Broadway, NYC, 10003. (212)260-0006. Quarterly. Jewish Education Service of North America, Inc.

UNITED SYNAGOGUE REVIEW (1943). 155 Fifth Ave., NYC, 10010. (212)533-7800. Ruth M. Perry. Biannually. United Synagogue of America.

UNSER TSAIT (1941). 25 E. 21 St., NYC, 10010. (212)475-0059. Jacob S. Hertz. Monthly. Yiddish. Jewish Labor Bund.

DER WECKER (1921). 45 E. 33 St., NYC, 10016. (212)686-1538. Elias Schulman. Bimonthly. Yiddish. Jewish Socialist Verband of America.

WOMEN'S AMERICAN ORT REPORTER (1966). 315 Park Ave. S., NYC, 10010. (212)505-7700. Elie Faust-Levy. Quarterly. Women's American ORT, Inc.

WOMEN'S LEAGUE OUTLOOK (1930). 48 E. 74 St., NYC, 10021. (212)628-1600. Yvette

Rosenberg. Quarterly. Women's League for Conservative Judaism.

WORKMEN'S CIRCLE CALL (1934). 45 E. 33 St., NYC, 10016. (212)889-6800. Walter L. Kirschenbaum. Bimonthly. Workmen's Circle.

YEARBOOK OF THE CENTRAL CONFERENCE OF AMERICAN RABBIS (1890). 21 E. 40 St., NYC, 10016. (212)684-4990. Elliot L. Stevens. Annually. Central Conference of American Rabbis.

YIDDISH (1973). Queens College, Kiely 802, 65-30 Kissena Blvd., Flushing, 11367. (718)520-7067. Joseph C. Landis. Quarterly. Queens College Press.

YIDDISHE HEIM (1958). 770 Eastern Pkwy., Brooklyn, 11213. (718)493-9250. Rachel Altein, Tema Guarary. Quarterly. English-Yiddish. Agudas Nshei Ub'nos Chabad.

YIDDISHE KULTUR (1938). 1123 Broadway, Rm. 305, NYC, 10010. (212)243-1304. Itche Goldberg. Monthly (except June–July, Aug.–Sept.). Yiddish. Yiddishe Kultur Farband, Inc.—YKUF.

YIDDISHE VORT (1953). 5 Beekman St., NYC, 10038. (212)791-1800. Joseph Friedenson. Monthly. Yiddish. Agudath Israel of America.

YIDDISHER KEMFER (1906). 275 Seventh Ave., NYC, 10001. (212)675-7808. Mordechai Strigler. Weekly. Yiddish. Labor Zionist Letters, Inc.

YIDISHE SHPRAKH (1941). 1048 Fifth Ave., NYC, 10028. (212)231-7905. Mordkhe Schaechter. Irregularly. Yiddish. Yivo Institute for Jewish Research, Inc.

YIVO ANNUAL OF JEWISH SOCIAL SCIENCE (1946). 1048 Fifth Ave., NYC, 10028. (212)535-6700. Irregularly. Yivo Institute for Jewish Research, Inc.

YIVO BLETER (1931). 1048 Fifth Ave., NYC, 10028. (212)535-6700. Editorial board. Irregularly. Yiddish. Yivo Institute for Jewish Research, Inc.

YOUNG ISRAEL VIEWPOINT (1952). 3 W. 16 St., NYC, 10011. (212)929-1525. Yaakov Kornreich. Monthly (except July, Aug.). National Council of Young Israel.

YOUNG JUDAEAN (1912). 50 W. 58 St., NYC, 10019. (212)303-8268. Mordecai Newman. Six times a year. Hadassah Zionist Youth Commission.

YUGNTRUF (1964). 3328 Bainbridge Ave., Bronx, 10467. (212)654-8540. Hershl Glasser. Quarterly. Yiddish. Yugntruf Youth for Yiddish.

NORTH CAROLINA

AMERICAN JEWISH TIMES–OUTLOOK (1934; reorg. 1950). PO Box 33218, Charlotte, 28233. (704)372-3296. Ruth Goldberg. Monthly. The Blumenthal Foundation.

OHIO

THE AMERICAN ISRAELITE (1854). 906 Main St., Rm. 505, Cincinnati, 45237. (513)621-3145. Phyllis R. Singer. Weekly.

AMERICAN JEWISH ARCHIVES (1947). 3101 Clifton Ave., Cincinnati, 45220. (513)221-1875. Jacob R. Marcus, Abraham J. Peck. Semiannually. American Jewish Archives of Hebrew Union College–Jewish Institute of Religion.

CLEVELAND JEWISH NEWS (1964). 13910 Cedar Rd., University Hts., 44118. (216)-371-0800. Cynthia Dettelbach. Weekly. Cleveland Jewish Publication Co.

DAYTON JEWISH CHRONICLE (1961). 118 Salem Ave., Dayton, 45406. (513)222-0783. Anne M. Hammerman. Weekly.

INDEX TO JEWISH PERIODICALS (1963). PO Box 18570, Cleveland Hts., 44118. (216)-321-7296. Miriam Leikind, Bess Rosenfeld, Jean H. Foxman. Semiannually.

OHIO JEWISH CHRONICLE (1921). 2831 E. Main St., Columbus, 43209. (614)237-4296. Judith Franklin, Steve Pinsky, Diane Levi. Weekly.

STARK JEWISH NEWS (1920). 2631 Harvard Ave. NW, 44709. (216)452-6444. Adele Gelb. Monthly. Canton Jewish Community Federation.

STUDIES IN BIBLIOGRAPHY AND BOOKLORE (1953). 3101 Clifton Ave., Cincinnati, 45220. (513)221-1875. Herbert C. Zafren. Irregularly. English-Hebrew-German. Library of Hebrew Union College–Jewish Institute of Religion.

YOUNGSTOWN JEWISH TIMES (1935). PO Box 777, Youngstown, 44501. (216)746-6192. Harry Alter. Fortnightly.

OKLAHOMA

SOUTHWEST JEWISH CHRONICLE (1929). 314-B N. Robinson St., Oklahoma City, 73102. (405)236-4226. E. F. Friedman. Quarterly.

TULSA JEWISH REVIEW (1930). 2205 E. 51 St., Tulsa, 74105. (918)749-7751. Dianna Aaronson. Monthly. Tulsa Section, National Council of Jewish Women.

PENNSYLVANIA

JEWISH CHRONICLE (1962). 5600 Baum Blvd., Pittsburgh, 15206. (412)687-1000. Joel Roteman. Weekly. Pittsburgh Jewish Publication and Education Foundation.

JEWISH EXPONENT (1887). 226 S. 16 St., Philadelphia, 19102. (215)893-5740. Albert Erlick. Weekly. Federation of Jewish Agencies of Greater Philadelphia.

JEWISH QUARTERLY REVIEW (1910). 250 N. Highland Ave., Merion, 19066. (215)-667-1830. Leon Nemoy, Bernard Lewis, David M. Goldenberg. Quarterly.

JEWISH TIMES OF THE GREATER NORTHEAST (1925). 2417 Welsh Rd., Philadelphia, 19114. (215)464-3900. Leon E. Brown. Weekly. Federation of Jewish Agencies of Greater Philadelphia.

NEW MENORAH (1979). 6723 Emlen St., Philadelphia, 19119. (215)849-5385. Arthur Waskow, Shana Margolin. Bimonthly. B'nai Or Religious Fellowship.

RHODE ISLAND

RHODE ISLAND JEWISH HISTORICAL NOTES (1954). 130 Sessions St., Providence, 02906. (401)331-1360. Michael Fink. Annually. Rhode Island Jewish Historical Association.

TENNESSEE

HEBREW WATCHMAN (1925) 4646 Poplar Ave., Suite 232, Memphis, 38117. (901)-763-2215. Herman I. Goldberger. Weekly.

TEXAS

JEWISH CIVIC PRESS (1965). PO Box 35656, Houston, 77235. (713)491-1512. Abner Tritt. Monthly.

JEWISH HERALD-VOICE (1908). PO Box 153, Houston, 77001. (713)630-0391. Joseph W. and Jeanne F. Samuels. Weekly.

JEWISH JOURNAL OF SAN ANTONIO (1973). 8434 Ahern, San Antonio, 78216. (512)-341-8234. Norma Grubman. Monthly. Jewish Federation of San Antonio.

TEXAS JEWISH POST (1947). PO Box 742, Fort Worth, 76101. (817)927-2831. 11333 N. Central Expressway, Dallas, 75243. (214)692-7283. Jimmy Wisch. Weekly.

VIRGINIA

UJF NEWS (1959). 7300 Newport Ave., Norfolk, 23462. (804)489-8040. Reba Karp. Weekly. United Jewish Federation of Tidewater.

WASHINGTON

JEWISH TRANSCRIPT (1924). 510 Securities Bldg., Seattle, 98101. (206)624-0136. Richard Gordon. Bimonthly. Jewish Federation of Greater Seattle.

M'GODOLIM: THE JEWISH QUARTERLY (1979). 2921 E. Madison St., #7, Seattle, 98112-4237. (206)322-1431. Keith S. Gormezano. Quarterly. Hebrew-English.

WISCONSIN

WISCONSIN JEWISH CHRONICLE (1921). 1360 N. Prospect Ave., Milwaukee, 53202. (414)271-2992. Arthur J. Stegeman. Weekly. Milwaukee Jewish Federation.

NEWS SYNDICATES

JEWISH PRESS FEATURES (1970). 15 E. 26 St., Suite 1350, NYC, 10010. (212)679-1411. Larry Yudelson. Monthly. Jewish Student Press Service.

JEWISH TELEGRAPHIC AGENCY, INC. (1917). 165 W. 46 St., NYC., 10036. (212)-575-9370. Murray Zuckoff. Daily.

SEVEN ARTS FEATURE SYNDICATE and WORLDWIDE NEWS SERVICE (WNS) (1923). 165 W. 46 St., Suite 511, NYC, 10036. (212)575-9370. John Kayston. Semiweekly.

CANADA

BULLETIN DU CONGRES JUIF CANADIEN (Région du Québec) (1952). 1590 Dr. Penfield Ave., Montreal, PQ H3G 1C5. (514)-931-7531. M. Mayer Levy. Quarterly. French. Canadian Jewish Congress.

CANADIAN JEWISH HERALD (1977). 17 Anselme Lavigne Blvd., Dollard des Ormeaux, PQ H9A 1N3. (514)684-7667. Dan Nimrod. Irregularly.

CANADIAN JEWISH NEWS (1960). 562 Eglinton Ave. E., Suite 401, Toronto, ONT M4P 1P1. (416)483-9331. Maurice Lucow. Weekly.

CANADIAN JEWISH OUTLOOK (1963). 6184 Ash St., #3, Vancouver, BC V5Z 3G9. (604)324-5101. Ben Chud, Henry Rosenthal. Monthly.

CANADIAN ZIONIST (1934). 1310 Greene Ave., Suite 800, Montreal, PQ H3Z 2B2. (514)934-0804. Glenna Uline. Five times a year. Canadian Zionist Federation.

JEWISH EAGLE (1907). 4180 De Courtrai, Rm. 218, Montreal, PQ H3S 1C3. (514)-735-6577. B. Hirshtal. Weekly. Yiddish-Hebrew-French.

JEWISH POST (1925). 117 Hutchings St., Winnipeg, MAN R2X 2V4. (204)694-3332. Matt Bellan. Weekly.

JEWISH STANDARD (1929). 67 Mowat Ave., Toronto, ONT M6K 3E3. (416)537-2696. Julius Hayman. Semimonthly.

JEWISH WESTERN BULLETIN (1930). 3268 Heather St., Vancouver, BC V5Z 3K5. (604)879-6575. Samuel Kaplan. Weekly.

JOURNAL OF PSYCHOLOGY AND JUDAISM (1976). 1747 Featherston Dr., Ottawa, ONT K1H 6P4. (613)731-9119. Reuven P. Bulka. Semiannually. Center for the Study of Psychology and Judaism.

OTTAWA JEWISH BULLETIN & REVIEW (1954). 151 Chapel St., Ottawa, ONT K1N 7Y2. (613)232-7306. Cynthia Engel. Biweekly. Jewish Community Council of Ottawa.

UNDZER VEG (1932). 272 Codsell Ave., Downsview, ONT M3H 3X2. (416)636-4024. Joseph Kligman. Quarterly. Yiddish-English. Achdut HaAvoda-Poale Zion of Canada.

WESTERN JEWISH NEWS (1926). 400-259 Portage Ave., Winnipeg, MAN R3C 2G6. (204)942-6361. Cheryl Fogel. Weekly. English-Hebrew.

WINDSOR JEWISH COMMUNITY BULLETIN (1938). 1641 Ouellette Ave., Windsor, ONT N8X 1K9. (519)973-1772. Joseph Eisenberg. Irregularly. Windsor Jewish Community Council.

Obituaries: United States[1]

ALROY, GIL CARL, professor, author; b. Czernowitz, Rumania, Nov. 7, 1924; d. NYC, May 19, 1985; in U.S. since 1954. Educ.: CCNY, Princeton U. (PhD). Prof., political science, Hunter College, since 1963. Author: *Behind the Middle East Conflict* (1975), *The Kissinger Experience* (1975), *The Middle East Uncovered* (1979), and other works.

BAAR, EMIL N., lawyer, communal worker; b. Vienna, Austria, Sept. 9, 1891; d. NYC, Nov. 11, 1985; in U.S. since 1893. Educ.: Columbia Coll., Columbia U. Law School. U.S. infantry, WWI; Lt., U.S. army reserve. Member, since 1926, and later sr. partner, Baar, Bennett & Fullen, NYC; justice, N.Y. State Supreme Court, 1951; special asst., N.Y. State Attorney General, 1955 and 1959. Bd. mem.: United Hospital Fund, Natl. Conf. of Christians and Jews, Brooklyn Museum, and other groups; mem.: Amer. Legion, Natl. Republican Club, N.Y. State and Amer. Bar Assns., B.P.O. Elks, and others. Trustee, Union of Amer. Hebrew Congs., since 1948; natl. chmn., UAHC bd. of trustees, 1959–63, and hon. life chmn. since 1964; pres., Union Temple of Brooklyn, 1941–49, and hon. life pres; pres., Jewish Hospital of Brooklyn, 1948–54, and hon. life chmn. of bd; pres., Jewish Braille Inst., 1966–72; bd. mem.: Hebrew Union Coll.–Jewish Inst. of Religion, Fed. of Jewish Philanthropies of N.Y., Brooklyn Jewish Community Council, World Union for Progressive Judaism. Recipient: hon. DHL, HUC-JIR; numerous awards, including Distinguished Service to Jewry Award, Fed. of Jewish Philanthropies; Synagogue Council of America Statesman Award; Maurice N. Eisendrath "Bearer of Light" Award.

BERNSTEIN, PHILIP S., rabbi, communal worker; b. Rochester, N.Y., June 25, 1901; d. Rochester, N.Y., Dec. 3, 1985. Educ.: Syracuse U., Jewish Inst. of Religion (rabbi, DD), Hebrew U. of Jerusalem, Cambridge U. (England). Rabbi, Temple B'rith Kodesh, Rochester, N.Y., 1926–73; rabbi emer. since 1973. Chief Jewish chaplain, U.S. armed forces, during WWII; adviser on Jewish affairs to commander of U.S. forces in Europe, in charge of organizing camps for displaced persons, 1946–47. Pres.: Rochester City Club, Rochester City Planning and Housing Council; mem.: Monroe County Human Relations Comm; active in behalf of workers' rights, low-cost housing, and family planning. Pres., Central Conf. Amer. Rabbis, 1950–52; hon. chmn., AIPAC, 1954–68; adviser and friend to Israeli prime ministers David Ben-Gurion and Golda Meir. Author: *Rabbis at War, What the Jews Believe*, and numerous magazine and journal articles. Recipient: many honors, including Rotary Man of the Year Award; Solomon Bublick Award, Hebrew U. of Jerusalem; chair in Jewish studies named in his honor at U. Rochester.

---

[1] Including Jewish residents of the United States who died between January 1 and December 31, 1985.

BOLTEN, SEYMOUR R., civil servant; b. NYC, July 17, 1921; d. Washington, D.C., June 6, 1985. Educ.: NYU, Harvard U. Served U.S. army, WWII; awarded Silver Star and Bronze Star. Joined CIA 1950; retired 1977; an authority on internatl. drug trade, he was believed to be the highest-ranking Jew among known CIA members; special adviser to the White House on narcotics, 1977–81; sr. adviser on law enforcement policy, U.S. Treasury, since 1981. Instrumental in organizing the President's Comm. on the Holocaust, to which he was White House liaison under Pres. Jimmy Carter. Recipient: Intelligence Medal of Merit; Distinguished Intelligence Medal.

BRESLOW, ISRAEL, labor leader, communal worker; b. Dashev, Russia, Apr. 26, 1906; d. NYC, July 28, 1985; in U.S. since early 1930s. A garment worker, he joined Dressmakers Union Local 22, ILGWU, 1937; elected to exec. bd. 1942; pres. of local, 1944–50; business agent, 1948–58; sec.-mgr., 1958–75 (retirement); v.-pres., ILGWU, 1962–75. Pres.: Jewish Forward Assn. and Radio Station WEVD-FM, 1973–76, 1978–81, 1983–85; Workmen's Circle, 1958–62, 1966–70; bd. mem.: Jewish Labor Com., YIVO Inst. for Jewish Research; active in Jewish Socialist Verband, Social Democrats USA, League for Industrial Democracy, Cong. for Jewish Culture. Author: articles in Yiddish in *Jewish Daily Forward* and *Der Wecker*, in English in Workmen's Circle *Call*. Recipient: Jewish Teachers Sem. Award; Prime Minister of Israel's Medal.

BULOFF, JOSEPH, actor; b. Vilna, Lithuania, Dec. 6, 1899; d. NYC, Feb. 27, 1985; in U.S. since 1927. A leading figure on the Yiddish and American stages, appeared in over 200 Yiddish plays, in a number of Broadway productions (including the original *Oklahoma!, My Sister Eileen,* and *Fifth Season*), in motion pictures, and on radio and TV. He traveled widely giving lecture-readings in Yiddish and English. Mem.: Hebrew Actors Union. Author: *The Chekhov Sketchbook* (1983); *Tales from the Old Marketplace* (1986). Recipient: Obie Awards for theatrical performances in *Hard to Be a Jew* (1973) and *The Price* (1979); Sholom Aleichem Award, Queens Coll.; Sam Levinson Memorial Award; Certificate of Honor and Manger Award, Tel Aviv U.; and many other honors.

CAREY, DAVID, actor, musician; b. Brookline, Mass., Nov. 16, 1943; d. NYC, Mar. 10, 1985. Devoted his brief career to Yiddish theater; taught music in Workmen's Circle schools and NYC's Hebrew Arts School; performed on the Yiddish stage; in 1978 cofounded, with Raymond Ariel, the Shalom Yiddish Musical Theater, which sought to attract a largely American-born, English-speaking audience. Mem. exec. bd., Hebrew Actors Union; mem.: Screen Actors Guild, Actors Equity, Workmen's Circle.

CERIER, MAURICE, communal worker; b. Boston, Mass., July 31, 1923; d. Manhasset, N.Y., Oct. 18, 1985. Fund-raiser, UJA of Greater N.Y., 1948–76; dir. of major gifts and asst. v.-pres., nat'l. UJA, since 1976.

CHARCHAT, ISAAC, businessman, communal worker; b. (?), Sweden, 1904; d. NYC, May 25, 1985; U.S. citizen since 1950. Pres., United Cargo Corp., Manhattan-based container shipping co., for over 20 years. First pres., Internatl. Synagogue of Kennedy Airport; treas., American-Israel Chamber of Commerce. Author: *A Constant Reminder* (1984), an autobiographical novel about anti-Semitism in Europe in the 1920s.

CHERNIAK, SAADIAH, communal worker; b. Kursk, Russia, Jan. 15, 1900; d. NYC, Dec. 1, 1985; in U.S. since 1941. Joined staff of Jewish Colonization Assoc., Istanbul, Turkey, 1923; later transferred to Paris office; exec. dir., Amer. Friends of the Alliance Israélite Universelle, 1948–82.

CHILEWICH, ARON, businessman, philanthropist; b. Pskov, Russia, Dec. 1, 1900; d. NYC, Sept. 2, 1985; in U.S. since 1939. An internatl. trader in hides, leather, and other commodities. A founder, Albert Einstein Coll. of Medicine; v. chmn., bd. of govs., Ben-Gurion U. of the Negev; founder and trustee, Sam and Esther Minskoff Cultural Center/Park East ESHI Day School; trustee, Park East Synagogue; active in behalf of many Jewish and Israeli causes, including the Hebrew U., Haifa U., Tel Aviv U., UJA, United Israel Appeal. Recipient: hon. doctorate, Ben-Gurion U. of the Negev; American Arbitration Assn. Award, and numerous other honors.

COHEN, OSCAR, communal worker; b. Dundas, Ont., Canada, June 1, 1908; d. NYC, June 8, 1985; in U.S. since 1946. Educ.: U.

Toronto. Served Canadian army 1941–46, achieving rank of lt. col. Staff mem., Canadian Jewish Cong., in charge of organizing European refugee rescue efforts, 1933–39; dir., Detroit Jewish Community Council, 1946–49; natl. staff mem., Anti-Defamation League, 1949–74, most of that time as dir., Program Div., in charge of developing education programs to combat anti-Semitism and racism and to advance democratic ideals and intergroup understanding. Among important works in human relations that he initiated or helped to develop were the U. of California's *Patterns of American Prejudice* study, John F. Kennedy's *A Nation of Immigrants*, and *American Jews: Their Story*, by Oscar Handlin. Recipient: Order of the British Empire (1945); Lifetime Achievement Award, Cornerhouse Found. (1974), and many other honors.

CRUSO, PINCHAS, communal worker; b. Romny, Russia, Sept. 15, 1889; d. NYC, Oct. 14, 1985; in U.S. since 1909. Spent several years in Palestine before coming to U.S. Served U.S. army, WWI, in France. A leading figure in Amer. Labor Zionist movement, in which he held many posts over the years: N.Y. sec., People's Tool Campaign (forerunner, Israel Histadrut Campaign); sec., Young Poale Zion; founder and first sec., League for Labor Palestine; founder and first managing ed., *Jewish Frontier*, 1934–75; pres., Labor Zionist Org. of Amer. (Poale Zion); field sec., Natl. Com. for Labor Israel. A frequent delegate to World Zionist Congresses; v.-pres., Amer. Zionist Council; mem., World Zionist Org. Actions Com. Author: numerous articles in English and Yiddish.

CUMMINGS, NATHAN, businessman, philanthropist; b. St. John, N.B., Canada, Oct. 14, 1896; d. Palm Beach, Fla., Feb. 19, 1985. After starting out in the food business in Canada, in 1939 he purchased a Baltimore, Md., wholesale food concern that he built into a leading internatl. conglomerate, Consolidated Foods Corp. Prominent art collector and museum patron; major benefactor: Mt. Sinai Medical Center, NYC; Memorial-Sloan Kettering Cancer Center, NYC. Supporter of the Israel Bond Org., the Amer. Jewish Com., Amer. Friends of the Israel Museum, Park Ave. Synagogue, NYC.

DWORKIN, ZALMAN S., rabbi; b. Rogachev, Russia, (?), 1900; d. NYC, Mar. 9, 1985; in U.S. since 1953. Educ.: Yeshivah Tomchei Tmimim in Lyubavichi and later in Rostov-on-the Don, Russia. Rabbi *(rav)* of Voranok, Ukraine, and Starodub, White Russia, 1924–39, during which time became expert *shohet;* found refuge during WWII in Samarkand, where he served as rabbi and head of underground yeshivah; held rabbinical posts in France and Ireland, 1946–53, and in Detroit, Mich., in 1953; headed Lubavitch Yeshivah in Pittsburgh, 1954–60; moved to Brooklyn in 1960, becoming rabbi of the Central Lubavitch Cong.; dean, Lubavitch Kollel–Graduate School; and chmn., worldwide Lubavitch Rabbinical Council *(Vaad Rabonei Lubavitch).*

EISENBERG, AZRIEL, educator, author; b. Dombrovitz, Russia-Poland, Aug. 29, 1903; d. NYC, Dec. 15, 1985; in U.S. since 1914. Educ.: NYU, Teachers Coll.–Columbia U. (PhD), Teachers Inst.–Jewish Theol. Sem. of Amer. Headed bds. of Jewish educ. in Cincinnati,1935–40; Cleveland,1940–46; and Philadelphia,1946–49, where he was also dean of Gratz Coll.; exec. v.-pres., Jewish Educ. Com. of N.Y. (forerunner of Bd. of Jewish Educ.), 1949–66; dir., World Council on Jewish Educ., 1966–68. Chmn.: Natl. Bible Contest, 1956–77; United Synagogue Comm. on Jewish Educ.; pres., Natl. Council for Jewish Educ.; mem.: Natl. Jewish Book Council, Jewish Publ. Soc. Publ. Com. Author and ed. of some 60 works on Jewish subjects, many for children. Recipient: hon. doctorates from JTS, Baltimore Hebrew Coll., Gratz Coll.; JWB Jewish Book Council Award; Pres. Zalman Shazar Award (Israel), and other honors.

FINER, MORRIS H., rabbi, communal worker; b. (?), (?), 1912; d. Jerusalem, Israel, June 23, 1985. Educ.: CCNY, Rabbi Isaac Elchanan Theol. Sem., Brooklyn Law School. Served as rabbi of congregations in Haverstraw and Astoria, N.Y., and Tulsa, Okla.; dir., communal service div., RIETS, 1944–78; moved to Israel, 1981. Mem.: Rabbinical Council of Amer.

FRANCK, ISAAC, communal worker, professor; b. Zozov, Russia, Mar. 15, 1909; d. Washington, D.C., May 14,1985; in U.S. since 1923. Educ.: NYU, U. Md. (PhD), Herzliah and Tarbut Hebrew Teachers Sems. Exec. dir., Jewish community councils of Detroit, Mich., 1941–46, and Brooklyn, N.Y., 1946–47; exec. sec., Amer. Fund for Israel Insts., 1947–49; exec. v.-pres., Jewish Community Council of Greater Washington, 1949–74; lect., later adj. prof., Amer. U., 1956–73; lect., Howard U., 1973–77; sr. research scholar, Kennedy Inst. of Ethics, Georgetown U., 1979–85; adj. prof., community and family medicine, Georgetown U., 1980–85. Sec.: Interreligious Com. on Race Relations, Washington Urban Coalition, 1962–73; D.C. Supt. of Schools Citizens Advisory Com., 1969–73; consultant to Voice of Amer. and other USIA programs. Author: numerous articles and book reviews in both Jewish and genl. pubs. Recipient: Stephen S. Wise Medallion, Amer. Jewish Cong, and other awards; an annual memorial lecture series was established in his name by Kennedy Inst. of Ethics, Georgetown U., and Jewish Community Council; library of Greater Washington Bd. of Jewish Educ. renamed the Isaac Franck Jewish Public Library.

FRANK, PHYLLIS, communal worker; b. Jersey City, N.J., Dec. 18, 1933; d. Silver Spring, Md., Jan. 1, 1985. Educ.: Simmons Coll. Pres., Jewish Community Council of Greater Washington, 1978–80; natl. v.-pres., Pioneer Women/Na'amat, 1982–85; mem., World Zionist Org. Actions Com., 1983–85; bd. mem.: Amer. Zionist Fed., Jewish Social Service Agcy. of Greater Washington. Recipient: Golda Meir Award, Pioneer Women; Pioneer Woman of the Year Award; many other civic and communal honors.

GOELL, THERESA B., archaeologist, architect; b. NYC, July 17, 1901; d. NYC, Dec. 18, 1985. Educ.: Radcliffe Coll., Cambridge U. (England), NYU Inst. of Fine Arts. Lived in Palestine 1930s, working on staff of Amer. School for Oriental Research and as architect of more than 200 buildings in Tel Aviv, Haifa, and Jerusalem; best known for archaeological work at Nimrud Dagh, Turkey, in 1950s, where she uncovered the tomb of Antiochus I.

GOITEIN, SHELOMO DOV, professor; b. Burgkunstadt, Germany, Apr. 3, 1900; d. Princeton, N.J., Feb. 6, 1985; in U.S. since 1957. Educ.: U. Frankfurt (PhD), U. Berlin. Teacher, hist. and Bible, Reali School, Haifa, Palestine, 1923–28; instr., later prof., hist. of Islam and the Muslim peoples, Hebrew U. of Jerusalem, 1928–48; sr. educ. officer, Mandatory Govt. of Palestine, 1938–48 (while retaining post at Hebrew U.); dir., School of Oriental Studies, Hebrew U., 1949–56; prof., Arabic, U. Pa., Philadelphia, 1957–71; named long-term visitor at Institute for Advanced Study, Princeton, N.J., 1971. Cofounder and pres. (1949–57), Israel Oriental Soc.; pres., Amer. Oriental Soc.; fellow: Medieval Acad. of Amer., Amer. Acad. for Jewish Research; bd. mem., Conf. of Jewish Social Studies; hon. fellow, Middle East Studies Assn.; sr. scholar, Assn. for Jewish Studies; mem., Amer. Philos. Soc. Author: *A Mediterranean Society: The Jewish Communities of the Arab World as Portrayed in the Documents of the Cairo Geniza* (4 vols.; the 5th and last vol. forthcoming); more than 500 books and articles in the fields of Islamic hist. and institutions, the documents of the Cairo Geniza, the Jews of Yemen (languages, life, hist.), biblical lit. and society, and teaching methodology (Bible, other Hebrew subjects, Arabic). Recipient: hon. doctorates from U. Chicago, Jewish Theol. Sem. of Amer., Gratz Coll., Spertus Coll., U. Pa.; Haskins Medal, Medieval Acad. of Amer.; Yitzhak Ben Zvi Prize, Jerusalem; Levi Della Vida Medal, U. Calif.; hon. mem., Société Asiatique, Paris; Harvey Prize, Technion, Haifa; hon. fellow, School of Oriental and African Studies, London; MacArthur Found. Award (a lifetime stipend made to "individuals of exceptional talent," 1983); Natl. Jewish Book Award (1984); Joseph Handleman Prize, Jewish Acad. of Arts and Sciences (1984).

GOLDBERGER, MILTON, editor, publisher; b. Memphis, Tenn., Apr. 11, 1906; d. Memphis, Tenn., May 26, 1985. Educ.: U. Tenn., Ohio State U. Editor, *The Hebrew Watchman* (Memphis), 1928–55; since 1955 publisher of shopping newspapers. Bd. mem: B'nai B'rith lodge, Memphis Zionist District, Baron Hirsch Cong. Coauthor: *Southern Jewry*.

GROSS, NATHAN K., businessman, communal worker; b. NYC, Jan. 16, 1911; d. NYC, Aug. 20, 1985. Founder and sr. partner, Jess E. Gross Co. (insurance). V.-pres., Union of Orthodox Jewish Congs., 1941–83, chmn. of the bd. since 1983, and chmn. its Joint Kashruth Comm. for over 3 decades; pres. and bd chmn., Cong. Ohab Zedek, Manhattan; bd. mem., Hebrew Free Burial Assn.

HANFT, BENJAMIN, publicist; b. NYC, Dec. 18, 1904; d. NYC, Nov. 8, 1985. Started out as newspaper reporter in the 1920s, later held public relations positions with various Jewish orgs.: Amer. Jewish JDC, natl. UJA, N.Y. UJA, Council of Jewish Feds. and Welfare Funds, Amer. Jewish Com., Amer. Jewish Cong., Amer. Friends of Hebrew U., and others. Founder, Jewish Publicity Dirs. Council.

KLEIN, EDWARD E., rabbi, communal worker; b. Newark, N.J., May 25, 1913; d. NYC, July 13, 1985. Educ.: NYU, Hebrew Union Coll.-Jewish Inst. of Religion (rabbi, DD). Asst. rabbi, Stephen Wise Free Synagogue, NYC, 1940–42; dir., Hillel Found., U. Calif., Berkeley, 1942–43; rabbi, Stephen Wise Free Synagogue, NYC, 1943–81; rabbi emer. since 1981; visiting lect., homiletics, HUC-JIR. Active in numerous civic-improvement, social, and Jewish causes: cochmn., League of West Side Orgs., 1952–56; Mayor's Appeal Bd. for Fair Housing Practices, 1958–62; Mayor's Adv. Com. on Higher Educ., 1966–68; chmn.: Lincoln Square Community Council; Planned Parenthood Clergy Adv. Comm., 1968–72; bd. mem., Amer. Found. on Nonviolence; mem. natl. adv. com., Religious Action Center, Washington. V.-pres., N.Y. Bd. of Rabbis; pres., HUC-JIR Alumni Assn. and mem. its Rabbinic Bd. of Alumni Overseers; mem., Social Action Comm., Union of Amer. Hebrew Congs.; chmn., Church and State Com., Central Conf. Amer. Rabbis. An early supporter of the civil rights movement, his synagogue was the first religious inst. in NYC to invite Dr. Martin Luther King, Jr., to its pulpit. Recipient: awards from the Council of Spanish-Amer. Orgs. of N.Y., Natl. Conf. of Christians and Jews, Jewish War Veterans–N.Y. Council, Ministerial Interfaith Assn. of Harlem, NYU Alumni Assn., Amer. Jewish Cong. (Stephen Wise Award, 1978).

KOENIGSBERGER, IRENE DINER, chemist, communal worker; b. NYC, Sept. 21, 1896; d. Chevy Chase, Md., Aug. 12, 1985. Educ.: Hunter Coll., Columbia U., NYU (PhD). The daughter of the dean of Fordham U. pharmacy school, she completed a doctorate in chemistry at age 19, in the course of her research discovering a method for determining the life of automobile tires and other rubber products. Employed by the War Dept. during WWI, she settled in Washington, D.C. A lifelong active member of B'nai B'rith Women: a founder and pres. of the Argo chap., of District 5, and of the B'nai B'rith Hillel Found. at George Washington U. A pet house at the BBW Home for Emotionally Disturbed Children in Jerusalem was established in her name. A founder of the Jewish Community Council of Greater Washington and, with her husband, of Temple Sinai in Washington, of which she was hon. v.-pres. Mem.: Hadassah, Natl. Council of Jewish Women, Amer. Technion Soc., and other orgs. Recipient: Hunter Coll. Distinguished Alumna Medal, 1980.

KUSEVITSKY, DAVID, cantor; b. Smorgon, Russia, (?), 1911; d. NYC, July 31, 1985; in U.S. since 1948. The youngest of 4 brothers who all became well-known cantors, he sang in and eventually led the choir of his oldest brother, Moshe, in Vilna. Drafted into the Polish army, he led the army choir. In mid-1930s became cantor of the Hendon Synagogue, London, England, and taught music at Jews' Coll. Assumed post of cantor of Temple Emanu-El, in the Borough Park section of Brooklyn, in 1948. Faculty mem., Cantors Inst., Jewish Theol. Sem. of Amer., since 1967. On Dec. 27, 1953, joined with brothers Moshe, Jacob, and Simcha in first joint U.S. recital, before an overflow audience in Carnegie Hall. Widely acclaimed for his beautiful tenor voice, vocal interpretation, and inspired teaching, he made numerous recordings, including "Cantorial Masterpieces" and "Gems of the Synagogue."

KUZNETS, SIMON, professor; b. Kharkov, Russia, Apr. 30, 1901; d. Cambridge, Mass., July 9, 1985; in U.S. since 1922. Educ.: Columbia U. (PhD). Fellow, Social Science Research Council, 1925–27; staff mem., Natl. Bureau Econ. Research, 1927–61. Asst. prof., assoc. prof., and prof., U. Pa., 1930–54; assoc. dir., War Production Bd.'s Bureau of Planning and Statistics, 1942–44; prof., Johns Hopkins U., 1954–60; prof., Harvard U., 1960–71. Pres.: Amer. Econ. Assn., Amer. Statistical Assn., Econometric Soc; a founder, Internatl. Assoc. for Research in Income and Wealth. Chmn., 1954–64, U.S. adv. com., Falk Project for Econ. Research in Israel; from 1964 on, mem. bd. trustees, Maurice Falk Inst. for Econ. Research in Israel. Author: numerous works, most notably *National Income and Its Composition, 1919 to 1938* (1941) and *Economic Growth of Nations* (1971). Regarded as a pioneer in the development of methods for measuring natl. income and econ. growth. Recipient:

Nobel Prize in Economics, 1971; hon. doctorates from Harvard, Princeton, Columbia, U. Pa., U.N.H., Hebrew U. of Jerusalem.

LAPSON, JUDAH, educator; b. Vinnitsa, Russia, Oct. 16, 1901; d. NYC, Dec. 27, 1985; in U.S. since 1911. Educ.: NYU; Teachers Inst.–Jewish Theol. Sem. of Amer. Served in the Jewish Legion of the British army, WWI. Dir., Hebrew Culture Council, Jewish Educ. Com. of N.Y. (succeeded Bureau of Jewish Educ.), 1929–69, in which capacity he fostered the introduction of Hebrew-language instruction in public and private high schools and colleges; founder, dir., and pres., Natl. Hebrew Culture Council, 1951–84; codir., Camp Achvah, 1929–44. Pres., NY State Fed. of Foreign Lang. Teachers, 1961. Pres., Menorah Soc., NYU, 1921–24; founder and natl. v.-pres., Avukah Intercollegiate Student Zionist Fed., 1924–28; exec. mem., ZOA, 1925–27; chmn., Palestine Educ. Com., 1930–41; managing ed., *Sheviley Hahinuch,* 1942–55; sec., Natl. Council for Jewish Educ., 1941–46, and Amer. Div. World Council for Jewish Educ., 1949–58; natl. cmdr., Amer. Veterans of the Jewish Legion, 1959–85; bd. mem., Alumni Assn., Teachers Inst., JTS. Author: *Hebrew for College Entrance* (1953), *Hebrew in Colleges and Universities* (1958). Recipient: hon. doctorate, Baltimore Hebrew Coll.; King George Medal (WWI); citations and awards from Histadruth Ivrith, Amer. Assn. of Teachers of Hebrew, Natl. Council of Jewish Educ., JTS, ZOA; Govt. of Israel Military Volunteers Ribbon and Aleh Decoration; Jabotinsky Centennial Medal.

MEYERHOFF, JOSEPH, businessman, philanthropist; b. (?), Russia, April 8, 1899; d. Baltimore, Md., Feb. 2, 1985; in U.S. since 1906. Educ.: U. Md. (LLB). Pres., bd. chmn., exec. com. chmn., Monumental Properties, 1933–78; bd. chmn., Magna Properties, since 1979. A real-estate developer who, by his own estimate, built more than 15,000 homes in the Baltimore area, 17,000 apartments in Md., Pa., Ga., and Fla., and 19 shopping centers in various states. Pres., Natl. Assn. Home Builders, 1946–47, and life mem. its bd. dirs.; chief benefactor, Joseph Meyerhoff Symphony Hall, Baltimore; pres., chmn., Baltimore Symphony Orchestra Assn.; benefactor: Baltimore Museum of Art, Baltimore Opera, and Peabody Inst. of Johns Hopkins U. Served on many civic and philanthropic bodies: Md. State Planning Comm., United Fund of Central Md., Md. State Bd. of Public Works, Provident Hosp. and Sinai Hosp., Baltimore. A generous supporter and worker in behalf of numerous Jewish causes and institutions in the U.S. and Israel: bd. chmn., Palestine Econ. Corp.; mem. exec. com., natl. UJA, its genl. chmn., 1961–64, and later hon. natl. chmn.; life trustee, United Israel Appeal; mem. bd. govs., Jewish Agency; bd. mem.: Associated Jewish Charities and Welfare Fund of Baltimore, Tel Aviv U., Hebrew U. of Jerusalem, Weizmann Inst. of Science, Technion-Israel Inst. of Technology, and Ben-Gurion U. of the Negev. Recipient: hon. doctorates from Baltimore Hebrew Coll., Dropsie U., Towson State U., U. Md., Johns Hopkins U., Tel Aviv U., Hebrew U., Weizmann Inst., and numerous other honors.

NAGEL, ERNEST, professor; b. Novemesto, Czechoslovakia, Nov. 16, 1901; d. NYC, Sept. 20, 1985; in U.S. since 1911. Educ.: CCNY, Columbia U. (PhD). Instr., asst. prof., assoc. prof., and prof. of philosophy, Columbia U., 1930–66; prof., Rockefeller U., 1966–67; named U. Prof., Columbia, 1967, and U. Prof. Emer., 1970. World-renowned philosopher of science, law, and social sciences. Fellow: Amer. Acad. Arts and Sciences, Amer. Phil. Soc. Author: *The Structure of Science* (1961) and many other works. Recipient: Guggenheim Fellowships, 1934, 1950; Distinguished Scholarship, Amer. Council of Learned Socs., 1959; Nicholas Murray Butler Gold Medal, Columbia U., 1980.

OLSHANSKY, CHARLES, communal worker; b. NYC, Jan. 3, 1913; d. Richmond, Va., Mar. 8, 1985. Educ.: Teachers Coll.–Columbia U. Dir. activities, Grand St. Settlement House, NYC, 1935–41; dir., USO-JWB, Newport News, Va., 1941–44; dir., USO-JWB, San Juan, P.R., 1944–45; dir., Jewish Community Center and Federation, Newport News, 1947–75; program coord., Peninsula Agency on Aging, Newport News, since 1975. Pres., Va. Assn. Social Workers; bd. mem.: Retired Seniors Volunteer Program, Newport News Girls Club, Peninsula Industrial Com. V.-pres., Middle Atlantic Section, Natl. Assn. Jewish Center Workers; bd. mem., Beth Sholom Home of E. Va. Recipient: War Dept.

Civilian Service Award; Brotherhood Citation, Natl. Conf. of Christians and Jews; Distinguished Humanitarian Award named in his honor by Peninsula Jewish Community.

PODOLOFF, MAURICE, sports executive; b. Elizabethgrad, Russia, Aug. 8, 1890; d. West Haven, Conn., Nov. 24, 1985; in U.S. since 1896. Educ.: Yale U., Yale Law School. In 1926, with his father and brothers, completed New Haven Arena and sponsored a professional hockey team; pres., Canadian-Amer. Hockey League, later the Amer. Hockey League, 1936–51. First pres., Basketball Assn. of Amer., 1946–49; commissioner, Natl. Basketball Assn., 1949–63. Credited with making basketball a major professional sport. Elected to Basketball Hall of Fame, 1974; honored by having the NBA's most-valuable-player award named for him—the Podoloff Cup.

RABB (RABINOWITZ), SIDNEY R., businessman, philanthropist; b. Boston, Mass., Oct. 20, 1900; d. Boston, Mass., Oct. 13, 1985. Educ.: Harvard Coll. Served U.S. Marine Corps, WWI. Went to work for an uncle's firm, Economy Grocery Stores, becoming genl. mgr. shortly thereafter, treas. in 1925, and bd. chmn. in 1930, a position he held until his death. The co. evolved into Stop & Shop Inc.—operator of supermarkets in the Northeast, Bradlees discount stores, and other retail outlets. A major benefactor of Beth Israel and Mass. Genl. Hosps. in Boston, Harvard U., Brandeis U., and other institutions, he served many causes in both the general and Jewish communities. Among his positions: mem. visiting com., Harvard Grad. School Business Admin. 1960–73; trustee, pres., v.-pres., Boston Public Library, 1957–80; trustee, Boston Symphony Orchestra, 1960–70; past pres., mem. exec. com., hon. life trustee, Beth Israel Hosp.; v.-chmn., mem. exec. com., Mass. Com. Catholics, Protestants, and Jews. Hon. life trustee, Combined Jewish Philanthropies; fellow, Brandeis U.; mem. adv. bd., Inst. of Jewish Law at Boston U. Law School; mem. natl. bd. govs., Israel Bond Org.; bd. mem., Kehillath Israel Synagogue, Brookline, Mass. Recipient: hon. degrees from Harvard Coll., Boston U., Brandeis U., Tufts U., Suffolk U., Northeastern U., and numerous awards, including Scopus Award, Amer. Friends of Hebrew U.; Natl. Community Service Award, Jewish Theol. Sem. of Amer.

REGUER, MOSHE ARON, professor; b. Brest Litovsk, Poland, Nov. 20, 1905; d. NYC, July 7, 1985; in U.S. since 1929. Educ.: Gymnasium, Brest Litovsk; Slobodker Yeshivah, Lithuania; Hebrew U., Jerusalem; Yeshiva U. (ordination, DHL). Instr., Hebrew Teachers Training School for Girls, NYC, 1935–38; instr., Jewish Studies, Yeshiva U., 1938–46; dir., Hebrew Teachers Inst., Montreal, 1946–51; instr., later asst. prof., of Hebrew, Yeshiva U., 1951–68; assoc. prof. Jewish studies, 1968–74. Mem.: Rabbinical Council of Amer. educ. and Israel comms.; N.Y. Bd. of Rabbis; Yeshiva U. Rabbinical Alumni and Teachers Inst. Com.

RISEMAN, MERVIN H., attorney, communal worker; b. Opelousas, La., Mar. 14, 1917; d. NYC, Aug. 14, 1985. Educ.: Tulane U., NYU (LLM). Served U.S. Navy, WWII, achieving rank of lt. cmdr. Practiced law in New Orleans, 1939–47, and in NYC since 1947. Bd. mem., Lenox Hill Neighborhood Assn. Mem. bd. govs. and natl. exec. council, Amer. Jewish Com., as well as former natl. sec. and v.-pres., chmn. Jewish Communal Affairs and Domestic Affairs comms., and pres. NY chapter; v.-pres. and trustee, Congregation Emanu-El NYC; chmn. and bd. mem., Greater NY Conf. on Soviet Jewry (Coalition to Free Soviet Jews); bd. mem., Natl. Conf. on Soviet Jewry; mem.: Natl. Jewish Community Relations Adv. Council; admin. council, Jacob Blaustein Inst. for the Advancement of Human Rights; v.-chmn., N.Y. Fed. of Reform Synagogues.

RIZ, YAAKOV, educator; b. Lutz, Poland, (?), 1922; d. Philadelphia, Pa., Dec. 20, 1985; in U.S. since 1951. Spent WWII years in Russia, where he was arrested as a Zionist and sentenced to 6 years in a slave labor camp; settled in Palestine, 1947, and fought with Palmach in War of Independence; principal, Workmen's Circle School, NE Philadelphia; founder, Jewish Identity Center, a storefront museum of the Holocaust and Jewish heritage, Philadelphia.

ROGINSKY, MOSHE, rabbi, communal worker; b. Navaredok, Russia-Poland, (?), 1909; d. NYC, Jul. 7, 1985; in U.S. since early 1950s. A teacher and head of yeshivahs, he spent most of WWII in Soviet Union, afterward living in Paris. Exec. dir., Ezras Torah, an internatl. relief org., since 1955. Author: works on talmudic law.

ROSENWALD, MARY KURTZ, violinist, philanthropist; b. (?), Latvia, Aug. 15, 1906; d. NYC, Nov. 13, 1985; in U.S. since 1935. Educ.: Hochschule für Musik in Berlin. Played first violin, Ballet Russe de Monte Carlo, before her marriage to William Rosenwald. Mem., Women's City Club of NY; trustee, Dalton Schools; bd. mem.: Musicians Found., Philharmonic Symphony Soc. of N.Y. Active in behalf of UJA-Fed., serving on its Gotham Women's Div. bd., 1974–85, and as a founding mem. of its European-Amer. Com., 1945–85. Recipient: Fritz Kreisler Prize for Violin (Berlin, Germany); Harriet H. Jonas Award, Amer. Jewish Com. (1972).

ROUSSO, LOUIS E., businessman, philanthropist; b. Monastir, Turkey, Sept. 15, 1895; d. NYC, Dec. 4, 1985; in U.S. since 1911. Educ.: Alliance Israélite Universelle. Starting as a presser in a NYC garment shop, eventually became a clothing manufacturer. Bd. chmn., Russ Togs, Inc., 1935–75. Major benefactor: Hebrew U., Jerusalem; Misgav Ladach Hosp., Jerusalem; Albert Einstein Coll. of Medicine of Yeshiva U. Past pres. and hon. life trustee, Sephardic Temple–Cong. Emeth Veshalom, Cedarhurst, N.Y.; past pres. and bd. chmn., Sephardic Home for the Aged; active in behalf of UJA-Fed., Israel Bonds, and other causes.

SALBERG, RITA, communal worker; b. NYC, Apr. 13, 1927; d. NYC, Aug. 21, 1985. Educ.: Brooklyn Coll. NYC schoolteacher for 14 years. Mem., N.Y. State Human Rights Comm. Natl. commissioner and mem. natl. exec. com. and N.Y. regional bd., Anti-Defamation League; v.-pres., Internatl. B'nai B'rith Women; v.-pres., Natl. Conf. on Soviet Jewry.

SCHLAMME, MARTHA, singer, entertainer; b. Vienna, Austria, ca. 1930; d. Jamestown, N.Y., Oct. 6, 1985; in U.S. since 1948. Known primarily for her interpretations of the music of Kurt Weill and her repertoire of folk songs in 12 languages, including Yiddish and Hebrew.

SCOOLER, ZVEE, actor, radio personality; b. Kamenetz-Podolsk, Russia, Dec. 25, 1899; d. NYC, Mar. 25, 1985; in U.S. since 1912. An actor on Broadway, Off Broadway, on the Yiddish stage, and in films, he made his debut in 1921 in *The Dybbuk*, with Maurice Schwartz's Yiddish Art Theater, remaining with the co. for 25 years. A popular Yiddish radio commentator, his weekly program *"Gram-Meister"* ("Rhyme-Master") aired for 50 years on NYC station WEVD. His acting credits included the entire 7-year Broadway run of *Fiddler on the Roof* (as Mordcha, the innkeeper) and the films *The Wall*, *The Apprenticeship of Duddy Kravitz*, *Hester Street*, *The Chosen*, and *The Pawnbroker*.

SEGAL, HENRY C., editor and publisher; b. Chillicothe, Ohio, Oct. 27, 1900; d. Cincinnati, Ohio, July 18, 1985. Educ.: Ohio State U. Reporter, Akron, Ohio *Press*, 1923; various positions, *Cincinnati Post*, 1923–28; managing ed., then ed. and publisher, *The American Israelite*—the oldest Amer. Jewish weekly in the U.S.—1928–82; part-time correspondent, the *New York Times*, for 30 years; journalism instr., U. Cincinnati. Adv. bd. mem., Big Brothers Assn.; founder and bd. mem., Jewish Community Center and JCRC, Cincinnati; bd. mem.: Rockdale Temple, United Jewish Social Agencies.

SIGAL, PHILLIP, rabbi, author; b. Toronto, Ont., Canada, Feb. 24, 1927; d. Grand Rapids, Mich., July 6, 1985; in U.S. since 1943. Educ.: Mesiftah Torah Vadaat, Yeshiva U., Columbia U., Jewish Theol. Sem. of Amer., U. Pittsburgh (PhD). Rabbi: Bridgeton, N.J., 1955–65; Bloomfield, N.J., 1965–72; Hillel dir., Pittsburgh, 1972–75; teaching asst., Pittsburgh Theol. Sem., 1976–79; rabbi, Grand Rapids, Mich., 1980–85. Chmn.: Bridgeton, N.J. Human Relations Comm.; Bloomfield, N.J. Comm. on Civil Rights; founder and pres., Cumberland County, N.J. Guidance Center. Author: *New Dimensions in Judaism* (1972), *Emergence of Contemporary Judaism* (3 vols., 1980–86); *Judentum* (1986). Recipient: hon. doctorate, JTS.

SKIRBALL, JACK H., motion picture producer, rabbi; b. Homestead, Pa., June 23, 1896; d. Los Angeles, Calif., Dec. 8, 1985. Educ.: Hebrew Union Coll.-Jewish Inst. of Religion, Western Reserve U. Asst. rabbi, Cleveland, Ohio, 1922–25; rabbi, Evansville, Ind., 1926–33; genl. mgr., production, Educ. Films Corp. of Amer., 1933–39; independent producer since 1938. Active in Boy Scouts, Amer. Red Cross, and other orgs. Former v.-chmn. bd. of govs., HUC-JIR, and bd. mem. for over 30 years; chmn. bd. of overseers, HUC-JIR

Los Angeles School; a founder and benefactor of that school and its Skirball Museum; benefactor, the Skirball Inst. on Amer. Values, Amer. Jewish Com., Los Angeles. Recipient: hon. doctorates from HUC-JIR and U. Southern Calif., and numerous other honors.

STEIN, LEONARD, businessman, communal worker; b. Harrisburg, Pa., June 22, 1918; d. Silver Spring, Md., July 1, 1985. Retail furniture merchant. Active in B'nai B'rith since his teens; pres.: Free State and Natl. Capital Assn. Lodges, 1960s; District 5, 1976–77; Natl. Capital BB Housing Found., 1970–85, in which position was instrumental in creating an apartment complex for low-income sr. citizens; mem. bd. of govs., BB Internatl., 1980–85.

STROOCK, ALAN M., attorney, communal worker; b. NYC, Nov. 12, 1907; d. NYC, Mar. 29, 1985. Educ.: Harvard Coll., Yale Law School. Law clerk for Justice Benjamin N. Cardozo, U.S. Supreme Court, 1934–36; assoc., then partner, in the firm that became Stroock & Stroock & Lavan, 1936–83; of counsel, 1984. Asst. corporation counsel of NYC, 1938; mem.: U.S. Comm. for UNESCO; various coms. for Harvard U.; bd. of trustees, Horace Mann School for Boys; life trustee, NYU. Bd. chmn. and pres. of the corp., Jewish Theological Sem. of Amer.; life trustee, Fed. of Jewish Philanthropies of N.Y.; v.-pres. and chmn. admin. com., Amer. Jewish Com., and a founder of *Commentary* magazine; chmn. bd. of trustees, Amer. Friends of the Alliance Israélite Universelle. Recipient: hon. doctorate, JTS.

THORNE, AHRNE, writer, editor; b. Lodz, Poland, Dec. 26, 1904; d. NYC, Dec. 13, 1985; in U.S. since 1940. An anarchist from his student days in Paris in the 1920s, he espoused a peaceful society free of religious and state domination; began writing for the *Freie Arbeiter Stimme*—the N.Y.-based Jewish anarchist journal—while living in Toronto in the 1930s. From 1940 on, in NYC, worked as a printer and free-lance writer, contributing articles in Yiddish to the *Jewish Daily Forward* and other publications, and in English to the *New Leader, Present Tense,* and *Midstream,* as well as translations into Yiddish from English, French, and German. Asst. ed., *Freie Arbeiter Stimme,* 1952–77, and ed., 1975–77, when the paper closed after 87 years of publication.

ULLMANN, JACOB W., business executive, philanthropist; b. NYC, Aug. 12, 1927; d. NYC, Feb. 5, 1985. Educ.: MIT, NYU, U. Mich. Sr. engineer, Oak Ridge Natl. Lab., 1950–66; technical asst. to v.-pres., Union Carbide Corp., since 1966. Pres., bd. chmn., and treas., Amer. Soc. for Technion-Israel Inst. of Technology, and mem. Technion's internatl. bd. of govs.; gov. and mem. bd. of dirs., Weizmann Inst. of Science; benefactor: Albert Einstein Coll. of Medicine, Ben-Gurion U. of the Negev, Hadassah. Recipient: hon. degree, Technion; Jabotinsky Centennial Medal.

WAIFE, MARIE, the last surviving child of Sholom Aleichem; b. Odessa, Russia, Oct. 29, 1892; d. NYC, Dec. 11, 1985; in U.S. since 1914. Educ.: U. Lausanne (Switzerland). Known for the gatherings she arranged on her father's *yahrzeit*—as requested in his will—at which his stories were read, and which were attended by leading figures in the arts. Author: *My Father, Sholom Aleichem* (1968).

WALD, ALBERT, attorney, communal worker; b. NYC, Feb. 21, 1889; d. NYC, Feb. 1, 1985. Educ.: CCNY, N.Y. Law School. As N.Y. state senator, 1933–35, sponsored N.Y.'s first minimum-wage law. Mem.: natl. council, Boy Scouts of Amer. and its lay com. on Jewish service; v.-pres., Union of Orthodox Jewish Congs. of Amer.; pres., Synagogue Council of Amer.; sec., Emet–Rabbi Herzog World Acad. (Jerusalem).

WILLEN, JOSEPH, communal worker; b. Kushnitza, Russia, June 22, 1897; d. NYC, July 6, 1985; in U.S. since 1905. Educ.: CCNY. Served U.S. army, WWI. Joined staff of Fed. of Jewish Philanthropies of N.Y. in 1919; served as its exec. v.-pres., 1941–67, and exec. consultant since 1967. Regarded as a pioneer in community organizing and fund raising, he developed the system of raising funds through a network of trade, professional, and community groups as well as other now common techniques. Dir., Community Council of Greater N.Y. and mem. its central planning bd.; mem.: natl. adv. bd., former India League of Amer.; India Famine Emergency Mission, 1947; bd. advisors, Vocational Advisory Service; Citizens' Budget Comm.; NYC Mayor's Com. on Unity; N.Y. State Finance Com. (WWII); Brandeis U. Graduate Social Welfare School bd. of overseers; Navy League of the U.S.; N.Y. Council Against Poverty; Presidents' Council, NYU Graduate School of Social Work; bd. mem.: N.Y. Urban League, United Neighborhood Houses, Pro Deo U. of Rome, Fountain House, Stockbridge School; consultant: Amer. Red Cross, Greater N.Y. Fund. Mem. bd. govs., Amer. Jewish Com., its former v.-pres., mem. Community Activities com., and chmn. Labor com.; bd. mem.: Council of Jewish Feds., Natl. Jewish Welfare Bd., Amer. Soc. for Technion, Technion-Israel Inst. for Technology (Haifa), Amer. Jewish JDC, Amer. Jewish Hist. Soc., Jewish Theol. Sem. of Amer. Recipient: hon. doctorates from Boston U. and JTS and many other honors.

ZUCKER, DAVID, businessman, communal worker; b. (?), Poland, (?), 1906; d. Miami Beach, Fla., July 28, 1985; in U.S. since 1923; founder, Danbar Press, a NYC printing concern. Pres., World Council of Synagogues; mem. bd. of overseers, Jewish Theol. Sem. of Amer.; v.-pres., United Synagogue of Amer. and pres. its N.Y. region; founder and benefactor, Center for Conservative Judaism in Jerusalem; founding mem., Zionist Org. of Amer.; bd. mem., Temple Israel, Great Neck, N.Y.

Calendars

SUMMARY JEWISH CALENDAR, 5747–5751 (Oct. 1986–Aug. 1991)

HOLIDAY	5747 1986			5748 1987			5749 1988			5750 1989			5751 1990		
Rosh Ha-shanah, 1st day	Sa	Oct.	4	Th	Sept.	24	M	Sept.	12	Sa	Sept.	30	Th	Sept.	20
Rosh Ha-shanah, 2nd day	S	Oct.	5	F	Sept.	25	T	Sept.	13	S	Oct.	1	F	Sept.	21
Fast of Gedaliah	M	Oct.	6	S	Sept.	27	W	Sept.	14	M	Oct.	2	S	Sept.	23
Yom Kippur	M	Oct.	13	Sa	Oct.	3	W	Sept.	21	M	Oct.	9	Sa	Sept.	29
Sukkot, 1st day	Sa	Oct.	18	Th	Oct.	8	M	Sept.	26	Sa	Oct.	14	Th	Oct.	4
Sukkot, 2nd day	S	Oct.	19	F	Oct.	9	T	Sept.	27	S	Oct.	15	F	Oct.	5
Hosha'na' Rabbah	F	Oct.	24	W	Oct.	14	S	Oct.	2	F	Oct.	20	W	Oct.	10
Shemini 'Azeret	Sa	Oct.	25	Th	Oct.	15	M	Oct.	3	Sa	Oct.	21	Th	Oct.	11
Simhat Torah	S	Oct.	26	F	Oct.	16	T	Oct.	4	S	Oct.	22	F	Oct.	12
New Moon, Heshwan, 1st day	S	Nov.	2	F	Oct.	23	T	Oct.	11	S	Oct.	29	F	Oct.	19
New Moon, Heshwan, 2nd day	M	Nov.	3	Sa	Oct.	24	W	Oct.	12	M	Oct.	30	Sa	Oct.	20
New Moon, Kislew, 1st day	T	Dec.	2	S	Nov.	22	Th	Nov.	10	T	Nov.	28	S	Nov.	18
New Moon, Kislew, 2nd day	W	Dec.	3							W	Nov.	29			
Hanukkah, 1st day	Sa	Dec.	27	W	Dec.	16	S	Dec.	4	Sa	Dec.	23	W	Dec.	12
		1987													
New Moon, Tevet, 1st day	Th	Jan.	1	M	Dec.	21	F	Dec.	9	Th	Dec.	28	M	Dec.	17
New Moon, Ṭevet, 2nd day	F	Jan.	2	T	Dec.	22				F	Dec.	29	T	Dec.	18
											1990				
Fast of 10th of Ṭevet	S	Jan.	11	Th	Dec.	31	S	Dec.	18	S	Jan.	7	Th	Dec.	27

	1987			1988			1989			1990			1991	
New Moon, Shevat	Sa	Jan.	31	W	Jan.	20	Sa	Jan.	7	Sa	Jan.	27	W	Jan.	16
Hamishshah-'asar bi-Shevat	Sa	Feb.	14	W	Feb.	3	Sa	Jan.	21	Sa	Feb.	10	W	Jan.	30
New Moon, Adar I, 1st day	S	Mar.	1	Th	Feb.	18	S	Feb.	5	S	Feb.	25	Th	Feb.	14
New Moon, Adar I, 2nd day	M	Mar.	2	F	Feb.	19	M	Feb.	6	M	Feb.	26	F	Feb.	15
New Moon, Adar II, 1st day							T	Mar.	7						
New Moon, Adar II, 2nd day							W	Mar.	8						
Fast of Esther	Th	Mar.	12	W	Mar.	2	M	Mar.	20	Th	Mar.	8	W	Feb.	27
Purim	S	Mar.	15	Th	Mar.	3	T	Mar.	21	S	Mar.	11	Th	Feb.	28
Shushan Purim	M	Mar.	16	F	Mar.	4	W	Mar.	22	M	Mar.	12	F	Mar.	1
New Moon, Nisan	T	Mar.	31	Sa	Mar.	19	Th	Apr.	6	T	Mar.	27	Sa	Mar.	16
Passover, 1st day	T	Apr.	14	Sa	Apr.	2	Th	Apr.	20	T	Apr.	10	Sa	Mar.	30
Passover, 2nd day	W	Apr.	15	S	Apr.	3	F	Apr.	21	W	Apr.	11	S	Mar.	31
Passover, 7th day	M	Apr.	20	F	Apr.	8	W	Apr.	26	M	Apr.	16	F	Apr.	5
Passover, 8th day	T	Apr.	21	Sa	Apr.	9	Th	Apr.	27	T	Apr.	17	Sa	Apr.	6
Holocaust Memorial Day	S	Apr.	26	Th	Apr.	14	T	May	2	S	Apr.	22	Th	Apr.	11
New Moon, Iyar, 1st day	W	Apr.	29	S	Apr.	17	F	May	5	W	Apr.	25	S	Apr.	14
New Moon, Iyar, 2nd day	Th	Apr.	30	M	Apr.	18	Sa	May	6	Th	Apr.	26	M	Apr.	15
Israel Independence Day	M	May	4	F	Apr.	22	W	May	10	M	Apr.	30	F	Apr.	19
Lag Ba-'omer	S	May	17	Th	May	5	T	May	23	S	May	13	Th	May	2
Jerusalem Day	W	May	27	S	May	15	F	June	2	W	May	23	S	May	12
New Moon, Siwan	F	May	29	T	May	17	S	June	4	F	May	25	T	May	14
Shavu'ot, 1st day	W	June	3	S	May	22	F	June	9	W	May	30	S	May	19
Shavu'ot, 2nd day	Th	June	4	M	May	23	Sa	June	10	Th	May	31	M	May	20
New Moon, Tammuz, 1st day	Sa	June	27	W	June	15	M	July	3	Sa	June	23	W	June	12
New Moon, Tammuz, 2nd day	S	June	28	Th	June	16	T	July	4	S	June	24	Th	June	13
Fast of 17th of Tammuz	T	July	14	S	July	3	Th	July	20	T	July	10	S	June	30
New Moon, Av	M	July	27	F	July	15	W	Aug.	2	M	July	23	F	July	12
Fast of 9th of Av	T	Aug.	4	S	July	24	Th	Aug.	10	T	July	31	S	July	21
New Moon, Elul, 1st day	T	Aug.	25	Sa	Aug.	13	Th	Aug.	31	T	Aug.	21	Sa	Aug.	10
New Moon, Elul, 2nd day	W	Aug.	26	S	Aug.	14	F	Sept.	1	W	Aug.	22	S	Aug.	11

CONDENSED MONTHLY CALENDAR
(1986–1988)

1985, Dec. 13–Jan. 10, 1986] TEVET (29 DAYS) [5746

Civil Date	Day of the Week	Jewish Date	SABBATHS, FESTIVALS, FASTS	PENTATEUCHAL READING	PROPHETICAL READING
Dec. 13	F	Tevet 1	New Moon; Hanukkah, sixth day	Num. 28:1–15 Num. 7:42–47	
14	Sa	2	Mi-kez; Hanukkah, seventh day	Gen. 41:1–44:17 Num. 7:48–53	Zechariah 2:14–4:7
15	S	3	Hanukkah, eighth day	Num. 7:54–8:4	
21	Sa	9	Wa-yiggash	Gen. 44:18–47:27	Ezekiel 37:15–28
22	S	10	Fast of 10th of Tevet	Exod. 32:11–14 34:1–10	Isaiah 55:6–56:8 (afternoon only)
28	Sa	16	Wa-yehi	Gen. 47:28–50:26	I Kings 2:1–12
Jan. 4	Sa	23	Shemot	Exod. 1:1–6:1	Isaiah 27:6–28:13 29:22–23 *Jeremiah 1:1–2:3*

Italics are for Sephardi Minhag.

1986, Jan. 11–Feb. 9] SHEVAṬ (30 DAYS) [5746

Civil Date	Day of the Week	Jewish Date	SABBATHS, FESTIVALS, FASTS	PENTATEUCHAL READING	PROPHETICAL READING
Jan. 11	Sa	Shevaṭ 1	Wa-'era'; New Moon	Exod. 6:2–9:35 Num. 28:9–15	Isaiah 66:1–24
18	Sa	8	Bo'	Exod. 10:1–13:16	Jeremiah 46:13–28
25	Sa	15	Be-shallaḥ (Shabbat Shirah); Ḥamishshah-'asar bi-Shevaṭ	Exod. 13:17–17:16	Judges 4:4–5:31 *Judges 5:1–31*
Feb. 1	Sa	22	Yitro	Exod. 18:1–20:23	Isaiah 6:1–7:6 9:5–6 *Isaiah 6:1–13*
8	Sa	29	Mishpaṭim	Exod. 21:1–24:18	I Samuel 20:18–42
9	S	30	New Moon, first day	Num. 28:1–15	

Italics are for Sephardi Minhag.

1986, Feb. 10–Mar. 11] ADAR I (30 DAYS) [5746

Civil Date	Day of the Week	Jewish Date	SABBATHS, FESTIVALS, FASTS	PENTATEUCHAL READING	PROPHETICAL READING
Feb. 10	M	Adar I 1	New Moon, second day	Num. 28:1–15	
15	Sa	6	Terumah	Exod. 25:1–27:19	I Kings 5:26–6:13
22	Sa	13	Teẓawweh	Exod. 27:20–30:10	Ezekiel 43:10–27
Mar. 1	Sa	20	Ki tissa'	Exod. 30:11–34:35	I Kings 18:1–39 *I Kings 18:20–39*
8	Sa	27	Wa-yakhel (Shabbat Shekalim)	Exod. 35:1–38:20 Exod. 30:11–16	II Kings 12:1–17 *II Kings 11:17–12:17*
11	T	30	New Moon, first day	Num. 28:1–15	

1986, Mar. 12–Apr. 9] ADAR II (29 DAYS) [5746

Civil Date	Day of the Week	Jewish Date	SABBATHS, FESTIVALS, FASTS	PENTATEUCHAL READING	PROPHETICAL READING
Mar. 12	W	Adar II 1	New Moon, second day	Num. 28:1–15	
15	Sa	4	Pekude	Exod. 38:21–40:38	I Kings 7:40–50
22	Sa	11	Wa-yikra (Shabbat Zakhor)	Levit. 1:1–5:26 Deut. 25:17–19	I Samuel 15:2–34 *I Samuel 15:1–34*
24	M	13	Fast of Esther	Exod. 32:11–14 34:1–10	Isaiah 55:6–56:8 (afternoon only)
25	T	14	Purim	Exod. 17:8–16	Book of Esther (night before and in the morning)
26	W	15	Shushan Purim		
29	Sa	18	Ẓaw (Shabbat Parah)	Levit. 6:1–8:36 Num. 19:1–22	Ezekiel 36:16–38 *Ezekiel 36:16–36*
Apr. 5	Sa	25	Shemini (Shabbat Ha-hodesh)	Levit. 9:1–11:47 Exod. 12:1–20	Ezekiel 45:16–46:18 *Ezekiel 45:18–46:15*

Italics are for Sephardi Minhag.

1986, Apr. 10–May 9] NISAN (30 DAYS) [5746

Civil Date	Day of the Week	Jewish Date	SABBATHS, FESTIVALS, FASTS	PENTATEUCHAL READING	PROPHETICAL READING
Apr. 10	Th	Nisan 1	New Moon	Num. 28:1–15	
12	Sa	3	Tazria'	Levit. 12:1–13:59	II Kings 4:42–5:19
19	Sa	10	Mezora' (Shabbat Ha-gadol)	Levit. 14:1–15:33	Malachi 3:4–24
23	W	14	Fast of Firstborn		
24	Th	15	Passover, first day	Exod. 12:21–51 Num. 28:16–25	Joshua 5:2–6:1, 27
25	F	16	Passover, second day	Levit. 22:26–23:44 Num. 28:16–25	II Kings 23:1–19, 21–25
26	Sa	17	Hol Ha-mo'ed, first day	Exod. 33:12–34:26 Num. 28:19–25	Ezekiel 37:1–14
27	S	18	Hol Ha-mo'ed, second day	Exod. 13:1–16 Num. 28:19–25	
28	M	19	Hol Ha-mo'ed, third day	Exod. 22:24–23:19 Num. 28:19–25	
29	T	20	Hol Ha-mo'ed, fourth day	Num. 9:1–14 Num. 28:19–25	
30	W	21	Passover, seventh day	Exod. 13:17–15:26 Num. 28:19–25	II Samuel 22:1–51
May 1	Th	22	Passover, eighth day	Deut. 15:19–16:17 Num. 28:19–25	Isaiah 10:32–12:6
3	Sa	24	Ahare mot	Levit. 16:1–18:30	Ezekiel 22:1–16
6	T	27	Holocaust Memorial Day		
9	F	30	New Moon, first day	Num. 28:1–15	

1986, May 10–June 7] IYAR (29 DAYS) [5746

Civil Date	Day of the Week	Jewish Date	SABBATHS, FESTIVALS, FASTS	PENTATEUCHAL READING	PROPHETICAL READING
May 10	Sa	Iyar 1	Kedoshim; New Moon, second day	Levit. 19:1–20:27 Num. 28:9–15	Isaiah 66:1–24
14	W	5	Israel Independence Day		
17	Sa	8	Emor	Levit. 21:1–24:23	Ezekiel 44:15–31
24	Sa	15	Be-har	Levit. 25:1–26:2	Jeremiah 32:6–27
27	T	18	Lag Ba'omer		
31	Sa	22	Be-ḥukkotai	Levit. 26:3–27:34	Jeremiah 16:19–17:14
June 6	F	28	Jerusalem Day		
7	Sa	29	Be-midbar	Num. 1:1–4:20	I Samuel 20:18–42

1986, June 8–July 7] SIWAN (30 DAYS) [5746

Civil Date	Day of the Week	Jewish Date	SABBATHS, FESTIVALS, FASTS	PENTATEUCHAL READING	PROPHETICAL READING
June 8	S	Siwan 1	New Moon	Num. 28:1–15	
13	F	6	Shavu'ot, first day	Exod. 19:1–20:23 Num. 28:26–31	Ezekiel 1:1–28 3:12
14	Sa	7	Shavu'ot, second day	Deut. 15:19–16:17 Num. 28:26–31	Habbakuk 3:1–19 *Habbakuk 2:20–3:19*
21	Sa	14	Naso'	Num. 4:21–7:89	Judges 13:2–25
28	Sa	21	Be-ha'alotekha	Num. 8:1–12:16	Zechariah 2:14–4:7
July 5	Sa	28	Shelaḥ lekha	Num. 13:1–15:41	Joshua 2:1–24
7	M	30	New Moon, first day	Num. 28:1–15	

Italics are for Sephardi Minhag.

1986, July 8–Aug. 5] TAMMUZ (29 DAYS) [5746

Civil Date	Day of the Week	Jewish Date	SABBATHS, FESTIVALS, FASTS	PENTATEUCHAL READING	PROPHETICAL READING
July 8	T	Tammuz 1	New Moon, second day	Num. 28:1–15	
12	Sa	5	Ḳoraḥ	Num. 16:1–18:32	I Samuel 11:14–12:22
19	Sa	12	Ḥuḳḳat, Balaḳ	Num. 19:1–25:9	Micah 5:6–6:8
24	Th	17	Fast of 17th of Tammuz	Exod. 32:11–14 34:1–10	Isaiah 55:6–56:8 (afternoon only)
26	Sa	19	Pineḥas	Num. 25:10–30:1	Jeremiah 1:1–2:3
Aug. 2	Sa	26	Maṭṭot, Mas'e	Num. 30:2–36:13	Jeremiah 2:4–28 3:4 *Jeremiah 2:4–28 4:1–2*

Italics are for Sephardi Minhag.

1986, Aug. 6–Sept. 4] AV (30 DAYS) [5746

Civil Date	Day of the Week	Jewish Date	SABBATHS, FESTIVALS, FASTS	PENTATEUCHAL READING	PROPHETICAL READING
Aug. 6	W	Av 1	New Moon	Num. 28:1–15	
9	Sa	4	Devarim (Shabbat Ḥazon)	Deut. 1:1–3:22	Isaiah 1:1–27
14	Th	9	Fast of 9th of Av	Morning: Deut. 4:25–40 Afternoon: Exod. 32:11–14 34:1–10	(Lamentations is read the night before.) Jeremiah 8:13–9:23 Isaiah 55:6–56:8
16	Sa	11	Wa-ethannan (Shabbat Naḥamu)	Deut. 3:23–7:11	Isaiah 40:1–26
23	Sa	18	ʻEkev	Deut. 7:12–11:25	Isaiah 49:14–51:3
30	Sa	25	Re'eh	Deut. 11:26–16:17	Isaiah 54:11–55:5
Sept. 4	Th	30	New Moon, first day	Num. 28:1–15	

1986, Sept. 5–Oct. 3] ELUL (29 DAYS) [5746

Civil Date	Day of the Week	Jewish Date	SABBATHS, FESTIVALS, FASTS	PENTATEUCHAL READING	PROPHETICAL READING
Sept. 5	F	Elul 1	New Moon, second day	Num. 28:1–15	
6	Sa	2	Shofeṭim	Deut. 16:18–21:9	Isaiah 51:12–52:12
13	Sa	9	Ki teze'	Deut. 21:10–25:19	Isaiah 54:1–10
20	Sa	16	Ki tavo'	Deut. 26:1–29:8	Isaiah 60:1–22
27	Sa	23	Niẓẓavim, Wa-yelekh	Deut. 29:9–31:30	Isaiah 61:10–63:9

1986, Oct. 4–Nov. 2] TISHRI (30 DAYS) [5747

Civil Date	Day of the Week	Jewish Date	SABBATHS, FESTIVALS, FASTS	PENTATEUCHAL READING	PROPHETICAL READING
Oct. 4	Sa	Tishri 1	Rosh Ha-shanah, first day	Gen. 21:1–34 Num. 29:1–6	I Samuel 1:1–2:10
5	S	2	Rosh Ha-shanah, second day	Gen. 22:1–24 Num. 29:1–6	Jeremiah 31:2–20
6	M	3	Fast of Gedaliah	Exod. 32:11–14 34:1–10	Isaiah 55:6–56:8 (afternoon only)
11	Sa	8	Ha'azinu (Shabbat Shuvah)	Deut. 32:1–52	Hosea 14:2–10 Micah 7:18–20 Joel 2:15–27 *Hosea 14:2–10* *Micah 7:18–20*
13	M	10	Yom Kippur	Morning: Levit. 16:1–34 Num. 29:7–11 Afternoon: Levit. 18:1–30	Isaiah 57:14–58:14 Jonah 1:1–4:11 Micah 7:18–20
18	Sa	15	Sukkot, first day	Levit. 22:26–23:44 Num. 29:12–16	Zechariah 14:1–21
19	S	16	Sukkot, second day	Levit. 22:26–23:44 Num. 29:12–16	I Kings 8:2–21
20–23	M-Th	17–20	Ḥol Ha-mo'ed	M Num. 29:17–25 T Num. 29:20–28 W Num. 29:23–31 Th Num. 29:26–34	
24	F	21	Hosha'na' Rabbah	Num. 29:26–34	
25	Sa	22	Shemini 'Aẓeret	Deut. 14:22–16:17 Num. 29:35–30:1	I Kings 8:54–66
26	S	23	Simḥat Torah	Deut. 33:1–34:12 Gen. 1:1–2:3 Num. 29:35–30:1	Joshua 1:1–18 *Joshua 1:1–9*
Nov. 1	Sa	29	Be-re'shit	Gen. 1:1–6:8	I Samuel 20:18–42
2	S	30	New Moon, first day	Num. 28:1–15	

Italics are for Sephardi Minhag.

1986, Nov. 3–Dec. 2]   HESHWAN (30 DAYS)   [5747

Civil Date	Day of the Week	Jewish Date	SABBATHS, FESTIVALS, FASTS	PENTATEUCHAL READING	PROPHETICAL READING
Nov. 3	M	Heshwan 1	New Moon, second day	Num. 28:1–15	
8	Sa	6	Noah	Gen. 6:9–11:32	Isaiah 54:1–55:5 *Isaiah 54:1–10*
15	Sa	13	Lekh lekha	Gen. 12:1–17:27	Isaiah 40:27–41:16
22	Sa	20	Wa-yera'	Gen. 18:1–22:24	II Kings 4:1–37 *II Kings 4:1–23*
29	Sa	27	Hayye Sarah	Gen. 23:1–25:18	I Kings 1:1–31
Dec. 2	T	30	New Moon, first day	Num. 28:1–15	

1986, Dec. 3–Jan. 1, 1987]   KISLEW (30 DAYS)   [5747

Civil Date	Day of the Week	Jewish Date	SABBATHS, FESTIVALS, FASTS	PENTATEUCHAL READING	PROPHETICAL READING
Dec. 3	W	Kislew 1	New Moon, second day	Num. 28:1–15	
6	Sa	4	Toledot	Gen. 25:19–28:9	Malachi 1:1–2:7
13	Sa	11	Wa-yeze'	Gen. 28:10–32:3	Hosea 12:13–14:10 *Hosea 11:7–12:12*
20	Sa	18	Wa-yishlah	Gen. 32:4–36:43	Hosea 11:7–12:12 *Obadiah 1:1–21*
27	Sa	25	Wa-yeshev; Hanukkah, first day	Gen. 37:1–40:23 Num. 7:1–17	Zechariah 2:14–4:7
Dec. 28–31	S-W	26–29	Hanukkah, second to fifth days	S Num. 7:18–29 M Num. 7:24–35 T Num. 7:30–41 W Num. 7:36–47	
Jan. 1	Th	30	New Moon, first day; Hanukkah, sixth day	Num. 28:1–15 Num. 7:42–47	

Italics are for Sephardi Minhag.

1987, Jan. 2–Jan. 30] TEVET (29 DAYS) [5747

Civil Date	Day of the Week	Jewish Date	SABBATHS, FESTIVALS, FASTS	PENTATEUCHAL READING	PROPHETICAL READING
Jan. 2	F	Tevet 1	New Moon, second day; Hanukkah, seventh day	Num. 28:1–15 Num. 7:48–53	
3	Sa	2	Mi-kez; Hanukkah, eighth day	Gen. 41:1–44:17 Num. 7:54–8:4	Zechariah 2:14–4:7
10	Sa	9	Wa-yiggash	Gen. 44:18–47:27	Ezekiel 37:15–28
11	S	10	Fast of 10th of Tevet	Exod. 32:11–14 34:1–10	Isaiah 55:6–56:8 (afternoon only)
17	Sa	16	Wa-yehi	Gen. 47:28–50:26	I Kings 2:1–12
24	Sa	23	Shemot	Exod. 1:1–6:1	Isaiah 27:6–28:13 29:22–23 *Jeremiah 1:1–2:3*

Italics are for Sephardi Minhag.

1987, Jan. 31–Mar. 1] SHEVAṬ (30 DAYS) [5747

Civil Date	Day of the Week	Jewish Date	SABBATHS, FESTIVALS, FASTS	PENTATEUCHAL READING	PROPHETICAL READING
Jan. 31	Sa	Shevaṭ 1	Wa-'era'; New Moon	Exod. 6:2–9:35 Num. 28:1–15	Isaiah 66:1–24
Feb. 7	Sa	8	Bo'	Exod. 10:1–13:16	Jeremiah 46:13–28
14	Sa	15	Be-shallaḥ (Shabbat Shirah); Ḥamishshah-'asar bi-Shevaṭ	Exod. 13:17–17:16	Judges 4:4–5:31 *Judges 5:1–31*
21	Sa	22	Yitro	Exod. 18:1–20:23	Isaiah 6:1–7:6 9:5–6 *Isaiah 6:1–13*
28	Sa	29	Mishpaṭim (Shabbat Sheḳalim)	Exod. 21:1–24:18 Exod. 30:11–16	II Kings 12:1–17 *II Kings 11:17–12:17* *I Samuel 20:18–42*
Mar. 1	S	30	New Moon, first day	Num. 28:1–15	

Italics are for Sephardi Minhag.

1987, Mar. 2–Mar. 30] ADAR (29 DAYS) [5747

Civil Date	Day of the Week	Jewish Date	SABBATHS, FESTIVALS, FASTS	PENTATEUCHAL READING	PROPHETICAL READING
Mar. 2	M	Adar 1	New Moon, second day	Num. 28:1–15	
7	Sa	6	Terumah	Exod. 25:1–27:19	I Kings 5:26–6:13
12	Th	11	Fast of Esther	Exod. 32:11–14 34:1–10	Isaiah 55:6–56:8 (afternoon only)
14	Sa	13	Tezawweh (Shabbat Zakhor)	Exod. 27:20–30:10 Deut. 25:17–19	I Samuel 15:2–34 *I Samuel 15:1–34*
15	S	14	Purim	Exod. 17:8–16	Book of Esther (night before and in the morning)
16	M	15	Shushan Purim		
21	Sa	20	Ki tissa' (Shabbat Parah)	Exod. 30:11–34:35 Num. 19:1–22	Ezekiel 36:16–38 *Ezekiel 36:16–36*
28	Sa	27	Wa-yakhel, Pekude (Shabbat Ha-ḥodesh)	Exod. 35:1–40:38 Exod. 12:1–20	Ezekiel 45:16–46:18 *Ezekiel 45:18–46:15*

Italics are for Sephardi Minhag.

1987, Mar. 31–Apr. 29]   NISAN (30 DAYS)   [5747

Civil Date	Day of the Week	Jewish Date	SABBATHS, FESTIVALS, FASTS	PENTATEUCHAL READING	PROPHETICAL READING
Mar. 31	T	Nisan 1	New Moon	Num. 28:1–15	
Apr. 4	Sa	5	Wa-yikra'	Levit. 1:1–5:26	Isaiah 43:21–44:24
11	Sa	12	Zaw (Shabbat Ha-gadol)	Levit. 6:1–8:36	Malachi 3:4–24
13	M	14	Fast of Firstborn		
14	T	15	Passover, first day	Exod. 12:21–51 Num. 28:16–25	Joshua 5:2–6:1, 27
15	W	16	Passover, second day	Levit. 22:26–23:44 Num. 28:16–25	II Kings 23:1–9, 21–25
16	Th	17	Hol Ha-mo'ed, first day	Exod. 13:1–16 Num. 28:19–25	
17	F	18	Hol Ha-mo'ed, second day	Exod. 22:24–23:19 Num. 28:19–25	
18	Sa	19	Hol Ha-mo'ed, third day	Exod. 33:12–34:26 Num. 28:19–25	Ezekiel 37:1–14
19	S	20	Hol Ha-mo'ed, fourth day	Num. 9:1–14 Num. 28:19–25	
20	M	21	Passover, seventh day	Exod. 13:17–15:26 Num. 28:19–25	II Samuel 22:1–51
21	T	22	Passover, eighth day	Deut. 15:19–16:17 Num. 28:19–25	Isaiah 10:32–12:6
25	Sa	26	Shemini	Levit. 9:1–11:47	II Samuel 6:1–7:17
26	S	27	Holocaust Memorial Day		
29	W	30	New Moon, first day	Num. 28:1–15	

1987, Apr. 30–May 28] IYAR (29 DAYS) [5747

Civil Date	Day of the Week	Jewish Date	SABBATHS, FESTIVALS, FASTS	PENTATEUCHAL READING	PROPHETICAL READING
Apr. 30	Th	Iyar 1	New Moon, second day	Num. 28:1–15	
May 2	Sa	3	Tazria', Mezora'	Levit. 12:1–15:33	II Kings 7:3–20
4	M	5	Israel Independence Day		
9	Sa	10	Aḥare mot, Ḳedoshim	Levit. 16:1–20:27	Amos 9:7–15 *Ezekiel 20:2–20*
16	Sa	17	Emor	Levit. 21:1–24:23	Ezekiel 44:15–31
17	S	18	Lag Ba-'omer		
23	Sa	24	Be-har, Be-ḥukkotai	Levit. 25:1–27:34	Jeremiah 16:19–17:14
27	W	28	Jerusalem Day		

1987, May 29–June 27] SIWAN (30 DAYS) [5747

Civil Date	Day of the Week	Jewish Date	SABBATHS, FESTIVALS, FASTS	PENTATEUCHAL READING	PROPHETICAL READING
May 29	F	Siwan 1	New Moon	Num. 28:1–15	
30	Sa	2	Be-midbar	Num. 1:1–4:20	Hosea 2:1–22
June 3	W	6	Shavu'ot, first day	Exod. 19:1–20:23 Num. 28:26–31	Ezekiel 1:1–28 3:12
4	Th	7	Shavu'ot, second day	Deut. 15:19–16:17 Num. 28:26–31	Habbakuk 3:1–19 *Habbakuk 2:20–3:19*
6	Sa	9	Naso'	Num. 4:21–7:89	Judges 13:2–25
13	Sa	16	Be-ha'alotekha	Num. 8:1–12:16	Zechariah 2:14–4:7
20	Sa	23	Shelaḥ lekha	Num. 13:1–15:41	Joshua 2:1–24
27	Sa	30	Ḳoraḥ; New Moon, first day	Num. 16:1–18:32 Num. 28:9–15	Isaiah 66:1–24 *Isaiah 66:1–24* *I Samuel 20:18, 42*

Italics are for Sephardi Minhag.

1987, June 28–July 26] TAMMUZ (29 DAYS) [5747

Civil Date	Day of the Week	Jewish Date	SABBATHS, FESTIVALS, FASTS	PENTATEUCHAL READING	PROPHETICAL READING
June 28	S	Tammuz 1	New Moon, second day	Num. 28:1–15	
July 4	Sa	7	Ḥuḳḳat	Num. 19:1–22:1	Judges 11:1–33
11	Sa	14	Balaḳ	Num. 22:2–25:9	Micah 5:6–6:8
14	T	17	Fast of 17th of Tammuz	Exod. 32:11–14 34:1–10	Isaiah 55:6–56:8 (afternoon only)
18	Sa	21	Pineḥas	Num. 25:10–30:1	Jeremiah 1:1–2:3
25	Sa	28	Maṭṭot, Mas'e	Num. 30:2–36:13	Jeremiah 2:4–28 3:4 *Jeremiah 2:4–28 4:1–2*

Italics are for Sephardi Minhag.

1987, July 27–Aug. 25]   AV (30 DAYS)   [5747

Civil Date	Day of the Week	Jewish Date	SABBATHS, FESTIVALS, FASTS	PENTATEUCHAL READING	PROPHETICAL READING
July 27	M	Av 1	New Moon	Num. 28:1–15	
Aug. 1	Sa	6	Devarim (Shabbat Hazon)	Deut. 1:1–3:22	Isaiah 1:1–27
4	T	9	Fast of 9th of Av	Morning: Deut. 4:25–40 Afternoon: Exod. 32:11–14 34:1–10	(Lamentations is read the night before.) Jeremiah 8:13–9:23 Isaiah 55:6–56:8
8	Sa	13	Wa-ethannan (Shabbat Nahamu)	Deut. 3:23–7:11	Isaiah 40:1–26
15	Sa	20	'Ekev	Deut. 7:12–11:25	Isaiah 49:14–51:3
22	Sa	27	Re'eh	Deut. 11:26–16:17	Isaiah 54:11–55:5
25	T	30	New Moon, first day	Num. 28:1–15	

1987, Aug. 26–Sept. 23]   ELUL (29 DAYS)   [5747

Civil Date	Day of the Week	Jewish Date	SABBATHS, FESTIVALS, FASTS	PENTATEUCHAL READING	PROPHETICAL READING
Aug. 26	W	Elul 1	New Moon, second day	Num. 28:1–15	
29	Sa	4	Shofetim	Deut. 16:18–21:9	Isaiah 51:12–52:12
Sept. 5	Sa	11	Ki teze'	Deut. 21:10–25:19	Isaiah 54:1–10
12	Sa	18	Ki tavo'	Deut. 26:1–29:8	Isaiah 60:1–22
19	Sa	25	Nizzavim, Wa-yelekh	Deut. 29:9–31:30	Isaiah 61:10–63:9

1987, Sept. 24–Oct. 23] TISHRI (30 DAYS) [5748

Civil Date	Day of the Week	Jewish Date	SABBATHS, FESTIVALS, FASTS	PENTATEUCHAL READING	PROPHETICAL READING
Sept. 24	Th	Tishri 1	Rosh Ha-shanah, first day	Gen. 21:1–34 Num. 29:1–6	I Samuel 1:1–2:10
25	F	2	Rosh Ha-shanah, second day	Gen. 22:1–24 Num. 29:1–6	Jeremiah 31:2–20
26	Sa	3	Ha'azinu (Shabbat Shuvah)	Deut. 32:1–52	Hosea 14:2–10 Micah 7:18–20 Joel 2:15–27 *Hosea 14:2–10* *Micah 7:18–20*
27	S	4	Fast of Gedaliah	Exod. 32:11–14 34:1–10	Isaiah 55:6–56:8 (afternoon only)
Oct. 3	Sa	10	Yom Kippur	Morning: Levit. 16:1–34 Num. 29:7–11 Afternoon: Levit. 18:1–30	Isaiah 57:14–58:14 Jonah 1:1–4:11 Micah 7:18–20
8	Th	15	Sukkot, first day	Levit. 22:26–23:44 Num. 29:12–16	Zechariah 14:1–21
9	F	16	Sukkot, second day	Levit. 22:26–23:44 Num. 29:12–16	I Kings 8:2–21
10	Sa	17	Ḥol Ha-mo'ed	Exod. 33:12–34:26 Num. 29:17–22	Ezekiel 38:18–39:16
11-13	S-T	18-20	Ḥol Ha-mo'ed	S Num. 29:20–28 M Num. 29:23–31 T Num. 29:26–34	
14	W	21	Hosha'na' Rabbah	Num. 29:26–34	
15	Th	22	Shemini 'Azeret	Deut. 14:22–16:17 Num. 29:35–30:1	I Kings 8:54–66
16	F	23	Simḥat Torah	Deut. 33:1–34:12 Gen. 1:1–2:3 Num. 29:35–30:1	Joshua 1:1–18 *Joshua 1:1–9*
17	Sa	24	Be-re'shit	Gen. 1:1–6:8	Isaiah 42:5–43:10 *Isaiah 42:5–21*
23	F	30	New Moon, first day	Num. 28:1–15	

Italics are for Sephardi Minhag.

1987, Oct. 24–Nov. 21] HESHWAN (29 DAYS) [5748

Civil Date	Day of the Week	Jewish Date	SABBATHS, FESTIVALS, FASTS	PENTATEUCHAL READING	PROPHETICAL READING
Oct. 24	Sa	Heshwan 1	Noah; New Moon, second day	Gen. 6:9–11:32 Num. 28:9–15	Isaiah 66:1–24
31	Sa	8	Lekh lekha	Gen. 12:1–17:27	Isaiah 40:27–41:16
Nov. 7	Sa	15	Wa-yera'	Gen. 18:1–22:24	II Kings 4:1–37 *II Kings 4:1–23*
14	Sa	22	Hayye Sarah	Gen. 23:1–25:18	I Kings 1:1–31
21	Sa	29	Toledot	Gen. 25:19–28:9	I Samuel 20:18–42

1987, Nov. 22–Dec. 21] KISLEW (30 DAYS) [5748

Civil Date	Day of the Week	Jewish Date	SABBATHS, FESTIVALS, FASTS	PENTATEUCHAL READING	PROPHETICAL READING
Nov. 22	S	Kislew 1	New Moon	Num. 28:1–15	
28	Sa	7	Wa-yeze'	Gen. 28:10–32:3	Hosea 12:13–14:10 *Hosea 11:7–12:12*
Dec. 5	Sa	14	Wa-yishlah	Gen. 32:4–36:43	Hosea 11:7–12:12 *Obadiah 1:1–21*
12	Sa	21	Wa-yeshev	Gen. 37:1–40:23	Amos 2:6–3:8
16-18	W-F	25-27	Hanukkah, first to third days	W Num. 7:1–17 Th Num. 7:18–29 F Num. 7:24–35	
19	Sa	28	Mi-kez; Hanukkah, fourth day	Gen. 41:1–44:17 Num. 7:30–35	Zechariah 2:14–4:7
20	S	29	Hanukkah, fifth day	Num. 7:36–47	
21	M	30	New Moon, first day; Hanukkah, sixth day	Num. 28:1–15 Num. 7:42–47	

Italics are for Sephardi Minhag.

1987, Dec. 22–Jan. 19, 1988] TEVET (29 DAYS) [5748

Civil Date	Day of the Week	Jewish Date	SABBATHS, FESTIVALS, FASTS	PENTATEUCHAL READING	PROPHETICAL READING
Dec. 22	T	Tevet 1	New Moon, second day; Hanukkah, seventh day	Num. 28:1–15 Num. 7:48–53	
23	W	2	Hanukkah, eighth day	Num. 7:54–8:4	
26	Sa	5	Wa-yiggash	Gen. 44:18–47:27	Ezekiel 37:15–28
31	Th	10	Fast of 10th of Tevet	Exod. 32:11–14 34:1–10	Isaiah 55:6–56:8 (afternoon only)
Jan. 2	Sa	12	Wa-yehi	Gen. 47:28–50:26	I Kings 2:1–12
9	Sa	19	Shemot	Exod. 1:1–6:1	Isaiah 27:6–28:13 29:22–23 *Jeremiah 1:1–2:3*
16	Sa	26	Wa-'era'	Exod. 6:2–9:35	Ezekiel 28:25–29:21

1988, Jan. 20–Feb. 18] SHEVAT (30 DAYS) [5748

Civil Date	Day of the Week	Jewish Date	SABBATHS, FESTIVALS, FASTS	PENTATEUCHAL READING	PROPHETICAL READING
Jan. 20	W	Shevat 1	New Moon	Num. 28:1–15	
23	Sa	4	Bo'	Exod. 10:1–13:16	Jeremiah 46:13–28
30	Sa	11	Be-shallah (Shabbat Shirah)	Exod. 13:17–17:16	Judges 4:4–5:31 *Judges 5:1–31*
Feb. 3	W	15	Hamishshah-'asar bi-Shevat		
6	Sa	18	Yitro	Exod. 18:1–20:23	Isaiah 6:1–7:6 9:5–6 *Isaiah 6:1–13*
13	Sa	25	Mishpatim (Shabbat Shekalim)	Exod. 21:1–24:18 Exod. 30:11–16	II Kings 12:1–17 *II Kings 11:17–12:17*
18	Th	30	New Moon, first day	Num. 28:1–15	

Italics are for Sephardi Minhag.

1988, Feb. 19–Mar. 18]   ADAR (29 DAYS)   [5748

Civil Date	Day of the Week	Jewish Date	SABBATHS, FESTIVALS, FASTS	PENTATEUCHAL READING	PROPHETICAL READING
Feb. 19	F	Adar 1	New Moon	Num. 28:1–15	
20	Sa	2	Terumah	Exod. 25:1–27:19	I Kings 5:26–6:13
27	Sa	9	Tezawweh (Shabbat Zakhor)	Exod. 27:20–30:10 Deut. 25:17–19	I Samuel 15:2–34 *I Samuel 15:1–34*
Mar. 2	W	13	Fast of Esther	Exod. 32:11–14 34:1–10	Isaiah 55:6–56:8 (afternoon only)
3	Th	14	Purim	Exod. 17:8–16	Book of Esther (night before and in the morning)
4	F	15	Shushan Purim		
5	Sa	16	Ki tissa'	Exod. 30:11–34:35	I Kings 18:1–39 *I Kings 18:20–39*
12	Sa	23	Wa-yakhel, Pekude (Shabbat Parah)	Exod. 35:1–40:38 Num. 19:1–22	Ezekiel 36:16–38 *Ezekiel 36:16–36*

Italics are for Sephardi Minhag.

1988, Mar. 19–Apr. 17] NISAN (30 DAYS) [5748

Civil Date	Day of the Week	Jewish Date	SABBATHS, FESTIVALS, FASTS	PENTATEUCHAL READING	PROPHETICAL READING
Mar. 19	Sa	Nisan 1	Wa-yikra' (Shabbat Ha-hodesh); New Moon	Levit. 1:1–5:26 Exod. 12:1–20 Num. 28:9–15	Ezekiel 45:16–46:18 *Ezekiel 45:18–46:15* *Isaiah 66:1, 23*
26	Sa	8	Zaw (Shabbat Ha-gadol)	Levit. 6:1–8:36	Malachi 3:4–24
Apr. 1	F	14	Fast of Firstborn		
2	Sa	15	Passover, first day	Exod. 12:21–51 Num. 28:16–25	Joshua 5:2–6:1, 27
3	S	16	Passover, second day	Levit. 22:26–23:44 Num. 28:16–25	II Kings 23: 1–9, 21–25
4	M	17	Hol Ha-mo'ed, first day	Exod. 13:1–16 Num. 28:19–25	
5	T	18	Hol Ha-mo'ed, second day	Exod. 22:24–23:19 Num. 28:19–25	
6	W	19	Hol Ha-mo'ed, third day	Exod. 34:1–26 Num. 28:19–25	
7	Th	20	Hol Ha-mo'ed, fourth day	Num. 9:1–14 Num. 28:19–25	
8	F	21	Passover, seventh day	Exod. 13:17–15:26 Num. 28:19–25	II Samuel 22:1–51
9	Sa	22	Passover, eighth day	Deut. 15:19–16:17 Num. 28:19–25	Isaiah 10:32–12:6
14	Th	27	Holocaust Memorial Day		
16	Sa	29	Shemini	Levit. 9:1–11:47	I Samuel 20:18–42
17	S	30	New Moon, first day	Num. 28:1–15	

Italics are for Sephardi Minhag.

1988, Apr. 18–May 16] IYAR (29 DAYS) [5748

Civil Date	Day of the Week	Jewish Date	SABBATHS, FESTIVALS, FASTS	PENTATEUCHAL READING	PROPHETICAL READING
Apr. 18	M	Iyar 1	New Moon, second day	Num. 28:1–15	
22	F	5	Israel Independence Day		
23	Sa	6	Tazria', Mezora'	Levit. 12:1–15:33	II Kings 7:3–20
30	Sa	13	Aḥare mot, Kedoshim	Levit. 16:1–20:27	Amos 9:7–15 *Ezekiel 20:2–20*
May 5	Th	18	Lag Ba-'omer		
7	Sa	20	Emor	Levit. 21:1–24:23	Ezekiel 44:15–31
14	Sa	27	Be-har, Be-ḥukkotai	Levit. 25:1–27:34	Jeremiah 16:19–17:14
15	S	28	Jerusalem Day		

1988, May 17–June 15] SIWAN (30 DAYS) [5748

Civil Date	Day of the Week	Jewish Date	SABBATHS, FESTIVALS, FASTS	PENTATEUCHAL READING	PROPHETICAL READING
May 17	T	Siwan 1	New Moon	Num. 28:1–15	
21	Sa	5	Be-midbar	Num. 1:1–4:20	Hosea 2:1–22
22	S	6	Shavu'ot, first day	Exod. 19:1–20:23 Num. 28:26–31	Ezekiel 1:1–28 3:12
23	M	7	Shavu'ot, second day	Deut. 15:19–16:17 Num. 28:26–31	Habbakuk 3:1–19 *Habbakuk 2:20–3:19*
28	Sa	12	Naso'	Num. 4:21–7:89	Judges 13:2–25
June 4	Sa	19	Be-ha'alotekha	Num. 8:1–12:16	Zechariah 2:14–4:7
11	Sa	26	Shelaḥ lekha	Num. 13:1–15:41	Joshua 2:1–24
15	W	30	New Moon, first day	Num. 28:1–15	

Italics are for Sephardi Minhag.

1988, June 16–July 14] TAMMUZ (29 DAYS) [5748

Civil Date	Day of the Week	Jewish Date	SABBATHS, FESTIVALS, FASTS	PENTATEUCHAL READING	PROPHETICAL READING
June 16	Th	Tammuz 1	New Moon, second day	Num. 28:1–15	
18	Sa	3	Korah	Num. 16:1–18:32	I Samuel 11:14–12:22
25	Sa	10	Hukkat	Num. 19:1–22:1	Judges 11:1–33
July 2	Sa	17	Balak	Num. 22:2–25:9	Micah 5:6–6:8
3	S	18	Fast of 17th of Tammuz	Exod. 32:11–14 34:1–10	Isaiah 55:6–56:8 (afternoon only)
9	Sa	24	Pinehas	Num. 25:10–30:1	Jeremiah 1:1–2:3

1988, July 15–Aug. 13] AV (30 DAYS) [5748

Civil Date	Day of the Week	Jewish Date	SABBATHS, FESTIVALS, FASTS	PENTATEUCHAL READING	PROPHETICAL READING
July 15	F	Av 1	New Moon	Num. 28:1–15	
16	Sa	2	Maṭṭot, Mas'e	Num. 30:2–36:13	Jeremiah 2:4–28 3:4 *Jeremiah 2:4–28 4:1–2*
23	Sa	9	Devarim (Shabbat Ḥazon)	Deut. 1:1–3:22	Isaiah 1:1–27
24	S	10	Fast of 9th of Av	Morning: Deut. 4:25–40 Afternoon: Exod. 32:11–14 34:1–10	(Lamentations is read the night before.) Jeremiah 8:13–9:23 Isaiah 55:6–56:8
30	Sa	16	Wa-etḥannan (Shabbat Naḥamu)	Deut. 3:23–7:11	Isaiah 40:1–26
Aug. 6	Sa	23	'Eḳev	Deut. 7:12–11:25	Isaiah 49:14–51:3
13	Sa	30	Re'eh; New Moon, first day	Deut. 11:26–16:17 Num. 28:9–15	Isaiah 66:1–24 *Isaiah 66:1–24 I Samuel 20:18, 42*

1988, Aug. 14–Sept. 11] ELUL (29 DAYS) [5748

Civil Date	Day of the Week	Jewish Date	SABBATHS, FESTIVALS, FASTS	PENTATEUCHAL READING	PROPHETICAL READING
Aug. 14	S	Elul 1	New Moon, second day	Num. 28:1–15	
20	Sa	7	Shofeṭim	Deut. 16:18–21:9	Isaiah 51:12–52:12
27	Sa	14	Ki teẓe'	Deut. 21:10–25:19	Isaiah 54:1–55:5
Sept. 3	Sa	21	Ki tavo'	Deut. 26:1–29:8	Isaiah 60:1–22
10	Sa	28	Niẓẓavim	Deut. 29:9–30:20	Isaiah 61:10–63:9

Italics are for Sephardi Minhag.

1988, Sept. 12–Oct. 11] TISHRI (30 DAYS) [5749

Civil Date	Day of the Week	Jewish Date	SABBATHS, FESTIVALS, FASTS	PENTATEUCHAL READING	PROPHETICAL READING
Sept. 12	M	Tishri 1	Rosh Ha-shanah, first day	Gen. 21:1–34 Num. 29:1–6	I Samuel 1:1–2:10
13	T	2	Rosh Ha-shanah, second day	Gen. 22:1–24 Num. 29:1–6	Jeremiah 31:2–20
14	W	3	Fast of Gedaliah	Exod. 32:11–14 34:1–10	Isaiah 55:6–56:8 (afternoon only)
17	Sa	6	Wa-yelekh (Shabbat Shuvah)	Deut. 31:1–30	Hosea 14:2–10 Micah 7:18–20 Joel 2:15–27 *Hosea 14:2–10* *Micah 7:18–20*
21	W	10	Yom Kippur	Morning: Levit. 16:1–34 Num. 29:7–11 Afternoon: Levit. 18:1–30	Isaiah 57:14–58:14 Jonah 1:1–4:11 Micah 7:18–20
24	Sa	13	Ha'azinu	Deut. 32:1–52	II Samuel 22:1–51
26	M	15	Sukkot, first day	Levit. 22:26–23:44 Num. 29:12–16	Zechariah 14:1–21
27	T	16	Sukkot, second day	Levit. 22:26–23:44 Num. 29:12–16	I Kings 8:2–21
28–30	W-F	17–19	Hol Ha-mo'ed	W Num. 29:17–25 Th Num. 29:20–28 F Num. 29:23–31	
Oct. 1	Sa	20	Hol Ha-mo'ed	Exod. 33:12–34:26 Num. 29:26–31	Ezekiel 38:18–39:16
2	S	21	Hosha'na' Rabbah	Num. 29:26–34	
3	M	22	Shemini 'Azeret	Deut. 14:22–16:17 Num. 29:35–30:1	I Kings 8:54–66
4	T	23	Simhat Torah	Deut. 33:1–34:12 Gen. 1:1–2:3 Num. 29:35–30:1	Joshua 1:1–18 *Joshua 1:1–9*
8	Sa	27	Be-re'shit	Gen. 1:1–6:8	Isaiah 42:5–43:10 *Isaiah 42:5–21*
11	T	30	New Moon, first day	Num. 28:1–15	

Italics are for Sephardi Minhag.

1988, Oct. 12–Nov. 9]   ḤESHWAN (30 DAYS)   [5749

Civil Date	Day of the Week	Jewish Date	SABBATHS, FESTIVALS, FASTS	PENTATEUCHAL READING	PROPHETICAL READING
Oct. 12	W	Ḥeshwan 1	New Moon, second day	Num. 28:1–15	
15	Sa	4	Noaḥ	Gen. 6:9–11:32	Isaiah 54:1–55:5 *Isaiah 54:1–10*
22	Sa	11	Lekh lekha	Gen. 12:1–17:27	Isaiah 40:27–41:16
29	Sa	18	Wa-yera'	Gen. 18:1–22:24	II Kings 4:1–37 *II Kings 4:1–23*
Nov. 5	Sa	25	Ḥayye Sarah	Gen. 23:1–25:18	I Kings 1:1–31

1988, Nov. 10–Dec. 8]   KISLEW (29 DAYS)   [5749

Civil Date	Day of the Week	Jewish Date	SABBATHS, FESTIVALS, FASTS	PENTATEUCHAL READING	PROPHETICAL READING
Nov. 10	Th	Kislew 1	New Moon	Num. 28:1–15	
12	Sa	3	Toledot	Gen. 25:19–28:9	Malachi 1:1–2:7
19	Sa	10	Wa-yeẓe'	Gen. 28:10–32:3	Hosea 12:13–14:10 *Hosea 11:7–12:12*
26	Sa	17	Wa-yishlaḥ	Gen. 32:4–36:43	Hosea 11:7–12:12 *Obadiah 1:1–21*
Dec. 3	Sa	24	Wa-yeshev	Gen. 37:1–40:23	Amos 2:6–3:8
4–8	S-Th	25–29	Ḥanukkah, first to fifth days	S Num. 7:1–17 M Num. 7:18–29 T Num. 7:24–35 W Num. 7:30–41 Th Num. 7:36–47	

Italics are for Sephardi Minhag.

1988, Dec. 9–Jan. 6, 1989]   TEVET (29 DAYS)   [5749

Civil Date	Day of the Week	Jewish Date	SABBATHS, FESTIVALS, FASTS	PENTATEUCHAL READING	PROPHETICAL READING
Dec. 9	F	Tevet 1	New Moon; Hanukkah, sixth day	Num. 28:1–15 Num. 7:42–47	
10	Sa	2	Mi-kez; Hanukkah, seventh day	Gen. 41:1–44:17 Num. 7:48–53	Zechariah 2:14–4:7
11	S	3	Hanukkah, eighth day	Num. 7:54–8:4	
17	Sa	9	Wa-yiggash	Gen. 44:18–47:27	Ezekiel 37:15–28
18	S	10	Fast of 10th of Tevet	Exod. 32:11–14 34:1–10	Isaiah 55:6–56:8 (afternoon only)
24	Sa	16	Wa-yehi	Gen. 47:28–50:26	I Kings 2:1–12
31	Sa	23	Shemot	Exod. 1:1–6:1	Isaiah 27:6–28:13 29:22–23 *Jeremiah 1:1–2:3*

Italics are for Sephardi Minhag.

SELECTED ARTICLES OF INTEREST IN RECENT VOLUMES OF THE AMERICAN JEWISH YEAR BOOK

The American Jewish Family Today	Steven Martin Cohen 82:136–154
Attitudes of American Jews Toward Israel: Trends Over Time	Eytan Gilboa 86:110–125
California Jews: Data from the Field Polls	Alan M. Fisher and Curtis K. Tanaka 86:196–218
A Century of Conservative Judaism in the United States	Abraham J. Karp 86:3–61
A Century of Jewish History, 1881–1981: The View from America	Lucy S. Dawidowicz 82:3–98
The "Civil Judaism" of Communal Leaders	Jonathan S. Woocher 81:149–169
The Demographic Consequences of U.S. Jewish Population Trends	U.O. Schmelz and Sergio DellaPergola 83:141–187
The Demography of Latin American Jewry	U.O. Schmelz and Sergio DellaPergola 85:51–102
Israelis in the United States: Motives, Attitudes, and Intentions	Dov Elizur 80:53–67
Jewish Education Today	Walter I. Ackerman 80:130–148
Jewish Survival: The Demographic Factors	U.O. Schmelz 81:61–117
Jews in the United States: Perspectives from Demography	Sidney Goldstein 81:3–59
The Labor Market Status of American Jews: Patterns and Determinants	Barry R. Chiswick 85:131–153
Latin American Jewry Today	Judith Laikin Elkin 85:3–49
Leadership and Decision-making in a Jewish Federation: The New York Federation of Jewish Philanthropies	Charles S. Liebman 79:3–76

Los Angeles Jewry: A Demographic Portrait — Bruce A. Phillips 86:126–195

The National Gallup Polls and American Jewish Demography — Alan M. Fisher 83:111–126

The 1981–1982 National Survey of American Jews — Steven Martin Cohen 83:89–110

Recent Jewish Community Population Studies: A Roundup — Gary A. Tobin and Alvin Chenkin 85:154–178

Reform and Conservative Judaism in Israel: A Social and Religious Profile — Ephraim Tabory 83:41–61

Religiosity Patterns in Israel — Calvin Goldscheider and Dov Friedlander 83:3–39

The Social Characteristics of the New York Area Jewish Community, 1981 — Paul Ritterband and Steven M. Cohen 84:128–161

Soviet Jewry Since the Death of Stalin: A Twenty-five Year Perspective — Leon Shapiro 79:77–103

Trends in Jewish Philanthropy — Steven Martin Cohen 80:29–51

OBITUARIES

Leo Baeck	By Max Gruenewald 59:478–82
Jacob Blaustein	By John Slawson 72:547–57
Martin Buber	By Seymour Siegel 67:37–43
Abraham Cahan	By Mendel Osherowitch 53:527–29
Albert Einstein	By Jacob Bronowski 58:480–85
Felix Frankfurter	By Paul A. Freund 67:31–36
Louis Ginzberg	By Louis Finkelstein 56:573–79
Jacob Glatstein	By Shmuel Lapin 73:611–17
Sidney Goldmann	By Milton R. Konvitz 85:401–03
Hayim Greenberg	By Marie Syrkin 56:589–94
Abraham Joshua Heschel	By Fritz A. Rothschild 74:533–44
Horace Meyer Kallen	By Milton R. Konvitz 75:55–80
Mordecai Kaplan	By Ludwig Nadelmann 85:404–11
Herbert H. Lehman	By Louis Finkelstein 66:3–20
Judah L. Magnes	By James Marshall 51:512–15
Alexander Marx	By Abraham S. Halkin 56:580–88
Reinhold Niebuhr	By Seymour Siegel 73:605–10
Joseph Proskauer	By David Sher 73:618–28
Maurice Samuel	By Milton H. Hindus 74:545–53
Leo Strauss	By Ralph Lerner 76:91–97
Max Weinreich	By Lucy S. Dawidowicz 70:59–68
Chaim Weizmann	By Harry Sacher 55:462–69
Stephen S. Wise	By Philip S. Bernstein 51:515–18
Harry Austryn Wolfson	By Isadore Twersky 76:99–111

Index

Abella, Rosalie, 206
Aberbach, David, 216
Abrahams, Charles, 217
Abram, Morris B., 37
Abrams, Alan, 205
Abrams, Herb, 206
Abu al-Abbas, Mohammed, 157, 158, 307, 308
Abu Nidal, 308
Achille Lauro, 156, 157, 158, 160, 227, 292, 296, 307, 308
Adams, James, 216
Adenauer, Konrad, 34
Adiv, Udi, 328
Adler, Cyrus, 344
Adler, Ruth, 216
Afn Shvel, 429
After Midnight, 216
Ages of Man, 216
Agudat Israel party (Israel), 319
Agudath Israel of America, 378
   Children's Division—Pirchei Agudath Israel, 378
   Girls' Division—Bnos Agudath Israel, 378
   Women's Division—N'Shei Agudath Israel of America, 378
   Young Men's Division—Zeirei Agudath Israel, 378
Agudath Israel World Organization, 379
Ain, Joe, 206
AIPAC (*see* American Israel Public Affairs Committee)
Aizenberg, Yevgeniy, 266
Akiva, Miriam, 251
Akzin, Benjamin, 329
Albany Jewish World, 429

Aleichem, Scholem, 259
Alert, 427
Algemeiner Journal, 429
Algeria, 150
Ali, Kamal Hassan, 295, 296
All Germany Will Remain Loyal to the Führer, 257
Alroy, Gil Carl, 436
Altarus, Jakob, 259
Altes, Frits Korthals, 233
ALYN—American Society for Handicapped Children in Israel, 401
The Ambivalent American Jew, 16
AMC Cancer Research Center, 398
America-Israel Cultural Foundation, Inc., 401
America-Israel Friendship League, Inc., 401
American Academy for Jewish Research, 371
American Arab Anti-Discrimination Committee, 127, 135
American Associates, Ben-Gurion University of the Negev, 401
American Association for Ethiopian Jews, 376
American Association of Rabbis, 379
American Biblical Encyclopedia Society, 371
American Committee for Shaare Zedek Hospital in Jerusalem, Inc., 402
American Committee for the Weizmann Institute of Science, 402
American Council for Judaism, 367
American Ex-Prisoners of War, 33
American Federation of Jewish Fighters, Camp Inmates and Nazi Victims, Inc., 371

American Federation of Jews from Central Europe, Inc., 396
American Friends of Haifa University, 402
American Friends of the Alliance Israélite Universelle, Inc., 376
American Friends of the Haifa Maritime Museum, Inc., 402
American Friends of the Hebrew University, 402
American Friends of the Israel Museum, 402
American Friends of the Jerusalem Mental Health Center—Ezrath Nashim, Inc., 402
American Friends of the Shalom Hartman Institute, 402
American Friends of the Tel Aviv Museum, 402
American Friends of the Tel Aviv University, Inc., 403
American Israel Public Affairs Committee, 403
American-Israeli Lighthouse, Inc., 403
The American Israelite, 433
American Jewish Alternatives to Zionism, Inc., 367
American Jewish Archives, 433
American Jewish Committee, 34, 129, 130, 132, 133, 153, 341–363, 367
American Jewish Congress, 129, 130, 135, 323, 324, 368
American Jewish Correctional Chaplains Association, Inc., 398
American Jewish Historical Society, 371
American Jewish History, 428
American Jewish Joint Distribution Committee, Inc.—JDC, 376
American Jewish League for Israel, 403
American Jewish Philanthropic Fund, 376
American Jewish Press Association, 371
American Jewish Public Relations Society, 409
American Jewish Society for Service, Inc., 398
American Jewish Times-Outlook, 433
American Jewish World, 429

American Jewish Year Book, 8n, 170n, 429
American Legion, 117
American Modernity and Jewish Identity, 3n
American ORT Federation, Inc.—Organization for Rehabilitation Through Training, 376
  American and European Friends of ORT, 376
  American Labor ORT, 376
  Business and Professional ORT, 377
  National ORT League, 377
  Women's American ORT, 377
American Physicians Fellowship, Inc. for Medicine in Israel, 403
American Red Magen David for Israel, Inc., 403
American Sephardi Federation, 396
American Society for Jewish Music, 371
American Society for Technion—Israel Institute of Technology, 403
American Sociological Review, 170n
American Veterans Committee, 33
American Veterans of Israel, 396
American Zionist, 429
American Zionist Federation, 403
American Zionist Youth Foundation, Inc., 404
  American Zionist Youth Council, 404
Americans for a Safe Israel, 131, 404
Americans for Progressive Israel, 404
America's Jews, 12, 12n
Amit Woman, 430
Amit Women, 404
Ampal—American Israel Corporation, 404
Amsterdam Council of Churches, 237
Al Anba, 328
Andropov, Yuri, 263
Angovich, Leib, 269
Angress, Werner, 257
The Annals, 3n
Anne Frank Foundation, 233
Annenberg Research Institute, 379
Ansky, S., 324
Anti-Defamation League of B'nai B'rith, 121, 133, 134, 368

Antisemitism After the Holocaust, 257
Antisemitism: From Hostility Toward Jews to the Holocaust, 257
Arafat, Yasir, 139, 141, 142, 143, 144, 145, 146, 148, 150, 155, 156, 157, 158, 159, 286, 289, 295, 307, 308, 309
Arens, Moshe, 313
Argov, Shlomo, 159
A.R.I.F.—Association Pour le Rétablissement des Institutions et Oeuvres Israélites en France, Inc., 377
Aris, Helmut, 261
Ariste, Paul, 269
Arizona Post, 427
Arlosoroff, Chaim, 328
Aronowitsch, Julia, 259–260
Arthur Ruppin—Diaries, Letters, Memoirs, 259
Arthurs, Harry, 206
Aryan Nations, 134
ARZA—Association of Reform Zionists of America, 404
Asch, Schalom, 259
Aspetsberger, Friedbert, 258
al-Assad, Hafez, 141, 146, 290
Associated American Jewish Museums, Inc., 372
Association for Jewish Studies, 379
Association for the Sociological Study of Jewry, 372
Association of Hillel/Jewish Campus Professionals, 379
Association of Jewish Book Publishers, 372
Association of Jewish Center Workers, 368
Association of Jewish Chaplains of the Armed Forces, 379
Association of Jewish Community Organization Personnel, 398
Association of Jewish Community Relations Workers, 368
Association of Jewish Family and Children's Agencies, 398
Association of Jewish Family and Children's Agency Professionals, 398
Association of Jewish Libraries, 372
Association of Orthodox Jewish Scientists, 379
Association of Yugoslav Jews in the United States, Inc., 396
At the Good Address, 239
At the Handles of the Lock, 216
Atlanta Jewish Times, 428
Atrakchi, Albert, 159
Attali, Jacques, 223
Attewell, Bill, 197
Aufbau, 430
Aus der Fuenten, Ferdinand, 227
Ausländer, Rose, 254
Avneri, Avraham, 307
Avrushmi, Yona, 311

Baar, Emil N., 436
Bach, H.I., 216
Bachi, Roberto, 59n
Badawi, Abdul Halim, 295
Baltimore Jewish Times, 428
Barak, Ehud, 289, 308
Bard, Mitchell, 128
Barda, Shimon, 311
Bar-Ilan University in Israel, 404
Barkai, Avraham, 165
Bar Kochba, 259
Barnica, Edgardo Paz, 300
Baron de Hirsch Fund, 398
Barrow, Dame Nita, 363
Barry, Marion, 121
Barulin, Alexander, 269
Bayerdörfer, Hans-Peter, 258
al-Baz, Osama, 295
Beatrix, Queen of the Netherlands, 234
Bechor, David, 328
Beckett, Samuel, 324
Beem, H., 239
Be'eri, Dan, 311
Begin, Menachem, 131, 277, 286
Beginning Again, 216
Beisky, Moshe, 283
Belkin, David, 270
Bell, Daniel, 17, 17n
Belman, Zinaida, 270
Ben-Ari, Yitzhak, 249
Bendon, Janet, 206

Benedictus, David, 216
Benima, Tamarah, 239
Bennett, William J., 130
Ben-Shimol, David, 311
Ben-Shushan, Avraham, 329
Bensimon, Doris, 221
Ben-Tov, Mordechai, 329
Benvenisti, Meron, 314
Ben-Yair, Meir, 302
Bercuson, David, 205
Bergman, Schmuel Hugo, 258
Bergner, Elisabeth, 262
Berkoff, Steven, 216
Berkoff, West and Other Plays, 216
Berlinger, Eliezer, 235, 236
Berman, Myer, 217
Bernfes, Alexander, 217
Bernstein, Philip S., 436
Berri, Nabih, 154
Bessin, Shira Herzog, 206
Betar Zionist Youth Movement, Inc., 404
Beth Medrosh Elyon (Academy of Higher Learning and Research), 379
The Better Beyond, 259
Beutel, Ben, 207
Bialkin, Kenneth, 24, 118, 132
Bick, Harry, 206
Biden, Joseph, 36
Bilarz, Rudolf, 247
Birobidzhaner Shtern, 269, 270
Bitburg and Beyond, 21n
Bitburg in Moral and Political Perspective, 21n
Bitzaron, 430
Blair, Lionel, 216
Blattman, Yona, 305
Blau, Eric, 204
Bloch, Stanley, 213
Bloemendaal, Hans, 238
Blond, Elaine, 218
Blood Libels, 216
Blum, Martha, 260
B'nai B'rith Hillel Foundations, Inc., 379
B'nai B'rith International, 398
  Anti-Defamation League of (*see* page 368)
  Career and Counseling Services, 399
  Hillel Foundations, Inc. (*see* page 379)
  Klutznick Museum (*see* page 372)
  Youth Organization (*see* page 379)
B'nai B'rith International Jewish Monthly, 427
B'nai B'rith Klutznick Museum, 372
B'nai B'rith Messenger, 427
B'nai B'rith Women, 399
B'nai B'rith Youth Organization, 379
Bnai Zion—The American Fraternal Zionist Organization, 397
Board of Deputies of British Jews, 209, 211, 212, 214
Bock, Gisela, 256
Boenisch, Peter, 34
Bole, William, 32n, 33n
Bolten, Seymour, 437
Bonjour Paris, 259
Bonner, Elena, 264
Book of Mercy, 216
Bookbinder, Hyman, 21n, 24, 136
Bor, Michael, 216
Boschwitz, Rudy, 145
Boston Jewish Times, 428
Bourguiba, Habib, 156
Bradley, Tom, 121
Bramson ORT, 380
Brandeis-Bardin Institute, 380
Brandeis University National Women's Committee, 410
Brandt, Willy, 248, 260
Brauchitsch, Eberhard von, 241
The Bread of Exile, 216
Breger, Marshall, 21n, 30, 31, 136
Brent East Labor party (Great Britain), 210
Breslow, Israel, 437
Brezhnev, Leonid, 263
Brith Abraham, 397
Brith Sholom, 397
Brodsky, Vladimir, 266
Brody, David, 30
Brody, Hyman, 217
Broek, Hans van den, 224
Bronfman, Charles, 206
Bronfman, Edgar, 133, 255, 267, 299, 324

Brooke, Reuben, 239
Brookner, Anita, 216
Brown, Robert McAfee, 32
Browne, Arthur, 123
Brownstein, Morton, 206
Brunner, Alois, 248
Buckley, William F., Jr., 25, 33
Budapest Jewish Theological Seminary, 272
Buffalo Jewish Review, 430
Bukhris, Albert, 302
Bulgaria, 271
Bulka, Reuven, 205
Bulletin Du Congres Juif Canadien (Canada), 435
Buloff, Joseph, 437
Burns, Arthur F., 252
Burt, Richard R., 34
Bush, George, 29, 161
Buthelezi, Gatsha, 300

Cahen, Joel, 234
Cahen, Max, 236
CAJE (*see* Coalition for Alternatives in Jewish Education)
Calmann, Marianne, 215
Calway, B. H., 231
Cameron, Elspeth, 206
Canada, 195–207
Canada and the Birth of Israel, 205
Canada-Israel Securities, Ltd., State of Israel Bonds, 412
Canadian Association for Ethiopian Jews, 203
Canadian Association for Labor Israel, 412
Canadian B'nai Brith, 412
League for Human Rights, 412
Canadian Foundation for Jewish Culture, 412
Canadian Friends of the Alliance Israélite Universelle, 412
Canadian Friends of the Hebrew University, 412
Canadian Jewish Congress, 203, 413
Canadian Jewish Herald, 435
Canadian Jewish News, 435
Canadian Jewish Outlook, 435
Canadian ORT Organization, 413
Women's Canadian ORT, 413
Canadian Sephardi Federation, 413
Canadian Young Judaea, 413
Canadian Zionist, 435
Canadian Zionist Federation, 413
Bureau of Education and Culture, 413
Canetti, Elias, 259
Cannon, Lou, 29
Cantors Assembly, 380
Caplan, Elinor, 195
Cardozo, A. Lopez, 238
Carey, David, 437
Cargas, Harry, 32
Carlebach, Ephraim, 207
The Carrière of Carpentras, 215
Carter, Jimmy, 27, 118
Catholic War Veterans, 33
CBS News, 31n
Ceausescu, Nicolae, 274, 275
Census of Population and Housing, 44n
Center for Contemporary Studies (Great Britain), 209
Center for Holocaust Studies, Documentation & Research, 372
Center for Information and Documentation on Israel (The Netherlands), 233
Center for Jewish Community Studies, 368
Central Conference of American Rabbis, 380
Central Council for Jewish Social Services (Great Britain), 213
Central Sephardic Jewish Community of America, 397
Central Yeshiva Beth Joseph Rabbinical Seminary, 380
Central Yiddish Culture Organization, 372
The Century of Moses Montefiore, 216
Cerier, Maurice, 437
A Certain People, 11n, 15
Chagall, Marc, 223, 259
Chaim Weizmann, 216
Charchat, Isaac, 437
Chazan, Stanley, 218
Chernenko, Konstantin, 248, 263

Cherniak, Saadiah, 437
Chernin, Martin, 206
Chicago JUF News, 428
Chilewich, Aron, 437
Chiswick, Barry R., 170n
Chlenov, Mikhail, 269
Christian Democratic Union (West Germany), 241
Christian Democrats (The Netherlands), 224
Christian Science Monitor, 30n
Christians and Jews: The Eternal Bond, 205
Christie, Douglas, 198
Church of Jesus Christ of Latter-day Saints, 319
The Churches and the Third Reich, Vol. 2, 256
Chwolson, D., 268
City of Hope National Medical Center and Beckman Research Institute, 399
CLAL (see National Jewish Center for Learning and Leadership)
Clark, Joe, 203
Cleveland College of Jewish Studies, 380
Cleveland Jewish News, 433
Clore, David, 217
Coalition for Alternatives in Jewish Education (CAJE), 380
Cohen, Albert, 207
Cohen, David, 206
Cohen, John, 218
Cohen, Leonard, 216
Cohen, Matt, 205
Cohen, Michal, 302
Cohen, Oscar, 437
Cohen, Steven, 3, 3n, 15, 15n, 16
Cole, Phyllis, 204
Collected Writings: Jubilee Edition, 259
The Coming Cataclysm, 205
Commentary, 15n, 18n, 124, 128, 430
Commission for Jewish Demography of the Jewish Social Welfare Organization (The Netherlands), 230
Commission for Racial Equality, 211
Commission on Social Action of Reform Judaism, 368

Committee to Bring Nazi War Criminals to Justice in U.S.A., Inc., 368
Communist party (France), 219, 220
Communist party (Israel), 328
Communist party (The Netherlands), 237
Communists on the Jewish Question, 258
Compulsory Sterilization Under Nazism, 256
Conference of Jewish Communal Service, 399
Conference of Presidents of Major American Jewish Organizations, 357, 368
Conference on Jewish Material Claims Against Germany, Inc., 377
Conference on Jewish Social Studies, Inc., 372
Congregation Bina, 372
Congress Monthly, 430
Connecticut Jewish Ledger, 427
Conservative Friends of Israel (Great Britain), 210
Conservative Judaism, 430
Consultative Council for Jews and Christians (The Netherlands), 232
Consultative Council of Jewish Organizations-CCJO, 368
Contemporary Jewry—Studies in Honor of Moshe Davis, 59n, 430
Coordinating Board of Jewish Organizations, 369
Corren, Asher, 213
Cortes, Hernandez, 300
Costa Rica, 300
Cotler, Irwin, 199
Council for a Beautiful Israel Environmental Education Foundation, 405
Council for Jewish Education, 380
Council of Jewish Federations, Inc., 399
Council of Jewish Organizations in Civil Service, Inc., 369
Craxi, Bettino, 158
Crosbie, John, 199
Cruso, Pinchas, 438
Cummings, Nathan, 438
Cutler, Philip, 206
The Czar's Fools, 259

Czechoslovakia, 271, 272
Czerski, Alexander, 251
Czerwinsky, Horst, 247

Daghani, Arnold, 217
Dam, C. van, 239
Danon, Tsadik, 276
David, Fritz Joseph, 251
Davids, Leo, 200
Davis, M., 49n
Davis, Morris Harold, 217
Dayton Jewish Chronicle, 433
Deaver, Michael, 25, 28, 34
Deborah, 236, 237
Deborah—Fools Dancing in the Ghetto, 259
The Deceived Generation, 257
Decter, Midge, 119
de Gunzberg, Baroness Aileen Minda Bronfman, 207
de Jong, Abraham, 239
Dekel, Michael, 313, 314, 329
Delganov, Elena, 213
Delganov, Viktor, 213
DellaPergola, Sergio, 8, 8n, 9, 10n, 11n, 44n, 45n, 165n, 221
Dellums, Ronald, 123
Dereckson, Uli, 152
De Rosa, Luigi, 165n
Deschenes, Jules, 199
Detroit Jewish News, 429
Deutsche National-Zeitung, 245
Diakonov, I., 269
Diaries and Letters, 258
Dietz, George, 134
Dine, Thomas, 135
Dinitz, Simcha, 158, 160
Dinkins, David, 35
Distinctions, 216
Dole, Robert, 27, 32, 135
Dollhopf, Helmut, 257
Dolman, Dick, 237
Dominitz, Yehuda, 320
Drache, Sharon, 205
Dregger, Alfred, 22, 30
Dropsie College for Hebrew and Cognate Learning (*see* Annenberg Research Institute)

Dror—Young Kibbutz Movement—Habonim, 405
    Chavurat Hagalil, 405
    Garin Yarden, 405
Drutz, Efim, 268
Dulzin, Arye, 320
Dumas, Roland, 220, 297
Durlacher, Gerhard, 239
Duynmeyer, Kerwin, 226
Dworkin, Zalman, 438

Eckardt, A. Roy, 33
Eckstein, Yechiel, 33
Economic Horizons, 430
Egypt, 143, 144, 146, 148, 149, 150, 151, 158, 159, 209, 228, 249, 285, 287, 294–297, 307
Ehre, Ida, 260
Ehrlich, Ernst, 255
Eiber, Ludwig, 257
Eichel, Larry, 131
Eichmann, Bernd, 256
Eikhenvald, Alexandra, 269
Einstein (Albert) College of Medicine (*see* Yeshiva University)
Eisenberg, Azriel, 438
Eitan, Rafael, 162, 294, 329
El Al, 308
Elboz, Annie, 217
El-Hanani, Arye, 330
Eliahu, Yosef, 302
Elias Canetti: Delusion as a Form of Life, 258
Elmakayis, Leah, 302
Else Lasker-Schüler: Biography of a German-Jewish Poet, 258
Elzas, Julius, 239
Emanuel, Gabriel, 204
Emerson, Steven, 128
Emunah Women of America, 405
Engels, Josef, 255
Eshel, Tamar, 300
Essas, Eliahu, 267
The Essene Odyssey, 216
Ethiopian Jews, American Association for, 376
Etzion, Yehuda, 310

European Economic Community (EEC), 298
Evan, 233, 234
Even, Judith, 40n
Eyrich, Heinz, 247
Ezrin, Hershell, 206

Fabius, Laurent, 219
Faerber, Meir, 259
Fahd, King of Saudi Arabia, 140, 143, 209
Falwell, Jerry, 27, 33, 131, 132
Family and Friends, 216
Farrakhan, Louis, 117, 120, 121, 122
Al-Faruj, Harun Ibn, 268
Fassbinder, Rainer Werner, 245
al-Fatah, 139, 145, 146, 147, 155, 309
Faurisson, Robert, 198
Featherman, David L., 170n
Federal Republic of Germany, 241–260
Federated Council of Israel Institutions —FCII, 405
Federation of Jewish Men's Clubs, Inc., 380
Fedorov, Yuri, 267
Fein, Leonard, 3, 3n
Feldman, Lily Gardner, 216
Felix Guttmann: A Jewish Fate in the Third Reich, 259
Fels-Kupferschmidt, Annie, 239
Fergusson, Ewen, 209
Ferkauf Graduate School of Psychology (*see* Yeshiva University)
Fern, Jakob, 259
Finer, Morris, 438
Finn, Ralph, 216
Fisch, Solomon, 217
Fischel, Lola, 252
Fischer, Franz, 227
Fischer, Stanley, 291
Fishel, John, 206
Fishman, Asher, 217
Fleeman, David B., 363
Fleming, Gerald, 215
Flemming, Liselotte, 251
Flick, Friedrich Karl, 241
Floating Down to Camelot, 216
For Tommy on His Third Birthday, 256

Forms of Prayer, 216
Forty Years After 1945, 233
Foxman, Abraham, 21n, 37, 37n
France, 219–223
Franck, Isaac, 438
Frank, Phyllis, 439
Franklin, Myrtle, 216
Franklin, Olga, 217
Free Democratic party (West Germany), 241
Free German Labor party (West Germany), 245
Free Sons of Israel, 397
Frenkel, Vladimir, 266
Frenzel, Karl, 247
Frey, Gerhard, 245
Friderichs, Hans, 241
Fridland, M., 268
Friedemann, Friedrich Georg, 258
Friedlaender, Albert, 261
Friedman, Howard I., 28, 126, 127, 261, 363
Friedman, Murray, 136
Friedman, Rosemary, 216
Friends of Pioneering Israel, 413
Frisner, Simon, 217
Fritta, Bedrich, 256
From Time Immemorial: The Origins of the Arab-Jewish Conflict in Palestine, 216
Frydman, Michal, 273
Fund for Higher Education, 405
Fyvel, Tosco, 217

Ganiram, Yitzhak, 310
Gans, Herbert, 15, 15n
Garbage, the City, and Death, 245
Garfinkel, Marvin, 206
Gelder, Sal van, 240
Generation Between Fear and Hope, 257
Genscher, Hans-Dietrich, 248, 249, 297
Genuth, Nitza, 40n
Gerhardt, Ernst, 251
German Democratic Republic, 261–262, 271
German-Israeli Research and International Development Fund, 250
German-Israeli Society, 250

The German Jews, 215
German People's Union, 245
Gershon, Karen, 216
Ghan-Firestone, Esther, 204
Gilbert, Martin, 216
Gilbert, Michael, 205
Gilels, Emil, 270
Gingrich, Newt, 27, 132
Ginsburg, Alexander, 259
Givat Haviva Educational Foundation, Inc., 405
Glanville, Brian, 216
Glazer, Nathan, 130
Glazier, Ian A., 165n
Glick, Srul Irving, 204
Glikson, P., 45n, 165n
Goell, Theresa, 439
Goeree, Jenny, 233, 234
Goeree, Lucas, 233, 234
Goitein, Shelomo Dov, 439
Golan, Gershon, 207
Gold, Phil, 206
Goldberger, Milton, 439
Goldblatt, Frank, 207
Goldbloom, Michael, 206
Goldbloom, Victor, 197, 206
Goldman, Raymond, 214
Goldmann, Nahum, 257
Goldscheider, Calvin, 9, 9n, 10n, 11, 11n, 12, 12n, 15
Goldsmith, Judy, 131
Goldstein, David, 216
Goldstein, Sidney, 8, 8n, 11, 11n, 165n, 170n
Goldstein, Zvi, 251
Goodman, Alan, 311
Goodstein, Reuben Louis, 217
Gorbachev, Mikhail, 151, 237, 263, 264, 265, 268, 271, 299, 322
Gordimer, Nadine, 254
Gordis, David M., 353n
Gordon, Milton, 11
Gore, Bernard, 217
Gorky, Maxim, 270
Gould, Julius, 216
Graetz, Heinrich, 257
Graham, Billy, 33, 34
Granot, Elazar, 329

Grant, James, 217
Gratz College, 381
Gray, William, 125
Gray Wolves (West Germany), 244
Grayek, Stefan, 273
Great Britain, 208–218
Greater London Council, 210
Greater Phoenix Jewish News, 427
Greenberg, Irving, 132
Greenblum, Joseph, 12n, 15n, 16n
Greens party (West Germany), 241
Gregory, Dick, 35
Grief Forgotten, 216
Grimm, Gunter, 258
Gromyko, Andrei, 263
Gronski, Ryszard Marek, 254
Gross, Nathan, 439
Grossman, D., 45n
Grossman, Larry, 195
Gruenewald, Max, 254
Grunzweig, Emil, 311
Gubbay, Lucien, 216
Gubenko, Yakov, 270
Guggenheim, Walter Gad, 251
A Guide to Jewish Amsterdam, 239
A Guide to Jewish Knowledge, 239
Gur-Arye, Binyamin, 328
Guttmann, Julius, 257

Haas, Wilhelm, 251
Habash, George, 146
Habonim-Dror North America, 405
Hacken, Vera, 259
Hadarom, 430
Hadashot, 322
Hadassah Magazine, 430
Hadassah, the Women's Zionist Organization of America, Inc., 405
Hashachar, 406
Hadassah-WIZO Organization of Canada, 413
Hadoar, 430
Haifa Maritime Museum, American Friends of, 402
Haifa University, American Friends of, 402
Hainowitz, Asher, 238
Hamizrah Hehadash, 45n

Hamtzan, 315
Hanft, Benjamin, 439
Hannah Arendt: A German Jewess in the Epoch of Totalitarianism, 258
Hannah Arendt-Karl Jaspers: Correspondence, 258
Hansen, Niels, 251
Harlap, S., 49n
Harnoi, Yosef, 311
Hart, Ronald James D'Arcy, 217
Härtling, Peter, 259
Hartman, Geoffrey, 21n
Hartt, Stanley, 206
Hashachar (*see* Hadassah)
Hashomer Hatzair, Socialist Zionist Youth Movement, 406
al-Hassan, Hani, 142
Hassan, King of Morocco, 150, 289
Haunschild, Hans-Hilger, 251
Haus, Gabriel, 217
Hayman, Ronald, 216
Heaven and Earth, 216
Hebrew Arts School, 372
Hebrew College, 381
Hebrew Culture Foundation, 373
Hebrew Manuscript Painting, 216
Hebrew Theological College, 381
Hebrew Union College—Jewish Institute of Religion, 381
  American Jewish Archives, 381
  American Jewish Periodical Center, 381
  Edgar F. Magnin School of Graduate Studies, 382
  Jerome H. Louchheim School of Judaic Studies, 382
  Nelson Glueck School of Biblical Archaeology, 382
  Rhea Hirsch School of Education, 382
  School of Education, 382
  School of Graduate Studies, 382
  School of Jewish Communal Service, 382
  School of Jewish Studies, 382
  School of Sacred Music, 382
  Skirball Museum, 382

Hebrew University, American Friends of, 402
Hebrew University, Canadian Friends of, 412
Hebrew Watchman, 434
Hechtman, Isaac, 207
Heidemann, Gerd, 241
Heilman, Samuel, 15
Hellfeld, Matthias von, 257
Helms, Jesse, 129, 131
Henry, Frances, 205
Heritage-Southwest Jewish Press, 427
Hermann Broch: A Biography, 258
Herring, Basil, 205
Hertzberg, Arthur, 15
Herut party (Israel), 286
Herut-U.S.A., Inc., 406
Herzliah-Jewish Teachers Seminary, 382
  Graduate School of Jewish Studies, 382
  Jewish People's University of the Air, 383
Herzog, Chaim, 298, 299, 300, 310, 324, 328
Hessing, Jakob, 258
Heth, Meir, 283
Heuberger, Georg, 254
HIAS, Inc., 377
Hilberg, Raul, 197
Hillel, Shlomo, 316
Hillel Foundations (B'nai B'rith), 379
Himmelfarb, Milton, 21n
Hirsch, Burkhard, 246
Hirsch, John, 206
Histadrut, 280, 281, 282, 300
Histadruth Ivrith of America, 373
History and Culture of Jews in the Rhineland, 258
The History of Anti-Semitism, 216
Hitler and the Final Solution, 215
Hochbaum, Martin, 135
Hochberg, Hy, 207
Hoenlein, Malcolm, 29, 30
Hofacker, Alfred von, 35
Hoffmann, Christhard, 257
Hoffmann, Elly, 251
Hogewoud, Frits J., 239

Holocaust—related groups:
  American Federation of Jewish Fighters, Camp Inmates and Nazi Victims, Inc., 371
  American Federation of Jews from Central Europe, Inc., 396
  Center for Holocaust Studies, Documentation & Research, 372
  Committee to Bring Nazi War Criminals to Justice in U.S.A., Inc., 368
  Conference on Jewish Material Claims Against Germany, Inc., 377
  Holocaust Center of Greater Pittsburgh, 373
  Jewish Restitution Successor Organization, 377
  Martyrs Memorial & Museum of the Holocaust, 374
  New York Holocaust Memorial Commission, 375
  Research Foundation for Jewish Immigration, Inc., 375
  St. Louis Center for Holocaust Studies, 375
  Simon Wiesenthal Center, 396
  Thanks to Scandinavia, Inc., 377
Holocaust Center of Greater Pittsburgh, 373
Honecker, Erich, 248, 262
Hooks, Benjamin, 125
Hope Center for the Retarded, 399
Hörner, Johann, 247
Horowitz, Aron, 205
Houphouet-Boigny, Felix, 299
House of Life: Jewish Cemeteries, 257
How Beautiful Is Your Love, 259
Howe, Geoffrey, 209
Humanistic Judaism, 429
Humanistic Judaism, Society for, 388
The Humanity of Jewish Law, 216
Hungary, 271, 272
Hussein, King of Jordan, 139, 141, 142, 144, 145, 146, 147, 148, 149, 150, 151, 152, 155, 158, 160, 209, 286, 287, 288, 289, 295, 298, 323

Ikle, Fred, 292
Ilan, Judith Onderwijzer, 239

Illiana News, 428
Images in Transition, 216
In Two Worlds, 239
Index to Jewish Periodicals, 433
Indian Jews (*see* Congregation Bina)
Indiana Jewish Post and Opinion, 428
Institute for Computers in Jewish Life, 383
Institute for Jewish Policy Planning and Research (*see* Synagogue Council of America)
Intermountain Jewish News, 427
International Conference of Jewish Communal Service (*see* World Conference of Jewish Communal Service)
International Council of Christians and Jews, 255
International Council on Jewish Social and Welfare Services, 399
Israel, 137–163, 196–197, 209, 220, 221, 246, 249–251, 271, 277–330, 355, 357
Israel and South Africa, 216
Israel (State of) Bonds, 408, 412
Israel Committee Nederland, 229
Israel Horizons, 430
Israel Museum, American Friends of, 402
Israel Quality, 430
Israeli-German Society, 250
I've Taken a Page in the Bible, 216
Ivri, David, 329
Izvestiia, 265, 268

Jackson, Jesse, 121, 123, 125
Jakobovits, Immanuel, 210, 212
Janah, Ibn, 268
Janmaat, Henk, 225
Janner, Greville, 212
Jansen, Hans, 232
Japanese American Citizens League, 33
Jaruzelski, Wojciech, 219, 273
JDC (*see* American Jewish Joint Distribution Committee)
Jerusalem, population, 39–113
Jerusalem Mental Health Center, American Friends of, 402

Jerusalem Post, 290, 314, 317, 323, 324
Jerusalem: Rebirth of a City, 216
A Jew in Breslau 1941, 256
Jewish Academy of Arts and Sciences, Inc., 373
Jewish Action, 430
Jewish Advocate, 428
Jewish Agency (see World Zionist Organization)
Jewish Americans, 11, 11n
Jewish Blind Society (Great Britain), 212
Jewish Book Annual, 430
Jewish Book Council (JWB), 374
Jewish Book World, 430
Jewish Braille Institute of America, Inc., 399
Jewish Braille Institute Voice, 430
Jewish Braille Review, 430
Jewish Cemeteries in Frankfort, 258
The Jewish Cemetery: Witness to History, Testimony to Culture, 258
Jewish Chautauqua Society, Inc., 383
Jewish Chronicle, 434
Jewish Chronicle (Great Britain), 210, 212
Jewish Civic Press (Georgia), 428
Jewish Civic Press (La.), 428
Jewish Civic Press (Texas), 434
Jewish Commitment: A Study in London, 216
Jewish Community News, 428
Jewish Community Voice, 429
Jewish Conciliation Board of America, Inc., 400
Jewish Continuity and Change, 9n
Jewish Current Events, 430
Jewish Currents, 430
Jewish Defense League, 135
Jewish Defense Organization, 135
Jewish Eagle (Canada), 435
Jewish Education, 430
Jewish Education in Media, Inc., 383
Jewish Education Service of North America, Inc., 383
Jewish Educational Development Trust (Great Britain), 215

Jewish Ethics and Halakkah for Our Time, 205
Jewish Exponent, 434
Jewish Floridian Group, 428
Jewish Forward, 430
Jewish Frontier, 430
Jewish Fund for Justice, 126, 400
Jewish Guardian, 431
Jewish Herald-Voice, 434
Jewish Historical Museum, 238, 239
Jewish Horizon, 429
Jewish Identity on the Suburban Frontier, 12n
Jewish Immigrant Aid Services of Canada (JIAS), 413
Jewish Information Bureau, Inc., 373
Jewish Journal (California), 427
Jewish Journal (Florida), 428
Jewish Journal (N.Y.), 431
Jewish Journal of San Antonio, 434
Jewish Labor Bund, 397
Jewish Labor Committee, 369
   National Trade Union Council for Human Rights, 369
   Women's Division of, 369
   Workmen's Circle Division of, 369
Jewish Ledger, 431
Jewish Life in Los Angeles, 7n
Jewish Media Service, JWB, 373
Jewish Ministers Cantors Association of America, Inc., 383
Jewish Museum, 373
Jewish Music Council (JWB), 374
Jewish Music Notes, 431
Jewish National Fund of America, 406
Jewish National Fund of Canada (Keren Kayemeth Le'Israel, Inc.), 413
Jewish News, 429
Jewish Observer, 431
The Jewish Paradox: Zionism and Judaism After Hitler, 257
Jewish Peace Fellowship, 369
Jewish Post (Canada), 435
Jewish Post and Renaissance, 431
Jewish Press (Nebraska), 429
Jewish Press (N.Y.), 431
Jewish Press Features, 434

Jewish Publication Society, 373
Jewish Quarterly, 215, 434
Jewish Reconstructionist Foundation, 383
  Federation of Reconstructionist Congregations and Havurot, 383
  Reconstructionist Rabbinical Association, 383
  Reconstructionist Rabbinical College (*see* page 387)
Jewish Record, 429
Jewish Reporter (Massachussetts), 428
Jewish Reporter (Nevada), 429
Jewish Restitution Successor Organization, 377
Jewish Social Studies, 431
Jewish Social Welfare Organization (The Netherlands), 232
Jewish Socialist (Great Britain), 215
Jewish Socialist Verband of America, 397
Jewish Spectator, 427
Jewish Standard, 429
Jewish Standard (Canada), 435
Jewish Star (California), 427
Jewish Star (New Jersey), 429
Jewish Student Press Service, 411
Jewish Teachers Association—Morim, 384
Jewish Telegraphic Agency Community News Reporter, 431
Jewish Telegraphic Agency Daily News Bulletin, 431
Jewish Telegraphic Agency, Inc., 434
Jewish Telegraphic Agency Weekly News Digest, 431
Jewish Theological Seminary of America, 384
  Albert A. List College of Jewish Studies, 384
  American Student Center in Jerusalem, 384
  Cantors Institute and Seminary College of Jewish Music, 384
  Department of Radio and Television, 384
  Graduate School, 384
  Jewish Museum (*see* page 373)
  Louis Finkelstein Institute for Religious and Social Studies, 384
  Melton Research Center for Jewish Education, 384
  National Ramah Commission, 385
  Prozdor, 385
  Rabbinical School, 385
  Schocken Institute for Jewish Research, 385
  University of Judaism, 385
Jewish Times, 428
Jewish Times of the Greater Northeast, 434
Jewish Transcript, 434
Jewish Veteran, 428
Jewish War Veterans of the United States of America, 33, 369
  National Memorial, Inc; National Shrine to the Jewish War Dead, 370
Jewish Week, 431
Jewish Weekly News, 428
Jewish Welfare Board (Great Britain), 212
Jewish Western Bulletin (Canada), 435
Jewish Women's League (West Germany), 253
Jews and Judaism in Literature, 257
The Jews and Martin Luther, 257
Jews' College (Great Britain), 215
Jews in the Bohemian Countries, 258
The Jews of Europe and the Inquisition of Venice, 1550–1670, 215
The Jews of Islam, 215
Jews Under the Swastika, 257
Jibril, Ahmed, 146, 152, 280, 305
John Paul II, Pope, 132, 231
Jolles, Benjamin, 218
Jones, Barry, 301
Jordan, 138, 141, 142, 143, 144, 145, 146, 147, 148, 149, 150, 151, 158, 160, 209, 249, 287, 288, 289, 292, 298
Journal of Jewish Communal Service, 429
Journal of Psychology and Judaism (Canada), 435
Journal of Reform Judaism, 431

Journal of the North Shore Jewish Community, 429
Judah L. Magnes Museum—Jewish Museum of the West, 373
Judaica Captioned Film Center, Inc., 374
Judaism, 431
Juliana, Queen of the Netherlands, 231
Just, Meir, 234, 235
Just-Dahlmann, Barbara, 256
JWB, 400
　　Jewish Book Council (*see* page 374)
　　Jewish Chaplains Council, 400
　　Jewish Media Service (*see* page 373)
　　Jewish Music Council (*see* page 374)
　　Lecture Bureau (*see* page 374)
JWB Circle, 431
JWB Jewish Book Council, 374
JWB Jewish Music Council, 374
JWB Lecture Bureau, 374

Kach party (Israel), 317
Kafka, Franz, 259
Kafka: Judaism, Politics and Literature, 216
Kagedan, Ian, 206
Kahan, Yitzhak, 329
Kahane, Meir, 302, 315, 316, 317
Kalb, Bernard, 147
Kalb, Marvin, 37
Kampe, Norbert, 257
Kandil, Abdel Hadi, 295
Kanievsky, Ya'acov Israel, 329
Kansas City Jewish Chronicle, 429
Kantrowitz, George, 207
Kaplan, Abraham, 204
Kaplan, Jacob, 222
Kastner, Israel, 325
Katz, Jakob, 259
Katzav, Moshe, 329
Kaufman, Gerald, 216
Kaufmann, Isidore, 325
Kayne, Harry, 218
Kayserling, Meyer, 344
Keegstra, James, 197, 198, 199, 205
Keim, Anton Maria, 256
Keller, Hans, 217
Kemp, Jack, 132

Kentucky Jewish Post and Opinion, 428
Keren Or, Inc., 406
Kessar, Israel, 281, 285
Kessler, Samuel, 260
Keun, Irmgard, 216
Keyes, Alan L., 363
Kholmiansky, Alexander, 266
Khoury, Elias, 151, 209, 298
Khoury, Ghazi, 228
Kibbutz Journal, 431
Kilgour, David, 203
King, W. L. Mackenzie, 205
Kinnock, Neil, 213
Kirchner, Peter, 261
Kirkland, Lane, 33
Kirkpatrick, Jeane, 27
Kissing America, 216
Kissinger, Henry, 27
Klappert, Bertold, 257
Klein, Edward, 440
Kliger, Samuil, 268
Kligman, Paul, 207
Klinghoffer, Leon, 157, 158, 307
Klönne, Arno, 257
Knobloch, Charlotte, 253
Koch, Edward, 122
Koenigsberger, Irene Diner, 440
Kohl, Helmut, 21, 22, 24, 27, 28, 29, 31, 32, 34, 35, 36, 117, 241, 242, 243, 248, 252, 253, 254, 255, 297
Köhler, Lotte, 258
Koifman, Yevgeniy, 267
Kok, Bert, 239
Kol Hat'nua, 431
Kollek, Teddy, 250, 318, 329
Kopelowitz, Lionel, 212
Kops, Bernard, 216
Kopuit, Maurits, 240
Korff, Modest Graf, 247
Kornfeld, Karl Heinz, 251
Kosher Directory, 431
Kosher Directory, Passover Edition, 431
Kosmin, Barry A., 211
Koteret Rashit, 305
Kovac, Teodor, 276
Kowarsky, Paul, 204
Kraft, Gerald, 253
Kraus, David, 329

Krausz, Armin, 216
Kreitmann, Esther, 259
Kremers, Heinz, 257
Krizons, Helmut George, 247
Krolik, Schlomo, 258
Kronitz, Leon, 207
Kujau, Konrad, 241
Kultur Un Lebn—Culture and Life, 431
Kundera, Milan, 324
Kusevitsky, David, 440
Kushner, Donn, 205
Kushner, Jeff, 206
Kutschmann, Walter, 248
Kuznets, Simon, 165n, 440
Kwaterko, A., 273
Kwinter, Monte, 195

Labor party (Israel), 284, 285, 286
Labor party (The Netherlands), 224
Labor Zionist Alliance, 406
Labor Zionist Movement of Canada, 414
Lahad, Antoine, 279
Lambert, Phyllis, 206
Lambsdorff, Otto Graf, 241
Lamishpahah, 431
Lamm, Hans, 253, 260
Lamm, Norman, 118
A Land of Two Peoples, 216
Lang, Jack, 222
Lanzmann, Claude, 274
Lapson, Judah, 441
Las Vegas Israelite, 429
The Last Arab Jews, 215
Lastman, Mel, 206
Lautenberg, Frank, 30
Laxer, Carl, 202
Layton, Irving, 206
Lazarus, Peter, 217
Lazerwitz, Bernard, 11
League for Labor Israel, 406
League for Yiddish, Inc., 374
Lear, Norman, 362
Lebanon, 137, 138, 139, 154, 160, 228, 246, 277–280, 290, 291, 305, 309
Lebensold, Fred, 207
Legal Decisions by Rhenish Rabbis Before the First Crusade, 258

Lehman, John, 292
Lehmann, Hermann, 217
Leo Baeck Institute, 253, 374
Leo Baeck Institute Year Book, 216
Leon, Phillip, 206
Le Pen, Jean-Marie, 220
Le Rider, Jacques, 258
Lerman, Tony, 215
Lerner, Motti, 325
Lester, Julius, 122
Levi Arthritis Hospital, 400
Levin, Hanoch, 325
Levin, S.S., 214
Levin, Yakov, 266
Levinas, Emmanuel, 258
Levine, Aaron, 205
Levinsky, Akiva, 319
Levisson, R.A., 236
Levitt, S., 205
Levkov, Ilya, 21n
Levy, Abraham, 216
Levy, Caren, 211
Levy, David, 281, 286
Levy, Herbert, 207
Levy, Mayer, 206
Lew, Dayan Meyer, 216
Lewis, Bernard, 215
Libbert, Laurence Joseph, 217
Liberal party (The Netherlands), 224
Libya, 150, 159
Lichtenstein, Erwin, 254
Lichtenstein, Heiner, 256
Liebermann, Max, 262
Lieberson, Stanley, 17
Liebman, Charles, 15, 16, 17, 17n
Liedel, Herbert, 257
Life of Siegmund Warburg, 223
Likud party (Israel), 284, 285, 289, 316
Lilith—The Jewish Women's Magazine, 431
Lipman, Sonia, 216
Lipman, V.D., 216
Lippmann, Walter, 260
Lipset, Seymour Martin, 135
Littell, Franklin, 32
Litvinovsky, Pinhas, 329
Livingstone, Ken, 210
Livni, Menachem, 310

Lockshin, Louis, 207
London Board for Shechita, 214
Long Island Jewish World, 37n, 431
Lorge, Ernst, 261
Lott, Trent, 27
Loury, Glenn C., 125
Love Is Not Love, 216
Lubbers, Ruud, 224
Lucas, Victor, 212
Luckner, Gertrud, 255
Ludwig, Franz, 35
Lurie, Leonard, 217
Lützeler, Paul Michael, 258

Mach, Dafna, 258
Machne Israel, Inc., 385
Mack, Julian, 345
Magnes, Judah, 345
Magonet, Jonathan, 215
Maier, Uri, 311
Mann, Paul, 207
Mapam party (Israel), 317
Marcus, Rachel, 330
The Mare, 259
Markisch, David, 259
Marks, Alfred, 216
Markx, Freddy, 238
Marshall, Louis, 342, 343, 344, 345
Martin Buber and Ludwig Strauss, 258
Martyrs Memorial & Museum of the Holocaust, 374
Marx, Herbert, 196
al-Masri, Taher, 148
al-Masri, Zafr, 312
Mayer, Jane, 29
Mayer, Robert, 217
Mazon, 126
McFarlane, Robert, 145
Meed, Benjamin, 21n
Meese, Edwin, III, 130
Meguid, Esmat Abdel, 296
Mehta, Zubin, 325
Meier-Ude, Klaus, 258
Memorial Foundation for Jewish Culture, Inc., 374
Memories: The Jewish East End, 215
Menczel, Puah, 251
Mendelssohn, Moses, 259

Mendes-Flohr, Paul, 216
Mengele, Josef, 248, 323
Merkos L'inyonei Chinuch, Inc. (The Central Organization for Jewish Education), 385
Mermelstein, Mel, 120
Mertes, Alois, 255
Mesh, Yakov, 267
Mesivta Yeshiva Rabbi Chaim Berlin Rabbinical Academy, 385
Metzenbaum, Howard, 30
Mexican American Legal Defense Fund, 33
Meyer, Daniel, 272
Meyerhoff, Joseph, 441
M'Godolim, 434
Miarri, Muhammad, 317
Michigan Jewish History, 429
Michman, Dan, 239
Michman, J., 239
Midstream, 124, 431
Migration Across Time and Nations, 165n
Mikardo, Ian, 210
Milhem, Mohammed, 151, 209, 298
Miller, Frank, 195, 196
Milstone, L., 205
The Miracle of the End of Wars, 258
Mirrer Yeshiva Central Institute, 385
Mirror of a People, 205
Missouri Jewish Post, 429
Mr. Wakefield's Crusade, 216
Mitterrand, François, 21, 22, 219, 221, 322
Mizrachi-Hapoel Hamizrachi Organization of Canada, 414
Modai, Yitzhak, 281, 282, 291, 292
Modern Jewish Studies Annual, 431
Moment, 17n, 18n, 131, 429
Mondale, Walter, 135
Monge, Luis Albert, 300
Montagu, Ewen Edward Samuel, 217
Moonman, Eric, 209, 212
Moore, George, 210
Mordechai, Yitzhak, 305
Morning Freiheit, 431
Morton, Harriet, 206
Mosco, Maisie, 216

Mottke the Thief, 259
Moynihan, Daniel Patrick, 36n
Mozes, Noah, 329
Mubarak, Hosni, 140, 143, 144, 145, 158, 209, 286, 287, 288, 295, 296, 307, 323
Mulroney, Brian, 195, 196, 301
Murphy, Richard W., 137, 144, 145, 146, 147, 148, 150, 152, 287, 288, 289
Murzhenko, Alexei, 267
Musa, Abu, 146
Musa, Saeed, 139
Mussner, Franz, 255
Mutius, Hans-Georg von, 257
My Life on the Silver Screen, 216
My School Time in the Third Reich, 258

Na'amat USA, the Women's Labor Zionist Organization of America, Inc., 406
Na'amat Woman, 432
Nachama, Estrongo, 261
Nachmann, Werner, 252, 259
Naftaniel, Ronny D., 233, 236
Nagel, Ernest, 441
Najes (West Germany), 253
Naouri, Rahamim, 223
Nashpits, Mark, 267, 323
National Association for the Advancement of Colored People, 117, 125, 126
National Association of Arab Americans, 127
National Association of Jewish Family, Children's and Health Professionals (*see* Association of Jewish Family and Children's Agency Professionals)
National Association of Jewish Vocational Services, 400
National Committee for Furtherance of Jewish Education, 385
National Committee for Labor Israel—Histadrut, 407
American Trade Union Council for Histadrut, 407
National Conference on Soviet Jewry, 357, 370
Soviet Jewry Research Bureau, 370
National Congress of Jewish Deaf, 400
National Council of Beth Jacob Schools, Inc., 386
National Council of Churches, 117
National Council of Jewish Prison Chaplains, Inc. (*see* American Jewish Correctional Chaplains Association, Inc.)
National Council of Jewish Women, 400
National Council of Jewish Women of Canada, 414
National Council of Young Israel, 386
American Friends of Young Israel Synagogues in Israel, 386
Armed Forces Bureau, 386
Employment Bureau, 386
Institute for Jewish Studies, 386
Young Israel Collegiates and Young Adults, 386
Young Israel Youth, 386
National Democratic party (West Germany), 244
National Foundation for Jewish Culture, 374
National Front (France), 219, 220
National Front (Great Britain), 208, 209
National Hebrew Culture Council, 375
National Jewish Center for Immunology and Respiratory Medicine, 401
National Jewish Center for Learning and Leadership—CLAL, 386
National Jewish Coalition, 131
National Jewish Commission on Law and Public Affairs, 130, 370
National Jewish Committee on Scouting, 401
National Jewish Community Relations Advisory Council, 122, 357, 370
National Jewish Daily and Israel Today, 427
National Jewish Girl Scout Committee, 401
National Jewish Hospitality Committee, 386

National Jewish Information Service for the Propagation of Judaism, Inc., 387
National Jewish Population Survey, 10
National Joint Community Relations Committee of Canadian Jewish Congress, 414
National Socialist Social Policy in World War Two, 256
National Union of Students (NUS), 210
National Yiddish Book Center, 375
Natkiel, Herman, 239
Navon, Yitzhak, 317
Near East Report, 428
Nechushtan, Yaakov, 228
Nederlands Israelietisch Kerkgenootschap, 234
Neiman, David, 124
Neither Your Honey Nor Your Sting, 216
Nekuda, 320
Nemon, Oscar, 217
Ner Israel Rabbinical College, 387
The Netherlands, 224–240
Netherlands Auschwitz Committee, 233
Netherlands Council of Churches, 228
Netherlands-Israel Friendship League, 229
Netherlands Palestine Committee, 228
Netherlands State Institute for War Documentations, 230
Netherlands Zionist Organization, 237
Netzer, Shraga, 329
Neville, Joseph, 218
New Israel Fund, 407
New Jewish Agenda, 370
The New Jewish Identity in America, 205
New Menorah, 434
New Republic, 122
New York Amsterdam News, 35n
New York Daily News, 26n, 32n, 33n
New York Holocaust Memorial Commission, 375
New York Post, 27n, 31n, 32n, 34n, 35n
New York Review of Books, 15n
New York Times, 23, 23n, 24n, 26n, 27n, 28n, 29n, 30n, 31n, 32n, 34n, 35n, 36n, 37n, 38n, 132, 265, 267, 286, 295

New York Times Book Review, 7n
New Yorker, 15n
Newens, Stan, 209
Newton, Elaine, 205
Niebuhr, Rheinhold, 347
Niepomniashchy, Mark, 266
Nieuw Israelietisch Weekblad (The Netherlands), 230, 238
al-Nimeiry, Gaafar, 161
Nir, Amiram, 329
Nir, Barak, 310
Nir, Shaul, 310
Nissim, Moshe, 315, 323
Nixon, Richard, 27
Noach, E. A., 239
Norman, Theodore, 215
North American Association of Jewish Homes and Housing for the Aging, 401
North American Jewish Students Appeal, 411
North American Jewish Students' Network, 411
North American Jewish Youth Council, 370
Northern California Jewish Bulletin, 427

Oberman, Sheldon, 205
O'Connor, John, Archbishop, 27, 118, 133
Odeh, Alex, 135
Official Writings: With an Essay by Klaus Hermsdorf, 259
Offman, Allan, 206
Ohio Jewish Chronicle, 433
Okamoto, Kozo, 152, 306
Oliver, Peter, 206
Olomeinu—Our World, 432
Olshansky, Charles, 441
Olszowski, Stefan, 299
Onderwijzer, A.S., 239
Opatoschu, Josef, 259
"Operation Moses," 320
Operation Moses, 216
Opposition to Nazism, 256
Or Chadash, 432
Organization of Petroleum Exporting Countries (OPEC), 139
ORT (*see* American ORT Federation)

ORT (see Canadian ORT Organization)
Ortega, Daniel, 300
Ott, Karl, 255
Ottawa Jewish Bulletin & Review, 435
Otto, Wolfgang, 248
The Otto Weininger Case, 258
Our Lost Illusions, 223
An Outstretched Arm, 215
Owens, Major R., 35
Ozar Hatorah, Inc., 387

Packwood, Robert, 135
Paikin, Harry, 207
Palestine Liberation Front, 146, 156, 157, 209
Palestine Liberation Organization (PLO), 139, 140, 141, 142, 144, 145, 146, 147, 148, 149, 150, 151, 155, 156, 157, 159, 196, 220, 227, 228, 229, 262, 287, 288, 289, 292, 298, 300, 307, 309, 316
Palestine National Council, 141, 147, 151, 287
Palestine National Salvation Front, 139
Palestine Solidarity Campaign, 210
Palm Beach Jewish World, 428
Paltzur, Esther, 307
Paltzur, Reuven, 307
Parfitt, Tudor, 216
Paris, Erna, 205
Park, Robert, 345
Paulus, Friedrich, 247
Pax Christi Nederland, 228
Pearl, Chaim, 239
Pearson, Lester, 205
PEC Israel Economic Corporation, 407
Pedagogic Reporter, 432
PEF Israel Endowment Funds, Inc., 407
Peli, Gilad, 311
Pereira, Hans Rodrigues, 232
Peres, Shimon, 34, 137, 138, 139, 141, 144, 149, 150, 151, 154, 162, 221, 265, 275, 277, 278, 281, 282, 283, 284, 285, 286, 287, 288, 289, 290, 291, 292, 293, 294, 295, 296, 297, 298, 299, 300, 303, 307, 312, 313, 314, 319, 321, 322, 324
Peretz, Martin, 121

Peretz, Yitzhak, 285, 318, 328
Perez, Isaac Leib, 259
Perlmutter, Nathan, 123, 127
Persecution, Exploitation, Extermination, 257
The Persecution of the Jews in the City of Utrecht, 239
Perspectives in American History, 165n
Peters, Joan, 216
Petlyura, Simon, 222
Petrified, Minimized, Forgotten: Concentration Camp Memorial Sites in the Federal Republic, 256–257
P'eylim—American Yeshiva Student Union, 387
The Philosophy of Judaism, 257
The Picture of Jews in German Child and Youth Literature from 1800 to This Day, 258
Pinhasi, Rafael, 329
Pioneer Women/Na'amat (see Na'amat USA)
The Play of Eizes: Life Story 1931–1937, 259
Pleticha, Heinrich, 258
Plisetskaia, Maia, 270
Ploeg, Adrian, 232
Poale Agudath Israel of America, Inc., 407
  Women's Division of, 407
Podoloff, Maurice, 442
Poland, 271, 273, 299
Poliakov, Leon, 216
A Political Life: Conversations with Leonard Reinisch, 258
Pollard, Jonathan Jay, 161, 162, 163, 293, 294
Poller, Arin, 40n
Polonsky, Gary, 206
Poppleworth, Justice, 209
Popular Front for the Liberation of Palestine, 146, 152, 305
Popular History of the Jews, 257
Popular Struggle Front, 146
Porush, Menahem, 329
Posen, Jakob, 255
Pouissant, Alvin, 122
Powell, Jody, 25
Pravda, 268, 270

Pregled (Yugoslavia), 276
Preiskel, Israel, 217
Present Tense, 432
Price, Abraham, 205
The Price of Fame, 216
Prince, Leslie, 217
Proceedings of the American Academy for Jewish Research, 432
Progressive Zionist Caucus, 407
Proofs of Affection, 216
Protestant Council of Churches, 234
Pullan, Brian, 215
Pullan, Harry, 207
Pushkin, Eliahu, 322

Qaddafi, Muammar, 120
Questle, Louis, 218
Quiet Neighbors: Prosecuting Nazi War Criminals in America, 119

Raab, Earl, 135
Rabb, Sidney, 442
Rabbinical Alliance of America (Igud Harabonim), 387
Rabbinical Assembly, 387
Rabbinical College of Telshe, Inc., 387
Rabbinical Council of America, Inc., 387
Rabbinical Council Record, 432
Rabin, Yitzhak, 138, 148, 153, 154, 278, 279, 281, 288, 290, 292, 293, 296, 301, 303, 306, 309, 312, 313
Rachmilewitz, Moshe, 329
Rahäuser, Kurt, 247
Rahman, Ahmed Abdel, 147
Rahman, Faiz Abu, 150
Raisman, Monty, 207
Rangel, Charles, 35
Raphael, Chaim, 215
Raphael, Frederic, 216
Rasky, Frank, 205
Ratuszniak, Zygmunt, 217
Rau, Johannes, 241
Ravid, Ilan, 162
Rayner, John, 214
Rayski, Adam, 223
Reagan, Maureen, 161

Reagan, Ronald, 21–38, 117–119, 135, 137, 140, 144, 145, 146, 147, 151, 153, 154, 156, 241, 242, 243, 248, 265, 292, 322
Recker, Marie-Luise, 256
Reconstructionist, 432
Reconstructionism (*see* Jewish Reconstructionist Foundation)
Reconstructionist Rabbinical College, 387
Reform Judaism, 432
Reform Synagogues of Great Britain, 214
Regan, Donald, 29, 34
Reguer, Moshe Aron, 442
Reich-Ranicki, Marcel, 258
Reinharz, Yehuda, 216
Religious Zionists of America, 407
  Bnei Akiva of North America, 407
  Mizrachi-Hapoel Hamizrachi, 408
  Mizrachi Palestine Fund, 408
  National Council for Torah Education of Mizrachi-Hapoel Hamizrachi, 408
  Noam-Mizrachi New Leadership Council, 408
The Reparation of Nazi Injustice by the Federal Republic of Germany, 257
Reporter, 432
Research Foundation for Jewish Immigration, Inc., 375
Research Institute of Religious Jewry, Inc., 388
Resnick, Mark, 206
Response, 432
Revolutionary Cells (West Germany), 244
Reyden, J.P. van der, 233
Reynolds, William Bradford, 126
Rhode Island Jewish Historical Notes, 434
Richard Wagner—Harbinger of Antisemitism, 259
Richmond, Theodore, 207
Riegner, Gerhart, 261, 262
Rifai, Zaid, 150
Rimler, Katrina, 204
Ringer, Herbert, 262

Riseman, Mervin, 442
Ritterband, Paul, 3, 3n
Rittner, Carol, 32
Riz, Yaakov, 442
The Road from Babylon, 215
Robertson, Pat, 33
Robertson, Ritchie, 216
Rocheman, Lionel, 204
Roginsky, Moshe, 442
Roisman, Lois, 126
Ron, Moshe, 329
Ronson, Lou, 206
Roodyn, Donald, 217
Rose, Alan, 261
Rose, Peter, 12
Rose, Richard, 204
Rosen, Moses, 275
Rosen, Shlomo, 330
Rosenberg, Stuart, 205
Rosenblatt, Zvi, 328
Rosenne, Meir, 363
Rosensaft, Menachem, 21n, 24, 31, 36, 36n
Rosenwald, Mary Kurtz, 443
Rossmeisl, Dieter, 257
Rote Armee Fraktion (West Germany), 244
Rotenberg, David, 195
Rotenstreich, Nathan, 18n
Rotstein, Siegmund, 262
Roumanian Jewish Federation of America, Inc., 397
Rousso, Louis, 443
Royal Society for the Prevention of Cruelty to Animals, 214
Rubens, Bernice, 216
Rubin, Abba, 216
Rübner, Tuvia, 258
Rudin, A. James, 32, 134
Rumania, 274, 275, 298
Ryan, Alan A., Jr., 119
Ryzhkov, Nikolai, 263

Sachar, Abram L., 362
As-Saiqa, 146
St. Louis Center for Holocaust Studies, 375
St. Louis Jewish Light, 429

Salberg, Rita, 443
Salgo, Laszlo, 272
Sali, Boyamu, 301
Saltzman, Morris, 206
Samkalden, Ivo, 240
San Diego Jewish Times, 427
Sandberg, Neil, 7n, 10n
Saner, Hans, 258
Saperstein, David, 28
Saudi Arabia, 140, 143, 209, 248, 249, 357
Schalit, Lionel, 217
Scheftelowitz, Elchanan, 251
Scheiber, Alexander, 272
Schick, Marvin, 125
Schiff, Jacob, 344, 345
Schimanowski, Gottfried, 257
Schindler, Alexander, 25, 27, 125
Schlamme, Martha, 443
Schluter, Poul, 297
Schmädeke, Jürgen, 256
Schmelz, U. O., 8, 8n, 9, 10n, 11n, 44n, 45n, 59n, 165n
Schmid, Hans-Dieter, 257
Schmidt, Helmut, 27
Schneider, Gerhard, 257
Schoeps, Julius H., 257
Scholder, Klaus, 256
Schonfield, Hugh, 216
Schoon, Simon, 232
Schulz, Harri, 247
Schuster, Aaron, 234
Schwanenfeld, Marianne von, 35
Schwartz, F., 239
Schwartz, Sidney H., 124
Schwarz, Walter, 257
Schwarzbard, Shalom, 222
Scooler, Zvee, 443
The Second World War, 256
The Secret of Anna Katz, 216
Secrets: Boyhood in a Jewish Hotel 1932–54, 216
Sefer Mitzvot Gadol, 205
Segal, Henry, 443
Segal, J. B., 215
Segal, Lord Samuel of Wytham, 217
Seib, Ferdinand, 258
Semel, Noam, 250

Senger, Valentin, 258
Seniora, Hanna, 150
Sentinel, 428
Sephardic House, 375
Sephardic Jewish Brotherhood of America, Inc., 397
Sese Seko, Mobutu, 299
Seven Arts Feature Syndicate and Worldwide News Service, 434
Sforim, Mendele Moicher, 259
Shahal, Moshe, 295
Shamai, Yaakov, 329
Shamir, Yitzhak, 138, 144, 162, 196, 209, 277, 284, 286, 287, 288, 289, 295, 298, 299, 300, 310, 313, 323, 324
Shapiro, Aumie, 215
Shapiro, Bernard, 200
Shapiro, Dmitri, 267
Shapiro, Michael, 215
Shapiro-Libai, Nitza, 300
Sharabaf, Uziahu, 310
Share, Hyman, 207
Sharon, Ariel, 285, 286, 303, 313
Shaw, Maxwell, 217
Shcharansky, Anatoly, 237
Shcharansky, Avital, 213, 237
Shebson, Pinchas, 217
Shefman, Alan, 206
Shemtov, Victor, 329
Shevardnadze, Eduard, 263, 264, 265, 299, 322
Sheviley Ha-Hinnukh, 432
Shifman, Ilya, 269
Shilo, Yigal, 326
Shindi, Wahi, 295
Shindler, Colin, 215
Shkolnik, Isaac, 267
Shkolnik, Itzhak, 213, 323
Shkolnik, Leonid, 269
Sh'ma, 432
Shmueli, A., 45n
Shmuessen Mit Kinder Un Yugent, 432
Sholem Aleichem Folk Institute, Inc., 388
Shomron, Dan, 329
Short Digest of Jewish Literature in the Middle Ages, 216
Shrayer, Leonid, 266

Shultz, George, 26, 34, 137, 138, 141, 143, 145, 147, 148, 153, 156, 160, 162, 287, 290, 291, 292, 293, 322, 362
Shvartsblat, Israel, 270
Sichrovsky, Peter, 259
Siegele-Wenschkewitz, Lenore, 257
Siegman, Henry, 28, 35, 35n, 132, 324
Siemers, Otto, 247
Sigal, John, 200
Sigal, Phillip, 207, 443
Signoret, Simone, 222, 223
Silberman, Charles, 7, 11n, 15, 127
Silbermann, Alphons, 246, 257, 259
Silberner, Edmund, 258
Silken, Sam, 217
Simon, Heinrich, 262
Simon, Marie, 262
Simon Wiesenthal Center (*see* Yeshiva University of Los Angeles)
Sinclair, Clive, 216
Sindermann, Horst, 261
Singer, Israel, 24, 30, 37
Sir Moses Montefiore, 1784–1885, 216
Sirat, René, 221, 222
Skirball, Jack, 443
Skirball Museum (*see* Hebrew Union College-Jewish Institute of Religion)
Sklare, Marshall, 11, 12n, 15, 15n, 16, 16n
Slawson, John, 350
Sobol, Yehoshua, 325
Social Democratic Party (West Germany), 241, 248
Society for Humanistic Judaism, 388
Society for the History of Czechoslovak Jews, Inc., 375
Society for the Protection of Animals (The Netherlands), 232
Society of Friends of the Touro Synagogue, National Historic Shrine, Inc., 388
Society of Israel Philatelists, 408
Soetendorp, Avraham, 235, 237
Sofaer, Abraham, 293
Sofer, Arnon, 314
Sofer, Ovadia, 265
Solarz, Stephen, 130

Sommer, Wilhem, 257
Sonntag, Jacob, 215
Sons of Italy, 33
South Africa, 124
South Yemen, 150
Southern Jewish Weekly, 428
Southwest Jewish Chronicle, 434
Sovetish haimland, 268, 269, 270
Soviet Jewry, National Conference on, 370
Soviet Jewry, Student Struggle for, 370
Soviet Jews, Union of Councils for, 370
Soviet Union, 145, 263–270
Speakes, Larry, 34
The Special Relationship Between West Germany and Israel, 216
Special Treatment, 205
Specter, Arlen, 31
Spectrum, 432
Sperber, Manes, 258
Spertus College of Judaica, 388
Springer, Axel, 251
Stage Struck, 216
Stark Jewish News, 433
Starkova, Klavdia Borisovna, 268
State of Israel Bonds, 408
Stauffenberg, Berthold von, 35
Stavitsky, Arkady, 270
Stavsky, Avraham, 328
Stein, Ernst, 255, 261
Stein, Herbert, 291
Stein, Leonard, 444
Stein, Richard, 233
Steinbach, Peter, 256
Steinberg, Henry, 206
Steinberg, Jack, 207
Sterling, Jeffrey, 217
Stern, Anne, 217
Stetham, Robert, 152
Stieg, Gerald, 258
Stilman, Abram, 207
Stippler, Elisabeth, 251
Stippler, Karl, 251
Stolar, Abe, 264
Stone, Chuck, 123
Stone, Peter, 218
Stoutenbeek, Jan, 239
Strassmann, Fritz, 251
Straus, Oscar, 344

Strauss, Herbert A., 257
Stripes Along the Sky, 239
Stroock, Alan, 444
Student Struggle for Soviet Jewry, 370
Studies in Bibliography and Booklore, 433
Studies in Social Sciences, 59n
Studies on the History of Dutch Jewry, 239
Sturm, Naftali, 251
Suall, Irwin, 134
Suffot, Ze'ev, 228
Sulzbach, Herbert, 217
Super, Arthur, 217
Surkis, Mordechai, 251
Swift, Steven, 216
Synagogue Council of America, 388
Synagogue Light, 432
Syria, 139, 146, 150, 152, 154, 155, 157, 159, 285, 289, 290
Szarota, Tomasz, 256
Szurmiej, Szymon, 254, 273
Szwejlich, Michael, 254

Tabbick, Jacqueline, 214
Tagesspiegel (West Germany), 254
Tal, Josef, 251
Talks and Tales, 432
Tamir, Avraham, 295
Tanenbaum, Marc H., 34n, 133, 255
Teeffelen, Toine van, 228
Teitelbaum, Max, 206
Tel Aviv Museum, American Friends of, 402
Tel Aviv University, American Friends of, 403
Tenenbaum, S. T., 205
Terry, Dixon, 134
Texas Jewish Post, 434
Thälmann, Ernst, 248
Thanks to Scandinavia, Inc., 377
Thatcher, Margaret, 151, 209, 213, 298
Theobald, Alfred Udo, 258
Theodor Herzl Foundation, 408
  Herzl Press, 408
  Theodor Herzl Institute, 408
Thieke, Friedrich Wilhelm, 36
Thijn, Ed van, 231
Thorne, Ahrne, 444

Three Times Three Links of a Chain, 259
Thursz, Daniel, 253
Tikhonov, Nikolai, 263
Time and Time Again, 216
Tishman, Peggy, 29
Tittmann, Sigmund, 251
Tobin, Gary, 127
To Death with the Railways of the Reich, 256
Torah Schools for Israel—Chinuch Atzmai, 388
Torah Umesorah—National Society for Hebrew Day Schools, 388
   Institute for Professional Enrichment, 388
   National Association of Hebrew Day School Administrators, 389
   National Association of Hebrew Day School Parent-Teacher Associations, 389
   National Conference of Yeshiva Principals, 389
   National Yeshiva Teachers Board of License, 389
Touati, Emile, 221
Touro College,
   College of Liberal Arts and Sciences, 389
   Division of Health Sciences, 389
   Flatbush Program, 389
   Graduate School of Jewish Studies, 389
   Institute of Jewish Law, 389
   Jacob D. Fuchsberg Law Center, 389
   Jewish People's University of the Air, 389
   School of General Studies, 390
   Yeshiva Ohr Hachayim, 390
Tradition, 432
The Transmigration of a Melody, 259
Treasures of a People, 205
Trends, 432
A Trust Betrayal, 205
Tulsa Jewish Review, 434
Tunisia, 221, 227, 292, 298
Turowicz, Jerzy, 274
Tutu, Bishop Desmond, 124
Tym, Minna, 217
Tzur, Ya'akov, 321, 322

Udovitch, Abraham L., 215
Uhlman, Fred, 217
UJF News, 434
Ukrainian National Association, 33
Uline, Glenna, 206
Ullmann, Jacob, 444
Under the Sign of Job, 258
Undzer Veg (Canada), 435
Unger, Wilhelm, 260
Unhealed Wounds, 205
Union of American Hebrew Congregations (UAHC), 122, 125, 126, 130, 133, 390
   American Conference of Cantors, 390
   Commission on Social Action of Reform Judaism (*see* page 368)
   National Association of Temple Administrators (NATA), 390
   National Association of Temple Educators (NATE), 390
   National Federation of Temple Brotherhoods, 390
   National Federation of Temple Sisterhoods, 390
   North American Federation of Temple Youth (NFTY), 390
   and Central Conference of American Rabbis: Commission on Jewish Education, 391
   and Central Conference of American Rabbis: Joint Commission on Synagogue Administration, 391
Union of Councils for Soviet Jews, 370
Union of Jewish Students (UJS), 210
Union of Jewish Students in Germany, 253
Union of Liberal and Progressive Synagogues (Great Britain), 214
Union of Orthodox Jewish Congregations of America, 391
   National Conference of Synagogue Youth, 391
   Women's Branch, 391
Union of Orthodox Rabbis of the United States and Canada, 391

Union of Sephardic Congregations, Inc., 391
United Charity Institutions of Jerusalem, Inc., 408
United Hellenic American Congress, 33
United Israel Appeal, Inc., 408
United Jewish Appeal, Inc., 377
  Rabbinic Cabinet, 377
  University Programs Dept., 378
  Women's Division of, 378
  Young Leadership Cabinet, 378
  Young Women's Leadership Cabinet, 378
United Jewish Teachers' Seminary, 414
United Lubavitcher Yeshivoth, 391
United Nations,
  Conference on Women, 197, 228, 238
  General Assembly, 227, 288
  Security Council Resolution 338, 142, 144, 145, 146, 288, 292
  Security Council Resolution 242, 141, 142, 144, 145, 146, 147, 148, 149, 288, 292
  Security Council Resolution 3379, 211
United Nations Interim Force in Lebanon, 277
United Order True Sisters, Inc., 397
United States Committee Sports for Israel, Inc., 408
United Synagogue (Great Britain), 211, 212
United Synagogue of America, 392
  Commission on Jewish Community and Public Policy, 392
  Commission on Jewish Education, 392
  Jewish Educators Assembly, 392
  Kadima, 392
  National Association of Synagogue Administrators, 392
  United Synagogue Youth of, 392
United Synagogue Review, 432
University Center for Jewish Studies (France), 222
University of Judaism, Los Angeles (*see* Jewish Theological Seminary)

Unlikely Tory: The Life and Times of Allan Grossman, 206
Unser Tsait, 432
USA Today, 31n

Vaad Mishmereth Stam, 392
Valensi, Lucette, 215
Veil, Simone, 252
Veisberg, Vladimir, 270
Victims and Neighbors, 205
Vigeveno, Paul, 239
Viguerie, Richard, 33
Virshuvsky, Anatoly, 266
Voevutskii, Igor, 268
Vogel, Hans-Jochen, 249
Voice of America, 161
Volvovsky, Leonid, 266
Vorontosov, Yuli, 265
Vrba, Rudolph, 198

Waife, Marie, 444
Wald, Albert, 444
Walk, Joseph, 256
Wallach, Yona, 329
Wallmann, Walter, 255
Wall Street Journal, 25, 26n, 29, 29n, 135
Warsaw Treaty Organization, 271
Warsaw Under the Swastika, 256
Washington Jewish Week, 428
Washington Post, 26n, 27n, 28, 29, 29n, 30n, 31n, 32n, 135
Waskow, Arthur, 131
Waxman, Mordecai, 133
Weber, Vin, 27
Webster, William, 134
Der Wecker, 432
We Do Not Know What Will Be Tomorrow, But We Know What Was Yesterday—Young Jews in Germany and Austria, 259
Weil, Wolf, 260
Weill, Kurt, 324
Weinberg, David, 206
Weinfeld, Morton, 200, 202
Weinreb, Friedrich, 258
Weiss, Avraham, 35
Weizman, Ezer, 282, 295, 328

Weizsäcker, Richard von, 37, 243, 249, 252, 255, 297
Wertheimer, Douglas, 205
Wesker, Arnold, 216
West Coast Talmudical Seminary, 393
Western Jewish News (Canada), 435
Western States Jewish History, 427
Weyel, Helene, 239
When God Invades Our Thoughts, 258
Wiesel, Elie, 24, 26, 29, 30, 118
Wiesemann, Falk, 258
Wiesenthal, Simon, 233
Wijsenbeek, Louis, 240
Will, George, 25
Willen, Joseph, 444
Willmot, Robert, 206
Windsor Jewish Community Bulletin, 435
Wingfield, Martin, 209
Wisconsin Jewish Chronicle, 434
Wisdom and Messiah, 257
Wiseman, Shloime, 207
Wisner, Heinz, 247
Wisse, Ruth, 15
WIZO-Nederland, 238
Wohl, Erwin, 251
Wohlgemuth, Isaiah, 256
Wolfson, Leonard, 217
Wollach, Zwi-Hermann, 260
Women's American ORT Reporter, 432
Women's League for Conservative Judaism, 393
Women's League for Israel, Inc., 409
Women's League Outlook, 432
Women's Social Service for Israel, Inc., 378
Workmen's Circle, 398
   Division of Jewish Labor Committee (see page 369)
Workmen's Circle Call, 433
World Confederation of Jewish Community Centers, 401
World Confederation of United Zionists, 409
World Conference of Jewish Communal Service, 371
World Council of Synagogues, 393
World Jewish Congress, 133, 371
World Union for Progressive Judaism, Ltd., 393
World Zionist Organization—American Section, 409
   Department of Education and Culture, 409
   North American Aliyah Movement, 409
   Zionist Archives and Library of the, 409
Wyschogrod, Michael, 255

Yad L'Achim, 319
Yad Vashem—German Rescuers of Jews, 256
Yagor, Yosef, 162
Yakirson, Shimon, 268, 269
Yavne Hebrew Theological Seminary, 393
Yearbook of the Central Conference of American Rabbis, 433
Yellin, Richard, 261
Yeshiva University, 393
   Albert Einstein College of Medicine, 394
   Alumni Office, 394
   Belfer Institute for Advanced Biomedical Studies, 394
   Benjamin N. Cardozo School of Law, 394
   Bernard Revel Graduate School, 394
   Brookdale Institute for the Study of Gerontology, 394
   David J. Azrieli Graduate Institute of Jewish Education and Administration, 394
   Ferkauf Graduate School of Psychology, 394
   Harry Fischel School for Higher Jewish Studies, 395
   Rabbi Isaac Elchanan Theological Seminary, 395
   Women's Organization, 395
   Wurzweiler School of Social Work, 395
   Yeshiva University of Los Angeles, 395
   Simon Wiesenthal Center, 396

Yeshiva University Museum, 375
Yeshivath Torah Vodaath and Mesivta Rabbinical Seminary, 396
　Alumni Association, 396
Yevtushenko, Yevgeniy, 264
Yiddish, 433
Yiddishe Heim, 433
Yiddishe Kultur, 433
Yiddishe Vort, 433
Yiddisher Kemfer, 433
Yiddisher Kultur Farband—YKUF, 375
Yidishe Shprakh, 433
Yinon, Noam, 311
YIVO Annual of Jewish Social Science, 433
YIVO Bleter, 433
YIVO Institute for Jewish Research, Inc., 376
　Max Weinreich Center for Advanced Jewish Studies, 376
Yosef, Ovadia, 320
You Can Be Your Own Rabbi, 205
Young, Andrew, 121
Young, Stuart, 213
Young Israel Viewpoint, 433
Young Judaean, 433
Youngstown Jewish Times, 433

Yudborovsky, Mordechai, 323
Yugntruf, 433
Yugntruf Youth for Yiddish, 412
Yugoslavia, 275, 276

Zaiger, Yitzhak, 329
Zamir, Yitzhak, 305, 311, 317
Zar, Moshe, 310
Zaritsky, Yosef, 329
Zbornik (Yugoslavia), 276
Zeevy, R., 45n
Zelichonok, Roald, 266
Zelkind, Leonid, 322
Zemans, Joyce, 206
Zentner, Christian, 256
Zichron Meir al Avelut, 205
Zimanas, Genrikas Oshervich, 270
Zimouki, Arye, 330
Zingeris, Emanuelis, 269
Zionist Federation (Great Britain), 211
Zionist Organization of America, 409
Zionist Organization of Canada, 414
Zislin, M., 268
Zitzerman, Saul, 206
Zmurid, Ahmed, 306
Zucker, David, 445
Zundel, Ernest, 197, 198, 199, 203
Zuria, Yosef, 311

3 1542 00147 1642

296.05 A512
1987
American Jewish year book.

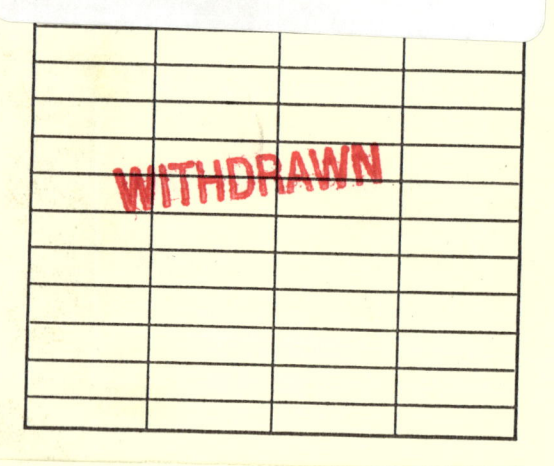

WITHDRAWN

Trexler Library
Muhlenberg College
Allentown, PA 18104

DEMCO